The O'Leary Series

Microsoft® Office XP

Volume II

Timothy J. O'Leary

Arizona State University

Linda I. O'Leary

InformationTechnology

McGraw-Hill Irwin

Boston   Burr Ridge, IL   Dubuque, IA   Madison, WI   New York
San Francisco   St. Louis   Bangkok   Bogotá   Caracas   Kuala Lumpur
Lisbon   London   Madrid   Mexico City   Milan   Montreal   New Delhi
Santiago   Seoul   Singapore   Sydney   Taipei   Toronto

McGraw-Hill Higher Education

A Division of The McGraw-Hill Companies

MICROSOFT® OFFICE XP, VOLUME II
Published by McGraw-Hill/Irwin, an imprint of the McGraw-Hill Companies, Inc. 1221 Avenue of the Americas, New York, NY, 10020. Copyright © 2002 by the McGraw-Hill Companies, Inc. All rights reserved. No part of this publication may be reproduced or distributed in any form or by any means, or stored in a database or retrieval system, without the prior written consent of The McGraw-Hill Companies, Inc., including, but not limited to, in any network or other electronic storage or transmission, or broadcast for distance learning.

Some ancillaries, including electronic and print components, may not be available to customers outside the United States.

Disclaimer: This book is designed to help you improve your computer use. However, the author and publisher assume no responsibility whatsoever for the uses made of this material or for decisions based on their use, and make no warranties, either expressed or implied, regarding the contents of this book, its merchantability, or its fitness for any particular purpose.

Neither the publisher nor anyone else who has been involved in the creation, production, or delivery of this product shall be liable for any direct, incidental, or consequential damages, such as, but not limited to, loss of anticipated profits or benefits resulting from its use or from any breach of warranty. Some states do not allow the exclusion or limitation of direct, incidental, or consequential damages, so the above disclaimer may not apply to you. No dealer, company, or person is authorized to alter this disclaimer. Any representation to the contrary will not bind the publisher or author.

This book is printed on acid-free paper.

domestic   1 2 3 4 5 6 7 8 9 0 QPD/QPD 0 9 8 7 6 5 4 3 2 1
international   1 2 3 4 5 6 7 8 9 0 QPD/QPD 0 9 8 7 6 5 4 3 2 1

ISBN 0-07-247248-0

Publisher: *George Werthman*
Sponsoring editor: *Dan Silverburg*
Developmental editor: *Sarah Wood*
Manager, Marketing and Sales: *Paul Murphy*
Project manager: *Jim Labeots*
Manager, new book production: *Melonie Salvati*
Freelance design coordinator: *Gino Cieslik*
Cover & interior design: *Maureen McCutcheon*
Cover image: *Digitalvision*
Photo research coordinator: *David A. Tietz*
Supplement coordinator: *Marc Mattson*
Senior producer, Media Technology: *David Barrick*
Compositor: *Rogondino & Associates*
Typeface: *10.5/13 New Aster*
Printer: *Quebecor World Dubuque Inc.*

Library of Congress Control Number 2001044377

INTERNATIONAL EDITION ISBN 0-07-112359-8
Copyright © 2002, Exclusive rights by The McGraw-Hill Companies, Inc. for manufacture and export.
This book cannot be re-exported from the country to which it is sold by McGraw-Hill.
The International Edition is not available in North America.

www.mhhe.com

InformationTechnology

Information Technology at McGraw-Hill/Irwin

At McGraw-Hill Higher Education, we publish instructional materials targeted at the higher education market. In an effort to expand the tools of higher learning, we publish texts, lab manuals, study guides, testing materials, software, and multimedia products.

At McGraw-Hill/Irwin (a division of McGraw-Hill Higher Education), we realize that technology has created and will continue to create new mediums for professors and students to use in managing resources and communicating information to one another. We strive to provide the most flexible and complete teaching and learning tools available as well as offer solutions to the changing world of teaching and learning.

McGraw-Hill/Irwin is dedicated to providing the tools for today's instructors and students to successfully navigate the world of Information Technology.

- **Seminar Series** McGraw-Hill/Irwin's Technology Connection seminar series offered across the country every year demonstrates the latest technology products and encourages collaboration among teaching professionals.

- **McGraw-Hill/Osborne** This division of The McGraw-Hill Companies is known for its best-selling Internet titles, *Internet & Web Yellow Pages* and the *Internet Complete Reference*. For more information, visit Osborne at **www.osborne.com**.

- **Digital Solutions** McGraw-Hill/Irwin is committed to publishing digital solutions. Taking your course online doesn't have to be a solitary adventure, nor does it have to be a difficult one. We offer several solutions that will allow you to enjoy all the benefits of having your course material online.

- **Packaging Options** For more information about our discount options, contact your McGraw-Hill/Irwin Sales representative at 1-800-338-3987 or visit our web site at **www.mhhe.com/it**.

APPROVED COURSEWARE

What does this logo mean?

It means this courseware has been approved by the Microsoft® Office User Specialist Program to be among the finest available for learning *Microsoft Word 2002, Microsoft Excel 2002, Microsoft Access 2002,* and *Microsoft PowerPoint 2002*. It also means that upon completion of this courseware, you may be prepared to become a Microsoft Office User Specialist.

What is a Microsoft Office User Specialist?

A Microsoft Office User Specialist is an individual who has certified his or her skills in one or more of the Microsoft Office desktop applications of Microsoft Word, Microsoft Excel, Microsoft PowerPoint®, Microsoft Outlook® or Microsoft Access, or in Microsoft Project. The Microsoft Office User Specialist Program typically offers certification exams at the "Core" and "Expert" skill levels.* The Microsoft Office User Specialist Program is the only Microsoft approved program in the world for certifying proficiency in Microsoft Office desktop applications and Microsoft Project. This certification can be a valuable asset in any job search or career advancement.

More Information:

To learn more about becoming a Microsoft Office User Specialist, visit www.mous.net

To purchase a Microsoft Office User Specialist certification exam, visit www.DesktopIQ.com

To learn about other Microsoft Office User Specialist approved courseware from McGraw-Hill/Irwin, visit http://www.mhhe.com/catalogs/irwin/cit/mous/index.mhtml

---

* The availability of Microsoft Office User Specialist certification exams varies by application, application version and language. Visit www.mous.net for exam availability.

Microsoft, the Microsoft Office User Specialist Logo, PowerPoint and Outlook are either registered trademarks or trademarks of Microsoft Corporation in the United States and/or other countries.

Who benefits from Microsoft, Office User Specialist certification?

Employers
Microsoft Office User Specialist ("MOUS") certification helps satisfy employers' needs for qualitative assessments of employees' skills. Training, coupled with MOUS certification, offers organizations of every size, the ability to enhance productivity and efficiency by enabling their employees to unlock many advanced and laborsaving features in Microsoft Office applications. MOUS certification can ultimately improve the bottom line.

Employees
MOUS certification demonstrates employees' productivity and competence in Microsoft Office applications, the most popular business applications in the world. Achieving MOUS certification verifies that employees have the confidence and ability to use Microsoft Office applications in meeting and exceeding their work challenges.

Instructors
MOUS certification validates instructors' knowledge and skill in using Microsoft Office applications. It serves as a valuable credential, demonstrating their potential to teach students these essential applications. The MOUS Authorized Instructor program is also available to those who wish to further demonstrate their instructional capabilities.

Students
MOUS certification distinguishes students from their peers. It demonstrates their efficiency in completing assignments and projects, leaving more time for other studies. Improved confidence toward meeting new challenges and obstacles is yet another benefit. Achieving MOUS certification gives students the marketable skills necessary to set them apart in the competitive job market.

To learn more about MOUS certification, visit www.mous.net

To purchase a MOUS certification exam, visit www.DesktopIQ.com

Brief Contents

Detailed Contents

EXCEL

Lab
4 Using Solver, Creating Templates, and Evaluating Scenarios EX4.1

Lab
5 Using Data Tables, Creating Macros, and Designing Onscreen Forms EX5.1

Lab

6   Creating and Using Lists and Web Pages

ACCESS

Lab

4   Working with Multiple Tables

Lab

5 Creating Custom Forms AC5.1

Lab

6 Creating Custom Reports, Macros, and Switchboards AC6.1

POWERPOINT

Lab
3 **Using Advanced Presentation**
Features PP3.1

Acknowledgments

The new edition of The O'Leary Series has been made possible only through the enthusiasm and dedication of a great team of people. Because the team spans the country, literally from coast to coast, we have utilized every means of working together including conference calls, FAX, e-mail, and document collaboration. We have truly tested the team approach and it works!

Leading the team from McGraw-Hill/Irwin are George Werthman, Publisher and Alexandra Arnold, Developmental Editor. Their renewed commitment, direction, and support have infused the team with the excitement of a new project.

The production staff is headed by James Labeots, Project Manager, whose planning and attention to detail has made it possible for us to successfully meet a very challenging schedule. Members of the production team include: Gino Cieslik, Designer; Pat Rogondino, Compositor; Susan Defosset, Copy Editor; Melonie Salvati, Production Supervisor; Marc Mattson, Supplement Coordinator; and David Barrick, Media Producer. We would particularly like to thank Pat and Susan—team members for many past editions—whom we can always depend on to do a great job.

Finally, we are particularly grateful to a small but very dedicated group of people who helped us develop the manuscript. Colleen Hayes, Susan Demar, and Kathy Duggan have helped on the last several editions and continue to provide excellent developmental and technical support. To Steve Willis and Carol Cooper who provide technical expertise, youthful perspective, and enthusiasm, my thanks for helping get the manuscripts out the door and meeting the deadlines.

Preface

Introduction

The 20th century not only brought the dawn of the Information Age, but also rapid changes in information technology. There is no indication that this rapid rate of change will be slowing— it may even be increasing. As we begin the 21st century, computer literacy will undoubtedly become prerequisite for whatever career a student chooses. The goal of the O'Leary Series is to assist students in attaining the necessary skills to efficiently use these applications. Equally important is the goal to provide a foundation for students to readily and easily learn to use future versions of this software. This series does this by providing detailed step-by-step instructions combined with careful selection and presentation of essential concepts.

About the Authors

Tim and Linda O'Leary live in the American Southwest and spend much of their time engaging instructors and students in conversation about learning. In fact, they have been talking about learning for more than 25 years. Something in those early conversations convinced them to write a book, to bring their interest in the learning process to the printed page. Today, they are as concerned as ever about learning, about technology, and about the challenges of presenting material in new ways, both in terms of content and the method of delivery.

A powerful and creative team, Tim combines his years of classroom teaching experience with Linda's background as a consultant and corporate trainer. Tim has taught courses at Stark Technical College in Canton, Ohio, Rochester Institute of Technology in upper New York state, and is currently a professor at Arizona State University in Tempe, Arizona. Tim and Linda have talked to and taught students from ages 8 to 80, all of them with a desire to learn something about computers and the applications that make their lives easier, more interesting, and more productive.

About the Book

Times are changing, technology is changing, and this text is changing, too. Do you think the students of today are different from yesterday? There is no doubt about it—they are. On the positive side, it is amazing how much effort students will put toward things they are convinced are relevant to them. Their effort directed at learning application programs and exploring the Web seems at times limitless. On the other hand, students can often be shortsighted, thinking that learning the skills to use the application is the only objective. The mission of the series is to build upon and extend this interest by not only teaching the specific application skills but by introducing the concepts that are common to all applications, providing students with the confidence, knowledge, and ability to easily learn the next generation of applications.

What's New in This Edition?

- **Introduction to Computer Essentials**—A brief introduction to the basics of computer hardware and software (Appears in Office XP, Volume I Only).

- **Introduction to Windows 2000**—Two hands-on labs devoted to Windows 2000 basics (Appears in Office XP, Volume I Only).

- **Introduction to the WWW: Internet Explorer and E-mail**—Hands-on introductions for using Internet Explorer to browse the WWW and using e-mail (Appears in Office XP, Volume I Only).

- **Topic Reorganization**—The text has been reorganized to include main and subtopic heads by grouping related tasks. For example, tasks such as changing fonts and applying character effects appear under the "Formatting" topic head. This results in a slightly more reference-like approach, making it easier for students to refer back to the text to review. This has been done without losing the logical and realistic development of the case.

- **Clarified Marginal Notes**—Marginal notes have been enhanced by more clearly identifying the note content with box heads and the use of different colors.

    Additional Information—Brief asides with expanded discussion of features.

    Having Trouble?—Procedural tips advising students of possible problems and how to overcome them.

    Another Method—Alternative methods of performing a procedure.

- Larger **Screen Figures** Make it easier to identify elements and read screen content.

- All **Numbered Steps** and bullets appear in left margin space making it easy not to miss a step.

- A **MOUS (*Microsoft Office User Specialist*) Skills** table, appearing at the end of each chapter, contains page references to MOUS skills learned in the lab.

- **Two new References**

    File Finder—Helps organize all data and solution files.

    MOUS (*Microsoft Office User Specialist*) Certification Guide—Links all MOUS objectives to text content and end-of-chapter exercises.

Same Great Features as the Office 2000 Series

- **Relevant Cases**—Four separate running cases demonstrate the features in each application. Topics are of interest to students—At Arizona State University, over 600 students were surveyed to find out what topics are of interest to them.

- **Focus on Concepts**—Each chapter focuses on the concepts behind the application. Students learn the essentials, so they can succeed regardless of the software package they might be using.

- **Steps**—Numbered procedural steps clearly identify each hands-on task needed to complete the step.

- **Screens**—Plentiful screen illustrations illustrate the completion of each numbered step to help students stay on track.

- **Callouts**—Meaningful screen callouts identify the results of the steps as well as reinforce the associated concept.

- **End-of-Chapter Material**

    Terminology—Questions and exercises test recall of the basic information and terminology in the lab.

    - Screen Identification
    - Matching
    - Multiple Choice

    Concepts—Questions and exercises review students' understanding of concepts and ability to integrate ideas presented in different parts of the lab.

    - Fill-In
    - Discussion Questions

    Hands-On Practice Exercises—Students apply the skills and concepts they learned to solve case-based exercises. Many cases in the practice exercises tie to a running case used in another application lab. This helps to demonstrate the use of the four applications across a common case setting. For example, the Adventure Travel Tours case used in the Word labs is continued in practice exercises in Excel, Access, and PowerPoint.

    - Step-by-Step
    - On Your Own
    - On The Web

- **Rating System**—The 3-star rating system identifies the difficulty level of each practice exercise in the end-of-chapter materials.

- **Working Together Labs**—At the completion of the brief and introductory texts, a final lab demonstrates the integration of the MS Office applications and the WWW.

Instructor's Guide

Instructor's Resource Kit

The **Instructor's Resource Kit** contains a computerized Test Bank, an Instructor's Manual, and PowerPoint Presentation Slides. Features of the Instructor's Resource Kit are described below.

- **Instructor's Manual** The Instructor's Manual contains lab objectives, concepts, outlines, lecture notes, and command summaries. Also included are answers to all end-of chapter material, tips for covering difficult materials, additional exercises, and a schedule showing how much time is required to cover text material.

- **Computerized Test Bank** The test bank contains over 1,300 multiple choice, true/false, and discussion questions. Each question will be accompanied by the correct answer, the level of learning difficulty, and corresponding page references. Our flexible Diploma software allows you to easily generate custom exams.

- **PowerPoint Presentation Slides** The presentation slides will include lab objectives, concepts, outlines, text figures, and speaker's notes. Also included are bullets to illustrate key terms and FAQs.

Online Learning Center/Web Site

Found at **www.mhhe.com/oleary**, this site provides additional learning and instructional tools to enhance the comprehension of the text. The OLC/Web Site is divided into these three areas:

- **Information Center** Contains core information about the text, supplements, and the authors.

- **Instructor Center** Offers instructional materials, downloads, additional exercises, and other relevant links for professors.

- **Student Center** Contains chapter competencies, chapter concepts, self-quizzes, flashcards, projects, animations, additional Web links, and more.

Skills Assessment

SimNet (Simulated Network Assessment Product) provides a way for you to test students' software skills in a simulated environment. SimNet is available for Microsoft Office 97, Microsoft Office 2000, and Microsoft Office XP. SimNet provides flexibility for you in your course by offering:

- Pre-testing options
- Post-testing options
- Course placement testing
- Diagnostic capabilities to reinforce skills
- Proficiency testing to measure skills
- Web or LAN delivery of tests.
- Computer-based training tutorials (new for Office XP)
- MOUS preparation exams

For more information on skills assessment software, please contact your local sales representative, or visit us at **www.mhhe.com/it**.

Digital Solutions to Help You Manage Your Course

PageOut is our Course Web Site Development Center that offers a syllabus page, URL, McGraw-Hill Online Learning Center content, online exercises and quizzes, gradebook, discussion board, and an area for student Web pages.

Available free with any McGraw-Hill/Irwin product, PageOut requires no prior knowledge of HTML, no long hours of coding, and a way for course coordinators and professors to provide a full-course Web site. PageOut offers a series of templates—simply fill them with your course information and click on one of 16 designs. The process takes under an hour and leaves you with a professionally designed Web site. We'll even get you started with sample Web sites, or enter your syllabus for you! PageOut is so straightforward and intuitive, it's little wonder why over 12,000 college professors are using it. For more information, visit the PageOut Web site at **www.pageout.net**.

Online courses are also available. Online Learning Centers (OLCs) are your perfect solutions for Internet-based content. Simply put, these Centers are "digital cartridges" that contain a book's pedagogy and supplements. As students read the book, they can go online and take self-grading quizzes or work through interactive exercises. These also provide students appropriate access to lecture materials and other key supplements.

Online Learning Centers can be delivered through any of these platforms:

McGraw-Hill Learning Architecture (TopClass)

Blackboard.com

Ecollege.com (formerly Real Education)

WebCT (a product of Universal Learning Technology)

McGraw-Hill has partnerships with WebCT and Blackboard to make it even easier to take your course online. Now you can have McGraw-Hill content delivered through the leading Internet-based learning tool for higher education. At McGraw-Hill, we have the following service agreements with WebCT and Blackboard:

Instructor Advantage Instructor Advantage is a special level of service McGraw-Hill offers in conjuction with WebCT designed to help you get up and running with your new course. A team of specialists will be immediately available to ensure everything runs smoothly through the life of your adoption.

Instructor Advantage Plus Qualified McGraw-Hill adopters will be eligible for an even higher level of service. A certified WebCT or Blackboard specialist will provide a full day of on-site training for you and your staff. You will then have unlimited e-mail and phone support through the life of your adoption. Please contact your local McGraw-Hill representative for more details.

Technology Connection Seminar Series

McGraw-Hill/Irwin's Technology Connection seminar series offered across the country every year demonstrates the latest technology products and encourages collaboration among teaching professionals.

Computing Essentials

Available alone, or packaged with the O'Leary Series, *Computing Essentials* offers a unique, visual orientation that gives students a basic understanding of computing concepts. *Computing Essentials* is one of the few books on the market that is written by a professor who still teaches the course every semester and loves it! While combining current topics and technology into a highly illustrated design geared to catch students' interest and motivate them in their learning, this text provides an accurate snapshot of computing today. When the book is bundled with software application lab manuals, students are given a complete representation of the fundamental issues surrounding the personal computing environment.

The text includes the following features:

- **A "Learn By Doing" approach** encourages students to engage in activity that is more interactive than the traditional learning pattern students typically follow in a concepts course. The exercises, explorations, visual orientation, inclusion of screen shots and numbered steps, and integrated Internet references combine several methods to achieve an interactive learning environment for optimum reinforcement.

- **Making IT Work For You** sections visually demonstrate how technology is used in everyday life. Topics covered include how find a job online and how to protect a computer against viruses. These "gallery" style boxes combine text and art to take students step-by-step through technological processes that are both interesting and useful. As an added bonus, the *CE 2001-2002 Making IT Work Video Series* has been created to complement the topics presented throughout the text.

- **On the Web Explorations** appear throughout the margins of the text and encourage students to go to the Web to visit several informative and established sites in order to learn more about the chapter's featured topic.

- **On the Web Exercises** present thought-provoking questions that allow students to construct articles and summaries for additional practice on topics relevant to that chapter while utilizing Web resources for further research. These exercises serve as additional reinforcement of the chapter's pertinent material while also allowing students to gain more familiarity with the Web.

- **A Look to the Future** sections provide insightful information about the future impact of technology and forecasts of how upcoming enhancements in the world of computing will play an important and powerful role in society.

- **Colorful Visual Summaries**, appearing at the end of every chapter, provide dynamic, graphical reviews of the important lessons featured in each chapter for additional reinforcement.

- **End-of-Chapter Review** material follows a three-level format and includes exercises that encourage students to review terms, concepts, and applications of concepts. Through matching, true/false, multiple choice, short answer completion, concept matching, and critical thinking questions, students have multiple review opportunities.

PowerWeb

PowerWeb is an exciting new online product available from McGraw-Hill. A nominally priced token grants students access through our Web site to a wealth of resources—all corresponding to computer literacy. Features include an interactive glossary; current events with quizzing, assessment, and measurement options; Web survey; links to related text content; and WWW searching capability via Northern Lights, an academic search engine. Visit the PowerWeb site at **www.dushkin.com/powerweb**.

Interactive Companion CD-ROM

This free student CD-ROM, designed for use in class, in the lab, or at home by students and professors alike, includes a collection of interactive tutorial labs on some of the most popular and difficult topics in information technology. By combining video, interactive exercises, animation, additional content, and actual "lab" tutorials, we expand the reach and scope of the textbook. The lab titles are listed below.

- Binary Numbers
- Basic Programming
- Computer Anatomy
- Disk Fragmentation
- E-mail Essentials
- Multimedia Tools
- Workplace Issues (ergonomics/privacy/security)
- Introduction to Databases
- Programming II
- Network Communications
- Purchasing Decisions
- User Interfaces
- File Organization
- Word Processing and Spreadsheets
- Internet Overview
- Photo Editing
- Presentation Techniques
- Computer Troubleshooting
- Programming Overview
- SQL Queries

As you begin each lab, take a few moments to read the **Case Study** and the **Concept Overview**. The case study introduces a real-life setting that is interwoven throughout the entire lab, providing the basis for understanding the use of the application. Also, notice the **Additional Information**, **Having Trouble?**, and **Another Method** boxes scattered throughout the book. These tips provide more information about related topics, help to get you out of trouble if you are having problems and offer suggestions on other ways to perform the same task. Finally, read the text between the steps. You will find the few minutes more it takes you is well worth the time when you are completing the practice exercises.

Many learning aids are built into the text to ensure your success with the material and to make the process of learning rewarding. The pages that follow call your attention to the key features in the text.

Each lab begins with a **Case Study**, which introduces a real-life setting that is interwoven throughout the lab, providing the basis for understanding the use of the application.

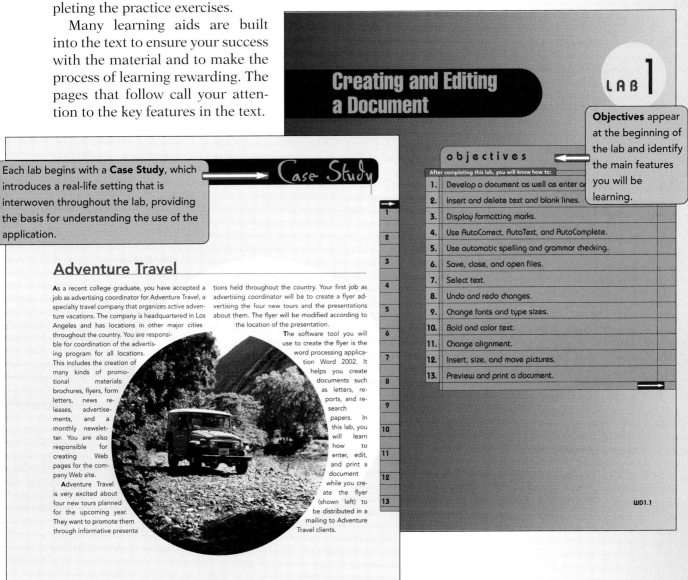

Creating and Editing a Document

LAB 1

Objectives appear at the beginning of the lab and identify the main features you will be learning.

objectives

After completing this lab, you will know how to:

1.	Develop a document as well as enter and
2.	Insert and delete text and blank lines.
3.	Display formatting marks.
4.	Use AutoCorrect, AutoText, and AutoComplete.
5.	Use automatic spelling and grammar checking.
6.	Save, close, and open files.
7.	Select text.
8.	Undo and redo changes.
9.	Change fonts and type sizes.
10.	Bold and color text.
11.	Change alignment.
12.	Insert, size, and move pictures.
13.	Preview and print a document.

WD1.1

Adventure Travel

As a recent college graduate, you have accepted a job as advertising coordinator for Adventure Travel, a specialty travel company that organizes active adventure vacations. The company is headquartered in Los Angeles and has locations in other major cities throughout the country. You are responsible for coordination of the advertising program for all locations. This includes the creation of many kinds of promotional materials: brochures, flyers, form letters, news releases, advertisements, and a monthly newsletter. You are also responsible for creating Web pages for the company Web site.

Adventure Travel is very excited about four new tours planned for the upcoming year. They want to promote them through informative presenta

tions held throughout the country. Your first job as advertising coordinator will be to create a flyer advertising the four new tours and the presentations about them. The flyer will be modified according to the location of the presentation.

The software tool you will use to create the flyer is the word processing application Word 2002. It helps you create documents such as letters, reports, and research papers. In this lab, you will learn how to enter, edit, and print a document while you create the flyer (shown left) to be distributed in a mailing to Adventure Travel clients.

Using Word Wrap

Now you will continue entering more of the paragraph. As you type, when the text gets close to the right margin, do not press ←Enter to move to the next line. Word will automatically wrap words to the next line as needed.

concept 6

Word Wrap

6 The **word wrap** feature automatically decides where to end a line and wrap text to the next line based on the margin settings. This saves time when entering text, as you do not need to press ←Enter at the end of a full line to begin a new line. The only time you need to press ←Enter is to end a paragraph, to insert blank lines, or to create a short line such as a salutation. In addition, if you change the margins or insert or delete text on a line, the program automatically readjusts the text on the line to fit within the new margin settings. Word wrap is common to all word processors.

> The **Concepts** that are common to all applications are emphasized— providing you with the confidence, knowledge, and ability to easily learn the next generation of applications.

1
● Press →.

● **Type:** about some of the earth's greatest unspoiled habitats and to find out how you can experience the adventure of a lifetime.

Your screen should be similar to Figure 1.22

word wrap continues text on next line when right margin boundary is reached

HAVING TROUBLE?
Do not worry about typing errors as you enter this text. You will correct them shortly.

> **Having Trouble?** notes help resolve potential problems as you work through each lab.

The program has wrapped the text that would overlap the beginning of the next line. You will continue the paragraph a second sentence.

1
● Click ☒ Close Window in the menu bar.

Another Method
The menu equivalent is File/Close and the keyboard shortcut is Ctrl + F4.

Your screen should be similar to Figure 1.28

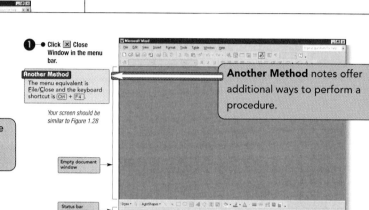

Empty document window

Status bar indicators blank

Figure 1.28

> **Another Method** notes offer additional ways to perform a procedure.

Because you did not make any changes to the document since saving it, the document window is closed immediately. If you had made additional changes, Word would ask if you wanted to save the file before closing it. This prevents the accidental closing of a file that has not been saved first. Now the Word window displays an empty document window, and the status bar indicators are blank because there are no open documents.

Opening a File

You asked your assistant to enter the remaining information in the flyer for you while you attended the meeting. Upon your return, you find a note from your assistant on your desk. The note explains that he had a little trouble entering the information and tells you that he saved the revised file as Flyer2. You want to open the file and continue working on the flyer.

Location to open files

Changes dialog box view

Figure 1.29

1
● Move to Z (second line of paragraph below tour list).

● Drag to the right until all the text including the space before the word "locations" is highlighted.

HAVING TROUBLE?
Hold down the left mouse button while moving the mouse to drag.

Additional Information
When you start dragging over a word, the entire word including the space after it is automatically selected.

Your screen should be similar to Figure 1.41

> Clear **Step-by-Step Instructions** detail how to complete a task, or series of tasks.

Announcing

New Adventure Travel Trips

Attend an Adventure Travel presentation to learn about some of the earth's greatest unspoiled habitats and find out how you can experience the adventure of a lifetime. This year we are introducing four new tours, offering you a unique opportunity to combine many different outdoor activities while exploring the world

Hike the Inca trail to Machu Picchu
Camp on safari in Tanzania
Climb Mt. Kilimanjaro
Explore the Costa Rican rain forests

Presentation d...
at 7 PM All...
The hotels ar...

text, including ending space, selected

> **Additional Information** notes offer brief asides with expanded coverage of content.

Figure 1.41

> **Screen captures** and **callouts** to features show how your screen should look at the completion of a step.

The cha...
be mo...
remov...

2
● Press Delete.

You also decide to delete the entire last sentence of the paragraph. You can quickly select a standard block of text. Standard blocks include a sentence, paragraph, page, tabular column, rectangular portion of text, or the entire document. The following table summarizes the techniques used to select standard blocks.

To Select	Procedure
Word	Double-click in the word.
Sentence	Press Ctrl and click within the sentence.
Line	Click to the left of a line when the mouse pointer is ⬦.
Multiple lines	Drag up or down to the left of a line when the mouse pointer is ⬦.
Paragraph	Triple-click on the paragraph or double-click to the left of the paragraph when the mouse pointer is ⬦.
Multiple paragraphs	Drag to the left of the paragraphs when the mouse pointer is ⬦.
Document	Triple-click or press Ctrl and click to the left of the text when the mouse pointer is ⬦.
	Use Edit/Select All or the keyboard shortcut Ctrl + Alt.

> **Tables** provide quick summaries of toolbar buttons, key terms, and procedures for specific tasks.

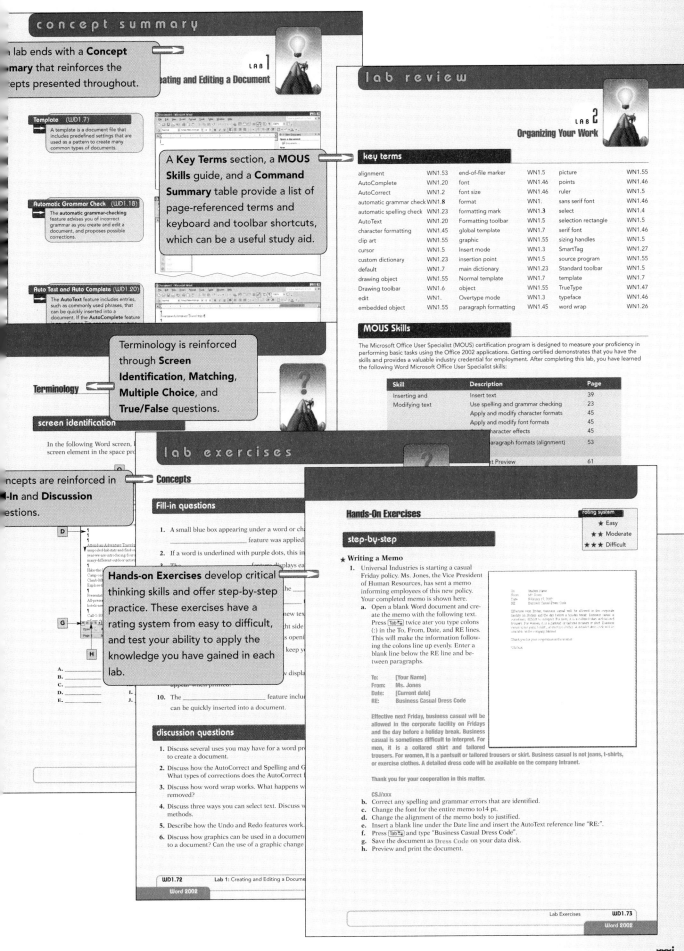

Each lab ends with a **Concept Summary** that reinforces the concepts presented throughout.

LAB 1
Creating and Editing a Document

Template (WD1.7)
A template is a document file that includes predefined settings that are used as a pattern to create many common types of documents.

A **Key Terms** section, a **MOUS Skills** guide, and a **Command Summary** table provide a list of page-referenced terms and keyboard and toolbar shortcuts, which can be a useful study aid.

Automatic Grammar Check (WD1.18)
The automatic grammar-checking feature advises you of incorrect grammar as you create and edit a document, and proposes possible corrections.

Auto Text and Auto Complete (WD1.20)
The **AutoText** feature includes entries, such as commonly used phrases, that can be quickly inserted into a document. If the **AutoComplete** feature

Terminology is reinforced through **Screen Identification, Matching, Multiple Choice**, and **True/False** questions.

Terminology

screen identification

In the following Word screen,
screen element in the space pro

LAB 2
Organizing Your Work

key terms

alignment	WN1.53	end-of-file marker	WN1.5	picture	WN1.55
AutoComplete	WN1.20	font	WN1.46	points	WN1.46
AutoCorrect	WN1.2	font size	WN1.46	ruler	WN1.5
automatic grammar check	WN1.8	format	WN1.	sans serif font	WN1.46
automatic spelling check	WN1.23	formatting mark	WN1.3	select	WN1.4
AutoText	WN1.20	Formatting toolbar	WN1.5	selection rectangle	WN1.5
character formatting	WN1.45	global template	WN1.7	serif font	WN1.46
clip art	WN1.55	graphic	WN1.55	sizing handles	WN1.5
cursor	WN1.5	Insert mode	WN1.3	SmartTag	WN1.27
custom dictionary	WN1.23	insertion point	WN1.5	source program	WN1.55
default	WN1.7	main dictionary	WN1.23	Standard toolbar	WN1.5
drawing object	WN1.55	Normal template	WN1.7	template	WN1.7
Drawing toolbar	WN1.6	object	WN1.55	TrueType	WN1.47
edit	WN1.	Overtype mode	WN1.3	typeface	WN1.46
embedded object	WN1.55	paragraph formatting	WN1.45	word wrap	WN1.26

MOUS Skills

The Microsoft Office User Specialist (MOUS) certification program is designed to measure your proficiency in performing basic tasks using the Office 2002 applications. Getting certified demonstrates that you have the skills and provides a valuable industry credential for employment. After completing this lab, you have learned the following Word Microsoft Office User Specialist skills:

Skill	Description	Page
Inserting and	Insert text	39
Modifying text	Use spelling and grammar checking	23
	Apply and modify character formats	45
	Apply and modify font formats	45
	character effects	45
	paragraph formats (alignment)	53
	Preview	61

Concepts are reinforced in
Fill-In and Discussion
questions.

Concepts

Fill-in questions

1. A small blue box appearing under a word or cha
_____ feature was applied

2. If a word is underlined with purple dots, this in

3. The _____ feature displays ea

Hands-on Exercises develop critical thinking skills and offer step-by-step practice. These exercises have a rating system from easy to difficult, and test your ability to apply the knowledge you have gained in each lab.

A. _____
B. _____
C. _____
D. _____
E. _____
I. _____
J. _____

10. The _____ feature includ
can be quickly inserted into a document.

discussion questions

1. Discuss several uses you may have for a word pr
to create a document.

2. Discuss how the AutoCorrect and Spelling and G
What types of corrections does the AutoCorrect f

3. Discuss how word wrap works. What happens w
removed?

4. Discuss three ways you can select text. Discuss w
methods.

5. Describe how the Undo and Redo features work.

6. Discuss how graphics can be used in a document
to a document? Can the use of a graphic change

Hands-On Exercises

rating system
★ Easy
★★ Moderate
★★★ Difficult

step-by-step

★ **Writing a Memo**

1. Universal Industries is starting a casual Friday policy. Ms. Jones, the Vice President of Human Resources, has sent a memo informing employees of this new policy. Your completed memo is shown here.

   a. Open a blank Word document and create the memo with the following text. Press [Tab] twice after you type colons (:) in the To, From, Date, and RE lines. This will make the information following the colons line up evenly. Enter a blank line below the RE line and between paragraphs.

   To: [Your Name]
   From: Ms. Jones
   Date: [Current date]
   RE: Business Casual Dress Code

   Effective next Friday, business casual will be allowed in the corporate facility on Fridays and the day before a holiday break. Business casual is sometimes difficult to interpret. For men, it is a collared shirt and tailored trousers. For women, it is a pantsuit or tailored trousers or skirt. Business casual is not jeans, t-shirts, or exercise clothes. A detailed dress code will be available on the company intranet.

   Thank you for your cooperation in this matter.

   CSJ/xxx

   b. Correct any spelling and grammar errors that are identified.
   c. Change the font for the entire memo to 14 pt.
   d. Change the alignment of the memo body to justified.
   e. Insert a blank line under the Date line and insert the AutoText reference line "RE:".
   f. Press [Tab] and type "Business Casual Dress Code".
   g. Save the document as Dress Code on your data disk.
   h. Preview and print the document.

Creating a Newsletter

LAB 4

objectives

After completing this lab, you will know how to:

1.	Create and enhance a WordArt object.
2.	Modify character spacing.
3.	Create horizontal rules.
4.	Collect and paste multiple items.
5.	Modify styles.
6.	Create newsletter-style columns.
7.	Use hyphenation.
8.	Create sidebars.
9.	Add borders and shading to paragraphs.
10.	Create and link text boxes.
11.	Insert symbols and drop caps.

Use the WordArt feature to create an attractive headline.

Newsletter-style columns make newsletters easy to read as well as attractive.

Text boxes, graphics, color, and borders enhance the appearance of the newsletter.

Adventure Travel Tours

The Adventure Travel Tours manager is very pleased with the research you did on Tanzania and Peru. The company plans to feature tours to these areas in the next few months and wants to provide much of the information you gathered to clients. A good way to present this type of information is through a monthly newsletter. Newsletters allow businesses to present timely information. Unlike a flyer, whose purpose is to quickly attract attention and provide a small amount of information, a newsletter is designed to provide detailed information. Because newsletters are generally several pages long, you have enough space to paint a picture and tell a story.

After discussing the plans for the upcoming newsletters with the Adventure Travel Tours manager, you have decided to make the African safari in Tanzania the focus of the next month's newsletter. In addition to using several topics from the material in the report on Tanzania, the newsletter will include various tips and facts about the country. You will also include some information about other upcoming tours and events.

In a newsletter, information must be easy to read and, more important, visually appealing. In this lab, you will use the WordArt and desktop publishing tools in Word 2002 to create the newsletter (shown left).

© Corbis

concept overview

The following concepts will be introduced in this lab:

1 **WordArt** WordArt is used to enhance your documents by changing the shape of text and adding special effects such as 3-D and shadows.

2 **Special Drawing Effects** Special drawing effects, such as shadows and 3-D effects, can be easily added to text and graphics, including WordArt objects, to enhance the appearance of your document.

3 **Collecting and Pasting** Collecting and pasting is the capability of the program to store multiple copied items in the Office Clipboard and then paste one or more of them into another document.

4 **Newsletter-Style Columns** Newsletter-style columns display text so that it flows from the bottom of one column to the top of the next.

5 **Hyphenation** The hyphenation feature inserts hyphens in long words that fall at the end of a line, splitting the word between lines.

6 **Text Box** A text box is a graphic object that is a container for text or graphics.

Creating a Newsletter Headline

A newsletter commonly consists of two basic parts: the headline and the body (see the following figure). The headline, also called the nameplate or banner, is the top portion of the newsletter. It generally contains the name, issue or volume number, and publication date. It may also include a company logo, a line that announces the main subject or article included in the newsletter, and a brief table of contents. The body, which is the text of the newsletter, is commonly displayed in a two- or three-column format. Article headings often include subheadings that help organize the newsletter topics. The headline is often visually separated from the body by horizontal lines, called rules. Your sample newsletter will include many of these features.

The first thing you want to do is to create a headline for the newsletter. The headline will display the name of the newsletter, The Adventure Traveler, the date of publication, and the volume number.

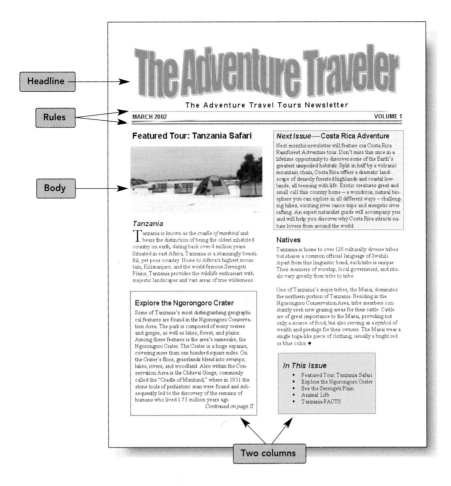

The text for the headline has already been entered for you.

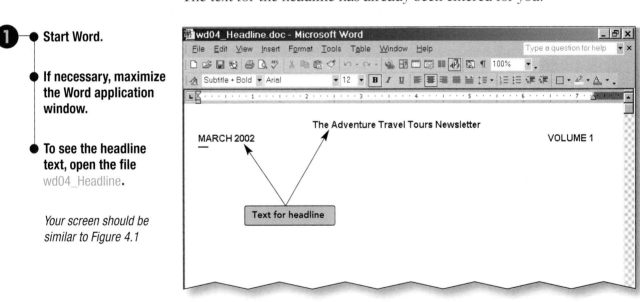

1

● **Start Word.**

● **If necessary, maximize the Word application window.**

● **To see the headline text, open the file** wd04_Headline.

Your screen should be similar to Figure 4.1

Figure 4.1

Using WordArt

You need to add the newsletter name at the top of the page headline. You will use the WordArt feature to make this name unique and more interesting.

WordArt

1 **WordArt** is used to enhance your documents by changing the shape of text and adding special effects such as 3-D and shadows. You can also rotate, flip, and skew WordArt text. The text that is added to the document using WordArt is a graphic object that can be edited, sized, or moved to any location in the document. In addition, it can be changed using the Drawing toolbar buttons.

You can use WordArt to add a special touch to your documents. However, you should limit its use to headlines in a newsletter or to a single element in a flyer. You want the WordArt to capture the reader's attention. Here are some examples of WordArt.

You will create a WordArt object consisting of the newsletter name for the headline. The Drawing toolbar is used to access the WordArt feature.

1 If necessary, display the Drawing toolbar.

● Click ◀ Insert WordArt.

Your screen should be similar to Figure 4.2

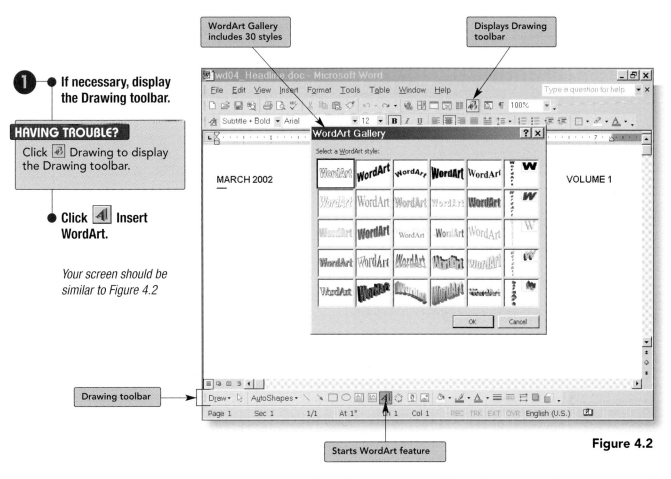

WordArt Gallery includes 30 styles

Displays Drawing toolbar

Drawing toolbar

Starts WordArt feature

Figure 4.2

In the WordArt Gallery dialog box, you first select one of the 30 styles or designs of WordArt you want to use for the headline. The styles consist of a combination of fonts, colors, and shapes and are just a starting point. As you will soon see, you can alter the appearance of the style by selecting a different color or shape, and by adding special effects.

2 ● Select **WordArt** (third row, second column).

● Click OK.

Your screen should be similar to Figure 4.3

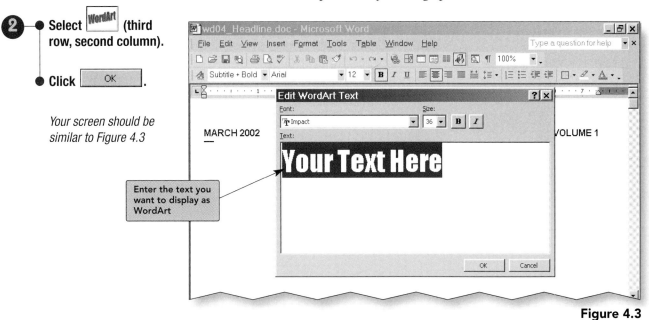

Enter the text you want to display as WordArt

Figure 4.3

Next, in the Edit WordArt Text dialog box, you need to replace the sample text with the text you want displayed using the selected WordArt design.

③ ● **Type** The Adventure
Traveler.

● **Click** [OK] .

*Your screen should be
similar to Figure 4.4*

Text you entered
appears in selected
WordArt style →

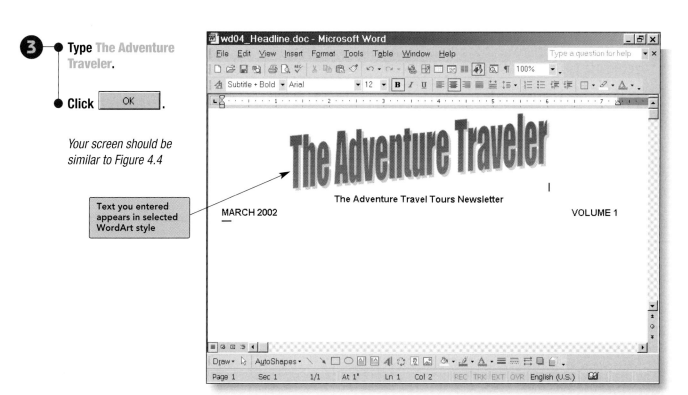

Figure 4.4

Another Method

To review these features,
refer to Concept 4: Text
Wrapping, in Lab 3.

Now the words you entered are displayed in the selected WordArt style in the document. When a WordArt object is first inserted in the document, it has a default wrapping style of In Line with Text, assuming the formatting of the line into which it was inserted, in this case, centered.

Changing the WordArt Shape and Size

Now that you can see how the selected style looks in the document, you want to change the WordArt shape to make it more interesting. You can select from 40 different shapes provided in the WordArt palette and apply the shape to the selected object.

Whenever a WordArt object is selected, the WordArt toolbar is displayed. The WordArt toolbar buttons (identified below) are used to modify the WordArt.

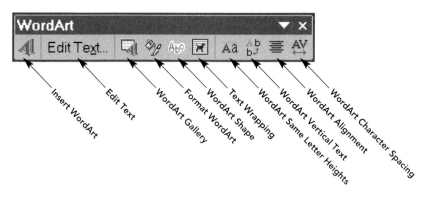

1 ● Select the WordArt
object.

● Click [Abc] WordArt
Shape.

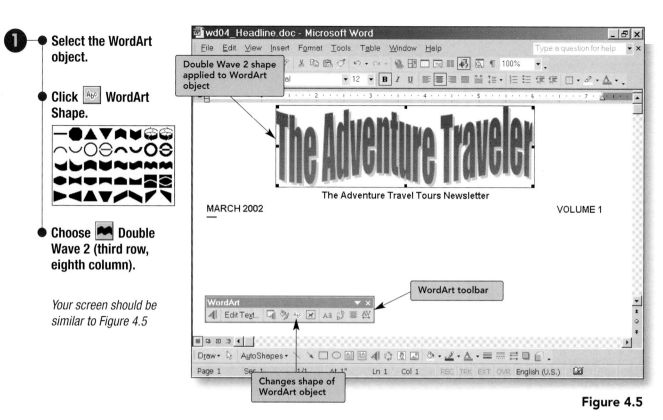

● Choose [●] Double
Wave 2 (third row,
eighth column).

*Your screen should be
similar to Figure 4.5*

Figure 4.5

The selected shape is applied to the WordArt object. You also want the
WordArt object to extend the full width of the text space between the margins. To do this you will increase its width.

2 ● Drag the middle sizing
handle of the WordArt
shape to increase the
width as shown in
Figure 4.6.

Another Method

You can also adjust the size
to exact measurements using
Format/WordArt/Size and
entering values to specify an
exact height and width.

*Your screen should be
similar to Figure 4.6*

Figure 4.6

The WordArt is now the full text width of the page.

Changing the WordArt Fill and Line Color

Next you want to change the color of the WordArt characters to match the colors used in the company logo. You can easily do this using some of the special effects options that can be applied to graphic objects.

concept 2

Special Drawing Effects

2 Special drawing effects, such as shadows and 3-D effects, can easily be added to text and graphics, including WordArt objects, to enhance the appearance of your document. When you draw an object, a border automatically appears around it. You can change the thickness and color of the border. You also can fill a drawing object with a solid color, a gradient color, texture, or a picture. Adding shadows or 3-D effects gives depth to an object.

Use these effects in moderation. You want to capture the reader's interest with your graphics but not detract from your message.

1 ● Click  Format WordArt.

● Open the Colors and Lines tab.

Another Method

The menu equivalent is Format/WordArt/Colors and Lines.

Your screen should be similar to Figure 4.7

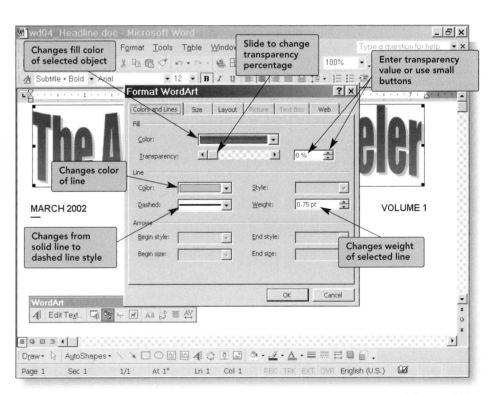

Figure 4.7

The default color and line settings for the selected WordArt design style are a purple gradient fill color set to 0 percent transparency with a light purple line color. When set, the transparency option makes the selected fill color less opaque, allowing the shadow color to bleed through. When set to zero, the color is solid or opaque. You want to use the corporate colors of green and blue in your newsletter. You will also set the transparency to 30 percent.

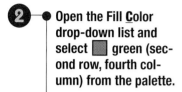

- Open the Fill **C**olor drop-down list and select ■ green (second row, fourth column) from the palette.

- Set the transparency to 30%.

Additional Information

You can type the transparency percentage in the text box, use the scroll buttons to increase/decrease the percentage or drag the slider to change the percentage. The result appears in the fill color box.

- Open the Line C**o**lor palette and select Light Turquoise (fifth row, fifth column).

- Click [OK].

Your screen should be similar to Figure 4.8

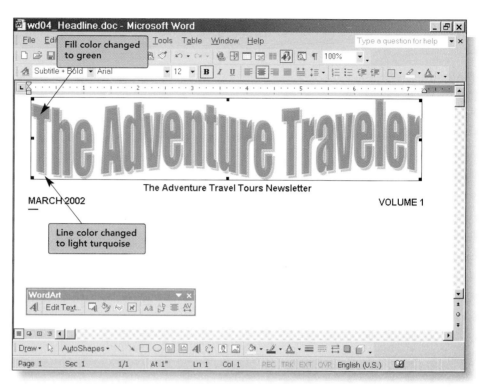

Figure 4.8

The selected fill and line colors are applied to the WordArt shape.

Modifying Character Spacing

Finally, you want to change the spacing of the characters in the WordArt object to be very close together. The character spacing for WordArt objects can be changed from the normal spacing (set at 100 percent) to closer together or wider apart. A larger percent value increases the spacing and a smaller percent value decreases the spacing. In addition, if the **kerning** setting is on, the spacing between particular pairs of letters it may be altered to improve the appearance of the text. You want to condense the spacing between characters as much as possible.

1 ● Click [AV] **WordArt Character Spacing.**

	Very Tight
	Tight
✓	Normal
	Loose
	Very Loose
	Custom: 100 %
✓	Kern Character Pairs

Additional Information
You can also specify a custom amount of spacing by entering a percent value in the Custom option.

2 ● **Choose Very Tight.**

Your screen should be similar to Figure 4.9

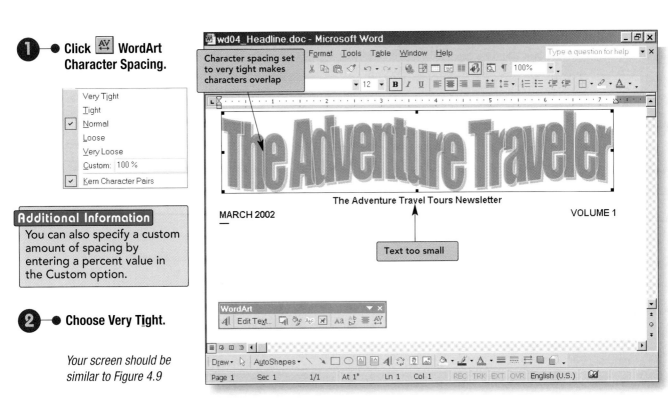

Figure 4.9

Now that the WordArt object is complete, the headline subtitle below it looks very small. You will make the font size larger and stretch the text to expand the character spacing.

3 ● **Select the subtitle line of text below the newsletter title.**

● **Choose Format/Font.**

● **Increase the point size to 14.**

● **Open the Character Spacing tab.**

Your screen should be similar to Figure 4.10

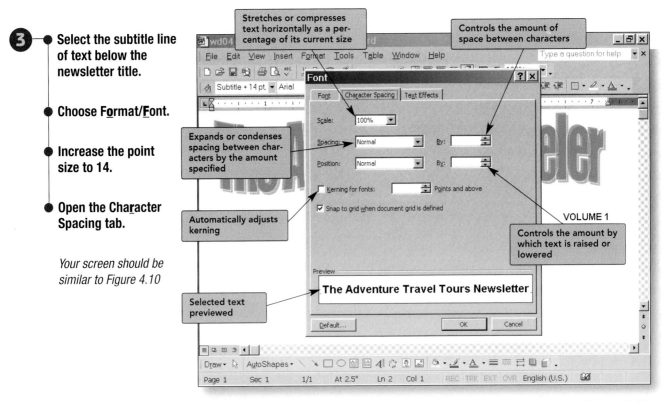

Figure 4.10

The Character Spacing tab is used to expand or condense the space between characters by a specified amount. You can also kern characters above a specified point size. Expanding or condensing characters changes the space by an equal amount regardless of the font design. You can also specify the amount of space by which you want to expand or condense the spacing. The default setting is 1 point.

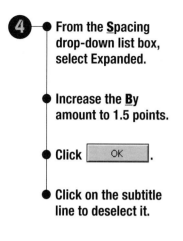

4 ● From the **S**pacing drop-down list box, select Expanded.

● Increase the **B**y amount to 1.5 points.

● Click [OK].

● Click on the subtitle line to deselect it.

Your screen should be similar to Figure 4.11

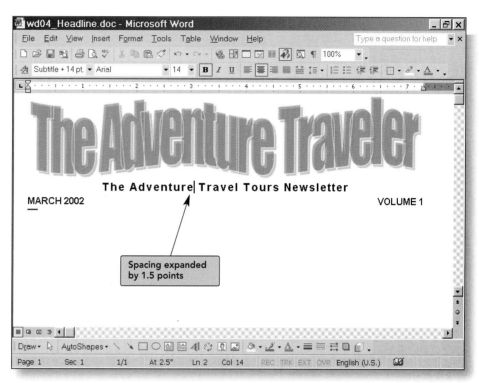

Figure 4.11

The spacing between characters has increased, making the headline subtitle more prominent.

Creating Horizontal Rules

Next you want the newsletter's issue identification information, which in this newsletter is the publication date and issue number, to be displayed between two horizontal lines or rules. Rules can be added to any side of a selected paragraph or object.

● Move to anywhere within the line of text containing the publication date and issue number.

● Choose Format/Borders and Shading.

● Open the Borders tab if necessary.

Your screen should be similar to Figure 4.12

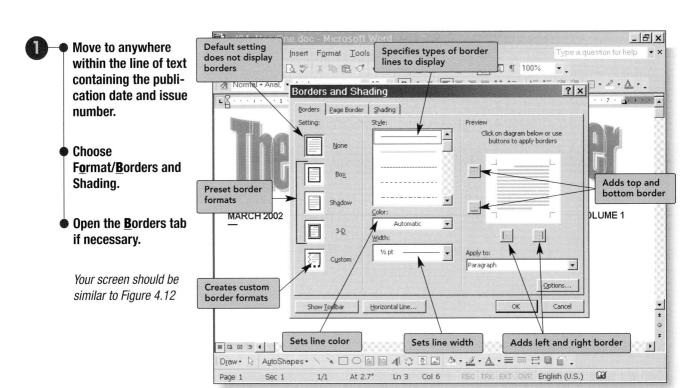

Figure 4.12

From the Borders and Shading dialog box, you can specify the style, color, weight, and location of the border. You can apply either a preset box border by selecting from the Settings options, or a custom border. You want to create a custom border that will display a 1.5-point single-line border in blue above the text, and a 3-point double-line border in blue below the text. As you specify the line settings, the Preview area will reflect your selections.

2

● Click 🔲 Custom.

Another Method

You can also specify border settings using the Tables and Borders toolbar.

● From the **W**idth drop-down list box, select 1½ pt.

● Open the **C**olor palette and select Light Blue (third row, sixth column).

● Click 🔲 Top Border.

The dialog box on your screen should be similar to Figure 4.13

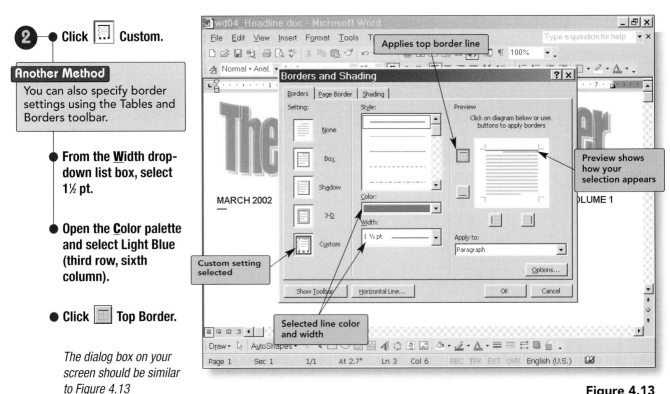

Figure 4.13

The Preview area of the dialog box shows how a top border line using the settings you specified will appear. Next you will add a double-line bottom border.

3
- From the Style list box, select ═════.

- From the Width drop-down list, select 3 pt.

- From the Color drop-down list, select Light Blue.

- Click ▦ Bottom Border.

HAVING TROUBLE?
Use the None option to remove all border lines, or remove individual lines by selecting the border location again.

- Click ▢ OK ▢ .

- Save the headline as Newsletter Headline.

Your screen should be similar to Figure 4.14

Another Method
You can also create a single horizontal line by typing ⊡ three times and pressing ⟵Enter and a double line by typing ⊡ three times and pressing ⟵Enter.

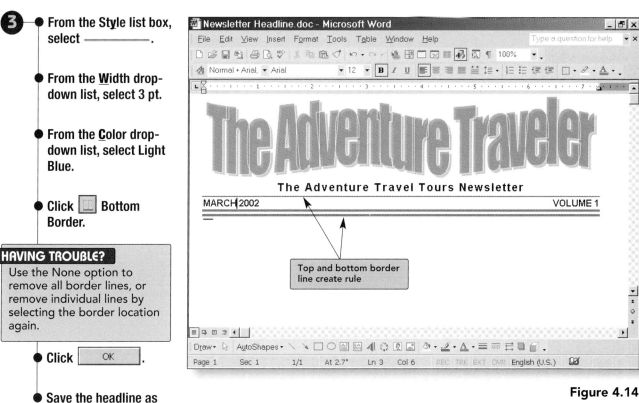

The Adventure Travel Tours Newsletter

MARCH 2002   VOLUME 1

Top and bottom border line create rule

Figure 4.14

The horizontal lines extend between the margins above and below the text in the color, style, and point size you specified. The newsletter headline is now complete and can be used with any newsletter.

Assembling the Newsletter from a Variety of Sources

Now you are ready to copy the headline into the document containing the text for the lead article of the newsletter. Following your manager's suggestions, you modified the report you wrote about Tanzania and Costa Rica by shortening the topic coverage and dividing the topics into several brief articles to be used in this and future newsletters. You saved the articles on different topics in separate files. In this month's newsletter, you will use the articles about the African Safari. You also have several other short topics to include in this month's newsletter saved in separate files. You will open files containing the main African safari articles and the other articles.

1
● **Open the file**
wd04_Newsletter
Articles.

● **If necessary, change
the view to Print
Layout and the zoom
to Page Width.**

● **Scroll through the text
to view the contents of
the document.**

● **Open the files** wd04_Be
an Adventure Traveler,
wd04_Costa Rica
Adventure, **and**
wd04_Tanzania Facts.

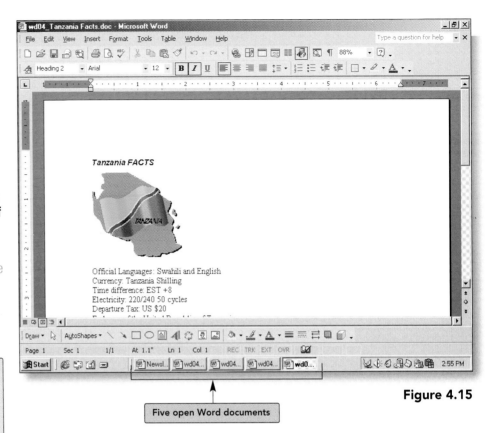

Five open Word documents

Figure 4.15

*Your screen should be
similar to Figure 4.15*

Using the Office Clipboard

You now have five open documents. You want to copy the newsletter banner into the document containing the African Safari article. In addition, you want to copy the information from the other three documents, Tanzania Facts, Costa Rica Adventure, and Be an Adventure Traveler, into this same file containing the lead article. You can copy and paste the selections one after the other, or you can use the Office Clipboard to collect multiple items and paste them into the document as needed.

concept 3

Collecting and Pasting

3 **Collecting and pasting** is the capability of the program to store multiple copied items in the Office Clipboard and then paste one or more of them into another document. For example, you could copy a chart from Excel, then switch to Word and copy a paragraph, then switch to PowerPoint and paste the two stored items into a slide in one easy step. This saves you from having to switch back and forth between documents and applications.

The Office Clipboard and the System Clipboard are similar but separate features. The major difference is that the Office Clipboard can hold up to 24 items whereas the System Clipboard holds only a single item. The last item you copy to the Office Clipboard is always copied to the System Clipboard. When you use the Office Clipboard, you can select the items in any order to paste from any of the items stored.

The Office Clipboard is available for all Office 2002 applications and non-Office programs if the Cut, Copy, and Paste commands are available. You can copy from any program that provides copy and cut capabilities, but you can only paste into Word, Excel, Access, PowerPoint, and Outlook.

Copying Multiple Objects to the Office Clipboard

First you will copy the headline to the Office Clipboard.

1 ● **Switch to the** wd04_ Newsletter Headline **document window**

● **Choose** **E**dit/Office Clip**b**oard.

● **If necessary, click** Clear All **to clear the contents of the Clipboard.**

● **Choose** **E**dit/Select **A**ll **to select the entire headline.**

● **Click** Copy.

Another Method

You can also use Ctrl + A to select the entire document and Ctrl + C to copy the selection to the Clipboard.

Your screen should be similar to Figure 4.16

Additional Information

The Office Clipboard is automatically activated if you copy or cut two different items consecutively in the same program; copy one item, paste the item, and then copy another item in the same program; or copy one item twice in succession.

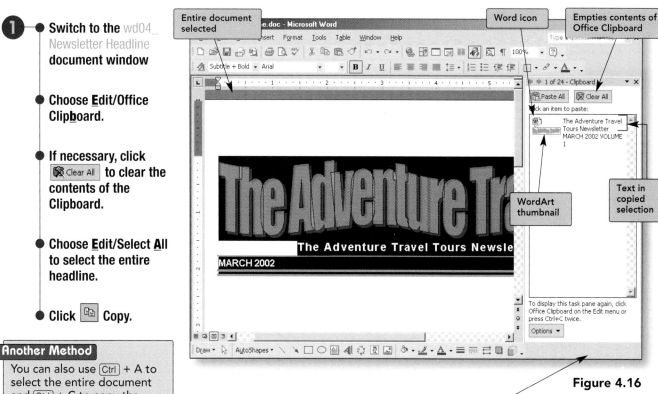

Figure 4.16

The ⊞ Office Clipboard icon appears in the system taskbar to show that the Clipboard is active. It also briefly displays a ScreenTip indicating that 1 out of a possible 24 items was collected as the selection is copied.

📋 1 of 24 - Clipboard

The Clipboard task pane displays a Word icon representing the copied item, a thumbnail of the WordArt, and the first few words in the selection.

Next you will copy the contents of the Be an Adventure Traveler and Tanzania Facts documents into the Office Clipboard. If you open the Office Clipboard in the task pane in one program or document, it does not automatically appear when you switch to another program or document. However, it is still active and will continue to store copied items.

2 ● **Switch to the** wd04_ Be an Adventure Traveler **document.**

● **Select the entire file.**

● **Click** 📋 **Copy.**

● **Double-click** 📋 **Clipboard in the system taskbar.**

Your screen should be similar to Figure 4.17

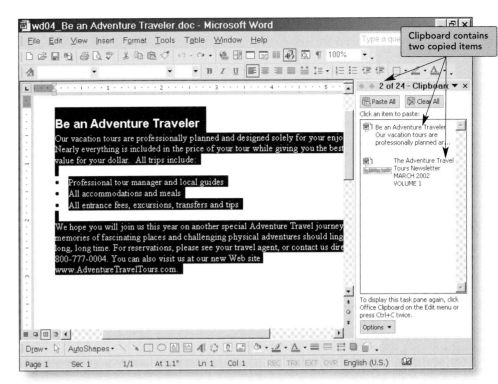

Figure 4.17

The second copied item was added to the Office Clipboard. The most recently added item is displayed at the top of the list.

3 ● **In a similar manner, copy the entire contents of the** wd04_ Tanzania Facts **and** wd04_Costa Rica Adventure **files to the Office Clipboard.**

● **Display the Office Clipboard task pane.**

Your screen should be similar to Figure 4.18

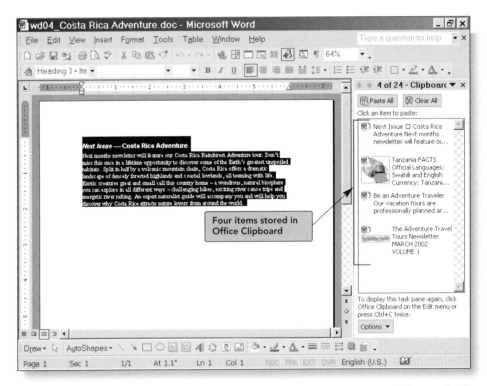

Figure 4.18

The Office Clipboard now contains four Word document icons.

Pasting Multiple Objects from the Office Clipboard

Now you are ready to paste the items into the main article document. You want to paste the headline first.

- **Switch to the** wd04_Newsletter Articles **document.**

- **If necessary, move to the beginning of the Featured Tour heading at the top of the document.**

- **Display the Office Clipboard task pane.**

- **Click on the newsletter headline item to paste it into the top of the document.**

Another Method

You could also select **P**aste from the item's shortcut menu.

Your screen should be similar to Figure 4.19

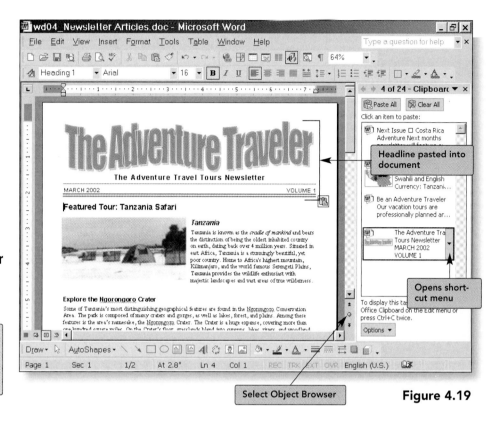

Figure 4.19

Another Method

You can also click 🔲 Select Object Browser and select the element to browse by from the menu.

Next you want to insert the information from the Be an Adventure Traveler file before the article about Animal Life. A quick way to move to specific elements in a document is to use **E**dit/**G**o To (or Ctrl + G), select the object type you want to go to (in this case Heading) and click Next or Previous to move to the next or previous occurrence.

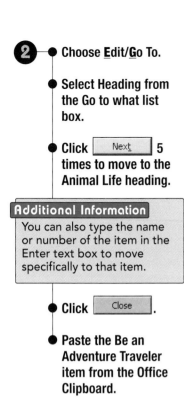

② ● Choose **E**dit/**G**o To.

● Select **Heading** from the Go to what list box.

● Click `Next` 5 times to move to the **Animal Life** heading.

Additional Information

You can also type the name or number of the item in the Enter text box to move specifically to that item.

● Click `Close`.

● Paste the **Be an Adventure Traveler** item from the Office Clipboard.

Your screen should be similar to Figure 4.20

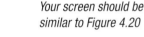

Second pasted item

Additional Information

The Office Clipboard Paste All option inserts the contents of all copied items in the order in which they were added to the Office Clipboard.

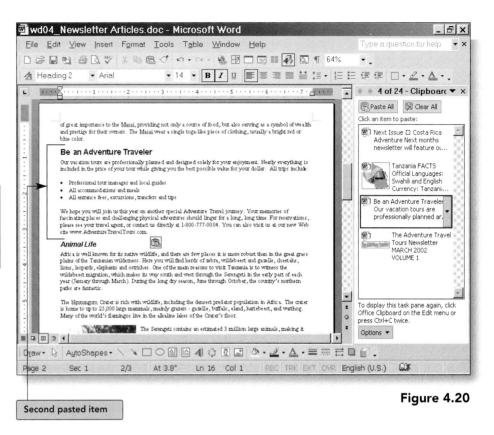

Figure 4.20

The text for the newsletter already fills almost two pages and you still have more information to add to the document. To make the articles fit into the two-page newsletter format better, you decide to reduce the font to 11 points.

Modifying Styles

Because you plan to add more articles to this document, you will make the font change by modifying the Normal style for this document. Then, as new information is added, it will automatically be formatted using the settings associated with the modified style.

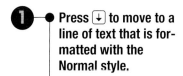

1 ● Press ↓ to move to a line of text that is formatted with the Normal style.

HAVING TROUBLE?
Normal will appear in the Style toolbar button.

● Click 🔏 Styles and Formatting.

Another Method
The menu equivalent is Format/Styles and Formatting.

● Point to the Normal style name in the Styles and Formatting task pane.

Your screen should be similar to Figure 4.21

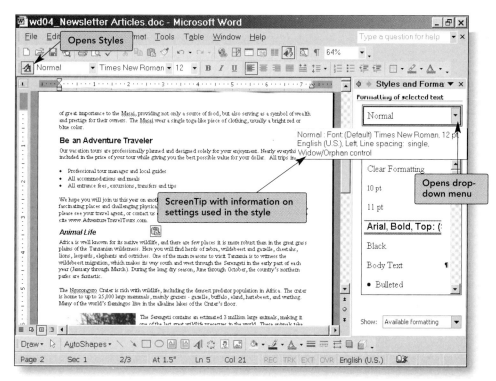

Figure 4.21

The Formatting of Selected Text box shows that the text of the current selection has the Normal style applied, and a ScreenTip displays information about the format settings used in the style.

2 ● Open the Formatting of Selected Text drop-down menu.

● Choose **M**odify.

Your screen should be similar to Figure 4.22

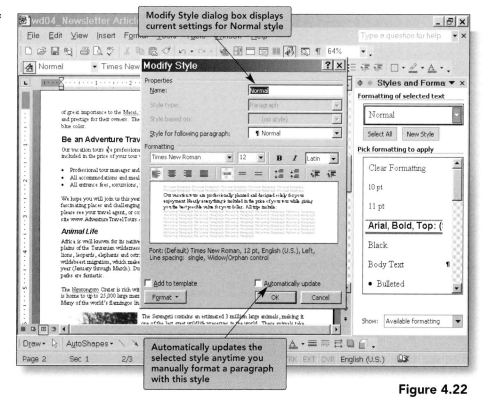

Figure 4.22

The current settings for the selected style are displayed in the Modify Style dialog box. After you modify the style, you can select Add to Template to add the modified style to the template used to create the document, which in this case is Normal. If you do not select this option, the Normal style is changed for the current document only. Selecting the Automatically Update option will automatically update the selected style anytime you manually format a paragraph with this style. It then applies the updated style to the entire document. You want to change the font size to 11 points for the current document only.

3 ● Select 11 from the size drop-down list box.

● Click [OK].

Your screen should be similar to Figure 4.23

New Normal style applied

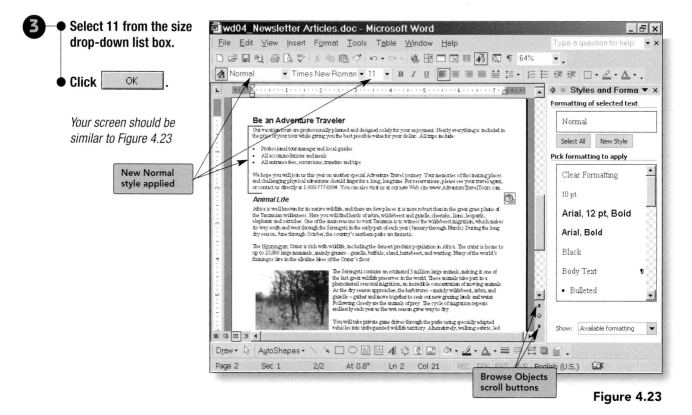

Browse Objects scroll buttons

Figure 4.23

The modified Normal style is applied to all paragraphs in the document that are formatted with the Normal style. Now you will insert the Costa Rica Adventure text above the Natives section in the document. Because you last specified Heading as the element to go to, you can quickly scroll the document by headings using the Browse Objects scroll buttons. These buttons scroll based on the last selected element type.

4 ● Click 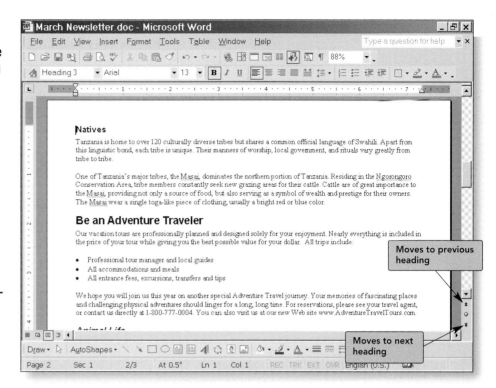 3 times (in the scroll bar) to move to the Natives heading on page 1.

● Display the Office Clipboard task pane.

● Paste the Next Issue - Costa Rica Adventure item from the Office Clipboard.

● Close the Office Clipboard task pane.

● Save the revised document as March Newsletter.

Your screen should be similar to Figure 4.24

Figure 4.24

The article content is pasted into the document and automatically converted to the new modified Normal style associated with this document.

Creating Newsletter-Style Columns

Now you are ready to format the newsletter articles so that they will be displayed in newsletter-style columns.

concept 4

Newsletter-Style Columns

4 **Newsletter-style columns** display text so that it flows from the bottom of one column to the top of the next. The Normal template has one column the full width of the margins, so the text appears to flow continuously from one page to the next. On occasion, the layout for your document may call for two or more columns on a page.

Newspapers, magazines, and newsletters are common applications for newsletter-style columns.

The optimum column width for reading comfort is 4.5 inches. In a newsletter, narrow columns help the reader read the articles more quickly, and you as the writer can fit information on a page in a visually pleasing arrangement. Note, however, that if you use more than four columns on an 8½-by-11-inch page, the columns will be too narrow and the page will look messy.

The Columns command on the Format menu is used to set the text format of a document to columns. With the Columns feature, you can change the text in the entire document to the new format. To affect only a portion of a document, you must divide the document into sections. Because you do not want the headline to appear in column format, you will create a section break below the headline.

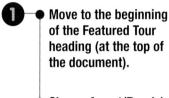

● **Move to the beginning of the Featured Tour heading (at the top of the document).**

● **Choose Insert/Break/Continuous.**

● **Click** OK **.**

HAVING TROUBLE?
Refer to Lab 3, Concept 2, to review section breaks.

Your screen should be similar to Figure 4.25

Section 2 of document

Figure 4.25

Although section break lines do not display in Print Layout view unless ¶ Show/Hide is selected, the status bar shows that the insertion point is positioned in section 2. The new section continues to the end of the document unless another section break is inserted.

Applying a Two-Column Layout

You want the newsletter to have two columns of text on the first page.

1 ● **Choose F**o**rmat/**
  Co**lumns.**

● **Select T**w**o from the**
  Presets area.

*Your screen should be
similar to Figure 4.26*

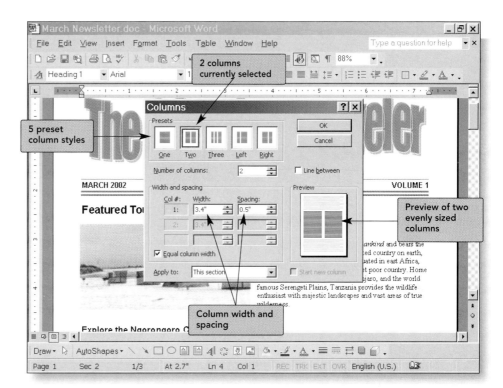

Figure 4.26

Using the Presets area, you can select up to three evenly spaced columns or
two unevenly spaced columns. If none of the preset styles is appropriate,
you can enter a number in the Number of Columns text box to create up to
14 columns.

The Number of Columns text box displays 2 as the selected number of
columns. Based on the number of columns you specify and your document's
left and right margin settings, Word automatically calculates the size of the
columns and the spacing between them. Using the default setting, the two
columns will be 3.4 inches wide, separated by 0.5 inch. The Preview box
shows how text will appear on the page using the specified column settings.

2 ● Click [OK].

● Scroll to the bottom of the document to see the entire newsletter, then return to the top of the document.

Your screen should be similar to Figure 4.27

2 evenly sized columns

Figure 4.27

The text is displayed as two evenly sized newsletter-style columns, with 0.5 inch of space between. The text at the bottom of the first column continues at the top of the second column. The column markers on the horizontal ruler show the size and spacing of each column.

Applying a Three-Column Layout

Next you would like the second page of the newsletter to be in three-column format. You want a second page to begin with the advertisement "Be an Adventure Traveler." To force a new page and section, you will insert a New Page section break. Then you will format the section to three columns. Another way to specify columns is to use the 🔳 Columns button on the Standard toolbar. It allows you to specify up to six columns using the default column definitions.

1 ● Move to the Be an Adventure Traveler heading.

● Choose **I**nsert/**B**reak/**N**ext Page/[OK].

● Click  Columns.

● Click on the third column from the left.

3 Columns

● Scroll the document to see the page in three-column layout.

Your screen should be similar to Figure 4.28

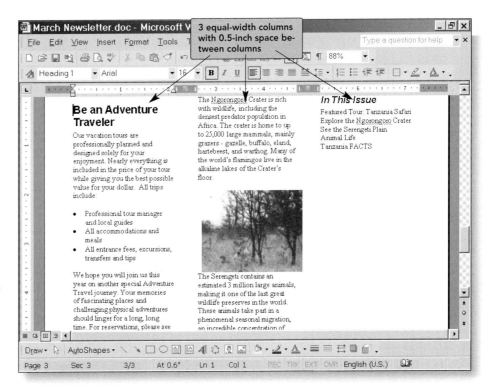

3 equal-width columns with 0.5-inch space between columns

Figure 4.28

Sizing Columns

The default width of 0.5 inch between the columns was appropriate for two columns, but seems too wide for three columns. You want to reduce the space between columns to 0.3 inch and maintain equal column widths.

1 ● Choose **F**ormat/**C**olumns.

● In the Width and Spacing section of the dialog box, reduce the **S**pacing to 0.3 for column 1.

● Select **E**qual Column Width.

● Click [OK].

Another Method

You can also drag the column marker in the ruler to adjust the column size and spacing between columns.

Your screen should be similar to Figure 4.29.

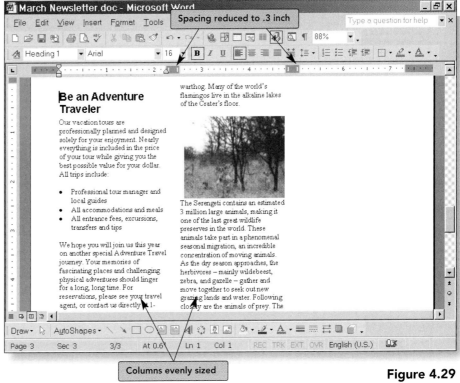

Spacing reduced to .3 inch

Columns evenly sized

Figure 4.29

The columns are equally sized with 0.3 inch between them. Because the columns are wider, there are only 2 full columns of text.

Using Hyphenation

Now that the layout is in columns, you notice that the lines have very un-even right margins. On lines of text where there are several short words, wrapping the text to the next line is not a problem. However, when long words are wrapped to the next line, a large gap is left on the previous line. To help solve this problem you will hyphenate the document.

concept 5

Hyphenation

5 The **hyphenation** feature inserts hyphens in long words that fall at the end of a line, splitting the word between lines. Because Word automatically moves long words that fall at the end of a line to the beginning of the next line, uneven right margins or large gaps of white space commonly occur in a document.

Using hyphenation reduces the amount of white space and makes line lengths more even, thereby improving the appearance of a document. The program inserts **optional hyphens**, which break the word only if it appears at the end of a line. Then, as you edit the document, the hyphenation is adjusted appropriately.

1 ● **Choose Tools/Language/ Hyphenation.**

Your screen should be similar to Figure 4.30

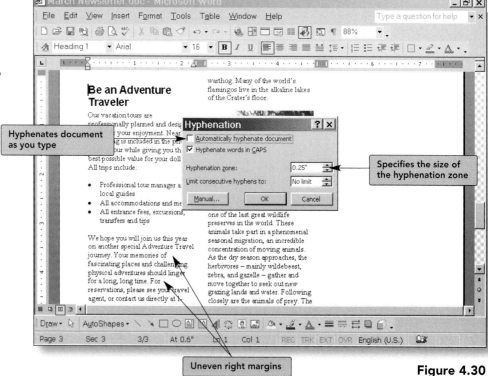

Figure 4.30

From the Hyphenation dialog box you can select the Automatically Hyphenate Document option, which lets Word set hyphenation for the entire document. You can also specify the size of the **hyphenation zone**, an unmarked space along the right margin that controls the amount of white space in addition to the margin that Word will allow at the end of a line. Making the hyphenation zone narrower (a smaller number) reduces the unevenness of lines by hyphenating more words, while making the zone wider (a larger number) hyphenates fewer words. Finally, you can specify whether words appearing in all capital letters should be hyphenated.

2 ● Select **A**utomatically Hyphenate Document.

● If necessary, specify a hyphenation zone setting of 0.25 inch.

● Click [OK].

● Save the document again.

Your screen should be similar to Figure 4.31

HAVING TROUBLE?

Depending on your printer, different words may be hyphenated.

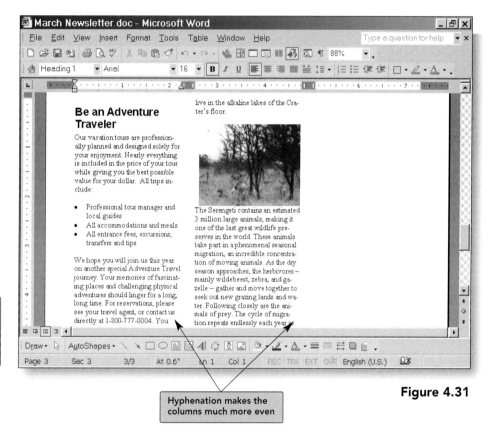

Hyphenation makes the columns much more even

Figure 4.31

Word has examined each line and determined where it is possible to hyphenate a word. Hyphenating the newsletter has made the column margins much less uneven. Word generally proposes accurate hyphenation. If you do not agree with how a word is hyphenated after it has been done, you can select the word and hyphenate it manually.

Creating Sidebars

You would like to set the Next Issue—Costa Rica Adventure article on the first page of the newsletter apart from the rest of the newsletter articles by adding a border and shading to the paragraph. An article you want to keep separate from other articles or information, and that highlights an article next to it, is called a **sidebar**. You can use a sidebar for such things as a list of contributors; addresses or contact information; a small self-contained story; a preview of the next issue; or a calendar or schedule.

Adding Borders and Shading to Paragraphs

First you will add the border around the article. To do this, you first select the text you want to include in the sidebar. When text is formatted into columns, you can use the mouse to move and select text just as in a document formatted with a single column. When you drag to select text in column layout, however, the selection moves from the bottom of one column to the top of the next.

1

● **Move to the Next Issue —Costa Rica Adventure heading (on the first page).**

● **Select the text from the heading to the end of the paragraph.**

● **Open the** ▣▾ **Border drop-down menu (on the Formatting toolbar).**

● **Choose** ▣ **Outside Border.**

Another Method

The menu equivalent is Format/Borders and Shading/Borders/Box.

Your screen should be similar to Figure 4.32

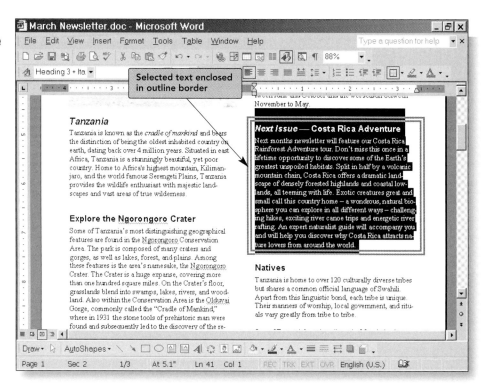

Figure 4.32

The last-used border style, in this case a double 3 pt weight blue line, surrounds the selection. You want to change the border style to a single line. Then, to make the sidebar stand out even more, you will add a shading color to the box.

2 • Choose Format/**B**orders and Shading/**B**orders.

• Change the line style to the single-line style in blue and 1½ pt. weight.

• Open the **S**hading tab.

Your screen should be similar to Figure 4.33

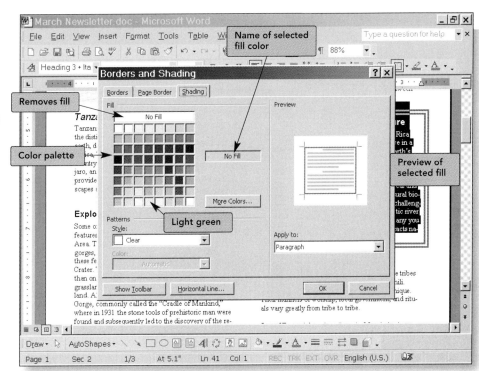

Figure 4.33

The Shading tab includes a color palette of fill colors. Selecting No Fill removes a previously selected fill. The name of the selected color appears in the text box to the right of the palette, and the preview area shows how the selection will appear. The More Colors option opens another dialog box of Standard and Custom colors from which you can select. The Apply To option allows you to apply the color to the paragraph or selected text. The default is to apply it to the paragraph containing the insertion point. If a selection is made, the color is applied to the entire selection.

3 • Select light green (last row, fourth column).

• Click 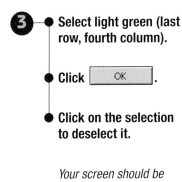 OK .

• Click on the selection to deselect it.

Your screen should be similar to Figure 4.34

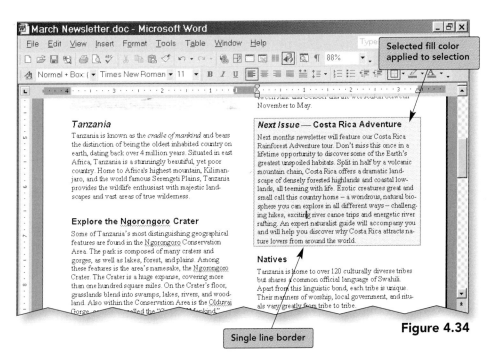

Figure 4.34

You also want to add the same border and shading to the Be an Adventure Traveler article on the third page. You can easily repeat the previous formatting by using the Repeat command.

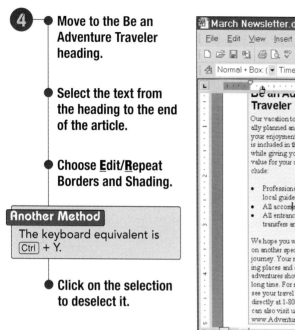

4
- Move to the Be an Adventure Traveler heading.

- Select the text from the heading to the end of the article.

- Choose **E**dit/**R**epeat Borders and Shading.

Another Method

The keyboard equivalent is Ctrl + Y.

- Click on the selection to deselect it.

Your screen should be similar to Figure 4.35

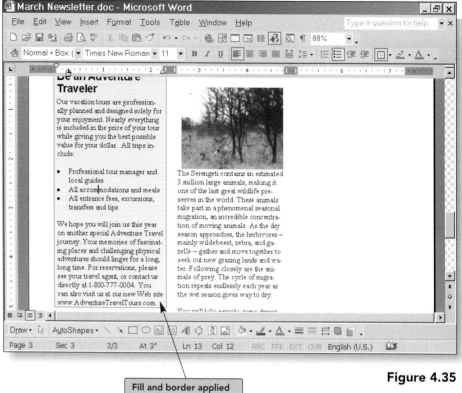

Fill and border applied

Figure 4.35

Creating Text Boxes

Next you want to add the information about the Tanzania Facts to the newsletter. Again, you would like to make this information stand out by displaying it as a sidebar. Another way to display information as a sidebar is to insert it in a text box.

Text Box

6 A **text box** is a graphic object that is a container for text or graphics. Because text boxes are graphic objects, you can place them on the page as you would a picture or WordArt, and move and resize them. You can also add drawing features to text boxes to enhance their appearance.

When using newsletter-style columns, the text scrolls from the bottom of one column to the top of the next. If you want your newsletter to have specific objects in fixed places on the page, it is best to use text boxes and link those that need to flow from one page to the next. When you link text boxes together, the large articles will automatically flow into the correct text boxes on the other pages in the newsletter. Text that is contained in a single text box or linked text boxes is called a **story**.

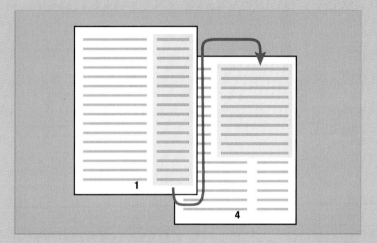

Generally, the first page of a newsletter should contain the beginnings of a main article and a secondary article, a sidebar with the newsletter contents, and perhaps a quote pulled from the article to capture the interest of someone just skimming the first page. The remainders of the articles are usually found on another page. All these elements can be entered into fixed text boxes in a template that you can use over and over so your newsletter looks the same every issue.

You will create a text box on the last page to contain the information about Tanzania and a map of the country.

1 ● **Display the Office Clipboard task pane.**

● **Paste the Tanzania Facts item at the end of the second column on the last page.**

● **Click** 🗙 Clear All **to clear the contents of the Office Clipboard.**

● **Close the Office Clipboard task pane.**

● **Select the text beginning with the heading "Tanzania FACTS" and ending with "$45."**

● **Click** 📰 **Text Box.**

● **Move the text box by dragging it to the top of the third column.**

Your screen should be similar to Figure 4.36

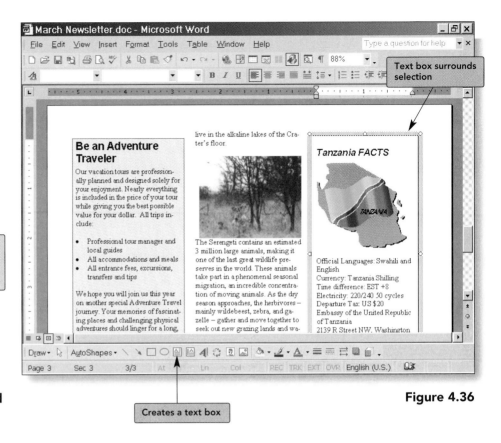

Figure 4.36

Creates a text box

The selected text is placed in a text box. The text is inserted using the new Normal font size of 11 points. In addition, the Text Box toolbar may be displayed. Its buttons (identified below) are used to link text boxes together so that text flows from one to the next. You will use this feature shortly.

Notice that when you moved the text box, all the objects inside the text box moved too. This is because the text box is a grouped object and is considered one graphic element. However, you can still format the text and size the graphic as separate items.

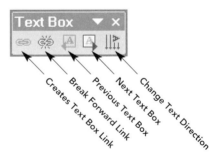

Formatting a Text Box

You will enhance the appearance of the text and text box next.

1 ● If necessary, adjust the size of the text box so it is the full width of the column and so all the text displays.

● Reduce the text size (excluding the heading) to 10 points and bold the text.

● Click 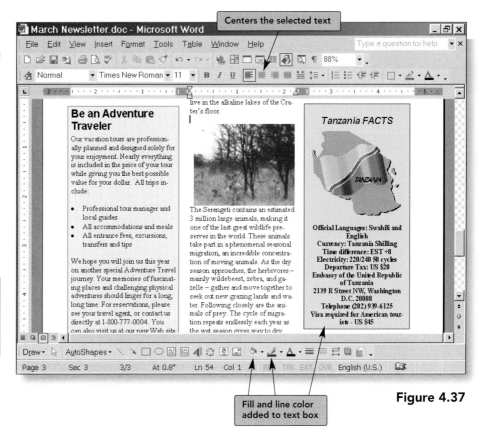 Fill Color and select gold from the color palette.

Additional Information

Because a text box is a drawing object, the Drawing toolbar buttons can be used to make these changes.

● Click ◢ ▾ Line Color and change the line color to blue.

● Center the entire contents of the text box.

● Deselect the text box.

Your screen should be similar to Figure 4.37

Figure 4.37

Next you want to include the listing of newsletter contents in a text box and move it to the first page of the newsletter.

2

- Select the heading "In This Issue" and the five lines of text that follow.

- Apply a text box to the selection.

- Fill the box with a color of your choice.

- Add a border with a color of your choice.

- Apply bullets to the five topics.

- Move the text box to the bottom of the column on page 2 as shown in Figure 4.38.

- Click outside the text box to deselect it.

Your screen should be similar to Figure 4.38

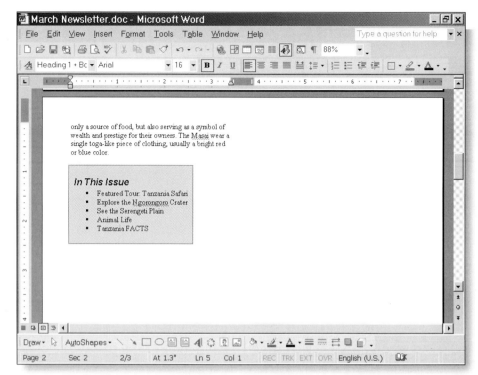

Figure 4.38

Now you would like to see the effects your changes have made to the layout and design of your newsletter.

3

- Change the zoom to Two Pages.

- Scroll down to see the third page.

- Scroll up to the first two pages again.

- Save the document again.

Your screen should be similar to Figure 4.39

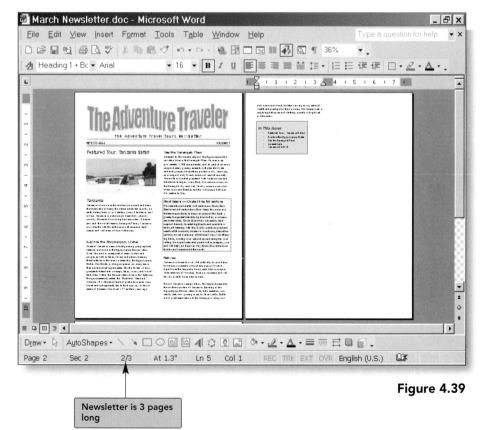

Newsletter is 3 pages long

Figure 4.39

The newsletter consists of three pages, with the second page only containing the end of the article on Natives and the text box. Once you have all the elements added to the newsletter, you will play with placement and size of the elements to make the entire newsletter fit on two pages.

Linking Text Boxes

As you look at the layout, you decide to make space on the first page by creating a linked text box for the two topics about the Ngorongoro Crater and the Serengetti Plain.

1 ● Change the zoom to Page Width.

● Move to the heading Explore the Ngorongoro Crater and select the text through the end of the See the Serengetti Plain article.

● Click 📧 Text Box.

● Add a light yellow fill color and blue border to the text box.

● Reduce the size of the text box until only the first article is displayed in it.

● Change the zoom to Whole Page and position the text box as shown in Figure 4.40.

Your screen should be similar to Figure 4.40

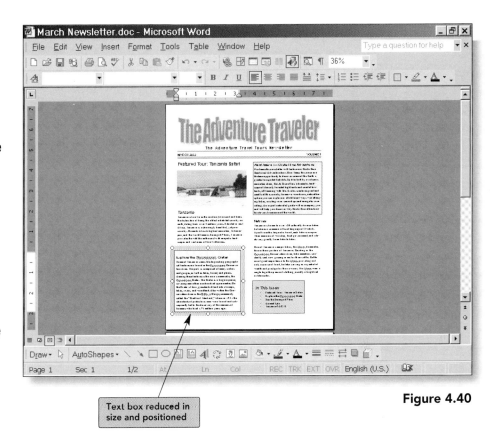

Text box reduced in size and positioned

Figure 4.40

Now you will create the second text box on page 2 where the remainder of the story will be displayed.

2

- **Change the zoom to Page Width.**

- **Move to the bottom of column 2 of page 2.**

- **Click 🖼 Text Box.**

- **Press ⌈Delete⌉ to remove the Drawing Canvas placeholder.**

Additional Information

When you create a text box without first selecting text, the Drawing Canvas appears and the mouse pointer changes to **+** so you can draw the text box.

- **Drag down and to the right to create a text box as shown in Figure 4.41.**

- **Add a light yellow fill color and blue border to the text box.**

Your screen should be similar to Figure 4.41

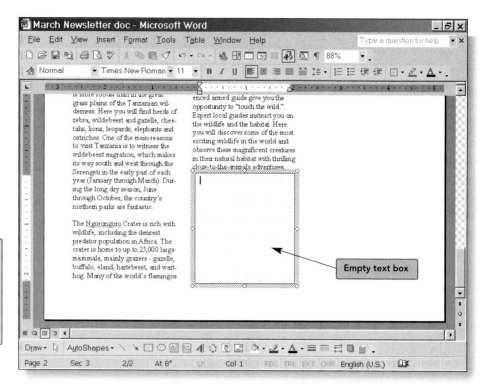

Figure 4.41

A text box created in this manner is inserted as a floating object. You want to change the wrapping style to Square. Then you will create a link between the two text boxes so that the overflow information from the first text box will flow into the empty text box. The text boxes to which you link must be empty—they cannot contain text.

3 • Choose For**m**at/Text
Bo**x**/Layout/Square/
OK .

Another Method
You can also right-click the
text box border and select
Format Text B**o**x from the
shortcut menu.

• Click on the Ngoron-
goro Crater text box on
page 1 to select it.

• Click 🔗 Create Text
Box Link (in the Text
Box toolbar).

Another Method
You can also select C**r**eate
Text Box Link from the
object's shortcut menu.

*Your screen should be
similar to Figure 4.42*

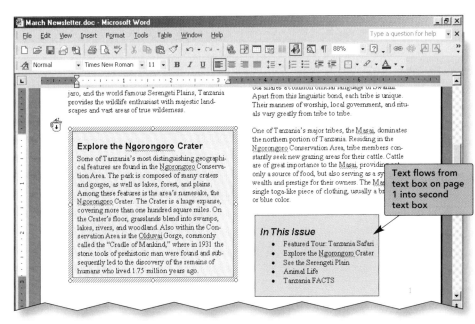

Figure 4.42

The mouse pointer changes to an upright pitcher 🫗 which indicates there
is text that is not showing that can flow into another text box. You decide to
go ahead and link the boxes.

4 • Scroll the document
and click on the blank
text box on page 2.

Additional Information
The mouse pointer changes
to a pouring pitcher 🫗 to
indicate that the text will be
poured into the text box.

• Increase the size of
the text box to fully
display the text.

• Size the text box to
the column width
and position it at the
bottom of the column.

*Your screen should be
similar to Figure 4.43*

Additional Information
To move between text boxes
in an article, select one of the
text boxes and then click 🔲
Next Text Box or 🔲
Previous Text Box on the Text
Box toolbar.

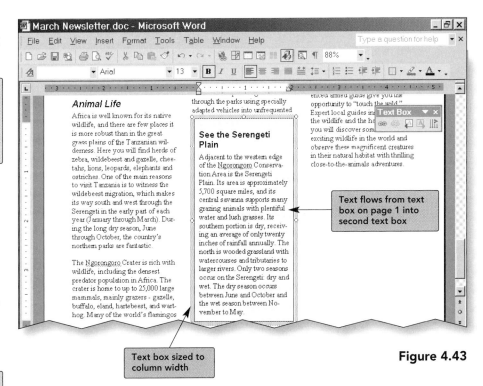

Figure 4.43

The overflow text from the first text box flows into the linked text box.

To indicate to the reader that the article is continued on another page, you will add a "Continued on" line to the bottom of the first text box and a "Continued from" line to the top of the second text box. You plan to use Roman numerals for the newsletter's page numbers and want the page reference to reflect this style.

4 ● **Move to the end of the first topic in the text box on page 1 and press** ⏎Enter.

HAVING TROUBLE?
If necessary, increase the length of the text box on page 1 to display the new line.

● **Type** Continued on page II.

● **Press** ⏎Enter **and type** Continued from page I.

● **Change the font style to italics and right-aligned for both lines.**

● **Change the zoom to Two Pages.**

● **Size and position the linked text boxes as shown in Figure 4.44.**

● **Save the newsletter again.**

Your screen should be similar to Figure 4.44

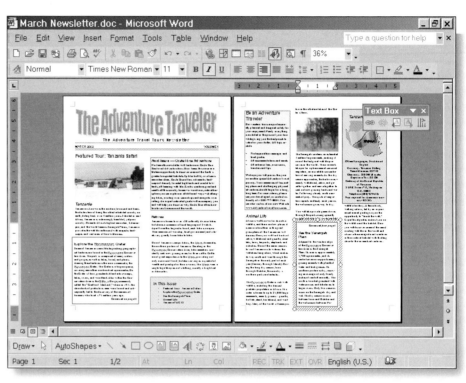

Figure 4.44

Finalizing the Newsletter

Now that the content and placement of articles in the newsletter is set, you want to add a few final touches to improve the appearance.

Inserting Symbols

One way to customize a newsletter is to place a small symbol at the end of each article to let the reader know that the article is finished and will not continue onto another page. You will add a symbol at the end of the article on page 1 and another at the end of the article on page 2.

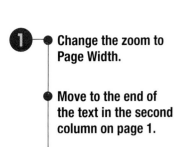

1 ● Change the zoom to Page Width.

● Move to the end of the text in the second column on page 1.

● Choose Insert/Symbol.

● If necessary, open the Symbols tab and select Symbol from the Font drop-down list.

● Select the diamond symbol (see Figure 4.44).

● Click [Insert].

Your screen should be similar to Figure 4.45

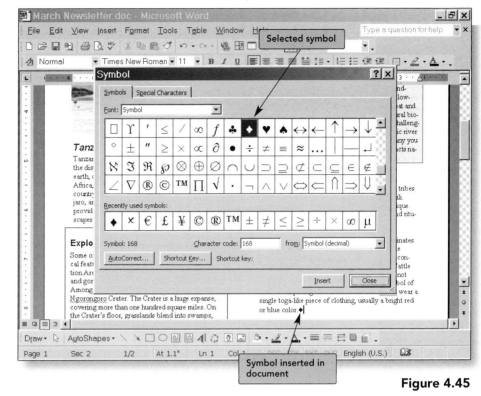

Figure 4.45

The dialog box remains open so you can insert additional symbols.

2 ● Move to the end of the text in column 3 on page 2 and insert the same symbol at this location.

● Click [Close] to close the dialog box.

Adding a Drop Cap

Finally, you would like to make the first letter of the first paragraph of the newsletter a drop cap. A **drop cap**, used most often with the first character in a paragraph, appears as a large uppercase character with the top part of the letter even with the line and the rest of the letter extending into the paragraph below it. The character is changed to a graphic object in a frame, and the text wraps to the side of the object.

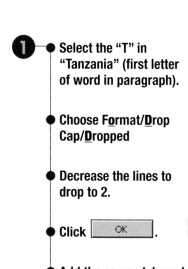

1
● Select the "T" in "Tanzania" (first letter of word in paragraph).

● Choose F**o**rmat/**D**rop Cap/**D**ropped

● Decrease the lines to drop to 2.

● Click ___OK___ .

● Add the same style and size drop cap to the "A" of "Africa" at the beginning of the article under Animal Life.

Another Method
You can use **E**dit/**R**epeat or F4 to quickly add the second drop cap.

Your screen should be similar to Figure 4.46

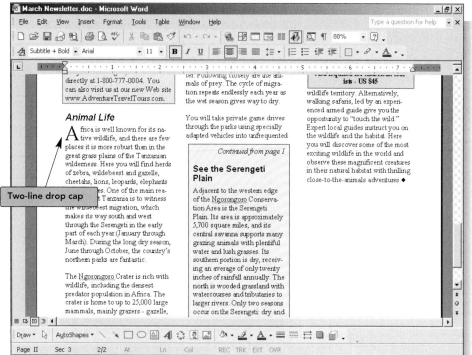

Figure 4.46

The drop-cap effect emphasizes the beginning of the paragraph and makes the columns appear more like those in a magazine.

Adjusting the Layout

Now you need to check the newsletter layout and move text and graphic elements around on the page until the newsletter has an orderly yet interesting appearance.

1
● Switch to Two Pages zoom and check the layout of the newsletter.

● Double-click on the photo of the lions to display the Format Picture dialog box.

● Open the Layout tab and click ___Advanced...___ .

● Open the Text Wrapping tab.

● Set the top and bottom distance from the text to 0.1 inch.

● Click ___OK___ two times.

Your screen should be similar to Figure 4.47

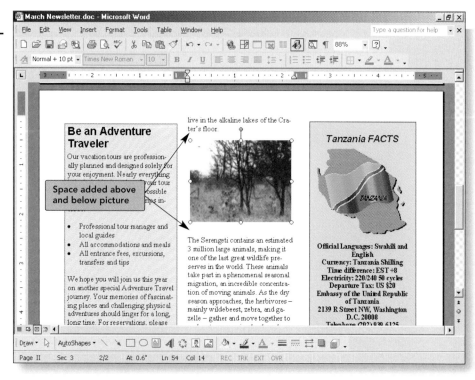

Figure 4.47

The added spacing around the pictures helps set it off from the running text. You will continue refining the layout.

2 ● Move the photo of lions to the top of column 2 on the second page.

● Insert a right-aligned page number in the footer using the uppercase Roman numeral format.

● Position and size the other graphic elements as needed so your newsletter is similar to that shown in Figure 4.46.

Your screen should be similar to Figure 4.48

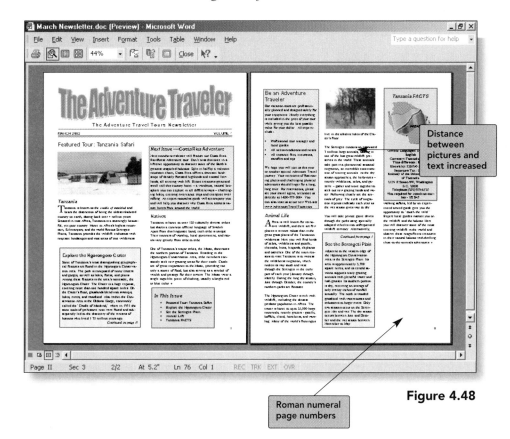

Figure 4.48

Roman numeral page numbers

Printing the Newsletter

As a final check before printing, it is a good idea to display the document in the Print Preview window to make sure that elements will print correctly.

1 ● Preview the document.

● If necessary, switch to Editing and make any changes to the layout as needed.

● Save the document again.

● Print the newsletter.

The printed copy of the newsletter should be similar to the document shown in the Case Study at the beginning of the Lab.

2 ● Exit Word, closing all open files.

Another Method

You can close all open documents without exiting the program by holding down ⇧Shift when opening the File menu and selecting Close All.

WordArt   (WD4.6)

WordArt is used to enhance your documents by changing the shape of text and adding special effects such as 3-D and shadows.

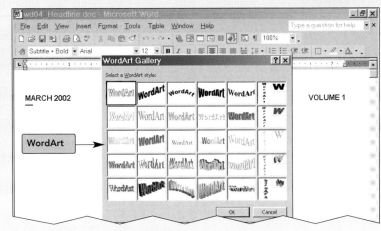

Special Drawing Effects   (WD4.10)

Special drawing effects, such as shadows and 3-D effects, can be easily added to text and graphics, including WordArt objects, to enhance the appearance of your document.

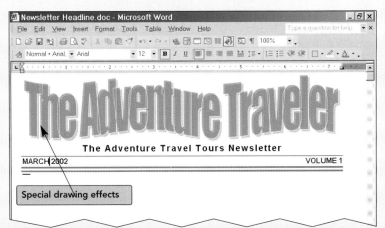

Collecting and Pasting   (WD4.16)

Collecting and pasting is the capability of the program to store multiple copied items in the Office Clipboard and then paste one or more of them into another document.

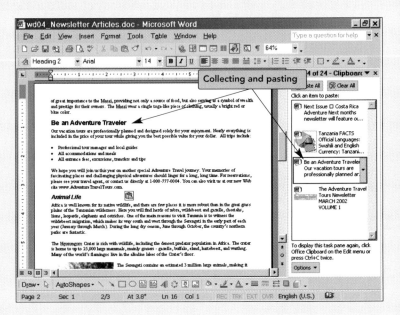

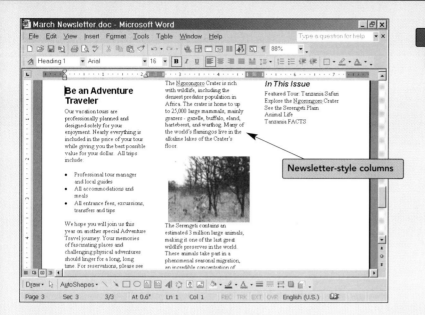

Newsletter-Style Columns (WD4.23)

Newsletter-style columns display text so that it flows from the bottom of one column to the top of the next.

Newsletter-style columns

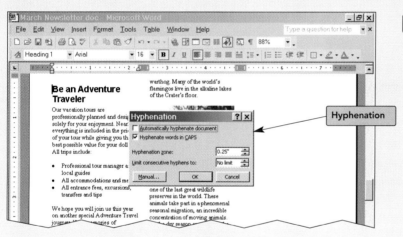

Hyphenation (WD4.28)

The hyphenation feature inserts hyphens in long words that fall at the end of a line, splitting the word between lines.

Hyphenation

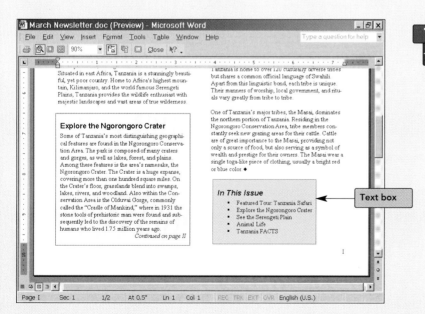

Text Box (WD4.33)

A text box is a graphic object that is a container for text or graphics.

Text box

lab review

LAB 4
Creating a Newsletter

key terms

collect and paste   WD4.16
drop cap   WD4.41
hyphenation   WD4.28
hyphenation zone   WD4.29
kerning   WD4.11
newsletter-style columns   WD4.23
optional hyphen   WD4.28

sidebar   WD4.29
story   WD4.33
text box   WD4.33
WordArt   WD4.6

mous skills

The Microsoft Office User Specialist (MOUS) certification program is designed to measure your proficiency in performing basic tasks using the Office XP applications. Getting certified demonstrates that you have the skills and provides a valuable industry credential for employment. After completing this lab, you have learned the following Microsoft Office User Specialist skills:

Skill	Description	Page
Inserting and Modifying Text	Insert, modify, and move text and symbols	WD4.17
Creating and Modifying Paragraphs	Modify paragraph formats	WD4.30
	Apply bullets, outline, and numbering format to paragraphs	WD4.36
Formatting Documents	Apply and modify column settings	WD4.23
	Modify document layout and Page Setup options	WD4.43
	Preview and print documents, envelopes, and labels	WD4.43
Managing Documents	Save documents using different names and file formats	WD4.15, WD4.23, WD4.29 WD4.36, WD4.40, WD4.43
Working with Graphics	Insert images and graphics	WD4.5, WD4.19

command summary

Command	Shortcut Keys	Button	Action
Edit/**R**epeat	Ctrl + Y		Repeats last action
Edit/Office Clip**b**oard			Activates Office Clipboard and displays the task pane
Edit/**G**oTo	Ctrl + G		Moves to specified location
Insert/**B**reak/Con**t**inuous			Inserts a section break and starts next section on same page as current section
Insert/**B**reak/**N**ext Page			Inserts a section break and starts next section on a new page
Insert/**S**ymbol			Inserts selected symbol
Insert/Te**x**t Box		▨	Inserts text box
F**o**rmat/**F**ont/Cha**r**acter Spacing			Changes spacing between characters
F**o**rmat/**B**orders and Shading			Adds borders and shadings to selection
		▢	Adds outside border
		▣	Adds top border
		▣	Adds bottom border
F**o**rmat/**C**olumns		▦	Specifies number, spacing, and size of columns
F**o**rmat/**D**rop Cap/**D**ropped			Changes character format as a dropped capital letter
F**o**rmat/**S**tyles and Formatting		▨	Displays Styles and Formatting taskbar from which you apply, create, or modify styles
F**o**rmat/**W**ordArt/Size		▨	Sizes, rotates, and scales WordArt object
F**o**rmat/**W**ordArt/Colors and Lines		▨	Applies fill and line color to WordArt object
F**o**rmat/Text B**o**x/Layout		▨	Changes wrapping style and alignment of text box
Tools/**L**anguage/**H**yphenation			Hyphenated document

Terminology

screen identification

In the following Word screen, letters identify important elements. Enter the correct term for each screen element in the space provided.

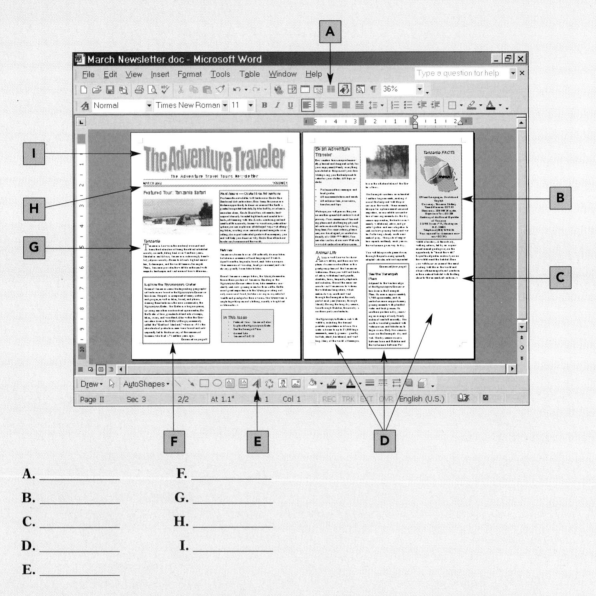

A. _____   F. _____

B. _____   G. _____

C. _____   H. _____

D. _____   I. _____

E. _____

matching

Match the item on the left with the correct description on the right.

1. [icon]   _____   **a.** adjusts the spacing between particular pairs of letters

2. drop cap   _____   **b.** creates a WordArt object

3. sidebar   _____   **c.** creates a linked text box

4. [icon]   _____   **d.** flows text from the bottom of one column to the top of the next

5. [icon]   _____   **e.** an unmarked space along the right margin that controls the amount of white space in addition to the margin that Word will allow at the end of a line

6. kerning   _____   **f.** sets apart an article from the article next to it

7. newsletter-style column   _____   **g.** adds a top border line to selection.

8. [icon]   _____   **h.** a large uppercase letter aligned with the top of a line and extending into the paragraph below it

9. [icon]   _____   **i.** creates a text box

10. hyphenation zone   _____   **j.** displays the Office Clipboard task pane

multiple choice

Circle the correct response to the questions below.

1. The feature that is used to enhance documents by changing the shape of text is called
   _____.
   a. WordArt
   b. WordWrap
   c. Art
   d. DrawShape

2. When an object that is _____ is moved, all objects inside the object move too.
   a. locked
   b. grouped
   c. fixed
   d. blocked

3. _____ adjusts the spacing between particular pairs of letters depending on the font design to improve the appearance of the text.
   a. Locking
   b. Floating
   c. Kerning
   d. Anchoring

lab exercises

4. Text that flows from the bottom of one column to the top of the next is said to be in _____ column format.
   a. newspaper
   b. newsletter-style
   c. adjusted
   d. fixed

5. Information you want to keep separate from other articles or information that highlights an article next to it is called a _____ article.
   a. sideline
   b. sidebar
   c. sidetrack
   d. sidestep

6. Word inserts _____ hyphens, which break the word only if it appears at the end of a line.
   a. fixed
   b. optional
   c. adjusted
   d. floating

7. You can also specify the size of the _____ zone, an unmarked space along the right margin that controls the amount of white space in addition to the margin that Word will allow at the end of a line.
   a. tab
   b. margin
   c. hyphenation
   d. border

8. _____ are graphic objects that are used to contain text or graphics.
   a. Text boxes
   b. List boxes
   c. Phrase boxes
   d. Display boxes

9. Text that is contained in a single text box or linked text boxes is called a(n) _____.
   a. article
   b. story
   c. item
   d. piece

10. A(n) _____, used most often with the first character in a paragraph, appears as a large uppercase character with the top part of the letter even with the line and the rest of the letter extending into the paragraph below it.
    a. decline character
    b. enlarged character
    c. drop cap
    d. character object

true/false

Check the correct answer to the following questions.

1. If you display the Office Clipboard in the task pane of one program or document, it automatically appears when you switch to another program or document.   True   False

2. Handles surround a WordArt object when it is selected.   True   False

3. You cannot change the thickness and color of a border.   True   False

4. WordArt can be changed using the Drawing toolbar buttons.   True   False

5. The Semitransparent option does not allow the shadow color to bleed through.   True   False

6. Kerning adjusts the spacing between particular pairs of letters depending on the font design.   True   False

7. Rules can be added to any side of a paragraph using the Lines toolbar.   True   False

8. When you link text boxes together, large articles will automatically flow into the correct text boxes on the other pages in a newsletter.   True   False

9. The last item you copy to the Office Clipboard is always copied to the Windows Clipboard.   True   False

10. The hyphenation feature inserts a hyphen in long words that fall at the end of a line to split the word between lines.   True   False

Concepts

fill-in

Complete the following statements by filling in the blanks with the correct terms.

1. The _____ feature is used to enhance your documents by changing the shape of text.

2. The _____ stores multiple copied items and the _____ holds one copied item.

3. A(n) _____ is a graphic object that is a container for text or graphics.

4. _____ reduces the amount of white space at the end of lines and makes line lengths more even to improve the appearance of a document.

5. _____ allow you to format a document to different column settings.

6. Text that flows from the bottom of one column to the top of the next is in _____ format.

7. A(n) _____ breaks a word only if it appears at the end of the line.

8. Text contained in linked text boxes is called a(n) _____.

9. _____ adjusts the spacing between pairs of letters based on the font design.

10. Shadows and 3-D effects are examples of _____.

1. How can WordArt enhance the look of a document? What types of documents are best suited for WordArt?

2. What types of special effects can be added to drawing objects? How do the special effects enhance the object?

3. How can newsletter-style columns enhance the look of a document? What types of documents are columns best suited for? How can the adjustment of widths, spacing, and hyphenation affect the layout?

4. How do linked text boxes differ from normal text boxes? When should you consider using a linked text box? When would it be appropriate to add a text box to a document?

Hands-On Exercises

step-by-step

Diet and Fitness Newsletter

★ **1.** The Lifestyle Fitness Club's newsletter for this month will focus on dietary concerns and fitness, along with this month's special sale item. The completed newsletter is shown here.

The Lifestyle Fitness Club

A Publication for Customers of The Lifestyle Fitness Club

FALL 2002   VOLUME I

Health

A Balanced Diet

Dietary advice for all types of athletes is the same as for the general public. That is, eat a well-balanced diet from a wide variety of foods in sufficient amounts to meet energy needs. Experts agree the key to healthy eating is the time-tested advice of balance, variety and moderation. In short, that means eating a wide variety of foods without getting too many calories or too much of any one nutrient.

Because people need more than 40 different nutrients daily for good health, it is important to eat a variety of foods. No single food supplies them all. Diets that include a wide variety of foods not only reap the nutritional benefits, but may also help prevent disease and consequently live longer. Recent studies have found that people who ate wide varieties of foods had a lower risk of premature death than those who ate the same food year after year.

Your daily food selection should include bread and other whole-grain products, fruits, vegetables, dairy products, and meat, poultry, fish and other protein foods. How much you should eat depends on your calorie needs. Nutrition experts like the American Dietetic Association recommend that we eat a diet low in fat and high in complex carbohydrates. Complex carbohydrates are foods such as pasta, rice, potatoes, and breads. Generally, nutritionists suggest that we consume no more than 30 percent to 35 percent of our calories as fat, at least 55 percent as carbohydrates, and the remainder as protein.

The Food Guide Pyramid shown below is a practical tool to help you make food choices that are consistent with the Dietary Guidelines for Americans.[1] Using the Pyramid en-

ables you to eat a variety of foods daily so that you can get the nutrients you need.

[1] The American Dietetic Association, www.eatright.org, 1/4/97

Fitness

Exercise and Weight Loss

The key to weight control is keeping energy intake (food) and energy output (physical activity) in balance. When you consume only as many calories as your body needs, your weight will usually remain constant. If you take in more calories than your body needs, you will put on excess fat. If you expend more energy than you take in, you will burn excess fat.

Exercise plays an important role in weight control by increasing energy output, calling on stored calories for extra fuel. Recent studies show that not only does exercise increase metabolism during a workout, but it causes your metabolism to stay increased for a period of time after exercising, allowing you to burn more calories. There are two basic forms of exercise: anaerobic and aerobic.

Anaerobic Exercise

Anaerobic activity is short in duration (0 to 2 minutes) and high in intensity. Anaerobic activities include activities such as racquetball, downhill skiing, weight lifting, sprinting, softball, soccer and football. This type of exercise requires immediate energy to be supplied by blood glucose and muscle glycogen, and focuses more on increasing muscle mass and building power.

Anaerobic exercise is very important in improving strength to perform daily activities and train for sporting events. Additionally anaerobic activity increases your metabolic rate for several hours after exercising, as well as your resting metabolic rate. The quickening of the metabolic rate may make it easier shed unwanted weight.

Aerobic Exercise

In the strictest sense, moderate-intensity activities that can be sustained for more than 2 minutes are called aerobic exercise. More commonly, aerobic exercise is defined as using the same large muscle group, rhythmically, for a period of 15 to 20 minutes or longer while maintaining 60-80% of your maximum heart rate. Examples of aerobic activities include cross-country skiing, biking rowing, jogging or walking

Aerobic exercise is highly effective in improving the cardiovascular system because it conditions the heart and lungs by increasing the oxygen available to the body and by enabling the heart to use oxygen more efficiently. Other benefits include:

- Reduction in body fat.
- Increased energy and general stamina
- Toned muscles and increased lean body mass.
- Reduced tension, depression, and anxiety
- Sleep better.

Special of the Month

The Ultra Rider Model UR-3200 Exercise Bike $499.00 (plus tax and shipping) Refer to the catalog for a full description

Student Name
Date

a. To create this newsletter, open the file wd04_Fitness Club Headline. Insert the [WordArt] WordArt object and center it below the main title. Enter the text **UPDATE** with top and bottom wrapping style.

b. Fill the WordArt object with orange and clear the Semitransparent check box. Change the line color to red. Apply the deflate shape and size appropriately.

c. Insert a shadow border of 3 points around the identification text.

d. Save the headline file as Fitness Headline2. Copy the entire file to the Clipboard. Close the file.

e. Open the file wd04_Fitness Club. Paste the headline text above the text in the Fitness Club file.

f. Move to the blank line below the bottom border line and insert a continuous section break.

g. Select the text below the bottom border and change to a two-column format. Then select the text beginning at the Fitness heading to the end of the document and format it to three columns. Change the spacing between the three columns to 0.3 for column 1 and choose equal column widths.

h. Apply automatic hyphenation to the entire document.

i. Create a text box that contains the text at the end of column 3 on page 2 beginning with the heading "Special of the Month" and ending with the word "description." Add a tan fill color and change the border color to black and increase the line weight to 3 pt.

j. Insert the clip art wd04_Exercise Bike beneath the "Special of the Month" heading. Size the graphic to fit the text box. Adjust the size of the text box to fully display the text.

k. Add the file wd04_Jogger clip art to the first paragraph below "Fitness" on page 2. Size the graphic to approximately 4 by 1.2 inches. Set the wrapping to Tight on both sides. Move the graphic to be displayed between the columns (see the figures for reference).

l. Add your name and the current date to the bottom of column 3 on page 2. Check the layout of your document and make adjustments as necessary. Save the document as Fitness Club Newsletter. Print the document.

Scenic Drives Newsletter

★ ★ **2.** The Adventure Travel agency devotes one issue of its newsletter annually to information about travel experiences from the car window. This year's car-window newsletter contains information on scenic drives around the United States and Canada. The completed newsletter is shown here.

The Adventure Travel Tours Newsletter

April 2002   VOLUME 2

This Adventure Travel Tours newsletter highlights several scenic drives in the US and Canada. For more information about the drives and accommodations call us at 1-800-555-0004 or visit our Web site at www.AdventureTravelTours.com.

Wisconsin's Kettle Moraine

The route follows the Kettle Moraine Scenic Drive developed and maintained by the Kettle Moraine State Forest staff. Along the way you're likely to learn more about glacial geology than you ever thought you'd know. You will travel many unmarked back roads, wandering all over in search of yet more glacial formations. It is likely to fill an enjoyable day of driving.

Lake Michigan

This drive tours the Lake Michigan shore from Sheboygan to Algoma, passing sand dunes, high bluffs, lighthouses, farms, and museums. The area's flavor and history are closely tied to the lake through fishing, sailing, and ship building. Special attractions: Kohler-Andrae State Park, Point Beach State Forest, the USS Cobia, lighthouses, museums, hiking, swimming, fishing, camping, wildlife watching.

Dahinda Illinois

Breathtaking fall scenery will usher you into this small community, a prime example of rural America at its finest; a small town with friendly folk always ready to visit. This is the only Scenic Drive stop along the Spoon River. The hilly timberland surrounding the river and nearby creeks, along with the vast area of river bottomland gives visitors a breathtaking view of Mother Nature's fiery fall colors.

Cohutta Loop

These 70 square miles of North Georgia wilderness are encompassed by the drive many refer to as the Cohutta Loop. For the outdoor enthusiast, this is heaven. The drive provides access to the largest wilderness area east of the Mississippi, abounds with walking trails and wildlife, and features occasional campgrounds as it follows the perimeter of the wilderness.

Columbia River

The Columbia River Gorge Loop is Oregon's most famous scenic drive. Drive along a two-lane country road that follows the contour of the land through open country and past towering basalt outcroppings. Along the route you'll find wineries that feature distinctive varieties, and picturesque surroundings. You will also pass dozens of waterfalls, and any number of hatcheries and dam fish ways for viewing the fall salmon runs.

Washington State

Washington has the fastest growing wine region in the country, the effects of its geography, climate, and soil create a classic combination for growing premium grapes to produce wines achieving world class status. Wine lovers can sample the newest releases from twenty-two wineries in the Yakima Valley Appellation at their annual "Spring Barrel Tasting" in late April. As the fruit begins to ripen in mid-September, wineries throughout the state celebrate the harvest season with open houses and special events.

Hood Canal

Washington state visitors are drawn by the wonders of the ancient rain forests, the wildness of its ocean beaches, and the mysteries of the Hood Canal. Rich native cultures have inhabited the land for thousands of years, and a heritage deeply rooted in logging and fishing is evident at every turn. The National Park, with its majestic mountains, vast glaciers, and wilderness trails, lures hikers and climbers. Rushing rivers, pristine lakes, distinctive wildlife, old growth forests, and magnificent vistas offer unlimited opportunities for fishers, naturalists, and photographers.

Upcoming Adventure Tours

January ◆ **Ski the Canadian Wilderness**: Fulfills everyone's desire to explore and participate in the majestic outdoors of northern Alberta, the Yukon, and the Northwest Territories.

June ◆ **Vancouver Island**: No matter where you travel on Vancouver Island or the Gulf Islands, there is an abundance of interesting things to do and see.

September ◆ **Amazon River Excursion**: Imagine yourself exploring the upper reaches of the exotic Amazon, one of the world's greatest ecosystems, on a multilevel riverboat with private rooms. Spend your days relaxing in comfort on the upper deck and walking through the forest surrounded by sights and sounds most people have only imagined.

Student Name
Date

a. To create this newsletter, open the file wd04_Scenic Drives and the file Newsletter Headline you saved in this lab.

b. In the Newsletter Headline file, change the date to the current month and year. Increase the volume number by one. Copy the text from the Newsletter Headline file to the top of the Scenic Drives file. Adjust the WordArt so that it is displayed a half inch below the top edge of the page.

c. Insert the clip art image wd04_Road below the first paragraph. Size the clip art appropriately. (about 3" × 2") Change the wrapping style for the graphic to Top and Bottom. Center it horizontally.

d. Select all the text below the clip art and format it to two equal columns. Apply hyphenation to the selected text.

e. Use bold and italics for each of the scenic drive headings. Use bold for the headline "Upcoming Adventure Tours" and the names of the upcoming adventure tours. Replace the hyphens with diamond (◆) symbols to separate the month and tour names.

f. Insert a column break before the Dahinda, Illinois heading and another column break before Washington State scenic drive heading. Insert another column break before "Upcoming Adventure Tours." (Hint: To insert a column break select Break from the Insert menu and choose Column break.)

g. Insert the picture of wd04_Canada at the beginning of the "January ◆ Ski the Canadian Wilderness" paragraph. Size it to fit across half the column and wrap the text to the right.

h. Add the picture wd04_MtDoug at the beginning of "June ◆ Vancouver Island" and wd04_Huts at the beginning of "September ◆ Amazon River Excursion." Size and format these pictures as you did the Canada picture.

i. Add your name and the current date to the bottom of column 2 on page 2. Check the layout of your document and make adjustments to the text as necessary. Save the document as Scenic Drives Newsletter. Print the document.

lab exercises

Cafe Promotion Newsletter

★ ★ **3.** The Downtown Internet Cafe would like to use a newsletter to promote itself. The newsletter will highlight some of the things people can do at the cafe and describe four coffees the cafe plans to feature this month. The completed newsletter is shown here.

Downtown Internet Cafe

A Newsletter for Coffee Lovers of the World

Spring 2002   Volume II

The Downtown Internet Cafe is a new concept in coffeehouses, combining the delicious aromas of a genuine coffeehouse with the fun of using the Internet. The Cafe offers the latest in technology while maintaining the atmosphere of an old time coffeehouse and much more. Enjoy flavored coffees, cappuccino, espresso, lattes, aromatic teas, and tempting desserts, while you challenge your mind playing on the Internet.

Things to Do in the Café

Things to Do in the Café

Sit comfortably at one of 30 Pentium - PC stations with access to the Internet via high-speed T1 modem connection. Our machines are equipped with the latest software for word processing, database, spreadsheets, and graphics software. And don't forget the games!

Our menu includes a fine selection of gourmet coffees, fresh salads, sandwiches, pastries and cookies to get you through the day. You can also purchase our freshly roasted and ground coffee to take home.

Services We Provide

Computer Use: Use the software and games on our computers for just $5.00 per hour.

Internet access: Use the WWW for just $8.00 per hour and $5.00 per half-hour.

Email Set Up: We will help you set up your e-mail account on mail servers providing the service for free.

VIP Membership: $100/month with unlimited access to the Internet. Laptops from the cafe are also provided to our privileged VIP customers.

Graphics: Scan your pictures/photos/logos at desired resolution.

Save Files: Save files on CDs, Zip drives and floppies.

Video Conferencing: We have 3 cameras available for video conferencing.

Printing: Color and black and white copies are available.

Web Page Development: Interested in developing a Web site? Let us help you set up your own Web site.

Subject Search: Let us know the subject you're looking for and we will do the

Coffee Reviews

Each month in our newsletter we will review the four coffees we are featuring in the café this month. The coffees are rated on a ten-point scale in a blind taste test. Stop by and enjoy a cup.

R & R Beans
Origin: Lake Toba area of North Sumatra Province, Sumatra, Indonesia.

Aroma: 7
Acidity: 6
Body: 6
Flavor: 8
Aftertaste: 6

Assessment: A solid, bordering-on-classic Sumatra profile: low-toned but rich, pleasantly pruny, its distinct pungency saved from bitterness by a sweetness that grows in power as the coffee cools.

Great Northern Gourmet Coffees
Origin: Lake Biwa region, Aceh Province, northern Sumatra

Aroma: 6
Acidity: 5
Body: 7
Flavor: 5
Aftertaste: 5

Assessment: Assuming classic and earthy are not mutually exclusive terms, this is a classically earthy Sumatra: a round, muted but full earth taste gently dominates the profile. Apparently the earth taste comes from drying the coffee directly on the ground rather than on tarpaulins. Although the earth tones are wonderfully soft, overall the profile suffers from a slight bitterness.

Timothy's World Coffee
Origin: Lake Toba area of North Sumatra Province, Sumatra, Indonesia.

Aroma: 7
Acidity: 7
Body: 8
Flavor: 6
Aftertaste: 6

Assessment: Rich, burgundy-like fullness, gathering under the back edges of the tongue, with just enough acidity to set off dark tickles and echoes. However, a slightly bitter and salty aftertaste gave away this coffee's weakness, which became abundantly clear as the cup cooled.

New World Coffee
Origin: Lake Toba area of North Sumatra Province, Sumatra, Indonesia.

Aroma: 9
Acidity: 5
Body: 6
Flavor: 7
Aftertaste: 6

Assessment: A rather refined profile, lighter and sweeter than most Sumatras, with clean hints of fruit and flowers under the usual Sumatra pungency.

Student Name
Date

a. To create the newsletter, open the file wd04_Coffee. Create a WordArt headline at the top of the document with the words The Downtown Internet Cafe. Choose an appropriate shape and adjust the size to fit between the margins.

b. Center and bold A Newsletter for Coffee Lovers of the World below the WordArt. Format the line to 14 point and expand the character spacing to 1.5 points. Type and bold Spring 2002 Volume II on the next line. Add a right tab at the right margin and indent "Volume II" to this position.

c. Add a blank line above the date and volume line. Add appropriately colored borders above and below the date and volume text line.

d. Apply hyphenation to all the text in the file.

e. Insert a blank line below the issue identification text and insert a continuous section break.

f. Select the text beginning at the heading "Things to Do in the Cafe," and ending at "by technical area." Apply two-column format. Insert a page break before the heading "Coffee Reviews."

g. Apply the heading 3 style to the headings "Things to Do in the Cafe," "Services We Provide," and "Coffee Reviews." Add italics and underlines to the names of the four featured coffees in the Coffee Reviews article.

h. Add an appropriate color to each heading for the types of services provided.

i. Insert the clip art wd04_Conversation above "Things to Do at the Cafe" heading. Set the wrapping to top and bottom. Change the size of the graphic to 2.5 × 2.5 inches.

j. Adding the clip art caused the Consulting text to move to page 2, so you would like to display the text in a text box. Select the heading Services We Provide and all the text under that topic. Create a text box and size it to fully display the text. Remove the blank lines between each service and resize the box until it is displayed down the right side of page 1 under the heading.

k. You want to draw attention to the services discussed in the text box using a fill effect. Apply a two-color fill effect of your choice to the text box. (Hint: access these options in the Colors and Lines tab of the format dialog box. Choose Fill Effects from the color drop down list and select the two colors option.

l. Apply a three-column format to the text on page 2 with spacing of 0.3 inch and equal columns.

k. Insert the clip art wd04_Coffee Beans in front of the "Coffee Reviews." Increase the size of the Coffee Reviews text to 22 points.

l. Insert the clip art wd04_Coffee Cup at the bottom of column 3 on page 2.

m. Add your name and the current date to the bottom of column 3 on page 2. Check the layout of your document and make adjustments to the text as necessary. Save the document as Internet Cafe Newsletter. Print the document.

Survival Newsletter

★ ★ **4.** The National Parks Service places newsletters for hikers in park stores. This month's newsletter highlights hikes and survival skills. The completed newsletter is shown here.

The National Parks Service

A Publication for People That Explore Our Great Country.

FALL 2001   VOLUME 10

Central Oregon Cascades Hikes

Come discover a new path along the Deschutes River near Bend, hike to a hidden cave overlooking Mt. Jefferson, or prowl a gold-mining ghost town near Eugene! With 47 easy day hikes suitable for the whole family, and there's a variety of tougher trails too, and lots of backpacking options.

Short Hikes in California's Central Coast

The central coast of California is a hiker's dream, with miles of trails with stunning coastal views, easily accessible and beautiful any time of the year. Try short hikes in San Luis Obispo, Santa Barbara, and Ventura counties, plus the scenic Channel Islands.

Day Hikes of the California Northwest

Ninety four wonderful day hikes located from Marin to Crescent City, to Mount Shasta. Including Trinity Alps, Russian, Marble Mountain, and Yolla Bolla

Wilderness Areas. The local geology, flora and wildlife makes the trips most enjoyable.

Best Easy Day Hikes Olympics

Olympic National Park is home to a vast network of hiking trails. Easy-to-follow trails that take you to some of the area's most spectacular scenery without taking you to physical extremes.

Hiking California

Boasting a mild climate, incredible diversity and thousands of miles of hiking trails, California has something for every hiker The hikes use routes varying from gentle inclines to rugged cross-country scrambles, including old favorites known to many and obscure routes known only to a few. Surveying the most awe-inspiring scenery in the state, trails will satisfy both beginning and veteran hikers.

Hiking the Cape Breton's Cabot Trail

Cape Breton's Cabot Trail includes 28 hiking trails from short hikes to longer day hikes. Discover whales, birds, animals, and flowers along the hiking trails.

Vermont and New Hampshire Hiking

Try some of the best hikes of Central Vermont, the Upper Valley of New Hampshire /Vermont. Including the Killington Peak Region the second highest peak in Vermont (4,242 '). Trails include surrounding region, the Long Trail and Appalachian Trail. Also the Mt. Ascutney Trails, in and around the Mt. Ascutney State Park. Hikes range from difficult to easy.

Utah's Favorite Hiking Trails

The Hikes range in length from a half-a-day stroll to Fisher Towers near Moab, to a four day walk around Brown Duck Mountain in the High Unitas area.

The National Parks Service

5 Basic Survival Skills

One of the most important elements to survival is between your ears.... your brain. Don't panic, use your wits and practice all elements of the 5 Basics before you may need to rely on them.

 **FIRE** can purify water, cook food, signal rescuers, provide warmth, light and comfort, help keep predators at a distance, and can be a most welcome friend and companion. Have a minimum of two ways to start a fire, one on your person at all times and the other in your gear.

 SHELTER is the means by which you protect your body from excess exposure from the sun, cold, wind, rain or snow. Anything that takes away or adds to your overall body temperature can be your enemy. Clothing is the first line of shelter protection, have the right clothes for the right environment. Always have a hat. Try and keep the layer closest to your body dry. Layers trap air and are warmer than one thick garment.

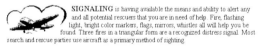 **SIGNALING** is having available the means and ability to alert any and all potential rescuers that you are in need of help. Fire, flashing light, bright color markers, flags, mirrors, whistles all will help you be found. Three fires in a triangular form are a recognized distress signal. Most search and rescue parties use aircraft as a primary method of sighting.

 FOOD/WATER are vital towards your survival. Ration your sweat not your water intake. Try to drink only in the cool of the evening. You can live up to three days without water. Do not eat plants you do not know. Never drink urine. Always assume that you will need extra food and water when you plan your trip. Pack energy bars and candy in your pockets at all time, just in case.

 FIRST AID is not just the basic medical needs, it is the primary way in which you act to survive. STOP means Sit, Think, Observe, and Plan. It is the most intelligent thing you can do when you realize you are lost or stranded. The most important element is to keep your brain functioning rationally; this is basic first aid for survival.

Student Name
Date

---

a. To create the newsletter, open the files wd04_Hikes, wd04_Park Headline, and wd04_Survival Skills. In the Park Headline file create a WordArt object with the text **The National Parks Service**. Color the WordArt green. Adjust the size of the WordArt appropriately.

b. Increase the font size of the remaining text to 14 points. Create a single green top border and a double green bottom border around the date and volume information.

c. Copy the text from the Hikes and Survival Skills documents to the Office Clipboard. Paste the Hikes text into the headline document one blank line below the bottom border.

d. Select all the text, excluding the headline, and format it to three columns with 0.3-inch spacing.

e. Bold the headlines for the different hikes.

f. Create a Next Page section break at the end of the paragraph on Utah's Favorite Hiking Trails. Add three blank lines to the top of page 2 and copy the WordArt object to the top of page 2.

g. Paste the Survival Skills text below the WordArt on page 2 and close the Office Clipboard. If necessary, change the format back to one column. Draw a double-line border under the WordArt on the second blank line. (You will need one blank line below the border to add more text.) Increase the size of the section heading and the five tips to 14 points and make them bold.

h. You would like to insert a clip art image in front of each tip. The pictures should be formatted tight to the text and appear on the left. Choose five appropriate clipart images from your ClipArt Gallery, or use the images wd04_Fire, wd04_Shelter, wd04_Signaling, wd04_Food&Water, wd04_First Aid. Add your name and the current date to the bottom of page 2. Check the layout of your document and make adjustments to the text as necessary. Save the document as National Parks Newsletter. Print the document.

Animal Angels Travel Newsletter

★ ★ **5.** Animal Angels, the volunteer group for the Animal Rescue Foundation, sends a monthly
★ newsletter to its members. This month's newsletter focuses on air travel issues. The completed
newsletter is shown here.

Animal Angels

The Animal Rescue Foundation rescues unwanted pets from local animal shelters and finds fosters homes for them until a suitable adoptive family can be found. The Animal Angels volunteer group produces this newsletter to keep you informed on issues related to the animals we are dedicated to saving. This month's newsletter is dedicated to air travel with animals.

Is Your Pet Up for the Flight?

Before you make any travel arrangements check with your vet. Animals that are very young or old, pregnant, ill, or injured should generally not travel. Sometimes the best decision is not to fly with pets. Some animals do not function well in unfamiliar surroundings, and an unhappy pet can make a trip miserable for everyone.

Most vets agree that your pet should not be tranquilized during the flight. It creates an unnecessary risk of suffocation!

Choosing a Pet-friendly Airline...

When making your reservations, inquire about the airline's Animal Welfare and Transport Policies. All airlines must comply with the basic guidelines set forth by the Animal Welfare Act, but standards still vary between carriers. Also keep in mind the US Department of Agriculture prohibits animals from being kept in the hold or on the tarmac for more than 45 minutes when temperatures are above 85F or below 45F.

Your airline should certainly adhere to these standards, but a good airline may prohibit animals on flights to cities where temperatures exceed these limits.

Continued from page 1

You should be sure to reserve a spot for your pet; many airlines carry a limited number of animals per flight. Try to arrange a nonstop flight, this reduces the time your pet spends in the hold, and eliminates the possibility that your pet is placed on the wrong flight.

Verify the policy on layovers and delays. If you must have a lengthy layover, or encounter a delay, make sure you will have access to your pet; a good airline will allow you to check on your pet in these circumstances.

You may also want to inquire about hand-carrying and counter-to-counter shipping. Hand-carrying assures that your pet will not be subjected to conveyor belt accidents. Counter-to-counter shipping ensures that your pet will be loaded right before departure and immediately after arrival. There is usually a fee for counter-to-counter shipping, but it may be worth the price for peace of mind.

Thanks to all of our loyal supporters whose donations have made it possible for us to provide vaccinations and medications for rescued animals.

Keep in mind that the more information a carrier provides in response to your questions, the more likely your pet will be well cared for!

Buying a Pet Carrier

❖ The carrier should have hard sides, ventilation on at least two sides, and exterior rims to prevent blocked airflow.

❖ The carrier must be large enough for the pet to stand, turn around, and lie down comfortably. Your pet should easily be able to stand, turn around, and lie down inside the carrier.

❖ It should also be marked with a large, highly visible label reading "Live Animal," at least one inch tall, including arrows indicating the carrier's upright position. Never lock your pet's carrier before departure, in an emergency, airline personnel may need access to your pet.

❖ Finally, both the pet and the carrier should be well marked with the owner's name, address, and phone number, and the pet's updated health certificate.

Student Name
Date

---

a. To create the newsletter, open the file wd04_Air Travel. Create and center a WordArt headline at the top of the document with the words **Animal Angels**. Choose a design and colors of your choice and adjust the size appropriately.

b. Insert a border line of your choice below the WordArt object.

c. Apply a two-line drop cap to the "T" in "The" in the beginning of first paragraph. Add color to the drop cap to match the WordArt object.

d. Beginning at the heading "Is Your Pet Up for the Flight?", select the text and apply a two-column format.

e. Since the entire article on selecting an airline does not fit on page 1, you decide to create a linked text box. Select the material from the heading "Choosing a Pet Friendly Airline…" to "for!" Create a text box and size it to the width of the second column on page 1. Move the bulleted paragraph to page 2.

f. Move the note on tranquilization to the space above the text box in the second column of page 1.

g. Move the graphic of the dogs and suitcases to the bottom of column 1 on page 1. Resize the image appropriately.

h. Create a second text box on page 2 and size it to the width of the left column. Link the text boxes. Resize the text boxes as necessary and add the text **continued from page 1** in italics and right-aligned at the top of the linked text box.

i. Change the border style on the text boxes to a line style of your choice. Then add color to each of the text boxes.

j. Adjust the layout as needed, and add your name and the date at the bottom of the second page.

k. Save the file as Air Travel Newsletter. Print the document.

on your own

Activity Newsletter

★ **1.** Prepare a two-page newsletter on an activity or club of interest to you. The newsletter should include the following features: WordArt, column format, linked text boxes, clip art and/or pictures. When you are finished, add your name and the current date to the last column on page 2. Check the layout of your document and make adjustments as necessary. Save the newsletter as Activity Newsletter and print the document.

Power Plant News

★★ **2.** As the Public Relations Officer for the local power company, you have been assigned a project to inform the public on issues related to the construction of a new power plant. As part of your campaign, you have been asked to create a newsletter to address community concerns. Your completed letter should have great visual appeal. Create a one-page newsletter with multiple graphic objects. Include your name and the date in the document. Save it as Power Plant Newsletter and print it.

Creating a Newsletter

★★ **3.** You are a physical education major and have written a report on water exercises. Open the file wd04_Water. Use this file to create a newsletter for students who use the pool at your school's recreation center. Use the features you have learned in Word, including WordArt, clip art, borders, colors, and text boxes, to create a newsletter that is both informative and visually appealing. When you are finished, add your name and the current date to the last column on page 2. Check the layout of your document and make adjustments as necessary. Save your file as Water Exercise Newsletter and print the document.

PTA Newsletter

★★★ **4.** You are a member of the PTA at the local elementary school. The budget for the year has just been released and the parents are trying to accommodate requests from the teachers and staff for equipment and supplies. The parents decide that a fund raiser will be necessary. In order to fund the purchases, the school has decided to hold an old-fashioned ice cream social. You have volunteered to put together a newsletter to be distributed to the students advertising the event. Your completed newsletter should include WordArt, column format, and other graphic features. Add your name and the date to the top of the newsletter, save the newsletter as PTA Newsletter, and print the document.

Garden Newsletter

★★★ **5.** The neighborhood that you live in has begun construction of a public garden in a previously vacant lot. You are the chairperson of the committee that raised the funds for the park. You and the other committee members have decided to distribute a newsletter updating the contributors and community on the park's progress. Your newsletter should have great visual appeal. Be sure to include WordArt and other graphic features, as well as photos of the garden. Add your name and the current date to the top of the newsletter. Save the document as Garden Newsletter and print it.

Creating a Personal Newsletter

Create a monthly newsletter with small articles on a topic of your choice. Use the Web or other resources to obtain information on your topic. Use the features you have learned in Word to create a newsletter that is both informative and visually appealing. Include features such as WordArt, clip art, borders, colors, and text boxes. When you are finished, add your name and the current date to the end of the document. Check the layout of your document and make adjustments as necessary. Save the document as My Newsletter and print it.

Creating Complex Tables and Merging Documents

objectives

After completing this lab, you will know how to:

1.	Use a template.
2.	Modify a field format.
3.	Insert graphics from the Web.
4.	Use the Draw Table feature to create and enhance a table.
5.	Merge cells.
6.	Change text orientation, table size, and page orientation.
7.	Insert a column.
8.	Perform calculations in a table.
9.	Add cell shading.
10.	Size rows and columns.
11.	Remove border lines.
12.	Create and modify a chart.
13.	Create an outline-style numbered list.
14.	Use the Mail Merge feature to create form letters.
15.	Print mailing labels and envelopes.

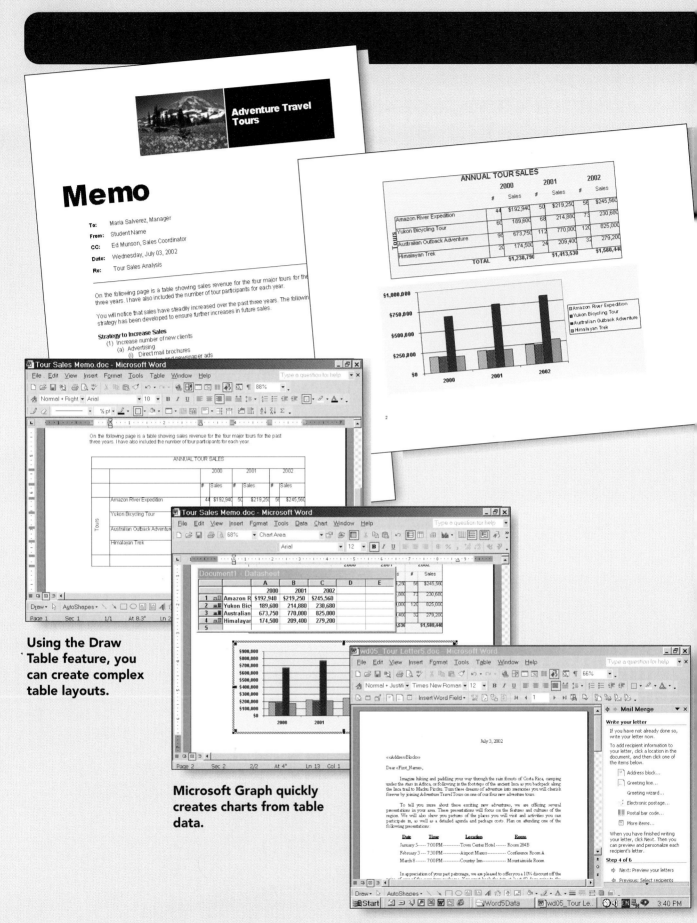

Using the Draw Table feature, you can create complex table layouts.

Microsoft Graph quickly creates charts from table data.

The Mail Merge feature helps you quickly generate a form letter.

Adventure Travel Tours

In addition to the four new tours, Adventure Travel Tours offers many established adventure tours. The four most popular tours are the Amazon River Expedition, the Yukon Bicycling Tour, the Australian Outback Adventure, and the Himalayan Trek. Your latest project for Adventure Travel Tours is to prepare a memo for the regional manager that contains a table showing the sales figures for these four major tours for the past three years. In addition, you want to include a strategy to increase sales for the four tours.

The manager has also asked you to personalize the letter you wrote about the new tours and presentations by including an inside address for each client and using his or her first name in the salutation. To do this, you will create a form letter. Form letters are common business documents used when the same information needs to be communicated to many different people. You will also create mailing labels for the letter and learn how to quickly address a single envelope.

© Corbis

Using a Template

You would like to create the sales-figure memo using one of the pre-designed document templates included with Word. The templates are designed to help you create professional-looking business documents such as letters, faxes, memos, reports, brochures, press releases, manuals, newsletters, resumes, invoices, purchase orders, and weekly time sheets. Once you create a document from a template, you can change different elements to give it your own personal style.

1 ● **Start Word.**

Additional Information
Word displays the last two templates that were used in the New From Template list.

● **Click** General Templates... **from the New Document task pane.**

● **Open the Memos tab.**

● **Select** Contemporary Memo.

Your screen should be similar to Figure 5.1

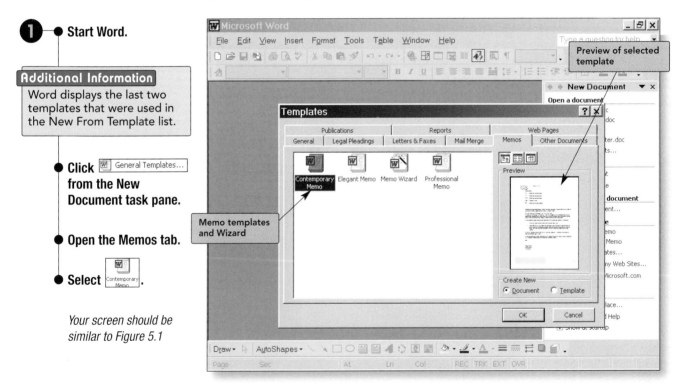

Figure 5.1

Word has several memo templates and a Memo Wizard that guides you step by step through creating a memo. Document templates have a .dot file extension and are stored in the Templates folder. When opened, the file type changes to a Word document (.doc). This prevents accidentally overwriting the template file when the file is saved.

The Preview area displays how the selected memo template looks. You will use the Professional Memo template to create your memo.

2 ● **Double-click** [Professional Memo].

● **Change the zoom to Page Width.**

Your screen should be similar to Figure 5.2

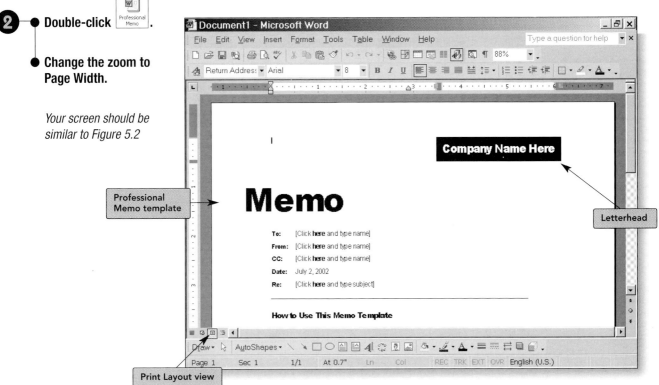

Figure 5.2

The memo template is opened as a Word document and is displayed in Print Layout view.

Replacing Template Placeholders

The template uses a single-row table to control the layout of the company letterhead. You will display the table gridlines and then replace the text in the table cell with the company name.

3

- If necessary, choose **Table/Show Gridlines.**

- Select the text **Company Name Here.**

- Type **Adventure Travel Tours.**

Your screen should be similar to Figure 5.3

Memo header

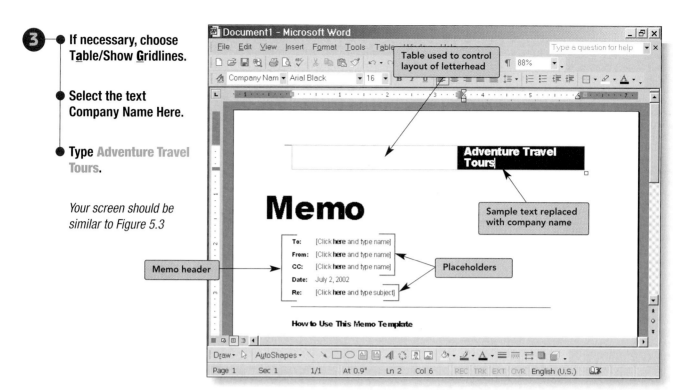

Figure 5.3

Additional Information

You can delete unwanted items from the memo template by selecting the object and pressing Delete.

The next area in the memo template you need to modify is the memo header, which includes the name of the recipient, the sender's name, a carbon or courtesy (CC) recipient, the date, and a subject line. Notice that the date is the current system date. The text in brackets is a **placeholder** that tells you what information to enter. To enter text, click on the placeholder and type the information you want to include in your document. This feature is found in most templates.

4

- Click the **To:** placeholder.

- Type **Maria Salverez, Manager.**

Your screen should be similar to Figure 5.4

Current system date

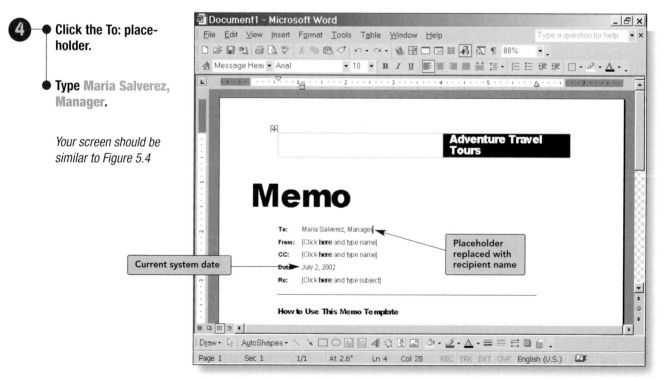

Figure 5.4

The placeholder is replaced with the name of the recipient. Notice that the Style list box displays "Message Header" as the default style; this sets the font to Arial and the size to 10 points.

5 ● **Replace the remaining four placeholders with the following:**

From: Your name

CC: Ed Munson, Sales Coordinator

Re: Tour Sales Analysis

Your screen should be similar to Figure 5.5

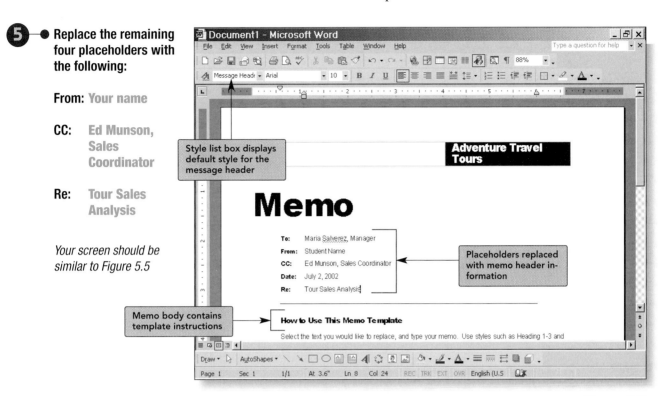

Figure 5.5

Next you want to enter the body of the memo. The memo template also includes instructions on how to use the template in the body of the memo. You will replace the template instructions with the information you want to include in the memo. However, because the template instructions are not placeholders, you first need to select the instructions to be deleted before typing the replacement text.

6 ● Click ¶ Show/Hide to turn on paragraph marks.

● Scroll the window to see the paragraph of template instructions in the body of the memo.

● Select the heading, the instructions paragraphs and the blank lines below the paragraph.

● Type the following text: On the following page is a table showing sales revenue for the four major tours for the past three years. I have also included the number of tour participants for each year.

● Press ←Enter twice.

Your screen should be similar to Figure 5.6

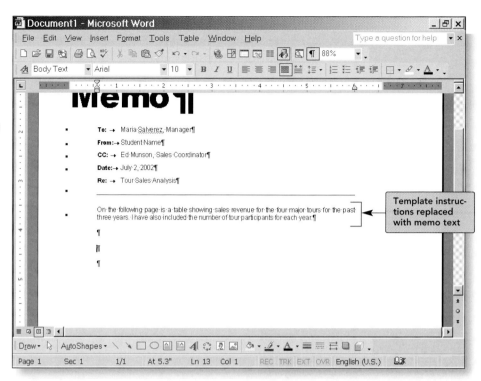

Figure 5.6

The template instructions are replaced with your own memo text.

Modifying Field Formats

The date in the memo template is a field that displays the current system date. You want to change the date format to include the day of the week. To do this, you need to edit the field format.

1 ● Right-click on the Date field.

● Choose **E**dit Field.

Your screen should be similar to Figure 5.7

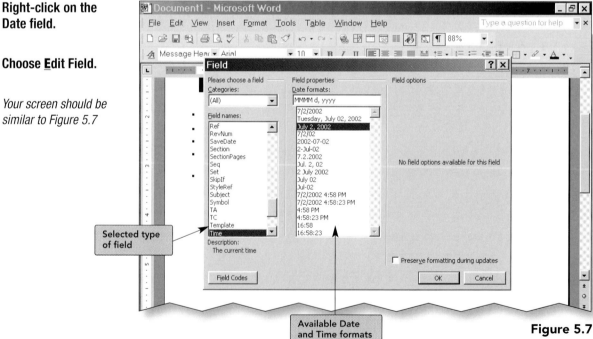

Figure 5.7

The Field dialog box displays a list of field names and formats for the selected field. Since the Date field is selected, the Time category is open and selected formats for date and time display in the Field Properties area.

2 • **From the Date formats list, select the format that includes the day of the week.**

• **Click** [OK] .

Your screen should be similar to Figure 5.8

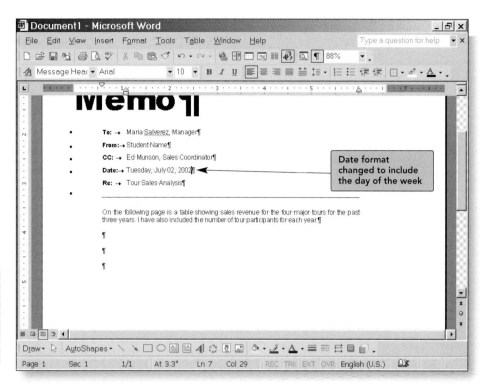

Figure 5.8

Inserting Graphics from the Web

Next you want to add a graphic to the letterhead. If the Clip Organizer does not include a suitable graphic, you can go to the Microsoft Design Gallery Live Web site and download a picture. You will use this resource to locate a graphic.

Note: This section requires an Internet connection. If you do not have this capability, insert the clip art graphic wd05_Mountain from your supplied data files and complete the instructions in Step 4 to size and position it.

1
● Click in the table cell to the left of the company name.

● Click 🔲 Insert Clip Art (on the Drawing toolbar).

● Click 🌐 Clips Online.

● Enter the information as needed to connect to the Internet.

HAVING TROUBLE?
If an End User license agreement appears, click Accept to continue.

Your screen should be similar to Figure 5.9

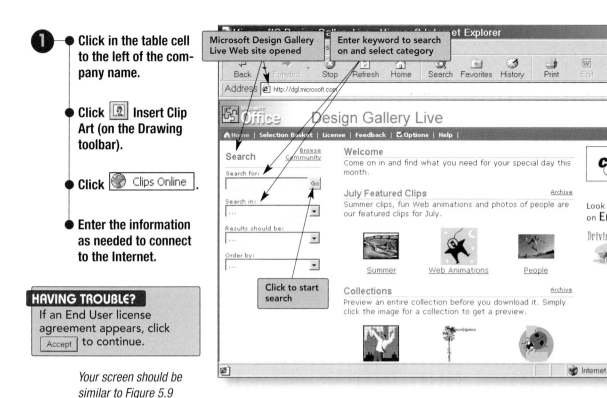

Figure 5.9

The browser on your system is started and the connection to the Microsoft Design Gallery Live Web site is made. The Design Gallery includes clip art, photos, sounds, and motion graphics that you can download and use in your documents. The easiest way to locate an item is to search on a keyword, just as you do in the Insert Clip Art task pane. You want to use a graphic of a mountain in the letterhead and will search using the keyword "mountain."

2
● In the Search For text box, type mountain.

● From the Search In drop-down list, select Nature.

● Click Go.

Another Method
You can also press ←Enter to start the search.

Your screen should be similar to Figure 5.10

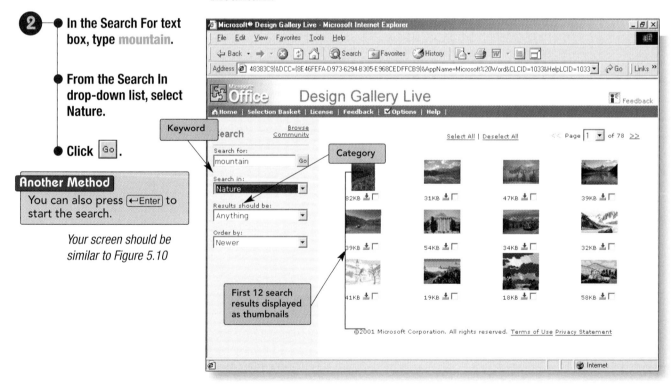

Figure 5.10

The Design Gallery displays the results of the search. Thumbnails of the first 12 items in the Nature category whose associated keyword matches the keyword you entered are displayed.

3 ● **Click on a thumbnail to see an enlarged view.**

● **Select a picture of your choice, preview it, and click ⬇ to download it.**

● **If you are prompted, select the MPF (Office XP) format type, and click Download Now!.**

Your screen should be similar to Figure 5.11

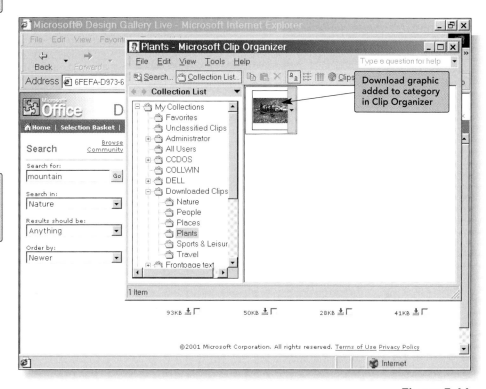

Figure 5.11

The picture is downloaded and added automatically to a category in the Clip Organizer on your system. The category it is added to is determined from the keywords associated with the picture. Next you want to insert the picture in the document.

4 ● Display the Word document window.

● Display the Clip Organizer window.

● Drag the picture into the left cell of the letterhead table.

Additional Information

You can also drag a thumbnail displayed in the Insert Clip Art task pane into the document to insert it.

● Close the Insert Clip Art task pane.

● Select the picture and reduce its size to approximately 1.25 inches high by 2 inches wide.

● Size and position the letterhead table similar to as shown in Figure 5.12.

HAVING TROUBLE?

Refer to Lab 3, page WD3.49 to review sizing and moving tables.

Your screen should be similar to Figure 5.12

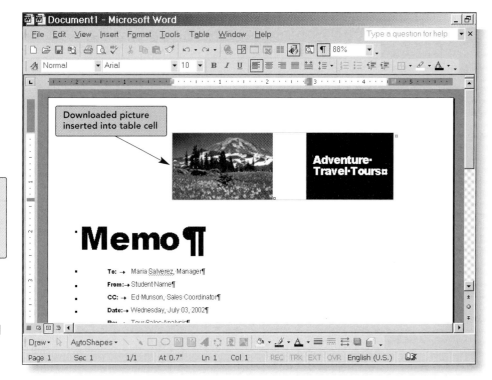

Figure 5.12

You will continue to refine the appearance of the letterhead later. For now, you want to save the changes you have made and continue to work on the memo content.

5 ● Close the Clip Organizer window.

● Close the browser window and, if necessary, disconnect from the Internet.

● Save the document as Tour Sales Memo.

Creating a Complex Table

Next you want to create a table to display the tour sales data below the memo text. The table will display the data vertically (in columns) for the three years and horizontally (in rows) for the four tours and a total. Your completed table will be similar to the one shown below.

Additional Information

Refer to Lab 3, Concept 7, to review tables.

ANNUAL TOUR SALES

		2000		2001		2002	
		#	Sales	#	Sales	#	Sales
Tours	Amazon River Expedition	44	$192,940	50	$219,250	58	$245,560
	Yukon Bicycling Tour	60	189,600	68	214,880	73	230,680
	Australian Outback Adventure	98	673,750	112	770,000	120	825,000
	Himalayan Trek	20	174,500	24	209,400	32	279,200
	TOTAL		$1,230,790		$1,413,530		$1,580,440

You will use the Draw table feature to create this table. The Draw Table feature can be used to create any type of table, but is particularly useful for creating a complex table like this.

1 ● **Move to the first blank line below the paragraph in the body of the memo.**

Your screen should be similar to Figure 5.13

Current style

Location to create table

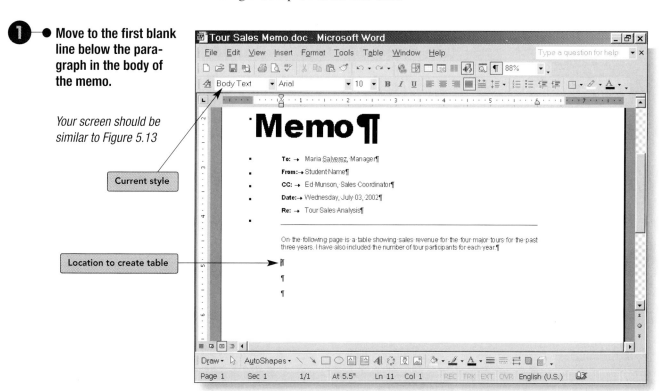

Figure 5.13

Notice that the Style list box shows "Body Text." The Body Text style includes formatting settings that will adversely affect the table that you are about to create at this location. You will change the style to Normal for the text after the memo body before creating the table. Then you will display the Drawing and Tables toolbar to help you create the table.

2 ● **Select the three blank lines.**

● **From the Style drop-down menu, choose Clear Formatting.**

Additional Information
Clearing formatting returns the style to Normal.

● **Click ¶ Show/Hide to hide the paragraph marks.**

● **Click ▦ Tables and Borders (on the Standard toolbar).**

Another Method
The menu equivalent is Table/Draw Table.

● **If necessary, move and dock the Tables and Borders toolbar below the Formatting toolbar.**

Your screen should be similar to Figure 5.14

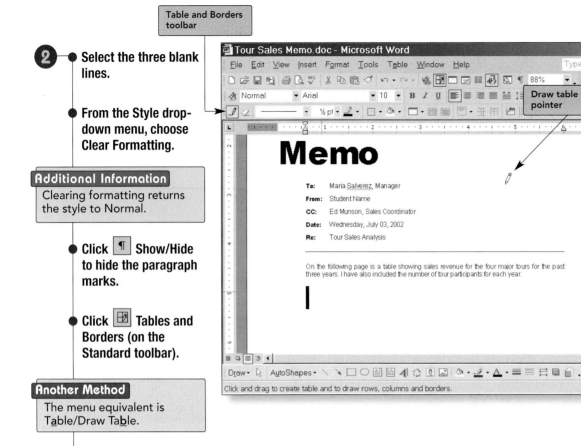

Figure 5.14

When the Tables and Borders toolbar is displayed, the Draw Table feature is automatically activated. Using Draw Table to create a table is like using a pen to draw a table. The mouse pointer changes to ✏ when positioned in the text area, and a dotted line appears to show the boundary or lines you are creating as you drag. First you define the outer table boundaries; then you draw the column and row lines.

The Tables and Borders toolbar buttons (identified below) are used to modify table settings.

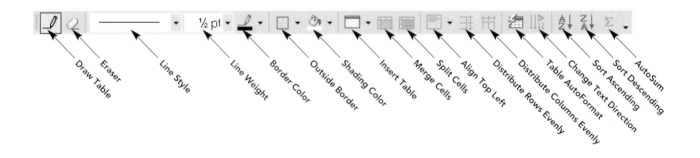

3 ● **Click below the paragraph and drag downward and to the right to create an outer table boundary of approximately 3 inches high by 6 inches wide (refer to Figure 5.15).**

● **Drag the right indent marker on the ruler to the right margin of the table.**

Your screen should be similar to Figure 5.15

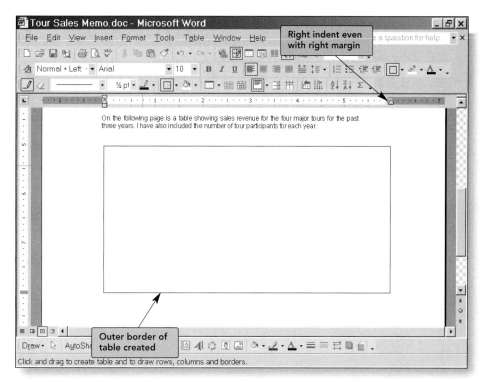

Figure 5.15

The outer border of the table is created. Next you need to add lines to create the columns and rows. When creating row or column lines, drag from the beginning boundary to the end to extend the line the distance you want. A dotted line appears in the ruler to show your position in the table as you draw. If you make an error, click 🔙 or 🖊 Eraser and drag over the line.

As you create the row and columns in the next step, refer to Figure 5.16 for placement. Do not be concerned if your table does not look exactly like Figure 5.16 when you are done as you will learn all about adjusting table rows and columns in following steps.

● Add four vertical column lines at positions 0.5, 3, 4, and 5 on the ruler (see Figure 5.16).

● Draw seven horizontal lines to create the rows as shown in Figure 5.16. (Lines 4, 5, and 6 begin at the first column.)

● Click 🖉 to turn off Draw Table.

Another Method

Typing in any cell will also turn off Draw Table.

Your screen should be similar to Figure 5.16

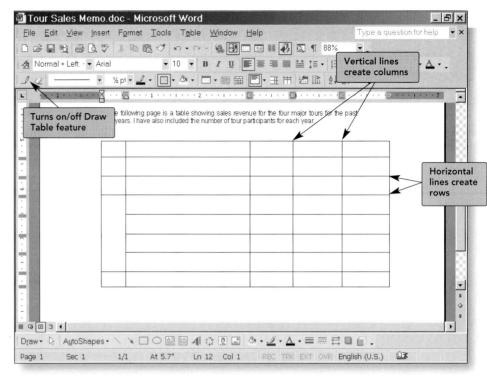

Figure 5.16

The table consists of eight rows and five columns. Now you are ready to enter information in the table.

● Enter the labels and data in the cells as shown in Figure 5.17. Incliude $ symbols in row 4 Sales Values only.

Your screen should be similar to Figure 5.17

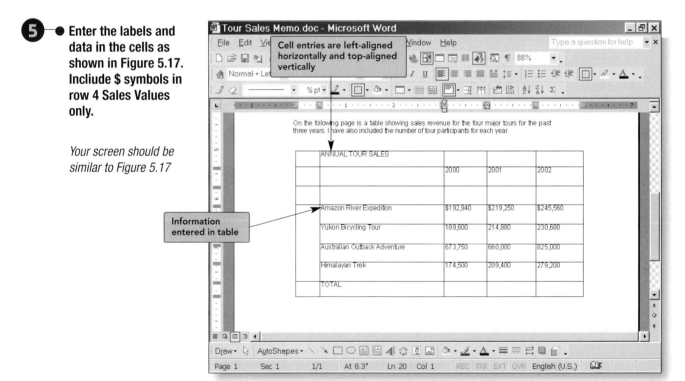

Figure 5.17

By default, entries in cells are left-aligned horizontally and top-aligned vertically in the cell space. You want to center the year headings and right-align the sales values.

Select cells C2 through E2, containing the year headings.

Click [≡] **Center.**

Select the cells containing the sales values and right-align the values.

Click in the table to deselect the cells.

Your screen should be similar to Figure 5.18

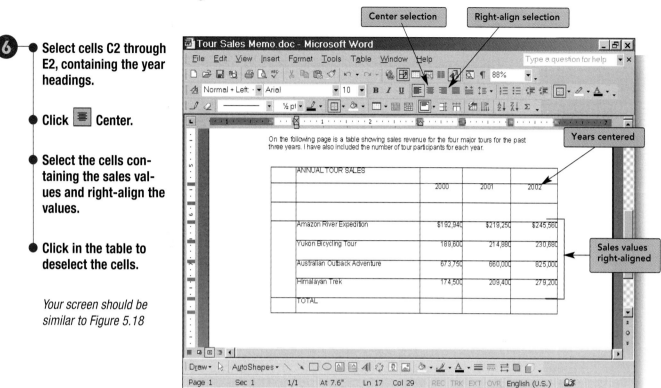

Figure 5.18

You will continue to add more formatting changes to improve the appearance of the table shortly.

Inserting a Column

You realize that you forgot to include columns for the number of people who took the tours in each year. To add this information, you need to insert three new columns to the left of the sales values. You can do this quickly using the Draw Table feature again.

1 ● Click  Draw Table.

● Using Figure 5.19 as a reference, drag to add three new columns at the 3.25, 4.25, and 5.25 positions extending from row 3 through row 7.

● Turn off the Draw Table feature.

Another Method

The Table/Insert/Columns to the left command will add a full height column to the left of the current column.

Your screen should be similar to Figure 5.19

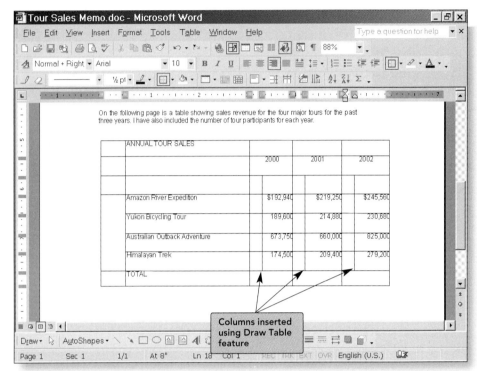

Figure 5.19

2 ● Choose Table/Table Properties/Table/Options/Automatically resize to fit contents.

● Click OK twice.

● Type # in cells C3, E3, and G3.

● Type Sales in cells D3, F3, and H3.

● Enter the following values in the cells specified.

If any of the sales values in your table wrap to a second line in a cell, this is because the cell width is too narrow to display the entry on a single line. In a Normal document template, the table properties are set to automatically resize to fit the cell contents. However, the Professional Memo template has this table property turned off. You will turn it on to fix this problem as well as to ensure that as you enter the data for the number of people in the tours, the columns will automatically resize to fit.

	Col C	Col E	Col G
Row 4	44	50	56
Row 5	60	68	73
Row 6	98	112	120
Row 7	20	24	32

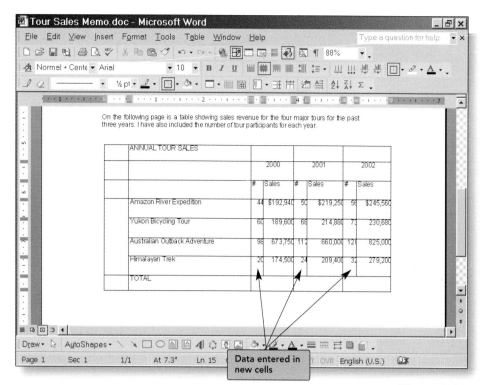

Figure 5.20

Performing Calculations in a Table

Now you want to calculate the sales revenue totals. Rather than adding the
values for each column of data and entering them in the Total row, you can
enter a formula to make this calculation for you.

concept 1

Formulas and Functions

1   Formulas and functions are used to perform calculations in tables. A **formula** is an expression that contains any combination of numbers, fields resulting in numbers, table references, and operators. **Operators** specify the type of calculation to perform. The most common operators are + (add), – (subtract), * (multiply), and / (divide).

To use the operators, follow the common arithmetic laws: multiply and divide before adding and subtracting, and calculate whatever is in parentheses first. For example, the formula, 125 + D3 * D5 will multiply the value in cell D3 by the value in cell D5 and then add 125. If you want to add 125 to D3 and then multiply the result by D5, put 125 and D3 in parentheses: (125 + D3) * D5.

A **function** is a prewritten formula. One function you may use frequently is the SUM function. SUM calculates the total of a column of numbers. Other functions include:

Function	Description
AVERAGE	Calculates the average of a column of numbers
COUNT	Totals the number of cells in the column
MAX	Displays the maximum value in the column
MIN	Displays the minimum value in the column

To reference cells in formulas and functions, use a comma to separate references to individual cells and a colon to separate the first and last cells in a block. For example C1, C5 references the values in cells C1 and C5, whereas C1:C5 references the values in cells C1, C2, C3, C4, and C5.

The calculated result of a formula or function is displayed in the table cell containing the formula or function. The result of the calculation is a field.

Therefore, if the data in the referenced cells of the formula or function changes updating the field quickly recalculates the result.

The formulas and functions in Word let you create simple tables and spreadsheets for your documents. For larger, more complex spreadsheets, use Excel and then paste the spreadsheet into your document.

Calculating a Sum

You will enter a formula to sum the sales revenue values in the 2000 column of data.

1 ● **Move to cell D8.**

● **Choose Table/Formula.**

Your screen should be similar to Figure 5.21

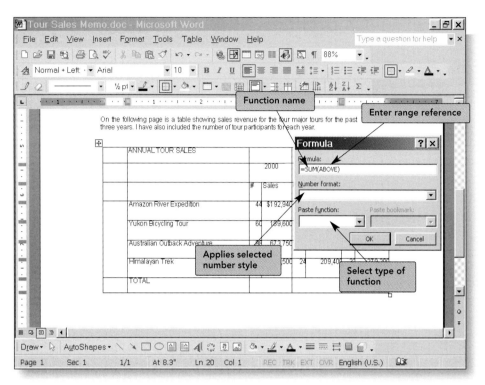

Figure 5.21

In the Formula dialog box, you enter the type of formula and the table cell references for the formula in the Formula text box. The function =SUM(ABOVE) is displayed by default because that is the only location of the cells containing values to sum. The range reference ABOVE will calculate a sum for all values directly above the current cell. Use the Paste Function list box to select the type of function you want, or type the function directly in the Function text box. From the Number Format drop-down list box, you can select a number style.

You want to sum the values in the range of cells D4 through D7 (D4:D7) and will replace ABOVE with the specific table cell references. You also want to format the numbers as currency.

2

● In place of the word **ABOVE** in the parentheses, enter **D4:D7**.

● Select **$#,##0.00;($#,##0.00)** from the Number Format drop-down list.

● Click [OK].

Your screen should be similar to Figure 5.22

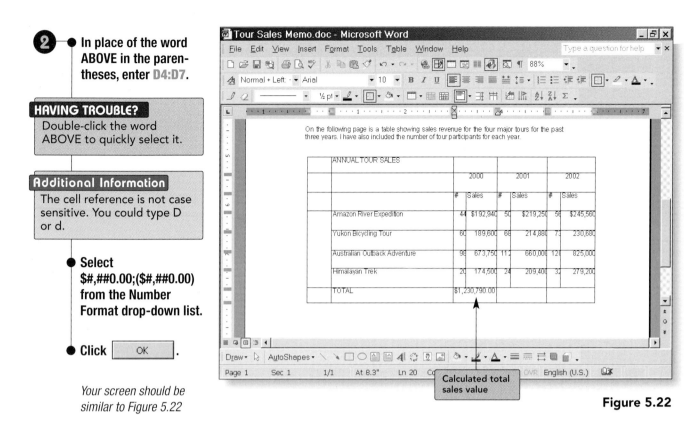

Calculated total sales value

Figure 5.22

Using the values in the specified cells of the table, the formula correctly calculates the result of $1,230,790.00. The value is displayed in the selected number format style. Because the SUM function is the most frequently used function, it has its own shortcut button. You will use the shortcut to calculate the sales total for 2001.

3

● Move to cell F8.

● Click Σ AutoSum.

Your screen should be similar to Figure 5.23

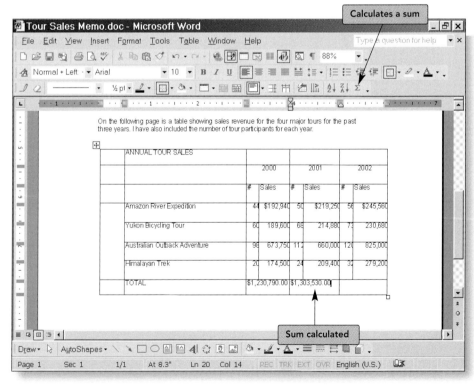

Calculates a sum

Sum calculated

Figure 5.23

Using the $\boxed{\Sigma}$ AutoSum button enters a SUM function that calculates the sum of all the numbers above the current cell. The calculated value of $1,303,530.00 is displayed in cell D8. It is also formatted as currency. This is because Word used the same format as the value in cell D4.

As you look at the total, you think it seems a little low and decide to check the values you entered for the year. You see that the Australian Outback Adventure value was entered incorrectly. It should be 770,000. Because the calculated result is a field, after changing the value in the cell, you can quickly update the calculation.

4 Change the entry in cell F6 to **770,000**.

Move to cell F8 and press F9 to update the field.

Another Method

You can also select Update Field from the field's shortcut menu.

Your screen should be similar to Figure 5.24

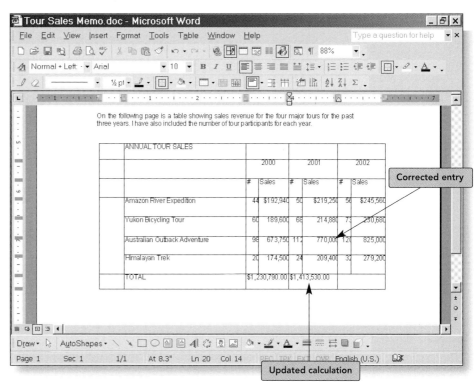

Figure 5.24

The correct calculated value of $1,413,530.00 is displayed in the cell. Next you need to enter the function to calculate the value for 2002. Additionally, you decide you do not want the two decimal places displayed for the three totals and will delete them.

Enter the function to calculate the total for 2002 in cell H8.

Click in the field and delete the decimal and two decimal places from each of the three calculated results.

Right-align the TOTAL label and total values.

Save the document again.

Your screen should be similar to Figure 5.25

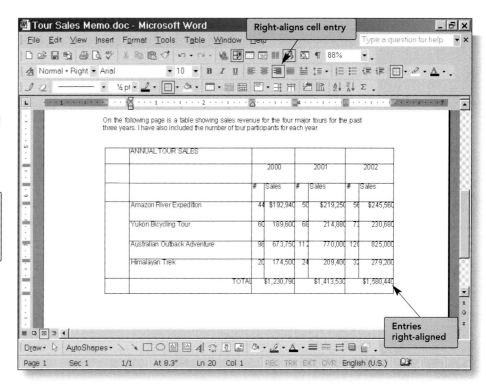

Figure 5.25

Formatting the Table

The table is really taking shape. Now that the content of the table is complete, you want to improve its appearance by enhancing the title, adding color, increasing the text size, and modifying the border lines.

Merging Cells

After looking at the table, you decide to display the title centered over all columns of the table. To do this, you will combine the cells in the row to create a single cell and then center the label within the cell.

● **Select row 1.**

Click at the left edge of the row to select the entire row.

● Click 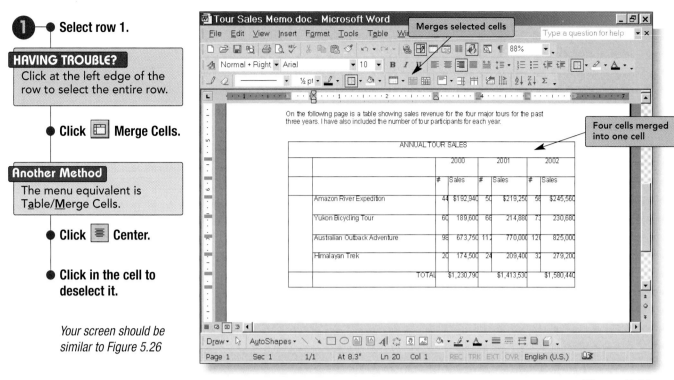 **Merge Cells.**

The menu equivalent is T**a**ble/**M**erge Cells.

● Click 🔳 **Center.**

● **Click in the cell to deselect it.**

Your screen should be similar to Figure 5.26

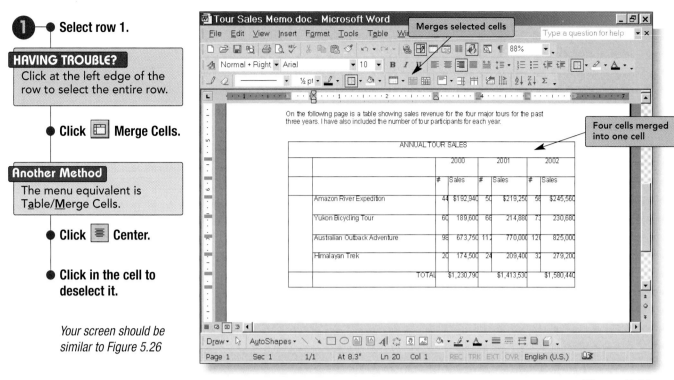

Figure 5.26

The four column dividers are eliminated, and the top row is one cell. The entry is centered in the cell space.

Changing Text Orientation

In cell A4 you want to display the heading "Tour." You also want the heading to appear centered and the orientation to be vertical within the cell space.

● **Enter** Tours **in cell A4.**

● Click 🔳 **Change Text Direction twice.**

The menu equivalent is F**o**rmat/**T**ext Direction/**O**rientation.

● Click 🔳 **Center.**

Your screen should be similar to Figure 5.27

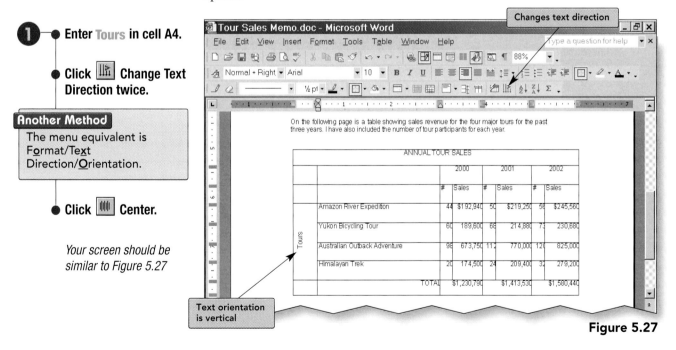

Figure 5.27

Adding Cell Shading

You will first add color shading to differentiate the areas of the table.

1 ● **Select the entire table.**

HAVING TROUBLE?

You can click ⊞, or drag, or use Table/Select/Table to select the entire table.

● **Open the** 🖌️ ▾ **Shading Color drop-down menu.**

● **Click** `More Fill Colors...`.

● **If necessary, open the Standard tab.**

Your screen should be similar to Figure 5.28

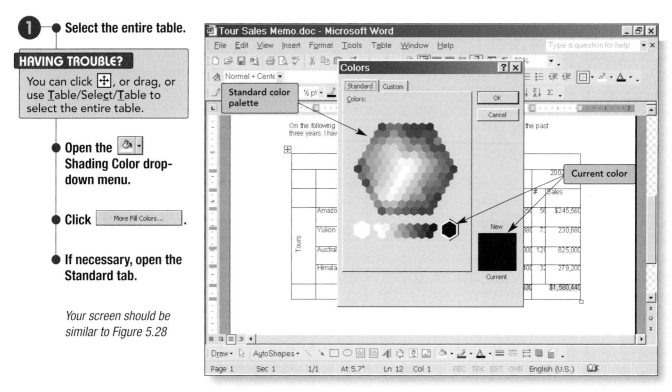

Figure 5.28

From the Colors dialog box, you can select from standard colors or create a custom color. The Standard tab palette includes many shade variations of the same colors that are included in the drop-down color palette list.

2 ● **Select a color of your choice from the standard color palette.**

● **Click** `OK`.

● **Select the tour names and sales values, and apply another color to the cells in this range.**

Your screen should be similar to Figure 5.29

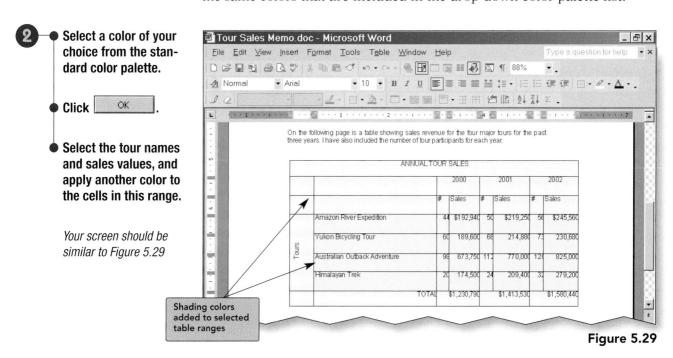

Figure 5.29

Next you want to enhance the text of the headings and the table data.

3

- Select the table title and increase the font size to 16 points, and add bold with a color of your choice.

- Select the year headings and increase the font size to 14 points, add bold and the same color as the title. Apply the same formats to the Tours label.

- Select the remaining text in the table and increase the font size to 12 points.

- Center and apply the same color to the # and Sales headings.

- Apply the same color and bold to the TOTAL label and values.

Your screen should be similar to Figure 5.30

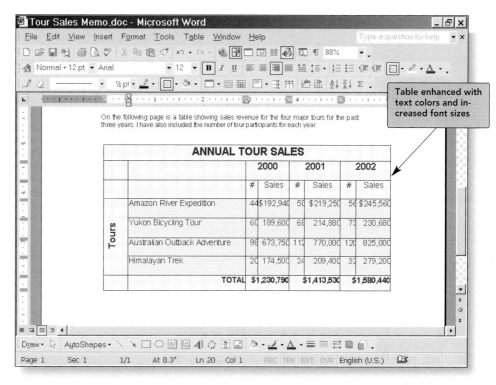

Figure 5.30

Changing Table Size and Page Orientation

Because the increased point size makes the table contents look crowded, you decide to make the entire table larger.

1

- Select the table.

- Drag the sizing handle to the right to increase the width of the table to the 7-inch position on the ruler.

Your screen should be similar to Figure 5.31

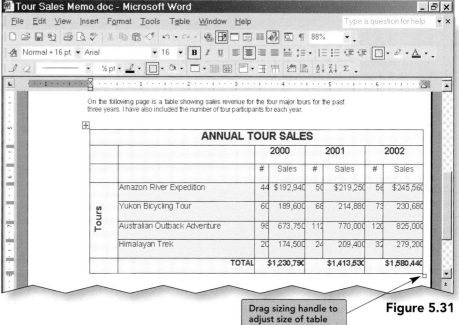

Drag sizing handle to adjust size of table

Figure 5.31

Now the table is too wide to fit easily within the width of the page. When text is wider than the width of the page, you can change the orientation of the page from **portrait**, in which text is printed across the width of the page, to **landscape**, in which text is printed across the length of the page.

Because the memo will look better in the current orientation of portrait, you decide to display the table on a separate page that will print in landscape orientation. To have different orientations within a document, you need to insert a section break first, and then apply the orientation to the section you want affected.

2 • **If necessary, insert a blank line above the table.**

• **Move to the blank line above the table.**

• **Insert a Next Page section break.**

• **Choose File/Page Setup/Landscape.**

• **Click** OK **.**

• **Change the zoom to Two Pages.**

Your screen should be similar to Figure 5.32

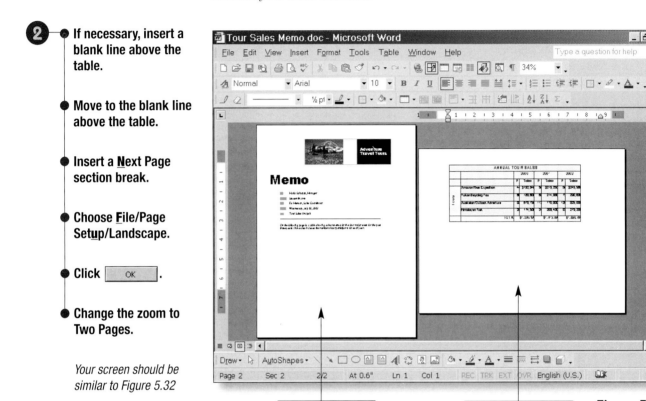

Portrait orientation   Landscape orientation

Figure 5.32

The entire table now easily fits across the width of the page.

Sizing Rows and Columns

You want to decrease the width of column A. To change the width of a column or row, point to the column divider line and drag it to the right or left to increase or decrease the column width, or up or down to increase or decrease the row height. A temporary dotted line appears to show your new setting.

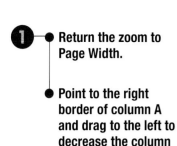

1 ● **Return the zoom to Page Width.**

● **Point to the right border of column A and drag to the left to decrease the column width to the minimum amount possible.**

Additional Information

The mouse pointer appears as ╋║╋ when you can drag to size a row or column.

Your screen should be similar to Figure 5.33

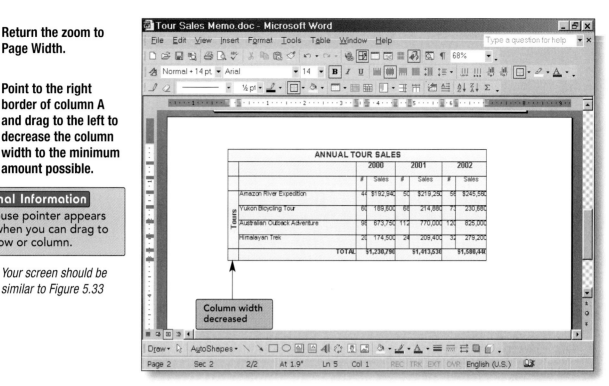

Figure 5.33

You also want to adjust the height of the rows to be equally sized.

2 ● **Select the entire table.**

● **Click** ⊞ **Distribute Rows Evenly.**

Another Method

The menu equivalent is Table/Autofit/Distribute Rows Evenly.

Your screen should be similar to Figure 5.34

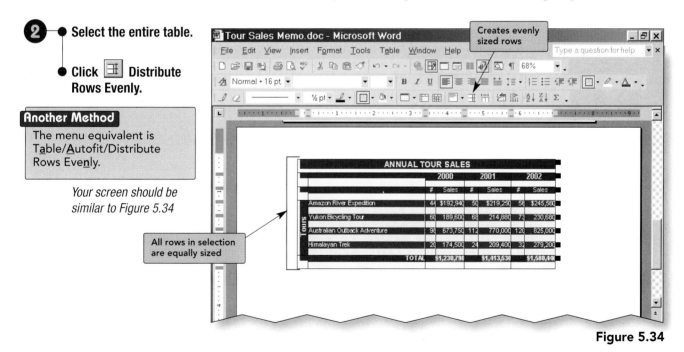

Figure 5.34

You also want the widths of the # columns to be the same and the widths of the Sales columns to be the same. However, because these columns are not adjacent, you cannot use the Distribute Columns Evenly feature. Instead, you need to specify the exact width for each column.

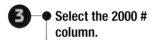

3 ● Select the 2000 # column.

● Choose T**a**ble/Table Pr**o**perties/Col**u**mn.

● Select Preferred **W**idth.

● Enter **.5** in the text box.

Your screen should be similar to Figure 5.35

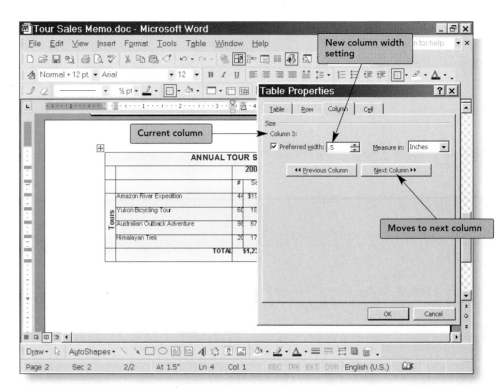

Figure 5.35

Notice the dialog box identifies the column as column number 3. You can continue specifying settings for the other columns by moving to the column and making the appropriate selections. When you are done, the new settings will be applied to the table.

4 ● Click **Next Column ▶▶** twice to move to column 5.

● Select Preferred Width to accept the last entered width setting.

● Move to column 7 and set the width to 0.5 inch.

● In a similar manner, set the column widths for columns 8, 6, and 4 to 1 inch.

● Click **OK**.

● Click on the table to deselect the column.

Your screen should be similar to Figure 5.36

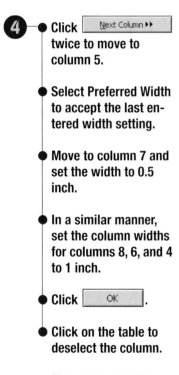

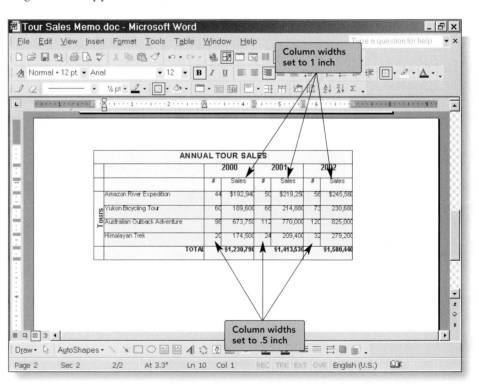

Figure 5.36

Removing Border Lines

When a table is created, single, black, 0.5-point solid-line borders are added by default around each cell. Once color and other formatting has been added to a table, you may no longer need all the border lines to define the spaces. You will remove the border line below row 1 first.

1 ● **Move to row 1.**

● **Open the** ▣▾ **Border drop-down menu.**

● **Click** ▣ **bottom border to clear the border line.**

Additional Information
The Border drop-down menu identifies the border lines that are used in a selected cell by highlighting them.

Your screen should be similar to Figure 5.37

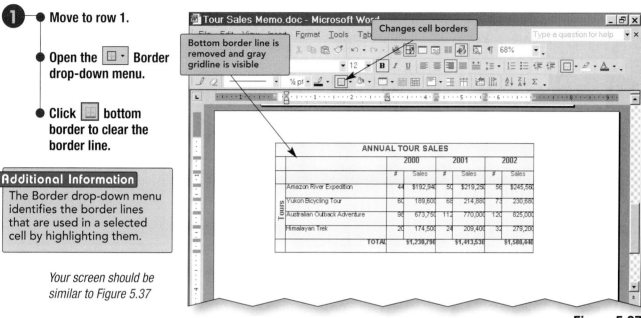

Figure 5.37

The border line is removed, but a gray gridline is still displayed. Gridlines are used to help you see the cell boundaries; however, they are not printed.

2 ● **Remove the border lines from the cells as shown in Figure 5.38.**

Your screen should be similar to Figure 5.38

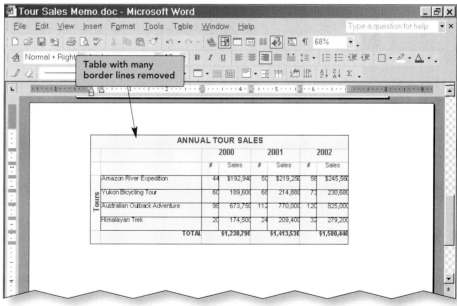

Figure 5.38

Finally, you want the table centered on the page.

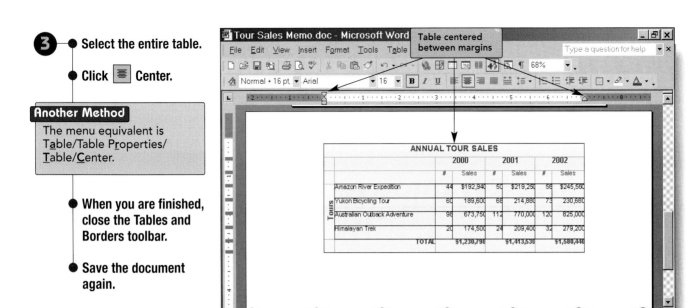

3 ● Select the entire table.

● Click 🔲 Center.

Another Method
The menu equivalent is
Table/Table Properties/
Table/Center.

● When you are finished,
close the Tables and
Borders toolbar.

● Save the document
again.

*Your screen should be
similar to Figure 5.39*

Figure 5.39

Creating a Chart

As you look at the data in the table, you decide to include a chart of the data
below the table, to better show the trends in sales.

concept 2

Charts

2 A **chart**, also called a graph, is a visual representation of numeric data. Presenting data as a chart provides more impact than the data alone and makes it easier to see trends and comparisons. Word
2002 includes a separate program, Microsoft Graph, designed to help you create 14 types of charts
with many different formats for each type.

Each type of chart represents the data differently and has a different purpose. It is important to select the type of chart that will provide the right emphasis to support the data. The basic chart types
are described below.

Type of Chart	Description
Area	Shows the relative importance of a value over time by emphasizing the area under the curve created by each data series.
Bar	Displays categories vertically and values horizontally, placing more emphasis on comparisons and less on time. Stacked-bar charts show the relationship of individual items to a whole by stacking bars on top of one another.
Column	Similar to a bar chart, except categories are organized horizontally and values vertically.
Line	Shows changes in data over time, emphasizing time and rate of change rather than the amount of change.
Pie	Shows the relationship of each value in a data series to the series as a whole. Each slice of the pie represents a single value in a data series.

Most charts are made up of several basic parts, as described in the following table.

Part	Description
X axis	The bottom boundary of the chart, also called the category axis, is used to label the data being charted; the label may be, for example, a point in time or a category.
Y axis	The left boundary of the chart, also called the value axis, is a numbered scale whose numbers are determined by the data used in the chart. Each line or bar in a chart represents a data value. In pie charts there are no axes. Instead, the data that is charted is displayed as slices in a circle or pie.
Legend	A box containing a brief description identifying the patterns or colors assigned to the data series in a chart.
Titles	Descriptive text used to explain the contents of the chart.

Pasting Data from a Table

To specify the data in the table to use in the chart, you will copy the sales labels in row 3, the four tour names in column B, and the sales values for the three years in columns D, F, and H.

1 ● Select cells B3 through H7.

● Click 🗐 Copy.

● Move to the blank line below the table.

● Press ↵Enter.

● Choose Insert/Object/ Microsoft Graph Chart.

● Click OK.

Your screen should be similar to Figure 5.40

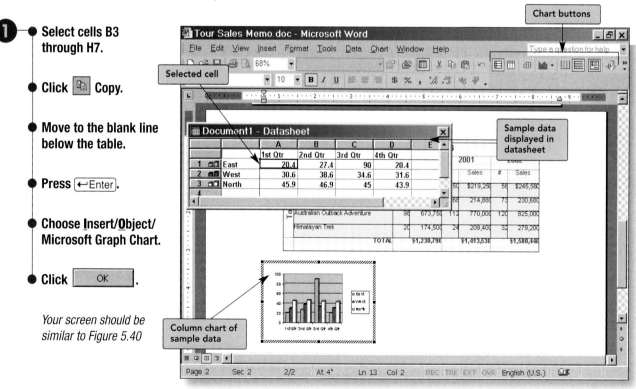

Figure 5.40

The Graph feature is activated and a table, called a **datasheet**, containing sample data is displayed in a separate window. A column chart using the sample data from the datasheet is inserted in the document. Notice that the datasheet displays the column letters A through E and row numbers 1 through 4 to label the cells in the table. The cell that is surrounded by the border is the selected cell and is the cell you can work in.

In addition to displaying sample data, the datasheet also contains place-holders for the row labels, which are used as the legend in the chart, and for the column labels, which are used as X-axis labels. The Standard toolbar also now includes buttons for working with charts.

Specifying the Chart Data

You need to replace the sample data in the datasheet with the data you copied from the table.

1 ● Click in the cell in the top left corner of the Datasheet window.

● Click 📋 Paste.

● Click on the selection to deselect it.

● Increase the size of the datasheet window to view all the data.

Your screen should be similar to Figure 5.41

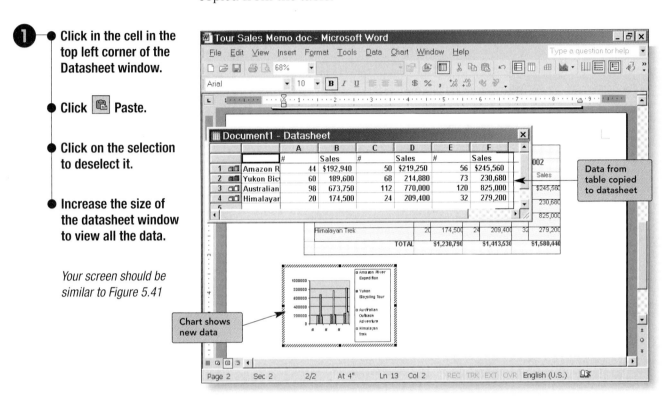

Figure 5.41

The data in the datasheet is updated to include the data from the table, and the chart reflects the change in data. Next you need to remove the three columns of data containing the number of participants and change the remaining column headings to reflect the three years.

2 ● **Right-click column A and choose Delete.**

● **Delete the other two columns with # in the heading row.**

● **In the first row of column A, replace "Sales" with 2000.**

● **In the same manner change the "Sales" headings in columns B and C to 2001 and 2002.**

Your screen should be similar to Figure 5.42

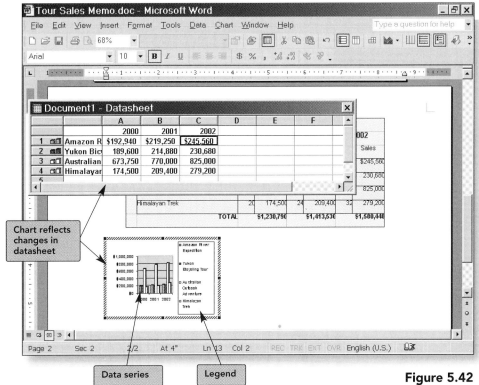

Chart reflects changes in datasheet

Data series

Legend

Figure 5.42

Each group of related data that is plotted in the chart is a **data series**. Each data series has a unique color or pattern assigned to it so that you can identify the different series. The **legend** identifies the color or pattern associated with each data series. As you can see, the values and text in the chart are directly linked to the datasheet, and any changes you make in the datasheet are automatically reflected in the chart.

Sizing the Chart

Now that the data is specified, you can close the datasheet. Then you will increase the size of the chart.

1 ● **Close the Datasheet window.**

● **Drag the right-corner and right-center sizing handles to increase the height and width of the chart.**

● **Click outside the chart to deselect it.**

HAVING TROUBLE?
If the chart moves to page 3, reduce its size so that it stays on page 2.

Your screen should be similar to Figure 5.43

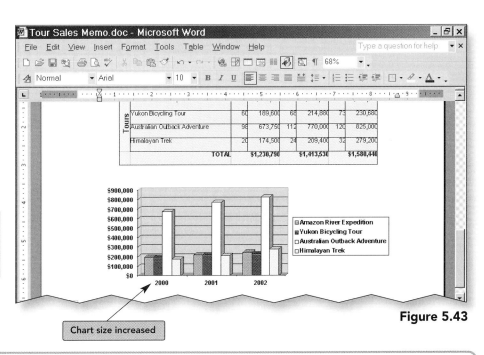

Chart size increased

Figure 5.43

Modifying the Chart

As you look at the chart, you decide you want to change it so the colors co-ordinate with the table in the memo. You also want to remove the 3-D effect on the chart, which is the default. To modify the chart, you need to activate the Graph application again. Then you can use the features on the Graph menu and toolbar to edit the chart.

1

- **Double-click on the chart.**

- **If the datasheet is open, close it.**

Another Method

The menu equivalent is Edit/Chart Object.

Your screen should be similar to Figure 5.44

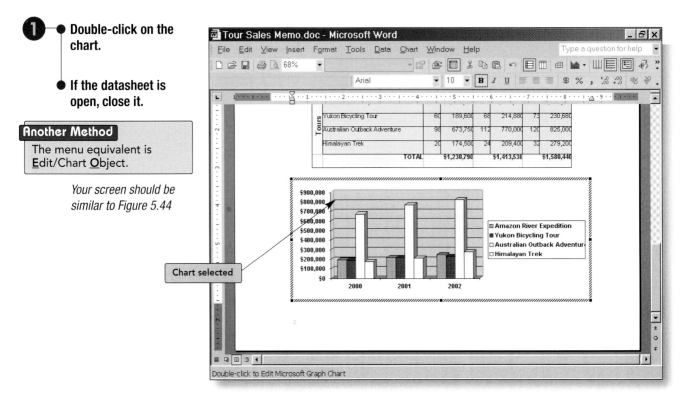

Figure 5.44

The chart object opens and the datasheet window is active. You want to change the color and appearance of the chart to match the colors in the table. First you will change the background color of the plot area.

2
- **Right-click on the area behind the columns of data.**

- **Choose F__o__rmat Walls.**

- **From the Area color palette, select the same color that you used behind the data in the table.**

- **Click** OK **.**

Your screen should be similar to Figure 5.45

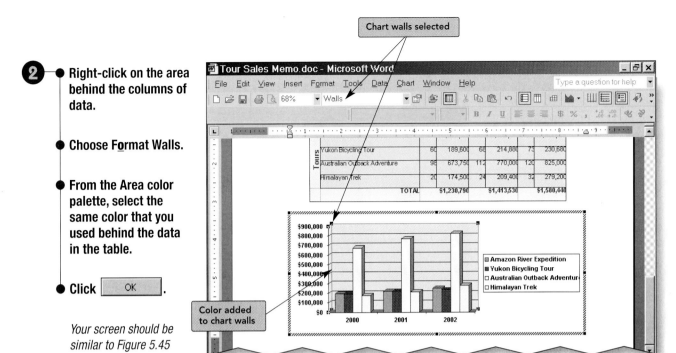

Figure 5.45

You also want to change the background color of the chart area.

3
- **Right-click on the white background of the chart.**

- **Choose F__o__rmat Chart Area.**

- **From the Area color palette, select the same color you used in the table.**

- **Click** OK **.**

Your screen should be similar to Figure 5.46

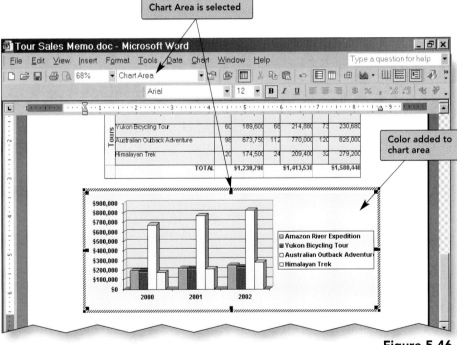

Figure 5.46

Next you will change the color of the columns.

4 ● **Right-click on any one of the Australian Outback Adventure columns.**

● **Choose F̲ormat Data Series.**

● **If necessary, open the Patterns tab.**

Your screen should be similar to Figure 5.47

Default settings for selected data series

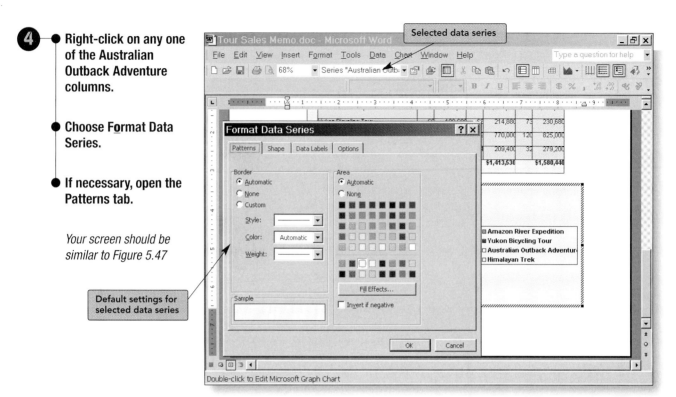

Figure 5.47

The Format Data Series dialog box is used to modify the appearance of the selected data series. The initial chart is created using the default chart colors. From the Patterns tab you can select different borders, fill colors, and patterns.

5 ● **From the Area color palette, select a color that coordinates with the table.**

● **Click** OK **.**

● **Repeat as needed for the other three data series.**

Your screen should be similar to Figure 5.48

Data series color changed

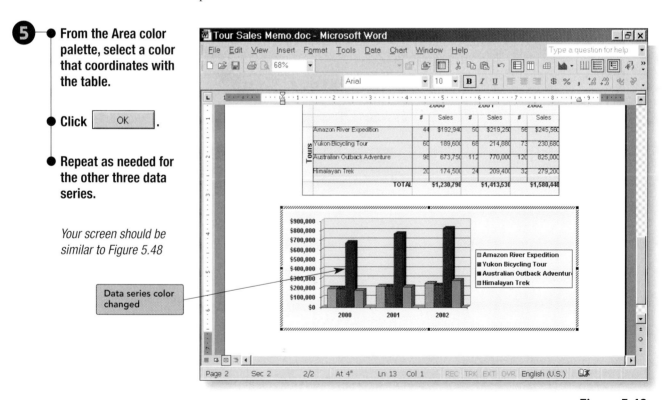

Figure 5.48

Next you want to change the type of column chart to display flat columns rather than 3-D columns.

6
- **Right-click on any one of the columns.**

- **Choose Chart Type.**

- **Select Clustered Column (row 1 column 1).**

- **Click [OK].**

Your screen should be similar to Figure 5.49

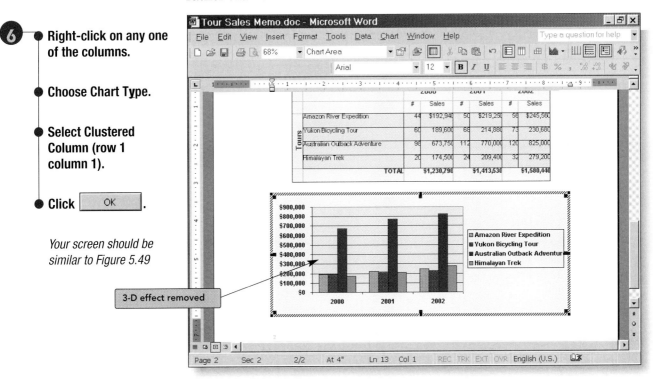

3-D effect removed

Figure 5.49

The 3-D effect has been removed from the columns. You also want to reduce the number of values that display on the Y axis. Currently because the values increment by 100,000, there are 9 values displayed. To reduce the number of values, you increase the incremental value.

7
- **Right-click anywhere on the Y axis.**

- **Choose Format Axis.**

- **If necessary, open the Scale tab.**

- **Type 250000 in the Major Unit text box.**

- **Click [OK].**

Your screen should be similar to Figure 5.50

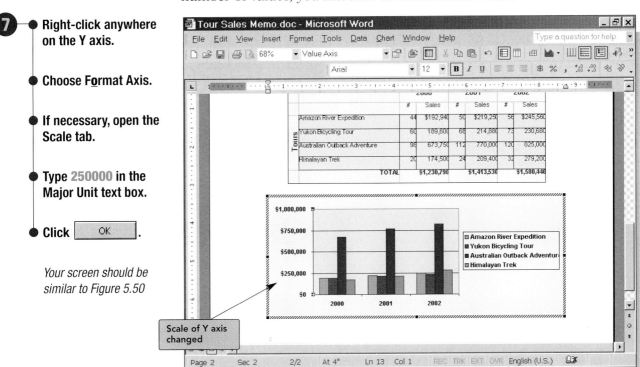

Scale of Y axis changed

Figure 5.50

There are now only four values displayed along the Y-axis.

The last two changes you want to make are to reduce the font size of the text in the legend and to center the chart object.

8

- **Right-click on the legend.**

- **Choose F̲ormat Legend.**

- **Open the Font tab and select 10 pt as the font size.**

- **Click** OK **.**

- **Click outside the chart to exit the Graph application.**

- **Select the chart object.**

- **Click** ≡ **Center.**

- **Deselect the chart object.**

- **Save the document again.**

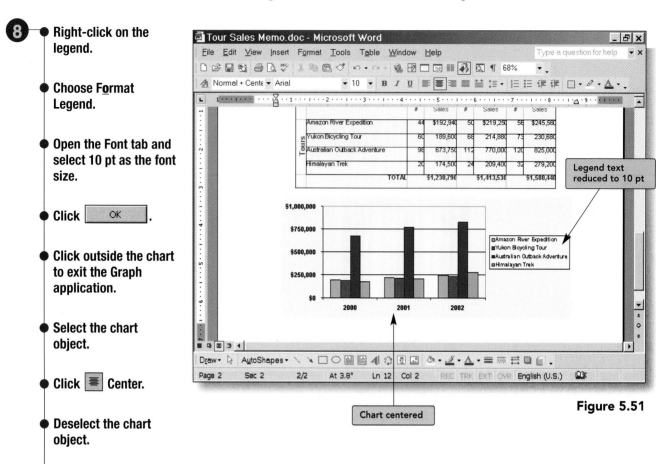

Figure 5.51

Your screen should be similar to Figure 5.51

The changes you made to the chart greatly improve its appearance.

Creating an Outline-Style Numbered List

Now that you have created the table and chart, you want to include in the memo a strategy on how to increase sales for the four major tours. First you will add a lead-in paragraph, and then you will enter the proposed strategy to increase sales.

1 ● Move to the end of the first paragraph in the memo.

● Set the zoom to Page Width.

● Press ←Enter.

● Change the style to Normal.

● Type: You will notice that sales have steadily increased over the past three years. The following strategy has been developed to ensure further increases in future sales.

● Press ←Enter twice.

Your screen should be similar to Figure 5.52

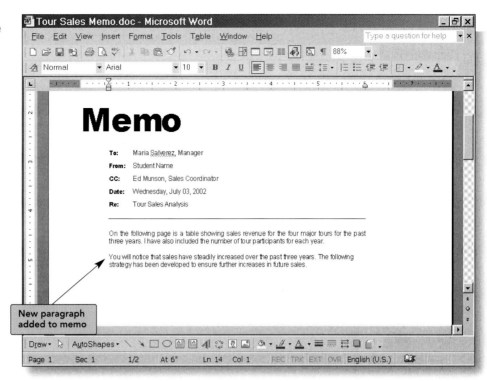

Figure 5.52

The strategy consists of several main points and corresponding subpoints. The best way to add this information to your memo is to use an outline-style numbered list.

2 ● Type Strategy to Increase Sales.

● Press ←Enter.

● Choose F**o**rmat/Bullets and **N**umbering.

● Open the O**u**tline Numbered tab.

Your screen should be similar to Figure 5.53

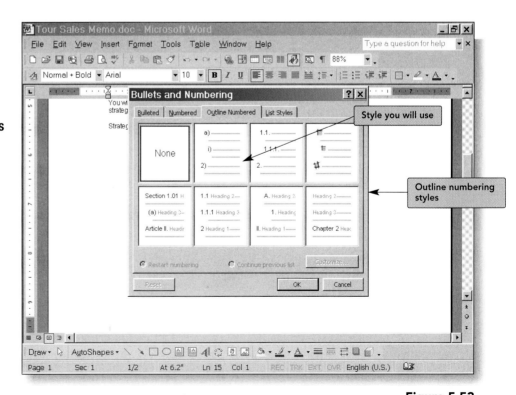

Figure 5.53

The Bullets and Numbering dialog box displays seven outline numbered-list styles. The first style to the right of None is the style you will use.

3 ● Select the first outline numbered-list style.

● Click [OK].

● Type Increase number of new clients.

● Press ←Enter.

Your screen should be similar to Figure 5.54

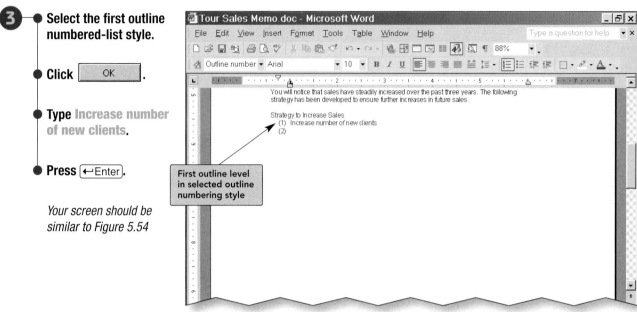

Figure 5.54

The outline number (1) in the selected style is inserted for the first line and the text following the outline number is automatically indented to the 0.25-inch position. The next line is automatically numbered (2) for the second entry at the same outline level. Next, however, you want to add the list of strategies for the first topic under the first topic heading. They will be entered at lower outline levels.

4 ● Press Tab.

● Type Advertising.

● Press ←Enter.

● Press Tab.

● Type Direct mail brochures.

● Press ←Enter.

● Type Magazine and newspaper ads.

● Press ←Enter.

● Type Web ads and specials.

● Press ←Enter.

Your screen should be similar to Figure 5.55

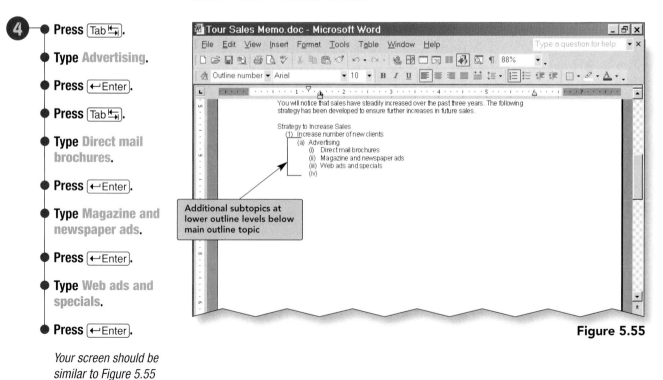

Figure 5.55

Each time you press $\boxed{\text{Tab}\rightleftharpoons}$ to indent a line, the next line indents to the 0.25-inch position and the outline numbering level is demoted to the next lower numbering level. That completes the first category. To add the second and third categories, you need to promote the outline numbering level by decreasing the indent.

5
- Press $\boxed{\text{⇧ Shift}}$ + $\boxed{\text{Tab}\rightleftharpoons}$.

- Enter the following three items:
  (b) Participate in "travel fairs"
  (c) Offer presentations to specialty groups (biking, hiking, etc.)
  (d) Expand Adventure Travel Web site

- Press $\boxed{\leftarrow\text{Enter}}$.

- Press $\boxed{\text{⇧ Shift}}$ + $\boxed{\text{Tab}\rightleftharpoons}$.

Your screen should be similar to Figure 5.56

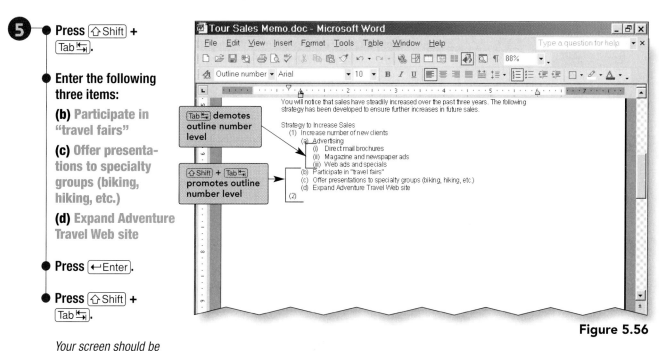

Figure 5.56

The outline level is at the first numbering level and you are ready to enter the second main strategy to increase sales by increasing repeat business.

6
- Complete the memo by entering the following topics at the levels shown:
  (2) Increase repeat business
  (a) Follow-up surveys
  (b) Thank-you letters
  (c) Newsletter

- Press $\boxed{\leftarrow\text{Enter}}$.

- Click to turn off Outline Numbering.

- Bold the heading above the outline numbered list.

Your screen should be similar to Figure 5.57

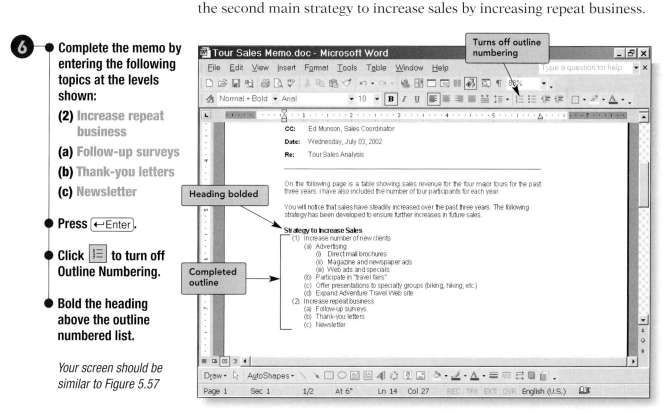

Figure 5.57

The memo is now complete. The final change you want to make is to fix the letterhead so there is no white space between the picture and the company name.

7

- **Move the right indent marker in the ruler for the left table cell to the right column margin.**

- **Drag the left border of the right cell to the left to increase the size of the cell.**

Your screen should be similar to Figure 5.58

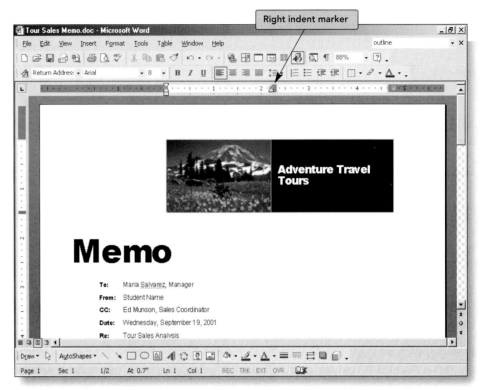

Right indent marker

Figure 5.58

8

- **Preview and then prin the memo.**

- **Save and close the file.**

The letterhead looks much better. Your completed memo should look like the memo shown here.

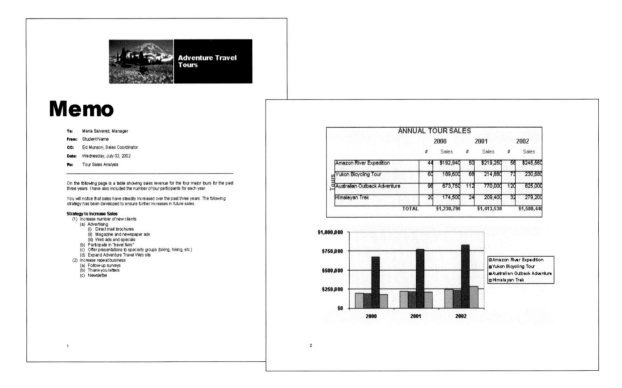

Note: If you are running short on time, this is an appropriate place to end this session.

Using Mail Merge

Recall that your second project is to personalize the letter you wrote about the new tours and presentations by including each client's name and address information in the inside address and his or her first name in the salutation. To do this you will use the Mail Merge feature to create a personalized form letter and mailing labels to be sent to all clients.

concept 3

Mail Merge

3 The **Mail Merge** feature combines a list of data (typically a file of names and addresses) with a document (commonly a form letter) to create a new document. The names and addresses are entered (merged) into the form letter in the blank spaces provided. The result is a personalized form letter.

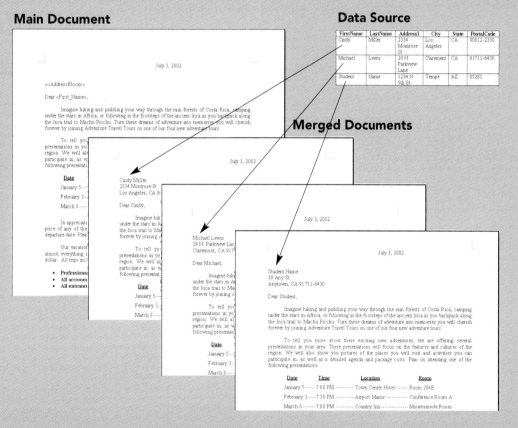

Mail Merge usually requires the use of two files: a main document and a data source. The **main document** contains the basic form letter. It directs the merge process through the use of merge fields. A **merge field** is a field code that controls what information is used from the data source and where it is entered in the main document. The **data source** contains the information needed to complete the letter in the main document. It is also called an **address file** because it commonly contains name and address data.

In addition to the templates, Word 2002 includes many wizards to help you create documents. A **wizard** asks you questions and then uses your answers to automatically lay out and format a document such as a newsletter or resume. You will use the Mail Merge Wizard to take you step by step through the process of creating a form letter. The four steps are:

1. Open or create a main document.

2. Open or create a data source with individual recipient information.

3. Add or customize merge fields in the main document.

4. Merge data from the data source into the main document to create a new, merged document.

Another Method

You can also use the icons on the Mail Merge toolbar instead of the Mail Merge Wizard to create a merge document. Choose **T**ools/Le**t**ters and Mailings/Show Mail Merge **T**oolbar.

You will open the tour letter as the main document and create the data source of clients' names and addresses. Then you will add the merge fields to the main document. When you perform the merge, Word takes the data field information from the data source and combines or merges it into the main document.

Creating the Main Document

You are going to use an existing letter as the main document. This letter is similar to the tour letter you saved as Tour Letter2 in Lab 2.

1 ● **Open the file** wd05_Tour Letter5.

● **If necessary, switch to Print Layout view and set the zoom to Page Width.**

● **Choose T**ools/Le**t**ters and Mailings/**M**ail Merge Wizard.

Your screen should be similar to Figure 5.59

Additional Information

Notice that the date in the letter on your screen is automatically updated to the current system date. This is because a Date field was entered in the document.

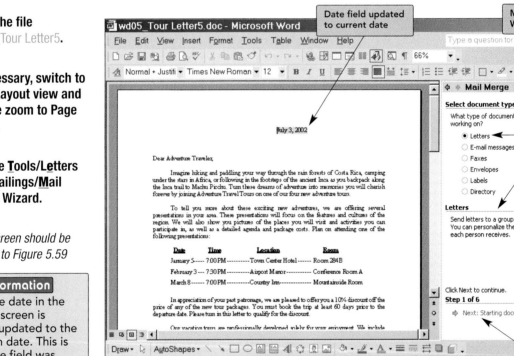

Figure 5.59

The Mail Merge task pane contains the wizard that will guide you through creating the form letter. The first selection you need to make is to specify the type of document you want to create. An explanation of the selected document type is displayed below the list of options.

2 • If necessary, select Letters.

• Click ⇨ Next: Starting document .

Your screen should be similar to Figure 5.60

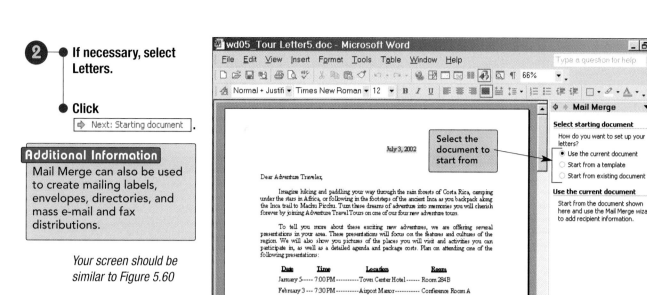

Figure 5.60

In the next step of the wizard, you need to identify the starting document. Since you already opened the file containing the letter you want to use, you will select the "use the current document" option.

3 • If necessary, select Use the current document.

• Click ⇨ Next: Select recipients .

Your screen should be similar to Figure 5.61

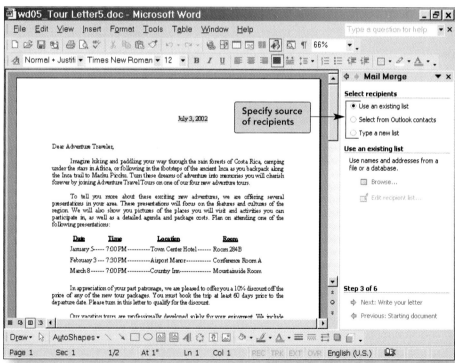

Figure 5.61

Creating the Data Source

Next you select the recipients to use as the data source for the mail merged document. You can use an existing list, select from your Outlook contacts, or type a new list.

You are going to type a new recipient list.

1 • Select **Type a new list**.

• Click ▦ Create... .

Your screen should be similar to Figure 5.62

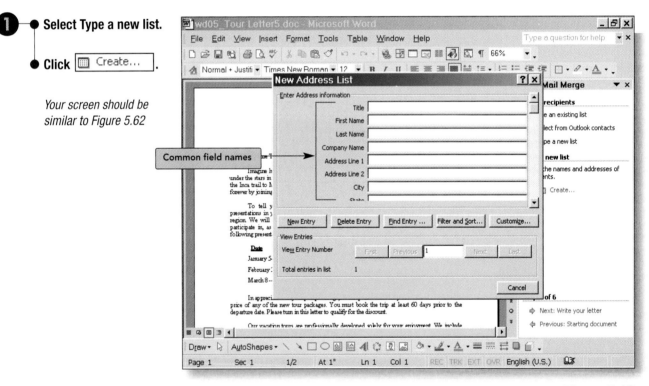

Figure 5.62

The New Address List dialog box is used to specify the field names for the data that will be entered in the recipient list.

concept 5

Field Names

5 **Field names** are used to label the different data fields in the recipient list. A field name can contain only letters, numbers, or the underline character. It can be a maximum of 40 characters and cannot contain spaces. The first character of a field name must be a letter. Field names should describe the contents of the data field.

Commonly used form-letter field names are displayed in the New Address List list box. You can remove from the list any field names that you do not need in your letter, or you can add field names to the list or rename the field names. In this case, you will remove several field names from the list.

2 ● Click [Customize...].

The dialog box on your screen should be similar to Figure 5.63

Field names to be removed

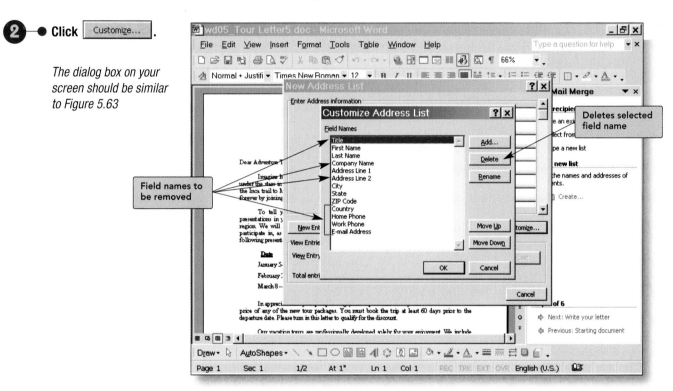

Figure 5.63

Additional Information

The [Move Up] and [Move Down] buttons let you rearrange the order of the fields.

Because you only need basic address information, you will remove any extra field names. Since the title field name is already selected, you will delete it first.

3 ● Click [Delete] to remove the Title field from the list.

● Click [Yes] to confirm the deletion.

● Select and remove the following field names: **Company Name, Address Line 2, Country, Home Phone, Work Phone and E-mail Address.**

● Click [OK].

Your screen should be similar to Figure 5.64

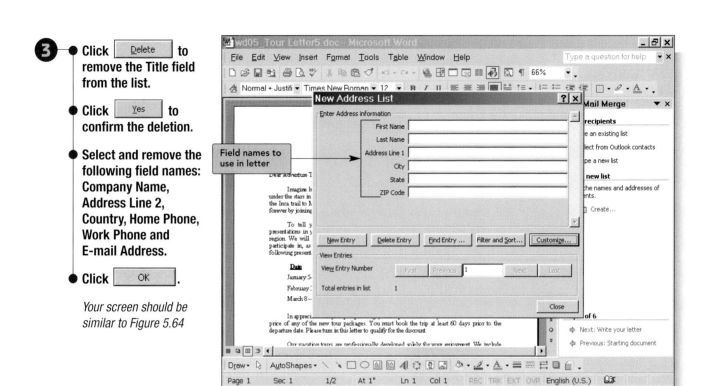

Figure 5.64

The New Address List dialog box now displays only the six field names to use in the letter, and text boxes for entering the data for each record. The data must be entered exactly as you want it to appear in the letter. If you do not have the information you need to complete a field, you can leave it blank. You will enter the data for the first field of the first record, the client's first name.

4 ● Click in the First Name field.

● Type **Cindy**.

● Press [Tab⇆] or [↵Enter].

● Enter the following information for the remaining fields of this record:

Last Name:	Miller
Address Line 1:	2334 Montrose St.
City:	Los Angeles
State:	CA
ZIP Code:	90012-2330

● If you see any errors in the field data, move back to the entry and edit it.

Your screen should be similar to Figure 5.65

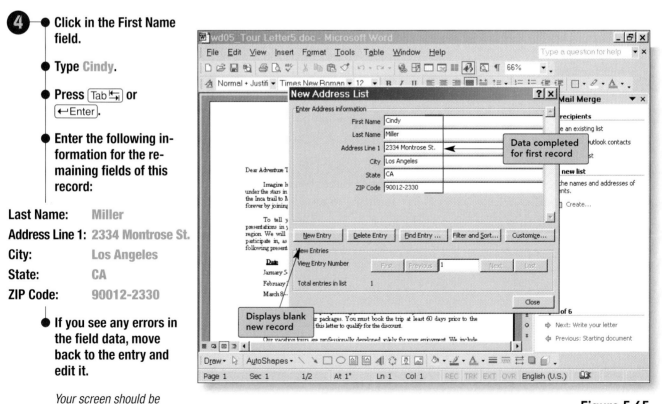

Figure 5.65

Next you will add this record to the data source file and display a new blank data form.

5 ● Click [New Entry].

● Enter the field data for the second record using the information:

First Name:	Michael
Last Name:	Lewis
Address Line 1:	29 N. Parkview Lane
City:	Claremont
State:	CA
ZIP Code:	91711-6430

Your screen should be similar to Figure 5.66

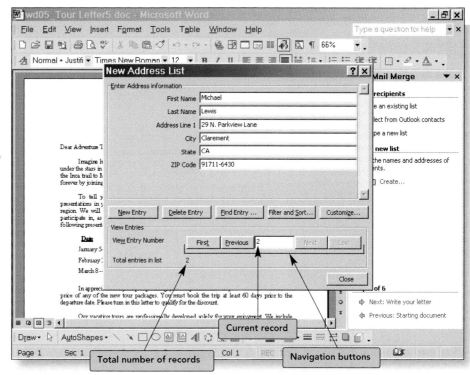

Figure 5.66

Notice that the View Entries area shows the number of records entered into the recipient list. The four record navigation buttons allow you to move among existing records in the list.

6 ● Click [New Entry].

● Enter your name and address as the third record in the data source.

● Use the record navigation buttons to move to each of the records and verify the data you entered. If necessary, correct any errors.

● Click [Close].

● Save the address list as *Client List* to your data file location.

Additional Information

The address list is saved as an .mdb file, which is a Microsoft Office Address List.

Your screen should be similar to Figure 5.67

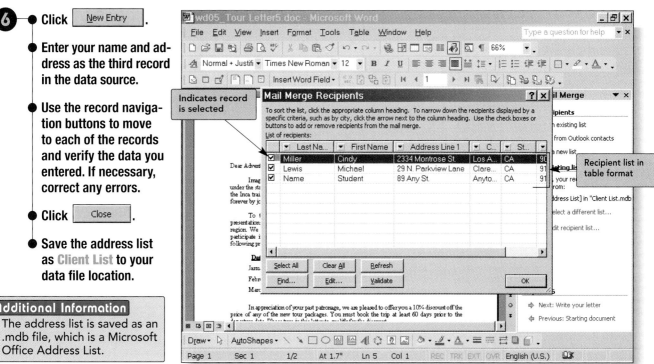

Figure 5.67

The Mail Merge Recipients dialog box is displayed along with the Mail Merge toolbar, shown below.

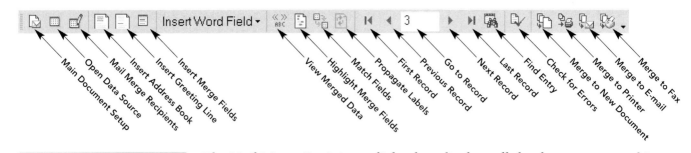

The number of records you enter in the data source file is limited only by your disk space. At any time, you can add more records using the Data Form as you just did.

The Mail Merge Recipients dialog box displays all the data you entered in a table format. The field names are displayed as the top row of the table, and each record is displayed as a row. You can sort the list or edit the data before you perform the merge. All the records are checked, indicating they are selected and will appear in the Mail Merge.

7 ● Click [OK].

Your screen should be similar to Figure 5.68

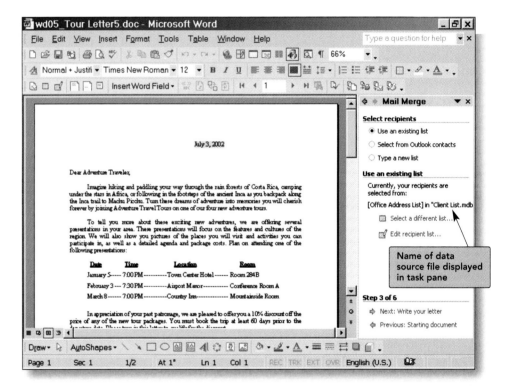

Figure 5.68

Now the list that you created appears as the current list in the task pane. You will use this recipient list and advance to the next step.

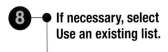

8 ● **If necessary, select Use an existing list.**

● **Click**

➡ Next: Write your letter .

Your screen should be similar to Figure 5.69

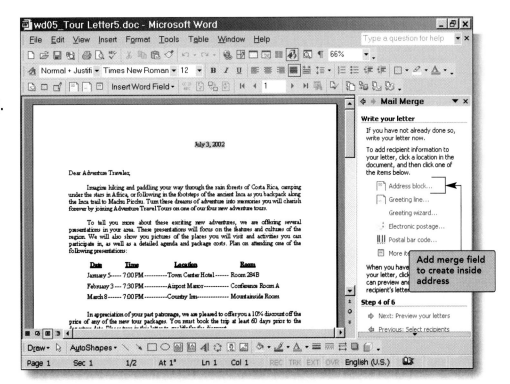

Figure 5.69

Entering Merge Fields in the Main Document

The next step is to create your letter, if you have not done so already, and to include the recipient information in it. How will Word know where to enter the client's name and other source data in the main document? Word uses merge fields to do this. Merge fields direct the program to accept information from the data source at the specified location in the main document. To prepare the letter to accept the fields of information from the data source, you need to add merge fields to the letter.

The letter needs to be modified to allow entry of the name and address information for each client from the data source. The inside address will hold the following three lines of information, which are the components of the address block:

First Name Last Name
Address Line 1
City, State Zip Code

The first line of the inside address, which will hold the client's full name, will be entered as line 5 of the tour letter. A merge field needs to be entered in the main document for each field of data you want copied from the data source. The location of the merge field indicates where to enter the field data. First you need to position the insertion point on the line where the client's name and address will appear.

① • **Move to the blank line above the salutation.**

• **Click** [≡ Address block...].

Your screen should be similar to Figure 5.70

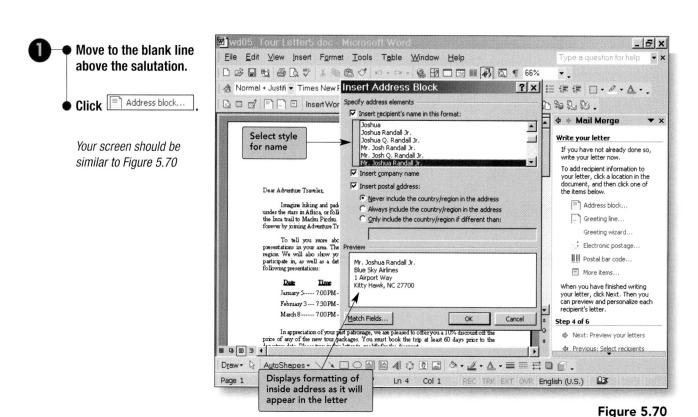

Select style for name

Displays formatting of inside address as it will appear in the letter

Figure 5.70

The Insert Address Block dialog box has many options for customizing the appearance of the fields. The Preview area displays how the Address Block will appear in the letter.

② • **Choose the example "Joshua Randall Jr." as the format for the recipient's name.**

• **Click Insert company name to deselect it.**

• **Click** [OK].

Another Method

You can also click ≡ Insert Address Block on the Mail Merge toolbar or ≡ Insert Merge Fields and insert the merge fields one at a time.

Your screen should be similar to Figure 5.71

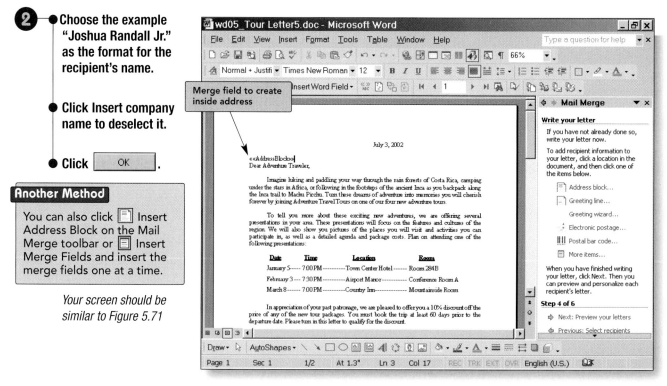

Merge field to create inside address

Figure 5.71

The merge field <<Address Block>> is displayed at the insertion point in the main document. It is a field code that instructs Word to insert the information from the data fields (from the data source) at this location in the main document when the merge is performed.

3 ● **Enter a blank line between the Address Block merge field and the salutation.**

● **Select "Adventure Traveler" in the salutation.**

● **Click 🖻 Insert Merge Fields (on the Mail Merge toolbar).**

● **Select the First Name merge field.**

● **Click ▭ Insert ▭.**

● **Click ▭ Close ▭.**

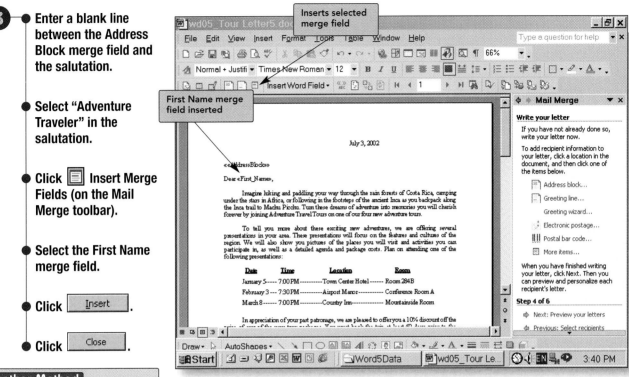

Figure 5.72

Another Method

You can also select the entire salutation and click
▭ Greeting line... in the Mail Merge task pane to access several options for formatting the salutation.

Additional Information

The same merge field can be used more than once in the main document.

Your screen should be similar to Figure 5.72

Using Mail Merge   **WD5.55**

Word 2002

Previewing the Merged Letter

The next step is to see how the form letter will appear with the merged data.

1 • **Click**

> ⇨ Next: Preview your letters

Another Method

You can also click 📝 View Merged Data on the Mail Merge toolbar.

Your screen should be similar to Figure 5.73

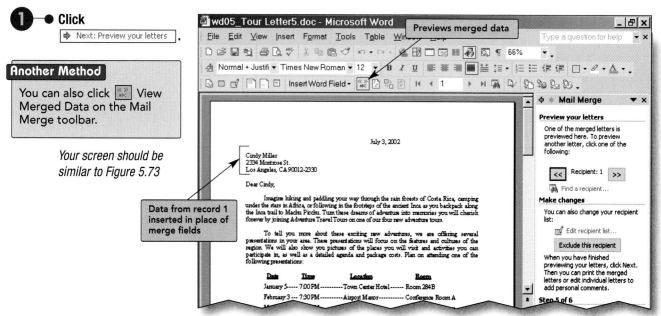

Figure 5.73

The data from the first record of the address list is displayed in place of the merge fields.

2 • **Click** >> **to see the address information for the next recipient in the letter.**

• **Change the zoom to Two Pages.**

Your screen should be similar to Figure 5.74

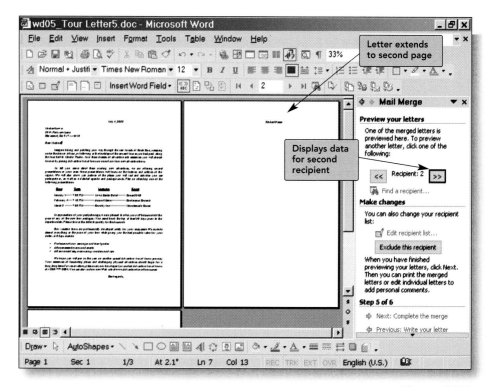

Figure 5.74

With the addition of the address information, the form letter no longer fits on one page. You can easily fix this using the shrink to fit feature to make the letter fit on one page.

3 ● Click  Print Preview.

● Click Shrink to Fit.

Your screen should be similar to Figure 5.75

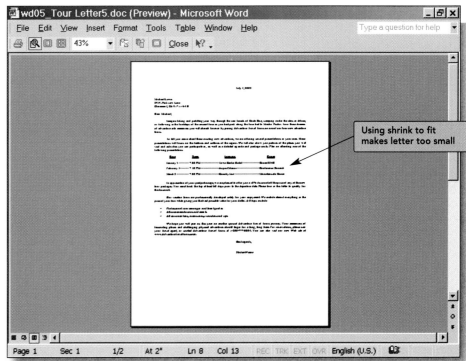

Using shrink to fit makes letter too small

Figure 5.75

The reduced letter now appears too small. You decide to undo the Shrink to Fit change and manually adjust the font size to make it more appropriate.

4 ● Choose **Edit/Undo Shrink to Fit**.

● **Close the Print Preview window.**

● **Select the letter only.**

● **Reduce the font size to 11 points.**

● **Deselect the selected text.**

● **Save the letter as** Tour Main Document.

Your screen should be similar to Figure 5.76

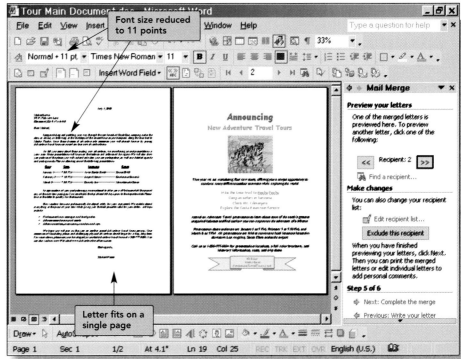

Font size reduced to 11 points

Letter fits on a single page

Figure 5.76

Performing the Merge

Now that you have created the main document and data source document, you are ready to combine them to create the new personalized tour letter. During this process a third file is created. The original main document and data source file are not altered or affected in any way. The third file is the result of merging the main document with the data source file.

1 ● Click

⇨ Next: Complete the merge .

Another Method

You can also click 🗐 Merge to New Document on the Mail Merge toolbar.

Your screen should be similar to Figure 5.77

Merged document

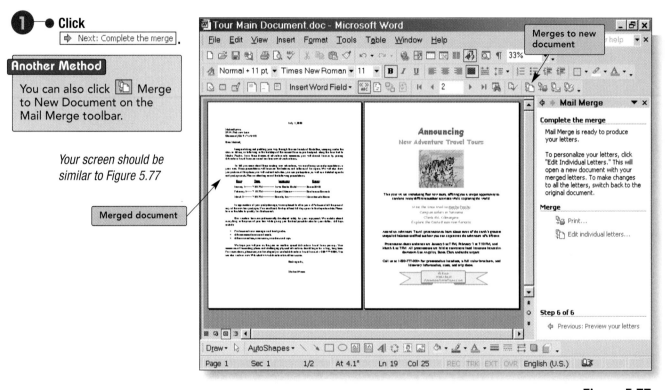

Figure 5.77

From the Mail Merge task pane box, you can personalize the letters before you print them. You can also direct the merge to output the form letters to e-mail or a fax if your system is set up to include these features. Finally, if you do not want every record in your data source to receive a copy of the form letter, you can specify a range of records to merge or criteria for records to meet.

Printing the Merged Letter

You can also specify the records you want to send a letter to. In this case, you only want to print the letter that contains your name and address, which is record 3.

1 ● Click .

● Click in the From field and type 3.

● Click in the To field and type 3.

● Click **OK**.

● Make the necessary selections from the Print dialog box for your system.

● Click **OK**.

Your printed output should be similar to that shown here.

2 ● Close the Mail Merge task pane.

● Close the Mail Merge toolbar.

● Return the zoom to Page Width.

● Save the merged document as Tour Merge Document to your data file location.

● Close all document windows, saving the files as necessary.

July 3, 2002

Student Name
89 Any St.
Anytown, CA 91711-6430

Dear Student,

Imagine hiking and paddling your way through the rain forests of Costa Rica, camping under the stars in Africa, or following in the footsteps of the ancient Inca as you backpack along the Inca trail to Machu Picchu. Turn these dreams of adventure into memories you will cherish forever by joining Adventure Travel Tours on one of our four new adventure tours.

To tell you more about these exciting new adventures, we are offering several presentations in your area. These presentations will focus on the features and cultures of the region. We will also show you pictures of the places you will visit and activities you can participate in, as well as a detailed agenda and package costs. Plan on attending one of the following presentations:

Date	Time	Location	Room
January 5	7:00 PM	Town Center Hotel	Room 284B
February 3	7:30 PM	Airport Manor	Conference Room A
March 8	7:00 PM	Country Inn	Mountainside Room

In appreciation of your past patronage, we are pleased to offer you a 10% discount off the price of any of the new tour packages. You must book the trip at least 60 days prior to the departure date. Please turn in this letter to qualify for the discount.

Our vacation tours are professionally developed solely for your enjoyment. We include almost everything in the price of your tour while giving you the best possible value for your dollar. All trips include:

- **Professional tour manager and local guides**
- **All accommodations and meals**
- **All entrance fees, excursions, transfers and tips**

We hope you will join us this year on another special Adventure Travel Tours journey. Your memories of fascinating places and challenging physical adventures should linger for a long, long time. For reservations, please see your travel agent, or contact Adventure Travel Tours at 1-800-777-0004. You can also visit our new Web site at www.AdventureTravelTours.com.

Best regards,

Now each time you need to send tour letters, all you need to do is edit the client data source file and issue the Merge command. Because the Date field was used, the date line will change automatically.

Printing Mailing Labels

Now that the form letter is ready to be sent to clients, you want to create mailing labels for the envelopes. To create mailing labels for your form letter, you will use the Mailing Label Wizard.

1 ● Choose **F**ile/**N**ew.

● Click 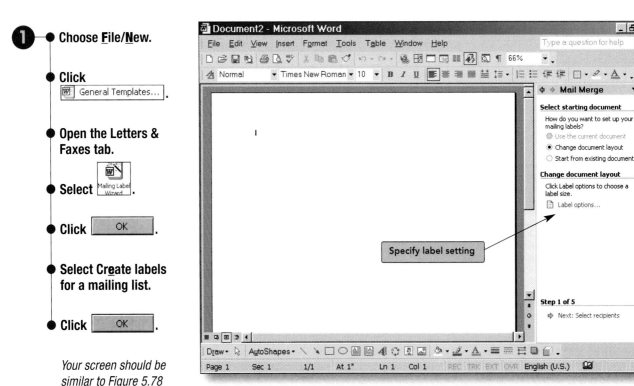 General Templates... .

● Open the Letters & Faxes tab.

● Select Mailing Label Wizard .

● Click OK .

● Select Cr**e**ate labels for a mailing list.

● Click OK .

Your screen should be similar to Figure 5.78

Specify label setting

Figure 5.78

The Mail Merge task pane displays with a blank document. The Wizard first needs to know how you want to set up the mailing labels. The default will use the new blank document as the starting document. You can also choose to use another existing document. The next step is to select a ready-to-use mail merge template.

2 ● Click ☐ Label options... .

Your screen should be similar to Figure 5.79

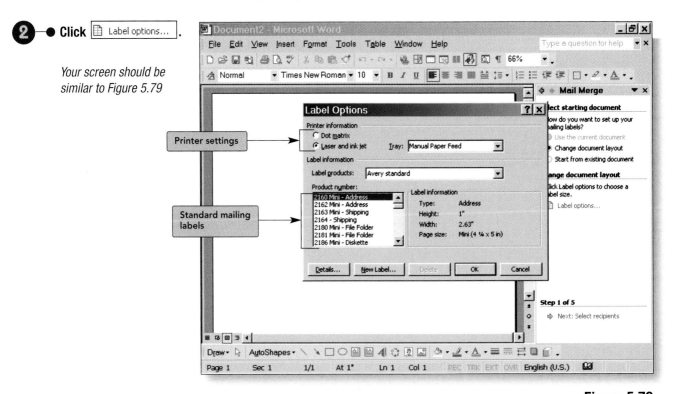

Printer settings

Standard mailing labels

Figure 5.79

The Label Options dialog box displays the type of printer and the manufacturer of mailing labels. Avery Standard is the default. The Product Number list shows all the types of labels for the selected manufacturer.

3 ● Select 5260-Address.

● Click OK.

Your screen should be similar to Figure 5.80

Blank label layout for selected type of label

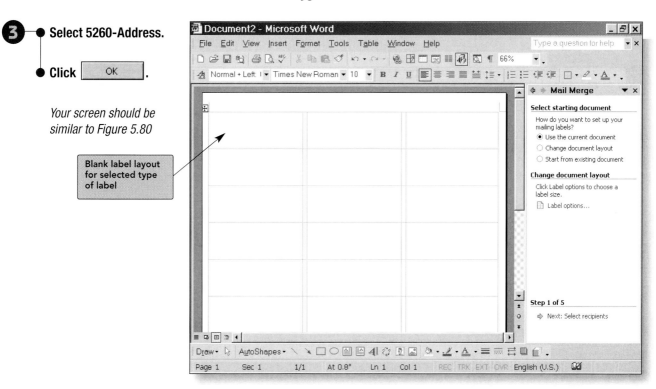

Figure 5.80

The main document is now set up to create mailing labels. You will use the Client List, which is the same data source you used for the merged letter.

4 ● Click ⇨ Next: Select recipients.

● Click 🔲 Browse….

● Select Client List from your data files.

● Click Open.

● From the Mail Merge Recipients dialog box, click OK.

● Click ⇨ Next: Arrange your labels.

Your screen should be similar to Figure 5.81

Recipient list identified

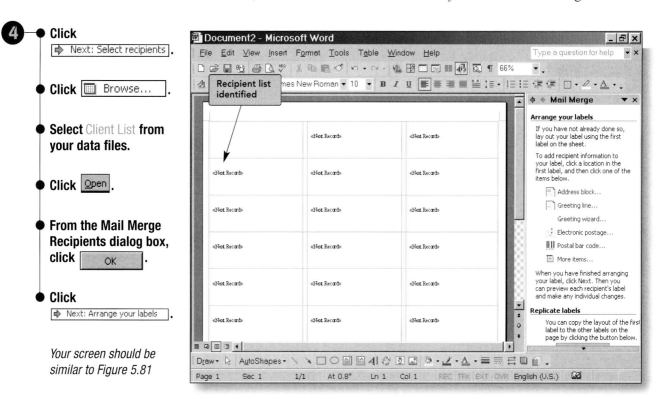

Figure 5.81

Next you set up the first label on the sheet and replicate that setup to the rest of the labels.

5
- Click 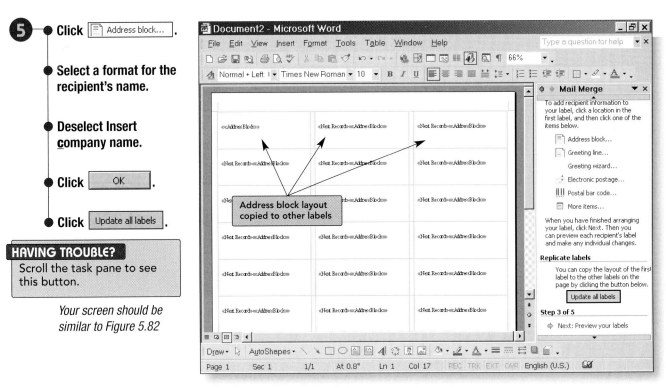 Address block... .

- Select a format for the recipient's name.

- Deselect Insert **c**ompany name.

- Click **OK** .

- Click Update all labels .

HAVING TROUBLE?
Scroll the task pane to see this button.

Your screen should be similar to Figure 5.82

Figure 5.82

Next you will preview the labels before you perform the merge.

6
- Click ▷ Next: Preview your labels .

HAVING TROUBLE?
You may need to scroll the task pane to see this option.

Your screen should be similar to Figure 5.83

Address block for three records in data source

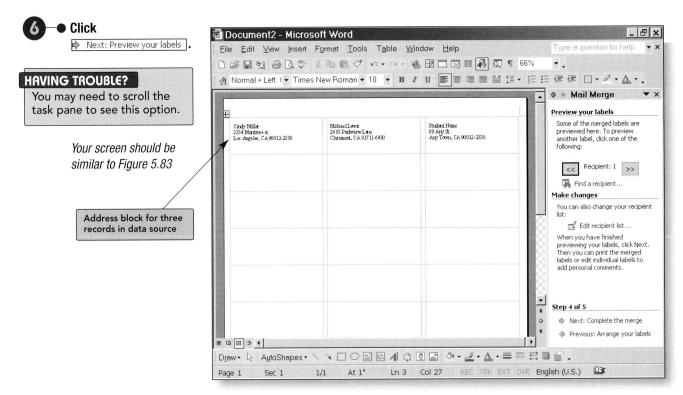

Figure 5.83

Check that the addresses fit on the label. The labels look good, so you can complete the merge and, if you wanted, print the labels. Instead, you will save the merged label file. Now when you send tour letters, you can create mailing labels using the same data source as the letter.

7

● **Click** ⇒ Next: Complete the merge .

● **Save the document as** Tour Mailing Labels.

● **Close the Mail Merge task pane and close the document.**

Preparing and Printing Envelopes

Sometimes you may want to quickly address a single envelope. To see how this feature works, you will address an envelope for one of the letters in the Tour Merge Document file.

1

● **Open the file** Tour Merge Document **file.**

● **If necessary, change the zoom to Page Width.**

● **Copy the inside address of the letter.**

● **Choose Tools/Letters and Mailings/ Envelopes and Labels.**

● **If necessary, open the Envelopes tab and select the entire entry in the Delivery Address text box.**

● **Press** Ctrl **+ V to paste the address in the Delivery Address text box.**

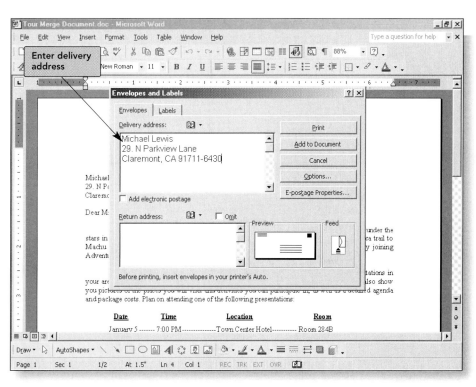

Figure 5.84

Additional Information

The Labels tab is used to create a mailing label rather than to print the address directly on the envelope.

Your screen should be similar to Figure 5.84

Another Method

You can also type an address directly in the Delivery Address text box.

To complete the information for the envelope, you need to add the return address. Then you will check the options for printing and formatting the envelope.

2 • **Enter your name and your school's address in the Return Address text box.**

• **Click** Options... .

• **If necessary, open the Envelope Options tab.**

Your screen should be similar to Figure 5.85

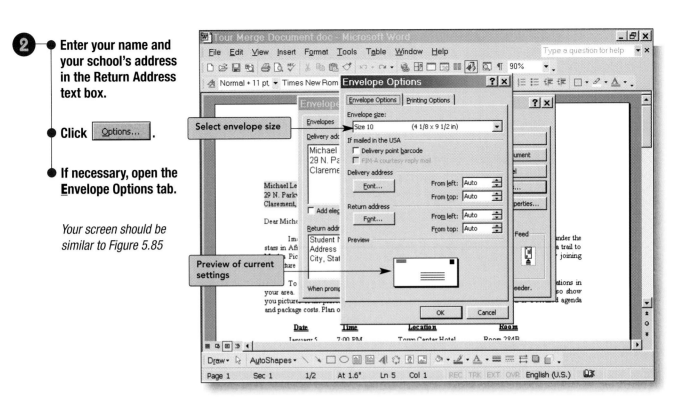

Figure 5.85

Using the Envelope Option dialog box, you can change the envelope size and the font and placement of the delivery and return addresses. The Preview area shows how the envelope will appear when printed using the current settings.

3 • **Open the Envelope Size drop-down list.**

Your screen should be similar to Figure 5.86

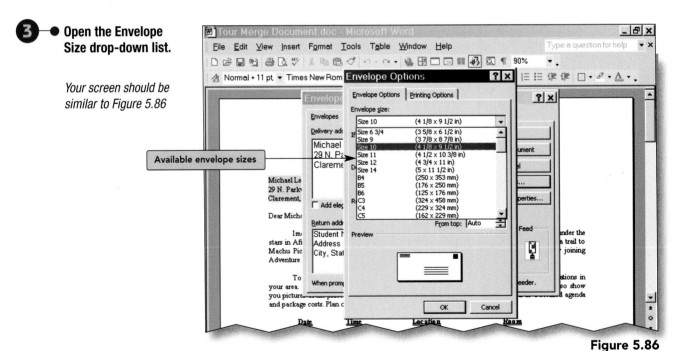

Figure 5.86

The default envelope size of 10 is for standard 8½-by-11-inch letter paper. This is the appropriate size for the letter. Next you will check the print options.

4 ● **Open the Printing Options tab.**

Your screen should be similar to Figure 5.87

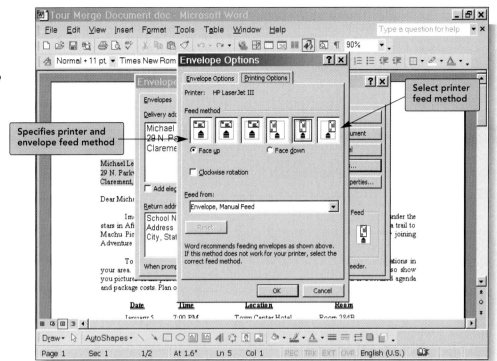

Figure 5.87

The options in this tab are used to specify how the envelope is fed into the printer. Word automatically selects the best option for the selected printer. You do not need to change any of the envelope options. Next you will print the envelope. Before printing, you would need to insert the correct size envelope in the printer. However, you will simply print it on a sheet of paper.

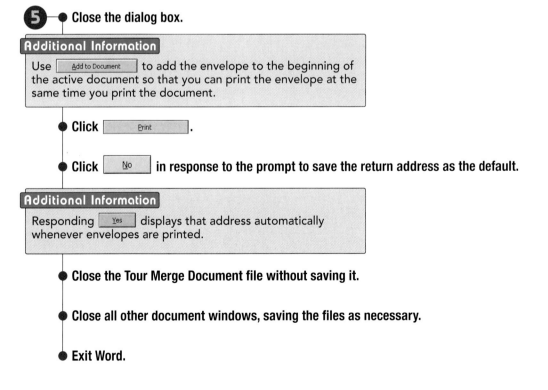

5 ● **Close the dialog box.**

Additional Information

Use [Add to Document] to add the envelope to the beginning of the active document so that you can print the envelope at the same time you print the document.

● **Click** [Print] **.**

● **Click** [No] **in response to the prompt to save the return address as the default.**

Additional Information

Responding [Yes] displays that address automatically whenever envelopes are printed.

● **Close the Tour Merge Document file without saving it.**

● **Close all other document windows, saving the files as necessary.**

● **Exit Word.**

LAB 5

Creating Complex Tables and Merging Documents

Formulas and Functions   (WD5.20)

Formulas and functions are used to perform calculations in tables.

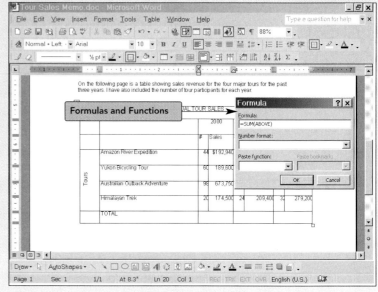

Charts   (WD5.32)

A chart, also called a graph, is a visual representation of numeric data.

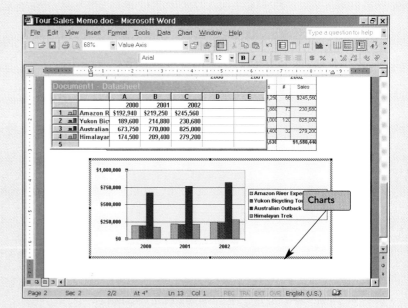

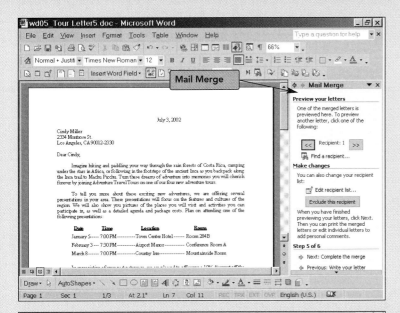

Mail Merge (WD5.45)

The Mail Merge feature combines a list of data (typically a file of names and addresses) with a document (commonly a form letter) to create a new document.

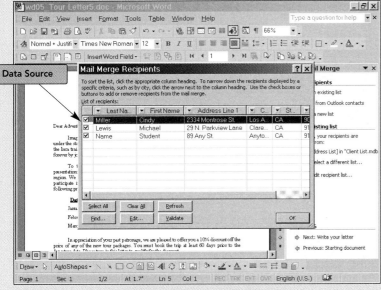

Data Source (WD5.48)

The data source file is a table of information that contains data fields in the columns and records in the rows.

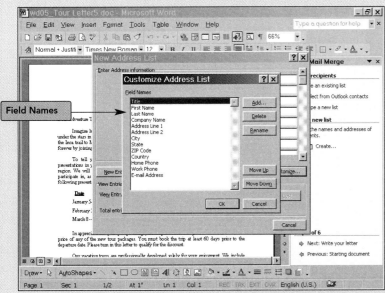

Field Name (WD5.49)

Field names are used to label the different data fields in the data source.

LAB 5

Creating Complex Tables and Merging Document

key terms

address file WD5.45	legend WD5.35
chart WD5.32	Mail Merge WD5.45
data field WD5.48	main document WD5.45
data series WD5.35	merge field WD5.45
data source WD5.45	operator WD5.20
datasheet WD5.33	placeholder WD5.6
field name WD5.49	portrait WD5.28
formula WD5.20	record WD5.48
function WD5.20	wizard WD5.46
landscape WD5.28	

mous skills

The Microsoft Office User Specialist (MOUS) certification program is designed to measure your proficiency in performing basic tasks using the Office XP applications. Getting certified demonstrates that you have the skills and provides a valuable industry credential for employment. After completing this lab, you have learned the following Microsoft Office User Specialist skills:

Skill	Description	Page
Inserting and Modifying Text	Enter and format Date and Time	WD5.8
Creating and Modifying Paragraphs	Apply bullet, outline, and numbering format to paragraphs	WD5.40
Formatting Documents	Modify document layout and Page Setup options	WD5.28
	Create and modify tables	WD5.13
	Preview and print documents, envelopes, and labels	WD5.59, WD5.63
Managing Documents	Create documents using templates	WD5.4
Working with Graphics	Insert images and graphics	WD5.9
	Create and modify diagrams and charts	WD5.32

command summary

Command	Button	Action
File/**N**ew/GeneralTemplates/ Letters & Faxes/Mailing Label Wizard		Starts Mailing Label Wizard to create mailing labels
Edit/Chart **O**bject/**E**dit		Opens Chart object for editing
View/**D**atasheet		Displays Datasheet table for Open Chart object
Insert/**O**bject/Microsoft Graph Chart		Creates a chart in the document
F**o**rmat/Bullets and **N**umbering/ **Ou**tline Numbered		Applies the selected outline number style to the text
F**o**rmat/Te**x**t Direction/**O**rientation	▯▯	Changes direction of text in a table
Tools/L**e**tters and Mailings/ **M**ail Merge Wizard		Starts Mail Merge Wizard
Tools/L**e**tters and Mailings/ Show Mail Merge **T**oolbar		Displays Mail Merge toolbar
Tools/L**e**tters and Mailings/ **E**nvelopes and Labels/**E**nvelopes		Creates and prints delivery and return address on envelopes
T**a**ble/Draw Ta**b**le	▱	Creates a table using Draw Table feature
T**a**ble/**I**nsert Columns		Inserts new columns in a table
T**a**ble/**M**erge Cells	▱	Merges cells in a table
T**a**ble/Sele**c**t/**T**able		Selects entire table
T**a**ble/**A**utofit/Distribute Rows Eve**n**ly	▯	Evenly sizes selected rows
T**a**ble/F**o**rmula		Inserts a formula into a table
T**a**ble/Show **G**ridlines		Displays gridlines in a table
T**a**ble/Table P**r**operties/**T**able/**C**enter		Centers the selected table
T**a**ble/Table P**r**operties/**T**able/**O**ptiona/ Automatically resi**z**e to fit contents		Automatically resizes columns in the table to fit text or graphic
T**a**ble/Table P**r**operties/Col**u**mn		Adjusts width of selected columns

Terminology

screen identification

In the following Word screen, letters identify important elements. Enter the correct term for each screen element in the space provided.

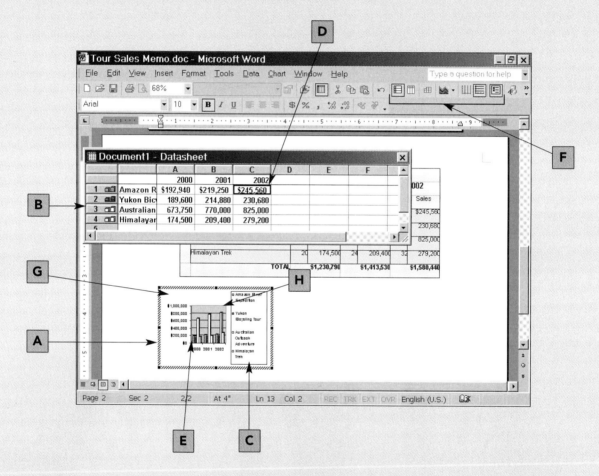

A. _____   E. _____

B. _____   F. _____

C. _____   G. _____

D. _____   H. _____

matching

Match the item on the left with the correct description on the right.

1. placeholder   _____   **a.** all the data fields that are needed to complete the information for one person

2. portrait   _____   **b.** orientation of the page, in which text is printed across the width of the page

3. address file   _____   **c.** each group of related data that is plotted in the chart

4. record   _____   **d.** contains the information needed to complete the letter in the main document

5. legend   _____   **e.** a table containing sample data

6. data series   _____   **f.** asks you questions and then uses your answers to automatically lay out and format a document

7. landscape   _____   **g.** orientation in which text is printed across the length of the page

8. data source   _____   **h.** text that marks the space and provides instructions for text to be entered in that location

9. datasheet   _____   **i.** the file that supplies the data in a mail merge

10. wizard   _____   **j.** identifies the color or pattern associated with each data series

multiple choice

Circle the correct response to the questions below.

1. A(n) _____ contains any combination of numbers, fields resulting in numbers, table references, and operators.
   a. expression
   b. calculation
   c. formula
   d. function

2. _____ orientation prints the text across the length of the page.
   a. Margin
   b. Picture
   c. Portrait
   d. Landscape

3. The _____ feature combines a list of data with a document to create a new document.
   a. Mail Format
   b. Mail Join
   c. Mail Manage
   d. Mail Merge

4. The _____ document contains the text that will become the basis of a form letter.
   a. letter
   b. data source
   c. address file
   d. main

5. The _____ contains the information needed to address and complete a form letter.
   a. letter
   b. data source
   c. address file
   d. main

6. All the data fields that are needed to complete the information for one person are called a _____.
   a. field
   b. record
   c. file
   d. row

7. _____ names are used to label each data field in the data source.
   a. Row
   b. Record
   c. Field
   d. File

8. A(n) _____ asks questions and then uses your answers to automatically lay out and format a document.
   a. template
   b. placeholder
   c. wizard
   d. merge

9. A formula uses _____ to specify the type of calculation to perform.
   a. cell references
   b. table references
   c. operators
   d. fields

10. A(n) _____ is used in the main document for each item from the data source that is inserted.
    a. placeholder
    b. record
    c. row
    d. data field

Check the correct answer to the following questions.

1. Text in a placeholder tells the user what information to enter.   True   False

2. A function is an expression that contains numbers only.   True   False

3. Text that is printed with landscape orientation is printed across the width of the page.   True   False

4. The Mail Merge feature combines a file of names and addresses with a document form letter to create a new document.   True   False

5. The data source document contains the basic form letter.   True   False

6. A merge field is a field code that controls what information is used from the main document and where it is entered in the data source.   True   False

7. The data source contains the information needed to complete the letter in the main document.   True   False

8. All the data fields that are needed to complete the information for one person are called a record.   True   False

9. Field names are used to label each data field in the data source.   True   False

10. A wizard asks you questions and then uses your answers to automatically lay out and format a document, such as a newsletter or resume.   True   False

lab exercises

Concepts

fill-in

Complete the following statements by filling in the blanks with the correct terms.

1. The left boundary of the chart is known as the _____.

2. The Graph feature activates a table called the _____.

3. Commonly used form-letter _____ are displayed in the New Address List list box.

4. The data source is a table of information that contains data _____ and _____ in the rows.

5. _____ requires the use of two files: a main document and a data source.

6. The data source can also be called the _____.

7. A(n) _____ is a visual representation of a chart.

8. SUM is a prewrittten _____.

9. A(n) _____ can only contain letter, numbers, or the underline character.

10. You can also use the icons on the Mail Merge toolbar instead of the Mail Merge _____ to create a merged document.

discussion questions

1. There are several methods you can use to create a table. Describe each and explain when they would be used.

2. What is the significance of using a column-and-row format in tables? How are the rows and columns labeled?

3. Describe the use of formulas and functions in tables. What advantage do they offer over entering fixed values?

4. Describe how the Mail Merge feature works. What are some advantages of using Mail Merge?

5. What steps are used to create a data source file? How is the data used in a main document?

step-by-step

Yoga Memo

★ 1. The Adventure Travel Tours manager has fielded several requests from clients seeking Yoga retreats. She has asked you to gather information on yoga packages the agency could offer. You did some research and found several resorts that offer such packages. You would like to send a memo to the manager with an update on your progress. The completed memo is shown here.

a. Open a new file with the Professional Memo template.

b. Replace "Company Name Here" with Adventure Travel Tours. Insert the wd05_Mountain picture in the left table cell. Size the picture and table appropriately.

c. Enter the following in the placeholders:

```
To:       Manager, Adventure Travel
From:     [Your Name]
CC:       Tour Director
Re:       Yoga Retreats
```

d. Remove the template instructions from the memo body and enter the following:

I researched several yoga retreats that meet our client requests. Now I am working on a document that will provide our agents with the information about the retreats. I plan to format the document as below. If you have any questions or would like me to provide additional information to the agents please let me know.

Kripalu Center for Yoga and Health

This Center emphasizes the gentle and slow Kripalu style of yoga on its 300 acres of meadows and hills. A variety of yoga programs are offered for beginners through advanced practitioners.

Memo

To:	Manager, Adventure Travel
From:	Student Name
CC:	Tour Director
Date:	September 27, 2001
Re:	Yoga Retreats

I researched several yoga retreats that meet our client requests. Now I am working on a document that will provide our agents with the information about the retreats. I plan to format the document as below. If you have any questions or would like me to provide additional information to the agents please let me know.

Kripalu Center for Yoga and Health

This Center emphasizes the gentle and slow Kripalu style of yoga on its 300 acres of meadows and hills. A variety of yoga programs are offered for beginners through advanced practitioners.

VALID DATES	PRICE/PERSON	MINIMUM STAY	YOGA
June 3 – Sept 7	$239/night	2 Nights	Kripalu
Dec 3 – Jan 23	$305/night	5 Nights	Svaroopa
April 1 – May 1	$363/night	4 Nights	Raja
Aug 6 – Aug 12	$415/night	6 Nights	Partner

e. Draw a table with the appropriate number of columns and rows to hold the following data. Place the table below the descriptive paragraph.

Valid Dates	Price/Person	Minimum Stay	Yoga
June 3–Sep 7	$239/night	2 Nights	Kripalu
Dec 3–Jan 23	$305/night	5 Nights	Svaroopa Yoga
April 1–May 1	$363/night	4 Nights	Raja Yoga
Aug 6–Aug 12	$415/night	6 Nights	Partner Yoga

f. Select each column and drag the right indent marker to the right edge of each column. Center cells B1 through D5.

g. Increase the font size of all the text in the memo to 12 points. Apply the Elegant AutoFormat to the table. Size the table rows and columns as necessary. Center the table in the memo.

g. Add color as you like to the memo. Save the document as Yoga Memo. Print the document.

Membership Memo

★ 2. The Lifestyle Fitness Club is preparing a memo containing a summary of membership data for the four stores. The most effective way to present the data is to use a table and chart. The completed memo with the table and chart are shown here.

a. Open a new file with the Professional Memo template.

b. Replace "Company Name Here" with Lifestyle Fitness Club. Adjust the size of the cell to display the text on one line.

c. Enter the following in the placeholders:

To:	Brian Birch, Owner
From:	[Your Name]
CC:	Kathy Roth, Assistant Manager
Re:	Membership Totals

d. Replace the template instructions from the memo body with the following: The data you requested comparing the total memberships for the years 1999 through 2001 for the four clubs is shown below.

e. Select all the blank lines below the sentence and clear the format (use Clear Formatting on the Style list).

f. Draw table approximately 2 by 6 inches. Add four columns and 6 rows to accommodate the information shown in the table below.

g. Enter the data into the table shown here.

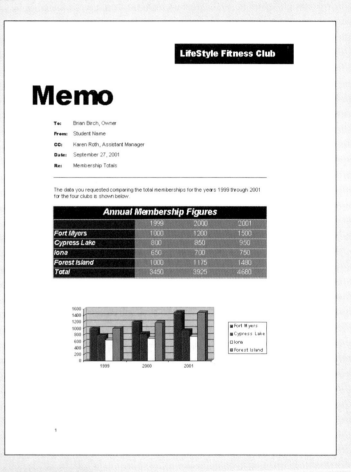

	Col. A	Col. B	Col. C	Col. D
Row 1		1999	2000	2001
Row 2	Fort Myers	1000	1200	1500
Row 3	Cypress Lake	800	850	950
Row 4	Iona	650	700	750
Row 5	Forest Island	1000	1175	1480
Row 6	Total			

h. In cell B6 enter a formula that sums the column, excluding the year in row 1. Enter the same type of formula in columns C and D.

i. Insert a new row at the top of the table. Merge the cells to make one cell. Center the table title Annual Membership Figures in the new cell. Increase the size of the title text to 16 points.

j. Increase the font size of the remaining table data to 12 points. Center-align the numbers and the year headings.

k. Select cells B2 through D7 and distribute the columns evenly. Select rows 2 through 7 and distribute the rows evenly. Format the table using colors and other effects of your choice. Center the table in the memo.

l. Add a chart below the table showing the growth for the four locations for the three years. Chart the data by columns. Adjust the size of the chart to match that of the table. Apply colors and patterns to match the table.

m. Format the memo as you like.

n. Save the document as Membership Memo. Print the document.

Video Club Membership Letter

★ ★ **3.** The Video Tower sends membership cards to all its new members. Since new people open new memberships every day, the owners would like you to create a form letter that can be used when the permanent membership cards are sent. One of your completed merge letters is shown here.

a. Open the file wd05_Video Tower Letter.

b. Using the Mail Merge Wizard, create a form letter from the current document. Create a data source file that contains the fields needed to enter the data shown below. Name the file Video Data Source. Enter the following records and one more that contains your name.

First name:	Stephanie	Rhett
Last name:	Manahan	Owens
Address1:	2931 Campus Dr.	3957 W. University Ave.
City:	St. John	Pleasant
State:	WI	FL
Zip Code:	53205-6911	33301-7985

c. In the Video Tower Letter document, create an inside address by inserting data source merge fields above the salutation. In the salutation replace "Member" with the First Name merge field.

d. Merge the data source and main document files. Save the merged letters as Video Merge Document. Print the letter that contains your name.

Letter (shown at right):

September 19, 2001

Student Name
555 Campus Lane
University Town, CA 55555

Dear Student:

Thank you for joining Video Tower and becoming one of our most valued members. Here's your new Video Tower card! Using your new card is as easy as 1-2-3:

1. Please sign your new card in ink with your usual signature.
2. If you have an old card or a temporary card, destroy it immediately.
3. Always carry your new Video Tower card with you.

Your new card identifies you as a member and guarantees you a pleasant experience at any of The Video Tower locations throughout the country.

You can begin using your new Video Tower card with your very next visit. In appreciation for becoming a Video Tower member, you will receive 10% off the first purchase you make in our multimedia shop. Please turn in this letter at the time the discount is given.

Additionally, each month you will receive The Video Tower Update, a newsletter about new products, movie trends, and upcoming events. The newsletter will also include announcements of special sale days for our members only. If you have questions about an event, call 1-800-555-9838 or come in and speak to the Customer Service representative.

We are the leading video store in the country with a tradition of personal, friendly service. As you use your new Video Tower membership card, you will discover the many conveniences that only our members enjoy.

We are delighted with the opportunity to serve you and we look forward to seeing you soon.

Sincerely,

The Video Tower Manager

Volunteer Recruitment Memo

★ ★ **4.** Animal Angels plans to send a letter to all the veterinarians in the area to enlist their help in the placement and care of homeless animals. Your completed form letter is shown here.

    a. Open the file wd05_Vet Letter to see the letter text. Create a WordArt object that contains the words Animal Angels. Center and place the WordArt at the top of the document. Enter three blank lines below the WordArt.

    b. Right-align the current date as a field. Enter four blank lines after the date.

    c. Use the active document to create a form letter. Create a data source named Vet Data Source that contains the following fields:

        Title
        First Name
        Last Name
        Address1
        City
        State
        Zip Code

    d. Enter the following records:

        Dr. Joel Allen
        316 River St.
        Claremont, NH 03702

        Dr. Matthew Smith
        452 Valley View Dr.
        Newport, NH 03706

        Dr. Deana Walter
        409 Laurel Rd.
        Claremont, NH 03707

    e. In the main document, insert fields representing the names and addresses above the first paragraph. Insert a salutation line that contains "Dear" and the title and last name from the data source file.

    f. Insert an appropriate closing to the letter and type your name as the sender.

    g. Merge the main document and the data source. Save the merge letters as Vet Merge Document. Print the letters.

Bonus Club Memo

★★ 5. The Downtown Internet Cafe manager asked you to create a letter to send to members of the bonus awards program. The body of the letter has already been created. One of the merge letters you will create is shown below.

   a. Open the file wd05_Cafe Bonus.

   b. Draw a table with the appropriate number of columns and rows to hold the following data. Place the table below the second paragraph. Enter the information shown below into the table.

Bonus Awards					
	Hours				
	20	50	75	100	150+
Award	Free coffee refill	Free bagel	One free hour online time	Two free hours online time	One free hour online time for each additional 25 hours
	Or free bagel	Or free half hour online time	Or free coffee and bagel	Or free coffee and bagel on next four visits	Or free coffee and bagel per visit for each additional 10 hours

   c. Apply format features you learned in this lab, including text alignment and colors to the table. Size the table rows and columns as necessary, and center the table.

   d. Use the wizard to create a form letter. Create a data source named Cafe Data Source that contains the following fields:

      Title
      First Name
      Last Name
      Address1
      City
      State
      Zip Code

   e. Create three records in the Cafe Data Source file.

   f. In the main document, insert fields representing the names and addresses above the first paragraph. Replace the word "Member" in the salutation line with the member's first name from the data source file. Insert your name in the closing.

   g. Merge the main document and the data source. Save the merged letters as Cafe Merge Document. Print the letters.

lab exercises

Leisure Activity Newsletter

★ 1. According to the Yankelovich study printed in the *Yankelovich Monitor Minute*, Americans are seeking more creative outlets through their home and family. You feel this information would be of interest to the people to whom you send a monthly newsletter. Use the information provided below to create an attractive table. Use the features you learned in the lab to enhance the appearance of the table. When you are finished, enter your name and the current date below the table. Save the document as Leisure Activities and print the document.

Activity	Boomers	Xers
Do-it-yourself projects	54%	50%
Home improvements	52	38
Gardening	39	18
Cooking from scratch	32	23
Raising children	53	29
Cooking for fun	39	33
They wish for more:		
Get-togethers with friends	52	43
Family get-togethers	49	37
Watching movies/videos	22	17

New Car Research

★ ★ 2. Your friend is excited about his new car and has gotten you interested in buying a new car. You have narrowed down your options to those shown below. Use the data to create a table that contains the make, model, fuel efficiency, and selling price. Add text to the document with a short description of the features that attract you to your favorite vehicle on the list. Enter your name and the current date at the end of the document. Save the document as New Car Info and print the document.

Make	Model	MPG (City/Hwy)	Retail
Toyota	Echo	34/41	$12,685
Honda	Insight	61/68	$19,716
Volkswagen	Jetta	42/49	$18,520
Nissan	Altima	21/28	$19,160

Hand Washing Data

★ ★ **3.** You work at the American Society for Microbiology and have received a request for data on hand washing. Create a memo using the Professional Memo Template. Add the paragraph below to the body of the memo. Address the memo to your instructor and include your name and the date in the memo placeholders. Then use the data below to create a table, with headings for city, sex, and percentage of hand washers. Include it in the memo you will send in response to the request. Add color and formatting of your choice to the table. Save your completed memo as Hand Washing and print it.

> Recent studies done by the American Society for Microbiology conclude that only 60% of Americans using public restrooms wash their hands. These findings are inconsistent with polling that suggested 98% of Americans wash their hands after using the restroom. Field observations demonstrate that the percentage of hand washers varies by city and sex. I have included the data from our studies in the table below.

City	% Women	% Men
Chicago	83	60
San Francisco	80	75
Atlanta	64	60
New Orleans	64	55
New York	49	35

Movie Data Research

★ ★ **4.** For your marketing class, you have been asked to create a report on historical movie promotions. To inform the rest of your team about the results of your research, use a Memo Template with appropriate fields and include a table, using the data below, that displays the current movies, the number of weeks they have been in theaters, and the gross revenue of each. Be sure to include a chart of your findings. When you are finished, format the table and chart in an attractive manner. Save the document as Movie Data and then print the document.

Movie	Weeks in Theater	Gross Revenue	Year
The Exorcist	24	$204 Billion	1973
Star Wars	21	$461 Billion	1977
Gone with the Wind	30	$200 Billion	1939

Frequent Flyer Letter

★ ★ **5.** Your job with a new low-cost airline company is to manage the company's frequent flyer program.
★   Use the features you learned in this lab to create a form letter to be sent to new customers of your
        airline's frequent flyer program. Put the program information provided below into a table, and
        then enhance the table. Enter your name as the signature name on the letter. Create at least three
        addresses in the data source file. When you are finished, save the document as Frequent Flyer Letter.
        Print the document.

Southwestern American Airlines Frequent Flyer Program Information
Flights to over 350 cities
Minimum award of 500 miles per flight
No deadline for accumulated flight miles
No blackout periods
Partners with international airlines to provide access to international flights with your award

on the web

Researching Job Opportunities on the Web

Use the Web to locate three advertisements for jobs of interest to you in your field. Using the
Letter Wizard, create a cover letter appropriate for each position. Include features you learned in
this and other tutorials to make a professional-looking document. Use Resume Wizard to create a
current resume for yourself. Include all the information that might help you secure one of the
positions you are interested in. When you are finished, save the document as Cover Letter and Resume.
Print the documents.

Creating a Web Site

LAB 6

objectives

After completing this lab, you will know how to:

1.	Plan and design a Web site.
2.	Use the Web Page Wizard.
3.	Preview a Web site.
4.	Create and size frames.
5.	Add backgrounds.
6.	Group objects.
7.	Use tables to control layout.
8.	Insert lines, animated graphics, and diagrams.
9.	Insert absolute and relative hyperlinks.
10.	Create a Web form.
11.	Use supporting folders.

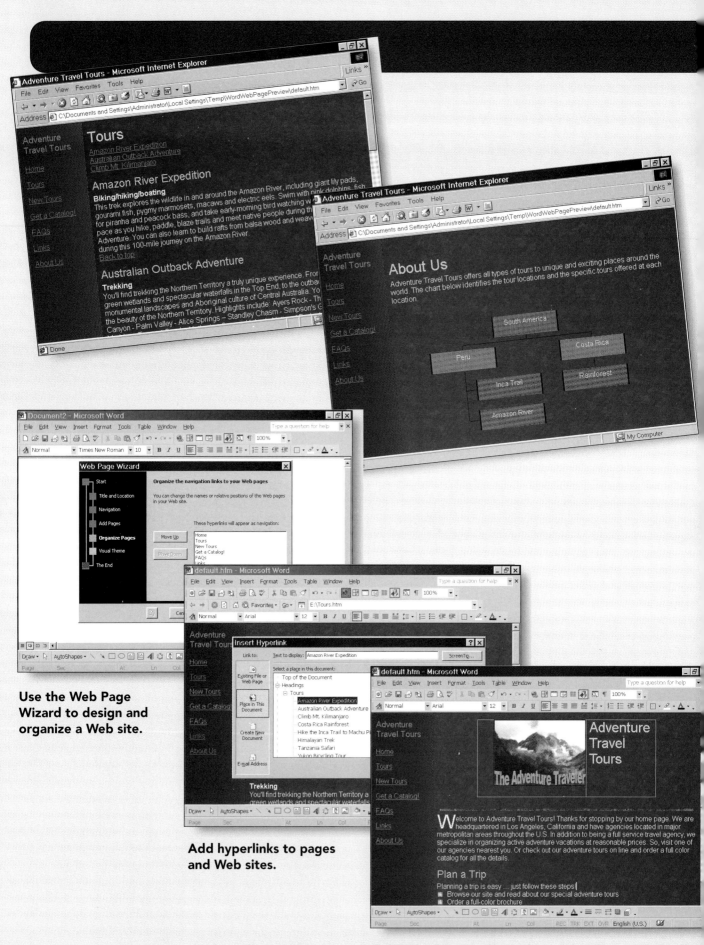

Use the Web Page Wizard to design and organize a Web site.

Add hyperlinks to pages and Web sites.

Enhance pages with graphics, animations and themes.

WD6.2

Adventure Travel Tours

The manager of Adventure Travel Tours has noticed that the company Web site has become disorganized as new items have been added to the site. In addition, the site has an inconsistent look—different colors and styles have been used as pages have been added. You have been asked to eval-uate the site for content, organ-ization, and style and to develop a new overall design and layout for the site as well as a new structure for the site content.

You are very excited about working on this project as you recently attended a seminar on Web page de-sign and layout. You learned about how to organize a site to make it both efficient and attractive. Additionally, the seminar demonstrated how these features could be created using Word. You will use Word to create the new Web site shown below.

© Corbis

concept overview

The following concepts will be introduced in this lab:

1	**Home Page**	The top-level or opening page of a Web site is called the home page.
2	**Frame**	A Web page can be divided into sections, called frames, that display separate Web pages.
3	**Group**	A group is two or more objects that are treated as a single object.
4	**Diagram**	A diagram is a graphic object that can be used to illustrate concepts and to enhance your documents.
5	**Absolute and Relative Links**	When you create a hyperlink in a document, you can make the path to the destination an absolute link or a relative link.
6	**Form**	Forms are used in Web pages to get information or feedback from users or to provide information. Using forms makes your Web site interactive.

Planning and Designing Web Sites

The Adventure Travel Tours Web site consists of several Web pages. These pages contain a list of tours, tour descriptions, a catalog request form, a newsletter, and links to other Web sites. Like all Web sites, the Adventure Travel Tours site opens with a home page that links to the additional pages.

concept 1

Home Page

1 The top-level or opening page of a Web site is called the **home page**. It is displayed by default when a user visits your Web site. A large site may have many home pages. The home page usually contains an introduction to the site along with hyperlinks that allow users to jump to another location on the same page, to another page in the same site, or to another page on a different site altogether.

Because the home page is the first page people see when visiting a site, it is very important that it is well designed. After looking at the existing home page and the organization of the Adventure Travel Tours site, you have decided to redesign the entire site.

When creating or authoring a Web page, you want to make the page both attractive and informative. You also want it to be easy to use, and you want it to work right. It is therefore important to plan the design of the Web site and the pages it will include. Web page design includes planning the text content of the page and the addition of elements such as graphic objects, images, art, and color, which can make the page both attractive and easy to use.

Graphic objects, images, art, and color are perhaps the most important features of Web pages. They entice the user to continue to explore the Web site. Other elements, such as animation, scrolling banners, blinking text, audio, and video can be added to a Web page to make it even more dynamic.

With all these elements, it is easy to add too many to a page and end up with a cluttered and distracting mess. Keep the following design tips in mind when authoring your own Web pages:

- The text content of your page is the single most important element. Text should be readable against the background. Check for proper spelling and grammar.

- Background colors and patterns add pizzazz to a page, but be careful that they do not make the page hard to read. Also keep in mind that more complex patterns take longer to download, and that many users have 256-color monitors, on which higher resolution colors will be lost.

- To speed up downloading, keep graphics simple and avoid busy animations and blinking text. A good suggestion is to keep the file size of images less than 100K. Smaller is even better.

- Page dimensions should be the same as the browser window size. Many users today have large monitors with the screen resolution set to 600 by 800 pixels. Some, however, still have 15-inch screens with the screen resolution set to 640 by 480 pixels. A page designed with 600 by 800 pixels will be too large for their screens. To solve this problem, many professional sites include a JavaScript program that determines the user's screen dimensions and dynamically resizes the page width. Older versions of browser programs may not support JavaScript; therefore, designing a Web page for 640 by 480 resolution is still the safest approach.

- In general, keep pages to no longer than two to three screens' worth of information. If a page is too long, the reader has to remember too much information that has scrolled off the screen.

- At the bottom of each page, include navigation links back to the home page and other major site pages so users will not get lost. Also include text links (alternative text) for users who have turned off graphics loading in their browsers to improve downloading speed.

- Get permission before using text, sounds, and images that are copyrighted. Copyright laws and infringement fines apply to pages posted on the Internet.

After a discussion with the marketing manager about the content and features that Adventure Travel Tours wants to include in the Web site, you drew a sample home page layout that you feel may be both interesting and easy to use (shown here). Your plans are to include separate pages for company information, tour descriptions and itinerary, frequently asked questions (FAQs), ordering catalogs and booking tours, a photo album, and links to other travel-related sites.

You have created a Word document containing the text for the home page. You have also prepared several other documents to use in the Web site, including the Web page you already created about the four new tours. Now you are ready to start creating the web site.

Using the Web Page Wizard

Word offers three ways to create Web pages. You can start with a blank Web page. You can convert an existing Word document to hypertext markup language (HTML), which you did in Working Together following Lab 3. Finally, you can use the Web Page Wizard to help you quickly create a Web site. The Web Wizard is a guided approach that helps you determine the content and organization of your Web site through a series of questions. Then it creates a Web site based on the answers you provide.

Starting the Web Page Wizard

1 **Start Word.**

From the New Document task pane, click 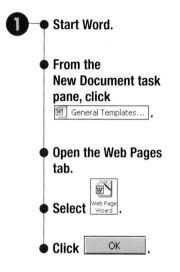 General Templates... **.**

Open the Web Pages tab.

Select Web Page Wizard **.**

Click OK **.**

Your screen should be similar to Figure 6.1

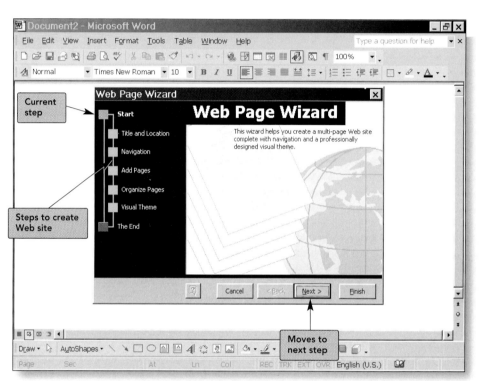

Figure 6.1

The opening dialog box of the Web Page Wizard briefly describes how the feature works. As the wizard guides you through creating the Web site, the left side of the window shows you which step you are on in the outline. The green box identifies the current step. Clicking Next > moves to the next step.

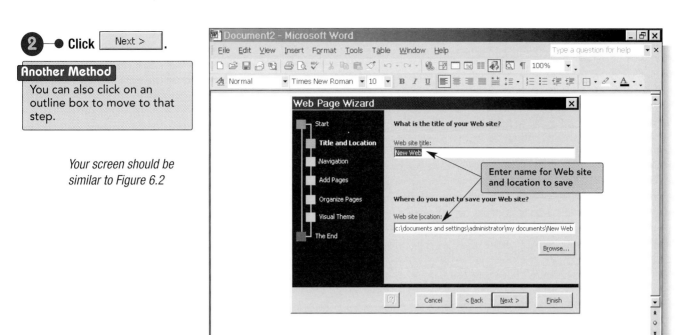

Figure 6.2

The second wizard dialog box asks you for the name of your Web site and the location where you want to save it.

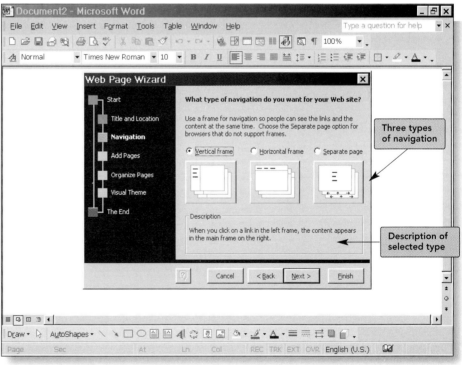

Figure 6.3

Setting Site Navigation

The third wizard dialog box asks you for the type of navigation you want to use. Most Web sites use frames to make navigation easier.

concept 2

Frame

2 A Web page can be divided into sections, called **frames**, that display separate Web pages. Because each one can display different information, frames not only make the Web site more organized but allow users to access the information more easily. The frames for a Web site are held in a special **frames page** container. The frames page serves as the file name for the collection of frames; it is invisible to the users viewing the Web site.

You can use frames to create a header for your Web site that appears on each page in the site. You can also create a table of contents in the left frame that displays hyperlinks to the main pages of a Web site. It stays on the screen while the right frame, often called the main frame, displays the contents of the page the hyperlink points to.

Table of contents frame on left, main frame on right

Header frame on top, table of contents frame on left, main frame on right

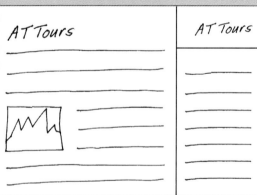

Main frame on left with two small frames on right

Although frames can make navigation in your Web site easier, having too many can make it difficult to read the screen. Use as few frames as possible. Many people have browsers that cannot display frames, so you may want to consider creating a nonframe version to accommodate those users.

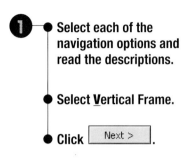

Additional Information

Refer to the discussion of hyperlinks in the Working Together section following Lab 3.

Your choices are to create a frame to the left or at the top of the home page. A vertical frame on the left side can display links to topics that, when selected, appear in the main frame on the right. A horizontal frame at the top of the screen can contain links to topics that, when selected, appear below the frame. You can also set up your Web site without frames so that the navigation is limited to browsers' Back and Forward buttons.

1 ● Select each of the navigation options and read the descriptions.

● Select **V**ertical Frame.

● Click [Next >].

Your screen should be similar to Figure 6.4

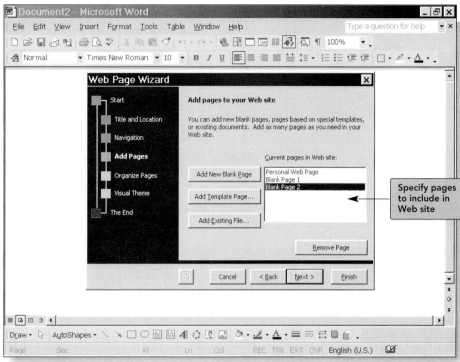

Figure 6.4

Creating Pages

The fourth wizard dialog box asks you to specify the pages to include in your Web site. By default, the wizard offers a Personal Web Page template and two blank pages. You want to remove the Personal Web Page template and include a home page using the text in the document ATT Home Page, which has already been created. You also want to include pages for the following: new tours, a list of all tours and descriptions, frequently asked questions (FAQs), ordering catalogs and booking tours, and links to other travel-related sites.

The three option buttons, described below, are used to specify the type of page to insert and the source of any contents you want included in the pages.

Option	Effect
Add New Blank Page	Creates a blank page
Add Template Page	Creates a page with suggested contents
Add Existing File	Creates a page containing the contents of the selected file

First you will remove the Personal Web Page and add a page using the text in the ATT Home Page document.

1 ● **Select Personal Web Page.**

● **Click** Remove Page .

● **Click** Add Existing File... .

● **If necessary, change the location to the location of your data files.**

● **Select the file** wd06_ATT Home Page.

● **Click** Open ▼ .

Your screen should be similar to Figure 6.5

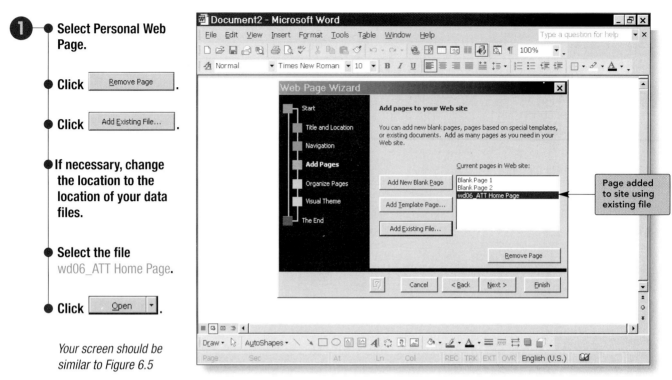

Figure 6.5

The list box displays the name of the file on which this page will be based. Next you want to add a page for the frequently asked questions. Word includes a template for a FAQs page.

2 ● **Click**  Add Template Page... .

Your screen should be similar to Figure 6.6

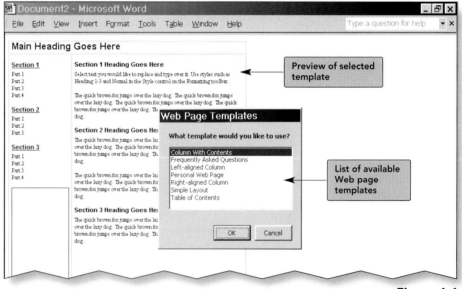

Figure 6.6

The Web Page Templates box lists the seven different templates you can use to create a Web page. The selected template is displayed behind the dialog box in the window. You want to use the Frequently Asked Questions template to create the FAQs page.

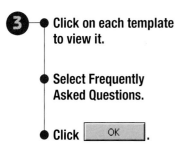

3 ● Click on each template to view it.

● Select Frequently Asked Questions.

● Click OK.

Your screen should be similar to Figure 6.7

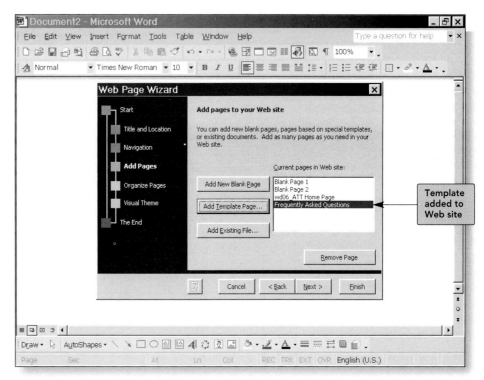

Figure 6.7

The page is added to the list and you are returned to the Web Page Wizard. Next you want to add two more pages from existing file content. The first is a list of all tours and a brief description, and the second is a Web page file about the new tours, similar to the one you created in the first Working Together lab. You will also add another blank page that you will add information to.

4 ● Click Add Existing File....

● If necessary, change the location to your data disk.

● Select wd06_Tour List.

● Click Open.

● In the same manner, add the wd06_New Tours.htm file to the list.

● Click Add New Blank Page to add another new blank page.

Your screen should be similar to Figure 6.8

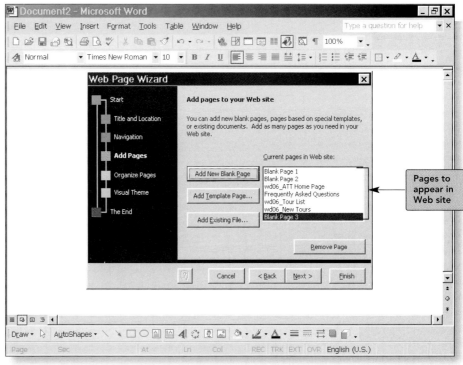

Figure 6.8

Organizing and Naming Pages

You are halfway finished with your Web site structure. The next step is to organize the Web pages.

 **Click** Next > .

Your screen should be similar to Figure 6.9

Figure 6.9

You need to specify the order in which the pages will appear as links in the table of contents frame. The ATT Home Page document contains the information you want displayed on the home page, so you need to move it to the top of the list. You want the Tours page second, the New Tours page third, a blank page fourth, the FAQs page fifth, and two more blank pages to be sixth and seventh.

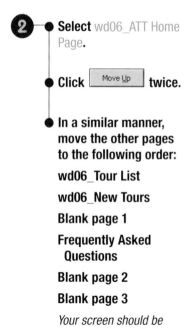

Select wd06_ATT Home Page.

Click Move Up **twice.**

In a similar manner, move the other pages to the following order:

wd06_Tour List

wd06_New Tours

Blank page 1

Frequently Asked Questions

Blank page 2

Blank page 3

Your screen should be similar to Figure 6.10

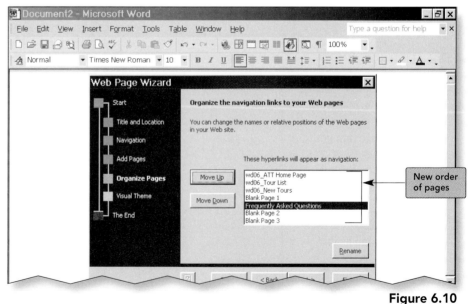

Figure 6.10

Now that the pages are in the right sequence, you want to give them more descriptive names. Each name will be used as the link in the contents frame. First you will rename the wd06_ATT Home Page to Home.

3 ● **Select** wd06_ATT Home Page.

● **Click** Rename .

● **Type** Home **in the Rename Hyperlink dialog box text box.**

● **Click** OK .

● **Using this same procedure, rename the remaining pages using the names shown below.**

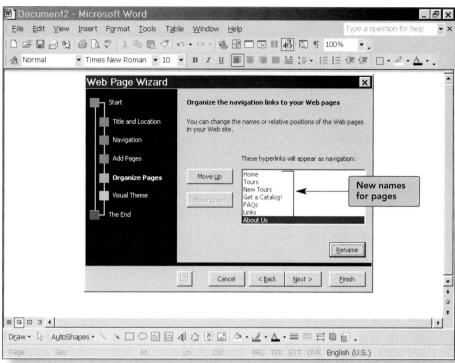

Figure 6.11

Old Name	New Name
wd06_Tour List	Tours
wd06_New Tours	New Tours
Blank page 1	Get a Catalog!
Frequently Asked Questions	FAQs
Blank page 2	Links
Blank page 3	About Us

Your screen should be similar to Figure 6.11

Selecting a Theme

Your Web site structure is almost finished. The last step in the process is to select a theme for the site. The theme you select here will be applied to all the pages in your site at once. You can also apply themes to individual pages, as you did in the first Working Together section.

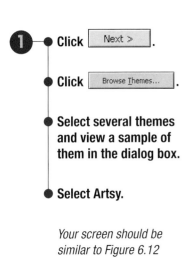

1 ● Click [Next >].

● Click [Browse Themes...].

● Select several themes and view a sample of them in the dialog box.

● Select Artsy.

Your screen should be similar to Figure 6.12

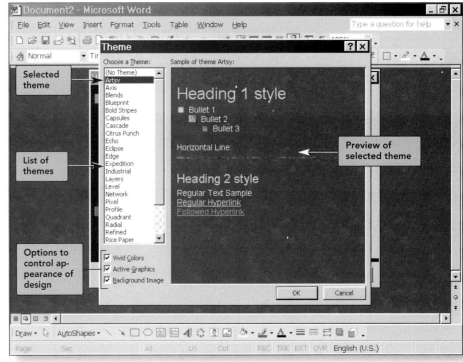

Figure 6.12

The three options under the Theme list box are used to control the appearance of the page. Choose Vivid Colors when you want to brighten the theme. Choose Active Graphics if you plan to include any animation. Background Image is selected by default. You want to brighten the theme colors and you plan to include animation. The name of the selected theme appears in the wizard text box. Now you are finished setting up the structure for the Web site and the last step is to create it.

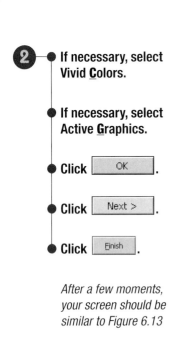

2 ● If necessary, select Vivid **C**olors.

● If necessary, select Active **G**raphics.

● Click [OK].

● Click [Next >].

● Click [Finish].

After a few moments, your screen should be similar to Figure 6.13

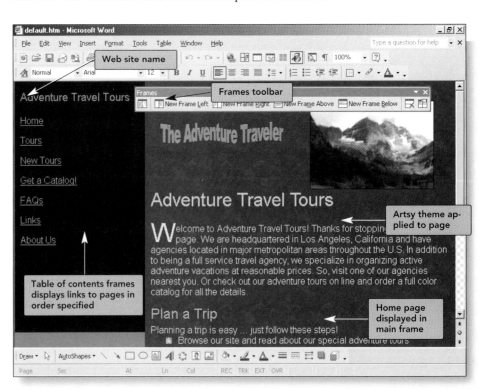

Figure 6.13

All the pages in the Web site are created and the home page is displayed. The Frames toolbar opens automatically. It can be used to add or delete frames to existing pages. The Web site name appears at the top of the contents frame, followed by the page names in the order you specified while using the wizard. Each page name is a link to the associated page. The design elements from the Artsy theme are applied to the page and affect the frame background, heading and body text styles, hyperlink colors, and bullets and horizontal lines.

Previewing the Web Site

Next you want to preview the site in a browser.

1 ● Choose **File/Web** Page Preview.

● **Maximize the browser window.**

Your screen should be similar to Figure 6.14

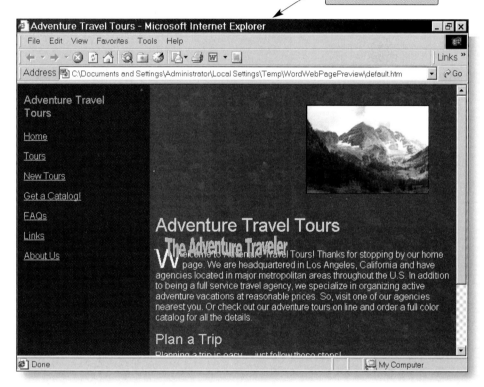

Browser loaded offline and current Web page is displayed

Figure 6.14

Additional Information
Offline viewing does not connect you to the Internet.

The browser on your system is loaded offline, and the Web page you are working on is displayed in the browser window. As you can see, the page appears different in the browser window than it did in the Word document window. It is important as you create your Web pages to preview them and make adjustments to the page so that they display correctly in the browser.

As you look at the home page, you decide you want to reduce the width of the contents frame and change its background color. You also want to combine the WordArt text with the picture and display the company name to the right of the picture. To view the other pages in the Web site, you click the links in the contents frame.

2 ● Click the **Tours** link in the contents frame.

Your screen should be similar to Figure 6.15

Table of contents frame is fixed in window

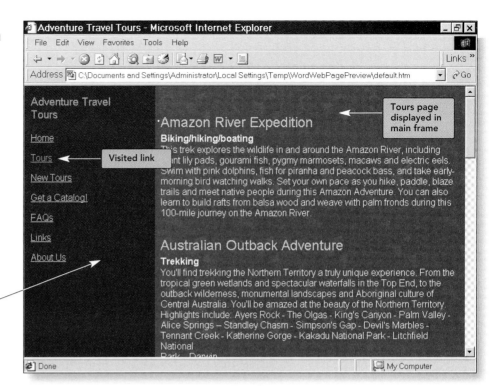

Figure 6.15

The Tours page is displayed in the main frame, while the table of contents remains fixed on the screen. This makes it easy to navigate to other pages within the site. Notice that the Tours link has changed to a different color, indicating it is a visited link. This page displays the contents of the wd06_Tour List file. Again you have several changes you want to make to this page.

3 ● Click the **New Tours** link.

● Click the **Get a Catalog!** link.

● Click the **FAQs** link.

Your screen should be similar to Figure 6.16

Followed links

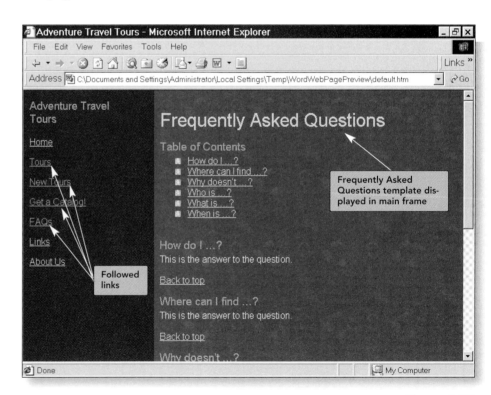

Figure 6.16

This page contains the Frequently Asked Questions template. Like other templates, it provides a suggested layout and ideas for content that you replace with your own information.

4 ● Click on the other links to view the associated pages.

● Click on the Word default.htm button in the taskbar to switch to the Word document window.

HAVING TROUBLE?
Point to the taskbar button to see the window name in a ScreenTip.

As you open the Web pages in Word, each page opens in a separate window. The window names are Default.htm:#, with the number representing the order in which they were opened. If only one window is open, it does not have a number.

Formatting a Web Page

You want the background of the table of contents frame to blend in better with the theme colors used in the main frame. Even though you applied a theme to the Web site, you can change the background of a page or frame. A **background** is a color or design that is displayed behind the text on the page. You can change the background to another color or select a background image, pattern, or texture, called a **wallpaper**.

Adding a Background

You will change the background of the contents frame to another color. Because you do not plan to add or remove frames, you can close the toolbar.

1 ● Close the Frames toolbar.

● Click in the contents frame to make it active.

● Choose Format/ Background/Fill Effects.

● Open the Gradient tab and select Two colors.

● Select Dark Blue as Color 1 and Gray–50% as Color 2.

● Select Vertical as the shading style.

● Select the bottom left Variants style.

Your screen should be similar to Figure 6.17

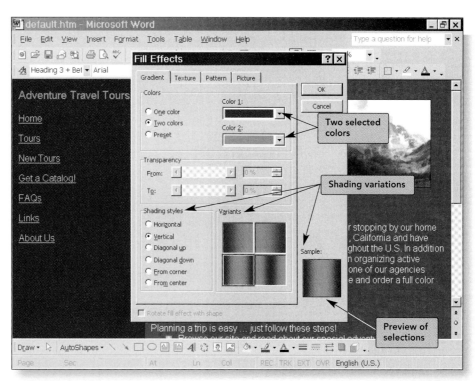

Figure 6.17

The Sample provides a preview of your selections.

2 ● **Click** `OK` **.**

Your screen should be similar to Figure 6.18

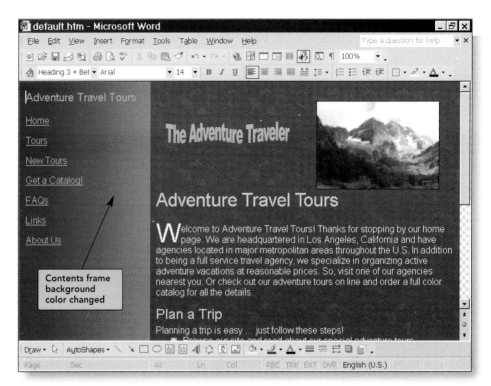

Contents frame background color changed

Figure 6.18

The selected background gradient is applied to the contents frame only.

Sizing a Frame

Next you need to adjust the width of the contents frame. Generally, you want the main frame to be as large as possible to display the maximum amount of page content. Reducing the size of the contents frame will make the main frame larger.

1 ● **Right-click on the contents frame and select Frame Properties from the Shortcut menu.**

● **Decrease the Width to 1.5 inches.**

● **Click** `OK` **.**

Another Method

You can also drag the frame divider line to adjust the frame width.

● **Click** 🖫 **Save to save the changes you have made to the contents frame page.**

Your screen should be similar to Figure 6.19

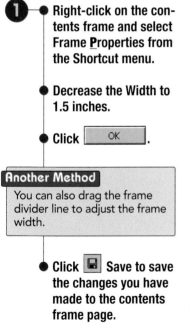

Contents frame size reduced

Figure 6.19

Grouping Objects

You decide that the home page would look better if the WordArt text were combined with the mountain picture. To do this, you will combine a WordArt object with a picture object by grouping them.

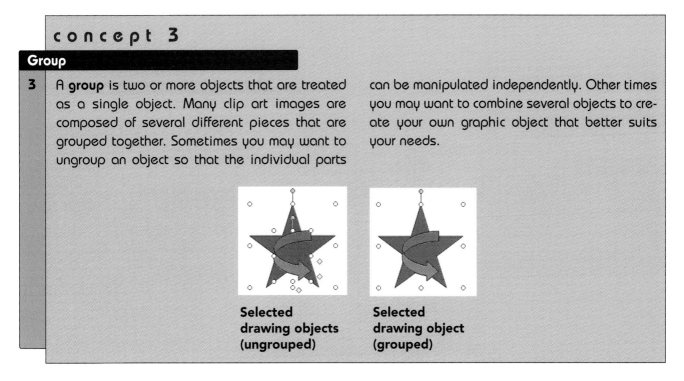

concept 3

Group

3 A **group** is two or more objects that are treated as a single object. Many clip art images are composed of several different pieces that are grouped together. Sometimes you may want to ungroup an object so that the individual parts can be manipulated independently. Other times you may want to combine several objects to create your own graphic object that better suits your needs.

**Selected
drawing objects
(ungrouped)**

**Selected
drawing object
(grouped)**

1 • Select and move the WordArt object over the picture object.

Your screen should be similar to Figure 6.20

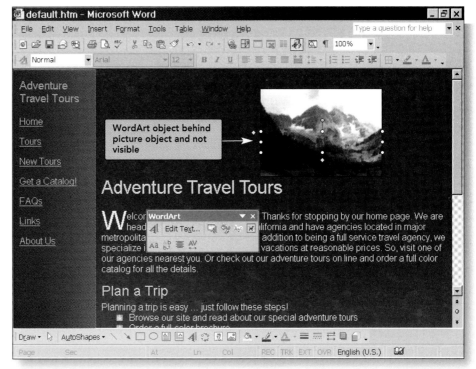

Figure 6.20

Notice that the WordArt object is not visible. This is because the objects were inserted as floating objects in the drawing layer so that they can be positioned precisely on the page, including in front of and behind other objects. As floating objects are added to a document, they stack in layers and may overlap. You can move floating objects up or down within a stack using the Order button on the drawing toolbar. Sometimes it is easy to lose a floating object behind another. If this happens you can press [Tab⇆] to cycle forward or [⇧Shift] + [Tab⇆] to cycle backward through the stacked objects until the one you want is selected. You need to move the WordArt object to the front of the stack.

2 ● Click [Draw ▾].

● Choose O**r**der/Bring to Fron**t**.

Another Method
You can also right-click on the object and select the order from the shortcut menu.

Your screen should be similar to Figure 6.21

Figure 6.21

The WordArt object is now at the top of the stack and is visible over the picture. You want the WordArt displayed centered at the bottom of the picture. You also want to group the two objects to create a single object.

3 ● Hold down [⇧Shift] and click on the picture.

● Click [Draw ▾].

● Choose **A**lign or Distribute/Align **B**ottom.

● Click [Draw ▾].

● Choose **A**lign or Distribute/Align **C**enter.

● Right-click on the selection and select **G**rouping from the shortcut menu.

● Choose **G**roup

Another Method
You can also select Group from the [Draw ▾] drop-down menu.

Your screen should be similar to Figure 6.22

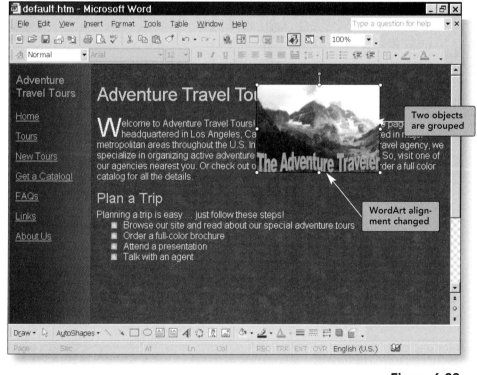

Figure 6.22

www.mhhe.com/oleary

The text is now centered at the bottom of the picture. Also, because you have grouped the two objects, when you move and size the object it will act as a single object.

Next you need to change the wrapping style of the object.

4 ● Change the text wrapping style to Top and Bottom.

HAVING TROUBLE?

Double-click the grouped object, open the Layout tab, and select the wrapping style.

● Click outside the object to deselect it.

Your screen should be similar to Figure 6.23

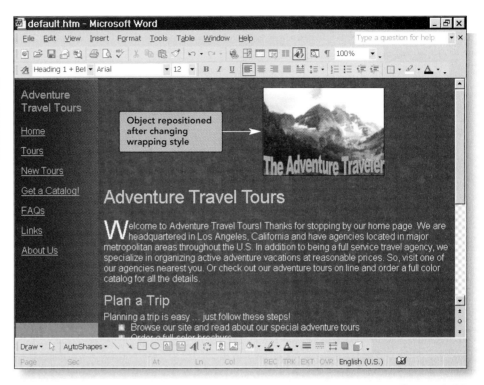

Figure 6.23

Using Tables to Control Page Layout

The next change you want to make is to display the company name to the right of the picture in the home page. Unlike a regular document, in which you could use columns to display text side by side, a Web page requires a table to control the page layout. The table allows you to place items in different locations on the Web page. You will create a one-row, two-column table to hold the two items. Then you will move the text and picture into the appropriate cells of the table.

1 ● Click on the blank line above the Adventure Travel Tours title.

● Click ▣ Insert Table and create a table that is 1 row by 2 columns.

● Select the picture, and cut and paste it into the left cell of the table.

● Select the company name, and cut and paste (or drag) this selection into the right cell of the table.

Your screen should be similar to Figure 6.24

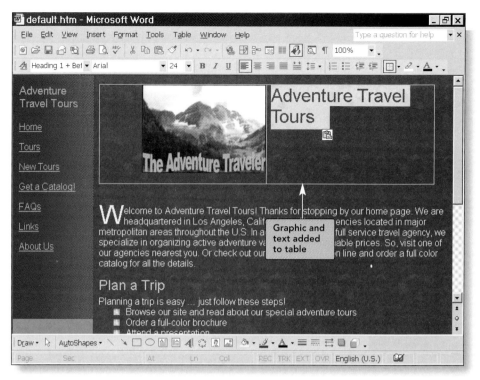

Figure 6.24

The picture and company name need to be in the center of the page. Since you are using the table as a layout tool, you need to center the table. You also want to turn off the display of the border lines.

2 ● Size the table as in Figure 6.25.

● Select the table and center it.

● Remove all the table border lines.

Your screen should be similar to Figure 6.25

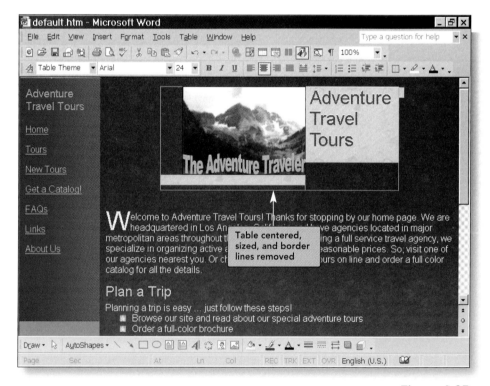

Figure 6.25

The table displays the picture and company name side by side, centered in the main frame. The table gridlines are still displayed.

Adding and Modifying Graphics

Graphics on a Web page add interest and present information in a more visually appealing manner. The major kinds of graphics found on Web pages include icons, lines or bars, bullets, photographs, and animated GIFs. You should be aware that some graphics, such as photographs, will take time to load in a browser window.

At the moment, Web browsers can display only two types of graphic files: GIF and JPG. These are compressed file formats that load fairly quickly in a browser window. If the graphics you create or add to your Web page are in a different format, Word converts them to GIF files when you save the Web page.

Inserting a Horizontal Line

You want to include a graphic horizontal line below the table on the home page to further separate the heading from the page content and to make the page more interesting. A line design is included with the theme, but because the Word document file you used for this page did not contain a horizontal line, the line in the theme was not used. You need to first add a horizontal line and then reapply the theme to change it to the graphic line associated with the theme.

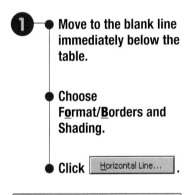

Move to the blank line immediately below the table.

Choose Format/Borders and Shading.

Click `Horizontal Line...` .

Another Method

You could also open the Clip Organizer and add a line from the Web Dividers category.

Your screen should be similar to Figure 6.26

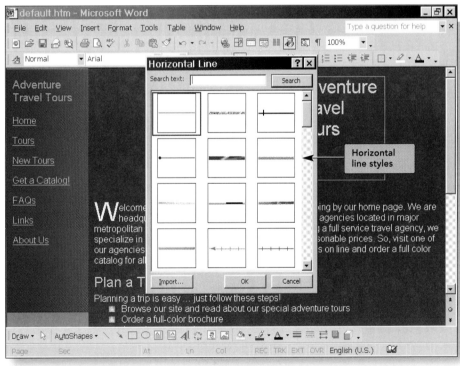

Figure 6.26

2 ● Select and insert any line style from the Horizontal Line dialog box.

Your screen should be similar to Figure 6.27

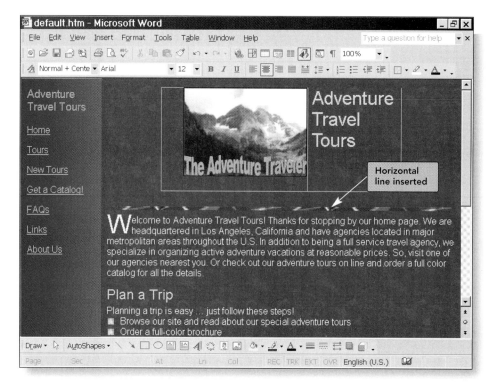

Horizontal line inserted

Figure 6.27

The selected line style is displayed the full width of the main frame. However, it is not the style that is associated with the theme. You will reapply the theme to update the line style to the one used in the theme. You will then need to remove the table border lines again.

3 ● Choose Format/Theme.

● If necessary, select the Artsy theme.

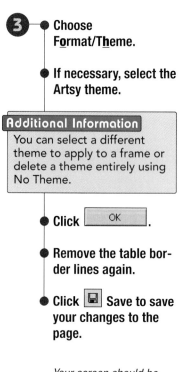

Additional Information

You can select a different theme to apply to a frame or delete a theme entirely using No Theme.

● Click ☐ OK ☐.

● Remove the table border lines again.

● Click 🖫 Save to save your changes to the page.

Your screen should be similar to Figure 6.28

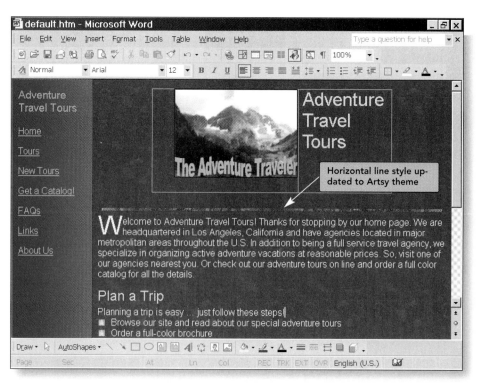

Horizontal line style updated to Artsy theme

Figure 6.28

A new horizontal line designed for use with the selected theme replaces the horizontal line you inserted.

Inserting Animated Graphics

Next you will work on the Links page. Because you still do not have all the content ready for this page, it is common practice to indicate that a page is under construction by inserting either text or a clever graphic. You will first replace the sample text on this page with a page title.

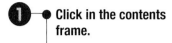

- Click in the contents frame.

- Press Ctrl and click **Links**.

- Replace the sample text with **Links** and apply the Heading 1 style to the word.

Additional Information

The styles associated with the theme are displayed in the Style drop-down list.

- Insert two blank lines below the heading.

Your screen should be similar to Figure 6.29

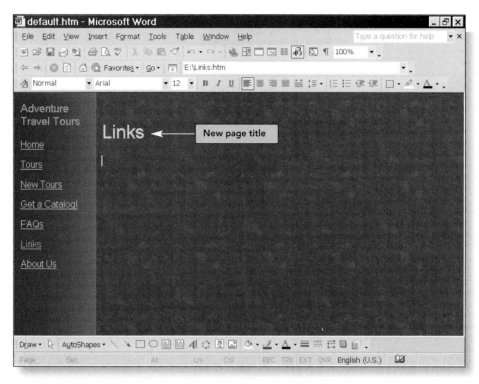

Figure 6.29

Next you will add two animated graphics to show that it is under construction.

2 ● **Insert the picture file** wd06_Construction.

● **If necessary, expand the object to fully display the graphic.**

● **Center the graphic on the page.**

● **Press** ⏎Enter.

● **In the same manner, add the picture file** wd06_Elephant Walking **and center it on the page.**

● **Save the page.**

Your screen should be similar to Figure 6.30

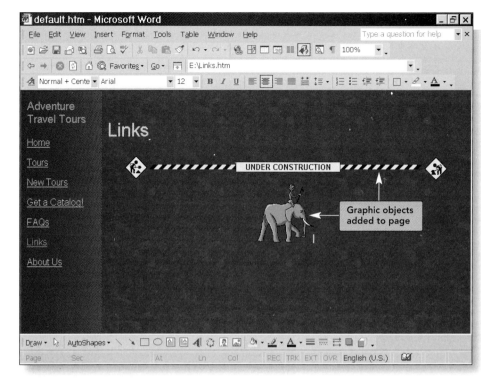

Figure 6.30

Because you are editing the Web page in Word, you cannot see the animation. To see the animation, you need to view the page in the browser. Since the browser is still open, you can simply switch to the browser window.

3 ● **Switch to the browser window.**

● **Click Links to display the page.**

Your screen should be similar to Figure 6.31

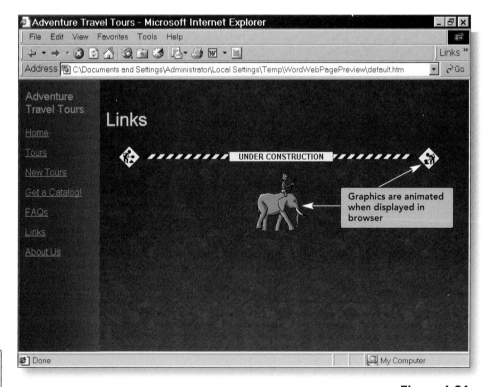

Figure 6.31

HAVING TROUBLE?
If the updated page is not displayed, click 🔄 in Internet Explorer or 🔄 in Netscape Communicator.

You should see the animation in the two graphics now.

Inserting a Diagram

The next page you will work on is the About Us page. On this page you want to include an overview to the tours and locations. You could type a list of locations and tours, but to make it more visually appealing you decide to create a diagram to display the information.

concept 4

Diagram

4   A **diagram** is a graphic object that can be used to illustrate concepts and to enhance your documents. Diagrams are based on text rather than numeric information. There are six predesigned diagrams you can use. The type of diagram you choose depends on the purpose of the diagram and the type of concept you want to illustrate. The table below describes the diagram types and uses.

	Type	Use
	Cycle	Shows a process that has a continuous cycle
	Target	Shows steps toward a goal
	Radial	Shows relationships of elements to a core element
	Venn	Shows areas of overlap between and among elements
	Pyramid	Shows foundation-based relationships
	Organization	Shows hierarchical-based relationships

Additionally, you can create flowcharts (or flow diagrams) using a combination of AutoShapes on the Drawing toolbar, including flowchart shapes and connectors. Flowcharts show a process that has a beginning and an end.

You will enter an introductory paragraph on the About Us page and then create a diagram to display the tour information.

1 ● Switch to the Word
document window.

● Open the About Us
page.

● Replace the sample
text with About Us and
apply a Heading 1 style.

● Insert a blank line
below the heading.

● Type: Adventure
Travel Tours offers all
types of tours to
unique and exciting
places around the
world. The chart
below identifies the
tour locations and the
specific tours offered
at each location.

● Press ⏎Enter.

● On the Drawing tool-
bar click ⬡ .

Another Method

The menu equivalent is
Insert/Diagram.

---

*Your screen should be
similar to Figure 6.32*

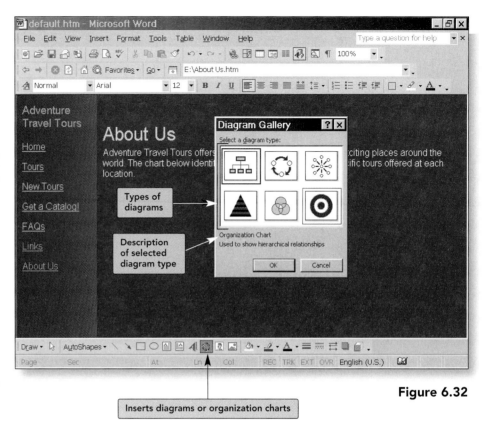

Figure 6.32

Inserts diagrams or organization charts

The Diagram Gallery dialog box asks you to select a type of diagram. The
best type of diagram to represent the tour information is an organization
chart. Typically, organization charts are used to illustrate a working unit
within a company; however, they can be used to illustrate any type of concept that consists of a hierarchal organization.

2
- Select each of the diagram types and read the descriptions.

- Select ⊞ Organization chart.

- Click ⟨ OK ⟩.

Your screen should be similar to Figure 6.33

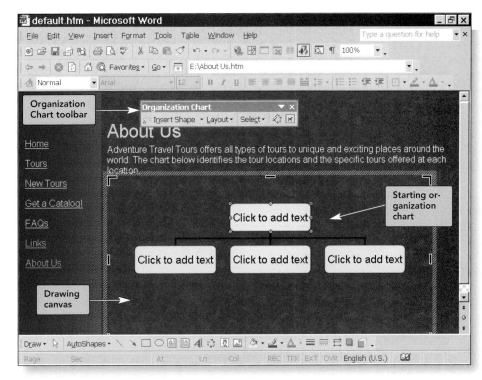

Figure 6.33

A starting organization chart consisting of boxes arranged in a hierarchy is displayed. A drawing canvas surrounds the entire chart and keeps all pieces of the chart together as a unit. The shapes you can use in an organization chart and what they represent are described below.

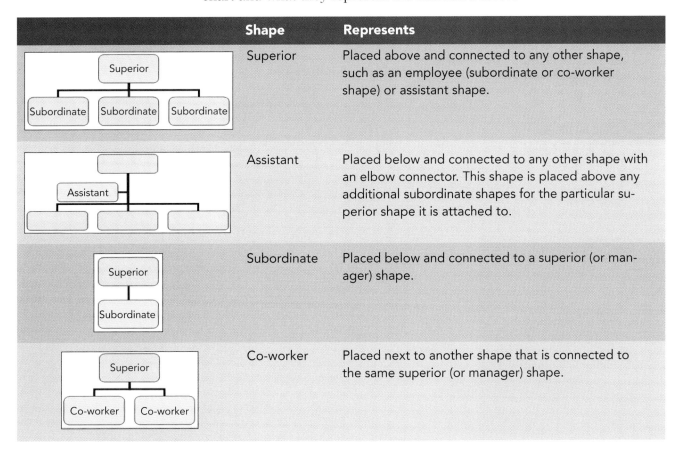

	Shape	Represents
	Superior	Placed above and connected to any other shape, such as an employee (subordinate or co-worker shape) or assistant shape.
	Assistant	Placed below and connected to any other shape with an elbow connector. This shape is placed above any additional subordinate shapes for the particular superior shape it is attached to.
	Subordinate	Placed below and connected to a superior (or manager) shape.
	Co-worker	Placed next to another shape that is connected to the same superior (or manager) shape.

Additionally, the Organization Chart toolbar is automatically opened. It contains buttons to add shapes, modify the layout, and enhance the chart.

You will create separate organization charts to illustrate the tour locations for each of the continents. The first chart you will create will show the South American tours. The completed diagram is shown below.

You will enter text for the first two levels. Since you only need two boxes at the second level, you will also delete a box.

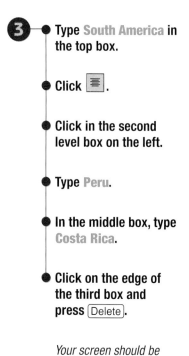

3 ● Type South America in the top box.

● Click [≡].

● Click in the second level box on the left.

● Type Peru.

● In the middle box, type Costa Rica.

● Click on the edge of the third box and press Delete.

Your screen should be similar to Figure 6.34

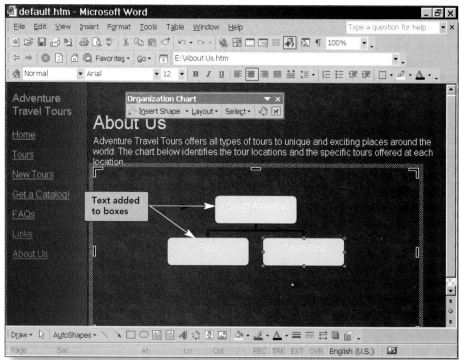

Figure 6.34

Next you need to add two subordinate shapes below the Peru shape to contain the names of the two tours. As you add shapes, the diagram will automatically resize to fit the drawing area. If you do not want the diagram to resize, you can expand the drawing canvas before adding more shapes. You can expand the drawing area by dragging the drawing canvas handles, or by using the options in the [Layout ▾] drop-down menu described below.

Option	Effect
Scale the Organization Chart	Increases the size of both the chart and the drawing canvas.
Fit Organization Chart to Contents	Reduces the size of the drawing canvas to fit the size of the chart.
Expand Organization Chart	Increases the size of the drawing canvas to add space around the chart.

You will let the chart resize to the current drawing canvas size, as there is still plenty of space.

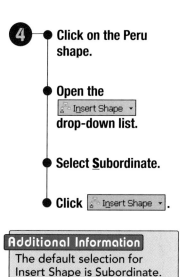

4 ● **Click on the Peru shape.**

● **Open the** [Insert Shape ▾] **drop-down list.**

● **Select Subordinate.**

● **Click** [Insert Shape ▾].

Additional Information
The default selection for Insert Shape is Subordinate.

Your screen should be similar to Figure 6.35

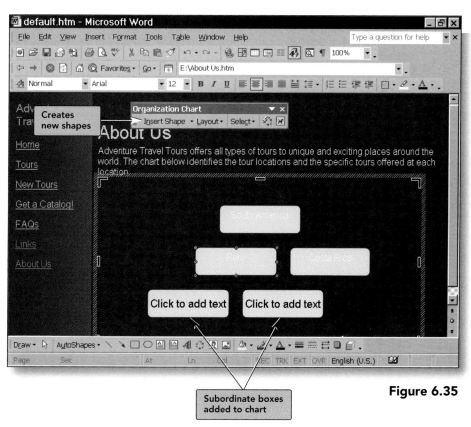

Creates new shapes

Subordinate boxes added to chart

Figure 6.35

The two new shapes are added in a horizontal line subordinate to the selected shape. You decide to change the layout of this grouping so the subordinate shapes line up in a column below the superior shape. The four types of layouts are described in the following table.

	Layout	Description
	Standard	Subordinate shapes line up horizontally below the superior shape.
	Both Hanging	Subordinate shapes hang in columns both to the left and right of the superior shape.
	Left Hanging	Subordinate shapes hang in columns to the left of the superior shape.
	Right Hanging	Subordinate shapes hang in columns to the right of the superior shape.

5 ● Open the Layout ▾ drop-down list.

● Select **R**ight Hanging.

Your screen should be similar to Figure 6.36

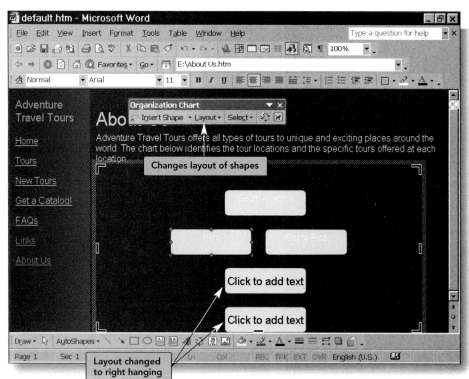

Figure 6.36

Now you will add the tour names to the two new subordinate shapes. Then you will add a subordinate shape below the Costa Rica shape for the Rainforest tour.

6 ● In the first subordinate
shape below Peru,
type Inca Trail.

● Enter Amazon River
in the second
subordinate shape.

● Add a subordinate
shape below Costa
Rica and include the
text Rainforest.

*Your screen should be
similar to Figure 6.37*

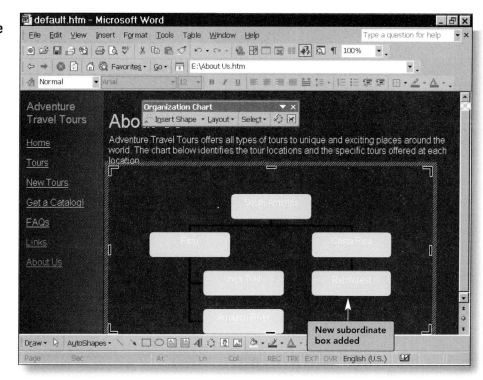

Figure 6.37

Finally, you want to change the style of the chart. There are 15 different
Autoformat styles consisting of different shape designs and colors from
which you can select.

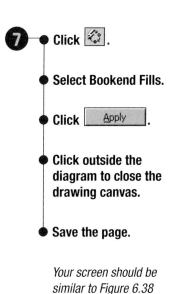

7 ● Click [icon].

● Select Bookend Fills.

● Click Apply.

● Click outside the
diagram to close the
drawing canvas.

● Save the page.

*Your screen should be
similar to Figure 6.38*

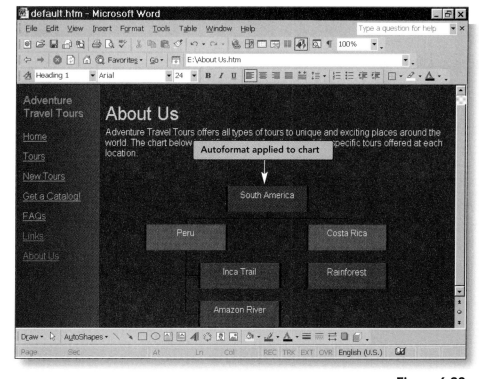

Figure 6.38

Inserting Hyperlinks

The next page you want to work on is Tours. The Tours page contains a brief description of several tours. You want to create a table of contents for the tour descriptions at the top of the page. Then you want to make each table of contents item a hyperlink so the reader can quickly go to a specific tour description in the page. The type of link you will create is a relative link.

concept 5

Absolute and Relative Links

5   When you create a hyperlink in a document, you can make the path to the **destination** (the element you go to from a hyperlink) an absolute link or a relative link. An **absolute link**, also called a **fixed link**, identifies the file location of the destination by its full address, such as c:\Word Data File\Sales.doc. Fixed links usually are used only if you are sure the location of the object will not change. A relative link identifies the destination location in relation to the location of the HTML file. A **relative link** is based on a path you specify in which the first part of the path is shared by both the file that contains the hyperlink and the destination file.

Hyperlinks to other Web sites should typically use a fixed file location that includes the full path to the location or URL of the page. All URLs have at least two basic parts. The first part presents the protocol used to connect to the resource. The **protocol** is the set of rules that control how software and hardware on a network communicate. The hypertext transfer protocol (http), shown in the example below, is by far the most common. The protocol is always followed by a colon (:). The second part of the URL presents the name of the server, the computer where the resource is located (for example, www.adventuretraveltours.com). This is always preceded by two forward slashes (//), and each part of the path is separated by a single forward slash (/).

$$\text{http://www.adventuretraveltours.com}$$

protocol   server

You will enter a heading at the top of the page and then create the links for the first three tour descriptions.

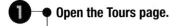

1 ● **Open the Tours page.**

● **Type** Tours **at the top of the page and apply the Heading 1 style to the word.**

● **Press** ⏎Enter**.**

● **Type the following three topic headings on separate lines:**

Amazon River Expedition

Australian Outback Adventure

Climb Mt. Kilimanjaro

● **Select the text "Amazon River Expedition."**

● **Click** 🖳 **Insert Hyperlink (on the Standard toolbar).**

Your screen should be similar to Figure 6.39

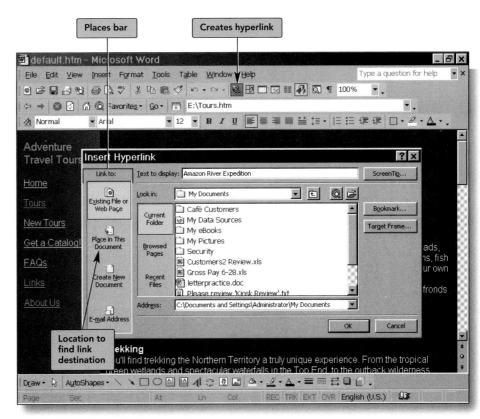

Figure 6.39

From the Insert Hyperlink dialog box, you first need to specify the type of link from the Places bar. The four options are described below.

Option	Effect
Existing File or Web Page	Creates a link in an existing Web page or file.
Place in This Document	Creates a link to a place in the active file.
Create New Document	Creates a link to a file that you have not created yet.
E-mail Address	Creates a link that allows users to create an e-mail message with the correct address in the To line.

Linking within the Document

You need to create a link to a location in the active document. Then you need to select the location in the document to which the link will jump. The list box will display a tree diagram showing an outline of the information in the current page. From the outline you select the heading you want to link to. If you wanted the linked information to display in a different frame, you would need to select the name of the frame in which you want the document to appear. By selecting the name from the list, you are creating a relative link.

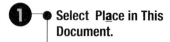

1
● Select Pl**a**ce in This Document.

● Select the "Amazon River Expedition" topic heading from the list box.

HAVING TROUBLE?
If the list of tour names is not displayed, click ⊞ next to Tours to expand the list.

Your screen should be similar to Figure 6.40

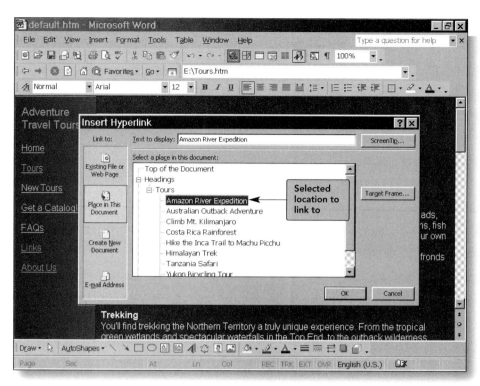

Figure 6.40

You can also assign a tip to be displayed when you point to the hyperlink using the ScreenTip option. If you do not enter text for the ScreenTip, Word uses the path to the file as the ScreenTip.

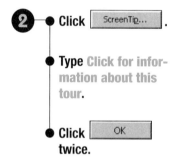

2
● Click ScreenTip... .

● Type Click for information about this tour.

● Click OK twice.

Additional Information
This type of link is also called a **target link** because it targets a heading or other object on a page.

Your screen should be similar to Figure 6.41

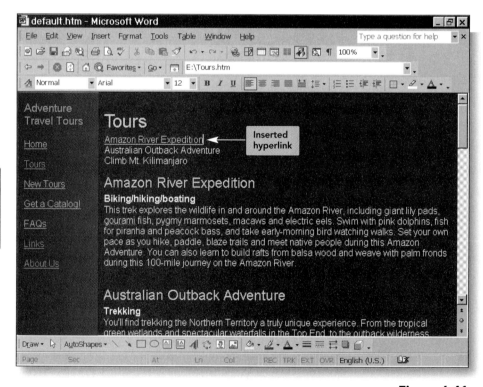

Figure 6.41

The text appears in the hyperlink colors associated with the theme. Next you will create hyperlinks for the other two topics, and then you will test them.

3 • In the same manner, create links and ScreenTips for the other two topics.

• Follow each of the links, ending with the Climb Mt. Kilimanjaro link.

Your screen should be similar to Figure 6.42

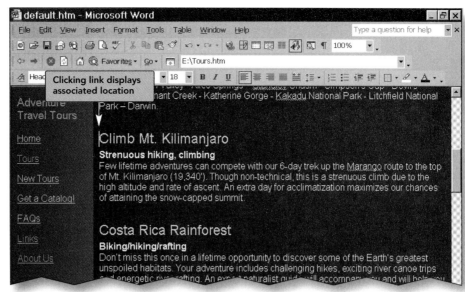

Figure 6.42

As you used each of the links, the section of the page associated with the link displays near the top of the frame. These links are relative links because they indicate a location to jump to relative to the location of the link. For example, if you move the text associated with the link to another location on the page, the link will still take you to the original location in the page, regardless of the information displayed at that location.

After each topic was displayed, you had to scroll back to the top of the page to access the listing again. To make navigation easier, include links back to the top of the page. This allows the reader to jump to the top instead of using the scroll bar.

4 • Move to the blank line below the Mt. Kilimanjaro description.

• Type Back to top.

• Select the text "Back to top" and create a link to the Tours heading.

Your screen should be similar to Figure 6.43

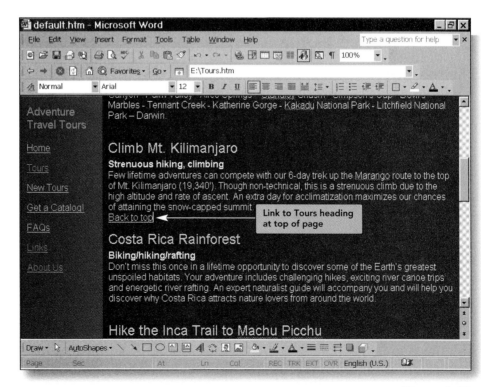

Figure 6.43

You want to include the same link below each of the descriptions. To do this quickly, you can copy the link.

5 • Copy the Back to top link (do not include the blank line at the end of the text).

• Use the Back to top link to return to the top of the page.

• Paste the Back to top link at the end of the Amazon River and Australian Outback tour descriptions.

• Test the links.

• Save the page.

Your screen should be similar to Figure 6.44

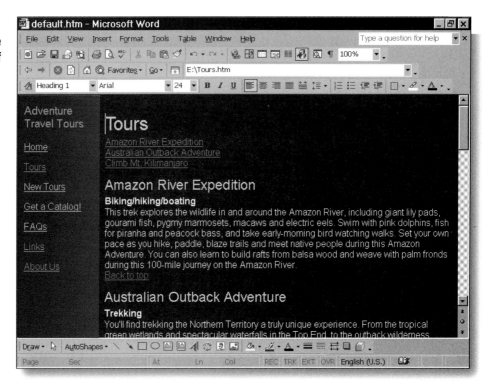

Figure 6.44

Linking to a Web Site

On the Links page, you want the first link to be to a Web site that provides weather reports for locations around the world. As these links are beyond your control, it is your responsibility to check these links periodically to ensure that they are still viable links.

First you will add a horizontal line below the page title and another heading then you will create the link to the Web site.

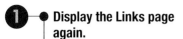

Web page window name

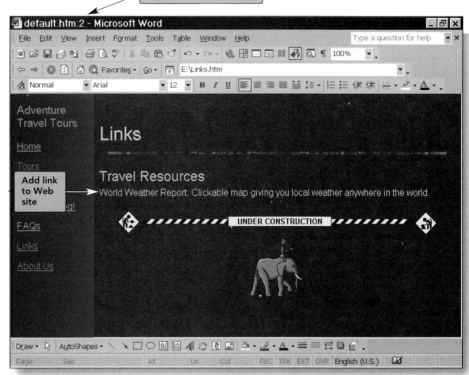

Figure 6.45

1 • Display the Links page again.

• On the blank line under Links, click ▣ ▾ Borders to open the Borders drop-down menu.

• Click 🔲 to insert the Artsy style horizontal line.

• Press ⏎Enter, type **Travel Resources**, and apply a Heading 2 style to the text.

• Press ⏎Enter.

• Type **World Weather Report: Clickable map giving you local weather anywhere in the world.**

• Press ⏎Enter.

Your screen should be similar to Figure 6.45

Next you will create the link to the World Weather Report page on the World Wide Web.

2
- Select the text "World Weather Report."
- Click  Insert Hyperlink.
- Select **E**xisting File or Web Page.
- In the Address text box, enter http://www.intellicast.com/LocalWeather/World/.
- Click OK.

Another Method

You could also click Web Page... to browse the Web to locate the site and enter the address if you are connected to the World Wide Web.

- Save the page.
- Switch to the browser window.
- Click Refresh.
- Point to the link.

Your screen should be similar to Figure 6.46

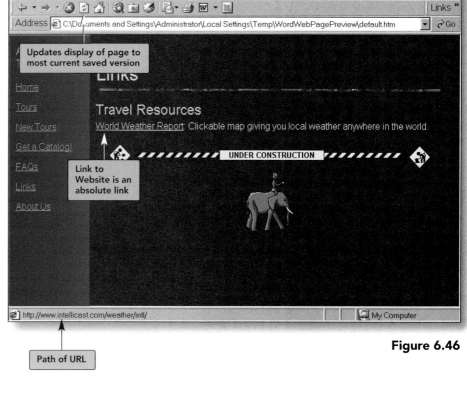

Figure 6.46

The status bar displays the full path of the URL. This link is an absolute link to a Web page document. Clicking on a hyperlink to a page directs the browser to get the page from the server and display it. You will try out this link at the end of the lab.

You also want to see how the ScreenTips you entered for the hyperlinks on the Tours pages work.

3
- Click Tours.
- Point to any of the topic hyperlinks.

Your screen should be similar to Figure 6.47

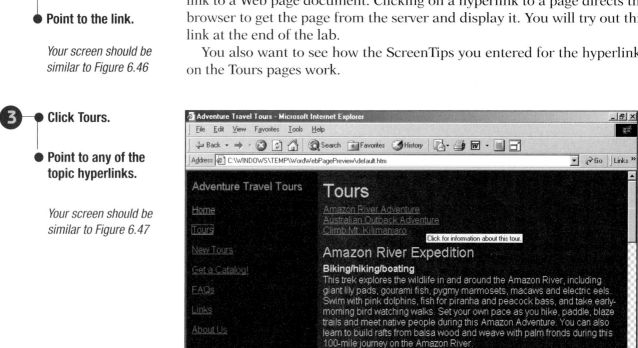

Figure 6.47

Linking to an E-mail Address

You also want to include a hyperlink on the home page, so readers can send an e-mail to Adventure Travel Tours to request specific information.

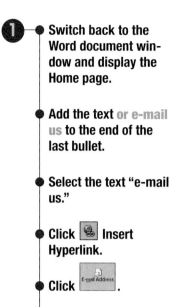

- **Switch back to the Word document window and display the Home page.**

- **Add the text** *or e-mail us* **to the end of the last bullet.**

- **Select the text "e-mail us."**

- **Click**  **Insert Hyperlink.**

- **Click** ⬚ **E-mail Address .**

- **In the E-mail address text box, type** frank.mandrake@ adventuretravel.com**.**

Another Method

If this e-mail address appears in the Recently used list you can select it rather than type in the address.

- **Click** ⬚ OK ⬚ **.**

- **Save the page.**

Your screen should be similar to Figure 6.48

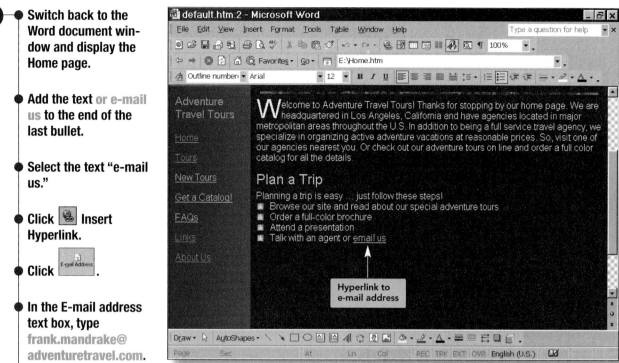

Figure 6.48

When the user clicks on the hyperlink, a new e-mail message window will open. The e-mail address you entered will appear in the To line. The user can then submit a question to the company.

Creating a Web Form

Finally, on the Get a Catalog! page, you want to add a form that allows users to order a catalog.

concept 6

Form

6 **Forms** are used in Web pages to get information or feedback from users or to provide information. Using forms makes your Web site interactive. The user completes the information requested in the form and then clicks a Submit button on the form, which sends the information in the form back to the Web server. The information is processed and a response is sent back to the user and displayed in another page in the browser window. For example, a company that sells golf clubs may provide a form in which users can enter the type of golf club they want to purchase. Then they submit the form, which sends their request to the Web server. The database is searched and the results of the search are returned to the user and displayed in a Web page. Other forms are used to collect information, as in the case of a customer survey. The information submitted from the form is stored on the site's Web server for later use. This type of form is often called a mailto form, because the results are submitted via an e-mail address.

Forms require additional support files and Web server support. When creating forms for use in a Web site, you should work with your network or Web site administrator.

After considering the information you need, you have designed the form shown below.

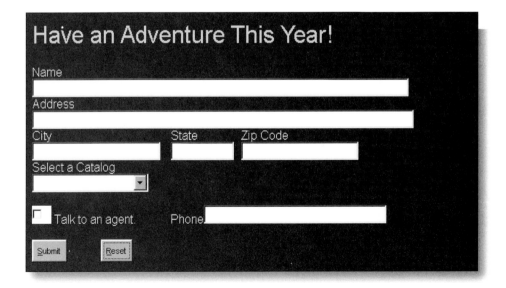

A form is created just like any other Web page document, with the addition of the form controls. **Controls** are graphic objects that are designed to automate the process of completing information in the form. There are 11 standard form controls that are used to enter different types of information. Just as in a paper form, there are fill-in boxes, check-off boxes, and selections from lists. You will use the following form controls:

Form Control	Use
☑ Check box	Allows selection of more than one item.
📇 Drop-down box	Displays available choices in a list.
[abl] Text box	Allows users to enter one line of text.
📇 Reset	Clears entries in the form.
📧 Submit	Submits the data in the form to the specified location.

You will enter a heading for the form and add text labels and controls to specify the information to be entered in the form.

1 ● Display the Get a Catalog! page.

● Replace the sample text with Have an Adventure This Year! and apply a Heading 1 Style.

● Press ⏎Enter twice.

● Type Name and press ⏎Enter.

● Display the Web Tools toolbar.

● If necessary, close the Web toolbar.

Your screen should be similar to Figure 6.49

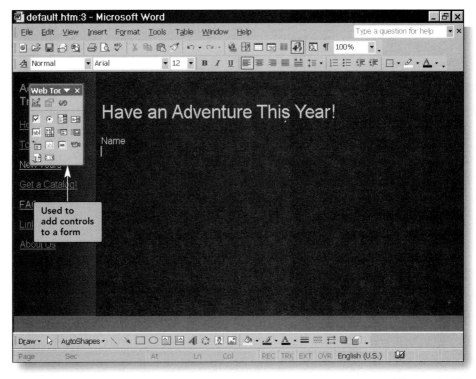

Used to add controls to a form

Figure 6.49

You use the Web Tools toolbar to add various form controls to a Web page.

Adding a Textbox Control

The first control you want to add to the form is a text box in which the user will enter his or her name.

1 ● Click [abl] Textbox.

● Size the text box object as shown in Figure 6.50.

Your screen should be similar to Figure 6.50

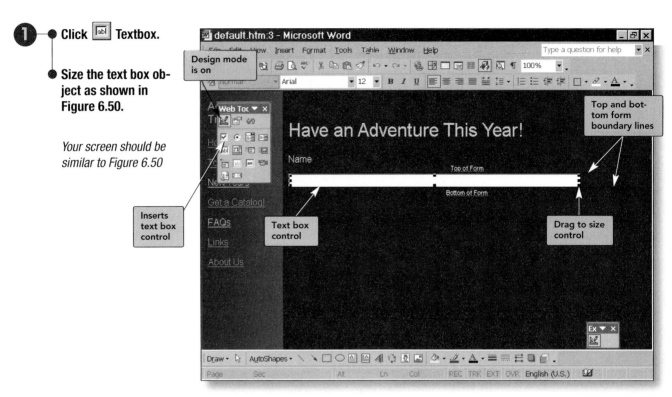

Figure 6.50

A blank Textbox control has been added to the form. Using a Web Tools button automatically turns on Design mode in which you can insert controls into the page. The button turns Design mode on and off.

Notice that a Top of Form and Bottom of Form boundary line is displayed above and below the control. The boundaries define the area containing the form controls and appear only in Design mode. As you continue to add more controls, they will appear within the boundaries. A Web page can have more than one form, each contained within its own form boundaries.

2

- Press ←Enter.

- Type Address and press ←Enter.

- Add and size another Textbox control as shown in Figure 6.51.

- Add the City, State, and Zip Code labels and Textbox controls as shown in Figure 6.51.

HAVING TROUBLE?
Use Tab↹ to separate the labels and controls.

Your screen should be similar to Figure 6.51

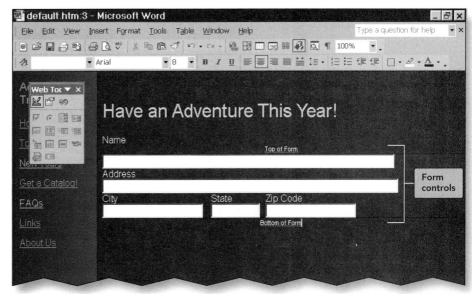

Figure 6.51

Adding a Drop-Down Box Control

Next you want to include a Drop-Down box control from which a catalog selection can be made. When inserting a Drop-Down box control, you also need to enter the list of items to be displayed when the Drop-Down box is opened. You will enter the names of the three catalogs in the list.

1

- On a blank line below the City control, type Select a Catalog.

- Press ←Enter.

- Click 🔲 Drop-Down Box.

- Click 🔲 Properties.

Your screen should be similar to Figure 6.52

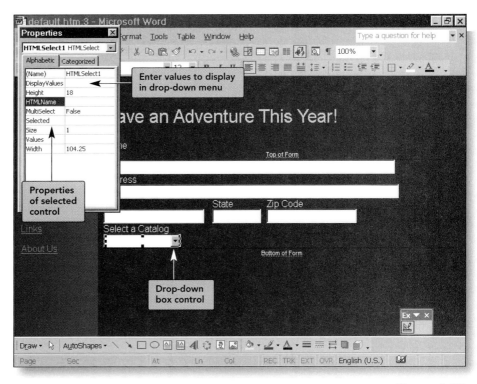

Figure 6.52

Additional Information
Control properties are also used to manage how data is communicated to the Web server.

In the Properties dialog box, you need to type the values you want to display when the Drop-Down box is opened. The values are separated with a semicolon without any blank spaces between titles.

Creating a Web Form   **WD6.45**

2

- **Click in the Display Values text box.**

- **Type African Adventures;South American Adventures;Far East Adventures.**

- **Click**  **to close the Properties dialog box.**

- **Press** ⏎Enter **twice.**

Your screen should be similar to Figure 6.53

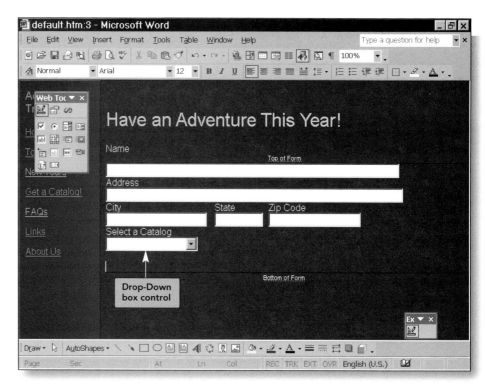

Figure 6.53

Adding a Checkbox Control

Last, you want to add a Checkbox control that allows the user to request that an agent call him or her with more information.

1

- **Click** ☑ **Checkbox.**

- **Click to the right of the control and enter a space.**

- **Type** Talk to an agent.

- **Press** Tab⇆ **twice.**

- **Add the label** Phone **and another Textbox control for a phone number, as shown in Figure 6.54.**

Your screen should be similar to Figure 6.54

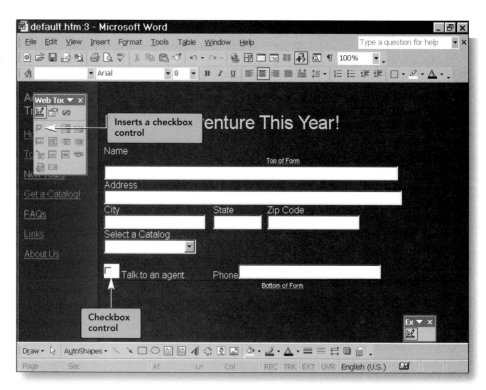

Figure 6.54

Adding Buttons

Now that all the necessary information is entered, you need to add two buttons: one to submit the form and another to clear it. A form should always include a Submit control, otherwise there is no way to send the information to the Web server. As part of the Submit button, you need to provide the e-mail address to which the form will be sent when submitted.

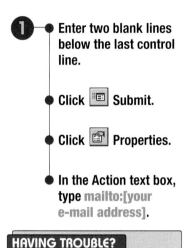

1 ● **Enter two blank lines below the last control line.**

● **Click** 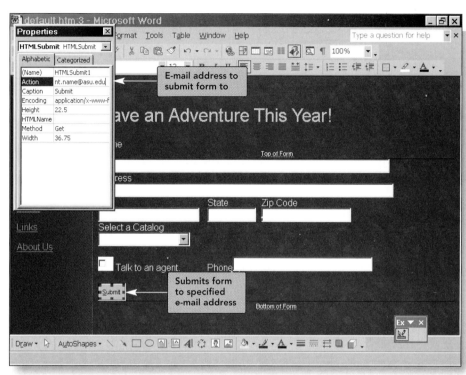 **Submit.**

● **Click** 🖳 **Properties.**

● **In the Action text box, type mailto:[your e-mail address].**

> **HAVING TROUBLE?**
> For example, mailto: sname@asu.edu.

Your screen should be similar to Figure 6.55

Figure shows a Properties window with E-mail address to submit form to, and Submits form to specified e-mail address.

Figure 6.55

Next you will add a button to clear the form.

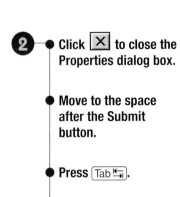

2 • Click ⊠ to close the Properties dialog box.

• Move to the space after the Submit button.

• Press ⌈Tab↹⌉.

• Click 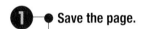 Reset.

• Click 🖾 Exit Design Mode

• Close the Web Tools toolbar.

Your screen should be similar to Figure 6.56

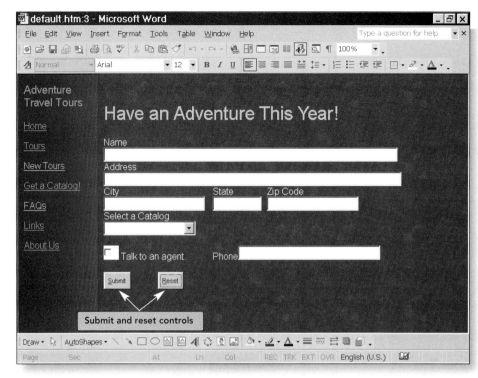

Figure 6.56

Previewing the Web Form

Now you want to preview the form.

1 • Save the page.

• Switch to the browser window.

• Display the Get a Catalog! page.

Your screen should be similar to Figure 6.57

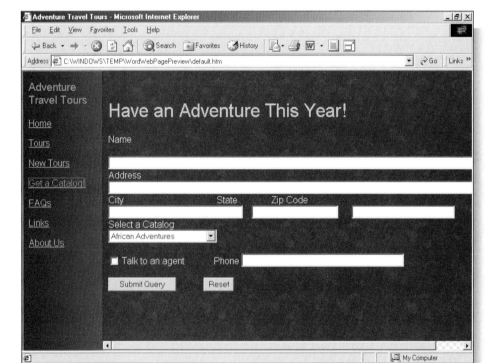

Figure 6.57

When you view the page in the browser, it may not appear exactly as it does in the Word document. For example, in Figure 6.57, the State and Zip Code labels do not display correctly over the boxes. Always view your Web pages in a browser and make any modifications before you make the pages public.

2 ● Return to the Word document and adjust the form as needed.

HAVING TROUBLE?
To edit a form, redisplay the Web tools toolbar and click 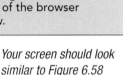 to turn on Design Mode.

● Move the Name label into the Form control boundary above the Textbox control.

● Enter a blank line between the Address and City control lines as in Figure 6.58.

● Save the form and redisplay it in the browser.

HAVING TROUBLE?
Don't forget to refresh the display of the browser window.

Your screen should look similar to Figure 6.58

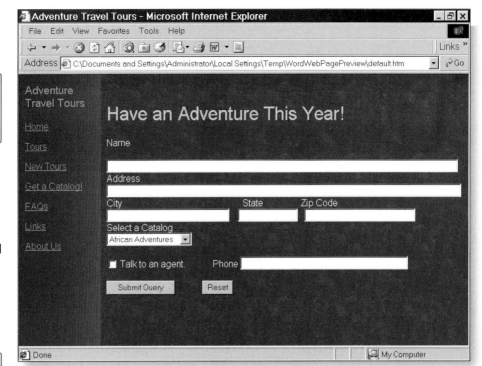

Figure 6.58

Next, you will use the form to request a catalog.

3 ● Move to each item in the form and enter the information requested for yourself. Select the Far East Adventures catalog.

HAVING TROUBLE?
Press [Tab ⇆] or click on a text box to move from one item to the next in the form.

● Print the completed form using the Print command on your browser (**F**ile/**P**rint).

● If you have Internet access, click the link to the World Weather Report on the Links page.

● Close the browser.

● Exit Word, saving all Web page documents when prompted.

Before making your Web site available for others to see, you should make sure that all of the links work correctly. In addition, because all browsers do not display the HTML tags in the same way, it is a good idea to preview your Web site using different browsers. Many of the differences in how browsers display a page are visual, not structural.

Using Supporting Folders

Each page in your Web site has a supporting folder that contains all the elements on the page, such as images and hyperlinks. You can view the folders that were created in the Exploring window.

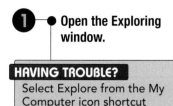

Open the Exploring window.

HAVING TROUBLE?
Select Explore from the My Computer icon shortcut menu.

Change the location to the location of your data files.

Your screen should be similar to Figure 6.59

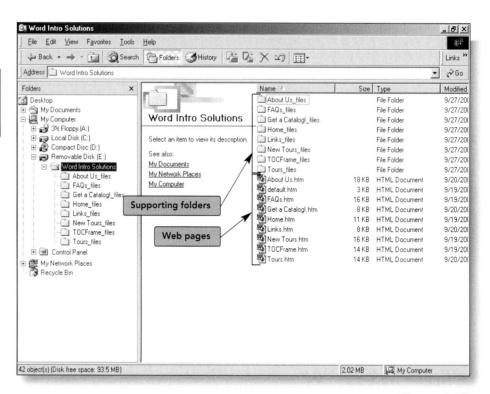

Figure 6.59

Also notice the document Default.htm included in the file list. This file is the frames page that controls the display of the frames for the Web site on the screen. If you want to view the Web site in Word again, open this file so that the pages will display correctly. Additionally, when creating Web sites, it is best to create them in their own folder so that the pages and supporting folders are organized in one location and so that files with the same names are not overwritten.

By default the name of the supporting folder is the name of the Web page plus an underscore (_) and the word "files." For example, the Links supporting folder name is Links_files. All supporting files, such as those for bullets, graphics, and background, are contained in the supporting folder. Any graphics that were added to the page that were not already JPG or GIF files are converted to that format.

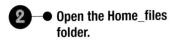

2 ● **Open the Home_files folder.**

Your screen should be similar to Figure 6.60

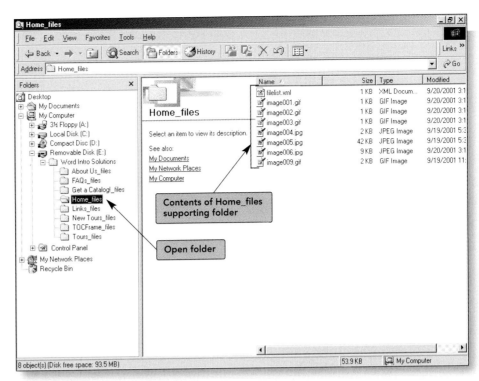

Figure 6.60

The Home_files folder contains nine graphic elements. Each graphic has been renamed "image000." The number is assigned in the order the element was added to the page.

3 ● **Close the Exploring window.**

When you move your files to place on a server, you need to include the HTML file and the associated supporting folder that contains all the elements on the page. If you do not, the page will not display correctly. If this folder is not available when the associated HTML page is loaded in the browser, the graphic elements will not be displayed.

concept summary

LAB 6
Creating a Web Site

Home Page (WD6.4)

The top-level or opening page of a Web site is called the **home page**.

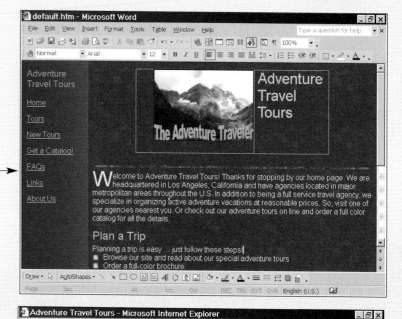

Home page

Frame (WD6.8)

A Web page can be divided into sections, called **frames**, that display separate Web pages.

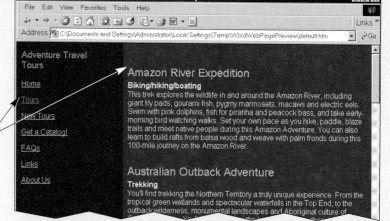

Frame

Group (WD6.19)

A group is two or more objects that are treated as a single object.

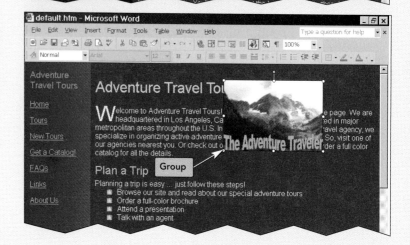

Group

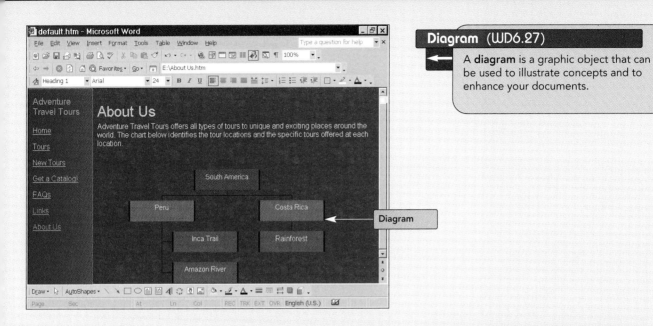

Diagram (WD6.27)

A **diagram** is a graphic object that can be used to illustrate concepts and to enhance your documents.

Diagram

Absolute and Relative Links (WD6.34)

When you create a hyperlink in a document, you can make the path to the destination an **absolute link** or a **relative link**.

Absolute and relative links

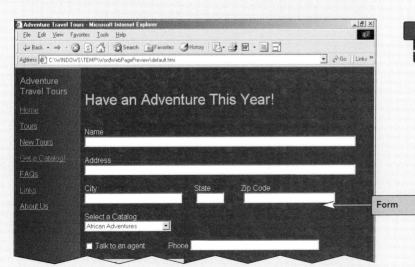

Form (WD6.41)

Forms are used in Web pages to get information or feedback from users or to provide information. Using forms makes your Web site interactive.

Form

LAB **6**

Creating a Web Site

key terms

absolute link WD6.34	fixed link WD6.34	home page WD6.4
background WD6.17	form WD6.41	protocol WD6.34
controls WD6.43	frame WD6.8	relative link WD6.34
destination WD6.34	frames page WD6.8	target link WD6.36
diagram WD6.27	group WD6.19	wallpaper WD6.17

mous skills

The Microsoft Office User Specialist (MOUS) certification program is designed to measure your proficiency in performing basic tasks using the Office XP applications. Getting certified demonstrates that you have the skills and provides a valuable industry credential for employment. After completing this lab, you have learned the following Microsoft Office User Specialist skills:

Skill	Description	Page
Creating and Modifying Paragraphs	Apply paragraph styles	WD6.35
Formatting Documents	Create and modify tables	WD6.21
Working with Graphics	Create and modify diagrams and charts	WD6.27
Workgroup Collaboration	Convert documents into Web pages	WD6.9

Command	Shortcut Key	Button	Action
Word			
File/New/General Templates /Web Pages/Web Page Wizard			Creates a new Web site
File/Web Page Preview			Displays saved Web page in a browser window
Insert/Diagram		⟳	Inserts a diagram
Format/Borders and Shading /Horizontal Line			Adds graphic horizontal line to Web page
Format/Background/Fill Effects			Applies background color to selection
Format/Theme			Applies a predesigned theme to Web page
Draw Drop-Down Menu			
Draw ▾ Order/Bring to Front			Brings object to front of stack
Draw ▾ Group			Creates a group from selected objects
Draw ▾ Ungroup			Ungroups a grouped object
Draw ▾ Regroup			Regroups an ungrouped object
Organization Chart Toolbar			
Insert Shape/Subordinate			Inserts a shape below the selected superior shape
Layout/Right Hanging			Hangs subordinate shapes to right of superior shape
Layout/Expand Organization Chart			Expands drawing canvas around organization chart
Web Tools Toolbar			
Checkbox		☑	Allows selection of more than one item
Drop-Down box		▤	Displays available choices in a list
Textbox		abl	A box where you can enter one line of text
Text Area		▥	A box where you can enter more than one line of text
Reset		▤	Clears entries in form
Submit		▥	Submits data in form to specified location

Terminology

screen identification

1. In the following Word screen, letters identify important elements. Enter the correct term for each screen element in the space provided.

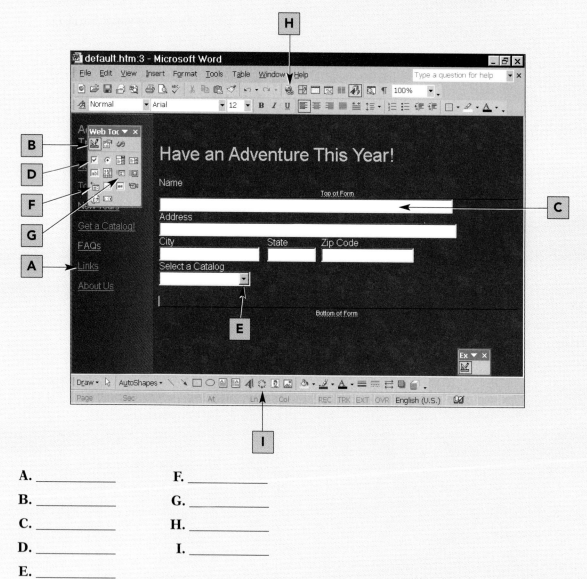

A. _____   F. _____

B. _____   G. _____

C. _____   H. _____

D. _____   I. _____

E. _____

Match the item on the left with the correct description on the right.

1. home page   _____ **a.**   two or more objects that are joined together as a single object

2. [icon]   _____ **b.**   creates an organization chart

3. hyperlink   _____ **c.**   allows users to jump to other locations

4. [icon]   _____ **d.**   below a superior shape

5. absolute link   _____ **e.**   identifies the location of a hyperlink by its full address

6. [icon]   _____ **f.**   creates a diagram

7. page   _____ **g.**   basic document of the World Wide Web

8. form   _____ **h.**   inserts a horizontal line

9. subordinate   _____ **i.**   an interactive element used to gather information from users

10. group   _____ **j.**   top-level page

Circle the correct response to the questions below.

1. _____ are based on text rather than numeric information.
   a. charts
   b. diagrams
   c. pages
   d. forms

2. A(n) _____ is two or more objects that are treated as a single object.
   a. combination
   b. group
   c. block
   d. collection

3. A Web page divided into sections that display separate Web pages is said to contain _____.
   a. panes
   b. sections
   c. frames
   d. forms

4. A(n) _____ is a color or design that is displayed behind the text on the page.
   a. window
   b. background
   c. backdrop
   d. environment

5. Images, patterns, or texture placed behind text on a Web page is called _____.
   a. wallpaper
   b. background
   c. backdrop
   d. imaging

6. A(n) _____ link identifies the file location of the destination page by its full address.
   a. relative
   b. absolute
   c. followed
   d. destination

7. The _____ diagram shows steps toward a goal.
   a. pyramid
   b. organization
   c. cycle
   d. target

8. The _____ shape is below and connected to any other shape with an elbow connector.
   a. subordinate
   b. superior
   c. co-worker
   d. assistant

9. _____ are commonly used in Web pages to get information or feedback from users.
   a. Links
   b. Text boxes
   c. Frames
   d. Forms

10. The top-level or opening page of a site is called the _____ page.
    a. introduction
    b. index
    c. home
    d. site

true/false

Circle the correct answer to the following questions.

1. A diagram can not be used to illustrate concepts.   True   False
2. Form controls are used to automate the input of information.   True   False

3. Controls can only be added when Design mode is on.	True	False
4. A Web page can be divided into forms that display separate Web pages.	True	False
5. An organization chart shows hierarchical-based relationships.	True	False
6. Wallpaper is a color or design that is displayed behind the text on the page.	True	False
7. A relative link identifies the file location of the destination by its full address.	True	False
8. Hyperlinks to other Web sites should typically use a fixed file location.	True	False
9. Backward slashes (\\) are used to separate the protocol from the rest of the address.	True	False
10. Web pages use frames to get information or feedback from users.	True	False

Concepts

fill in

Complete the following statements by filling in the blanks with the correct answers.

1. The top-level or opening page of a Web site is called the _____.

2. A(n) _____ is two or more objects that are treated as a single object.

3. _____ are used to make it easier to navigate in a Web site.

4. A graphic object that can be used to illustrate concepts is a(n) _____.

5. An organization chart is used to illustrate _____ relationships.

6. A(n) _____is a color or design that is displayed behind the text on the page.

7. A(n) _____ is a graphic object that automates a procedure.

8. Hyperlinks to other Web sites should typically use a fixed file location that includes the full path to the location or address of the page, called the _____.

9. When you create a Web page, all the elements on the page are stored in a(n) _____.

10. _____ are used in Web pages to get information or feedback from users or to provide information.

discussion questions

1. Discuss three attributes of a well-designed Web page.

2. Discuss frames and their advantages and disadvantages.

3. Discuss absolute and relative hyperlinks and when to use them.

4. Discuss supporting folders and why they are created.

5. Discuss diagrams and provide examples of when you use the different types.

Hands-On Exercises

step-by-step

The Sports Company Web Site

★★ ★ **1.** The Sports Company is a discount sporting goods store. You are working on a summer internship with the company and have been asked to help design and build a Web site for the company. This site will contain fitness-related information and links to products the company sells over the Internet. Much of the information for the site has already been saved in Word document files. When you are finished, the completed home page and Newsletter page should look similar to the ones shown here.

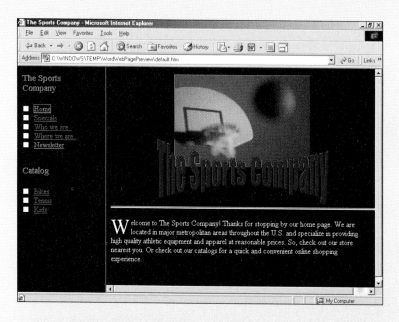

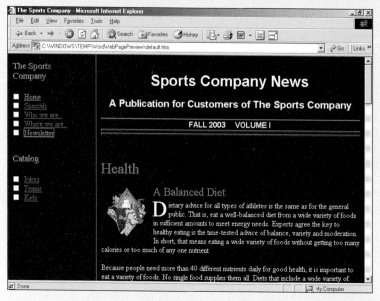

a. Open the file wd06_Home Page Text in Word. Reduce the size of the photo to approximately 2 by 3 inches. Center the WordArt above it. Center the whole graphic object on the page. Change the text wrapping style to Top and Bottom.

b. Center the WordArt object below the title as shown in the example. If necessary change the order so the photo is behind the WordArt. Group the objects.

c. Center the graphic object on the page. Change the text wrapping style to Top to Bottom. Reduce the size of the object to approximately 2 by 3 inches.

d. Save the document as Home Page Text2. Close the file.

e. You will use the Web Page Wizard to create the rest of the Web site. Start the wizard and enter the title **The Sports Company**. Specify a new folder as the location to save the Web site.

f. Select Vertical Frame for type of navigation.

g. Remove the Personal Web Page. Add the Home Page Text2 and wd06_SCNewsletter files. Add four new blank pages.

h. Move the Home Page Text2 file to the top of the list and rename the page **Home**. Rename the 6 blank pages with these titles: **Specials**, **Who we are . . .**, **Where we are . . .**, **Bikes**, **Tennis**, and **Kids**. Rename the SCNewsletter to **Newsletter** and move the newsletter page above Bikes.

i. Choose the Refined theme with vivid colors and active graphics, but without the Background Image. Finish the wizard. Preview the Web site. Switch back to Word.

j. Change the color of the WordArt to match the theme. Insert a horizontal line below the graphic and above the text in the main frame. If necessary, reapply the theme to update the horizontal line to the theme line. Add a drop cap to the W in the main frame using the Wrap 2 Lines setting.

k. Insert a blank line above "Bikes" in the table of contents frame and insert the word **Catalog**. Format the word as a Level 3 heading.

l. Delete the blank lines between the first five links. Insert a bullet in front of each link. In the same manner, insert bullets before the last three links. Adjust the spacing and bullets as necessary. Adjust the size of the contents frame as needed.

m. Open the Newsletter page and delete the graphic at the top of the page. Change the color of the lines above and below Fall 2003 to match the theme. Make any other necessary adjustments to the layout and spacing.

n. Create a link to the American Dietetic Association at www.eatright.org. Insert the link on the line following the sentence below the Food Pyramid. Add your name as a link to your e-mail address at the end of the newsletter

o. Preview the Web site and make any necessary adjustments to the pages. Print the Home page and the Newsletter page. Close all documents.

Animal Angels Web Site

★★ **2.** Animal Angels, the volunteer group for the Animal Rescue Foundation, would like a Web page to help attract volunteers and inform people about abandoned and adoptable pets. The home page has already been started and saved as an HTML document. You will enhance the page and add links to other pages. The completed home page and form are shown here.

a. Open the file wd06_Pets Home Page in Word. Create links from the text in the left column to the headings in the center column. Insert a Return to Top link after each section in the middle column.

b. In the "Pets Available for Adoption" section, insert one image of each kind of animal after the names (you can use wd06_Puppies, wd06_Cat, wd06_Parrots, and wd06_Lizard or one image of your choice). Size the images appropriately. Change the font size and left align the categories. Create a link from each of the pictures to four new pages that have the same location. (Hint: Use the Create New Document option on the Insert Hyperlink dialog box.) Name the new pages the same as the animal. Choose the Edit New Document Later option so that the new pages do not open.

c. Apply the Blends theme to the Web page.

d. Preview the page in your Web browser. Adjust any layout problems as needed.

e. Insert some blank lines above both the right and left columns to move them down below the Animal Angels title in the center column. Make the Pets of the Day and Upcoming Events Heading 3 style.

f. Insert an image of your choice above the links in the right column to add visual interest. Replace the Animal Angels title with a WordArt design of your choice.

g. Create a link called **Become a member** at the end of the list in the left column to a new page. Name the file **Member** and open the file for editing. Apply the Fixed theme with vivid colors to the new page.

h. On the Member page, you will create a form in which users can enter information so that Animal Angels can put them on its mailing list. Enter and center the title **Become an Animal Angel**. Apply the Heading 1 style.

i. Open the Web Tools toolbar. Enter the following text in the document.

For more information on becoming an Animal Angel please fill in the following fields. We will mail you a membership package. If you have a question please provide your e-mail address and a note in the comment box and we will be happy to e-mail a reply to you.
Full Name:
Street Address:
City:
State:
Zip Code:
E-mail Address:
Comments:

j. Insert text boxes next to the labels. Use the Text Area control for the Comments. Size and position the text boxes appropriately based on the type of input. Insert Reset and Submit buttons at the bottom of the form.

k. Close the Web Tools toolbar. Add the text **Questions? Contact** followed by your name as a link to your e-mail address at the end of the form.

l. Save the changes you have made to the pages and print the home and form pages.

Updating The Downtown Internet Cafe Site

★★ **3.** Evan, the owner of the Downtown Internet Cafe, has not updated its Web site in quite some time. He feels the old site is dated and would like you to completely redesign the site. He would like to have a list of services the cafe offers, as well as an online coffee store. Evan has provided you with all the new content and some recent photos taken at the cafe. Your completed Web pages should be similar to those shown here.

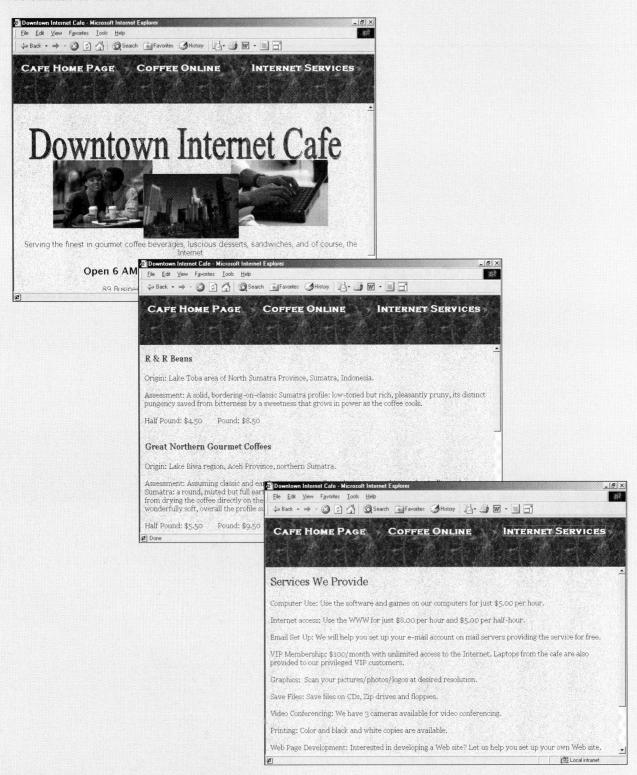

a. Begin the Web site using the Web Page Wizard. Title the Web page Downtown Internet Cafe. Choose horizontal navigation. Rename the default web pages: Cafe Home Page, Coffee Online, and Internet Services. Add the Layers visual theme with vivid colors and background image and finish the wizard.

b. Examine the new layout and add the Layers theme to the horizontal frame across the top of the site. Decrease the size of the frame to approximately 1 inch.

c. Delete the "Main Heading Goes Here" text. Insert a WordArt object (the example uses the style in the first column, fourth row) with the text Downtown Internet Cafe. Change the font to Times New Roman. Size and center the object as shown in the example figure. Change the shadow color to gray. (Hint: The shadow color options are available on the Drawing toolbar under the Shadow Settings menu). You now decide to change the fill color from Paper bag to Brown Marble. Change the wrapping style to Behind Text.

d. Delete all the default text below the photos. You now decide that some recent photos from the cafe would be appropriate for the site. Insert the files wd06_Computer, wd06_City, and wd06_Patrons. Change the layout to Behind Text. Arrange them as shown in the example and group the photos. Use Web page preview to examine the changes you have made so far. Save the file as a Web page called Downtown Internet Cafe Site.

e. With the new photos in place you feel the horizontal frame could use some formatting changes. Delete the Cafe name from the frame. Remove the table borders and use the brown marble texture to fill in the background.

f. Change the font color of the hyperlinks to white, the font to Copperplate Gothic Bold and use a 16 pt font size. Preview your changes in your browser.main window of the Coffee Online page. Close the wd06_Online Coffee file.

g. You like the changes you have made to the layout and now decide to change the content. Enter and center the following text below the photos:

Serving the finest in gourmet coffee beverages, luscious desserts, sandwiches
and, of course, the Internet.

Open 6 AM to 11 PM every day of the week!

89 Business Parkway, Suite 102, Chicago, IL, 86512
(555) 555-CAFE

h. Preview your changes in your browser. Return to the document and adjust the text until it displayed appropriately in the Web preview. You are happy with the page so far and decide to create the Coffee Online and Internet Services pages.

i. Click on the Coffee Online page to begin editing it. Delete the default text. Insert the file wd06_Coffee Online. Remove the sentence above the R&R Beans heading. Preview your changes in your browser. Make any necessary layout adjustments.

j. Click on the Internet Services page to begin editing it. Delete the default text. Insert the file wd06_Services. Make the first sentence a Heading 2 style. Return to the Home page.

k. You like the layout of the Home page, but would like to emphasize the text at the bottom of the page. Apply the Lucida Sans font to the text. Bold the sentence that gives the cafe hours. Increase the font size of this line to 16 pt.

l. Add your name as an e-mail address link as the contact at the bottom of the home page. Save the file and print the pages.

Creating a Personal Web Site

★★ ★ **4.** Now that you have practiced your Web page design skills you have decided to create a Personal Web Site. You will create a home page that highlights your interests and include a mini-biography. Be sure to include pictures and graphics and utilize the many formatting techniques available to you. You will also create a page about one of your insterests or hobbies. Although your completed home page will be personalized, it should be similar to that shown here.

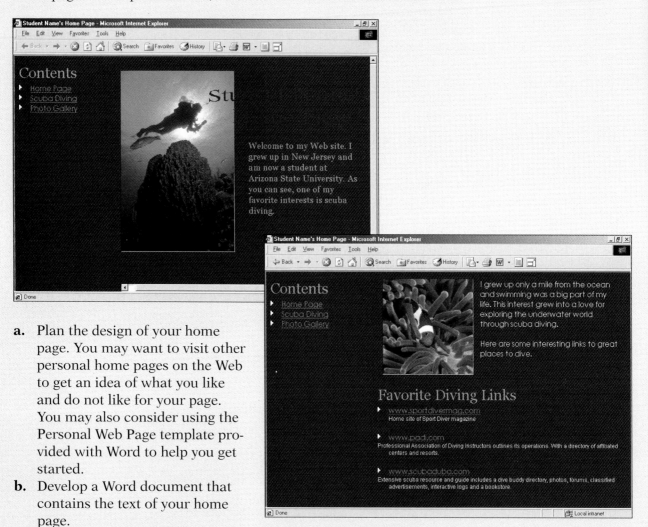

a. Plan the design of your home page. You may want to visit other personal home pages on the Web to get an idea of what you like and do not like for your page. You may also consider using the Personal Web Page template provided with Word to help you get started.

b. Develop a Word document that contains the text of your home page.

c. If necessary, save the Word document as an HTML document, or if you use the template, copy and paste the information from your document into the appropriate locations.

d. Apply a theme of your choice. Modify the background colors or theme to suit your design.

e. Add clip art, pictures, and animation to your home page. If you have access to a scanner, you can scan pictures to insert. You can also use the Web to locate graphics and animations. Use tables as necessary to align your text and pictures or clip art.

f. Add a link from your home page to another page. Include a brief description of the content. This page should be formatted similarly to your home page.

g. If possible, load your home page to a server so others can enjoy your work.

h. Save the file as My Home Page and print both pages.

Computer Virus Web Site

5. You are a graduate student and have received an assistantship to work with a university professor. The professor has assigned students a research project on computer viruses. You have been asked to create a Web page for inclusion on the class Web site that describes computer viruses and includes links to Web sites that discuss viruses. The pages you will create should be similar to the pages shown here.

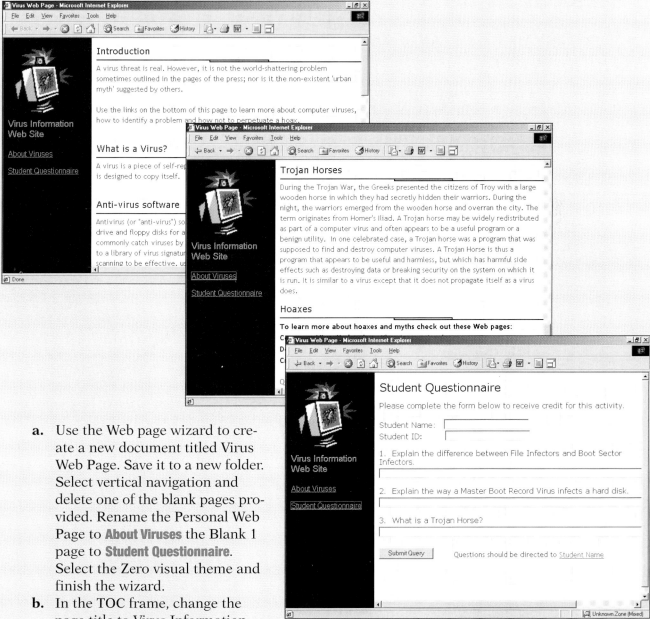

a. Use the Web page wizard to create a new document titled Virus Web Page. Save it to a new folder. Select vertical navigation and delete one of the blank pages provided. Rename the Personal Web Page to **About Viruses** the Blank 1 page to **Student Questionnaire**. Select the Zero visual theme and finish the wizard.

b. In the TOC frame, change the page title to Virus Information Web Site. Change the theme of the main frame from the Zero theme to the Modular theme.

c. You have already prepared the text for the main page and would like to insert it now. Select all the text in the main frame and insert the file wd06_Virus Text Page. Delete the blank line above the Instruction heading. Insert a horizontal line below the Introduction heading. If necessary, reapply the Modular theme to format the horizontal line appropriately.

d. Copy and paste the horizontal line below each of the headings in the main frame. Insert four blank lines above the title in the TOC frame. Insert the graphic file wd06_Virus. Change the wrapping style to Top and Bottom. Size and center the graphic over the title.

e. View the Web page in Web Page Preview and make any necessary layout adjustments so that the page displays correctly in your browser.

f. In the Hoaxes section of the main frame add the following text:

To learn more about hoaxes and myths check out these Web pages.
Computer Virus Myths—http://kumite.com/myths/
Don't Spread That Hoax!—http://www.nonprofit.net/hoax/hoax.html
Create Your Own Hoaxes—http://www.cao.com/hoax/

g. Next you will create the student questionnaire. Click on the Student Questionnaire hyperlink. Change the main frame to the Modular visual theme. Delete the default text. Enter and center the title **Virus Questionnaire**. Apply the Heading 1 style.

h. Below the title, create the form by entering the following text. Add controls as appropriate (see the example at the beginning of the exercise).

Please complete the form below to receive credit for this activity.
Student Name
Student ID
1. Explain the difference between File Infectors and Boot Sector Infectors.
2. Explain the way a Master Boot Record Virus infects a hard disk.
3. What is a Trojan Horse?

i. Insert a submit button that links to your e-mail address. Apply the Heading 4 style to the form directions and text box labels. Check your changes in Web Page Preview. make any required layout adjustments.

j. Your page is almost finished. All you need to do is finish adding the text to the Virus Home Page. Insert the file wd06_Trojan Horses below the Trojan Horse heading. The file also contains information on antivirus software—move this paragraph under the appropriate heading. The new paragraphs have different formatting. Select both paragraphs and choose Clear Formatting from the Styles and Formatting Drop Down Menu.

k. Check your changes in Web Page Preview and make any needed layout adjustments. Print the two pages.

Revising Your Personal Web Site

★ 1. To complete this problem, you must have completed Step-by-Step Exercise 4 in this lab and created your personal Web site. After designing your home page, you would like to know how others feel about what you added to your page. A good way of asking for input is to use a feedback form. With this form you can ask visitors to respond to questions. Create a feedback form in the same visual style as your home page. Enhance the page using lines, borders, and pictures as appropriate. Link the feedback form to your home page. Print the form page.

Creating a Fan Site

★ 2. Because the Web is open to anyone who has a computer and Internet access, there are many unofficial Web sites for popular television shows. People create Web pages to let others know what they like or dislike about a show. Design and create a Web site with the title My TV Site for the show of your choice. Include clip art, pictures, and animation to enhance the site. Link your site to other official and unofficial Web sites for the same or similar shows. Create frames that are appropriate for your design. Create additional pages that are links from your home page that give your views of the characters on the show. Print the pages.

Enhancing Adventure Travel Tours' Web Page

★★ 3. To complete this problem, you must have created the Adventure Travel Tours Web site in this lab. Open the Adventure Travel Web site. Create links to the other topics on the Tours page and add additional Back to Top links. Use a table to make the list of tour links display in two columns at the top of the page. Add a link to a new page that provides a detailed itinerary for one of the tours. (Use the Web to get itinerary information.) Add additional links and descriptions on the Links page that would be of interest to travelers. Add information to the FAQs page using information provided in the wd06_Tour FAQs document. Add an organizational chart and text to the About Us page that includes length of time in business, number of locations, philosophy, and objectives. Edit the hyperlink on the New Tours page to display the Presentations Locations.htm page you created in the first Working Together tutorial, if available. Apply the Nature theme to this page. Adjust the layout on all the pages as necessary. Print the Itinerary and Tour FAQs pages.

Creating a School Club Website

★★ 4. The members of a club at your school have asked you to create a Web site that will inform fellow
★ students and club members about their activities. Choose a club or an organization you are familiar with and create a Web site titled Club Website that includes information on the club history, its recent activities (include photos), faculty sponsor, calendar of events, and a mascot of your choice. Be sure to include an organizational chart for the club officers and links to your school's home page. The club has also asked that the site be colorful and include photos. When you have completed the site, print the home page.

Expanding the Animal Angels Web Site

★★ 5. To complete this exercise you must have completed Step-by-Step Exercise 4 in Lab 4 and Step-by-
★ Step Exercise 2 in Lab 6. You have been asked by the Animal Angels to include the monthly newsletter as a feature on the Web site. You decide that the newsletter should be reformatted for the Web. Reformat the content for the Web site and include new graphics. Apply a theme of your choice to the page and make any necessary adjustments to the layout. Finally, print the new page.

lab exercises

Evaluating Web Design

Do some research on the Web on the topics of your choice. Once you have some ideas of good and bad page design, create a Web page titled Web Evaluation that gives information on Web page design. Consider using frames to hold the lists of links to pages you felt were of good design as well as pages that in your opinion had bad page design. Add clip art, pictures, and animation to your page as needed. Use an appropriate background color or wallpaper. When you are finished, print the page(s) you created.

Using Solver, Creating Templates, and Evaluating Scenarios

Objectives

After completing this lab, you will know how to:

1.	Use Solver.
2.	Create and use workbook templates.
3.	Protect a worksheet.
4.	Open and use multiple workbooks.
5.	Link workbooks.
6.	Create and use Scenarios.
7.	Create a Scenario Summary.
8.	Create and modify 3-D shapes.
9.	Display the current date and time.

2003 Forecast.xls

Student Name

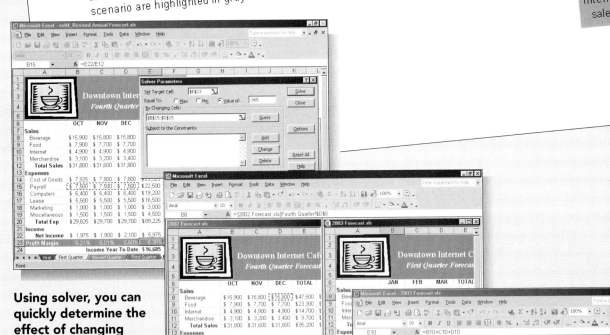

Scenario Summary 7/24/2002 17:33		Current Values:		Most Likely		Worst Case		Best Case	
Changing Cells:									
Internet JAN		$	4,410	$	4,900	$	4,410	$	4,410
Internet FEB		$	6,100	$	4,900	$	4,410	$	6,100
Internet MAR		$	6,100	$	4,900	$	4,410	$	6,100
Lease MAR		$	6,200	$	6,000	$	6,200	$	6,200
Result Cells:									
Profit Margin JAN		3.77%		5.25%		3.77%		3.77%	
Profit Margin FEB		8.70%		5.25%		3.77%		8.70%	
Profit Margin MAR		8.09%		5.25%		3.13%		8.09%	
Profit Margin TOTAL		6.91%		5.25%		3.56%		6.91%	

Notes: Current Values column represents values of changing cells at time Scenario Summary Report was created. Changing cells for each scenario are highlighted in gray.

Profits from high Internet sales

Using solver, you can quickly determine the effect of changing values in two or more cells on another cell.

Creating links between workbooks allows changes you make on one file to be automatically reflected in the other file.

Using Scenario Manager, you can analyze various possible outcomes to help plan for the future.

Downtown Internet Café

After further discussion with Evan, the owner of the Downtown Internet Café, you continued to refine the forecast analysis. You suggested several formatting changes to the worksheet and revised some values. You continued to use Goal Seek to determine the monthly payroll expense needed to achieve monthly profit margins of 6 percent for the third quarter.

Evan wants you to further determine a fixed payroll expense for the fourth quarter that will achieve a quarterly profit margin of 6.5 percent. You will use the Solver tool to determine the values.

Once the annual forecast for 2002 is complete, Evan wants you to use the same procedure to create the forecast for 2003. You will use the 2002 annual forecast worksheet to create a template for the next year's forecast, and then you will use the template to create the first-quarter forecast for that year.

Additionally, you have been asked to create three different scenarios that will show the best, worst, and most likely scenarios for the 2003 first-quarter forecast.

1	**Solver** Solver is a tool used to perform what-if analyses to determine the effect of changing values in two or more cells on another cell.
2	**Workbook Template** A workbook template is a workbook file that contains predesigned worksheets that can be used as a pattern for creating similar worksheets in new workbooks.
3	**Worksheet Protection** Worksheet protection prevents users from changing a worksheet's contents by protecting the entire worksheet or specified areas of it.
4	**Arrange Windows** The Arrange Windows feature displays all open workbook files in separate windows on the screen, in a tiled, horizontal, vertical, or cascade arrangement.
5	**Link Workbooks** A link creates a connection between files that automatically updates the data in one file whenever the data in the other file changes.
6	**Scenario** A scenario is a named set of input values that you can substitute in a worksheet to see the effects of a possible alternative course of action. Scenarios are designed to help forecast the outcome of various possible actions.

Analyzing the Worksheet

After seeing how the payroll values changed each month to achieve higher second- and third-quarter profit margins, Evan would like you to do a similar analysis on the fourth quarter. First you want to look at the current profit margin value for the fourth quarter.

1 ● **Open the workbook file** ex04_Revised Annual Forecast.

● **Make the Fourth Quarter sheet active.**

● **Select cell E23.**

Your screen should be similar to Figure 4.1

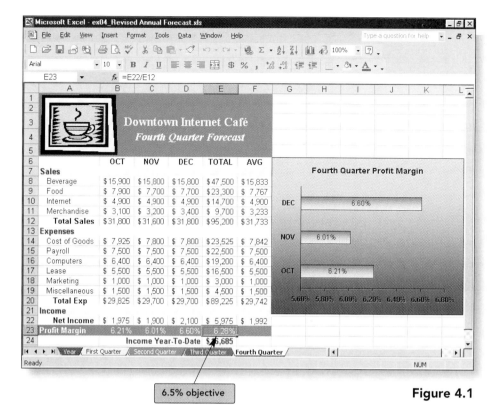

6.5% objective

Figure 4.1

The current profit margin for the fourth quarter is 6.28 percent. This time, Evan would like to keep the payroll expenses constant for the quarter while achieving a 6.5 percent quarterly profit margin.

While you are making changes to the quarterly worksheet, you will display the Watch Window to see how the changes affect the Annual Profit Margin.

2 ● **Move to the Year sheet.**

● **Select cell N23.**

● **Open the Watch Window.**

● **Set it to watch cell N23.**

● **Size and position the Watch Window as in Figure 4.2.**

HAVING TROUBLE?
To open the Watch Window, use Tools/Formula Auditing/Show Watch Window.

Your screen should be similar to Figure 4.2

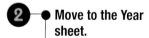

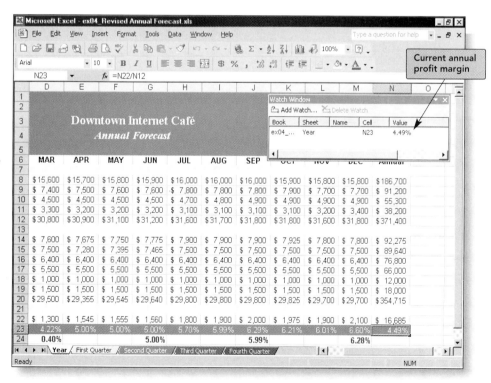

Current annual profit margin

Figure 4.2

Using Solver

Although you could manually perform What-If analysis or use the Goal Seek feature to determine the desired profit margin value, it would be much quicker to use the Solver tool.

concept 1

Solver

1. **Solver** is a tool used to perform what-if analyses to determine the effect of changing values in two or more cells, called the **adjustable cells**, on another cell, called the **target cell**. Solver calculates a formula to achieve a given value by changing one of the variables that affect the formula. To do this, Solver works backward from the result of a formula to find the numbers. The cells you select must be related through formulas on the worksheet. If they are not related, changing one will not change the other.

Solver can also produce three types of reports about the solution: Answer, Sensitivity, and Limits. In an Answer report, the original and final values of the target cell and adjustable cells are listed along with any constraints and information about the constraints. Information about how sensitive the solution is to small changes in the target cell formula or in the constraints is provided in a Sensitivity report. A Limits report includes the original and target values of the target cell and adjustable cells. It also lists the lower limit, the smallest value that the adjustable cell can take while holding all other adjustable cells fixed and still satisfying the constraints and upper or greatest value.

---

1 • Display the Fourth Quarter sheet.

• Choose **T**ools/Sol**v**er.

• Move the Solver Parameters dialog box to the lower right corner of the screen.

Your screen should be similar to Figure 4.3

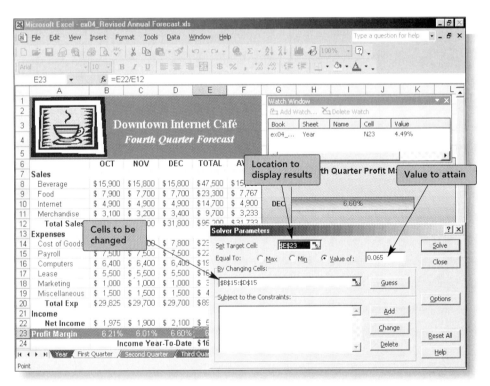

Figure 4.3

In the Solver Parameters dialog box, you need to supply three items of information: the target cell where the result will appear, the desired result value, and the cell or cells that will be changed to achieve the result.

Lab 4: Using Solver, Creating Templates, and Evaluating Scenarios

www.mhhe.com/oleary

The cell reference of the cell containing the formula you want to solve is entered in the Set Target Cell text box. The cell reference of the active cell, E23, is already correctly entered in this box.

The number you want as the result of the formula is entered in the Equal To text box. You can set the number to be a maximum, minimum, or an exact number. The maximum option sets the target cell to the highest possible number, while the minimum option sets the target cell for the lowest possible number.

The final information needed is the cell or cell range whose contents can be changed when the formula is computed. This range is entered in the By Changing Cells text box. In the fourth quarter, you are looking for a value of 6.5 percent by changing the values in the range of cells B15 through D15.

2

- Select **V**alue of.

- Type **.065** in the Value Of text box.

- Specify the range B15 through D15 in the **B**y Changing Cells text box.

HAVING TROUBLE?
You can minimize the dialog box using the ![button] button and select the range by high-lighting it in the worksheet.

Your screen should be similar to Figure 4.4

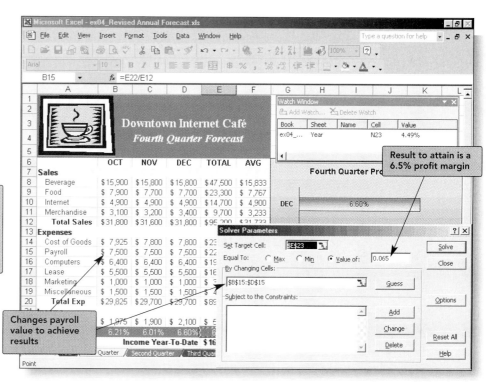

Figure 4.4

Now you are ready to have Solver find the values to meet the parameters you specified:

3 ● Click [Solve].

Your screen should be similar to Figure 4.5

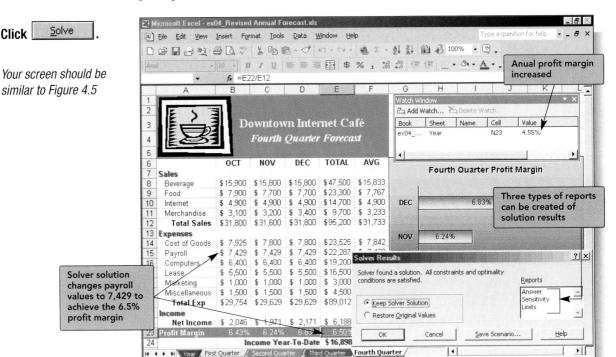

Figure 4.5

The Solver Results dialog box tells you that Solver found a solution. The new payroll numbers are entered in the worksheet range and the worksheet is automatically recalculated. By setting the payroll expense to $7,429, the monthly profit margins vary and the quarterly or total profit margin is 6.5 percent. As you can see in the Watch Window, the effect of changing the payroll expenses for the fourth quarter has affected the annual profit margin. The profit margin for the year increased from 4.49 to 4.55 percent due to the reduction of payroll expenses in the fourth quarter.

Creating an Answer Report

From the Solver Results dialog box, you can choose whether to keep the solution or restore the original values. In addition, you can have Solver create Answer, Sensitivity, and Limits Reports. You decide to keep the solution and create an Answer Report.

1 ● Select Answer from the **R**eports list box.

● Click OK .

● Make the Answer Report 1 sheet active.

Your screen should be similar to Figure 4.6

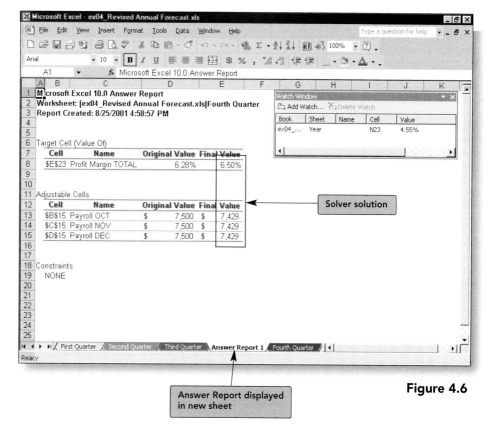

Answer Report displayed in new sheet

Figure 4.6

The Answer Report 1 sheet displays the Answer report that was generated. The target cell section of the report shows the original profit margin value of 6.28 percent and the final value of 6.50 percent. The Adjustable Cells area shows the original and final values for each cell that was changed to achieve the profit margin of 6.50 percent. The final value entered in each adjustable cell will be the same number even if the original values were different in each cell.

The forecast for 2002 is now complete.

2 ● Close the Watch Window.

● Make the Year sheet active.

● Move to cell A6 and save the current workbook file as 2002 Forecast.

Creating a Custom Template

After seeing the effects of your analyses on the Year sheet, Evan has found Solver to be a valuable tool for planning and managing operations. He has asked you to create a new workbook containing a forecast for the following year. You could create this new forecast workbook by starting all over again, specifying the formats and formulas. However, as the current workbook already contains this information, you decide to use it as a model or template for future forecasts.

concept 2

Workbook Template

2 A workbook **template** is a workbook file that contains predesigned worksheets that can be used as a pattern for creating similar sheets in new workbooks. Templates can contain text, graphics, formats, page layouts, headers and footers, functions and formulas, and macros.

Templates are useful in any application where input and output are required using the same format. By not having to redesign the worksheet form each time the report is needed, you save time and increase accuracy. You can go back to the original design repeatedly by saving the workbook containing the data under a different file name than the one you used to save the workbook template.

Excel saves a workbook template using a special file format with the file extension .xlt. Workbook templates are also stored in a special Templates folder. To use a workbook template, you select the template file name from the General tab of the New File dialog box. When you save the workbook after entering data in the template, Excel automatically displays the Save As dialog box so that you can specify the new file name. It also changes the file type to an Excel workbook (.xls). This ensures that you do not unintentionally save over the template file.

Designing the Template

A well-designed template allows you to enter information into the appropriate locations while protecting formulas and basic formats. Since the basic workbook design you want to use for your template is already in place, you will modify the worksheets in the workbook to create the template. The first steps are to eliminate the Answer Report 1 sheet and to change the values in the quarter sheets to zeros.

- • **Delete the Answer Report 1 sheet.**

- • **Select the First Quarter through Fourth Quarter sheets.**

HAVING TROUBLE?
Hold down ⇧Shift to extend the sheet selection.

- • **Enter 0 in cells B8 through D11 and cells B15 through D19 in the First Quarter sheet.**

- • **Move to cell A23.**

Your screen should look like Figure 4.7

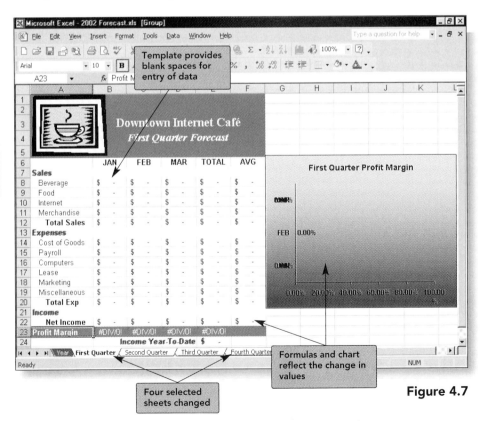

Figure 4.7

By replacing the values with 0, the underlying formulas remain intact. The selected cell format displays cells containing zero values with a dash symbol. All other worksheet cells containing formulas as well as the chart reflect the change in the values.

2 ● **Look at each of the three other quarter sheets to verify that the values have been replaced.**

● **Make the Year sheet active.**

Your screen should look like Figure 4.8

> Values in Year sheet are zero because the cells contain links to the quarter sheets

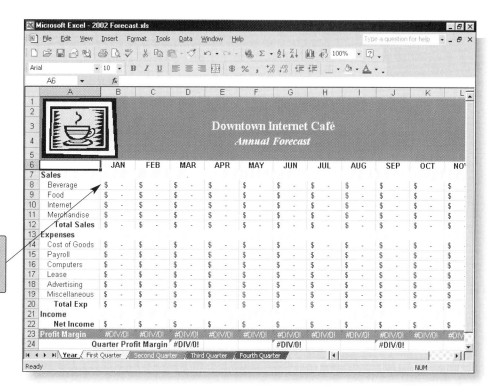

Figure 4.8

Because the Year sheet contains formulas that link to the values in the quarter sheets, this sheet also displays zero values. Now, whenever you are creating another annual forecast, you will simply enter the new values in place of the blanks in the quarter sheets and the annual sheet will automatically be completed.

Protecting the Worksheet

Now that all the values have been removed and the template is ready to use, you want to prevent unwanted changes to the worksheets that would cause headings and formulas to be altered or cleared. To do this, you can protect the worksheet.

Protection

3 Excel includes two levels of **protection** that control what information can be changed in a workbook. Worksheet protection prevents users from changing a worksheet's contents by protecting the entire worksheet or specified areas of it. When a worksheet is protected, all cells and graphic objects on it are locked. The contents of a locked cell cannot be changed. If you want to leave some cells unlocked for editing, such as in a worksheet that you use as an entry form, you can lock cells containing labels and formulas but unlock the entry fields so that other users can fill them in. This type of protection prevents you from entering or changing an entry in any locked cells.

Workbook-level protection prevents changes to an entire workbook in two ways. First, you

can protect the structure of a workbook so that sheets cannot be moved or deleted or new sheets inserted. Second, you can protect a workbook's windows. This prevents changes to the size and position of windows and ensures that they appear the same way each time the workbook is opened.

In addition, you can include a **password** that prevents any unauthorized person from either viewing or saving changes to the workbook. Two separate passwords can be used: one to open and view the file and another to edit and save the file. If you use a password, you must remember the password in order to turn protection off in the future.

Initially all cells in a worksheet are locked. However, you can enter data in the cells because the worksheet protection feature is not on. When protection is turned on, all locked cells are protected. Therefore, before protecting this sheet, you need to unlock the areas in the worksheet where you want to allow users to make changes to information.

The only area of the Year sheet that needs to be unprotected is the subtitle where the year will be entered when the template is used. You will unlock the cell containing the subtitle and add protection to the rest of the worksheet.

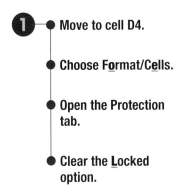

● Move to cell D4.

● Choose F**o**rmat/C**e**lls.

● Open the Protection tab.

● Clear the **L**ocked option.

Your screen should be similar to Figure 4.9

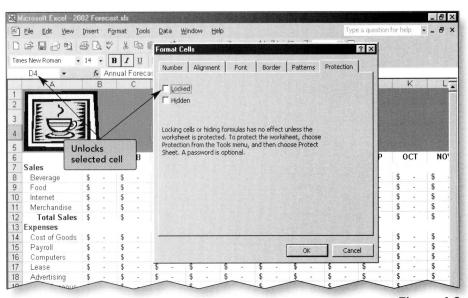

Figure 4.9

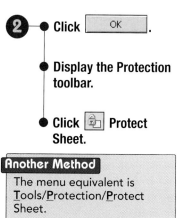

2 ● Click [OK].

● **Display the Protection toolbar.**

● **Click**  **Protect Sheet.**

Another Method

The menu equivalent is Tools/Protection/Protect Sheet.

Your screen should be similar to Figure 4.10

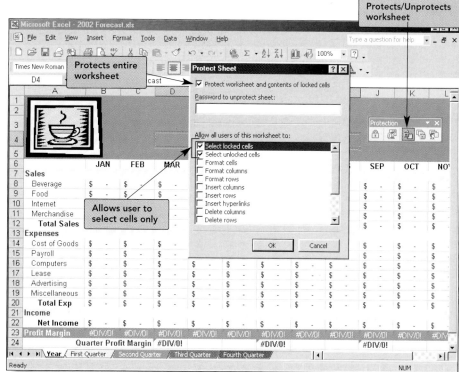

Figure 4.10

In the Protect Sheet dialog box, you select the options that you want to enable for all users of the template. The Select locked cells and Select unlocked cells options are enabled by default. Leaving these selected and the others unselected provides complete protection for the worksheet.

3 ● Click [OK].

Next, you need to unlock the data entry areas of the quarter sheets before you turn on protection for those sheets.

4

● **Select the First Quarter through Fourth Quarter sheets.**

● **Select cells B8 through D11 and B15 through D19.**

HAVING TROUBLE?
Hold down [Ctrl] to select non-adjacent ranges.

● **Choose F̲ormat/C̲ells.**

● **Clear the L̲ocked option in the Protection tab.**

● **Click** [OK].

Your screen should be similar to Figure 4.11

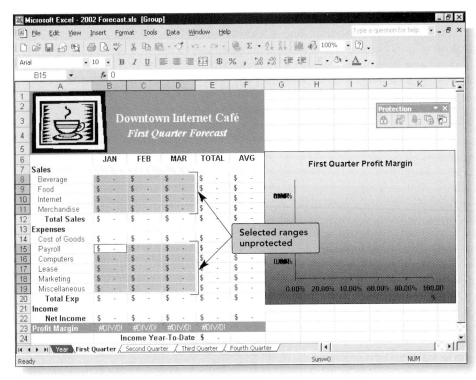

Figure 4.11

When protecting worksheets, you must protect each sheet individually. You will ungroup the sheets and protect each sheet.

5

● **Select U̲ngroup sheets from the sheet tab shortcut menu.**

Another Method
You can also hold down [⇧ Shift] while clicking a sheet tab to ungroup sheets.

● **If necessary, make the First Quarter sheet active.**

● **Click** 🔒 **Protect Sheet.**

● **Click** [OK].

● **In a similar manner protect the other three quarter sheets.**

Your screen should be similar to Figure 4.12

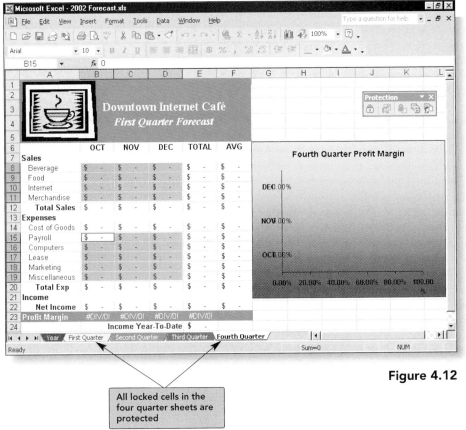

Figure 4.12

All locked cells in the four quarter sheets are protected

Now all locked cells in the four quarter sheets are protected. Only those cells you unlocked prior to turning on protection can be changed. To test this out, you will try to make an entry in a protected cell.

6 ● **Type any character in cell B6.**

Your screen should be similar to Figure 4.13

Locked cell is protected and cannot be changed

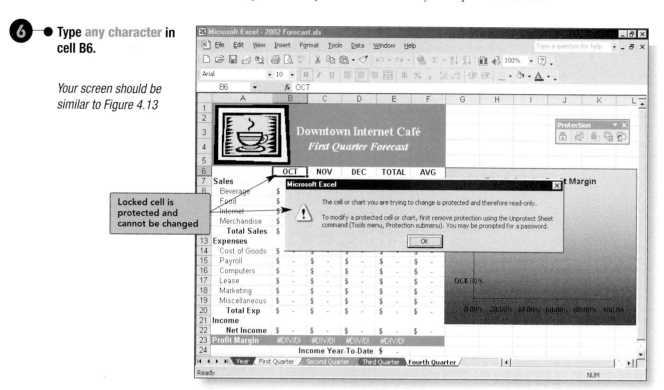

Figure 4.13

The warning dialog box informs you that you cannot change entries in locked cells. Next, you will enter a value in an unlocked cell.

7 ● **Click** OK **to clear the message.**

● **Type 1250 in cell B8 and press ←Enter.**

Your screen should be similar to Figure 4.14

Entry in un-locked cell is accepted

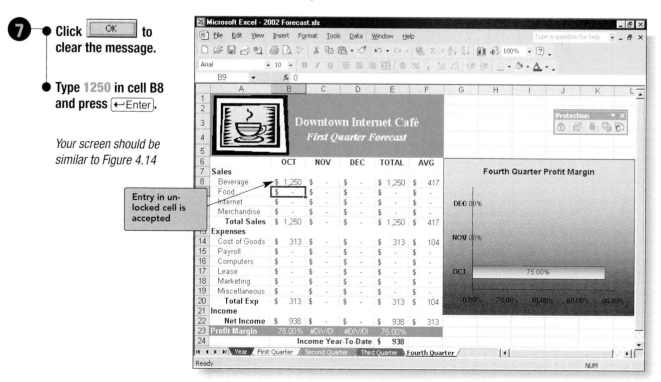

Figure 4.14

The entry is accepted because the cell was unlocked before protection was applied to the sheet.

Saving the Template

Now that the sheets are protected, you will save this workbook as a template file. First, you will clear the test entry and move the cell pointer to the location in the worksheet where you want it to appear when opened.

1 ● Click  Undo to remove the test entry.

● Move to cell B8 in each of the other quarter sheets.

● Move to cell D4 in the Year sheet.

● Close the Protection toolbar.

● Choose **F**ile/Save **A**s.

● Enter the new name, Forecast Template, in the File **N**ame text box.

● From the Save As **T**ype list box, select Template (*.xlt).

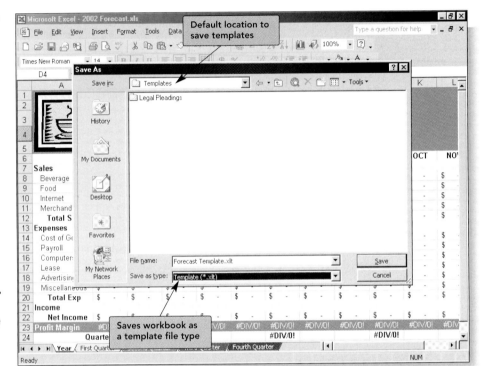

Figure 4.15

Additional Information
You cannot save a workbook as a template by typing the file extension .xlt in a file name. You must select the Template (.xlt) file type from the Save As Type list box.

Your screen should be similar to Figure 4.15

Templates are saved by default to the Templates folder on your system. You can also save templates to other locations just like any other workbook file.

2 ● Click [Save].

● **Close the** Forecast Template **file.**

HAVING TROUBLE?
If a file already exists with this name, click [Yes] to replace it.

The Forecast Template workbook is now ready to use.

Using the Template

Now you will use the Forecast Template file to create a new 2003 forecast workbook for the Downtown Internet Café.

1 ● Choose **File/New**.

● Click 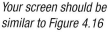 on the New Workbook task pane.

Your screen should be similar to Figure 4.16

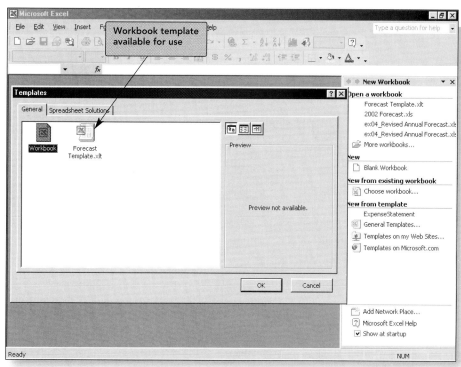

Figure 4.16

> **Additional Information**
> Only templates saved to the Template folder will be listed.

> **Additional Information**
> Your General tab may display additional icons depending on how many and what kind of templates have been created and saved in Excel.

The Forecast Template file name appears in the General tab of the Templates dialog box. You will open the template and change the subtitle in the Year sheet to display the year 2003.

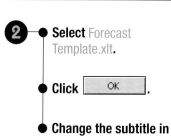

2 ● Select Forecast Template.xlt.

● Click ___OK___ .

● Change the subtitle in cell D4 of the Year sheet to 2003 Annual Forecast.

Your screen should be similar to Figure 4.17

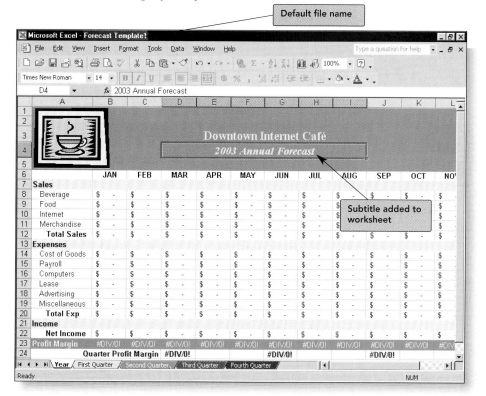

Figure 4.17

Before continuing, you want to save the revised template file as a new workbook file for use in entering the 2003 forecast data. Notice the file name in the title bar is Forecast Template1. Excel automatically adds a number to the file name when the template is opened to prevent you from accidentally overwriting the template when saving. Additionally, when using a template to create a new workbook file, even if you use the Save command, Excel automatically displays the Save As dialog box so that you can specify a new file name.

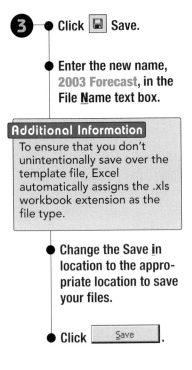

3 ● Click ⊟ Save.

● Enter the new name, **2003 Forecast**, in the File **N**ame text box.

Additional Information

To ensure that you don't unintentionally save over the template file, Excel automatically assigns the .xls workbook extension as the file type.

● Change the Save **i**n location to the appropriate location to save your files.

● Click ▭ **S**ave ▭.

Your screen should be similar to Figure 4.18

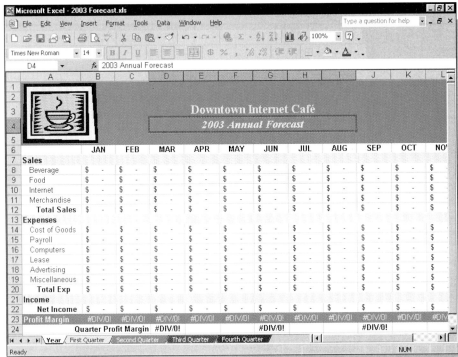

Figure 4.18

Working with Multiple Workbooks

Evan wants you to focus on the 2003 first-quarter forecast. Because he expects all sales and expenses to remain the same as the December 2002 values, you can obtain this data from the 2002 Forecast workbook. To do this, you want to copy the data from one workbook to the other. In Excel, you can open multiple workbook files at the same time. Each workbook is opened in its own window. You can also open additional separate windows to display different parts of the active workbook. The open windows can be arranged so that you can see them simultaneously to make it easy to work with data in multiple workbooks at the same time.

Additional Information

Use the **N**ew Window command on the **W**indow menu to display a second window for the active workbook.

Opening a Second Workbook File

You will open the workbook file containing the 2002 forecast data you saved earlier.

1 ● **Open the** 2002 Forecast **workbook file.**

Your screen should be similar to Figure 4.19

Active workbook contains cell selector

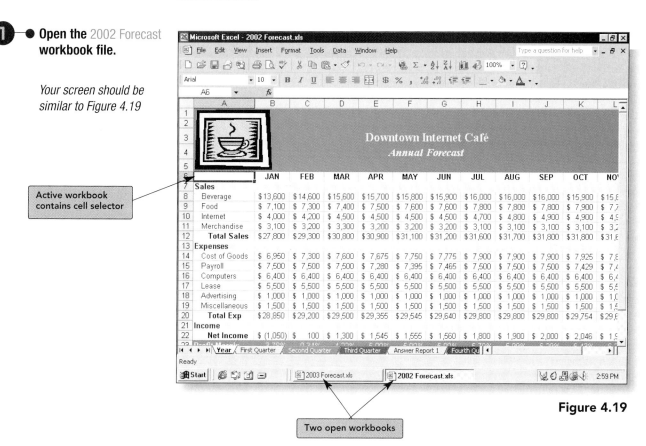

Figure 4.19

Two open workbooks

Now there are two active workbook files and the taskbar displays a button for each open window. The 2002 Forecast workbook file window is open on top of the 2003 Forecast workbook file window. The newly opened file is the **active workbook** file. It is the file that will be affected by changes and the file that contains the cell selector.

Arranging Windows

The way the workbooks are currently displayed makes it difficult to work with both files simultaneously. To make it easier to work with both files at the same time, you can change the arrangement of the windows.

concept 4

Window Arrangements

4 Open workbook windows can be arranged in different ways on the screen to make it easy to view and work with information in different workbooks. When new workbook windows are opened, they appear in the same size and on top of any other open windows. Open windows can be arranged in the following ways:

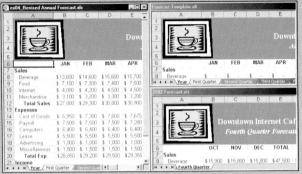

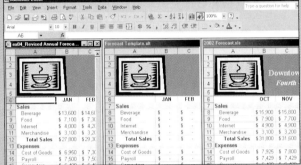

Tiled: The windows are displayed one after the other in succession, across and down the screen.

Vertical: The windows are displayed side by side.

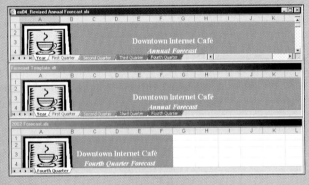

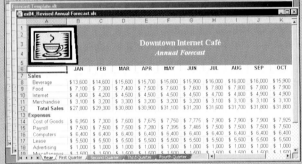

Horizontal: The windows are displayed one above the other.

Cascade: The windows are displayed one on top of the other, cascading down from the top of the screen.

You decide that the easiest way to work with the two files is to tile them.

Lab 4: Using Solver, Creating Templates, and Evaluating Scenarios

www.mhhe.com/oleary

1 ● Choose **W**indow/**A**rrange.

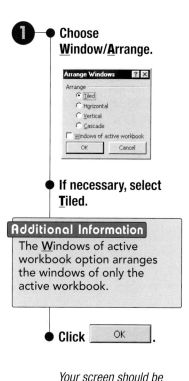

● If necessary, select **T**iled.

Additional Information

The **W**indows of active workbook option arranges the windows of only the active workbook.

● Click [OK].

Your screen should be similar to Figure 4.20

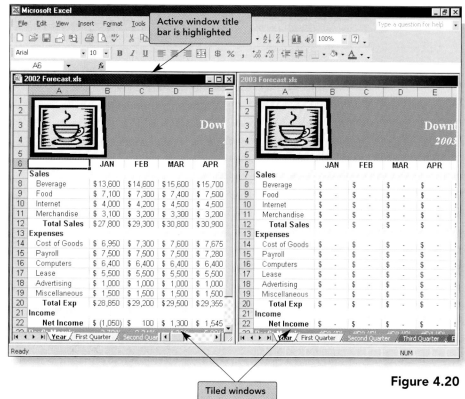

Figure 4.20

The two workbook windows appear next to each other. The title bar of the active workbook file is highlighted. You want to see the December values in the Fourth Quarter sheet of the 2002 forecast and the First Quarter sheet from the 2003 forecast.

2 ● Display the Fourth Quarter sheet in the 2002 Forecast workbook.

● Click in the 2003 Forecast workbook window to make it active.

● Display the First Quarter sheet.

Your screen should be similar to Figure 4.21

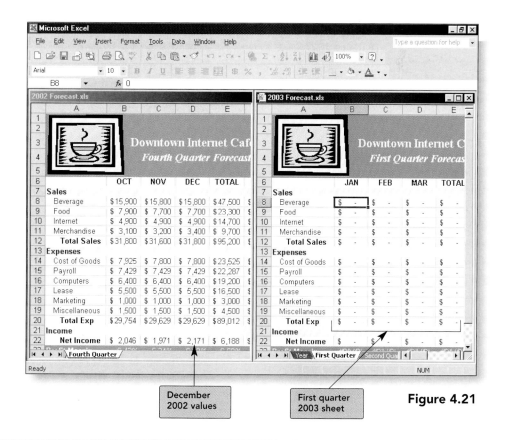

Figure 4.21

Linking Workbooks

You want to use the December data from the 2002 forecast workbook in the first quarter of the 2003 forecast workbook. Additionally, you want the data in the 2003 forecast to update automatically if the data in the 2002 forecast changes. To do this, you will create a link between the two workbook files.

concept 5

Link Workbooks

5 A **link** creates a connection between files that automatically updates the linked data in one file whenever the data in the other file changes. The link between the workbook files is formed by entering an **external reference** formula in one workbook that refers to a cell in another workbook. When data in a linked cell changes, the workbook that is affected by this change is automatically updated when it is opened.

The formula is entered in the workbook that receives the data. This workbook file is called the **dependent workbook**. The workbook that supplies the data is called the **source workbook**. The cell containing the external reference formula (the **dependent cell**) refers to the cell (the **source cell**) in the source file that contains the data to be copied.

An external reference formula uses the following format:

$$= [\text{workbook file reference}]\text{sheet reference!cell reference}$$

The file reference consists of the file name of the source file followed by the name of the worksheet. The cell reference of the cell or range of cells containing the number to be copied into the dependent workbook follows the file reference. The two parts of the formula are separated by an exclamation point.

You will create a link between the two workbook files by entering external reference formulas in the 2003 First Quarter worksheet that reference the cells containing the values in the Fourth Quarter sheet of the 2002 Forecast workbook. The 2002 Forecast workbook is the source workbook, and the 2003 Forecast workbook is the dependent workbook.

The first external reference formula you will enter will link the beverage sales numbers. To create an external reference formula, you copy the contents of the source cell to the Clipboard, switch to the dependent workbook, and then use the Edit/Paste Special command to create the external reference formula link in the specified cell of the dependent workbook.

The source cell is cell D8 of the Fourth Quarter sheet in the 2002 Forecast workbook. You will copy this source cell and paste it into the dependent cell.

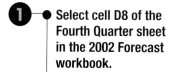

1
- Select cell D8 of the Fourth Quarter sheet in the 2002 Forecast workbook.

- Click  Copy.

- Select cell B8 in the First Quarter sheet of the 2003 Forecast workbook.

- Choose **E**dit/**P**aste **S**pecial.

Your screen should be similar to Figure 4.22

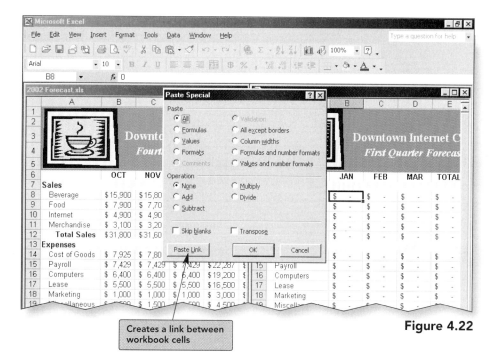

Creates a link between workbook cells

Figure 4.22

From the Paste Special dialog box, you specify how much of the cell contents you want pasted. You can paste either the entire cell contents (including formatting), or selected attributes associated with the cell, such as only the formula, value, format, comments, validation, or column width of the cell. You can also perform an addition, subtraction, multiplication, or division operation on the pasted cell. You can also create a link to the source cell contents so that when the source cell is changed, the linked cell is automatically changed as well.

2
- Click Paste Link.

Additional Information

The 🖺 Paste Options button also includes the **L**ink Cells option.

Your screen should be similar to Figure 4.23

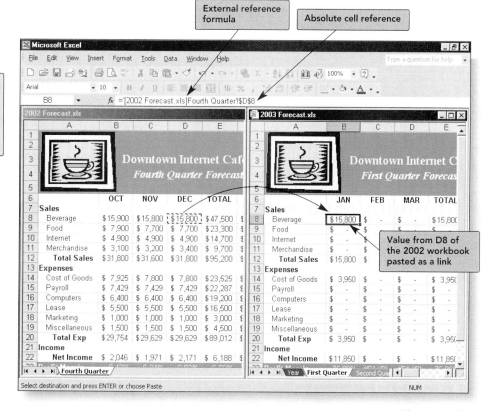

External reference formula

Absolute cell reference

Value from D8 of the 2002 workbook pasted as a link

Figure 4.23

The link has been established and an external reference formula has been entered into the selected cell of the dependent workbook. The formula is displayed in the formula bar, and the number in cell D8 of the source workbook is entered into the dependent workbook and displayed in cell B8. Notice that Excel uses absolute references in the external reference formula.

Next, you want to create a link between the other December values in the source workbook. To do this quickly, you can copy the external reference formula down the column and across the rows. However, you must first change the cell reference D8 in the external reference formula to a mixed reference of ($D8) so that it will adjust appropriately as the formula is copied.

3 ● **In cell B8 of the 2003 Forecast workbook edit the absolute reference (D8) in the formula to $D8.**

● **Copy the external reference formula in cell B8 to cells C8 and D8 and cells B9 through D11.**

● **Copy the external reference formula in cell B8 to the range B15 through D19.**

● **Click cell D19 to deselect the range.**

Your screen should be similar to Figure 4.24

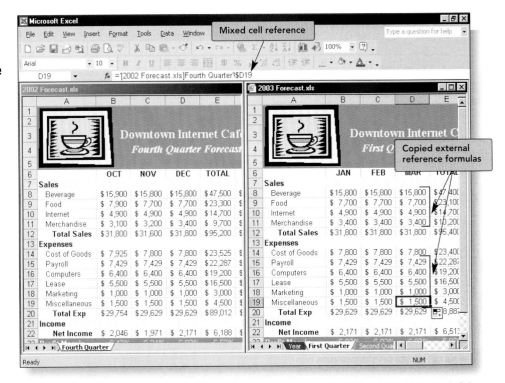

Figure 4.24

The First Quarter data for 2003 is now complete. It is the same as the December 2002 data. Because the data in the worksheets is linked, a change in the December 2002 worksheet values will automatically be reflected in the First Quarter 2003 worksheet.

Lab 4: Using Solver, Creating Templates, and Evaluating Scenarios

www.mhhe.com/oleary

Updating Linked Data

Evan advises you that the lease for the café will increase to $6,000 a month beginning in October of 2002. You want to enter this new amount and see the effect of this change.

1 ● **Enter 6,000 into cells B17, C17, and D17 in the Fourth Quarter sheet of the 2002 Forecast workbook.**

Your screen should be similar to Figure 4.25

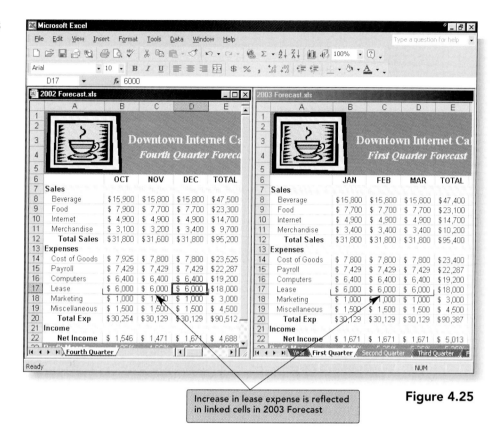

Increase in lease expense is reflected in linked cells in 2003 Forecast

Figure 4.25

All affected formulas are recalculated. Because the workbooks are linked, the change in the 2002 Forecast is automatically reflected in the 2003 Forecast. Once an external reference formula is entered in a worksheet, whenever the data in the cell referenced in the source file changes, the dependent file is automatically updated if it is open. However, if the dependent file is not open, it is not updated. To ensure that a dependent file gets updated when you open the source file, Excel displays an alert message asking if you want to update references to unopened documents. If you respond Yes, Excel checks the source documents and updates all references to them so that you will have the latest values from the source worksheet.

You do not need to obtain any further data from the 2002 Forecast workbook at this time. You can close it and enlarge the 2003 Forecast window to make it easier to work with.

2
- Save the 2002 Forecast and close the workbook.

- Maximize the 2003 Forecast window.

Your screen should be similar to Figure 4.26

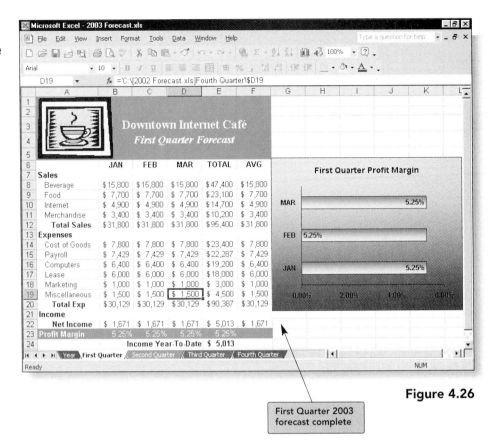

First Quarter 2003 forecast complete

Figure 4.26

Evaluating Scenarios

Evan has reviewed the First Quarter Forecast and is comfortable with it. While he realizes that sales and costs may be higher or lower than those presented, Evan believes the most likely scenario, or set of values, is reflected in the First Quarter worksheet. He has asked you to evaluate a best-case scenario and a worst-case scenario.

concept 6

Scenario

6 A **scenario** is a named set of input values that you can substitute in a worksheet to see the effects of a possible alternative course of action. Scenarios are designed to help forecast the outcome of various possible actions. You can create and save different groups of scenario values on a worksheet and then switch to any of these scenarios to view the results.

For example, if you want to create a budget forecast based on various revenue values, you could define the potential values and then switch between the scenarios to perform what-if analyses. You can also create reports in separate sheets that summarize the scenarios you create.

Lab 4: Using Solver, Creating Templates, and Evaluating Scenarios

www.mhhe.com/oleary

The current workbook reflects the most likely scenario. Evan has identified the best-case scenario as one where sales from Internet use increase 25 percent above the current estimate of $4,900 in February and March and all other values remain unchanged. His worst-case scenario is if Internet sales decrease 10 percent below the current estimate for the entire quarter and the lease in March increases from $6,000 to $6,200.

Adding Scenarios

You are going to use the Scenario tool to evaluate the alternative scenarios by changing the values for Internet Sales for January (cell B10), February (cell C10), and March (cell D10), and for March Lease Expense (cell D17). You could create separate worksheets to evaluate each scenario. However, using the Scenario Manager tool, you can create different scenarios and insert these scenarios directly into the workbook to see how each affects the worksheet.

1 ● **Move to cell B10.**

● **Choose**
Tools/Scenarios.

● **Move the Scenario Manager dialog box to the right of column F.**

Your screen should be similar to Figure 4.27

Most likely Internet sales

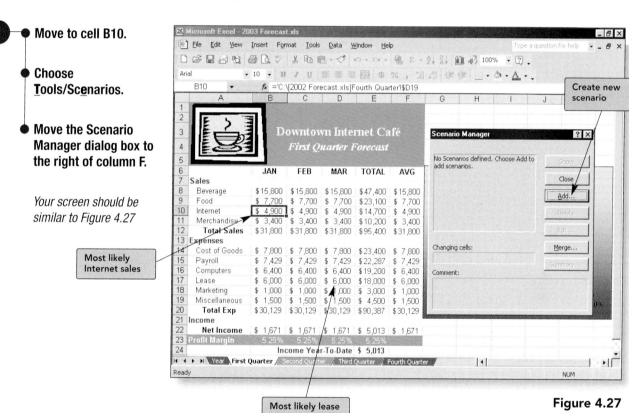

Most likely lease expense

Figure 4.27

The Scenario Manager dialog box is used to add, delete, and edit scenarios. There are no scenarios named yet. First, you will define the most likely scenario.

2 ● Click [Add...].

Your screen should be similar to Figure 4.28

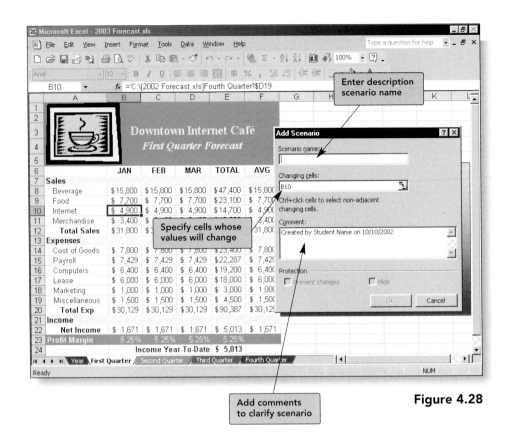

Figure 4.28

In the Add Scenario dialog box you enter a name for the first scenario and the range of cells that will contain the changing values in the Changing Cells text box.

3 ● Type **Most Likely** in the Scenario Name text box.

● Specify the range B10 through D10 and cell D17 as the changing cells in the Changing Cell text box.

Additional Information

Click [▦] to reduce the dialog box and select the range from the worksheet. Hold down [Ctrl] while selecting nonadjacent cells.

Your screen should be similar to Figure 4.29

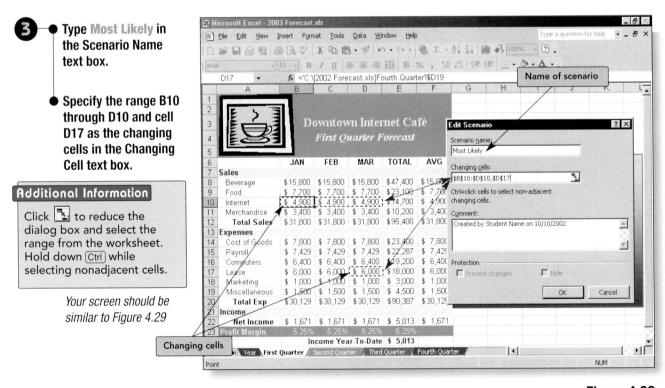

Figure 4.29

It is often helpful to add a comment to clarify the data included in the scenario. The default comment in the Comment text box displays the text "Created by [name] on [date]." You will include additional information to clarify the meaning of the scenario.

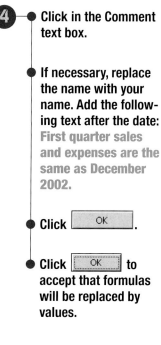

4 • **Click in the Comment text box.**

• **If necessary, replace the name with your name. Add the following text after the date:** First quarter sales and expenses are the same as December 2002.

• **Click** OK **.**

• **Click** OK **to accept that formulas will be replaced by values.**

Your screen should be similar to Figure 4.30

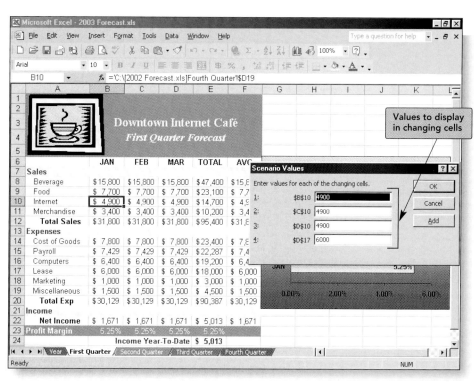

Figure 4.30

Additional Information

It is always a good idea to create a scenario of your original data as this will allow you to redisplay this information at any time.

The Scenario Values dialog box is used to enter the values to be varied for the different scenarios. The current worksheet values are displayed. These are the values you want to use for the Most Likely scenario.

5 ● Click [OK].

Your screen should be similar to Figure 4.31

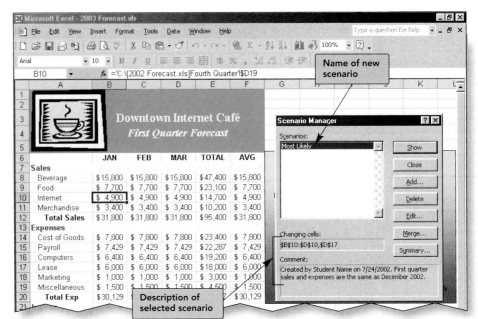

Name of new scenario

Description of selected scenario

Figure 4.31

You are returned to the Scenario Manager dialog box and the name of the new scenario is displayed in the Scenarios list box.

Next, you will create the worst-case scenario. You already calculated that a 10 percent decrease in Internet Sales for the three months would be 4410. Additionally the lease expense would increase to 6200.

6 ● Click [Add...].

● In the Scenario Name text box, type Worst Case.

● In the Comment text box, change the name if necessary and enter the following: Internet Sales are 10% less than the most likely values for February and March and March Lease increases to $6,200.

● Click [OK] twice.

● Enter 4410 in the $B10, $C10, and $D10 changing cells text boxes.

● Enter 6200 in the D17 changing cells text box.

Your screen should be similar to Figure 4.32

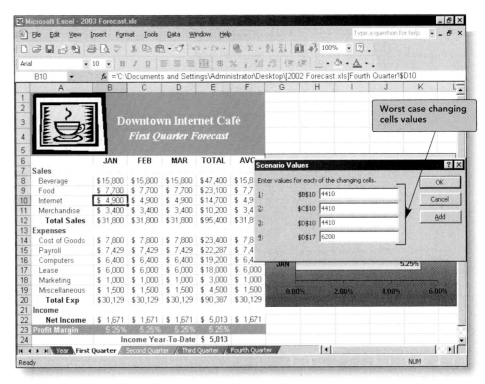

Worst case changing cells values

Figure 4.32

Next, you will create the best-case scenario. In this scenario, Evan anticipates that Internet Sales will increase 25 percent for February and March above the most likely values and the March lease expense will remain the same. You could create the scenario in the same way by entering the new values in the changing cells. Another way, however, is to use Solver to calculate the expected values for you and then create the scenario from the Solver result. Because you will be changing values in the worksheet, you will need to unprotect the sheet first.

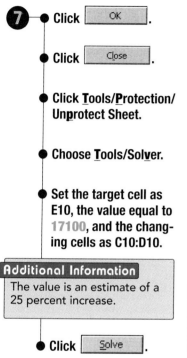

7 ● Click **OK**.

● Click **Close**.

● Click **Tools/Protection/Unprotect Sheet.**

● Choose **Tools/Solver.**

● Set the target cell as **E10**, the value equal to **17100**, and the changing cells as **C10:D10.**

Additional Information

The value is an estimate of a 25 percent increase.

● Click **Solve**.

Your screen should be similar to Figure 4.33

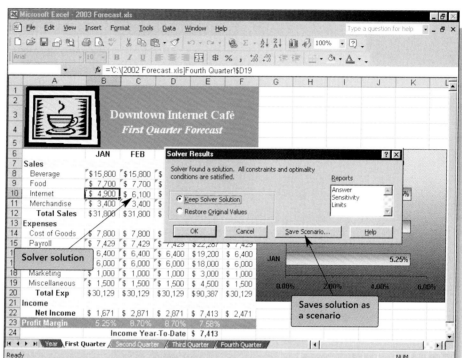

Figure 4.33

The Solver solution increases the February and March Internet sales to 6100. You will create the scenario from these results. You will also not keep the Solver solution, as you want the original values maintained in the worksheet.

8 • Click [Save Scenario...].

• Enter the scenario name of Best Case.

• Click [OK].

• Select Restore Original Values.

• Click [OK].

Your screen should be similar to Figure 4.34

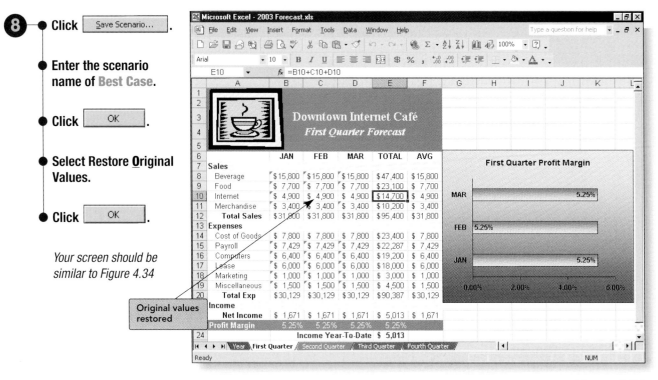

Figure 4.34

The original values are displayed in the worksheet again and the Solver results have been stored as a scenario.

Using Scenarios

There are now three different scenarios in the worksheet. You want to see the effect of the worst-case and best-case scenarios.

1 • Choose Tools/Scenarios.

• From the Scenario Manager dialog box, select Worst Case.

• Click [Show].

• Move the Scenario Manager dialog box down so that you can see the chart.

Your screen should be similar to Figure 4.35

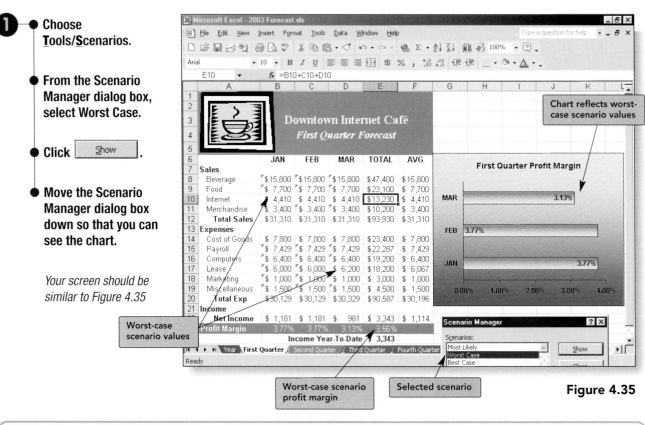

Figure 4.35

The worksheet displays the worst-case values. These values result in a total profit margin of 3.56 percent and the chart reflects the change in monthly profit margins.

2 In a similar manner, display the Best Case scenario.

HAVING TROUBLE?
If Excel did not update the chart, move the Scenario Manager box slightly to refresh the window.

Your screen should be similar to Figure 4.36

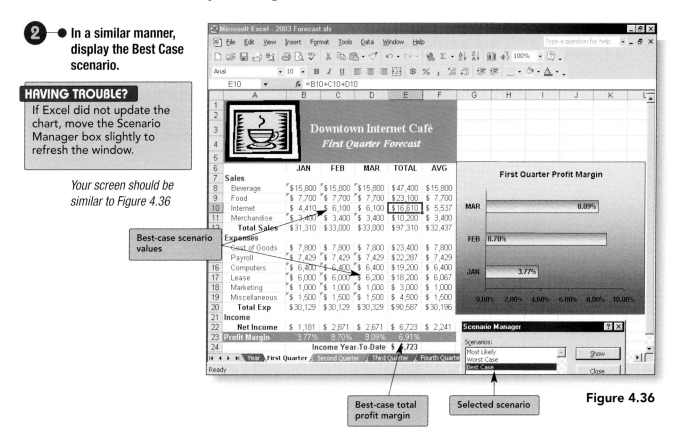

Best-case scenario values

Best-case total profit margin

Selected scenario

Figure 4.36

The best-case values are displayed in the worksheet. The total profit margin is now 6.91 percent. You now only need to edit the scenario to add a comment.

3 ● Click [Edit...].

● In the Comment text box, if necessary change the name and enter the following: **Internet Sales increase 25% for February and March above the most likely values and March lease expense remains the same.**

● Click [OK] twice.

● Move the Scenario Manager dialog box up to row 5.

Your screen should be similar to Figure 4.37

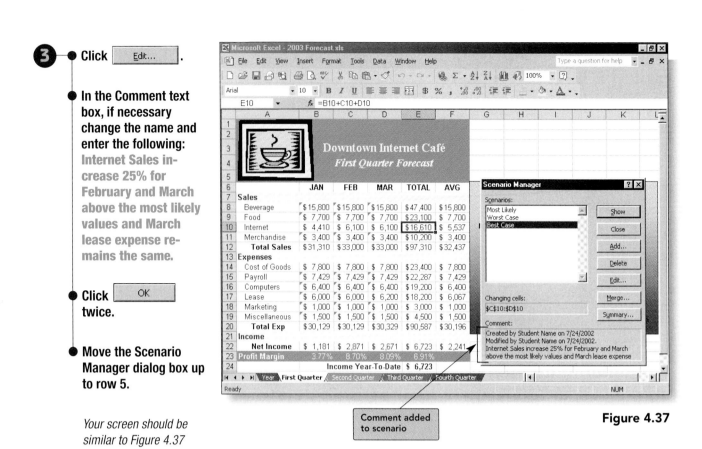

Comment added to scenario

Figure 4.37

Creating a Scenario Report

Another way to evaluate the scenarios is to create a summary report that will display the effect on the profit margins for each scenario.

1 ● Click [Summary...].

● Specify the range B23 through E23 (containing the profit margin values) as the range of cells whose results you want summarized.

● Click [OK].

Your screen should be similar to Figure 4.38

Scenario summary displayed in its own sheet

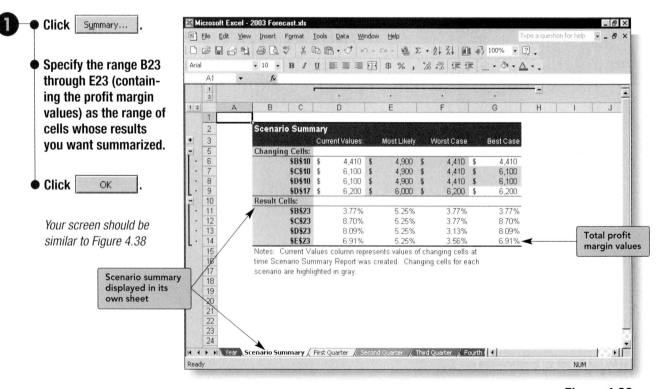

Total profit margin values

Figure 4.38

The Scenario Summary report is created and displayed in a separate sheet. It displays the values for the three scenarios and the results on the profit margin for each scenario. As you can see from the summary, the most likely scenario yields a constant 5.25 percent profit margin. The best-case scenario yields higher profit margins, with a total profit margin of 6.91 percent for the quarter. The worst-case scenario yields lower profit margins, with a total profit margin of 3.56 percent.

The report however, is hard to understand because it uses cell references as the labels. To clarify the meaning of the report, you will edit the row labels.

2 ● **Enter the labels in the following cells:**

C6	Internet JAN	**C11**	Profit Margin JAN
C7	Internet FEB	**C12**	Profit Margin FEB
C8	Internet MAR	**C13**	Profit Margin MAR
C9	Lease MAR	**C14**	Profit Margin TOTAL

● **Best Fit column C.**

● **Save the workbook.**

Your screen should be similar to Figure 4.39

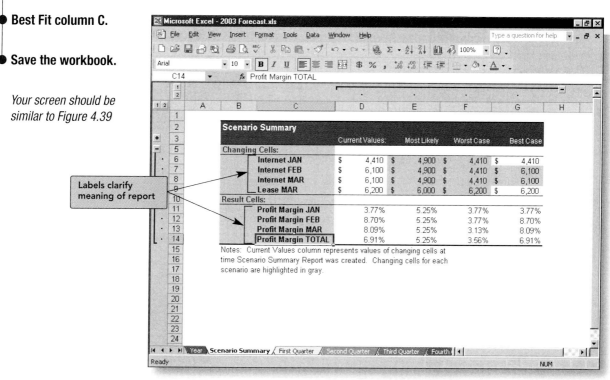

Figure 4.39

You have now completed best- and worst-case scenarios for the year 2003, as Evan requested. However, before printing the Scenario Summary worksheet and giving it to Evan, you want to add some 3-D graphics to the worksheet to emphasize the best-case profit margin scenario.

Enhancing the Report

To emphasize the impact of Internet sales, you want to add a three-dimensional (3-D) shape to the Scenario Summary report to draw attention to the rising profits. A **3-D shape** is a line, AutoShape, or free-form drawing object that has a three-dimensional effect applied to it.

Creating a 3-D Effect

The first object you want to create is a text box that identifies the Internet promotion as the focus of the high-sales scenario.

1
- If necessary, click 🖊 Drawing to display the Drawing toolbar.

- Click **AutoShapes ▾** and from the Block Arrows shapes choose Up Arrow.

- Click anywhere in the blank area under the Notes text.

- Insert the text **Profits from high Internet sales**.

> **HAVING TROUBLE?**
> Choose Add text from the arrow's Shortcut menu.

- Change the font orientation to horizontal and horizontal alignment to center and text orientation to horizontal.

- Expand the width of the arrow to display each word on a line.

> **HAVING TROUBLE?**
> Use Format/AutoShape/Alignment to change the text alignment and orientation.

Your screen should be similar to Figure 4.40

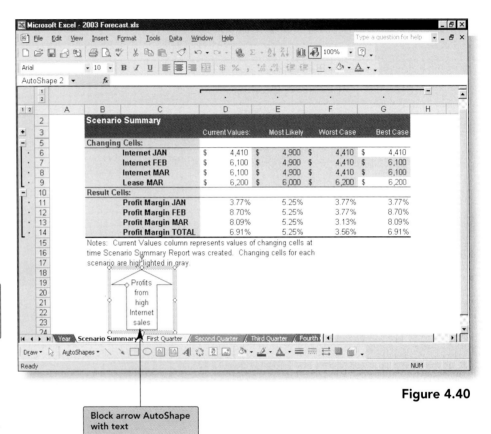

Block arrow AutoShape with text

Figure 4.40

Now you want to apply a 3-D effect to the text box. Excel includes many 3-D options you can use to change the depth (the extrusion) of the object and its color, rotation, angle, direction of lighting, and surface texture. When you change the color of a 3-D effect, only the 3-D effect of the object is changed, not the object itself.

2

● **Click** 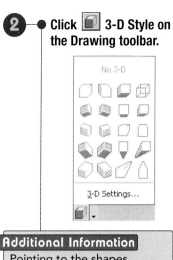 **3-D Style on the Drawing toolbar.**

Additional Information
Pointing to the shapes displays the name of the 3-D shape in a ScreenTip.

● **Choose 3-D Style 11 (3rd row, 3rd column).**

Your screen should be similar to Figure 4.41

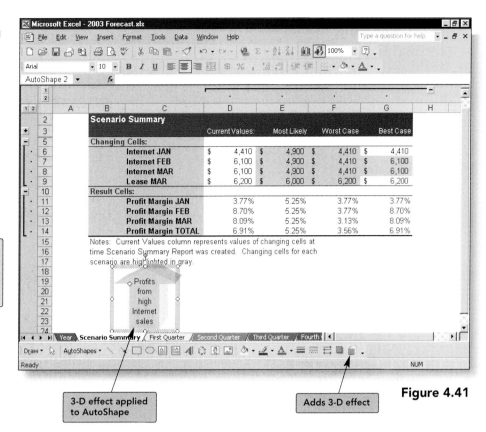

3-D effect applied to AutoShape

Adds 3-D effect

Figure 4.41

Enhancing a 3-D Object

Next, you want to change the fill color.

1

● **Open the** 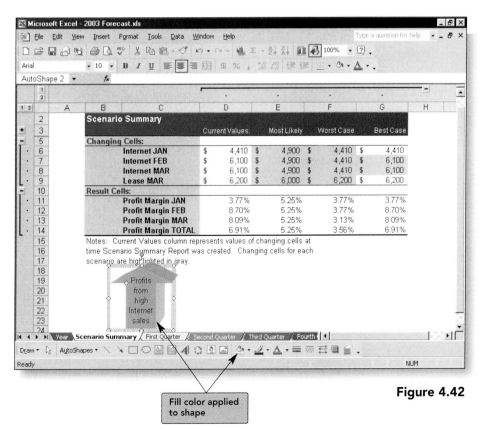 **Fill Color drop-down menu and select Pale Blue.**

Your screen should look like Figure 4.42

Fill color applied to shape

Figure 4.42

You would also like to see how the 3-D effect would look with different settings applied to it, such as a different lighting effect and a different box color.

2 → ● Click 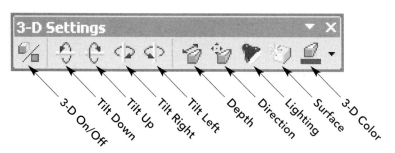 3-D Style and select 3-D Settings.

The 3-D Settings toolbar buttons (identified below) are used to modify the depth (the extrusion) of the 3-D effect and its color, rotation, angle, direction of lighting, and surface texture.

3 → ● Click ▼ Lighting and select a lighting option you like.

● From the 3-D Color menu select a color you like.

● Close the 3-D Settings toolbar.

Your screen should be similar to Figure 4.43

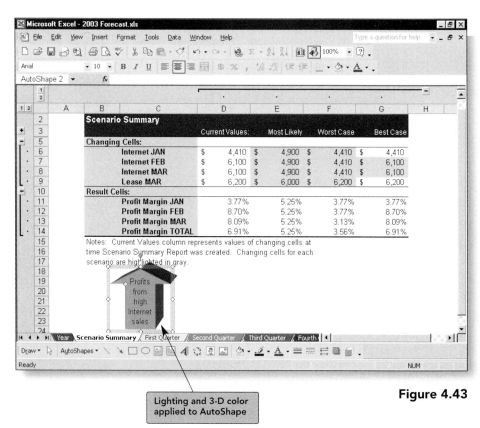

Lighting and 3-D color applied to AutoShape

Figure 4.43

Finally, you want to move the 3-D text box so that it points to the best-case result cells.

4 Drag the arrow to point to the bottom-center of the best-case result column.

Your screen should be similar to Figure 4.44

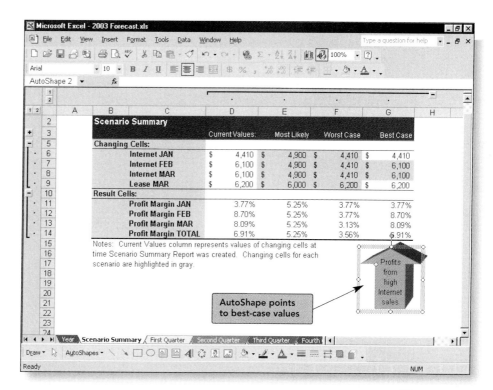

Figure 4.44

Displaying the Current Date and Time

You would also like to include a date and time stamp on the Scenario Summary worksheet to identify when the values were entered and the scenarios applied. You could just enter the current date and time on the worksheet, but you want to ensure that it reflects exactly when the most recent changes and analyses are done. To have the date and time automatically update whenever a worksheet is recalculated, the NOW date function is used.

Using the Insert Function Feature

You will enter the function in cell B3. You could enter the function directly by typing it. However, another way is to use the Insert Function feature. This feature simplifies entering functions by prompting you to select a function from a list and then helps you enter the arguments correctly.

1 **Move to cell B3 on the Scenario worksheet.**

Click f_x **Insert Function.**

Another Method

The menu equivalent is Insert/Function and the keyboard shortcut is ⇧Shift + F3.

Your screen should be similar to Figure 4.45

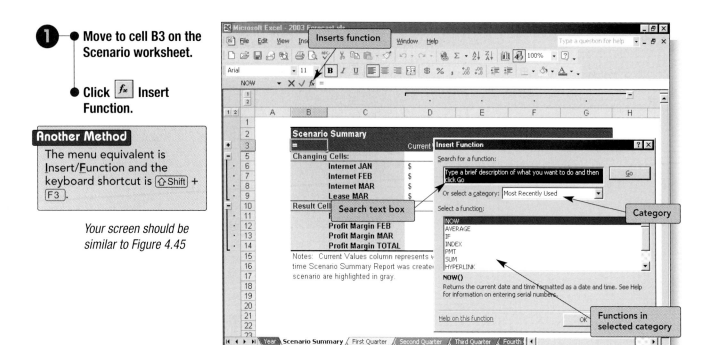

Figure 4.45

The NOW function may not be displayed in the most recently used category. Any function you want to use can be found by typing a description of what you want to do in the Search text box or by selecting a category.

2 **From the Or select a category drop down list, select Date & Time.**

Scroll the Select a Function list and select NOW.

Click OK .

Your screen should be similar to Figure 4.46

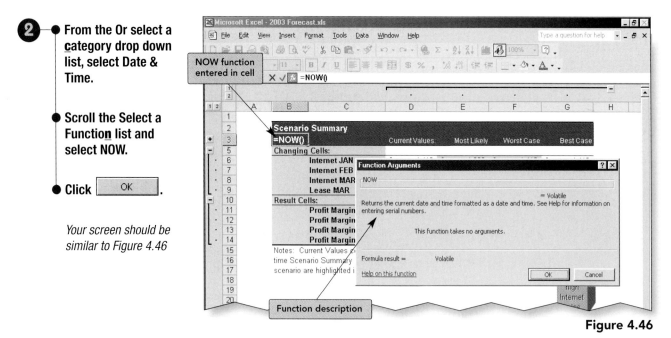

Figure 4.46

The Function Arguments dialog box displays a message telling you that this function displays the current date and time, and requires no arguments. To complete the function,

3 ● Click OK .

Your screen should be similar to Figure 4.47

NOW function re-
sults displayed

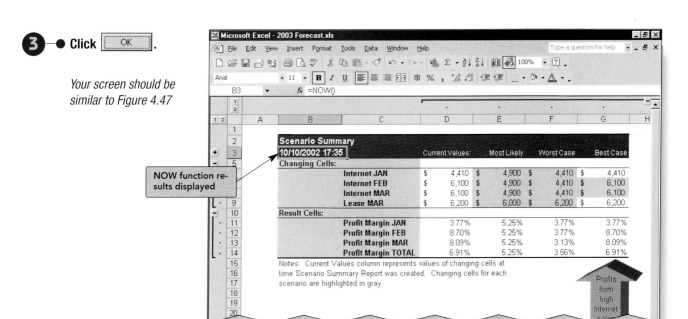

Figure 4.47

The current date and time are displayed in cell B3. A final change you want to make is to move the Note at the bottom of the Scenario Summary to the right. Rather than cutting and pasting the cell contents, you will insert blank cells before the cells and shift the existing cells to the right.

4 ● Select cells A15:A17.

● Choose **I**nsert/C**e**lls/
Shift Cells R**i**ght/
OK .

Your screen should be similar to Figure 4.48.

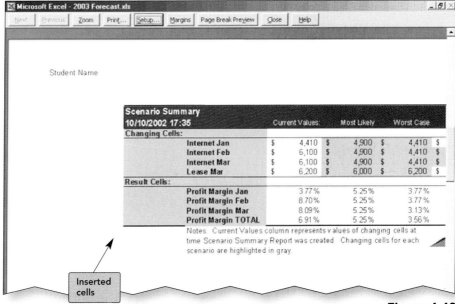

Inserted
cells

Figure 4.48

Three new cells have been inserted and the existing cells have shifted to the right. Now you are ready to print the worksheet.

5 ● **Preview then print the worksheet centered horizontally in landscape orientation. Include your name and the worksheet name in a custom header.**

● **Save the worksheet and exit Excel.**

LAB 4

Using Solver, Creating Templates, and Evaluating Scenarios

Solver (EX4.6)

Solver is a tool used to perform what-if analyses to determine the effect of changing values in two or more cells on another cell.

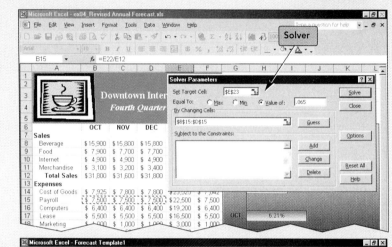

Workbook Template (EX4.10)

A workbook template is a workbook file that contains predesigned worksheets that can be used as patterns for creating similar worksheets in new workbooks.

Worksheet Protection (EX4.12)

Worksheet protection prevents users from changing a worksheet's contents by protecting the entire worksheet or specified areas of it.

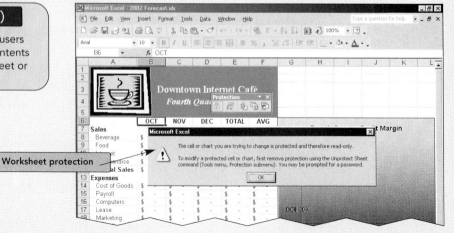

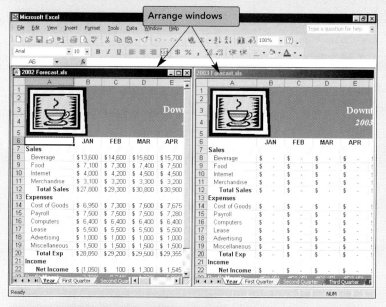

Arrange Windows (EX4.20)

The Arrange Windows feature displays all open workbook files in separate windows on the screen in a tiled, horizontal, vertical, or cascade arrangement.

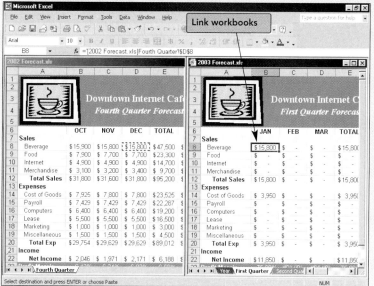

Link Workbooks (EX4.22)

A link creates a connection between files that automatically updates the data in one file whenever the data in the other file changes.

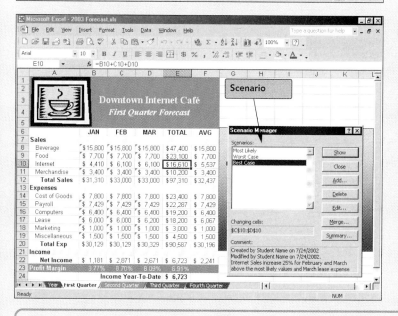

Scenario (EX4.26)

A scenario is a named set of input values that you can substitute in a worksheet to see the effects of a possible alternative course of action. Scenarios are designed to help forecast the outcome of various possible actions.

key terms

3-D shape   EX4.36

active workbook   EX4.19

adjustable cell   EX4.6

arrange windows   EX4.20

cascade   EX4.20

dependent cell   EX4.22

dependent workbook   EX4.22

external reference formula   EX4.22

horizontal   EX4.20

link   EX4.22

password   EX4.12

protection   EX4.12

scenario   EX4.26

Solver   EX4.6

source cell   EX4.22

source workbook   EX4.22

target cell   EX4.6

template   EX4.

tiled   EX4.20

vertical   EX4.20

mous skills

The Microsoft Office User Specialist (MOUS) certification program is designed to measure your proficiency in performing basic tasks using the Office XP applications. Getting certified demonstrates that you have the skills and provides a valuable industry credential for employment. After completing this lab, you have learned the following Microsoft Office User Specialist skills:

Skill	Description	Page
Managing Workbooks	Manage workbook files and folders	EX4.16
	Create workbooks using templates	EX4.9
	Save workbooks using different names and file formats	EX4.16
Creating and Revising Formulas	Use statistical, date and time, financial, and logical functions in formulas	EX4.39

Command	Shortcut Keys	Button	Action
Edit/Delete/Shift Cells Left			Deletes selected cells and shifts remaining cells to the left
Edit/Delete/Shift Cells Up			Deletes selected cells and shifts remaining cells up
Edit/Delete Sheet			Deletes selected worksheets from a workbook
Insert/Cells/Shift Cells Right			Moves existing cells to the right when new cells are inserted
Insert/Cells/Shift Cells Down			Moves existing cells down when new cells are inserted
Tools/Protection/Protect Sheet		🔒	Prevents unauthorized users from changing a worksheet's contents
Tools/Scenarios			Creates and saves sets of data used to perform what-if analyses
Tools/Solver			Calculates a formula to achieve a given value by changing one of the variables that affects formulas
Window/Arrange			Arranges open windows side-by-side, vertically, horizontally, or tiled

Terminology

screen identification

In the following worksheet, several items are identified by letters. Enter the correct term for each item in the spaces provided.

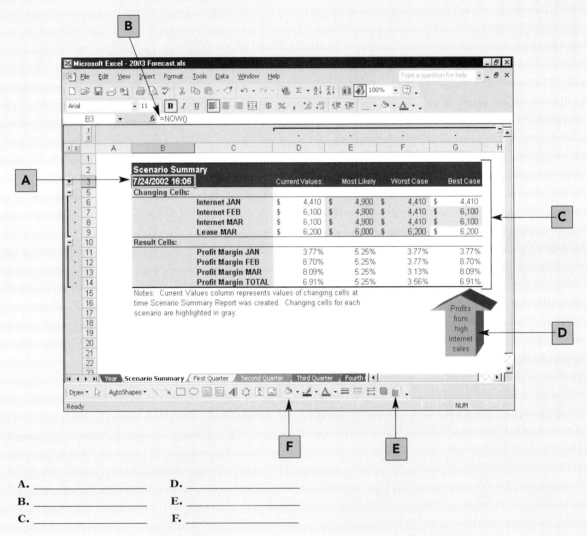

A. _____   D. _____

B. _____   E. _____

C. _____   F. _____

matching

Match the lettered item on the right with the numbered list on the left.

1. Solver _____ a. creates a connection between files that automatically updates the data in one file when a change is made in another file

2. source workbook _____ b. determines the effects of changed values in adjustable cells

3. scenario _____ c. cell containing the external reference formula

4. cascade _____ d. forecasts the outcome of various possible actions

5. target cell _____ e. object that has a three-dimensional effect applied to it

6. template _____ f. cell containing value you want to solve for

7. 3-D shape _____ g. prevents unauthorized users from viewing or changing a workbook

8. password _____ h. supplies the data in a linked workbook

9. dependent cell _____ i. used as a pattern for creating new workbooks

10. link _____ j. windows displayed one on top of another

multiple choice

Circle the correct response to the questions below.

1. A(n)_____is a named set of input values that you can substitute in a worksheet.
   a. scenario
   b. Solver
   c. adjustable cell
   d. template

2. In the external reference formula [Forecast.xls]Year$N$8, the name in brackets is _____.
   a. the source file
   b. the destination file
   c. the active file
   d. the current worksheet

3. The workbook that supplies that data is called the _____.
   a. source workbook
   b. dependent workbook
   c. link
   d. dependent cell

4. A(n)_____creates a connection between files that automatically updates the linked data in one file when a change is made in another file.
   a. password
   b. source file
   c. link
   d. external reference

5. _____ calculate(s) a formula to achieve a given value.
   a. Target Cells
   b. Formulas
   c. Solver
   d. Source Cells

6. The _____ tool lets you view varying values applied to a worksheet:
   a. Scenario
   b. Solver
   c. What-If
   d. Goal-Seek

7. The _____ command permanently deletes a selected worksheet.
   a. Clear Sheet
   b. Remove Sheet
   c. Delete Sheet
   d. Clear Contents

8. _____ prevents user from changing the contents of a worksheet.
   a. Locking cells
   b. Protecting a worksheet
   c. Unlocking cells
   d. A password

9. The _____ tool is used to find the value needed in one cell by changing the values in one or more other cells in the worksheet.
   a. Query
   b. Solver
   c. Value Analysis
   d. Look Up

10. The workbook file that receives linked data is called the _____.
    a. source workbook
    b. reference workbook
    c. dependent workbook
    d. external workbook

true/false

Circle the correct answer to the following questions.

1. A Scenario Summary shows the results of all scenarios created for a worksheet.	True	False
2. Templates cannot contain graphics.	True	False
3. Cells you select as variables in Solver must be related through formulas on a worksheet.	True	False
4. You can save a workbook as a template by adding the .xlt extension to the file name.	True	False
5. Solver can produce six types of reports about a solution.	True	False
6. When the worksheet is protected, the contents of locked cells cannot be changed.	True	False

7. A password prevents unauthorized users from viewing or saving changes
to a workbook.   True   False

8. The horizontal window arrangement displays windows side by side.   True   False

9. Whenever data containing an external reference formula are changed
in the dependent workbook, data in the linked cell in the source workbook
are automatically changed as well.   True   False

10. You cannot save different scenarios.   True   False

Concepts

Fill-In questions

Complete the following statements by filling in the blanks with the correct terms.

a. Use _____ to change the settings of a 3-D shape.

b. You can create and save different groups of _____ values.

c. Before protecting a worksheet, _____ those cells whose contents you want to change.

d. The _____ function automatically updates the date and time whenever a worksheet is
recalculated.

e. The cell containing a formula you want to solve is called the _____.

f. The command for the Excel workbook template file extension is _____.

g. You cannot save a workbook as a _____ by typing the file extension .xlt.

h. Once a(n)_____ formula is entered in a worksheet the _____file is automatically
updated if it is open.

i. The _____ dialog box is used to add, delete, and edit scenarios.

j. A _____ prevents unauthorized users from opening a workbook.

Discussion Questions

1. Discuss how templates can be used to make workbook creation easier. What types of templates do
you think would be most helpful, and what should these templates contain?

2. Discuss what happens to formulas that are linked to another workbook when the original
workbook is updated. When would it be appropriate to link data between workbooks?

3. Discuss how Solver and scenarios are used in a worksheet. How can they help with the analysis
of data?

Hands-On Exercises

Step by Step

Nursery Revenue Analysis

★ **1.** The West Side Plant Nursery has a six-month income worksheet that it uses to track the amount of income from different sources. The company would like to create a template that they can use each year to track the information. Your completed worksheet will be similar to the one shown here.

   a. Open the file ex04_West Side Income.

   b. Make a copy of Sheet1. Rename sheet1 **First Six Months** and Sheet 1(2) **Second Six Months**. Add tab colors.

   c. Delete the other blank sheets from the workbook.

   d. Modify the month column labels in the Second Six Months sheet to reflect the last six months of the year.

   e. Add the column label Annual Total in cell I4. Best Fit the column. Change the font color of the new label to light orange. Enter formulas in the Anual total column to calculate the totals for the year.

   f. Extend the worksheet formatting to the new column. Re-center the worksheet titles. Fix the border lines appropriately.

   g. Select both sheets. Select cells A3 and B5 through G11 and unlock the cells. Deselect the selection. Protect both worksheets.

   h. Ungroup the worksheets. Move to cell B5 of the First Six Month sheet.

   i. Save the workbook as a template with the name West Side Income.xlt. Close the workbook. Open the workbook template and enter sample data in both worksheets. Enter the current year in cell A3.

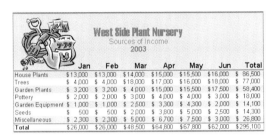

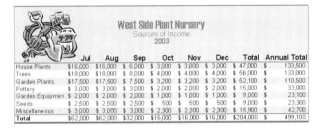

j. Enter your name and the current date using the NOW function in cells A15 and A16, respectively, of both sheets.

k. Preview the workbook. Center the worksheets horizontally. Print the worksheets in landscape orientation, each on a single page.

l. Save the workbook as West Side Income1.xls.

Adventure Travel Tours Revenue Analysis

★ 2. Adventure Travel Tours has begun a new marketing program that emphasizes their tour packages. They expect this campaign to increase the annual income earned in this division by as much as 15 percent over last year's earnings. You have been asked to create a Scenario Summary that analyzes quarterly profits in three scenarios. The company would also like to create a template to allow easy analysis of next year's performance. Your completed worksheets and scenario summary should be similar to those shown here.

a. Open the file ex04_Travel Analysis.

b. Make a copy of Sheet1. Rename sheet1 **Yearly Income** and Sheet1(2) **Projected Income**. Add color to the sheet tabs.

c. Delete the other blank sheets from the workbook.

d. Change the subtitle of the Projected Income Sheet to **Projected Annual Sources of Income**.

e. The company expects to see a total profit margin increase to $6,300,000 (approximately 10 percent of last year's earnings) in the Tour Package category. They have determined that Worst Case increases would be $6,020,000 (5 percent). The Best Case scenario puts the profits at $6,600,000 (15 percent). Use Solver to calculate the quarterly profits needed to achieve these goals. Create a scenario for each case with the appropriate title and comments. Remember to save the original data in the worksheet.

f. Create a Scenario Summary for the total tour packages. Delete the notes below the summary table. Delete the cell references and replace them with the names of the quarters (B7=First Quarter).

g. Add the worksheet title **Tour Packages Scenarios** centered over the Summary table. Change the formatting of the summary to match the other sheets. Print the summary.

Student Name   8/27/02

ADVENTURE TRAVEL
Annual Sources of Income

	1st Qtr	2nd Qtr	3rd Qtr	4th Qtr	Total
Car Rentals	$ 114,650	$ 114,875	$ 116,500	$ 119,145	$ 465,170
Airlines	$ 215,000	$ 218,750	$ 219,995	$ 225,390	$ 879,135
Tour Packages	$ 1,125,530	$ 1,350,655	$ 1,500,675	$ 1,755,850	$ 5,732,710
Hotels	$ 650,000	$ 650,545	$ 695,655	$ 705,115	$ 2,701,315
Total	$ 2,105,180	$ 2,334,825	$ 2,532,825	$ 2,805,500	$ 9,778,330

Student Name   8/27/02

TOUR PACKAGES SCENARIOS

Scenario Summary

Changing Cells:	Current Values:	Expected	Worst Case	Best Case
First Qtr	$ 1,125,530	$ 1,267,353	$ 1,125,530	$ 1,342,353
Second Qtr	$ 1,350,655	$ 1,492,478	$ 1,350,655	$ 1,567,478
Third Qtr	$ 1,500,675	$ 1,642,498	$ 1,500,675	$ 1,717,498
Fourth Qtr	$ 1,755,850	$ 1,897,673	$ 1,755,850	$ 1,972,673
Result Cells:				
Total	$ 5,732,710	$ 6,300,000	$ 5,732,710	$ 6,600,000

h. Move the Summary worksheet to the third tab position. Include your name and the date in a custom header on all sheets. Save the workbook as ATT Revenue Analysis. Print the workbook with the best case values showing centered horizontally in landscape orientation.

i. Because this format will be useful in making projections for next year you want to save it as a template. Delete the data from both worksheets. Delete the Scenario Summary worksheet. Unlock cell B2 and the data entry areas in both sheets. Protect both sheets.

j. Save the workbook as a template with the name ATT Analysis Template. Close the workbook.

k. Open a new workbook using the template. Add the current year to the subtitle line. Copy the best case scenario projected income data from the ATT Revenue Analysis workbook into the yearly Income sheet of the new workbook. Best Fit column F and restore protection.

l. Print the Yearly Income sheet. Save the workbook as ATT Revenue Analysis2.

Personal Budget Analysis

★ ★ **3.** You have just graduated from college, started your first professional job, and purchased a new car and house. With all the new financial obligations you have, you decide to create an annual budget to help you meet your obligations as well as save to purchase new furniture for your home. You estimate your furniture will cost around $4200. You have already started a worksheet containing the labels and the monthly expenses. Your complete budget will be similar to the one shown here.

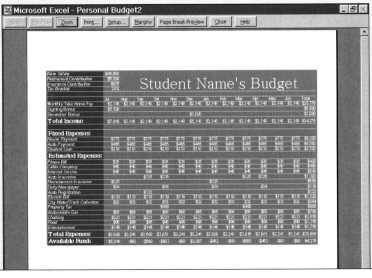

a. Open the file ex04_Personal Budget.

b. Add your name followed by Budget as the title at the top of the worksheet. Center and merge the title over the worksheet. Increase the font size to 14.

c. Calculate and enter the monthly take-home pay in cell B10. Use the formula =(B4-B5-B6-(B4*B7))/12. Copy this value into all the cells of row 10. Your yearly income will be calculated in N10.

d. Calculate the total expenses and available funds for rows 31 and 32.

e. After doing all the calculations, you realize that you are going to be short of funds for this year. Using Solver, reduce the clothing, food, and entertainment expenses to achieve a target value (cell N31) equal to your income. Keep the Solver solution in the worksheet. Looking over the solution, you realize that the values for these three categories are inappropriate and you would never be able to stay on budget. However, you know that, as part of your employment negotiations, you are going to receive a $5,500 signing bonus and a December bonus of $3,000.

f. Insert three rows below the Monthly Take Home Pay row. Label the new rows **Signing Bonus**, **December Bonus**, and **Total Income**. Enter **5,500** in July for the signing bonus and **3,000** in December. Total the income rows.

g. Adjust the formula in row 35 to calculate the new available funds.

h. Use Solver again to calculate the amount you can spend to equal your income. The solution gives you more than enough each month to meet your expenses. However, you would like to calculate a more realistic value for these cells. To do this, restore the original values and solve for $30,000. Keep the Solver solution.

i. Apply fill colors, font colors, and other features of your choice to enhance the worksheet.

j. Save the workbook as Personal Budget2. Print the worksheet in landscape orientation on one page.

University GPA Analysis

★★**4.** You are working in the university's graduation office. As part of your job, you have been asked to create a worksheet comparing college GPA's for the past four years. The school is concerned about inflated GPA's and would like to know what the trend is by major and overall. Additionally, you will create a base and two scenarios for increases in GPA's. Your completed worksheet will be similar to the one shown here.

a. Open the file ex04_School GPA.

b. Move to cell B4 in the Average GPA's worksheet. Enter the formula

`=(Business!B4+Education!B4+'Fine Arts'!B4+Engineering!B4)/4`

to calculate the total freshman class GPA's for the four colleges for 2001.

c. Copy the formula to cells C4 through E4. Then copy the formulas from B4 through E4 to B7 through E7.

d. Enter a formula in cell B8 that calculates the average of cells B4 through B7. Copy the formula through cell E8. Enter a formula that calculates the average of cells B4 through E4 in cell F4. Copy the formula through cell F8.

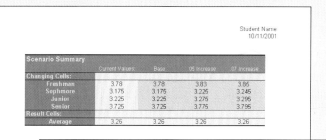

lab exercises

e. Next, you want to calculate the percent change for each class over the four years. Copy the worksheet from cells A1 through F8 to cells A11 through A18. Change the title to **Percent Increase** in cell A11. Delete the 2001 data in B14 through B18.

f. Enter the formula **=(C4-B4)/C4** in cell C14 to calculate the percent change from 2001 to 2002 for the freshman class. Copy the formula to calculate the percentages for the rest of the data.

g. Enter the formula **=(E4-B4)/E4** in cell F14 to calculate the total percent change over the four years. Copy the formula down the column through row 18. Format B14:F18 to display as percents.

h. In cell G2, enter the title **Projected** and, in cell G3, enter **2005**.

i. To calculate a base for your scenario, enter the formula **=E4+(E4*F14)** in cell G4. Copy the formula to cells G5 through G7. Format the column to two decimal places. Calculate the average in G8. Complete the border and color formatting as needed.

j. Create a scenario for the base values. Label this the **Base** scenario and use cells G4 through G7 as your changing cells. Add the comment **Projected GPA based on average for the previous years**. (Choose [OK] when the message to convert formula to fixed values appears.)

k. Create a scenario for a .05 increase and another for a .07 increase. Label and insert comments to the scenarios appropriately. Use the data in the following table for changing the cell values.

.05 Increase	.07 Increase
3.83	3.85
3.225	3.245
3.275	3.295
3.775	3.795

l. Create a Scenario Summary report using cell G8 as the result cell. Delete the note below the report. Add and format a title. Replace the cell references with appropriate labels. Change the text and fill colors to match the other sheets.

m. Add your name and the current date to a header in the Average GPA's worksheet and the Scenario Summary worksheet.

n. Save the workbook as GPA Analysis. Print the Average GPA worksheet showing the scenario values for a .07 percent increase centered horizontally. Print the Scenario Summary worksheet.

Animal Rescue Foundation Contribution Projections

★ ★ **5.** The Animal Rescue Foundation, a nonprofit animal rescue agency, relies on donations to cover all ★ its expenses. You would like to do some analysis on the data and project the amount that will be needed for next year based on scenarios that the committee feels are likely. Your completed income analysis will be similar to the one shown here.

a. Open the file ex04_ARF Contributions to see last year's income.

b. Copy the Fall-Winter sheet to a new sheet and rename the tab for the new sheet Analysis. Delete column H.

c. Merge cells A3 through G3 when you center the new title Analysis and Projections.

d. Enter the labels 2001 Income, 5% Increase, 10% Increase, 10% Decrease, 5% Decrease, and Current Scenario in cells B5 through G5. Adjust the size of the columns to fully display the labels.

e. Enter the reference formula =Spring-Summer!H6+Fall-Winter!H6 in cell B6. Copy the formula down the column to cell B11.

f. Use the number in cell B6 to calculate the values for cells C6 through F6.
Copy the formulas down the columns to row 11.

g. Copy and paste just the values from column B to column G.

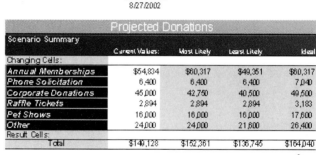

h. Create the following scenarios using cells G6 through G11 as the changing cells and the following calculated values in the worksheet:

Most Likely

Annual Memberships	10% increase
Phone Solicitation	Current
Corporate Donations	5% decrease
Raffle Tickets	Current
Pet Shows	Current
Other	Current

Least Likely

Annual Memberships	10% decrease
Phone Solicitation	Current
Corporate Donations	10% decrease
Raffle Tickets	Current
Pet Shows	Current
Other	10% decrease

Ideal

Annual Memberships	10% increase
Phone Solicitation	10% increase
Corporate Donations	10% increase
Raffle Tickets	10% increase
Pet Shows	10% increase
Other	10% increase

i. Create a Scenario Summary displaying the results for cell G12. Delete the note below the summary report. Change the cell references to appropriate labels.

j. Create a 3-D object that highlights the Ideal scenario in the Scenario Summary worksheet. Add and format a worksheet title.

k. Enter your name and the current date in a header of the Analysis and Scenario Summary worksheets.

l. Print the Analysis worksheet centered horizontally in landscape orientation on one page with the Most Likely scenario displayed. Print the Scenario Summary worksheet centered horizontally in landscape orientation.

m. Save the workbook as ARF Analysis.

Fitness Club Revenue Tracking

★ 1. As the accounting manager of the Lifestyle Fitness Club, you have decided to create a workbook template to track the revenues from memberships, classes, equipment and clothing sales, and special events for each quarter. Create a worksheet for the first quarter with row labels that reflect revenue sources. Include a title and column labels for the months in the first quarter. Calculate totals where appropriate. Copy the worksheet to three other sheets to be used for the next three quarters, and appropriately adjust the column labels and title. Unlock the cells that will be used for value inputs. Enter your name and the current date as a footer for each sheet. Add worksheet protection and save as a template. Use the template to enter sample data in the First Quarter sheet. Save the file as LFC Revenue Analysis and print the worksheet.

LocalNet Growth Projections

★ 2. You have been hired as a consultant by a local internet service provider (ISP) LocalNet, to help the ISP project expected growth over the next five years based on its research. Assume that the company currently has 15 percent of the local market. The current number of customers is 3,500 and available research estimates an increase of 2 percent in year 2; 4 percent in year 3; 7 percent in year 4; and 12 percent in year 5. Create a worksheet that shows the current customer figure and the projected increases for the next five years. Use these numbers to create revenue figures based on a yearly profit of $75 per customer. Create scenarios with the calculated values as the baseline, a 2 percent decrease in customers and revenue per year as the worst case, and an additional 4 percent increase per year as the best case. Create a Scenario Summary report. Create a 3-D object that highlights the best case scenario in the Scenario Summary worksheet. Enter your name and the current date in all the worksheets. Save the file as LocalNet Projections. Print the worksheets.

Spring Break Scenarios

★★ 3. Now that your personal budget is complete, you have decided to do some analysis to determine whether a trip during spring semester break is possible. Use the budget you created in Lab 3, On Your Own, exercise 1, and evaluate your yearly budget to determine whether you will have enough money to pay for a spring break trip next year. Use Solver to determine the number of hours you need to work to earn enough money for the trip in addition to the rest of your expenses. Create three scenarios: one showing the current values, a second showing a 5 percent decrease in entertainment expenses, and a third showing a decrease in one of your other expenses. Create a Scenario Summary. Enter your name and the current date in a header for all the worksheets. Save the file as Spring Break Analysis. Print the worksheets.

Art Department Expense Projections

★ ★ **4.** The College of Fine Arts would like you to use the data you collected in Lab 3, On Your Own,
★ exercise 2, to do some analysis for the coming year. They would like to refurbish one lab and
purchase new equipment for one department. Use the information you collected in the previous
exercise and create three scenarios: one showing the current values, a second showing a 5 percent
decrease in expenses, and a third showing a decrease in another expense category. Create a
Scenario Summary. Enter your name and the current date in a header for all the worksheets. Save
the file as Art Equipment Analysis. Print the worksheets.

Small Business Expansion Projections

★ ★ **5.** You believe the small business you created in Lab 3, On Your Own, exercise 4, could see greater
★ profits with an additional location. Use the information you gathered in the previous workbook
and the Solver to determine what variables would increase profits by 25 percent. Create three
scenarios to determine the effects of a 5 percent, 10 percent, and 15 percent increase in profits in
each quarter on the total yearly profits. Create a Scenario Summary. Add 3-D shapes and use the
NOW function in the summary. Save your file as Expansion Projections. Print the summary.

On the Web

Stock Portfolio Analysis

You have been studying the stock market in your economics class and would like to evaluate a
portfolio of four different stocks. Using the Web or other news source, choose four stocks listed
on the New York Stock Exchange and enter the following information about each stock in
separate sheets of a workbook: stock exchange number, cost per share, brokerage fee, total cost
per share, price/earnings ratio, dividend return percentage, and week-ending price. Track your
stocks (or use historical values) for a month. Create scenarios of good, bad, and expected market
changes in the current month-ending price over the next month. Enter your name and the current
date in headers in the worksheets. Save the file as Stock Analysis. Print the workbook.

Using Data Tables, Creating Macros, and Designing Onscreen Forms

LAB 5

Objectives

After completing this lab, you will know how to:

1.	Use the PMT function.
2.	Use a data table.
3.	Add controls.
4.	Create a macro with the Visual Basic Editor.
5.	Create a macro with the Macro Recorder.
6.	Name a range.
7.	Use the IF function.
8.	Create a form.
9.	Add cell comments.
10.	Document a file.

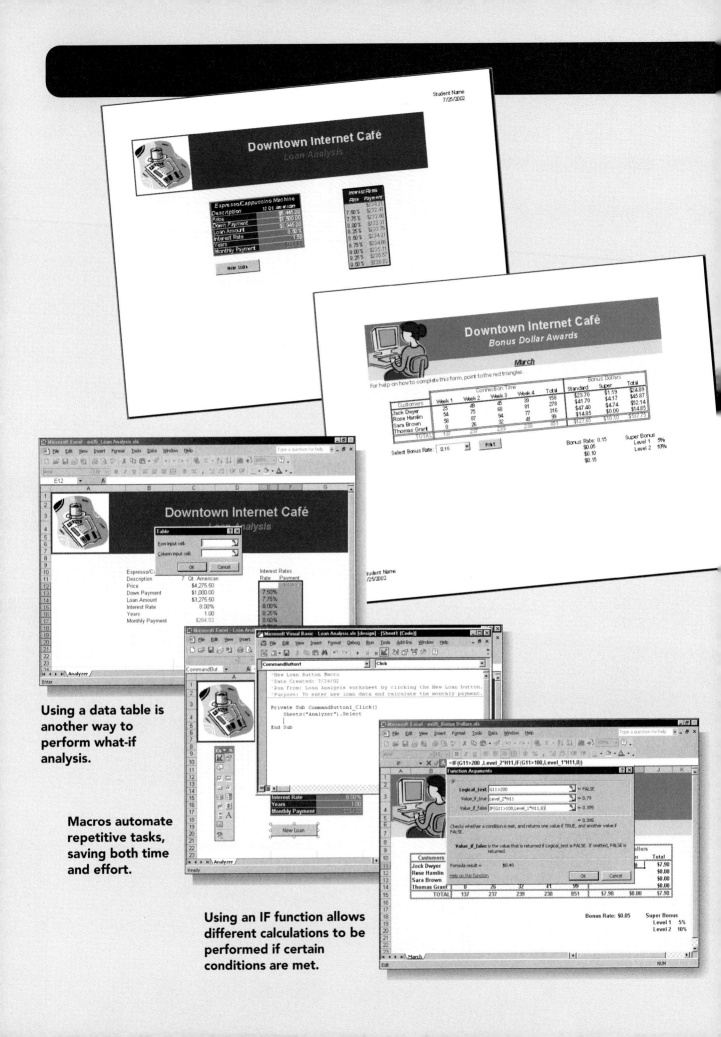

Using a data table is another way to perform what-if analysis.

Macros automate repetitive tasks, saving both time and effort.

Using an IF function allows different calculations to be performed if certain conditions are met.

Downtown Internet Café

Evan, the owner of the Downtown Internet Café, has been impressed with your use of Excel to forecast the café's future through 2002. He has two more projects for you. First, he is considering the purchase of a new espresso/cappuccino machine to replace the current one, which is leased. Evan plans to finance the purchase and would like you to evaluate several different loan options. You will create a loan analysis spreadsheet that incorporates Excel's PMT function, macros, and Data Table feature.

Next, Evan would like you to develop a spreadsheet to calculate and record customer Bonus Dollars. Bonus Dollars are awarded to customers based on their monthly Internet connection-time usage and can be redeemed for more connection time or other merchandise at the café. They are an incentive for customers to extend their stay at the café and, of course, spend more money while they're there. You will create an onscreen form to calculate and record customer Bonus Dollars. The completed loan analysis and Bonus Dollars form are shown on the opposite page.

1	**Data Table**	A data table is a range of cells that is used to quickly calculate multiple what-if versions in one operation and to show the results of all variations together in the worksheet.
2	**Macro**	A macro is a stored series of keystrokes and commands that are executed automatically when the macro is run.
3	**Controls**	Controls are graphic objects that are designed to help the user interact with the worksheet.
4	**Visual Basic Editor**	The Visual Basic Editor is a tool used to write and edit macros attached to Excel workbooks.
5	**Macro Recorder**	The Macro Recorder automatically creates a macro by recording a series of actions as macro commands.
6	**Form**	A form is a formatted worksheet with blank spaces that can be filled in online or on paper.
7	**IF Function**	The IF function checks to see if certain conditions are met and then takes action based on the results of the check.
8	**Comments**	Comments are notes attached to cells that can be used to clarify the meaning of the cell contents, provide documentation, or ask a question.

Calculating a Loan Payment

Evan has researched different kinds of commercial espresso/cappuccino machines and would like to see an analysis of what the monthly loan payments would be for different down payments, interest rates, and repayment periods for each kind. You have already started to create the analysis by entering some descriptive labels and formats in a worksheet. You will open the workbook file and continue to work on the loan analysis.

1 ● **Start Excel and open the workbook file** ex05_Loan Analysis.

● **If necessary, maximize the application and worksheet windows.**

Your screen should be similar to Figure 5.1

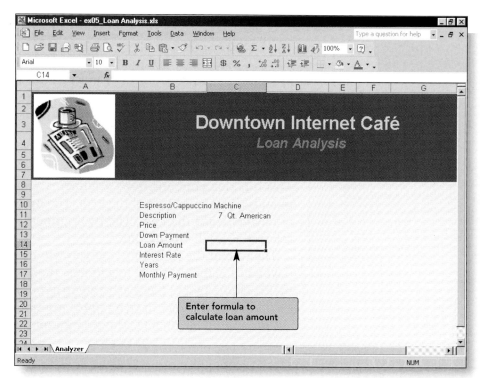

Figure 5.1

Much of the structure and formatting for the worksheet has already been completed. To continue to create the worksheet, you need to enter a formula to calculate the loan amount. The amount of the loan is the price of the item minus the down payment. Then you will enter the data for the first espresso/cappuccino machine Evan is considering.

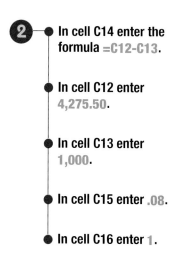

2 ● **In cell C14 enter the formula** =C12-C13.

● **In cell C12 enter** 4,275.50.

● **In cell C13 enter** 1,000.

● **In cell C15 enter** .08.

● **In cell C16 enter** 1.

Your screen should be similar to Figure 5.2

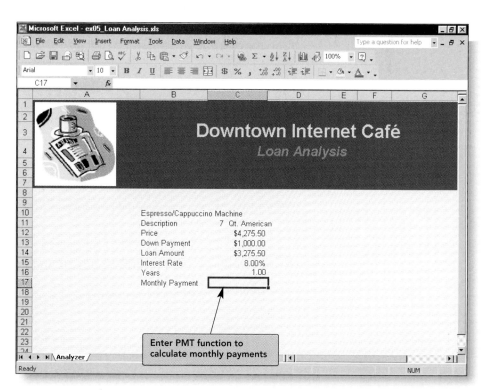

Figure 5.2

Using the PMT Function

The next thing that needs to be entered is the monthly payment. To calculate this value, you use the PMT function. The PMT function calculates a periodic payment on a loan. The value returned includes the loan amount and interest but no taxes, reserve payments, or fees sometimes associated with loans. The PMT function uses the following syntax:

PMT(rate, nper, pv)

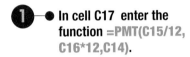

Additional Information

When using the PMT function, it is important to use consistent units for specifying rate and nper.

This function contains three arguments: rate, nper, and pv. The **rate** argument is the interest rate of the loan. The **nper** argument is the total number of payments for the loan. The **pv** argument is the amount of the loan, also referred to as the **principal**.

The rate in the PMT function you will use to calculate the monthly loan payment for the espresso machine is the yearly interest rate (C15) divided by 12. This converts the yearly rate to a monthly rate. The nper argument is the length of the loan in years (C16) multiplied by 12 to calculate the number of monthly payments. The pv argument is the loan amount in cell C14.

1 ● **In cell C17 enter the function =PMT(C15/12, C16*12,C14).**

HAVING TROUBLE?

You can use the Insert Function feature to help enter this function.

Your screen should be similar to Figure 5.3

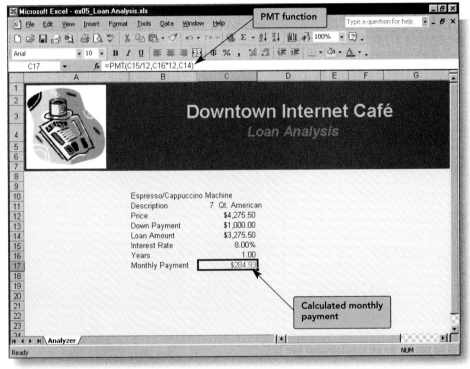

Figure 5.3

Excel calculates the monthly payment and displays it in cell C17.

Using a Data Table

You used an 8 percent interest rate to calculate the loan payments for the espresso/cappuccino machine, but you are aware that interest rates will vary, depending on which loan institution finances the purchase and when the loan is obtained. Therefore, you want to set up a data table that shows the effect of different interest rates on the monthly loan payment amount.

concept 1

Data Table

1 A **data table** is a range of cells that is used to quickly calculate multiple what-if versions in one operation and to show the results of all variations together in the worksheet. Data tables perform a type of what-if analysis in which one or more variables are changed to see the effect on the formulas that include these variables.

Espresso/Cappuccino Machine Description	
Price	$4,275.50
Down Payment	$1,000.00
Loan Amount	$3,275.50
Interest Rate	8.00%
Years	1.00
Monthly Payment	$284.93

One-variable Table Varying Interest Rates Only	
	$284.93
7.50%	$284.17
7.75%	$284.55
8.00%	$284.93
8.25%	$285.31
8.50%	$285.69
8.75%	$286.07
9.00%	$286.45
9.25%	$286.83
9.50%	$287.21

Two-variable Table Varying Interest Rates and Length of Loan			
$284.93	1.50	3.00	4.00
7.50%	$192.97	$101.89	$79.20
7.75%	$193.34	$102.26	$79.58
8.00%	$193.71	$102.64	$79.96
8.25%	$194.09	$103.02	$80.35
8.50%	$194.46	$103.40	$80.74
8.75%	$194.84	$103.78	$81.12
9.00%	$195.21	$104.16	$81.51
9.25%	$195.59	$104.54	$81.90
9.50%	$195.96	$104.92	$82.29

A **one-variable data table** can contain one or more formulas, and each formula refers to one input cell. An **input cell** is a cell in which a list of values is substituted to see the resulting effect on the related formulas. Input values can be listed down a column (**column-oriented**) or across a row (**row-oriented**).

A **two-variable data table** uses only one formula that refers to two different input cells, one column-oriented and one row-oriented. The purpose of this table is to show the resulting effect on the formula when the values in both of these cells are changed.

Creating a One-Variable Data Table

Since you are interested in seeing the effects of changing the interest rate only, you will create a one-variable data table. When designing a one-way data table, the input values and formulas must be in contiguous rows or columns. First, you need to set up the data table in an unused portion of the worksheet by entering a title and column headings and a series of interest rate percentages.

1

- In cell E10 enter the title **Interest Rates**.

- In cell E11 enter the column heading **Rate** and in cell F11 enter **Payment**.

- In cell E13 enter **7.5%** and in cell E14 enter **7.75%**.

- Select the range E13 through E14 and drag the fill handle through cell E21.

    Your screen should be similar to Figure 5.4

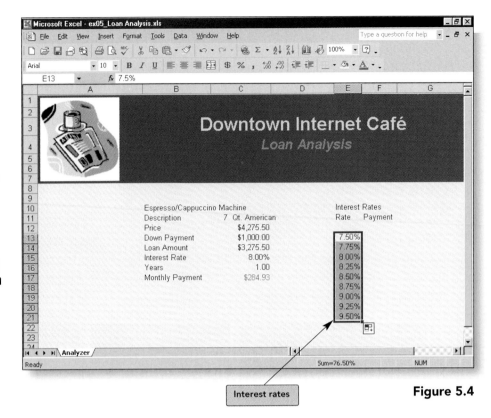

Interest rates

Figure 5.4

Dragging the fill handle filled column E with interest rates that range from 7.5 percent to 9.5 percent in 0.25 percent increments.

Next, you enter the monthly payment formula to be used in calculating the various payments in cell F12. The formula is always entered in the row above the first input value and one cell to the right of the column of values. Rather than just copying this formula from the monthly payment cell in the loan analysis section of the worksheet, you will define the new formula as equal to that cell. This way, the data table formula will be automatically updated if the original formula (the one in the loan analysis section of the worksheet) is changed.

Additional Information

If the input values are listed across the row, the formula is entered in the column to the left of the first value and one cell below the row of values.

2 ● **In cell F12 enter =C17.**

Your screen should be similar to Figure 5.5

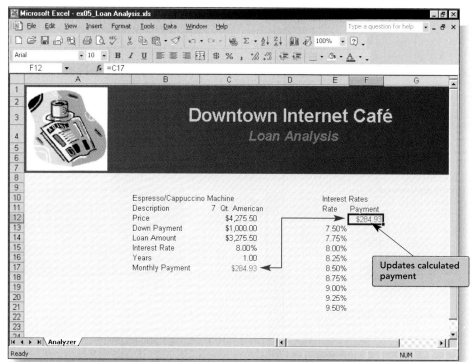

Figure 5.5

Finally, you need to define the range of cells that comprise the data table. In this case, the data table range consists of all cells except the ones containing the title and headings.

3 ● **Select the range E12 through F21.**

● **Choose Data/Table.**

Your screen should be similar to Figure 5.6

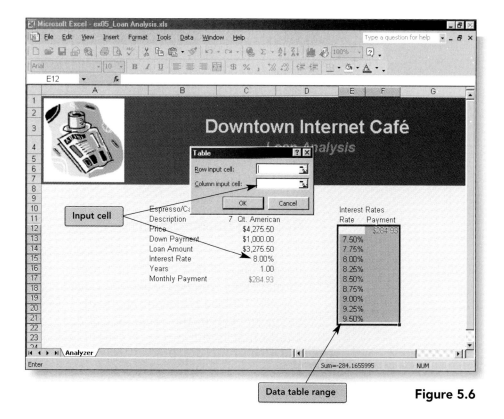

Figure 5.6

You use the Table dialog box to define the input cell in which values from the data table are substituted. Because the values in the data table are listed down a column, the input cell is entered as a Column Input Cell. In this case, the input cell is cell C15, the Interest Rate cell from the loan analysis section of the worksheet.

4 ● **Enter C15 in the Column Input Cell text box.**

Another Method
You can also define the input cell by reducing the dialog box and selecting the input cell in the worksheet.

● **Click** [OK] **.**

● **Deselect the table.**

Your screen should be similar to Figure 5.7

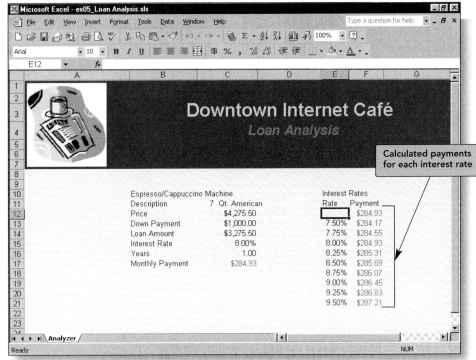

Figure 5.7

The data table shows the calculated monthly payments for each interest rate.

Automatically Formatting Worksheet Data

To quickly improve the appearance of the worksheet, you will apply an autoformat to the worksheet data and data table. An **autoformat** is a built-in combination of formats that can be applied to a range of cells. The autoformats consist of a combination of number formats, fonts and attributes, colors, patterns, borders, frames, and alignment settings.

Applying an Autoformat

To use an autoformat, you first specify the range you want affected by the formatting. In this case, you want to apply an autoformat to cells B10 through C17. You can select the range or you can let Excel select the range for you. To have Excel automatically select the range, the cell selector must be on any cell in the range. Excel determines that the range you want to autoformat is the range of cells that includes the active cell and is surrounded by blank cells.

1 ● **Move to any cell in the worksheet data.**

● **Choose Format/AutoFormat**

Your screen should be similar to Figure 5.8

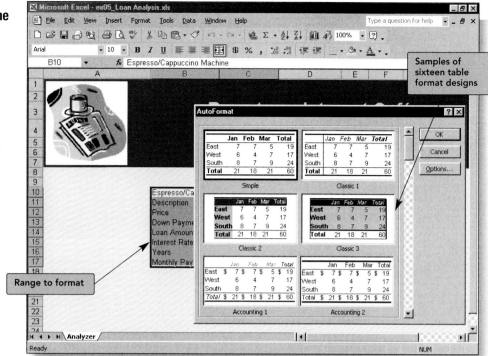

Figure 5.8

Additional Information

Use the None table format (located at the bottom of the list) to remove an existing AutoFormat.

The range B10 through C17 is correctly selected as the range to format. The AutoFormat dialog box displays samples of the sixteen different table format designs with the names assigned to the design below the sample.

You decide the Colorful 1 table format would be appropriate for the data.

2 ● **Scroll the list and select Colorful 1.**

● **Click** OK .

Your screen should be similar to Figure 5.9

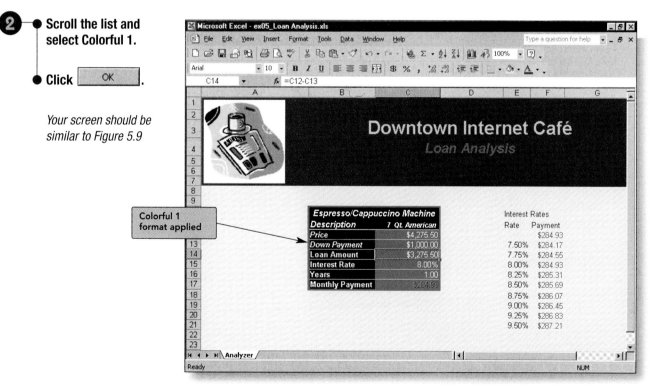

Figure 5.9

The Colorful 1 AutoFormat has been applied to the worksheet range. This format includes borderlines, fill and font colors, and adjustment of column widths to fit the entries in the selected range.

3 ● **Format the data table in cells E10 through F21 to the Classic 3 AutoFormat.**

● **Save the workbook as Loan Analysis.**

Your screen should be similar to Figure 5.10

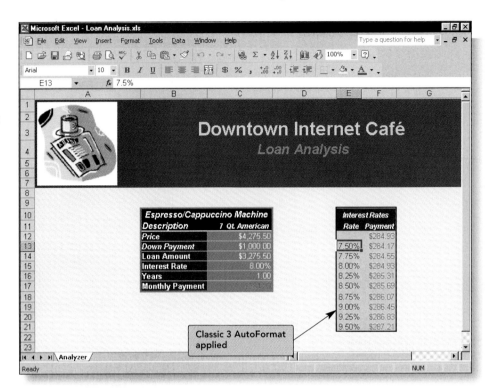

Figure 5.10

Automating Tasks with Macros

You now have the analysis worksheet for the espresso/cappuccino machine that Evan requested with a data table that calculates different interest rates for the loan. After showing the worksheet to Evan, he says he would like to see the same loan analysis applied to other espresso/cappuccino machines he is currently considering. He also wants to use it for other purchases he is considering.

Rather than enter the loan information for each item in the worksheet, you decide to create a macro that will automate the data entry process.

2 A **macro** is a stored series of keystrokes and commands. When the macro is executed, or **run**, the stored actions are performed automatically. Macros are very useful for replacing a series of commands that are performed repeatedly. Instead of performing the same actions every time you need to perform a task, you use the macro, which performs the task automatically for you.

Some macros are very simple and are merely a duplicate of a series of keystrokes. For exam-

ple, a macro can be written that selects a range of cells. A more complex macro may perform a command, such as copying data from one cell to another or changing column widths. Even more complex macros can be written that let you create customized functions that combine math expressions, Excel functions, and programming code to perform special calculations. Other macros can be used to create your own customized menus and dialog boxes.

A macro for your loan analysis worksheet will not only help you enter the information, but will also come in handy if someone else needs to use this worksheet to enter loan information, especially if that person does not know what cells to select in order to obtain the necessary data.

Changing the Macro Security Level

When a workbook contains macros, a macro virus warning may be displayed when the file is opened advising you that macros are detected and asking you to confirm that you want them enabled. This is because macros can contain viruses that may adversely affect your system. As a protection, Excel includes three security levels—high, medium and low.

1 ● Choose **Tools/Macro/Security**

Your screen should be similar to Figure 5.11

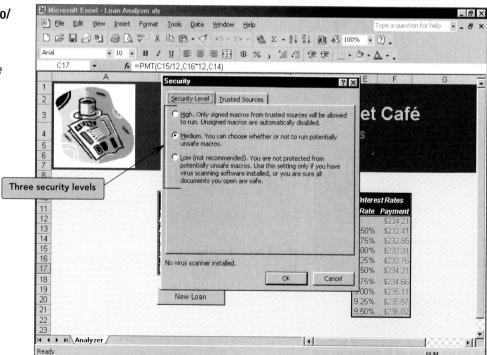

Three security levels

Figure 5.11

Initially, the security level is set to medium. Changing the setting to High provides the greatest amount of protection. This setting automatically disables macros if they are not digitally signed. A **digital signature** is an electronic encryption-based stamp of authentication that confirms the macro or document originated from the signer and has not been changed. The current security level, Medium, allows the user to decide to enable or disable unsigned macros. This is an appropriate level for this workbook.

2 ● If necessary, change the security level to <u>M</u>edium.

● Click 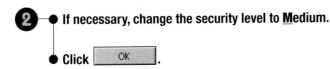 .

Creating a Command Button

One of the most common ways to run a macro is to create a command button in the worksheet that, when clicked, runs the macro instructions. You will create the command button before creating the macro so that the macro instructions can be assigned to the button. A command button is one of many different controls that can be added to a worksheet.

concept 3

Controls

3   **Controls** are graphic objects that are designed to help the user interact with the worksheet. They can be used to display or enter data, perform an action, or make the sheet easier to read. Controls include property settings that affect how they behave and work. The properties associated with many controls can be changed to customize the control for your own use. Examples of controls are check boxes, list boxes, option buttons, and command buttons.

    Excel includes two ways to add controls to a worksheet: the Forms toolbar or the Control Toolbox toolbar. The controls on the Forms toolbar are for use with existing Excel macros and work best on worksheets that will be used only in Excel. The Control Toolbox controls are ActiveX controls that allow you to make the controls "active" by writing a macro using Microsoft Visual Basic or scripts in Microsoft Script Editor that customize the behavior of the control. The Control Toolbox controls are for when the worksheet will be used in interaction with other Office programs or on an Internet location.

You decide to create the command button using the Control Toolbox.

1
- Display the Control Toolbox toolbar and move it into column A.
- Click ☐ Command Button.
- Click on cell B19 to create the button.
- Move and size the command button to cover cells B19 and B20.

Your screen should be similar to Figure 5.12

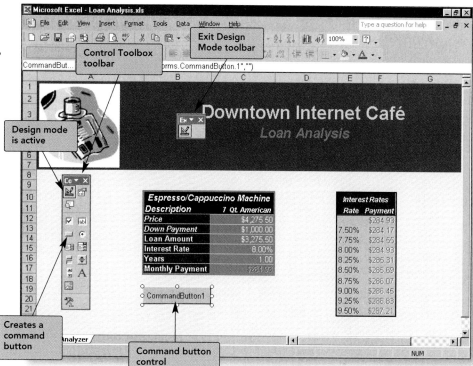

Figure 5.12

When you first create a control, Excel automatically changes to design mode so that you can modify the control. The Exit Design mode toolbar is automatically displayed. The first thing you need to do is change the default button name to a more descriptive name.

2
- Right-click the command button to open the shortcut menu.
- Choose CommandButton Object/Edit.
- Select the default button name and replace it with New Loan.
- Click outside the button object to deselect it.

Additional Information

You can also change a command button's font attributes by selecting Properties from the button's shortcut menu and selecting font and color settings.

Your screen should be similar to Figure 5.13

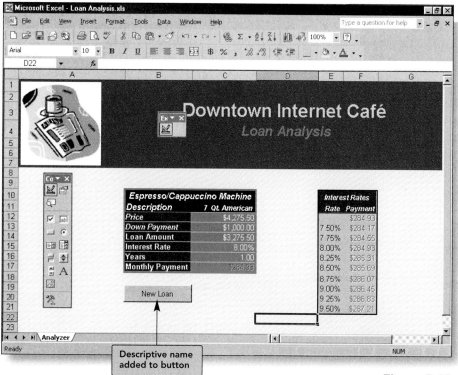

Figure 5.13

Create a Macro Using the Visual Basic Editor

After creating the command button, you use the Visual Basic Editor to create the macro instructions to automate the process of entering the new loan data.

concept 4

Visual Basic Editor

4 The **Visual Basic Editor** is an application used to write and edit macros attached to Excel workbooks. Although Visual Basic is a programming language, you can enter information into the Visual Basic Editor just as you would in a word processor—by typing to enter text, pressing ←Enter to end a line, using the arrow keys to move around the screen, and pressing Delete and Backspace to remove and correct text.

The types of information you enter into the Visual Basic Editor are called **statements**. A statement is a complete instruction that tells Excel to execute a specific task. A series of statements is a **Sub procedure**. A Sub procedure begins with a statement that starts the macro (when the command button is pressed) and ends with one that closes the macro (an End Sub statement). Sub procedures can also include remarks about the macro (such as its name and

purpose) and functions (such as returning values to the procedure).

The **syntax**, or rules of grammar of a Sub procedure statement, is as follows:

Object ("x").Property

The **object** is the item that the statement will affect (such as a cell, cell range, worksheet, or workbook). The object is enclosed in parentheses and surrounded by quotes.

The **property** is the action you want to perform on the object. The property consists of reserved words that have special meaning and direct Excel to perform the specified action. The object is separated from the property by a period. For example, the statement to tell Excel to select the range C2 through C10 is:

Range("C2:C10").Select

It is very important to plan a macro before creating it to ensure that the Visual Basic statements are in the exact order in which you want them to be executed. It is often helpful to write out the macro steps and then try them out manually in Excel before entering them in the Visual Basic Editor. You want this macro to perform the following actions:

1. Make the Analyzer sheet active.

2. Clear the cell ranges C11 through C15.

3. Display an input box that describes the information to be entered in cells C11, C12, C13, C15, and C16.

4. Move to cell C17.

Now you are ready to start the Visual Basic Editor and create the command button macro.

1

- **Double-click the New Loan command button.**

- **If necessary, close the Project Explorer window along the left side of the Visual Basic window and maximize the Code window on the right.**

Your screen should be similar to Figure 5.14

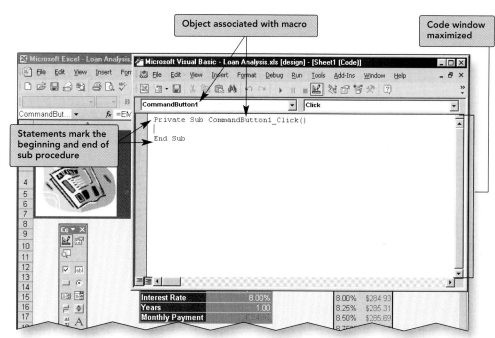

Figure 5.14

Additional Information

"Sub" is an abbreviation for "Sub procedure."

The Code window is used to write, display and edit the macro statements or code. It already contains the Sub and End Sub statements for the command button macro. You will enter the macro statements between the Sub statements. First, however, you want to include several **remark statements** that describe the macro and include overall procedural documentation. Remark statements always begin with an apostrophe, which tells Excel to ignore the information on that line.

2

- **Enter a blank line above the Private Sub line in the window.**

- **Type 'New Loan Button Macro on the newly inserted blank line.**

- **Press ←Enter.**

HAVING TROUBLE?

If you forgot to enter the apostrophe, a Compile error message is displayed. Click ⟨ OK ⟩ to clear the message and edit the line.

Your screen should be similar to Figure 5.15

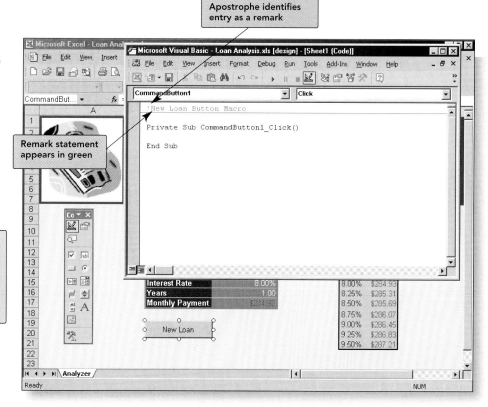

Figure 5.15

Remark lines generally appear in green type to distinguish them from the procedure statements.

3 ● **In the same manner, enter the following three additional remarks:**

'Date Created: today's date

'Run From: Loan Analysis worksheet by clicking the New Loan button.

'Purpose: To enter new loan data and calculate the monthly payment.

HAVING TROUBLE?
Remember to begin each remark statement with an apostrophe and press ⏎Enter to move to the next line.

Your screen should be similar to Figure 5.16

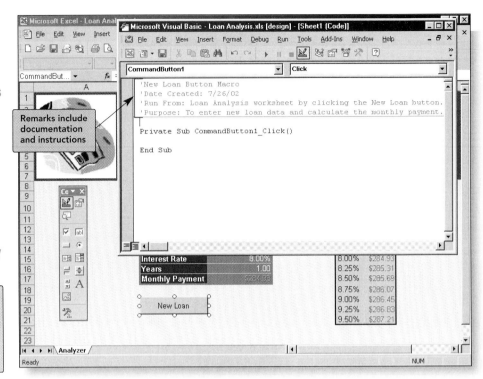

Remarks include documentation and instructions

Figure 5.16

Next, you will enter the Sub procedure statements. To differentiate the Sub statements from the rest of the code, you should indent them using [Tab↹]. Once you indent the first Sub statement line, the subsequent lines are automatically indented the same number of spaces. As you are typing, the Visual Basic Editor displays a list of acceptable statement properties. You can select the property you want from the list or continue typing it yourself. Additionally, the first letter of reserved words that are not inside parentheses will be automatically capitalized.

4 ● **Move the insertion point to the blank line between the Private Sub and End Sub statements.**

● **Press** Tab⇥.

● **Type** Sheets("Analyzer"). Select.

● **Press** ↵Enter.

HAVING TROUBLE?
If a Visual Basic statement is not entered using the correct syntax, an error message box is displayed and the error is identified in red. You must correct the error before you can move to the next line.

Your screen should be similar to Figure 5.17

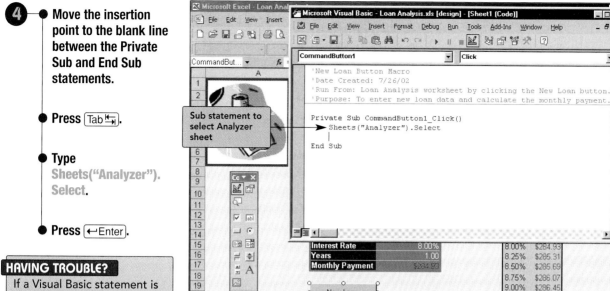

Figure 5.17

You will continue entering the Visual Basic statements. The reserved word "InputBox" instructs Excel to display a box containing instructions on how to enter the data. The text in parentheses following InputBox is the text that will appear when the InputBox is displayed. You will also include an "Enter" statement that allows the user to Press ↵Enter as an alternative to clicking ▢ OK ▢. To save time, you can copy the statements and then edit them. You can also type cell references and reserved words in lowercase. Reserved words are automatically capitalized and extra spaces are removed.

⑤──● In the same manner, enter the following Sub statements each on separate lines:

Range("C11:C13").Select

Selection.ClearContents

Range("C15:C16").Select

Selection.ClearContents

Range("C11").Value = InputBox("Enter the type of machine.", "Enter")

Range("C12").Value = InputBox("Enter the price.", "Enter")

Range("C13").Value = InputBox("Enter the down payment.", "Enter")

Range("C15").Value = InputBox("Enter the interest rate.", "Enter")

Range("C16").Value = InputBox("Enter the number of years to repay the loan.", "Enter")

Range("C17").Select

Your screen should be
similar to Figure 5.18

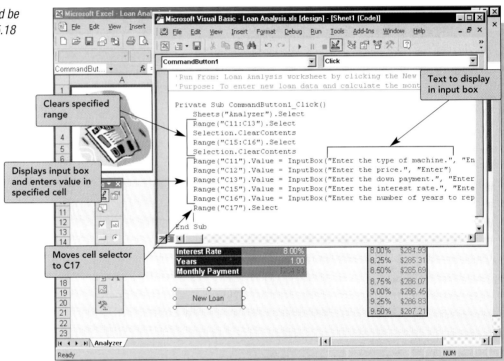

Figure 5.18

You are finished creating the command button macro. You will close the Visual Basic window and return to the worksheet to try out the command button. Before testing a new macro, it is a good idea to save the workbook file first in case the macro performs some unexpected actions.

6 ● **Click** ⊠ **Close (in the title bar of the Visual Basic window).**

Another Method

The menu equivalent is File/Close and Return to Microsoft Excel. The keyboard shortcut is Alt + Q.

● **If necessary, maximize the Excel window.**

● **Click** 📝 **Exit Design Mode on the Control Toolbox toolbar.**

● **Close the Control Toolbox toolbar.**

● **Save the workbook as Loan Analyzer.**

Your screen should be similar to Figure 5.19

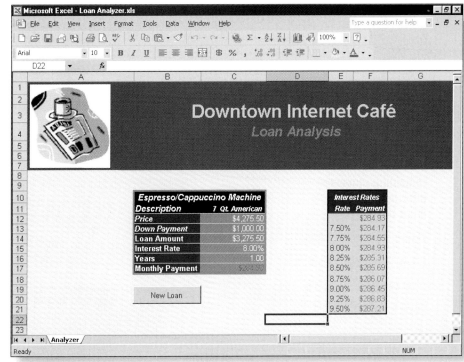

Figure 5.19

Running the Macro

The next step is to test the macro by clicking on the command button to run it. You will enter new loan information for another coffee machine that Evan is considering. The machine is 12 Qt. American that costs $5,445. Evan plans to make a down payment of $1,500 and to borrow the rest at 8.5 percent for 1.5 years.

1 ● **Click the New Loan command button.**

● **Type 12 Qt. American in the input box.**

Additional Information

You can interrupt the execution of a macro at any time by pressing Esc.

Your screen should be similar to Figure 5.20

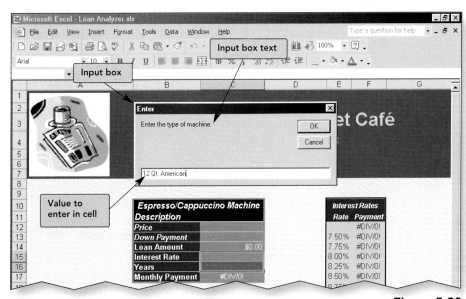

Figure 5.20

You can complete the entry by pressing [←Enter] or clicking [OK]. Since your hands are already on the keyboard, it is quicker to press [←Enter]. As you complete the entry, it is displayed in the appropriate worksheet cell. You will continue entering the remaining information in the input boxes.

2 ● **Press** [←Enter].

● **Using the following information, enter the remaining requested information in the input boxes.**

Price: 5445

Down Payment: 1500

Interest Rate: 8.5%

Loan Length: 1.5

HAVING TROUBLE?
Enter the interest rate as 8.5% or .085.

HAVING TROUBLE?
If your macro did not run correctly, you will need to correct or debug any statement errors.

Your screen should be similar to Figure 5.21

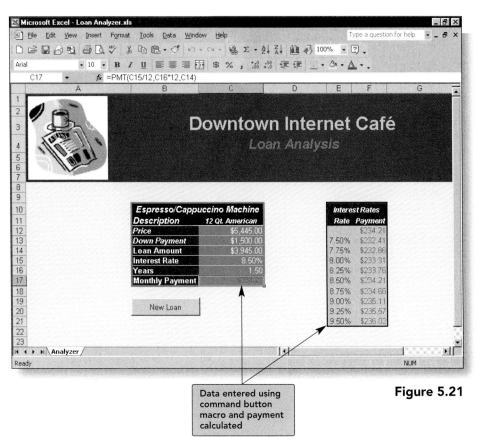

Data entered using command button macro and payment calculated

Figure 5.21

The worksheet now shows the loan analysis for the new set of information. Notice that the data table has also been recalculated based on the new monthly payment.

Using the Macro Recorder

Next, you want to create a macro that will print the worksheet. Instead of entering the Visual Basic instructions manually, you will use the Macro Recorder.

concept 5

5 The **Macro Recorder** automatically creates a macro by recording a series of actions as macro commands. When the recorder is on, Excel automatically records every action you perform and stores it as a Visual Basic statement. You can then easily select the recorded macro by name and play it back, or execute it, as often as you like.

The Macro Recorder method of creating macros is much easier than the Visual Basic

Editor method, and both types of macros can be viewed and changed via the editor. However, it is recommended that the Macro Recorder method be used for short procedures only (such as basic worksheet functions like formatting and printing), because it can be difficult to decipher and troubleshoot complex Visual Basic statements after they have been recorded.

Additional Information

The worksheet will print when you are finished recording the macro, so make any needed printer setup preparations before you begin.

You will use Macro Recorder to create a separate macro that prints the worksheet in landscape orientation.

1 ● **Choose Tools/Macro/Record New Macro.**

Your screen should be similar to Figure 5.22

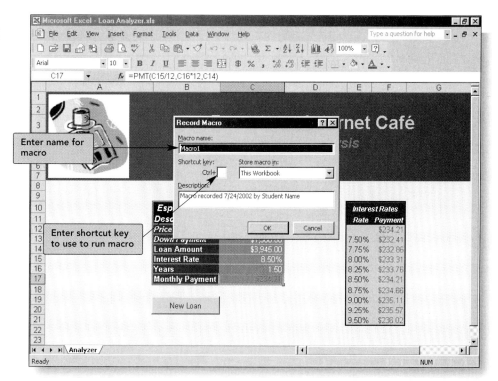

Figure 5.22

You use the Record Macro dialog box to name the macro, assign a shortcut key that will start the macro, select a location where it will be stored if other than in the active workbook, enter a description of the macro, and start the recording. You decide to name your macro PrintAnalysis and assign a shortcut key of Ctrl + ⇧Shift + P to it. You will leave the rest of the selections as they are.

2 ● Type PrintAnalysis in the Macro name box.

● Click in the Shortcut Key text box.

● Hold down ⇧Shift and type P.

● Click OK .

Your screen should be similar to Figure 5.23

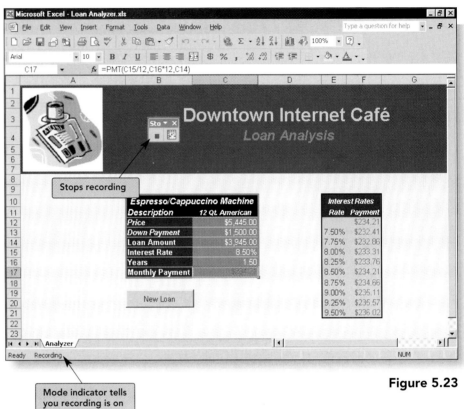

Figure 5.23

Stops recording

Mode indicator tells you recording is on

The message "Recording" is displayed in the status bar and the Stop Recording toolbar appears. Now any action you perform will be recorded as a macro.

3 • Choose **F**ile/Page
Set**u**p.

• Open the Page tab.

• Select **L**andscape.

• Open the
Header/Footer tab.

• Click [**C**ustom Header...].

• In the **R**ight section
enter *your name*.

• Press [←Enter].

• Type the current date.

• Click [OK].

• Click [Prin**t**...].

• Click [OK].

• Click [■] Stop Recording.

Another Method

The menu equivalent is
Tools/**M**acro/**S**top Recording.

*Your printed worksheet
should be similar to that
shown here.*

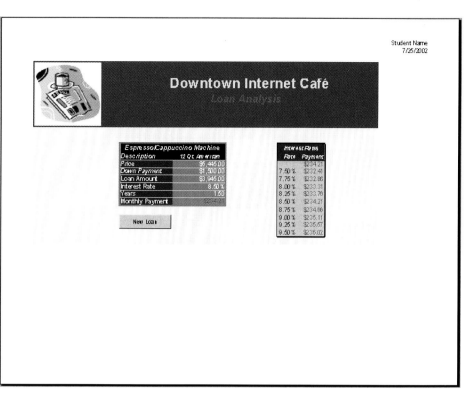

Editing a Macro

Sometimes, after recording a macro, you may want to change or customize it. You will look at the macro statements for the macro that was just recorded.

1 ● Choose **Tools/Macro/Macros**.

> **Another Method**
> The keyboard shortcut is [Alt] + [F8].

● Select **PrintAnalysis**.

● Click [Edit].

> **Additional Information**
> You can delete a macro by selecting it and clicking [Delete].

Your screen should be similar to Figure 5.24

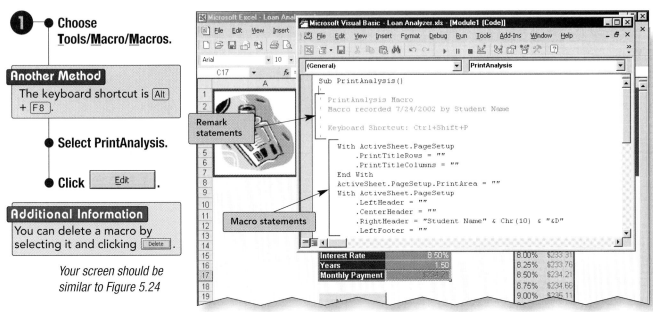

Figure 5.24

The Visual Basic code window for the selected macro is displayed. It contains the recorded macro statements for all settings that are on by default in the page setup dialog box as well as those you changed. You can edit the macro statements just as you did when creating the command button macro. In this case, you want to add a remark statement about the purpose of the macro to the documentation. Notice that there are several blank lines that begin with an apostrophe. These are predefined as remark lines and you do not need to type the apostrophe when adding text to the line.

2 ● On the blank line above the Keyboard Shortcut line, type **Purpose: Prints the loan analysis.**

Your screen should be similar to Figure 5.25

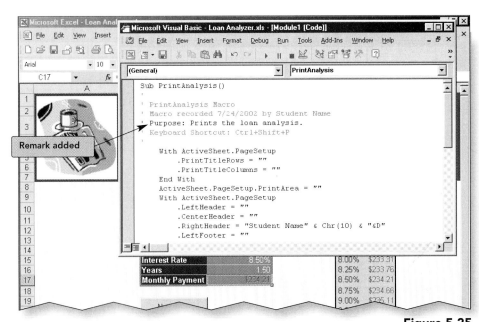

Figure 5.25

Lab 5: Using Data Tables, Creating Macros, and Designing Onscreen Forms

You will test the macro next by executing it with the shortcut key you assigned.

Additional Information

You can also run the macro from within Visual Basic Editor using Run/Run Sub/UserForm or F5.

3 ● **Close the Visual Basic window.**

● **Save the workbook again.**

● **Press** Ctrl + ⇧ Shift + P.

Additional Information

The worksheet blinks while the macro is in progress.

Another Method

The menu equivalent is Tools/ Macro/Macros/PrintAnalysis/ Run.

● **Close (and save if needed) the workbook.**

The macro was executed, and the worksheet is printed a second time in landscape orientation.

Creating a Form

Your second project is to create a form that records customer monthly connection times and calculates Bonus Dollars earned by each customer. Bonus Dollars are awarded to customers based on their monthly connection time use and can be applied toward any other purchases at the Café.

concept 6

Form

6 A **form** is a formatted worksheet with blank spaces that can be filled in online on an individual computer or on a network, or printed and completed on paper. The steps in creating a form are the same for both purposes. However, certain elements are more appropriate for one than for the other. For example, color and shading are more effective on online forms, while simplicity of design and layout is very important in printed forms. In addition, online forms can contain formulas that immediately calculate results such as totals, whereas printed forms would need to include blank spaces where the calculations would be entered manually.

The first step when creating a form is to decide what should appear on the form and what information will be entered into the form. When customers sign on to the computers, they enter their names, and the system tracks the time between sign-on and sign-off. Obtaining connection times for each customer is just a matter of checking the computers' logs. The Bonus Dollar form needs to be designed to accept input of customer connection times and to calculate Bonus Dollars earned. Although Evan wants the form to be electronic, he also wants to be able to print it out for reference.

You have already started designing the form by entering much of the text, many of the formulas, some formatting to improve the appearance, and some sample data. To see what has been done so far,

1 ● **Open the workbook file** ex05_Bonus Dollars.

● **If necessary, maximize the worksheet.**

Your screen should be similar to Figure 5.26

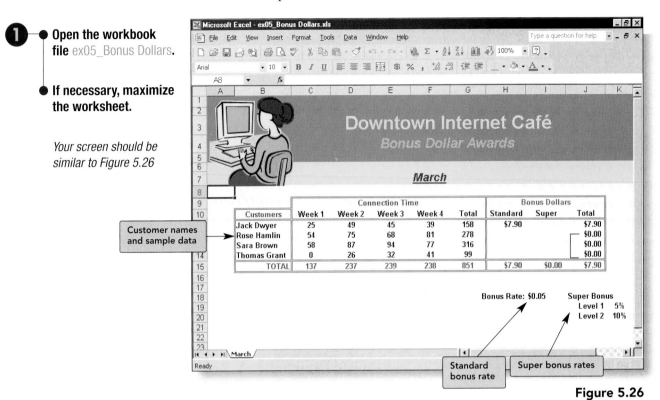

Figure 5.26

The worksheet displays the names of four customers and their connection time in minutes for each week in columns C through F.

The last three columns will be used to calculate and display customer Bonus Dollars. The Downtown Internet Café awards Bonus Dollars based on total connection time. A Standard Bonus is applied to every customer at a rate of $.05 per minute of connection time. An additional Super Bonus is awarded at two different levels for those customers who stay connected more than 100 minutes. The bonus awards are explained in the following table.

Bonus	Award
Standard Bonus	Total connection time multiplied by $.05
Super Bonus Level 1	If total connection time is greater than 100 minutes but less than or equal to 200 minutes, Standard Bonus + 5%
Super Bonus Level 2	If total connection time is greater than 200 minutes, Standard Bonus + 10%

Naming Ranges

The formula to calculate the Standard Bonus for Jack Dwyer has already been entered.

1 Move to H11.

Your screen should be similar to Figure 5.27

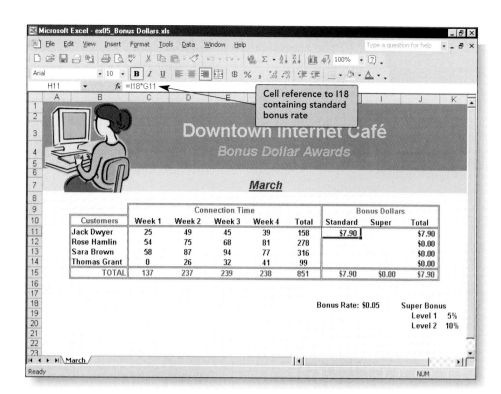

Cell reference to I18 containing standard bonus rate

Figure 5.27

The formula references cell I18. This cell contains the Standard Bonus rate amount of $.05 per minute. To make the formula easier to read and understand, you will assign a name to this cell. A **name** is a description of a cell or range of cells that can be used in place of cell references. The name can be used any time a cell or range is requested as part of a command or in a formula or function.

2 Move to I18.

• Choose
Insert/Name/Define.

Your screen should be similar to Figure 5.28

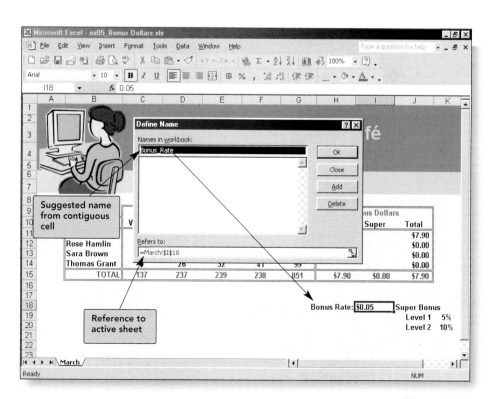

Suggested name from contiguous cell

Reference to active sheet

Figure 5.28

The Define Name dialog box is used to name, modify, and delete range names. In the Names in workbook text box, Excel has proposed the name Bonus_Rate. Excel automatically proposes a name for the cell or range using the contents of the active cell if it contains text, or the cell above or to the left of the active cell if the active cell does not contain text. If none of the proposed names is appropriate, you can name the range by typing the name into the text box. In this case, the proposed name is the contents of the cell to the left of the active cell. Excel replaced the blank space between the words with an underline character.

The Refers To text box displays the reference for the active cell. The reference includes the sheet name and cell reference. By default Excel makes named cell references absolute. The Names in workbook list box is empty because this worksheet does not contain any names yet. In this case, both the name and the cell reference are acceptable.

3 ● Click [OK] .

Your screen should be similar to Figure 5.29

Name box displays range name rather than cell reference

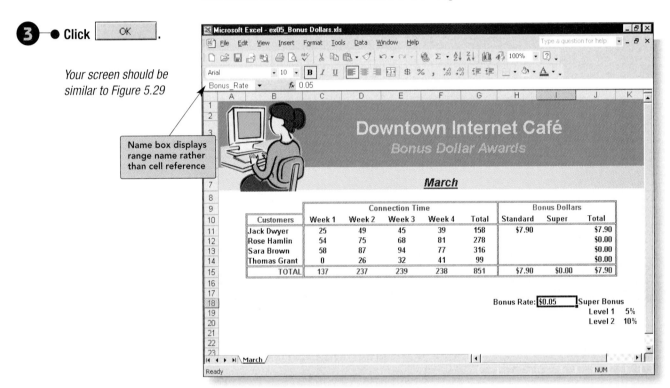

Figure 5.29

In place of the cell reference in the Name box of the formula bar, the range name is displayed.

Now you need to replace the cell reference in the formula in cell H11 with the name.

4 ● Move to H11.

● Change to Edit mode.

● Select (highlight) the cell reference I18 in the formula.

● Choose Insert/Name/Paste.

Your screen should be similar to Figure 5.30

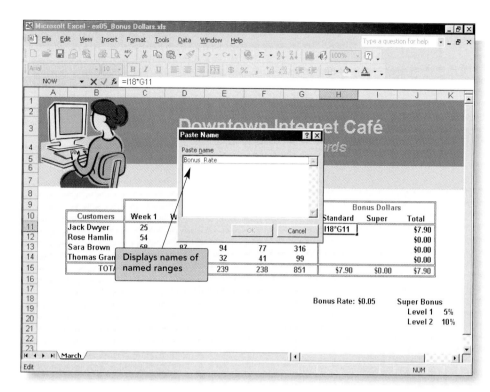

Figure 5.30

From the Paste Name dialog box you select the range name you want to use in place of the selected cell reference.

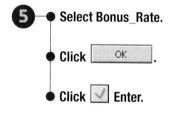

5 ● Select Bonus_Rate.

● Click ▭ OK ▭.

● Click ☑ Enter.

Your screen should be similar to Figure 5.31

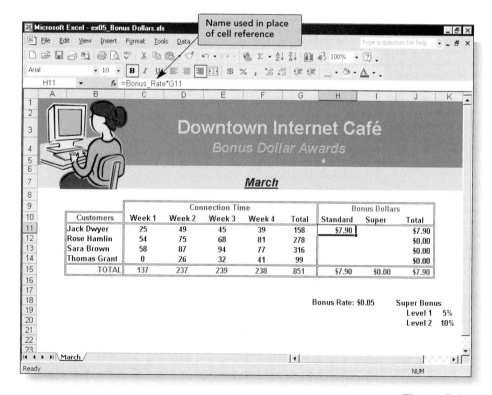

Figure 5.31

The selected range name has replaced the reference to cell I18 in the formula. Using a name makes the formula easier to understand.

Next you will name the Super Bonus levels in cells J19 and K20 that will be used in the formula to calculate the Super Bonus. You will name both cells at the same time using the labels in E19 and E20 as the names.

6 • **Select J19 through K20.**

• **Choose Insert/Name/Create.**

Your screen should be similar to Figure 5.32

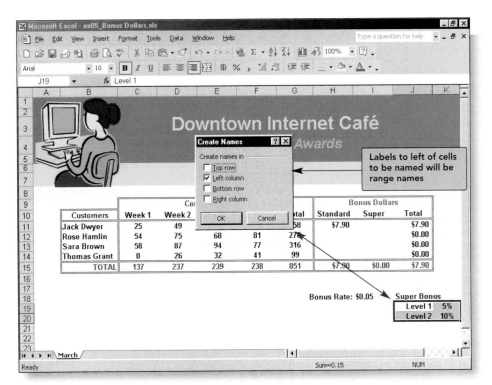

Figure 5.32

The Create Names dialog box lets you specify the location of the labels you want to use for names in relation to the cells to be named. In this case, you want to use the labels in the column to the left (K), which is the default. You will accept the default and then move to the cells to verify that the names have been created.

7 Click [OK].

● Move to K19 and note that Level_1 is displayed in the Name box.

● Move to K20 and note that Level_2 is displayed in the Name box.

● Save the workbook as Bonus Dollars.

Your screen should be similar to Figure 5.33

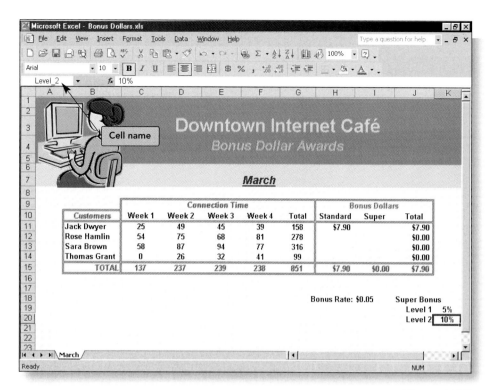

Figure 5.33

Using the IF Function

Now you are ready to enter a formula in cell I11 to calculate the Super Bonus. For any customer with more than 100 minutes of connection time, the Super Bonus is calculated using one of two levels. The highest level is for those with more than 200 minutes. Those customers receive a Super Bonus equal to 10 percent of their Standard Bonus. The other level is for those with less than or equal to 200 minutes who receive a Super Bonus equal to 5 percent of their Standard Bonus. You will use the IF function to calculate the Super Bonus.

concept 7

IF Function

7 The **IF function** checks to see if certain conditions are met and then takes action based on the results of the check. The syntax for this function is:

IF(logical_test,value_if_true,value_if_false)

This function contains three arguments: logical_test, value_if_true, and value_if_false. The logical_test argument is an expression that makes a comparison using logical operators. **Logical operators** are used in formulas and functions that compare numbers in two or more cells or to a constant. The result of the comparison is either true (the conditions are met) or false (the conditions are not met). The logical operators are:

Symbol	Meaning
=	Equal to
<	Less than
>	Greater than
<=	Less than or equal to
>=	Greater than or equal to
<>	Not equal to
NOT	Logical NOT
AND	Logical AND
OR	Logical OR

The logical test argument asks the question, "Does the entry in this cell meet the stated conditions?" The answer is either True (Yes) or False (No). The second argument, value_if_true, provides directions for the function to follow if the logical test result is true. The third argument, value_if_false, provides directions for the function to follow if the logical test result is false.

First you will enter the formula to calculate the discount earned for a connection time of 200 minutes or more. Then you will modify the function to include the other conditions.

1 • Move to cell I11.

• Click 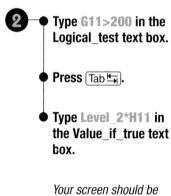 Insert Function.

• Select IF from the Most Recently Used or Logical Function categories.

• Click OK.

Your screen should be similar to Figure 5.34

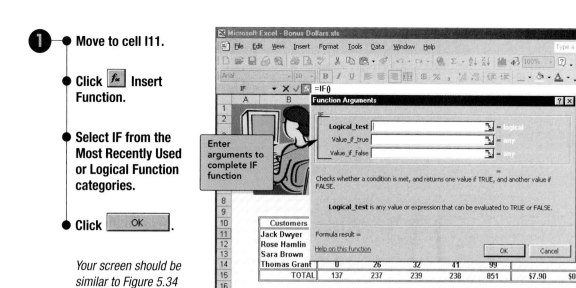

Figure 5.34

The IF Function Arguments dialog box contains three text boxes, one for each IF statement argument. The logical test is whether the total connection time for a customer is greater than 200 and the value_if_true argument provides directions for what to do if the logical test is true. In this case, the value_if_true directions are to multiply the value in cell H11 times the value in the cell named Level_2. To enter these arguments,

2 • Type G11>200 in the Logical_test text box.

• Press Tab ⇥.

• Type Level_2*H11 in the Value_if_true text box.

Your screen should be similar to Figure 5.35

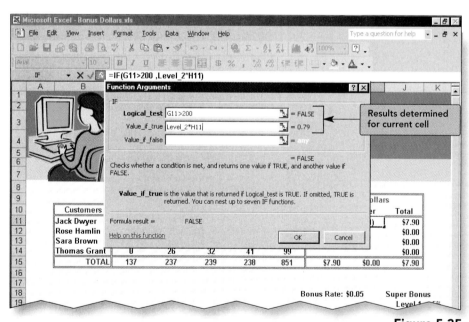

Figure 5.35

Notice that the Formula palette is already determining whether the conditions are true or false for the current customer based on the values in the referenced cells. In this case, because the value in G11 is less than 200, the logical test result is false and a Level 2 bonus would be 0.79 if true.

Next, you need to enter the value_if_false argument. It contains instructions that are executed if connection time is less than or equal to 200 minutes. If that connection time is greater than 100, then the Level_1 amount is used to calculate the Super Bonus, otherwise connection time is less than or equal to 100 and the Super Bonus is 0. To enter this condition, you include a second IF statement that will apply the Level 1 bonus. The arguments for the second IF statement are enclosed in their own set of parentheses. This is called a **nested function**.

3 ● **In the Value_if_false**
text box enter
IF(G11>100,Level_1*
H11,0).

Your screen should be
similar to Figure 5.36

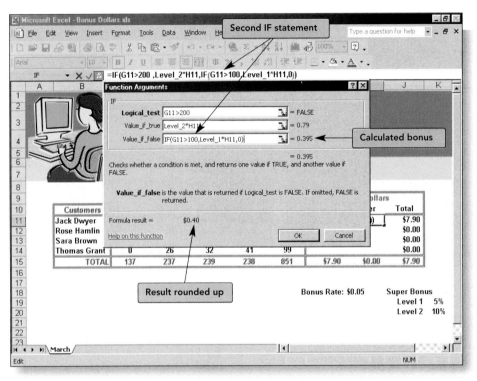

Figure 5.36

Now the calculated result is $0.395 for the current customer. The formula result will be rounded up to $0.40.

4 ● Click [OK].

Your screen should be similar to Figure 5.37

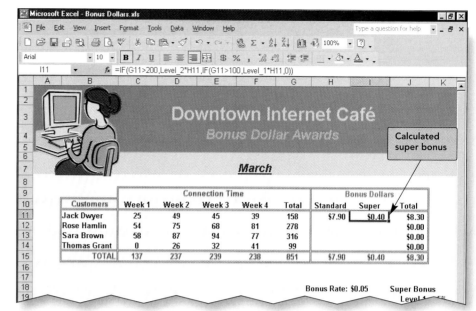

fx =IF(G11>200,Level_2*H11,IF(G11>100,Level_1*H11,0))

Calculated super bonus

March

| Customers | Connection Time | | | | | Bonus Dollars | | |
	Week 1	Week 2	Week 3	Week 4	Total	Standard	Super	Total
Jack Dwyer	25	49	45	39	158	$7.90	$0.40	$8.30
Rose Hamlin	54	75	68	81	278			$0.00
Sara Brown	58	87	94	77	316			$0.00
Thomas Grant	0	26	32	41	99			$0.00
TOTAL	137	237	239	238	851	$7.90	$0.40	$8.30

Bonus Rate: $0.05   Super Bonus
                       Level 1 5%

Figure 5.37

The Super Bonus for Jack Dwyer is $0.40. The IF function determined that the number in cell G11 was less than 200 but greater than 100. Therefore, the Super Bonus was calculated using Level_1, or 5 percent. Next, you will enter formulas to make these same calculations for the other three customers.

5 ● Copy cells H11 through I11 using the fill handle to the range H12 through I14.

● Click cell H12 to deselect the range.

Your screen should be similar to Figure 5.38

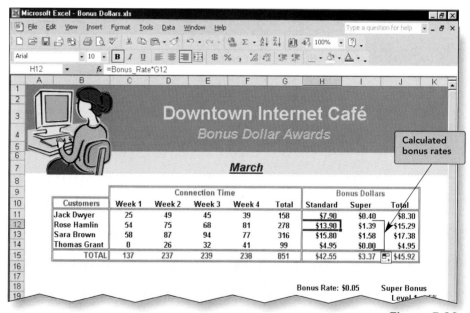

H12   fx =Bonus_Rate*G12

Calculated bonus rates

March

| Customers | Connection Time | | | | | Bonus Dollars | | |
	Week 1	Week 2	Week 3	Week 4	Total	Standard	Super	Total
Jack Dwyer	25	49	45	39	158	$7.90	$0.40	$8.30
Rose Hamlin	54	75	68	81	278	$13.90	$1.39	$15.29
Sara Brown	58	87	94	77	316	$15.80	$1.58	$17.38
Thomas Grant	0	26	32	41	99	$4.95	$0.00	$4.95
TOTAL	137	237	239	238	851	$42.55	$3.37	$45.92

Bonus Rate: $0.05   Super Bonus
                       Level 1 5%

Figure 5.38

Because the named references in the copied formulas are absolute, they copied correctly. Both Rose and Sara earned Super Bonus awards of 10 percent because the values in cells G12 and G13 are greater than 200. Thomas did not earn a Super Bonus because the value in cell G14 is less than 100.

Adding a Combo Box Control

Evan really likes the layout of the form. A change needs to be made, however, to the Standard Bonus rate. During some months the bonus rate may be raised to $0.10 or $0.15 per minute. The formulas to calculate the bonuses will need to be adjusted to use the other two bonus rates during those months. You could create two additional forms that would each have a different bonus rate in cell I18. This would require that the correct form used for that month's input be based on the bonus rate for that month. A simpler way to deal with this problem is to add a combo box control to the form.

Adding controls to forms makes it easier to fill out a form and increases the accuracy of the information entered in it. This is because many of the controls can include a list of options from which the user selects. Although controls are most effectively used in online forms, they can also be used in printed forms. For example, controls such as buttons and check boxes can be printed blank and then filled in by the user.

A combo-box control displays a text box and button that will display a drop-down list with the items that can be selected. The first step in creating a combo-box control is to enter the items you want to appear in the combo-box drop-down list in a columnar range. You will enter the three bonus amounts as items to be used.

1 ● **In cells H19 through H21 enter the numbers .05, .10, and .15.**

Additional Information
Cells H19:H21 were preformatted to currency.

● **Display the Control Toolbox toolbar.**

● **If necessary, move the toolbar to the left side of your screen.**

Your screen should be similar to Figure 5.39

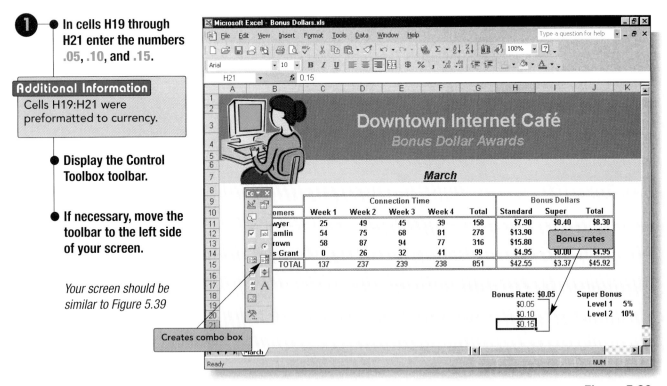

Figure 5.39

Now you are ready to add the combo box control to the form.

 **Click** 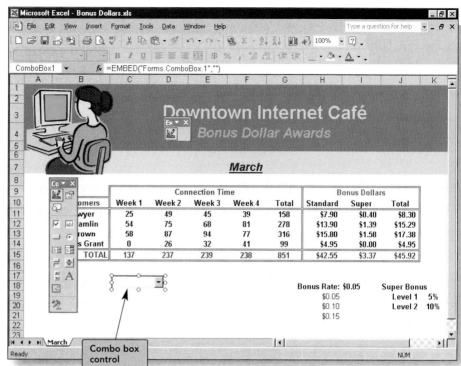 **Combo Box on the Control Toolbox toolbar.**

● **Click over cell C17 to create a combo box.**

Additional Information
The combo box is a selected object that can be sized or moved like any other object.

Your screen should be similar to Figure 5.40

Combo box control

Figure 5.40

Design mode is active, so you can modify the settings associated with the selected control. You need to specify the information to be displayed in the combo-box drop-down list and the location of the cell to link the selection to. You do this by setting the properties of the combo box.

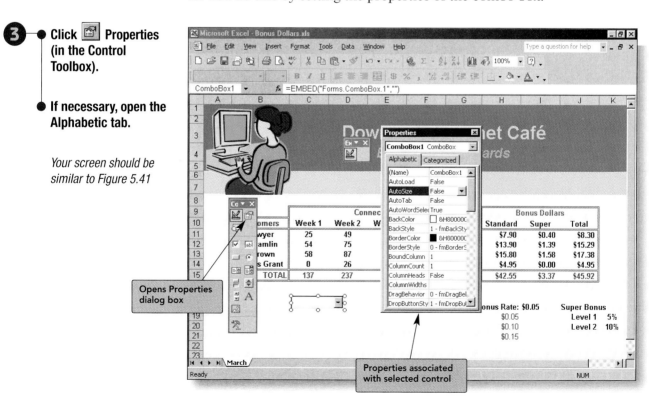

● **Click** 🖾 **Properties (in the Control Toolbox).**

● **If necessary, open the Alphabetic tab.**

Your screen should be similar to Figure 5.41

Opens Properties dialog box

Properties associated with selected control

Figure 5.41

The Alphabetic tab displays the properties for the selected control in alphabetical order. The ListFillRange option is used to specify the location of the cells containing the information to be displayed in the combo-box drop-down list, and the LinkedCell option is used to specify the cell to receive the selection.

4 ● **Scroll the list to locate the ListFillRange property box.**

● **Enter the range H19:H21 as the ListFillRange.**

● **Enter cell I18 as the LinkedCell.**

Your screen should be similar to Figure 5.42

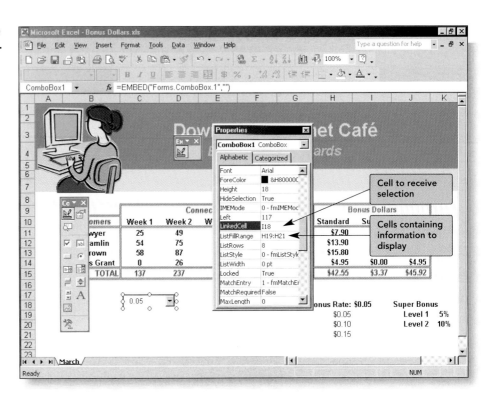

Figure 5.42

You are finished defining the properties and want to add a label next to the combo box and then try it out.

5 • Click ⊠ to close the Properties dialog box.

• Enter the label Select Bonus Rate: in cell B17 to identify the combo box.

Additional Information
Cell B17 was preformatted to be right aligned.

• Reposition the combo box control as needed to align with the label (see Figure 5.43).

• Click 🔍 Exit Design mode.

• Close the Control Toolbox toolbar.

• Open the combo box drop-down list.

• Select $0.15.

• Save the workbook.

Your screen should be similar to Figure 5.43

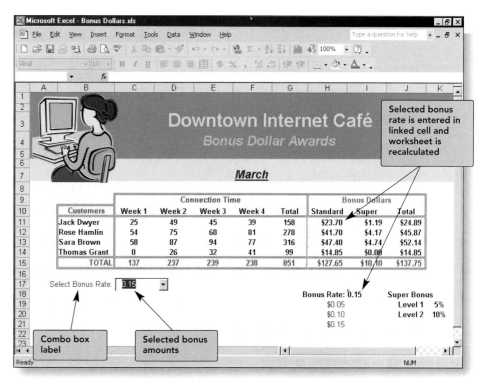

Figure 5.43

The selection you made from the combo box is entered in the bonus rate cell, I18, and the worksheet is recalculated using the new bonus rate.

Adding Comments

Now you will prepare the form to be used for entry of the same information for other months. Since someone else will most likely use the form, it is a good idea to include instructions on how to use it. Typically, these instructions are a combination of text entries and comments.

concept 8

Comments

8 **Comments** are notes attached to cells that can be used to help clarify the meaning of the data, provide documentation, or ask a question. Using comments is a good method of adding instructions that do not interfere with the appearance of the worksheet.

A comment appears as a note box attached to the cell. You can move and resize a comment box just as you would any other type of graphic object. If you move the cell that contains a comment, the associated comment box moves with it.

You will add one text entry and two cell comments that will provide the instructions for this form.

1 ● **Move to cell A8.**

● **Enter** For help on how to complete this form, point to the red triangles.

● **Format A8 to a font color of Dark Red and bold.**

● **Insert a blank row below row 8.**

Your screen should be similar to Figure 5.44

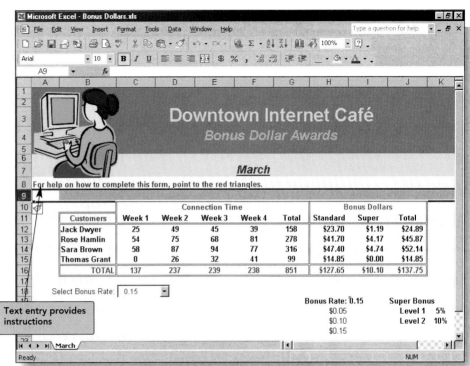

Figure 5.44

Next, you will add the cell comments using the Reviewing toolbar. The first comment will appear in cell F7 and will direct users to update the month.

2 ● **Display the Reviewing toolbar.**

● **If necessary, move the toolbar to the lower-right corner of the worksheet.**

● **Move to F7.**

● **Click** 🔲 **New Comment in the Reviewing toolbar.**

Another Method
The menu equivalent is Insert/Comment.

Your screen should be similar to Figure 5.45

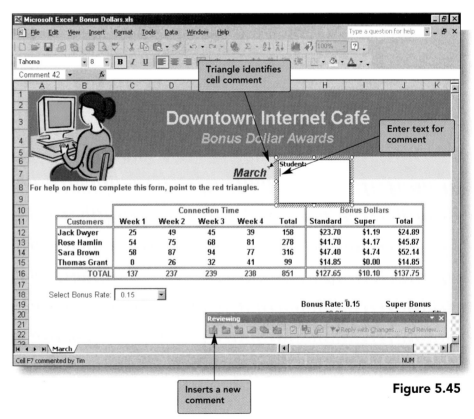

Figure 5.45

By default, the comment box includes the user name. You will delete the text for the comment.

3 ● Select the user name and press Delete.

● Type Enter the month.

● Size the comment box to fit the text.

● Click on any cell to complete the comment.

● Point to the red triangle in cell F7.

Your screen should be similar to Figure 5.46

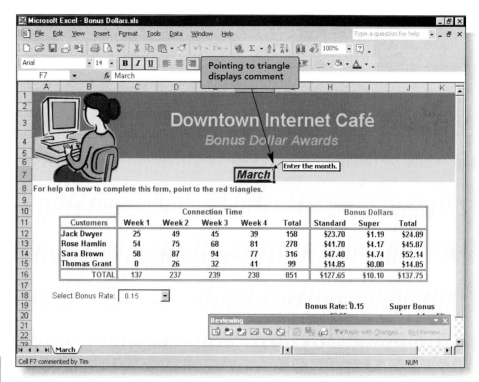

Figure 5.46

The comment is displayed in a comment text box. The second comment will be entered in cell C12.

4 ● Add a comment to C12 containing the text Enter weekly connection times here.

● Size the comment box to fit the text.

● Add a comment to B18 containing the text Select this month's bonus rate.

● Size the comment box to fit the text.

● Click 📇 Show All Comments.

Your screen should be similar to Figure 5.47

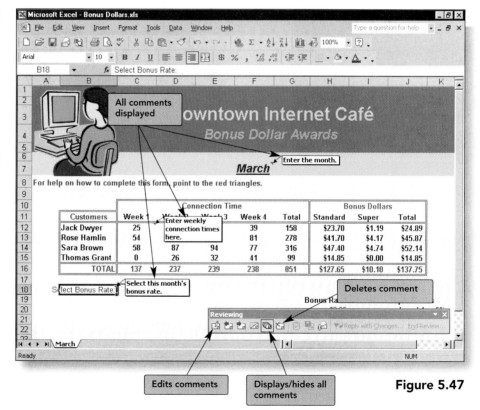

Figure 5.47

The three comments you entered are displayed. If comments overlay one another, you can move them around just like any other graphics object. However, when you hide and redisplay the comments they return to the default location.

5 ● **Click** 🔲 **Hide All Comments.**

Another Method

The menu equivalent, View/Comments, will display all comments or hide all displayed comments.

● **Close the Reviewing toolbar.**

● **Save the workbook.**

Your screen should be similar to Figure 5.48

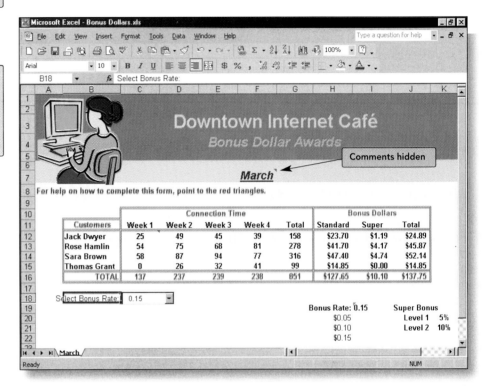

Figure 5.48

Finalizing the Form

A well-designed form is simple to use and uncluttered in design. To make the form easy to use, you will add a command button to print the output. To simplify the design you will hide non-essential items. Then you will prepare the workbook to be saved as a template to be used each month to record the customer's bonus dollar earnings. You will clear the sample data, unlock all data entry areas, and protect the worksheet. You will also add documentation to the workbook to clarify the purpose of the template.

Simplifying the Form

You will first add a command button to print the output then you will hide any non-essential information in the form to simplify its appearance.

1 ● Add a command button macro over cell
E18.

● Label the button
PrintForm.

● With the command
button selected,
record a macro to
print the worksheet in
landscape orientation,
centered horizontally
on the page. Include a
custom footer that dis-
plays your name and
date only.

● Exit Design Mode and
close the Control
Toolbox.

*Your screen should be
similar to Figure 5.49*

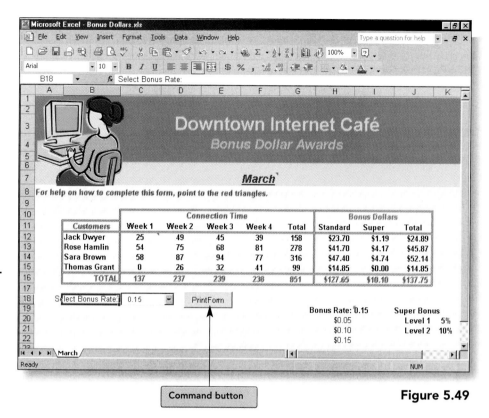

Command button

Figure 5.49

Users of this form do not need to see the list of rates and the two bonus levels. To simplify the form, you will hide this information.

2 ● Select rows 19
through 22.

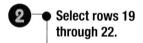
Additional Information

Click the row number to
quickly select an entire row.

● Choose Format/Row/
Hide.

Additional Information

To redisplay hidden rows,
select the rows above and
below the hidden rows and
use Format/Row/Unhide.

*Your screen should be
similar to Figure 5.50*

Rows 19
through 22
hidden

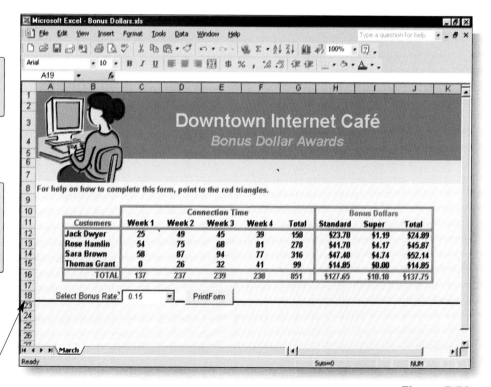

Figure 5.50

Preparing the Template

Each month the form will be used to record the customer's Bonus Dollar earnings. You need to clear the sample data and protect the worksheet. Finally, you will save it as a template file. You also want to include the file documentation so that users of the template will understand the purpose of the file.

First, you will clear the contents of the entry areas and unlock these cells for editing. Then you will protect the worksheet.

1 ● Clear the contents of cell F7 and cells C12 through F15.

● Unlock cell F7.

● Unlock the cells for weekly connection times (cells C12 through F15).

● Use **Edit/Go To** to move cell I19 that displays the selected bonus rate.

● Unlock cell I19.

● Protect the worksheet.

Your screen should be similar to Figure 5.51

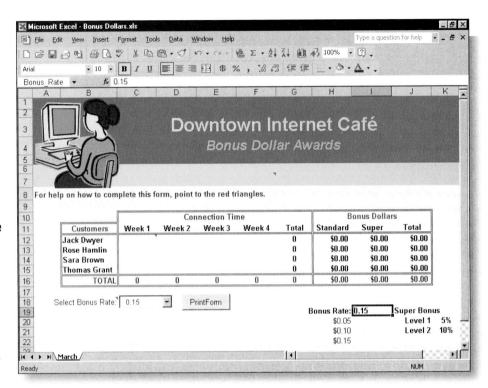

Figure 5.51

Next, you will enter basic documentation regarding the worksheet file.

2 • **Choose**
File/Properties.

• **If necessary, open the**
Summary tab.

• **In the Subject text**
box, type Monthly
record of connection
times and bonuses.

• **Enter** your name **into**
the Author text box.

• **In the Comments text**
box type Point to the
red triangles for in-
structions. Select the
bonus amount for the
month from the
Bonus Rate drop-
down list.

Your screen should be
similar to Figure 5.52

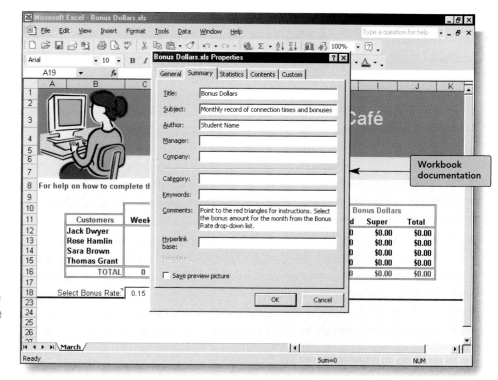

Figure 5.52

You are now ready to save the form as a workbook template.

3 • **Click** OK **to close the Properties dialog box.**

• **Move to cell A9.**

• **Save the workbook as a template using the file name** Monthly Bonus Form **to your data file location.**

• **Close the workbook and exit Excel.**

Using Data Tables, Creating Macros, and Designing Onscreen Forms

Data Table (EX5.7)

A data table is a range of cells that is used to quickly calculate multiple what-if versions in one operation and to show the results of all variations together in the worksheet.

Macro (EX5.13)

A macro is a stored series of keystrokes and commands that are executed automatically when the macro is run.

Controls (EX5.14)

A control is a graphic object that is designed to help the user interact with the form.

Visual Basic Editor (EX5.16)

The Visual Basic Editor is a tool used to write and edit macros attached to Excel workbooks.

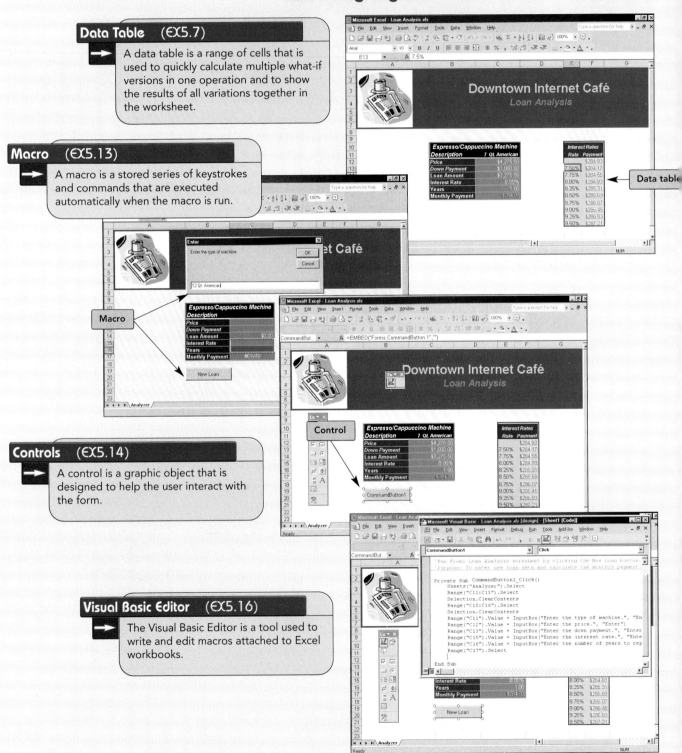

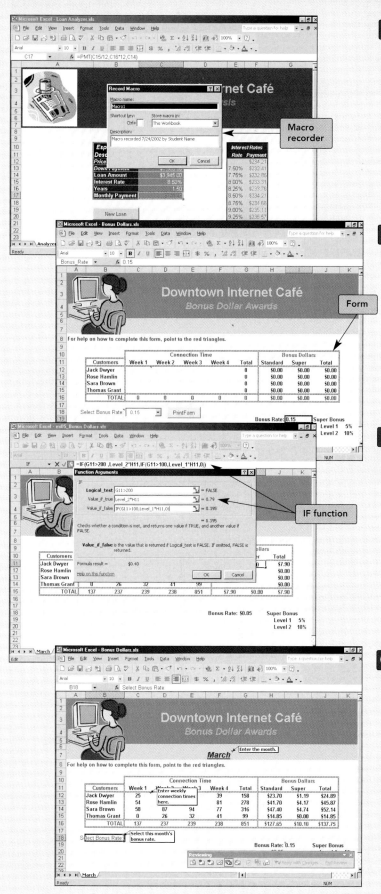

Macro Recorder   (EX5.23)

The Macro Recorder automatically creates a macro by recording a series of actions as macro commands.

Form   (EX5.27)

A form is a formatted worksheet with blank spaces that can be filled in online or on paper.

IF Function   (EX5.34)

The IF function checks to see if certain conditions are met and then takes action based on the results of the check.

Comments   (EX5.41)

Comments are notes attached to cells that can be used to clarify the meaning of the cell contents, provide documentation, or ask a question.

Using Data Tables, Creating Macros, and Designing Onscreen Forms

key terms

AutoFormat EX5.10	macro EX5.13	rate EX5.6
column-oriented EX5.7	Macro Recorder EX5.23	remark statement EX5.17
comment EX5.41	name EX5.29	row-oriented EX5.7
control EX5.14	nested function EX5.36	run EX5.13
data table EX5.7	nper EX5.6	statement EX5.16
digital signature EX5.14	object EX5.16	Sub procedure EX5.16
form EX5.27	one-variable data table EX5.7	syntax EX5.16
IF function EX5.34	principal EX5.6	two-variable data table EX5.7
input cell EX5.7	property EX5.16	Visual Basic Editor EX5.16
logical operator EX5.34	pv EX5.6	

mous skills

The Microsoft Office User Specialist (MOUS) certification program is designed to measure your proficiency in performing basic tasks using the Office XP applications. Getting certified demonstrates that you have the skills and provides a valuable industry credential for employment. After completing this lab, you have learned the following Microsoft Office User Specialist skills:

Skill	Description	Page
Formatting and Printing Worksheets	Modify row and column settings	EX5.46
	Use automated tools to format worksheets	EX5.10
Creating and Revising Formulas	Use statistical, date and time, financial, and logical functions in formulas	EX5.33
Workgroup Collaboration	View and edit comments	EX5.41

command summary

Command	Shortcut Key	Button	Action
Edit/Cle**a**r/Co**mm**ents			Deletes comment in selected cell
View/**C**omments			Displays all comments or hides all displayed comments
Insert/**N**ame/**D**efine			Assigns a name you specify to a cell or range of cells
Insert/**N**ame/**P**aste			Places the selected cell or cell range name in the formula bar or lists names in the worksheet
Insert/**N**ame/**C**reate			Creates a range name using the text in cells
Insert/**C**omment		🖼	Inserts a new comment in selected cell
Insert/**E**dit Comment		🖼	Edits comment in selected cell
F**o**rmat/**R**ow/**H**ide			Hides selected rows or columns
F**o**rmat/**R**ow/**U**nhide			Displays rows and columns that were previously hidden
F**o**rmat/**A**utoformat			Applies selected table format
Tools/**M**acros/**M**acros/<Macro name>/**R**un			Runs selected macro
Tools/**M**acros/**M**acros/<Macro name>/**E**dit			Opens selected macro in Visual Basic Editor for editing
Tools/**M**acro/**R**ecord New Macro			Records a series of actions as a macro
Tools/**M**acro/**S**top Recording		■	Stops the recording of a macro
Tools/**M**acro/**S**ecurity			Sets security level associated with macros in a workbook
Data/**T**able			Creates a data table based on specified input values and formulas
Visual Basic Editor			
File/**C**lose and Return			Closes the Visual Basic Editor window and returns to the active Excel worksheet
Run/**R**un Sub/UserForm	F5		Runs macro

lab exercises

Terminology

screen identification

In the following worksheet, several items are identified by letters. Enter the correct term for each item in the spaces that follow.

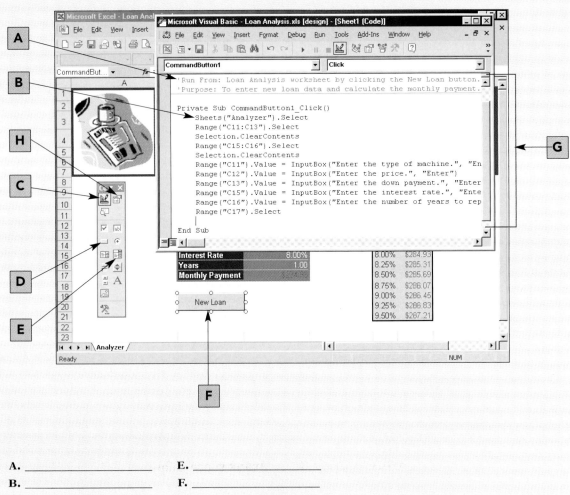

A. _____   E. _____
B. _____   F. _____
C. _____   G. _____
D. _____   H. _____

Match the letter on the right to the item in the numbered list on the left.

1. digital signature _____ **a.** descriptive statements in a macro

2. macro _____ **b.** a note attached to a cell

3. nested function _____ **c.** authentication that confirms a macro

4. controls _____ **d.** rules of grammar in a Sub procedure statement

5. data table _____ **e.** a function within another function

6. remark statements _____ **f.** a stored series of keystrokes and commands

7. statements _____ **g.** information in the Visual Basic Editor

8. syntax _____ **h.** graphic objects with properties in a worksheet

9. logical operators _____ **i.** compares numbers in two or more cells or to a constant

10. comments _____ **j.** a what-if analysis in which variables are used to see the effect on formulas

multiple choice

Circle the correct response to the questions below.

1. A(n)_____ begins with a statement that starts a macro.
   a. Sub procedure
   b. property
   c. remark statement
   d. nested function

2. The _____ automatically creates a macro by recording a series of actions.
   a. Visual Basic Editor
   b. nested function
   c. Macro Reader
   d. none of the above

3. A(n)_____is a formatted worksheet with blank spaces that can be filled in online.
   a. template
   b. form
   c. object
   d. cell

4. When a macro is _____, the actions within it are performed automatically.
   a. recorded
   b. executed
   c. stored
   d. opened

5. A _____ data table can be row- or column-oriented.
   a. multivariable
   b. two-variable
   c. single-variable
   d. one-variable

6. An Excel form can contain _____.
   a. text
   b. graphics
   c. cell comments
   d. all of the above

7. A macro created with the Visual Basic Editor must be attached to a(n) _____.
   a. object
   b. command button
   c. cell
   d. control box

8. A range name must start with _____.
   a. a letter
   b. a number
   c. a backslash
   d. any of the above

9. A(n) _____ argument is an expression that makes a comparison using logical operators.
   a. if_then
   b. logical_test
   c. and_or
   d. logical_if

10. _____ are used in formulas and functions that compare numbers in two or more cells.
    a. Logical operators
    b. Function arguments
    c. Nested functions
    d. Combo boxes

true/false

Circle the correct answer to the following questions.

1.	When a macro is executed the stored actions are performed automatically.	True	False
2.	The properties of controls cannot be changed or customized.	True	False
3.	Comments are attached to functions.	True	False
4.	A form created in Excel can only be used online.	True	False
5.	The result of an IF argument is either true or false.	True	False
6.	High security automatically disables macros if they are not digitally signed.	True	False
7.	A range name can only include letters and numbers.	True	False
8.	An apostrophe identifies a statement as a remark.	True	False

9. The IF function requires six arguments.   True   False
10. The only way to execute a macro is to use a command button.   True   False

Concepts

fill-in questions

Complete the following statements by filling in the blanks with the correct terms.

1. A range _____ can consist of any combination of 255 characters.

2. _____ are used in formulas and functions that compare values in two or more cells.

3. Excel uses the _____ computer programming language for macros.

4. A _____ appears as note box attached to a cell.

5. An _____ is a cell in which a list of values is substituted to see the resulting effect on the related formulas.

6. The steps in creating a(n)_____ are the same for online or paper completion.

7. The _____ can be used any time a cell or range is requested.

8. A(n)_____ control displays a text box and a button that will display a drop-down list.

9. The _____function checks to see if certain conditions are met and takes actions based on the results.

10. Graphic objects that are designed to help the user interact with the worksheet are called
_____.

discussion questions

1. Discuss different ways in which a data table can be used. When would you use a one-variable data table? When would a two-variable table be more appropriate?

2. Discuss some spreadsheet functions that you could automate with a macro. Would it be more appropriate to use the Visual Basic Editor or the Macro Recorder to create each of these macros?

3. Discuss what range names are and when it is appropriate to use them. Give some examples.

Hands-On Exercises

step by step

Animal Rescue Foundation Volunteer Rewards

★ 1. After viewing the revenue analysis you provided (Lab 4, Step by Step, 5), Samuel Johnson and the other Animal Rescue Foundation board members have begun the budget planning for the next year. They have realized that daily operation of the agency depends on the volunteers. To repay them for their time, the board has decided to implement a rewards program with some of the budget surpluses you have anticipated. You have been asked to create a worksheet to track the number of hours people have worked and determine their award level. Your completed worksheets should be similar to the one shown here.

a. Open the workbook file ex05_ARF Volunteers. Enter the data shown below into the worksheet.

Row		Col B	Col C	Col D	Col E
33	Pennington, Neil	75	62	8	79
34	Wilson, Aaron	35	40	23	39
35	Tranthorn, Ellie	27	35	19	12
36	Clark, Jamel	61	30	28	58
37	Ferguson, Robby	99	12	0	43
38	Carey, Ronnie	105	42	50	103

b. Sort the list in ascending order by name.

c. Enter formulas to calculate the average and total hours for the year in columns F and G.

d. Enter the labels Star Level 1, Star Level 2, and Star Level 3 right-aligned in cells I40 through I42. In cells J40 through J42, enter 300, 200, 100 as the award levels.

e. Use the Name Range command to name the values for the star levels.

f. In cell H5 enter the following formula to calculate the award level for the volunteers:
IF(G5>=Star_Level_1,1,IF(G5>=Star_Level_2,2,IF(G5>=Star_Level_3,3,0))).

g. Change the value in cell B5 to 450 and then to 0 to check the formula. Return the value to 235. Copy the formula down the column.

h. Select the entire worksheet excluding the star values. Enter your name and the current date in a header, center the worksheet horizontally.

i. Print the selection. Save the workbook as ARF Bonus Awards.

Student Name   September 8, 2002

Animal Angels Volunteers

	1st Qtr	2nd Qtr	3rd Qtr	4th Qtr	Average	Total	Level
Bell, Patricia	45	34	102	235	104	416	1
Carey, Ronnie	105	42	50	103	75	300	1
Carver, Kathi	30	83	3	3	29.75	119	3
Chorley, Besty	68	2	235	96	100.25	401	1
Clark, Jamul	61	30	28	58	44.25	177	3
Cody, Martin	28	66	6	45	36.25	145	3
Dickson, Diane	70	18	88	27	50.75	203	2
Edwards, Mike	12	20	61	28	30.25	121	3
Ferguson, Robby	99	12	0	43	38.5	154	3
Forester, Kimberly	30	63	34	44	42.75	171	3
Franklin, Stacey	57	98	93	80	82	328	1
Fulton, Anne	12	18	68	122	55	220	2
Garcia, Maria	5	23	61	36	31.25	125	3
Gatens, Chris	0	100	58	85	60.75	243	2
Henderson, James	9	76	51	60	49	196	3
Ingram, Helen	29	12	33	12	21.5	86	0
Isbell, Sonya	46	65	47	3	40.25	161	3
Johnson, Thaman	3	30	20	6	14.75	59	0
Jones, April	70	83	38	79	67.5	270	2
Kelly, William	12	76	63	94	61.25	245	2
Kettonhoeffer, Bill	4	59	57	8	32	128	3
Kullman, Rodney	28	30	35	16	27.25	109	3
La Paglia, Sally	39	10	12	134	48.75	195	3
Lee, Su	56	6	5	0	16.75	67	0
Legge, Cristan	3	81	73	34	47.75	191	3
Lopez, Andrew	86	34	5	156	70.25	281	2
Marcus, Danielle	3	19	24	2	12	48	0
Merwin, Michael	44	9	95	37	46.25	185	3
Nelson, Faith	9	112	6	0	31.75	127	3
Pennington, Neil	75	62	8	79	56	224	2
Peterson, Tracey	83	3	165	0	62.75	251	2
Pierce, Kai	6	98	4	75	45.75	183	3
Tranthorn, Ellie	27	39	19	12	24.25	97	0
Wilson, Aaron	35	40	23	39	34.25	137	3

Grade Book Maintenance

★ 2. You are a graduate assistant and have been assigned to work for a university professor. You are responsible for maintaining the grade book and have decided to create a worksheet that will calculate the students' final grades. You started the workbook by entering the row and column labels and the points earned for a sample set of students in four categories. You need to add formulas that will total the students' points on a summary worksheet and then use this new total to calculate the grade for the course. Your completed workbook should be similar to that shown here.

a. Open the file ex05_Grades.

b. Set cell D6 of the Summary sheet equal to the total on the Homework sheet (H6). Copy the formula down the column to insert the total homework points for all the students in the Summary sheet.

c. Repeat this step for the Projects, Quizzes, and Exams columns.

d. Enter a formula in row H of the Summary sheet to calculate the students' total points for the four categories.

Grade Book for Spring 2003

ID #	Last Name	First Name	Homework	Projects	Quizzes	Exams	Total	Percent	Letter
003874	Altiveros	Elaine	93	312	34	215	654	79.27%	C
004875	Brown	Stephanie	102	340	48	283	773	93.70%	A
000606	Colburn	Melissa	78	309	31	165	583	70.67%	C
009690	Davis	Kylie	110	331	51	275	767	92.97%	A
000943	Douglas	Mary	74	290	29	235	628	76.12%	C
002773	Dwyer	Jen	113	326	42	272	753	91.27%	A
009873	Gott	Linda	65	278	29	248	620	75.15%	C
007747	Hardy	Thomas	68	252	27	233	580	70.30%	C
002981	Hobson	Scott	110	329	42	282	763	92.48%	A
002637	Holt	Michelle	71	287	29	263	650	78.79%	C
002779	Jackson	Nicholas	103	340	48	281	772	93.58%	A
004994	Lopez	Marlene	78	302	29	198	607	73.58%	C
001572	Meese	Theresa	75	262	26	214	577	69.94%	C
004919	Mittelstadt	Jennifer	81	293	30	214	618	74.91%	C
003789	Oestreich	Kenneth	108	319	37	227	691	83.76%	B
002563	Pawlowski	Helen	57	232	26	202	517	62.67%	D
001326	Plumm	Kelly	109	320	41	265	735	89.09%	B
004662	Reboton	Erin	113	321	44	272	750	90.91%	A
002679	Riley	Russell	96	312	35	235	678	82.18%	B
000983	Shumacker	Michael	99	317	41	223	680	82.42%	B
007503	Smith	Shawn	85	311	34	249	679	82.30%	B
007843	Steele	Blaine	105	318	39	243	705	85.45%	B
006472	Williamson	Paul	77	246	24	220	567	68.73%	D

| Total Points Possible: | | | 120 | 345 | 60 | 300 | 825 | | |

Student Name
9/2/2001 12:18

e. Name cell H30 **Points_Possible**. Enter the formula **=H6/Points_Possible** in cell I6. Copy the formula down the column for the other students. Apply the percentage format with two decimal places.

f. Enter the following IF statement in cell J6
=IF(I6>0.899,"A",IF(I6>0.799,"B",IF(I6>0.699,"C",IF(I6>0.599,"D",E)))). You can use the insert function feature or type the IF statement directly into the cell. Copy the IF statement down the column for the other students.

g. Enter your name and the current date using the NOW function below the worksheet data.

h. Preview the Summary worksheet. Make any necessary formatting changes. Remove the header from the worksheet. Set the orientation to landscape.

i. Horizontally center the worksheet. Save the workbook as Gradebook and print the worksheet.

Wilson Electronics Financial Analysis   Do Not Use

★★ **3.** You have been hired as a salesperson for the Wilson Electronics Company. You want to be able to give your customers up-to-date and accurate information on the cost of high end electronics you sell. Many times customers have financing issues that are easily answered with what-if analysis on the terms of the payment plans you can give them. To automate the process, you plan to use a data table containing the model information and a table to calculate the different payments. The completed worksheet will be similar to the one shown here.

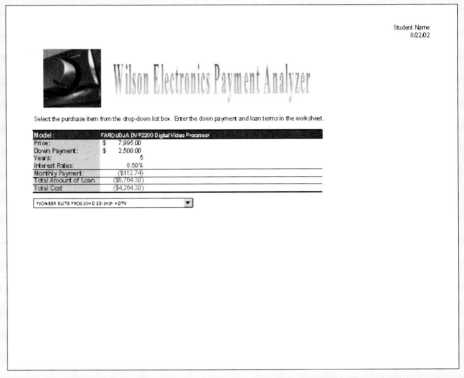

a. Open the file ex05_Electronics Analyzer.

b. Instead of typing in the model and price of the item each time, you want to be able to choose it from a drop down list that links to a data table. The information for the data table has already been created in cells C24 through D41. Enter the number **1** in cell C23. You will use the Choose function. In cell B12 enter **=CHOOSE(C23,D25, D26,D27,D28,D29, D31,D32,D33,D35, D36,D38,D39,D40,D41)** to select the items in the data table based on the number entered in cell C23.

c. Create a similar choose function in cell B13 to display the price associated with each item.

d. Enter sample data for the down payment of **$500** in cell B14, **2** for the years in cell B15, and **.0725** for the interest rate in cell B16.

e. Enter the payment function **=PMT(B16/12,B15*12,B13-B14)** in cell B17. To calculate the total amount of the loan, enter the formula **= B17*(B15*12)**. To calculate the total cost, enter the formula **=B14-B14**. ~~=B18+B14~~ =B18-B14

f. To see how the calculator works, enter 8 in cell C23.

g. Since each customer orders a different item, you would like to create a combo box that will allow you to quickly select the item rather than have to type the reference number in the cell. Using the Forms toolbar Combo Box button, create a combo box below cell D6. Set the Link Cell to C23 and the input range to **D24 through D41.**

h. Hide the Forms toolbar. Adjust the size and placement of the combo box and display it below the form data. Select an item from the combo box list.

i. Hide rows 18 though 36.

j. Apply an AutoFormat to enhance the worksheet. Adjust the column widths and layout as necessary. If necessary, change the alignment of cell B12 to left aligned

k. In cell A10, enter directions on how to use the form. Include cell comments to inform the user how to use the form.

k. To see how the worksheet works, enter the following for changing variable values:

Select	Pioneer Elite PRO510HD 53-inch TV
Down payment:	2,500
Years:	5
Interest Rate:	.085

l. Include your name and the current date in a header and print the worksheet in landscape orientation. Save the worksheet as Electronics Analyzer.

Currency Exchange Calculator

★ **4.** You work for Johnson & Scannell, an investment company that handles a lot of foreign accounts.
★ The company does a lot of currency exchanging and you would like to create a worksheet that will help employees quickly calculate the conversion. You have already created a worksheet that has the calculations for U.S. dollars to Canadian dollars. So that the worksheet works for any type of foreign currency, you will create a command button to ask the user to input the country's currency, the current exchange rate, and the U.S. dollar amount. The completed Exchange Rate worksheet and Visual Basic code window will be similar to the ones shown here.

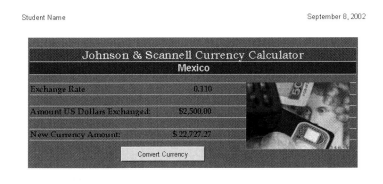

a. Open the Excel workbook file ex05_Currency Exchange. Open the Control Toolbox toolbar and create a command button positioned as shown in the example. Edit the command button to display the words Convert Currency.

b. Start the Visual Basic Editor to create the Command Button macro.

```
'Used to calculate US dollars to a different currency
'Written by Student Name
'Last Modified Current Date
'Run from Currency worksheet by clicking the Convert Currency button
'User enters the country, exchange rate from US dollars and the amount of US currency


Private Sub CommandButton1_Click()
    Sheets("Currency").Select
    Range("A3,B5,B7").Select
    Selection.ClearContents
    Range("A3").Value = InputBox("What country's currency?", "Enter")
    Range("B5").Value = InputBox("What is today's exchange rate from dollars?", "Enter")
    Range("B7").Value = InputBox("How much US money do you want to exchange?", "Enter")
    Range("A1").Select

End Sub
```

c. Enter the following remarks above the Sub procedure header:

'Used to calculate US dollars to a different currency
'Written by [Student Name]
'Last Modified [Current Date]
'Run from Currency worksheet by clicking the Convert New Currency button
'User enters the country, exchange rate from US dollars, and the amount of US currency

d. Inside the Sub and End Sub statements enter the following:

Sheets("Currency").Select
Range("A3,B5,B7").Select
Selection.ClearContents
Range("A3").Value = InputBox("What country's currency?", "Enter")
Range("B5").Value = InputBox("What is today's exchange rate from dollars?", "Enter")
Range("B7").Value = InputBox("How much US money do you want to exchange?", "Enter")
Range("A1").Select

e. Print the text in the code window and close the Visual Basic window. Exit design mode and close the Control Toolbox toolbar.
f. If necessary, change your macro security level to medium.
g. Click the command button and enter the following to check the accuracy of your command button. (The calculator should return $803.57.)

Country: Australia
Rate: $0.56
US Money: $450.00

h. Enter your name and the current date in a header and print the worksheet showing the exchange of Mexican pesos.
j. Save the workbook as Currency Converter.

Adventure Travel Tours Package Analysis

★ **5.** Adventure Travel Tours agents work hard to sell travel packages. To give their customers the best
★   possible fares, ATT agents make reservations based on group rates. Because the rates are
       calculated as a percentage of the previous year's sales, you would like to create a worksheet that
       will show the effects of a change in sales from –5 to 10 percent. The completed Adventure Travel
       Sales worksheet will be similar to the one shown here.

a. Open the file ex05_ATT Sales. Enter functions to calculate the totals.

b. Enter the values **–5%** to **10%** at 1% increments starting in K4 to be used for the values in a combo box.

c. Create a combo box that contains these values and display the combo box over cell C13. Link the combo box to cell J5. Enter the label **Increase Percentage** in cell A13.

d. Copy cells A3 to F11 to cell A15. Change the title in row 15 to **Number of Packages Needed in 2003**. Merge the title over the data.

e. In cell B18 enter the formula **=B6*(1+J5)**. Copy the formula through the cell range B18:E22.

f. Adjust the formatting as needed to make the worksheet attractive.

g. Enter comments to tell the user how to use the worksheet.

h. Hide columns J and K. Set the percentage increase to 3%.

i. Enter your name and the current date in a header, center the worksheet horizontally and print the worksheet.

j. Save the workbook as ATT Sales2.

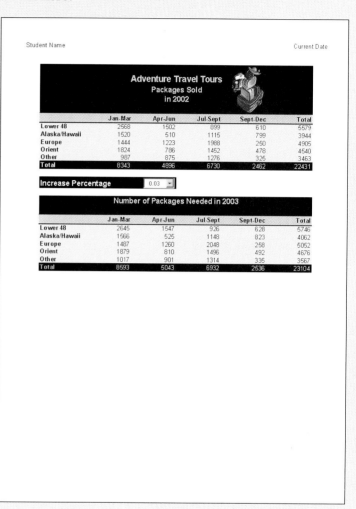

On Your Own

Creating a Personal Macro Library

★ **1.** In a blank new worksheet, use the Macro Recorder to record five macros for procedures that you use frequently and for which using a macro would save you time. For example, you may want to create a macro to modify the contents of the selected cell to 16 points, a selected font style, bold, and centered. Make sure that the macros are available to other open worksheets by using the Tools/Macros/Macros command. Add descriptions of the macros in the worksheet. Put the macro shortcut keys you assigned in cell comments. Enter your name and the current date in the worksheet. Test your macros by opening a new workbook and running the macros. Save the file as Macros and print both the macro and new worksheet.

401K Analysis

★ ★ **2.** The company you work for will contribute 3 percent of your gross pay to an individual retirement account (IRA). You can add up to another 15 percent of your gross pay to the same IRA. Create a worksheet with the following columns: Gross Wages, Employer Contribution, My Contribution, and Total Contribution. Enter your gross wages and create a formula to calculate the company contribution. In a column to the right, enter the numbers 0 to 10. Format them as percentages. Create a combo box that uses the percentages and calculates your contribution for the My Contribution column. Total the contributions. Use the combo box to see how much of your gross pay you can contribute to the IRA. Select the value you think is most appropriate for you. Enter your name and the current date in the worksheet. Save the file as My 401K and print the worksheet.

Furniture Purchase Analysis

★ ★ **3.** You have been furniture shopping for family room furniture and have your decision down to three groupings from different stores. Part of your decision is what the monthly payments will be based on the terms offered at the stores. The three stores offer different interest rates over a 3-year payment period. Using the information shown below and the features you learned in this lab, create a workbook to calculate the monthly payments for different interest rates. Use an AutoFormat to enhance the appearance of the worksheet. Save it as Furniture Loan Analysis. Print the analysis for the furniture grouping you want to purchase. Include your name and the current date in a header.

	Store 1	Store 2	Store 3
Purchase Total	$15,975	$22,320	$18,470
Down payment	$1,500	$2,000	$1,000
Interest rate	12%	8.5%	9%

Sports Company Credit Card Incentives

★★ **4.** The Sports Company has decided to offer its own credit card. As an incentive to get employees to promote the card, the company offers to give employees $1.00 for each card application they file. If an employee files 25 or more applications, a bonus is added. Create a worksheet for four employees that tracks the number of applications filed per week. Total the number of applications by employee and for the month. Calculate the amount the employee earned by multiplying the total by $1.00. Use a linking cell for the $1.00 bonus value so that you can increase or decrease it to see the effect. Use an IF statement to calculate a 10 percent bonus for employees who file 25 applications, and a 20 percent bonus for employees who file 50 or more applications. Create a combo box with $1.00, $1.50, and $2.00 in it. Unlock the data entry cells in the worksheet. Protect the worksheet. Select the $2.00 bonus amount. Enter your name and the current date in a header of the worksheet. Apply an AutoFormat of your choice to enhance the sheet. Save the file as Sports Company Credit Card and print the worksheet.

★Speeding Fine Calculator

★ **5.** You have been hired to work for the local traffic court. Create a worksheet that the clerks can use to calculate the amount of a speeding ticket. The worksheet should contain the following information: actual speed limit, speed offender was traveling, and number of tickets offender has received. The worksheet should calculate miles above speed limit, cost of ticket ($10.00 for each mile), court costs ($53.20), and additional charges ($20.00 for each offense). Use the Visual Basic Editor window and write the statements to ask the clerk to enter the actual speed limit, the speed offender was traveling, and number of tickets. Calculate the cost of the speeding ticket. Apply an AutoFormat of your choice to enhance the sheet. Enter your name and the current date in a header of the worksheet. Save the file as Speeding Fines and print the worksheet.

On the Web

Personal Computer Comparison Shopping

You are interested in buying a computer. Use the Internet to find prices for similar features for computers manufactured by different companies. Using the features you learned in this tutorial, create a worksheet that allows you to compare multiple computers on the same worksheet. Use a combo box to change the loan interest rate you have to pay for financing the purchase. Link the down payment, number of years, and interest rates to cells that can vary. Format the worksheet in an attractive manner. Enter your name and the current date in a header and print the worksheet. Save the workbook as Computer Comparisons.

Creating and Using Lists and Web Pages

LAB 6

objectives

After completing this lab, you will know how to:

1.	Create a list.
2.	Use a data form to add records.
3.	Create and use hyperlinks.
4.	Save a workbook in a new folder.
5.	Find and Replace information.
6.	Sort data.
7.	Filter records.
8.	Print selected areas.
9.	Save a worksheet as a Web page.

Creating a list is useful for organizing related information.

Using a data form speeds up entering and locating records in a list.

Sorting the information in a list displays the information you need in the specified order, alphabetically, numerically or by date.

Downtown Internet Café

The form you created to track the Downtown Internet Café's customer Internet connection times and Bonus Dollar awards is working quite well. Evan would now like to have a separate worksheet that contains the café customers' contact information so that he can use it to send out the Bonus Dollars discount coupons. This type of information can be entered into a worksheet as a list. While using Excel to create the list, you will learn about locating, modifying, ing, sorting, and filtering records in the list.

Now you have two workbooks containing data pertaining to

the Downtown Internet Café customers. To make it easier to work with the two workbooks, you will create a hyperlink in one workbook to open the other workbook. You will also save them to a separate folder.

The second project Evan has asked you to look into is to make the Bonus Dollars worksheet available to customers on the Web site to check their award status. To do this you will convert it to a Web page. A printout of a filtered list and the Bonus Dollars Web page are shown on the preceding page.

© Corbis

concept overview

The following concepts will be introduced in this lab:

1	**List**	A list or database is an organized collection of related information that is entered into a series of worksheet rows and columns.
2	**Find and Replace**	The Find and Replace feature helps you quickly find specific information and automatically replace it with new information.
3	**Sort**	You can sort data in a specified sequence, alphabetically, numerically, or by date.
4	**Filter**	A filter is a restriction you place on records in a list to quickly isolate and display a subset of records.
5	**Web Page**	A Web page is a document that can be used on the World Wide Web (WWW) and displayed in a browser.

Creating a List

You want to create an Excel worksheet that will contain the café's customer contact information and Internet connection times. In order to manipulate the data the way you want to, you decide to format this worksheet as a list.

concept 1

List

1 A **list** or **database** is an organized collection of related information that is entered into a series of worksheet rows and columns. Each row contains a **record**, which is all the information about one person, thing, or place. Each column is a **field**, which is the smallest unit of information about a record.

The first row in a list must contain column labels that serve as field names. A **field name** is a descriptive label used to identify the data stored in the field. The field names are used to create reports and find and organize data stored in the list. All other contiguous rows contain the records. The area containing the records is called the **list range.**

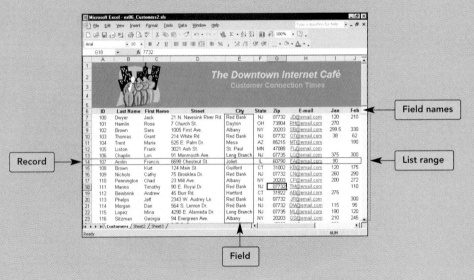

You have already entered many of the field names to create the structure for the list and have saved it in a workbook file named Customer List.

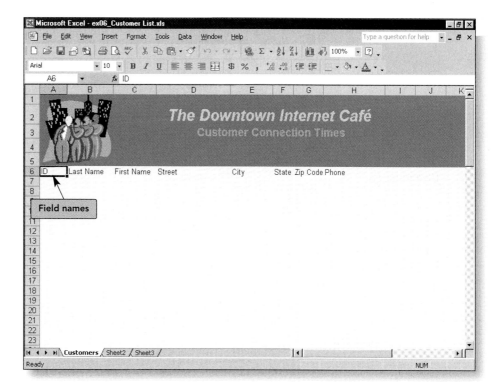

Figure 6.1

Row 6 contains the field names for the customer information that will be entered in the list.

Defining Field Names

You decide to change the phone field to a field for each customer's e-mail address. Additionally, you still need to add field names for the months that will be used to record the monthly connection times for each customer. In addition, it is a good idea to use formatted column labels for field names to help differentiate the labels from the data in the list. You will center, bold, and add a blue fill color to all the field name labels.

1 ● **Replace the entry in H6 with** E-mail.

Additional Information
Field names must be text entries.

● **Enter** Jan **in cell I6.**

● **Drag the fill handle of cell I6 to extend the range through December (cell T6).**

● **Center, bold, and add the Pale Blue fill to the entire range A6 through T6.**

● **Move to A6.**

Your screen should be similar to Figure 6.2

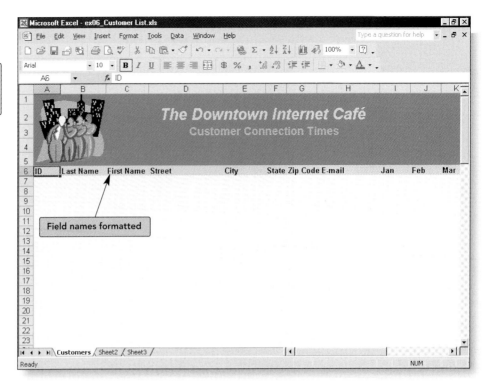

Figure 6.2

You are now ready to begin entering the information for the first record in row 7.

Entering Records

You have the customer information and connection time data for the first two months of the year and want to enter this information into the list range. The first record in the list must begin in the row immediately below the row of field names. Although you can enter the record information by typing it directly in the cells, Excel includes a special form, called a **data form**, that makes it easy to enter database records. Excel generates the data form from the field labels. When using the data form, the cell selector must be on any cell in the row containing the field labels in order to identify the location of the labels.

1 ● Choose **D**ata/F**o**rm.

● Click [OK] to use the first row in the selection as the labels.

Your screen should be similar to Figure 6.3

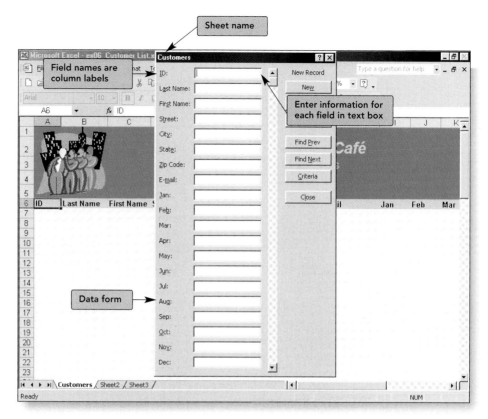

Figure 6.3

Notice that the Data Form dialog box has the name of the worksheet as its title and the column labels as its field names. In the text box to the right of each label, you enter the record information for that field.

When entering the data in a list, it is important that the data are entered consistently. For example, if you abbreviate the word "Street" as "St", it should be abbreviated in the same way for each record where it appears. Also be careful not to include blank spaces before or after an entry as this can cause problems when trying to locate information in the list. When a field entry is complete, use [Tab⇆] to move to the next field entry box or click on the box you want to move to. Use [⇧Shift] + [Tab⇆] to move to a previous box. Do not use the [↓] and [↑] keys to move within the data form as this will display the next or previous record or a blank new form.

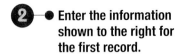

2 ● Enter the information shown to the right for the first record.

ID	100
Last Name	Dwyer
First Name	Jack
Street	21 N. Navesink River Dr.
State	NJ
E-mail	JD@email.com
Feb	210

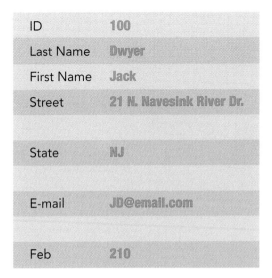

HAVING TROUBLE?
If you press ↓ a new record form is displayed. Press ↑ or Find Prev to return to the previous record.

Additional Information
Connection time is recorded in minutes.

Your screen should be similar to Figure 6.4

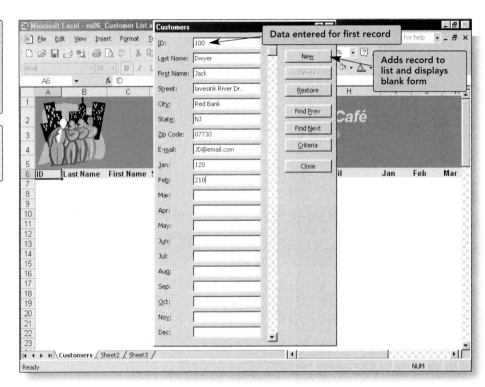

Figure 6.4

The data for the first record is complete. You will add it to the list and display another blank entry form to add the information for another record. You will add three more records and then you will close the data form.

3 ● Click [New].

Another Method

You can also press [Enter] or [↓] to move to a new entry form if you are on the last record.

● **Enter the information shown to the right for the next three records.**

Additional Information

While you are adding a record, you can make changes and correct mistakes. You can also undo all changes by clicking [Restore], as long as you do it before clicking [New] or closing the data form.

	Record 2	Record 3	Record 4
ID	101	102	103
Last Name	Hamlin	Brown	Thomas
First Name	Rose	Sara	Grant
Street	7 Church St.	1005 First Ave.	159 Branch Ave.
City	Dayton	Albany	Red Bank
State	OH	NY	NJ
Zip	73094	20203	07730
Phone	RH@email.com	SB@email.com	GT@email.com
Jan	270	299.5	38
Feb		330	62

● Click [Close].

● **Best-fit the Street column width so that the entire data entry is visible.**

● **Move to G.**

Your screen should look similar to Figure 6.5

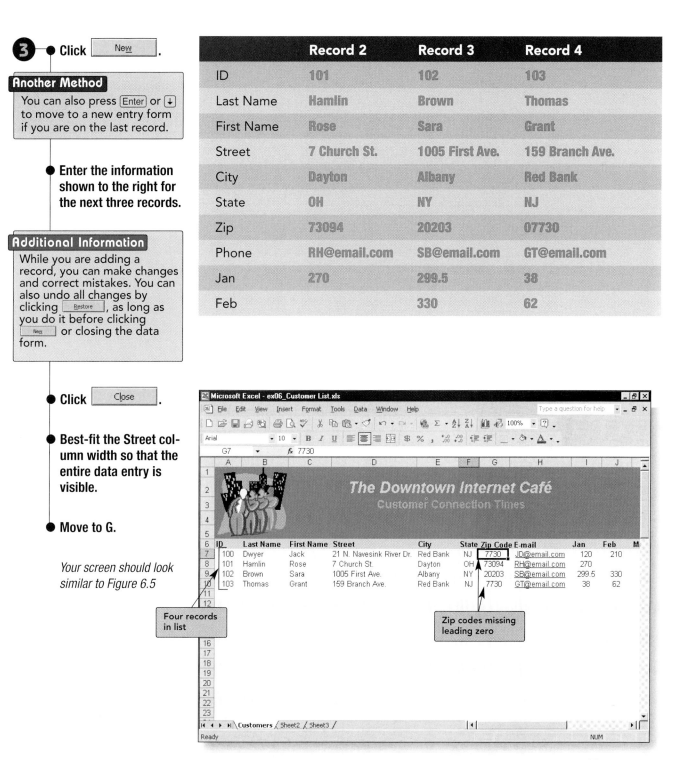

Figure 6.5

The field information for the first four records is displayed in the list range.

Editing Records

Notice that the zip codes for the first and last records do not display the leading zero (07730). This is because Excel drops leading zeros for numeric data. Since this field will not be used in calculations, you can change the format for the field to text so that numeric entries will appear as entered. Since you will be adding many more records to the database, you will extend the format for this field beyond the records that are currently entered.

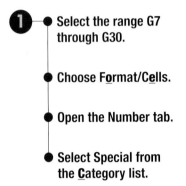

1 ● Select the range G7 through G30.

● Choose F**o**rmat/C**e**lls.

● Open the Number tab.

● Select Special from the **C**ategory list.

Your screen should look similar to Figure 6.6

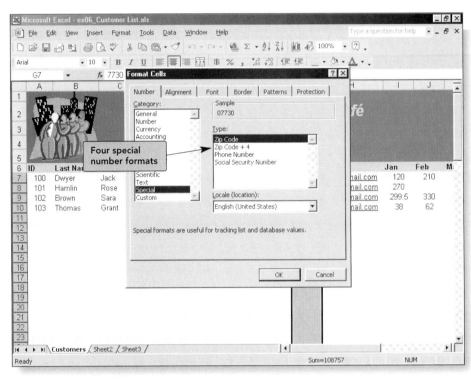

Figure 6.6

There are four special formats that are designed particularly for use in lists where numeric data is frequently entered but not used for calculations. You want to format the selection to the standard zip code format.

2 ● From the **T**ype list box, select Zip Code

● Click ___OK___.

Your screen should look similar to Figure 6.7

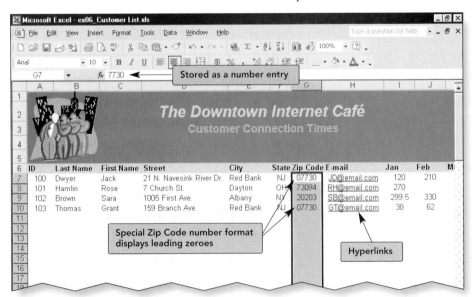

Figure 6.7

The number entries appear as they were entered because they are format-ted as a special number entry. However, the entries are stored as numbers without the zero.

Working with Hyperlinks

Notice the addresses in the E-mail column are underlined and in blue. This is because they were automatically identified as an e-mail address and for-matted as a hyperlink. A **hyperlink** is a connection to a location in the cur-rent document, in another document, or to a Web site. It allows the user to jump to the referenced location by clicking on the hyperlink text when reading the document on the screen.

The automatic identification of Internet or network paths and the con-version to hyperlinks is a feature common to all Office programs. Sometimes you may not want the item to be automatically formatted as a hyperlink. You can turn off this feature using **S**top Automatically Creating Hyperlink from the  AutoCorrect Options button menu. You can also remove the hyperlink autoformatting from an individual cell by selecting **R**emove Hyperlink from the shortcut menu.

Using a Hyperlink

In this case, clicking on the hyperlink opens a new e-mail message window to allow you to send a message to the address. You think this would be a pretty convenient method of notifying customers of special sales as well as their Bonus Dollar status.

Another Method
You can also use **T**ools/**A**utocorrect Options and clear the "Internet and network paths with hyperlinks" option in the AutoFormat As You Type tab.

① ● **Click on the e-mail hyperlink for the first record.**

Additional Information
The mouse pointer appears as 🖑 when pointing to a hyperlink.

Your screen should be similar to Figure 6.8

HAVING TROUBLE?
Your new message window may be different than shown depending on the e-mail program on your system.

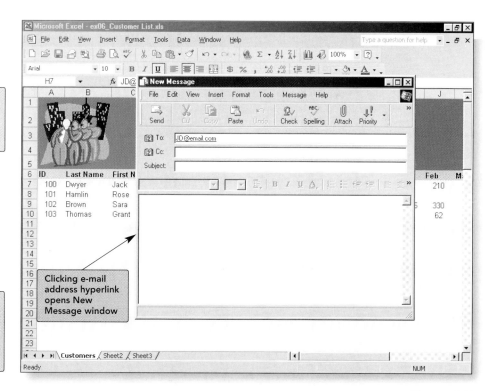

Figure 6.8

The new message window for the e-mail application on your system opens and is already addressed to the selected address. You will learn more about e-mailing in the Working Together 2 lab.

To select a cell containing a hyperlink without activating the hyperlink, click and hold on the cell until the mouse pointer changes to ✛ to indicate it will select the cell rather than jumping to the hyperlink destination.

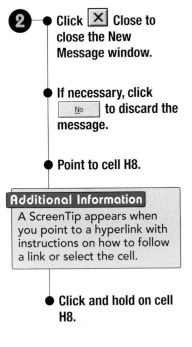

2 ● Click ⊠ Close to close the New Message window.

● If necessary, click [No] to discard the message.

● Point to cell H8.

Additional Information
A ScreenTip appears when you point to a hyperlink with instructions on how to follow a link or select the cell.

● Click and hold on cell H8.

Your screen should look similar to Figure 6.9

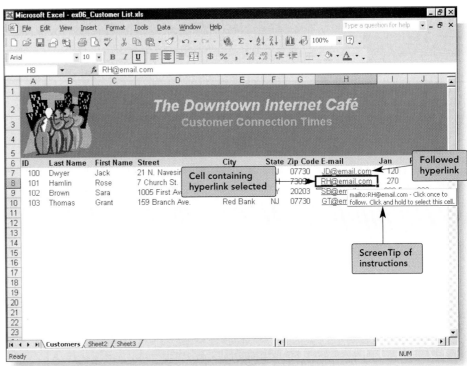

Figure 6.9

The cell containing the hyperlink is now selected and can be edited as needed. Notice that the color of the hyperlink you used in cell H7 is purple and the color of the hyperlink in the other cells is the default color of blue. The change in color indicates the link has been followed.

Creating a Hyperlink between Workbooks

Now that you see how convenient the hyperlink will be, you decide to add a hyperlink from the customer list worksheet to the Bonus Dollars workbook (created in Lab 5. Adding this hyperlink will make it easy to switch to the appropriate sheet in the Bonus Dollars workbook and copy the customers' total monthly connection times into the list. You will link to the Bonus Dollars workbook file and will display the hyperlink in cell K5, above the March column of data.

● Move to K5.

● Click 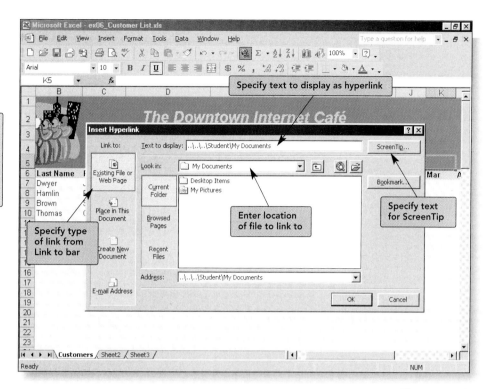 Insert Hyperlink

Another Method

The menu equivalent is Insert/Hyperlink and the keyboard shortcut is Ctrl + K. You can also select Hyperlink from a cell's shortcut menu.

Your screen should be similar to Figure 6.10

Figure 6.10

From the Insert Hyperlink dialog box, you first need to specify the type of link from the Link to bar. The four options are described below.

Option	Effect
E**x**isting File or Web Page	Creates a link in an existing Web page or file
Pl**a**ce in This Document	Creates a link to a place in the active file
Create **N**ew Document	Creates a link to a file that you have not created yet
E-**m**ail Address	Creates a link that allows users to create an e-mail message with the correct address in the To line

You want to create a link to a location in another workbook file.

2 ● **If necessary, select E̲xisting File or Web Page from the Link to bar.**

● **Specify the location of your Excel solution files in the Look in location.**

● **Select** Bonus Dollars **from the file list.**

Next, you want to enter the text that the hyperlink will display in the worksheet. If you do not enter anything in the "Text to Display" box, the hyperlink automatically displays the path of the linked file. You will also put instructions in the hyperlink ScreenTip.

3 ● **Replace the entry in the Text to Display text box with** March.

● **Click** ScreenTip... .

● **Type** Click to open the March Bonus Dollars worksheet.

● **Click** OK .

Your screen should be similar to Figure 6.11

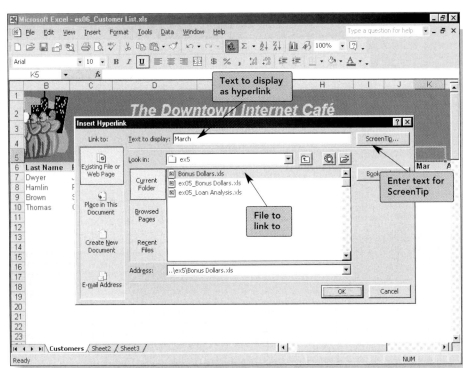

Figure 6.11

In the future, as you record each month's bonus dollar awards using the Monthly Bonus Form template, you plan to maintain the completed monthly worksheets in a single workbook file. When the workbook contains many worksheets, you will want to make sure that the user is taken directly to the worksheet containing the data for the appropriate month. To do this, you create a bookmark to that location in the linked workbook file.

4 ● Click [B̲ookmark...].

● If necessary, click [E̲nable Macros].

Your screen should be similar to Figure 6.12

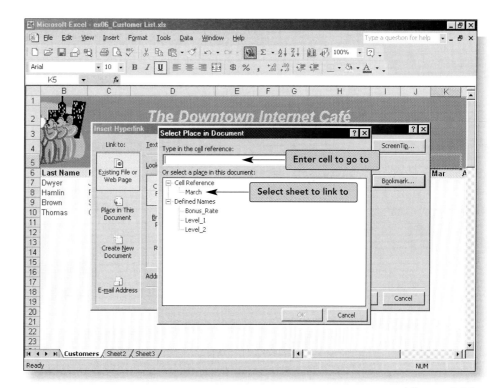

Figure 6.12

In the Select Place in Document dialog box you select a specific location to which you want the user to be taken in the linked document. The list box displays a tree diagram showing the outline of the information in the workbook and named ranges. From the outline, you select the location to which you want to link. In this case, you want the cell pointer positioned on the first customer's total connection time data (G12).

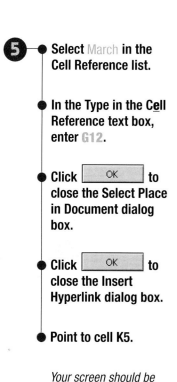

5 ● Select March in the Cell Reference list.

● In the Type in the Cell Reference text box, enter G12.

● Click [OK] to close the Select Place in Document dialog box.

● Click [OK] to close the Insert Hyperlink dialog box.

● Point to cell K5.

Your screen should be similar to Figure 6.13

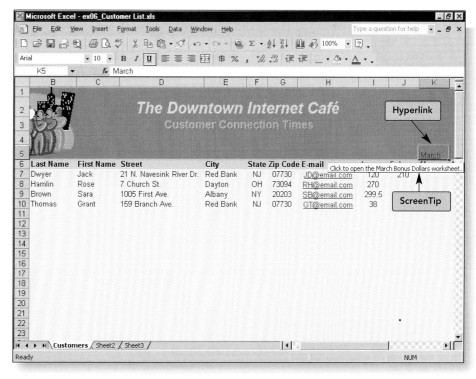

Figure 6.13

The text you entered for the hyperlink is displayed in the cell. It appears underlined and in the default hyperlink colors. The ScreenTip displays the text you entered. Because the hyperlink text is difficult to see, you will first change the text color and bold the entry. Then you will use the hyperlink.

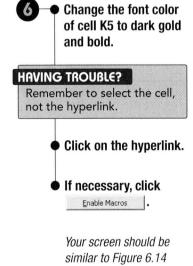

6 ● Change the font color of cell K5 to dark gold and bold.

● Click on the hyperlink.

● If necessary, click

    Enable Macros .

Your screen should be similar to Figure 6.14

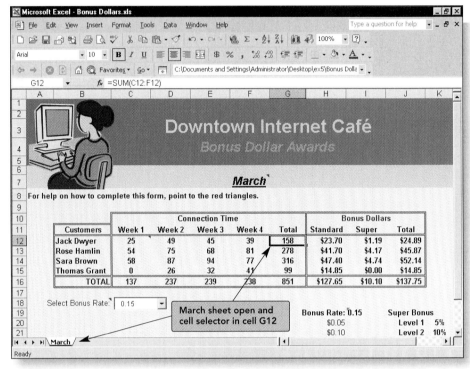

March sheet open and cell selector in cell G12

Figure 6.14

The Bonus Dollars workbook is open and the cell selector is in the location you specified as the bookmark. The user can now copy the customer monthly Internet connection totals from the Bonus form to the Customers worksheet.

Once both workbooks are open, you can switch back and forth between them or tile the two workbooks so that you can see them both simultaneously. You will tile the windows and copy the March total values into the list.

7 ● Choose
Window/**A**rrange/**T**iled

● Scroll the Bonus
Dollars sheet to dis-
play column G.

● Copy the total values
in cells G12:G15.

● Scroll the Customer
List worksheet to see
column K.

● Paste the copied val-
ues into cells K7:K10.

● From the 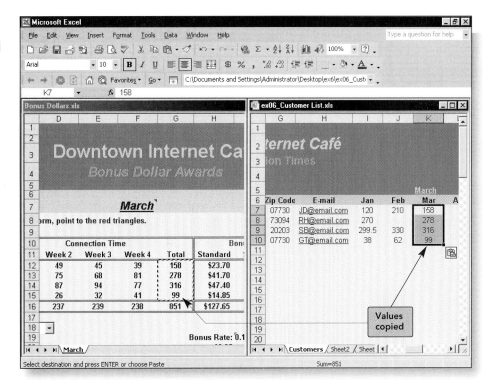 Paste
Options button, select
Values only.

*Your screen should be
similar to Figure 6.15*

Figure 6.15

Saving to a New Folder

Since the workbooks you have been creating recently are to track customer
information, you decide to save them in a separate folder from the rest of
the café's financial workbooks. You will save the ex06_Customer List file as
Customer1 to a new folder named Café Customers.

1 ● Choose **F**ile/Save **A**s.

● Type Customer1 as
the File name.

● If necessary, change
the location to where
you save your files.

● Click 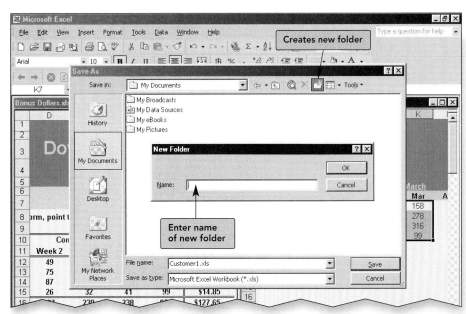 Create New
Folder in the Save As
dialog box.

*Your screen should be
similar to Figure 6.16*

Figure 6.16

The New Folder dialog box enables you to create and name a new folder.

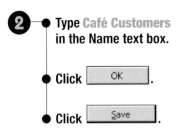

2 ● Type Café Customers in the Name text box.

● Click [OK].

● Click [Save].

Your screen should be similar to Figure 6.17

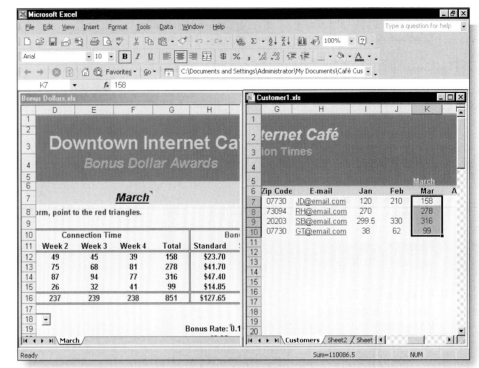

Figure 6.17

The Customer1 workbook is saved in the new folder.

3 ● Save the Bonus Dollars **workbook to the new folder.**

● Close the Bonus Dollars **workbook.**

● Close the Customer1 **workbook.**

● Turn off the display of the Web toolbar.

Finding and Replacing Information

You have continued to work on the café customer list by adding additional records. You will open the workbook file and continue working on the list.

1 Open the workbook file ex06_Customers2.

● Maximize the window.

● Use the data form to add your data to the list as a new record using ID number **999**. Enter connection times of **210**, **270**, and **240** for the Jan, Feb, and Mar fields. All other information can be fictitious.

● Close the data form.

● Scroll to see your record in row 40.

Your screen should be similar to Figure 6.18

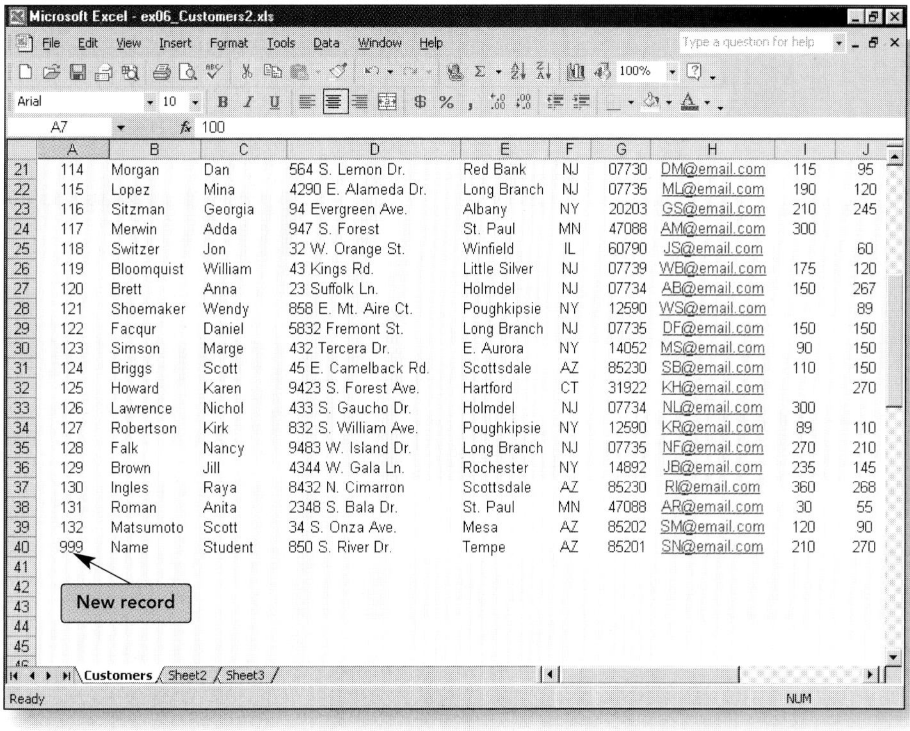

Figure 6.18

As you look over the records in the list and check the information against the customer registration information, you notice that the address for one of the café's customers, Frank Liston, was entered incorrectly. The street address should be 3021 Ash St. instead of 302. You have also been notified of a zip code change; 07730 is now 07732. Also, the January connection time for Jill Brown should be 135, not 235.

You could correct the data just by changing the appropriate cells directly on the worksheet. However, the larger your list becomes, the more difficult it will be to find the data you want to modify. Therefore, you'll practice using the other data location and modification methods to make the necessary changes.

concept 2

Find and Replace

2 The **Find and Replace** feature helps you quickly find specific information and automatically replace it with new information. The Find command locates all occurrences of the text or numbers you specify. The Replace command is used with the Find command to locate the specified entries and replace the located occurrences with the replacement text you specify. You can also find cells that match a format you specify and replace the format with another. Finding and replacing data and formats is both fast and accurate, but you need to be careful when replacing that you do not replace unintended matches.

Finding Information

First, you will locate and correct the incorrect data using the Find command. This command can be used to locate data in any type of worksheet, not just in a list.

1 ● **Choose Edit/Find.**

Another Method
The keyboard shortcut is Ctrl + F.

● **If necessary, click** Options >> **to display the additional search options.**

Your screen should be similar to Figure 6.19

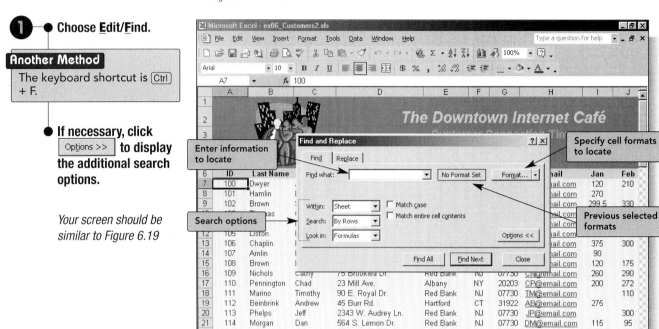

Figure 6.19

In the Find and Replace dialog box, you enter the information you want to locate in the Fi**n**d what text box. It must be entered exactly as it appears in the worksheet.

The additional options in the Find dialog box can be combined in many ways to help locate information. They are described in the table below.

Option	Effect
Within	Searches the active worksheet or workbook.
Search	Specifies the direction to search in the worksheet: By Columns searches down through columns and By Rows searches to the right across rows.
Look in	Looks for a match in the specified worksheet element; formulas, values, comments.
Match case	Finds words that have the same pattern of uppercase letters as entered in the Find what text box. Using this option makes the search **case sensitive**.
Match entire cell contents	Looks for an exact and complete match of the characters specified in the Find what text box.
Format	Used to specify a cell format to locate and replace. A sample of the selected format is displayed in the Preview box.

To enter the address to find and to search using the default options,

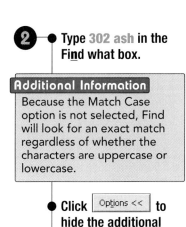

2 ● **Type 302 ash in the Find what box.**

Because the Match Case option is not selected, Find will look for an exact match regardless of whether the characters are uppercase or lowercase.

● **Click** `Options <<` **to hide the additional search options.**

● **Click** `Find Next`.

Your screen should be similar to Figure 6.20

Clicking `Find All` displays all text or format matches in a list. Selecting an item from the list moves the cell selector to the cell containing the entry.

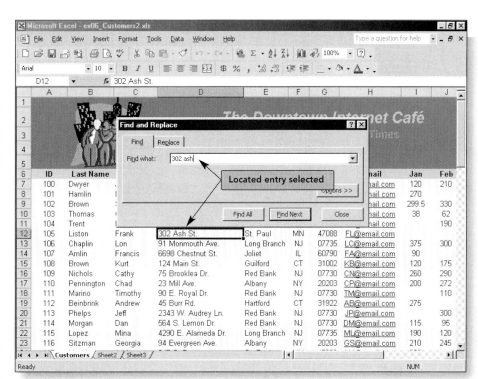

Figure 6.20

The cell containing this entry is located and displayed. You can now edit the cell to display the correct address information.

3 ● **Double-click on the cell.**

● **Change the address to 3021 Ash St.**

Your screen should be similar to Figure 6.21

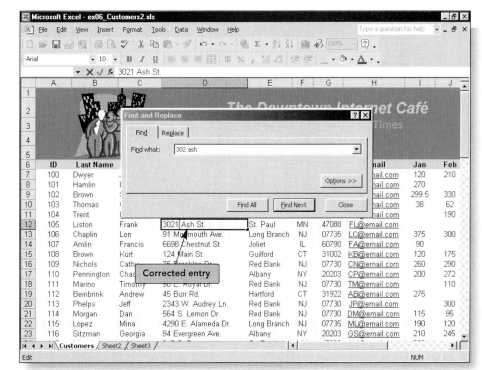

Figure 6.21

Replacing Information

Next, you'll use the Replace command to update the zip code. Once again, this command can be used on any type of worksheet to change cell data. The replacement text must be entered exactly as you want it to appear.

1 ● **Open the Replace tab.**

Another Method

The menu equivalent is Edit/Replace and the keyboard shortcut is [Ctrl] + H.

● **Type 7730 in the Find what box.**

Additional Information

You do not enter the leading zero in the zip code to find because the values are stored without the zero.

● **Type 07732 in the Replace with box.**

● **Click** [Find Next].

● **Click** [Replace].

Your screen should be similar to Figure 6.22

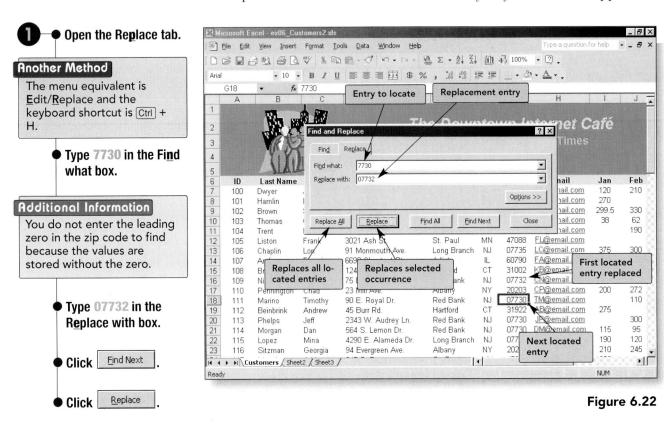

Figure 6.22

The original zip code entry is replaced with the new zip code. The program immediately continues searching and locates a second occurrence of the entry. You decide the search is locating the values accurately and that it will be safe to replace all finds with the replacement value.

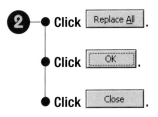

2 ● Click | Replace All |.

● Click | OK |.

● Click | Close |.

*Your screen should be
similar to Figure 6.23*

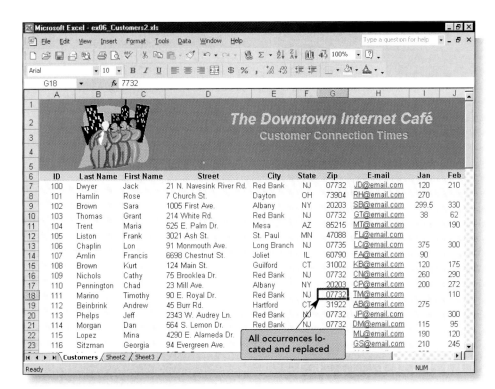

All occurrences lo-
cated and replaced

Figure 6.23

All matches are replaced with the replacement text and the dialog box is closed. It is much faster to use Replace All than to confirm each match separately. However, exercise care when using Replace All because the search text you specify might be part of another word and you may accidentally replace text you want to keep.

Using the Data Form to Locate and Change Data

Since the data you are working with has been defined as a database list, you can also use the Data Form to find and modify records. You'll use this method to make the final change to your data, correcting the connection time for Jill Brown.

1 ● Choose **D**ata/F**o**rm.

● Click [Criteria].

Your screen should be similar to Figure 6.24

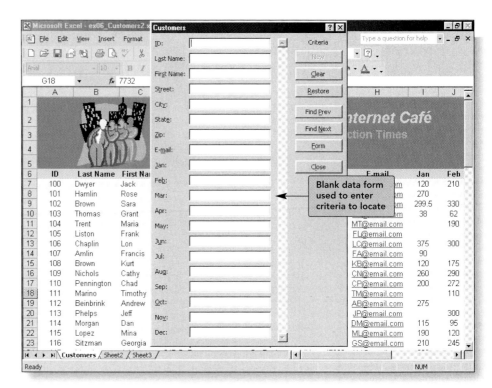

Blank data form used to enter criteria to locate

Figure 6.24

A blank data form is displayed in which you can enter the **criteria** or conditions for the record to meet in order to be located. The more precise and unique the criteria you enter, the fewer matches will be located. In this case, you'll enter the customer's last name, Brown, to locate and display the record for Jill Brown.

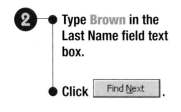

2 ● Type Brown in the Last Name field text box.

● Click [Find Next].

Your screen should be similar to Figure 6.25

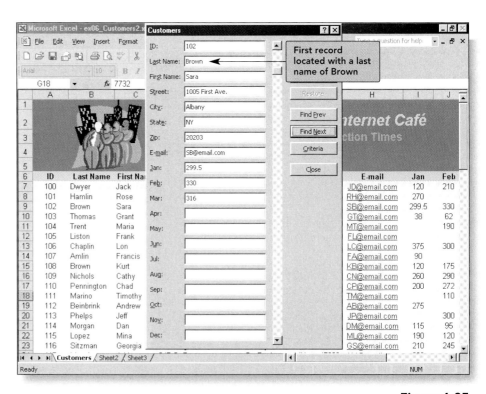

First record located with a last name of Brown

Figure 6.25

The first located record with a last name of Brown, Sara Brown, is displayed in the data form. Because there are several records with a last name of Brown, the located record is not the record you want to edit. You want to find the record for Jill Brown.

3 • Click Find Next two more times until Jill Brown's record is displayed.

• Double-click the Jan field text box to highlight the current value, 235.

• Type 135.

• Click Close.

• Scroll the list to see Jill Brown's record in row 36.

Your screen should be similar to Figure 6.26

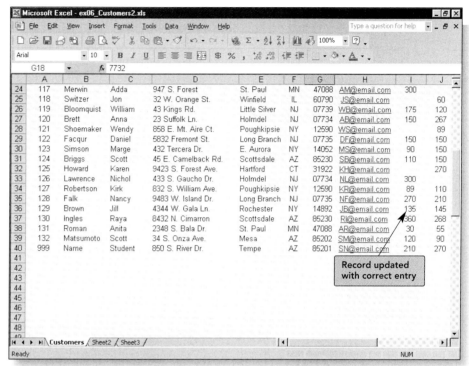

Figure 6.26

The record for Jill Brown is updated and now contains the correct value, 135, in the January connection time field.

Now that your data entries are error-free, you're ready to move on to sorting the data in a logical order.

Sorting Data

Currently, the records in the list are in the order in which you entered them. However, you feel that they would be easier to work with if they were displayed in alphabetical order by last name. To do this, you can sort the records in the list.

Sort

3 You can **sort** data in a specified sequence, al-phabetically, numerically, or by date. Sorting data often helps you find specific information quickly. The data in a worksheet can be sorted into ascending (A to Z, 1 to 9, earliest date to most recent date) or descending (Z to A, 9 to 1, most recent date to earliest date) order. When you sort, Excel rearranges the rows, columns, fields, or individual cells according to the sort order you specify.

A single sort operation can be based on up to three columns or fields of data. When a sort is done on more than one column or field, it is called a **multilevel sort**. For example, if you wanted to rearrange a list of employee data to begin with those who have worked for the com-pany the longest, you could sort it in ascending order by date and then by name.

Sorting on a Single Field

For the first sort, you want the records arranged in ascending alphabetical order by last name. The cell selector needs to be in any cell in the field to be sorted.

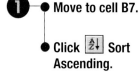

1 ● Move to cell B7.

● Click 🔼 Sort Ascending.

Your screen should be similar to Figure 6.27

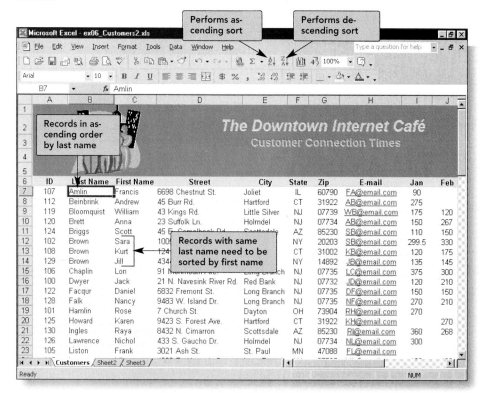

Figure 6.27

The records in the database range are rearranged to display in ascending al-phabetical order by last name. However, notice that although the records for Sara, Kurt, and Jill Brown are sorted correctly by last name, they are not sorted correctly by first name.

Sorting on Multiple Fields

You want the records that have the same last name to be further sorted by first name. To do this, you will perform a multilevel sort.

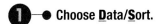
Choose Data/Sort.

Your screen should be similar to Figure 6.28

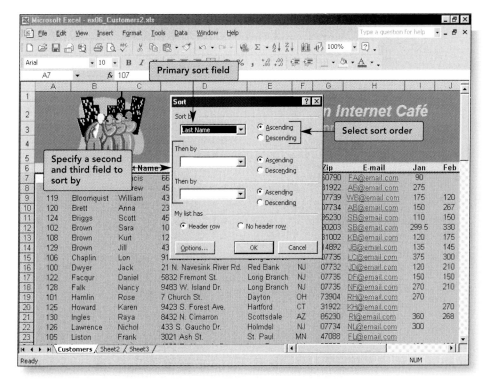

A multilevel sort uses the first field name selected in the Sort By section of the dialog box as the primary sort field; all other fields are sorted in order after the primary sort is performed. The Sort By text box correctly displays the name of the field on which the primary sort will be performed. Additionally, because the default setting is Ascending sort order, this option does not need to be changed. You need to specify the secondary sort field as the First Name field.

Select First Name from the first Then by drop-down list.

Your screen should be similar to Figure 6.29

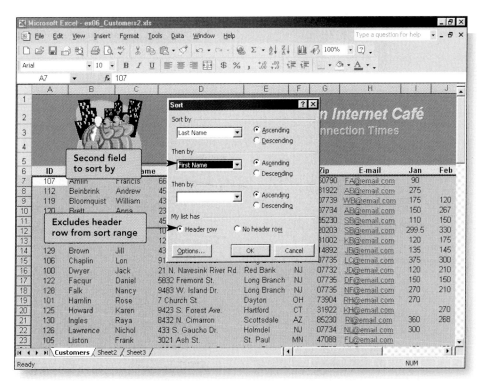

Figure 6.29

When a sort is performed, Excel assumes that you want all data except the uppermost row contained in contiguous rows and columns surrounding the selected cell to be sorted. The first row is not included in the sort range because the default setting assumes that the first row contains column labels or field names that you do not want included in the sort. If your data did not include a column label or field name as the first row in the range, you would need to choose the No header ro**w** option to change the setting to include this row in the sort. Since this worksheet includes field names in the first row, the Header **r**ow option is correctly specified already.

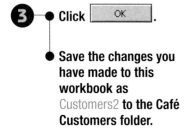

Click OK .

Save the changes you have made to this workbook as Customers2 **to the Café Customers folder.**

Your screen should be similar to Figure 6.30

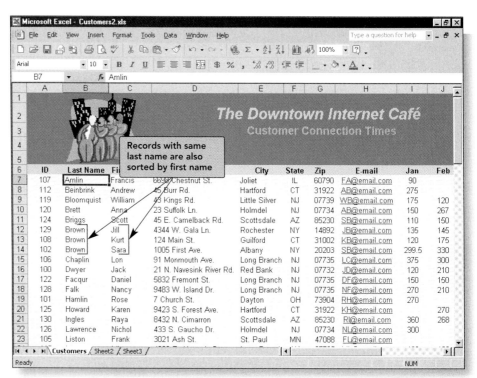

Figure 6.30

The records are now in sorted order first by last name and second by first name within same last names. As you can see, sorting is a fast, useful tool. The original sort order remains in effect until you replace it with a new sort order. If the order in which you enter records in a list is important, include a field for a unique record number. Then you can return to the entry order by sorting on the number field.

Filtering Data

Evan has informed you that he is sending out "valued customer" e-mail notes to the in-state customers who have been connecting at the café since the beginning of the year. He has asked you for a printout of the connection times and e-mail address information for those customers. Rather than creating a separate worksheet, you can filter the database range in the current worksheet to show only the requested records.

Filter

4 A **filter** is a restriction you place on records in the list to quickly isolate and display a subset of records. A filter is created by specifying a set of limiting conditions, or criteria, that you want records to meet in order to be displayed. A filter is ideal when you want to display the subset for only a brief time and then return immediately to the full set of records. You can print the filtered records as you would any worksheet. A filter is only temporary, and all records are redisplayed when you remove the filter.

Unlike the Sort feature, the filter feature does not rearrange a list. It just temporarily hides rows that do not meet the specified criteria. Data in a filtered list can be edited, formatted, charted, or printed.

Filtering on a Single Criteria

You will filter the list to display only NJ residents first.

1 ● **Choose**
Data/Filter/AutoFilter.

Your screen should be similar to Figure 6.31

Drop-down list used to select filter criteria

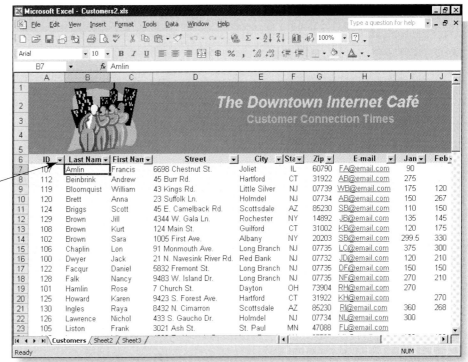

Figure 6.31

Drop-down list arrows appear next to each field name. These enable you to select the field or fields and field criteria you want to use to filter the list. The first criterion you want the records in your database range to meet is in the State field.

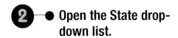

2 ● **Open the State drop-down list.**

Your screen should be similar to Figure 6.32

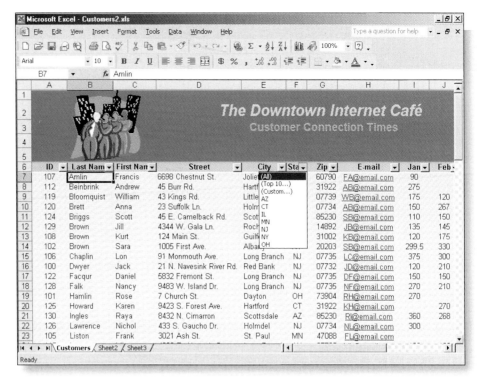

Figure 6.32

The drop-down list contains the current values in the field. In addition, you can select from these options:

Option	Effect
(All)	Displays all records regardless of the value in this field
(Top 10)	Displays the records with the highest values in this field
(Custom)	Used to specify ranges of values that a record must meet to be displayed
(Blanks)	Displays only those records that do not contain a value in this field
(NonBlanks)	Displays only those records that contain a value in this field

You want to specify that only records that have a state value of NJ are displayed.

3 ● Choose NJ from the drop-down list.

Your screen should be similar to Figure 6.33

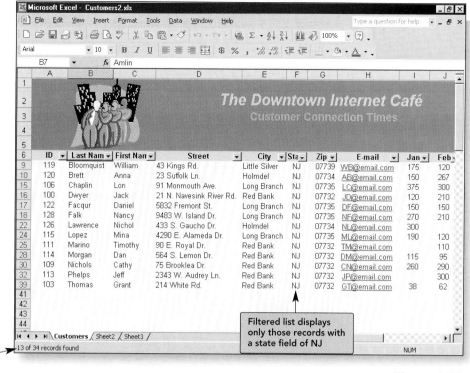

Number of records in filtered list

Filtered list displays only those records with a state field of NJ

Figure 6.33

Only those records for customers in New Jersey are displayed. However, not all of these customers have been online at the café all three months. Therefore, you want to specify further criteria to accept only "nonblanks" in the month field.

4 ● Open the Mar drop-down list.

● Choose (NonBlanks).

● In a similar manner, choose (NonBlanks) for January and February.

Your screen should be similar to Figure 6.34

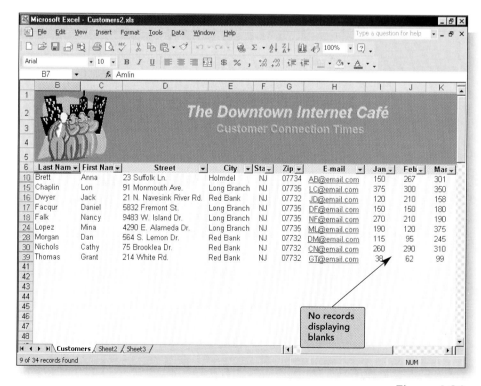

No records displaying blanks

Figure 6.34

Only the records that meet the specified criteria are displayed.

Creating a Custom Filter

You would also like to see the same information for the other out-of-state customers. To do this, you could change the State criteria and print each filter result. However, a faster way is to create a custom filter for the State field.

1 ● **From the State drop-down list, select (Custom...).**

Your screen should be similar to Figure 6.35

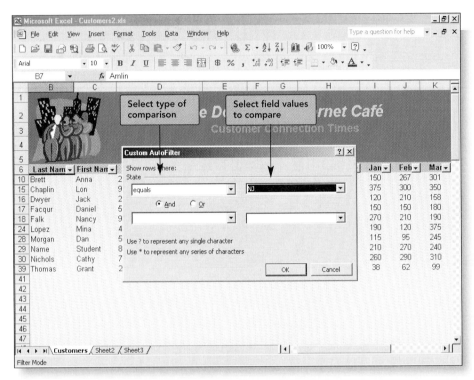

Figure 6.35

The Custom AutoFilter dialog box is used to specify a filtering operation that makes comparisons between two values. The type of comparison to make is specified in the box on the left, and the value to compare to is specified in the box on the right. You can include a second set of criteria by selecting the **A**nd or **O**r options and specifying the settings in the lower row of boxes. The AND and OR operators are used to specify multiple conditions that must be met for the records to display in the filtered list. The AND operator narrows the search, because a record must meet both conditions to be included. The OR operator broadens the search, because any record meeting either condition is included in the output.

You want to display records for all states except New Jersey.

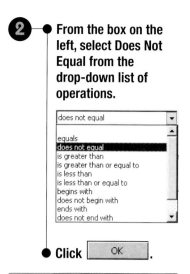

2 From the box on the left, select Does Not Equal from the drop-down list of operations.

does not equal

equals
does not equal
is greater than
is greater than or equal to
is less than
is less than or equal to
begins with
does not begin with
ends with
does not end with

● Click [OK].

Additional Information

Your record may appear in the filtered list if your state field entry is not NJ.

Your screen should be similar to Figure 6.36

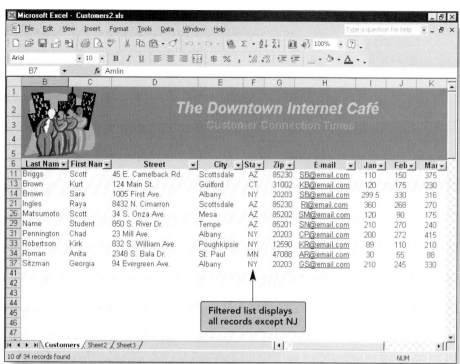

B7 — *fx* Amlin

The Downtown Internet Café
Customer Connection Times

Last Name	First Name	Street	City	State	Zip	E-mail	Jan	Feb	Mar
Briggs	Scott	45 E. Camelback Rd.	Scottsdale	AZ	85230	SB@email.com	110	150	375
Brown	Kurt	124 Main St.	Guilford	CT	31002	KB@email.com	120	175	230
Brown	Sara	1005 First Ave.	Albany	NY	20203	SB@email.com	299.5	330	316
Ingles	Raya	8432 N. Cimarron	Scottsdale	AZ	85230	RI@email.com	360	268	270
Matsumoto	Scott	34 S. Onza Ave.	Mesa	AZ	85202	SM@email.com	120	90	175
Name	Student	850 S. River Dr.	Tempe	AZ	85201	SN@email.com	210	270	240
Pennington	Chad	23 Mill Ave.	Albany	NY	20203	CP@email.com	200	272	415
Robertson	Kirk	832 S. William Ave.	Poughkipsie	NY	12590	KR@email.com	89	110	210
Roman	Anita	2348 S. Bala Dr.	St. Paul	MN	47088	AR@email.com	30	55	88
Sitzman	Georgia	94 Evergreen Ave.	Albany	NY	20203	GS@email.com	210	245	330

Filtered list displays all records except NJ

Customers / Sheet2 / Sheet3 /

10 of 34 records found   NUM

Figure 6.36

Now the filtered list displays records for all states except New Jersey that have connection time usage in all three months. As expected, only a few out-of-state customers meet this requirement.

Printing Selected Areas

You are finished filtering the data, and you've got the information Evan requested. However, you do not want the worksheet printout to include the months that do not yet have any connection data in them, so you will set a **print area** that specifies the area of the worksheet to print. The print area can be one or more ranges of cells.

Setting a Print Area

You will include only the list fields through March. To define a print area, you first select the cell range that you want to print.

1 ● Select NJ from the
AutoFilter drop-down
list to display the NJ
records again.

● Select A6 through col-
umn K of the last row
of displayed records.

● Choose **F**ile/**Prin**t
Area/**S**et Print Area.

*Your screen should be
similar to Figure 6.37*

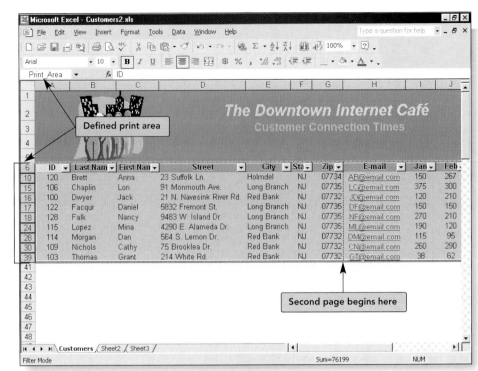

Figure 6.37

A print area is highlighted and a page break line shows where the selected
range will print on a second page. You need to change the orientation to
landscape so that the range will print on one page.

2 ● Click 🔍 Print
Preview.

● Change the worksheet
orientation to
Landscape.

● Add a right-aligned
header that displays
your name and the
current date, on a
single line.

● If necessary, click
Zoom to view the
whole page.

*Your screen should be
similar to Figure 6.38*

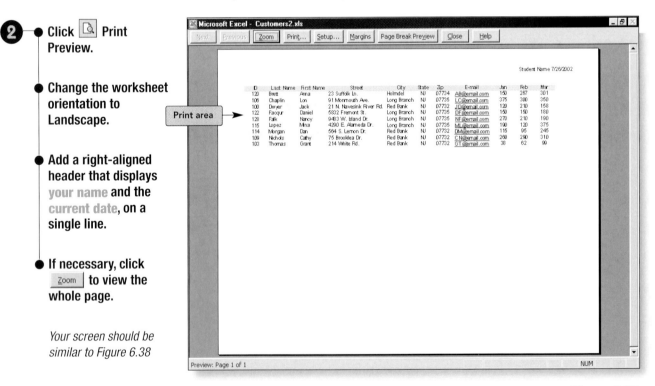

Figure 6.38

The preview window displays only the information contained in the defined
print area. The print area is saved with the worksheet and will be used automatically whenever you print the worksheet.

Printing Nonadjacent Ranges

However, as you look at the preview, you realize Evan will not need the address information either, since the promotion is being sent by e-mail. You want to print the name fields and the e-mail address and connection time fields only. To do this, you select a range to print and use the Selection option in the Print dialog box to specify a temporary print area.

1 ● **Close the preview window.**

● **Select A6 through the last row of records in column C and H6 through the last row of records in column K.**

HAVING TROUBLE?
Hold down [Ctrl] to select nonadjacent ranges.

● **Choose File/Print/Selection.**

● **Click** Preview **.**

● **Scroll down to see the second page.**

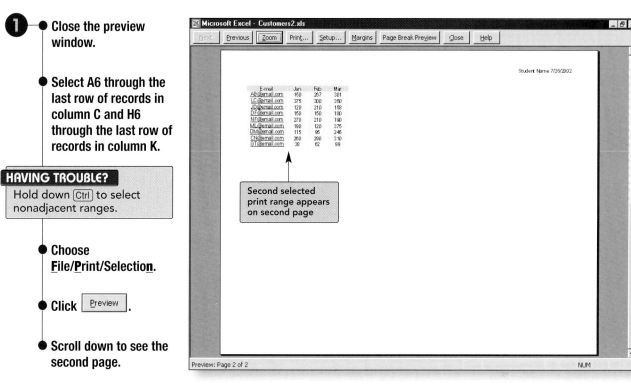

Figure 6.39

Your screen should be similar to Figure 6.39

The first selection appears on the first page and the second selection on the second page. Each nonadjacent selection begins printing on a new page. To fix this, you need to hide the columns you do not want to print and then define a single print range.

2

- Close the preview window.

- Select and hide columns D through G.

HAVING TROUBLE?
Use Format/Column/Hide to hide the selected columns.

- Select A6 through K39.

- Click 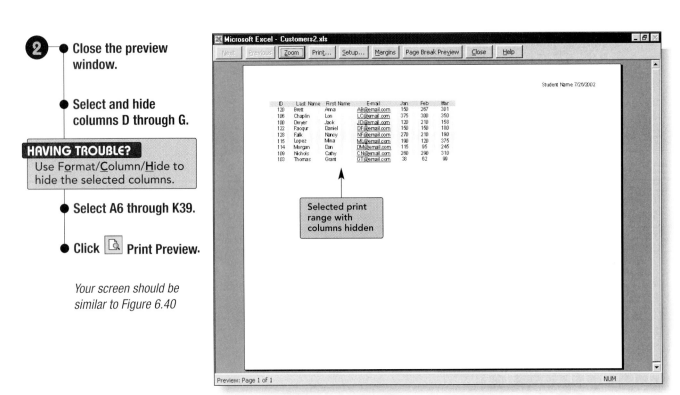 Print Preview.

Your screen should be similar to Figure 6.40

Selected print range with columns hidden

Preview: Page 1 of 1

Figure 6.40

Finally, the printout is how you want it to appear, except you no longer need to use landscape orientation.

3

- Change the orientation to Portrait.

- Center the worksheet horizontally on the page.

- Print the worksheet.

Additional Information
The AutoFilter drop-down buttons do not print.

Evan now has the information in the printout that he needs.

Clearing Print Areas

You can now unhide the columns and remove the AutoFilter from the database range and continue working on it.

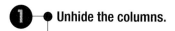

1 ● **Unhide the columns.**

● **Choose
Data/Filter/AutoFilter.**

● **Move to cell A7.**

*Your screen should be
similar to Figure 6.41*

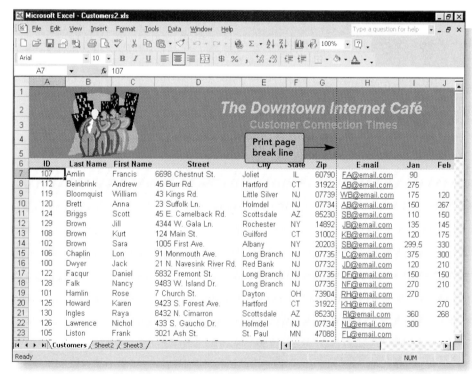

> Removing filter
> displays all
> records

Figure 6.41

The filter is removed and all records are again displayed. The dotted lines
indicate where a page break will occur when the worksheet is printed using
the defined print area. Since the print area did not work for the data you
wanted to print, you will remove it.

2 ● **Choose File/Print
Area/Clear Print Area.**

● **Save the workbook.**

*Your screen should be
similar to Figure 6.42*

> The Downtown Internet Café
> Customer Connection Times

> Print page
> break line

Figure 6.42

The single page break line indicates where the second page would begin if
the entire worksheet were printed in portrait orientation.

Creating a Web Page

The second project Evan has asked you to look into is to make the Bonus Dollars worksheet available to customers on the Café's Web site so that they can check their award status. To do this, you will convert the Excel worksheet to a Web page.

Previewing the Web Page

Note: This section of the lab assumes that a Web browser is installed on your computer.

You have made several changes to the worksheet that were needed before it could be used on the Web. You replaced the Customer name with the ID number and removed the Select Bonus Rate combo box and the Print Command button from the form.

1  **Open the workbook file** ex06_Bonus Dollars Web.

Your screen should be similar to Figure 6.43

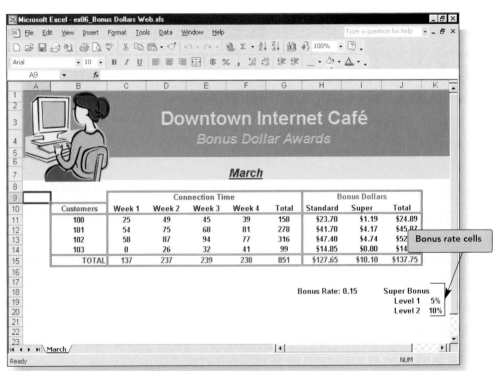

Figure 6.43

The only information remaining below the form are the Bonus Rate cells used to calculate the Bonus Dollars. Before you convert the worksheet, you want to preview how it will look first.

2 ● Choose File/Web Page Preview

● Maximize the browser window.

Your screen should be similar to Figure 6.44

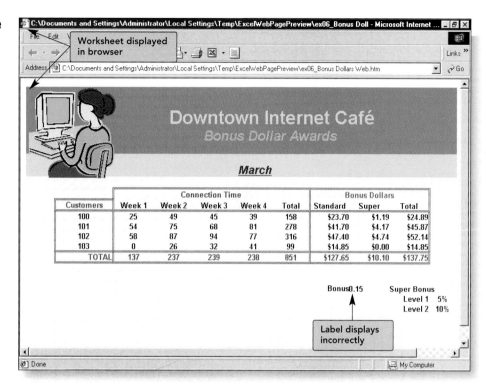

Figure 6.44

The browser opens on your system and displays the worksheet. The name of the worksheet appears in the browser window title bar. Most of the information looks pretty good, except for the display of the Bonus Rate label.

Saving the Worksheet as a Web Page

You will go ahead and convert the worksheet to a Web page and then make the needed adjustments.

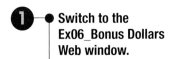

1 ● Switch to the Ex06_Bonus Dollars Web window.

HAVING TROUBLE?
Click on the appropriate button in the taskbar to display the worksheet or press [Alt] + [Tab↹] to display the previously viewed window.

● Choose **F**ile/Save as Web Page.

Your screen should be similar to Figure 6.45

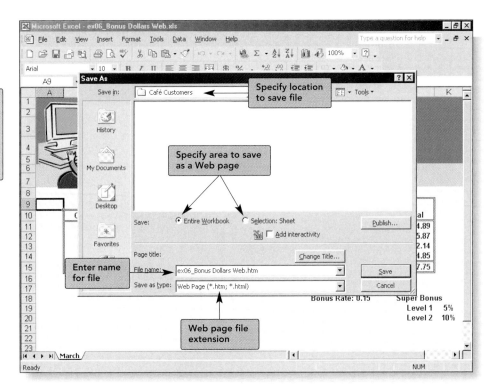

Figure 6.45

Additional Information
You can also preselect a range to use as the area to save as a Web page.

In the Save As dialog box, enter a name for the Web page file, choose the location where you want the file saved, and specify whether you want to use the entire workbook or just the current selection as your Web page contents. The default file name is the same as the workbook file name with the Web page file extension of .htm or html. Excel converts a worksheet to a Web page by adding hypertext markup language (HTML) coding to the document. You can also add a title to your Web page from this dialog box. You will specify the current worksheet as the contents for the Web page.

2

- Select S**e**lection:Sheet.

- Change the file name to March Bonus Dollars.

- Specify the Café Customers folder as the location to save the file.

- Click [S**a**ve].

Your screen should be similar to Figure 6.46

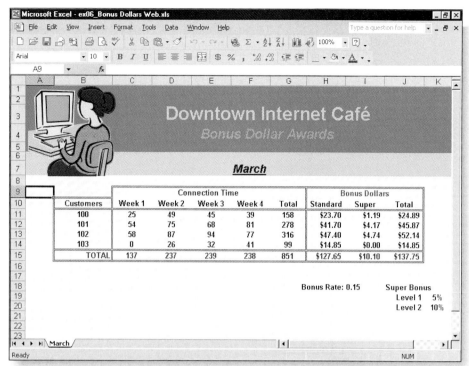

Figure 6.46

Next, you will make the changes to the Bonus Rate cell so that it displays correctly and then preview the Web page to check how it looks again.

3

- Move the contents of cell H18 to G18.

- Left-align the entry.

- Fix the fill color of cell H18.

- Format cell I18 as Currency with two decimal places.

- Choose **F**ile/We**b** Page Preview.

Your screen should be similar to Figure 6.47

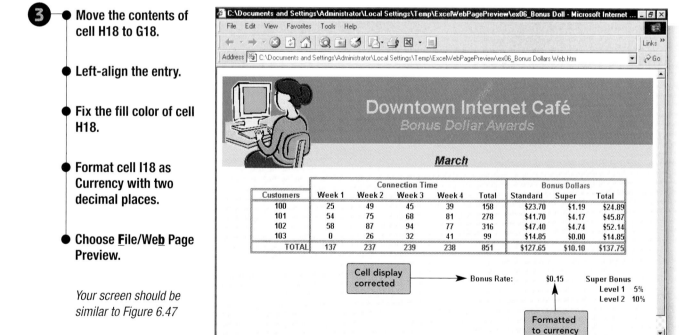

Figure 6.47

The revised worksheet is displayed in your browser window. You like the way this looks and need to resave the changes you made to the worksheet to update the Web page file.

4 ● Close the browser application.

● Choose File/**S**ave as Web Page.

● Select R**e**publish:Sheet.

● Click [**S**ave].

● Close all open workbooks without saving changes and exit Excel.

Using Supporting Folders

Each Web page you create has a folder that contains all the elements on the page, such as images and hyperlinks.

You will use the Windows Exploring window to see the Web page and folder that were created.

1 ● Open the Exploring window.

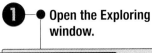
Select E**x**plore from the My Computer icon shortcut menu.

● Change the location to the location where you saved the Web page.

● Select the March Bonus Dollars.htm **file.**

Your screen should be similar to Figure 6.48

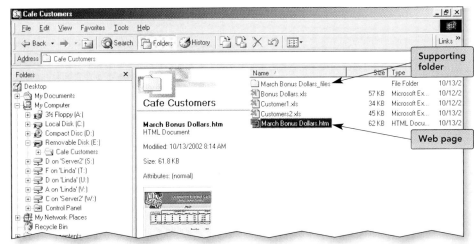

Figure 6.48

The Web page file and its supporting folder are saved in the Café Customers folder. By default, the name of the supporting folder is the name of the Web page plus an underscore (_) and the word "files." All supporting files, such as those for bullets, graphics, and background are contained in the supporting folder. Any graphics that were added to the page that were not already JPEG or GIF files are converted to that format. To see the files in the supporting folder,

2 ● Open the March Bonus Dollars_files **folder.**

● **If necessary, expand the Name column to fully display the file names.**

Your screen should be similar to Figure 6.49

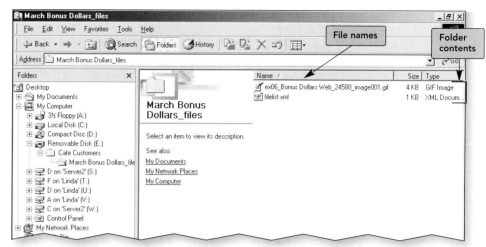

Figure 6.49

The Web page contains one graphic element. The graphic has been renamed "image001."

When you move your files to place on a server, you need to include the HTML file and the associated supporting folder that contains all the elements on the page. If this folder is not available when the associated HTML page is loaded in the browser, the graphic elements will not be displayed.

3 ● Close the Exploring window.

Discussion Comments

When working with a Web page or other Office file that can be opened with a browser, the **Web discussion** feature can be used. This feature allows users to attach comments to the document that can be read and responded to by all reviewers. The **discussion comments** are stored in a database on a discussion server and appear with the document. A **discussion server** is a computer that stores discussion text and information about the location of the file being discussed. The file must be available on the discussion server or another server location for access by all reviewers.

LAB **6**

Creating and Using Lists and Web Pages

List   (EX6.4)

A list or database is an organized collection of related information entered in sequential rows and columns.

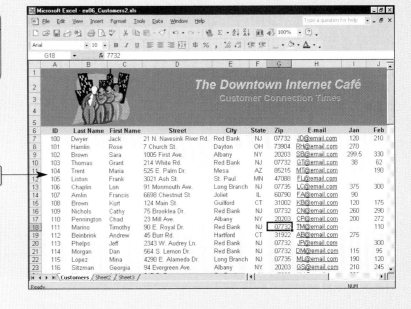

List

Find and Replace   (EX6.19)

The Find and Replace feature helps you quickly find specific information and automatically replace it with new information.

Find and Replace

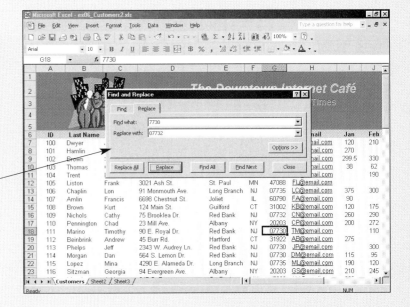

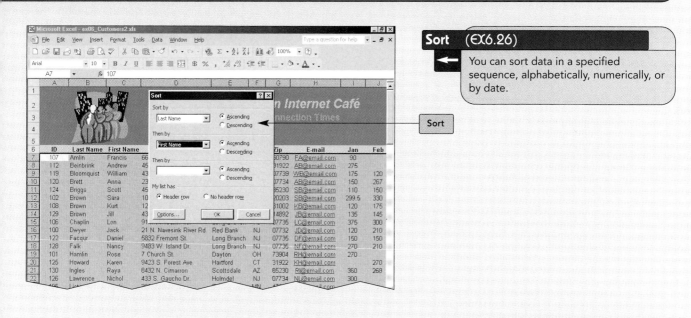

Sort

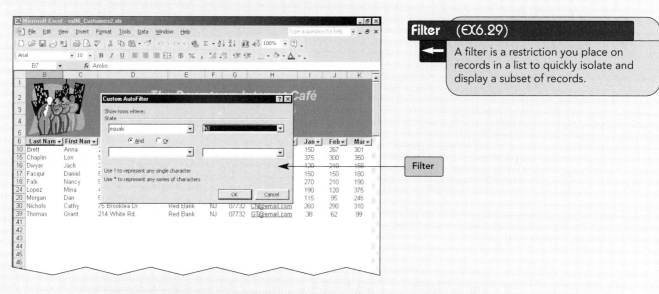

Filter

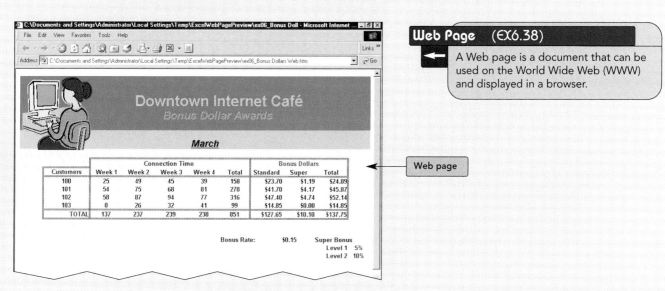

Web page

LAB 6

Creating and Using Lists and Web Pages

key terms

browser   EX6.38

case sensitive   EX6.20

criteria   EX6.24

data form   EX6.6

database   EX6.4

discussion comments   EX6.43

discussion server   EX6.43

field   EX6.4

field name   EX6.4

filter   EX6.29

Find and Replace   EX6.19

HTML (Hypertext Markup Language)   EX6.38

hyperlink   EX6.11

list range   EX6.4

list   EX6.4

multilevel sort   EX6.26

print area   EX6.33

record   EX6.4

sort   EX6.26

Web Page   EX6.38

mous skills

The Microsoft Office User Specialist (MOUS) certification program is designed to measure your proficiency in performing basic tasks using the Office XP applications. Getting certified demonstrates that you have the skills and provides a valuable industry credential for employment. After completing this lab, you have learned the following Microsoft Office User Specialist skills:

Skill	Description	Page
Working with cells and cell data	Find and replace cell data and formats	EX6.19
	Work with a subset of data by filtering lists	EX6.29
Managing Workbooks	Manage workbook files and folders	EX6.17
Formatting and Printing Workbooks	Modify page setup options for worksheets	EX6.33
	Preview and print worksheets and workbooks	EX6.34
Workgroup Collaboration	Convert worksheets into Web pages	EX6.38
	Create hyperlinks	EX6.11
	View and edit comments	EX6.43

Command	Shortcut Key	Button	Action
File/Save as Web Page			Creates a Web page from the entire active workbook or the current worksheet selection
File/Web Page Preview			Displays the active workbook as a Web page in the browser without actually publishing it
File/Print Area/Set Print Area			Sets area of worksheet to be printed
File/Print Area/Clear Print Area			Clears print area
Edit/Find	Ctrl + F		Searches for a specified entry
Edit/Replace	Ctrl + H		Searches for a specified entry and replaces it with another specified entry
Insert/Hyperlink	Ctrl + K	🔗	Inserts a new hyperlink or modifies the selected hyperlink
Insert/Hyperlink/Remove Link			Removes hyperlink settings from selected cell
Tools/AutoCorrect Options/AutoFormat As You Type/Internet and network paths with hyperlinks			Turns on/off feature to automatically format Internet and network paths as hyperlinks
Format/Cells/Category/Special			Applies the selected special format to the number entries
Data/Sort			Arranges data alphabetically, numerically, or by date
Data/Filter/AutoFilter			Displays records based on specified criteria
Data/Form			Displays a data form dialog box for record entry and modification

Terminology

screen identification

In the following worksheet, several items are identified by letters. Enter the correct term for each item in the spaces that follow.

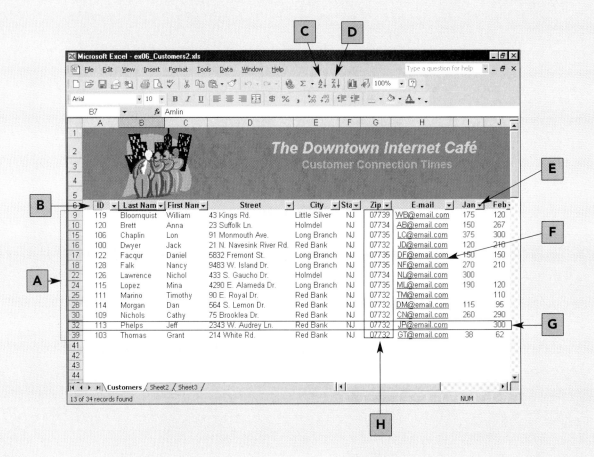

A. _____   E. _____

B. _____   F. _____

C. _____   G. _____

D. _____   H. _____

matching

Match the letter on the right to the item in the numbered list on the left.

1. Web page   ____ **a.** a connection to a location in another document

2. field   ____ **b.** displays a subset of records according to specified criteria

3. descending   ____ **c.** Web page programming language

4. filter   ____ **d.** Z to A order

5. list   ____ **e.** displayed in each row of a list

6. sort   ____ **f.** used to enter information in a list

7. hyperlink   ____ **g.** a document that can be displayed in a browser

8. record   ____ **h.** the smallest unit of information about a record

9. data form   ____ **i.** organizes data in a specified sequence

10. HTML   ____ **j.** a database

multiple choice

Circle the correct response to the questions below.

1. A _____ is one unit of information in a list.
   a. field
   b. record
   c. sort
   d. database

2. The _____ from the list appear as the column labels in a data form.
   a. record names
   b. column letters
   c. field names
   d. cell references

3. The sort feature lets you sort up to _____ fields in a list at a time.
   a. 2
   b. 1
   c. 3
   d. 4

4. The _____ option in a filter field drop-down list enables you to specify ranges of values that the record must meet to be displayed.
   a. Criteria
   b. Range
   c. Values
   d. Custom

5. The quickest way to locate a record in a large list is to use the _____ feature.
   a. Find
   b. Criteria
   c. Replace
   d. Sort

6. A sort that is performed on more than one column or field is called a:
   a. multiple sort
   b. advanced sort
   c. multi-level sort
   d. selective sort

7. Use a _____ to quickly jump to another location in a document.
   a. Web page
   b. hyperlink
   c. browser
   d. filter

8. The programming language used in Web pages is:
   a. HTLM
   b. HTXT
   c. HTML
   d. HXLS

9. To locate and change data in a list, use the_____.
   a. Find command
   b. Replace command
   c. Data form
   d. All of the above

10. To print nonadjacent ranges on the same page,
    a. move the columns between the areas you do not want to print and select the range
    b. select the nonadjacent ranges and print the selections
    c. define a print area
    d. hide the columns between the areas you do not want to print and select the range

true/false

Circle the correct answer to the following questions.

1. You can erase any changes you made to a record in the data form by clicking ⟲, as long as you do it before proceeding to the next record or closing the dialog box.   True   False

2. A browser is used to display Web pages.   True   False

3. A print area is saved with the worksheet.   True   False

4. A data form cannot be used to locate records.   True   False

5. A sort displays a subset of records.   True   False

6. A filter rearranges data according to the criteria you specify.   True   False

7. A discussion comment is saved with the worksheet.   True   False

8. Field names are entered in the first row of a list.	True	False
9. Nonadjacent ranges can only be printed on separate pages.	True	False
10. You must first create a new folder in Windows Explorer before you can save a workbook in it.	True	False

Concepts

fill-in questions

Complete the following statements by filling in the blanks with the correct terms.

1. Converting a worksheet to a Web page changes the file type to _____.

2. A _____ is used to enter records into a list.

3. _____ adds drop-down lists to the field names in a list.

4. _____ a list to display records in a specified order.

5. _____ order displays records in Z to A alphabetical order.

6. Apply a _____ to a list to display a subset of records.

7. The two types of filter functions are _____ and _____.

8. Define a _____ to print the same selection each time you print the worksheet.

9. Use a _____ to specify operations that make comparisons between two values.

10. A _____ folder is created when you save a worksheet as a Web page.

discussion questions

1. Discuss different ways that an Excel list can be used.

2. Discuss the differences between the AutoFilter function and the Custom Filter function. When would you use AutoFilter? When would the custom filter be more appropriate?

3. Discuss how a worksheet is converted to a Web page and used.

lab exercises

Hands-On Exercises

step by step

Kodiak Construction Database

★ 1. The Kodiak Construction Company uses an Excel list to keep track of jobs for the year and the permit fees paid on them. They have asked you to do some analysis on the data so that they can better see trends and make any needed adjustments. Your completed analysis of the list will be similar to the one shown on the facing page.

  a. Open the workbook file ex06_Kodiak Database.

  b. Format the Phone field using the special phone number format.

  c. You have been given invoices for three new jobs. Using the data form, enter the following three new records into the database.

Job Number	04025	04026	04027
Date	04/23/04	04/26/04	04/28/04
Category	Residential	Residential	Commercial
Site Address	2983 Club House Dr	20234 Midway Ave	467 Broadway Rd
Contact	Leware, Edward	Williams, Gary	Student Name
Phone	555-1763	555-0031	555-2763
Permit Fees	$55.00	$350.00	$1,075.00

  d. Close the data form and scroll to the end of the list.

  e. The Accounting department has requested a list of jobs whose permit fees were more than $1000. Filter the database to display these records only. Print the filtered list in landscape orientation, centered horizontally.

  f. Marketing has also requested a copy of the job list sorted by category. Sort the list on Category. Print all the fields except the Permit Fees field.

  g. Change the layout to Portrait and include your name and the current date in the header.

  h. Save the workbook as Kodiak Database Update.

Kodiak Construction
Jobs Database

Job Number	Date	Category	Site Address	Contact	Phone
30055	01/11/04	Commercial	420 McCormick Dr	Forester, Kimberly	555-7521
09851	01/12/04	Commercial	639 Bear Claw Rd	Paul, Timothy	555-2454
98374	01/15/04	Commercial	33 Arrowhead Rd	Vaughn, James	555-7483
00983	02/13/04	Commercial	5623 Scott Dr	Anderson, Tom	555-2734
34592	02/16/04	Commercial	7020 Green Valley Way	Merwin, Michael	555-6853
46191	03/07/04	Commercial	23418 Placer Cr	Carothers, Daryl	555-1324
30141	03/09/04	Commercial	2351 Live Oak Dr	Ross, Cathy	555-4314
09834	03/10/04	Commercial	4512 Brandling Ave	Stansbury, Thomas	555-1287
00123	04/07/04	Commercial	41523 Mount Marapai Rd	Kenson, Lois	555-0267
92364	04/10/04	Commercial	1873 Rosser St	Young, Luanne	555-0153
15623	04/18/04	Commercial	90842 Rolling Ridge Ave	Davis, Dorothy	555-0931
04027	04/28/04	Commercial	467 Broadway Rd	Name, Student	555-2763
98753	01/04/04	Residental	3200 Sunflower Dr	Jones, April	555-3443
00083	01/06/04	Residental	11440 N Deer Hill	Sierra, Judy	555-7464
03652	01/06/04	Residental	2154 Congress Ave	Kelly, William	555-7674
98345	01/12/04	Residental	78343 Horizon Rd	Henderson, James	555-4245
28974	01/12/04	Residental	2489 Green Brier Pkwy	Thomas, Susanne	555-9313
89120	01/17/04	Residental	2873 Pinnacle Pass	Carilisi, Sarah	555-2384
00095	02/10/04	Residental	2983 E Hwy 78	Mattson, Linda	555-2938
12654	02/13/04	Residental	1024 Gurley Peaks	Staley, Jeff	555-1982
09852	02/23/04	Residental	934 Hillside Dr	Richards, Mike	555-2094
22523	02/28/04	Residental	12004 Upper Sky Pkwy	Rhodes, Edna	555-1983
22083	03/23/04	Residental	845 Willow Creek Rd	Eaton, Gloria	555-1236
00376	03/30/04	Residental	5637 Hilltop Rd	Boyer, Keith	555-1828
04025	04/23/04	Residental	2983 Club House Dr	Leware, Edward	555-1763
04026	04/26/04	Residental	20234 Midway Ave	Williams, Gary	555-0031

Kodiak Construction
Jobs Database

Job Number	Date	Category	Site Address	Contact	Phone	Permit Fees
98374	01/15/04	Commercial	33 Arrowhead Rd	Vaughn, James	555-7483	$ 3,300.00
00983	02/13/04	Commercial	5623 Scott Dr	Anderson, Tom	555-2734	$ 9,830.00
34592	02/16/04	Commercial	7020 Green Valley Way	Merwin, Michael	555-6853	$ 2,240.00
09852	02/23/04	Residental	934 Hillside Dr	Richards, Mike	555-2094	$ 1,500.00
46191	03/07/04	Commercial	23418 Placer Cr	Carothers, Daryl	555-1324	$ 7,522.00
09834	03/10/04	Commercial	4512 Brandling Ave	Stansbury, Thomas	555-1287	$ 10,023.00
00123	04/07/04	Commercial	41523 Mount Marapai Rd	Kenson, Lois	555-0267	$ 8,700.00
04027	04/28/04	Commercial	467 Broadway Rd	Name, Student	555-2763	$ 1,075.00

Wilson Electronics Employee Database

★ **2.** Part of your job in the Personnel department at Wilson Electronics is to maintain the employee sales database. Recently, in order to boost sales, the company has been running a rewards program for their employees based on sales performance. In addition to the standard database maintenance, you have been asked to examine the employee database and determine the appropriate rewards. Your completed analysis and update of the database should be similar to that shown here.

a. Open the file ex06_Wilson Employees.

b. The employee data for several new employees has not been included in the database. Use the data form to enter the records shown below.

Employee #	Last Name	First Name	Department	Total Sales
45925	Phillips	Jennifer	Audio	$752.98
08420	Schwartz	Grant	Small Appliances	$1230.79
64301	Thurman	Andy	Electronics	$1951.50
00345	Wood	Cyrus	Computers	$5,450.97

c. Apply an ascending sort to the Last Name column to alphabetize your list.

d. As you work with the database, you realize that a change in department structure has not yet been included. The Large Appliances department has been restructured and is now called Kitchen and Home. Use Find and Replace to make this change to the file.

e. There have been some personnel changes since the last database update. Eugene Radden and Tony Patel are no longer with the company. Find and remove their records from the database. Joann Keifer recently got married. Change her last name to **Hancock**.

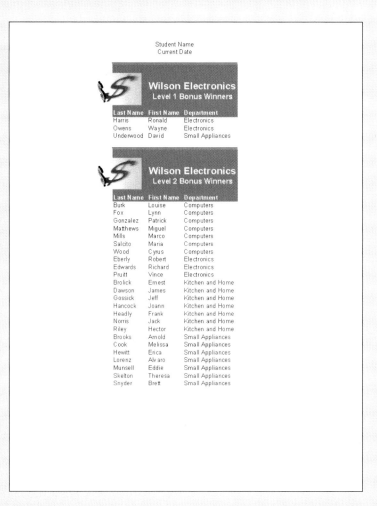

f. You have finished making the necessary changes to the database and can now begin your analysis. Use a multilevel sort to display the records first by department and then by last name.

g. Now that you have the data organized, you need to filter the records to determine which employees have earned rewards. There are two awards levels. Those who have sales of at least $2000 receive $75, those with sales of at least $4000 receive $150. Use AutoFilter and apply a custom filter to determine those employees whose sales are greater than or equal to $2000 but less than $4000. Copy this filtered sheet to a new sheet and name it **Bonus Winners**. Best Fit columns.

h. Use AutoFilter on the Employee Sales sheet and apply a custom filter to determine those employees whose sales are greater than or equal to $4000. Copy this information to the Bonus Winners sheet below the other information separated by a blank row.

i. Apply an AutoFormat of your choice to the new sheet. Change the subtitle to **Level 1 Bonus Winners**.

j. Insert the copy of the title and field name above the second group of records. Best Fit the columns. Change the subtitle to **Level 2 Bonus Winners**.

k. You need to print the list of winners to post in the break room, but some of the information included in your new sheet is confidential. Define a print area to include only the employees' last and first names and their department.

l. Adjust the formatting so that the printout will include the title information and graphic. Print the Bonus Winners worksheet with your name and the current date centered on a separate line in a header. Center the worksheet horizontally.

m. Remove the filter from the sales worksheet. Save your completed workbook as **Wilson Employee Rewards**.

Lifestyle Fitness Club Employee Database

★★ 3. You work in Human Resources at the Lifestyle Fitness Club. One of your duties includes maintaining an Excel database of employee information. Your supervisor requested some payroll information that will be used to determine pay raises. You have been asked to provide an analysis of jobs and pay rates. Your completed analysis will be similar to the one shown here.

a. Open the file ex06_LFC Database.

b. Using the data form, enter a new record into the database. Use your name as the employee. Enter **9999** as your employee number, the current date as the Hire Date, **Sales Associate** as your job title, **10.00** as your pay rate and **20** as your Hours.

c. Use the data form to edit the entry for Kimberly Kieken. Her last name is now **Larson**.

d. Sort the list to display the records by pay rate first, job title second, and hire date third. Filter the list to exclude records with a pay rate of salary. Add your name and the current date to the footer. Print the sorted list in landscape orientation.

e. Filter the list again to display only those records with a hire date before November 2000. Print the filtered sheet.

f. Remove the filter.

g. Save your completed workbook as LFC Analysis.

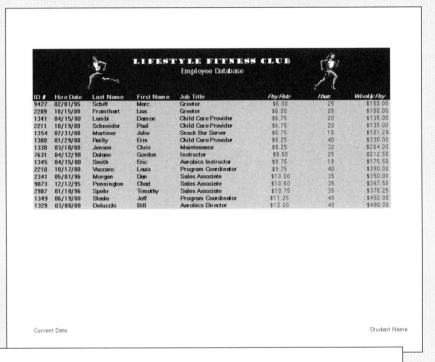

Adventure Travel Tours Client Database

★ ★ **4.** As a travel agent at Adventure Travel Tours you maintain an Excel database of your clients. You
★ have recently created several new tour packages and would like to inform your clients about them.
Your database includes information about where customers have traveled in the six areas your
new packages cover. You would like to target those who have already traveled in the new areas of
your packages. Some of your completed worksheets will be similar to those shown here.

a. Open the file ex06_ATT
Client List.

b. Merge and center Your
Name Client List under
the company name at
the top of the work-
sheet. Increase the font
size to 14 and apply the
same font color as the
main title.

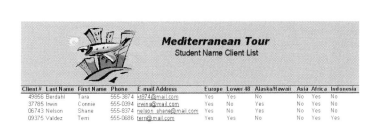

c. The data for one of your
clients has changed
since you last worked
with the workbook. Use
the data form to locate
the record for Debby
Shaw. Change her e-
mail address to
debby_shaw@
mail.com.

d. One of your new
packages is a tour of
Indonesia. Filter the
list to display those
clients who have
traveled to Indonesia
in the past. Insert a
new sheet and name
it Indonesia Tour.
Copy the filter re-
sults (including the
title) to the new
sheet. Best Fit the
columns. Change the
title to Indonesia Tour.

e. Print the Indonesia
Tour sheet centered
horizontally in land-
scape orientation.

f. You have another tour package that explores the Mediterranean and then ventures into Africa. You need to display a list of clients who have traveled to Africa and Europe. In the Client List sheet, display all the records in the Indonesia category again. First filter for those who have traveled to Europe. Then filter the list to determine which of those clients have traveled to Africa.

h. Insert a new sheet titled Mediterranean Tour. Copy the filtered Client List sheet to the new sheet. Best Fit the columns. Change the title to Mediterranean Tour. Print the Mediterranean Tour sheet centered horizontally in landscape orientation.

i. Return to the Client List sheet and remove the filter. Save your completed worksheet as ATT Client List2.

Animal Rescue Foundation Donation Inventory

★ ★ ★ **5.** The Animal Rescue Foundation relies on donations to furnish foster homes with the supplies they need. They have started to record the donation information in an Excel workbook so that they can keep an inventory of goods. You have been asked to update and maintain this inventory and furnish the board of directors with an inventory that calls attention to supply shortages. The directors have also asked you to create a Web page so that foundation members can see the inventories and make donations accordingly. Your completed worksheets should be similar to those shown here.

a. Open the file ex06_ARF Inventory.

b. The inventory consists of a list of items showing the quantity on hand and the desired quantity. You need to add a column that will identify the need status of each item. Add the label Status in cell E9. Adjust the formatting as needed.

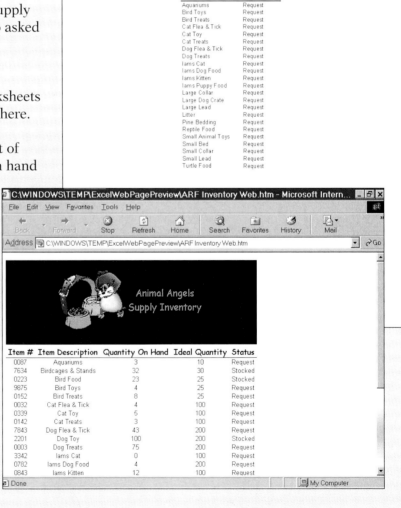

c. In order to indicate a need for an item, you will enter a formula that will calculate when an item's on-hand amount is less than half of the ideal amount, and display either stocked or request based on the determination. Enter the formula =IF(C10<(D10/2), "Request","Stocked") in cell E10. Copy the formula to the rest of the cells in that column.

d. You now have a list that displays which items need to be restocked. Now you need to print a list of low stock items for the board. Display only those items with "Request" status.

e. The board does not need most of the information in the sheet. They would like a list with the item description and the status. Hide columns A, C, and D. Add the title Inventory in cell E2 and Shortages in E3. Apply formatting of your choice. Preview the sheet. Add your name and the current date to a custom header and print the sheet centered horizontally.

f. Unhide the columns. Delete the titles in cells E2 and E3. Remove the AutoFilter. Save your completed workbook as ARF Inventory2.

g. You have been asked to create a Web page with the inventory information. Preview the Web page. Fix and enhance the formatting of the sheet as needed.

h. Save the Supply Inventory as a Web page called ARF Inventory Web.

i. Create a folder named ARF Inventory to contain the workbook files.

on your own

Statters Suppliers Database

★ 1. Statters Office Supply needs you to create a database to hold supplier information such as company name, location, sales representative, product category (such as paper, furniture, computers, small electronics, and so on). Enter a list of at least 20 records in an Excel worksheet with the appropriate fields. Format the worksheet in an attractive manner. Sort the list by the supplier's state. Filter the list to display suppliers of the same category of product. Enter a function to count the number of records and include an appropriate label. Print the filter results with your name and the current date as a header. Save the workbook as Statter's Suppliers.

Kids Express Inventory Analysis

★ ★ 2. The Kids Express Toy Company needs help with its inventory. Create a worksheet that has 20 inventory records. The records should contain a product identification number, description, wholesale distributor, wholesale price, retail price, and quantity on hand. Format the worksheet in an attractive manner. Sort the records by distributor. Filter the records to display a selected distributor and total the quantity on hand for that distributor. Enter your name and the current date as a header to the filter results and print them. Filter the list next to find all items with a retail price higher than a selected value. Enter your name and the current date as a header to the filter results and print them. Save the workbook as Toy Inventory.

Baseball League Roster

★ ★ **3.** You have a summer internship working in your town's community activities department. You have been asked to create a database of players enrolled in the summer baseball program in order to divide them into the various teams. Create a database that lists the players' name, address, phone number, age, and position. Format the worksheet in an attractive manner. Enter 30 records in the list. Include your name as one of the records and a position of pitcher. Sort the database by player name, position, and age. Filter the list to show only pitchers. Enter your name and the current date as a header to the worksheets. Print the filter results. Save the workbook as Summer Baseball League.

Cleaning Service Customer List

★ ★ **4.** Desert Rescue Cleaning wants to keep track of its customers with an Excel worksheet database. Create a worksheet database that includes the customers' ID number, cleaning address with suite or apartment number, contact name, phone number, and square footage. Format the worksheet in an attractive manner. Enter 15 records into the database. Enter your name as the contact for the first record. Sort the database contact name. Filter the list to display only those records with a square footage larger than a specified value. Enter functions to display the minimum and maximum square footage values. Include appropriate labels. Enter your name and the current date as a header to the worksheets. Print the filter results. Save the workbook as Cleaning Company Customers.

★ ★
★ **5.** After analyzing your budget to see if you will have enough money to take a trip over spring break (step-by-step exercise 3 of Lab 4), you tell your friends about the results. They would also like to analyze their budgets. To make the worksheet available to your friends, you decide to create a template of the worksheet and make it available on your Web site for them to use. Clear out your personal data to create the template and preview it as a Web page. Make any necessary adjustments to the worksheet and then save it as an interactive Web page as Budget Analysis. Try out the worksheet to make sure it works in the browser and modify again as needed. Print the blank worksheet in the browser.

You decide to convert your Stock Analysis worksheet (On Your Web, Lab 4) to a Web page for use by your friends. Clear out your stock data to create the template and preview it as a Web page. Make any necessary adjustments to the worksheet so that it displays correctly in the browser. Include instructions on how to use the worksheet. Include a link to a Web site that provides stock information. Save the worksheet as an interactive Web page as Stock Analysis Web. Try out the worksheet to make sure it works in the browser and connects you to the stock Web site. Modify it again as needed. Print the blank worksheet in the browser with your name in a header.

Working with Multiple Tables

LAB 4

objectives

After completing this lab, you will know how to:

1.	Create a table using the Table Wizard.
2.	Create an input mask.
3.	Create a lookup field.
4.	Copy and import data.
5.	Set required properties.
6.	Add a calculated field to a query.
7.	Create a crosstab query.
8.	Define table relationships and enforce referential integrity.
9.	Print a database relationships report.
10.	Use subdatasheets.
11.	Back up and restore a database.

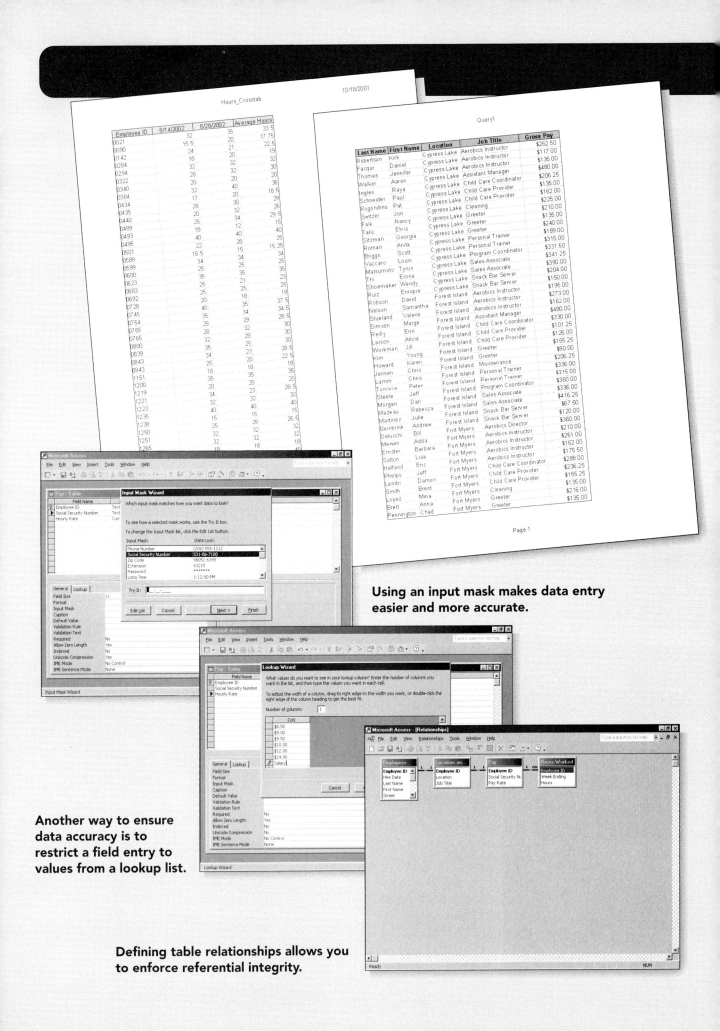

Using an input mask makes data entry easier and more accurate.

Another way to ensure data accuracy is to restrict a field entry to values from a lookup list.

Defining table relationships allows you to enforce referential integrity.

Lifestyle Fitness Club

You have created an employee database and several queries and reports related to this database for the Lifestyle Fitness Club; this has made recordkeeping at the club much easier than it used to be when everything was done manually. Based on the success of this database, the club owners would like you to use Access to store the employees' salary information. They would like this information kept in a separate data table, and they want to be able to use it along with the other employee data tables to calculate gross weekly salaries.

In creating the new table and

queries, you will learn about features, such as applying input masks and required properties to fields, that ensure the correct information is entered. You will also learn how to run one query that shows table data in tabular format and another that includes a field to calculate your numerical data. Since you will be sharing employee information between data tables, you will also learn how to establish relationships, enforce referential integrity between data, and print a report that shows the database relationships. The crosstab and relationships reports are shown on the previous page.

© Corbis

Concept Overview

The following concepts will be introduced in this lab:

1.	**Input Mask**	An input mask is a field property that controls where data is entered in a field, the kind of data, and the number of allowable characters.
2.	**Lookup Field**	A lookup field provides a list of values from which the user can choose to enter data into that field.
3.	**Copy and Import**	Selections can be copied or duplicated to new locations in a database, between databases, or to other applications; or imported from another application and converted into a format that can be used in a table.
4.	**Required Property**	The Required property specifies whether a value is required in a field.
5.	**Calculated Field**	A calculated field displays the result of a calculation in a query.
6.	**Crosstab Query**	A crosstab query summarizes table data and displays it in a tabular format.
7.	**Relationship**	A relationship establishes the association between common fields in two tables.
8.	**Subdatasheet**	A subdatasheet is a data table that is nested in another data table and that contains data related or joined to the table where it resides.

Creating a Table with the Table Wizard

The owners of the Lifestyle Fitness Club have asked you to create a new data table that will hold the employees' pay rate information. You know that the Table Wizard contains a sample data table that is very similar to what you need, so you decide to use it to create the new table.

The Table Wizard helps you create a new data table by leading you step-by-step through selecting the type, or category, of table you want to create (personal or business), the table design you want to use and the fields that you want to include. You can select fields from more than one sample table, and you can delete the fields you do not want once the table is created. The Wizard will also assign the primary key field for you and create a related data-entry form, if desired. You will create the new employee salary table in the Club Employees database.

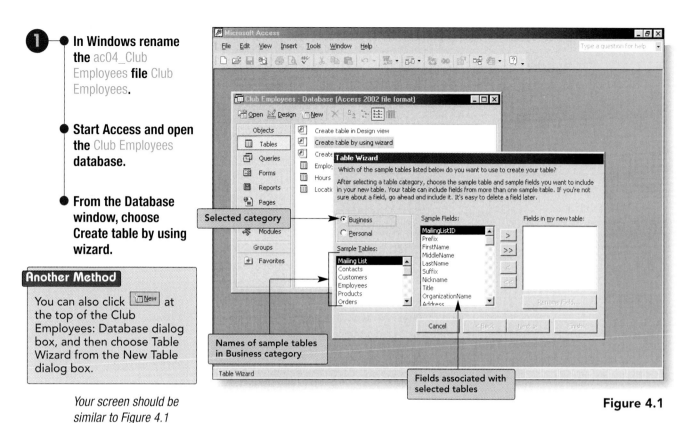

1 ● **In Windows rename the** ac04_Club Employees **file** Club Employees**.**

● **Start Access and open the** Club Employees **database.**

● **From the Database window, choose Create table by using wizard.**

Another Method

You can also click [📖New] at the top of the Club Employees: Database dialog box, and then choose Table Wizard from the New Table dialog box.

Your screen should be similar to Figure 4.1

Selected category

Names of sample tables in Business category

Fields associated with selected tables

Figure 4.1

From the first screen of the Table Wizard, you select the table category, sample table, and sample fields you want to use. The Business category is already selected, which is the appropriate category for the database you are creating. The sample table you want to use for your database is named Time Billed.

2 ● **From the Sample Tables list select Time Billed.**

Your screen should be similar to Figure 4.2

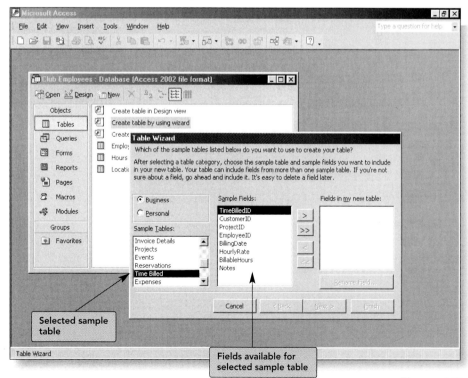

Selected sample table

Fields available for selected sample table

Figure 4.2

Now the sample fields reflect field names that would be used in the selected type of table. You will use two of the fields from the sample table in your new Pay data table: EmployeeID and HourlyRate. Then you will rename the fields Employee ID and Hourly Rate so that they are exactly the same as the corresponding field names in the employee data tables you created earlier.

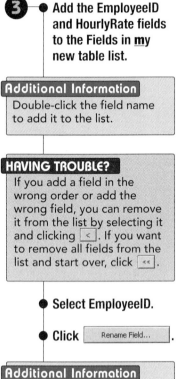

3 ● **Add the EmployeeID and HourlyRate fields to the Fields in my new table list.**

Additional Information
Double-click the field name to add it to the list.

HAVING TROUBLE?
If you add a field in the wrong order or add the wrong field, you can remove it from the list by selecting it and clicking [<]. If you want to remove all fields from the list and start over, click [<<].

● **Select EmployeeID.**

● **Click** [Rename Field...] **.**

Additional Information
In the Rename Field dialog box, you can edit the existing name or give the field an entirely new name.

● **Insert a blank space before ID in the field name.**

● **Click** [OK] **.**

● **In a similar manner, rename the HourlyRate field Hourly Rate.**

Your screen should be similar to Figure 4.3

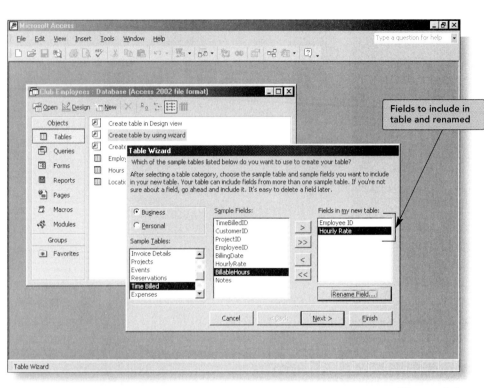

Fields to include in table and renamed

Figure 4.3

The fields you want included in the new table are now specified, and you are ready to go to the next step in the Table Wizard where you will specify the name for the new table and a primary key field. You want to rename the table Pay and let the Table Wizard set the primary key (which is the default).

Click [Next >].

● **Type Pay as the new table name.**

Your screen should be similar to Figure 4.4

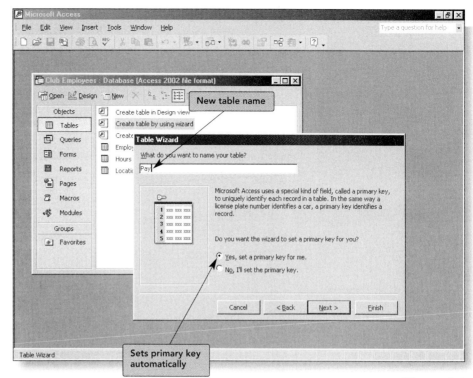

Figure 4.4

In the next Wizard dialog box you will specify how the new table is related to other tables in the database. You will learn about relationships and have a chance to define some later in this lab, but for now you will not establish a relationship between the tables.

● **Click** [Next >].

● **Click** [Next >].

Your screen should be similar to Figure 4.5

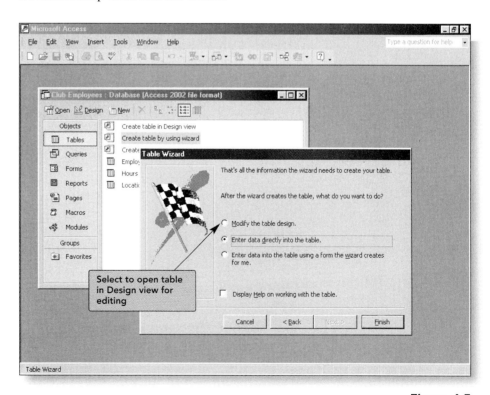

Figure 4.5

In the final Table Wizard dialog box, you specify what you want to do after the table is created. Your selection will determine in what view the Wizard opens your table. You want to check the field properties and modify them if necessary, and you will create the data entry form yourself after you have set up the table the way you want it.

6 ● Select **M**odify the table design.

● Click [**F**inish].

Your screen should be similar to Figure 4.6

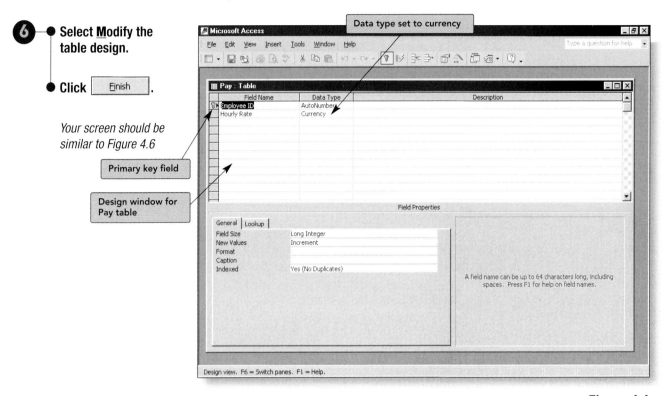

Figure 4.6

Your new Pay table is created and displayed in Design view. Notice that the Hourly Rate field has been automatically assigned the Currency data type. Also, the Employee ID field has been assigned the primary key, which is what you want.

Controlling Field Input

As you recall from previous labs, you use Design view to add and remove fields, as well as to change the properties of each field, such as its name, size, and data type. You can also apply an input mask and provide lookup values to ensure that the entries made in a field are valid. You will learn about these features next.

Changing Field Properties

First, you want to make a few quick adjustments to the field properties assigned by the Table Wizard. When it created the table, the Table Wizard automatically assigned the AutoNumber data type to the Employee ID field, which will automatically increment the data entries in this field; however, the numbers assigned to club employees are not necessarily in sequential numerical order. You will change the Employee ID data type to Text and the field size to 4, as it is in the other employee tables. You also want to add a field that will contain the employees' social security numbers for payroll purposes.

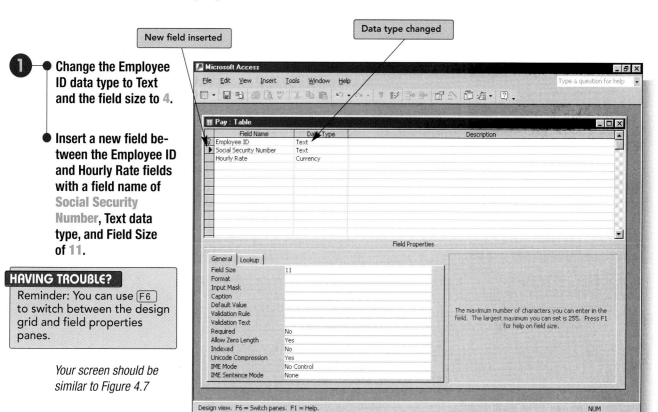

Change the Employee ID data type to Text and the field size to 4.

Insert a new field between the Employee ID and Hourly Rate fields with a field name of Social Security Number, Text data type, and Field Size of 11.

HAVING TROUBLE?
Reminder: You can use [F6] to switch between the design grid and field properties panes.

Your screen should be similar to Figure 4.7

Figure 4.7

Creating an Input Mask

Most people know that a social security number is always nine digits, typically in the format ###-##-####. However, when someone has to enter several records in one sitting, it is very easy to make a mistake and enter a letter or punctuation mark instead of a digit, the wrong number of digits, or the hyphens in the wrong place. To make the task of entering each club employee's social security number a bit easier, as well as to ensure that the entry is made in the proper format, you decide to apply an input mask to the Social Security Number field.

concept 1

Input Mask

1 An **input mask** is a field property that controls where data is entered in a field, the kind of data, and the number of allowable characters.

The input mask format consists of **literal characters**, such as hyphens and parentheses, that display just as they are, and **mask characters** that define the characteristics of the input mask. Any character that is not a mask character is a literal character. If you want to use one of the mask characters as a literal, precede it with a (\) backslash.

The following mask characters are used to define input masks:

Character	Description
0	Requires that a digit from 0–9 be entered.
9	An entry is not required, but if an entry is made, it must be a digit or space.
#	An entry is not required, but if an entry is made, it must be a digit, space, + (plus sign), or – (minus sign).
L	Requires that a letter from A–Z be entered.
?	An entry is not required, but if an entry is made, it must be a letter from A–Z.
A	Requires that a letter or digit be entered.
a	An entry is not required, but if an entry is made, it must be a letter or digit.
&	An entry is required, and it can be any character or a space.
C	An entry is not required, but if an entry is made, it can be any character or a space.
. , : ; - /	A decimal placeholder and thousand, date, and time separators.
<	Converts entries to all lowercase.
>	Converts entries to all uppercase.
!	Displays the input mask from right to left at the point where the ! is inserted, rather than from left to right.
\	Displays the character that follows as a literal character (for example, \A is displayed as just A).

You will define an input mask to ensure that the correct number and type of characters are entered into the Social Security Number field. Because input masks are sometimes complicated, Access includes a Wizard to help you define the input mask. Alternatively, you can type it in directly.

1 ● **Click the Input Mask property box.**

HAVING TROUBLE?

If the Input Mask Wizard is not installed on your system, type 000-00-000;;_ in the Input Mask text box and proceed to step 5 below Figure 4.14.

● **Click** ⋯ **at the end of the property box.**

● **Click** Yes **when you are asked to save the table.**

Your screen should be similar to Figure 4.8

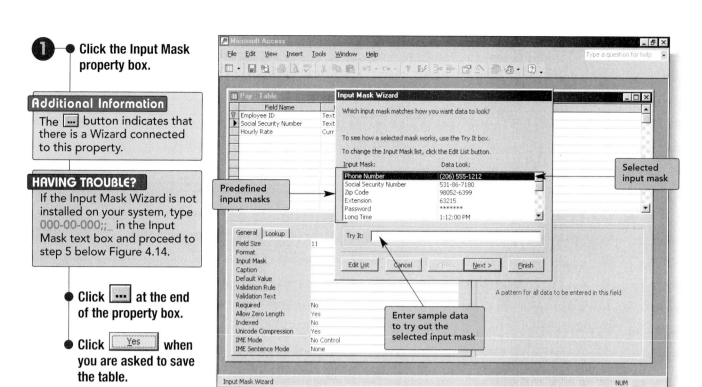

Figure 4.8

The Input Mask Wizard dialog box lists ten predefined masks. You can also use this dialog box to try out one of the masks or create your own custom masks for the Input Mask Wizard to display. For your purposes, the Social Security input mask is exactly what you want.

2 ● **Select Social Security Number.**

● **Click the Try It box.**

Your screen should be similar to Figure 4.9

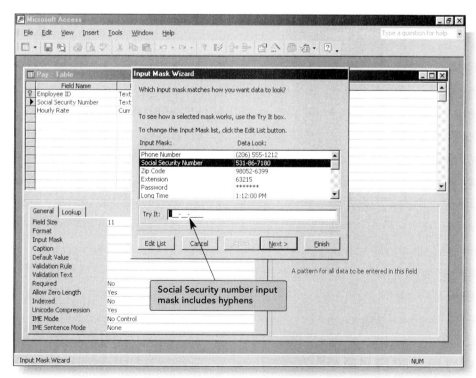

Figure 4.9

Notice that the input mask automatically inserted hyphens in the correct locations for a social security number. This means the social security number can be entered without having to type the hyphens as well. If, however, the user types the hyphens or enter the hyphens in the wrong place, the input mask will automatically correct the error. You decide to test the mask by entering a social security number a few different ways.

3 ● **Position the insertion point at the beginning of the Try It box.**

● **Type 123456789.**

● **Clear the entry and type 123-45-6789.**

Additional Information

Press Esc to clear the entry.

● **Clear the entry and type 12-345-6789.**

Your screen should be similar to Figure 4.10

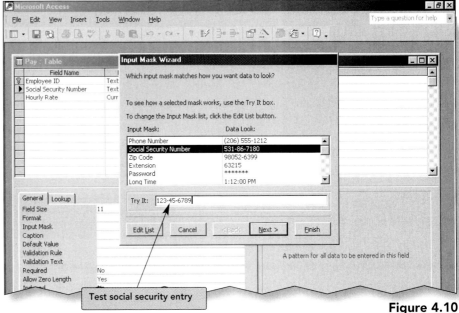

Figure 4.10

In each case, the hyphens were automatically entered in the proper location. Now you want to see what happens when you make an incorrect entry.

4 ● **Clear the entry and type 12345678.**

● **Press ←Enter.**

Your screen should be similar to Figure 4.11

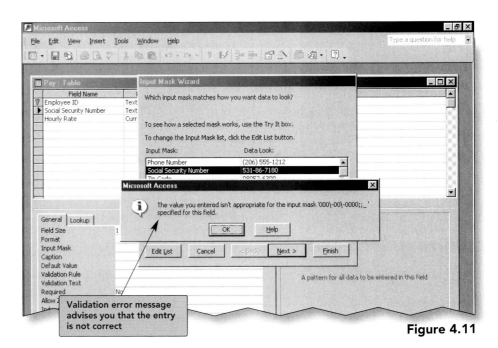

Figure 4.11

A validation error message is displayed advising you that you have made an invalid entry. Now that you have seen how this feature works, you can clear the incorrect entry and continue defining the input mask.

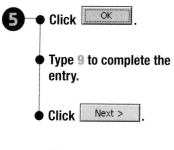

5 ● Click [OK].

● Type **9** to complete the entry.

● Click [Next >].

Your screen should be similar to Figure 4.12

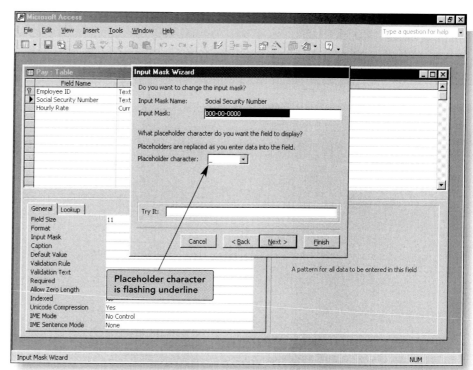

Figure 4.12

The sample entry is accepted and the next Input Mask Wizard dialog box is displayed. Next you need to specify the placeholder character you want to display as data is entered into the field. The default is the standard flashing underline, which is acceptable, so you can proceed to the next step.

6 ● Click [Next >].

Your screen should be similar to Figure 4.13

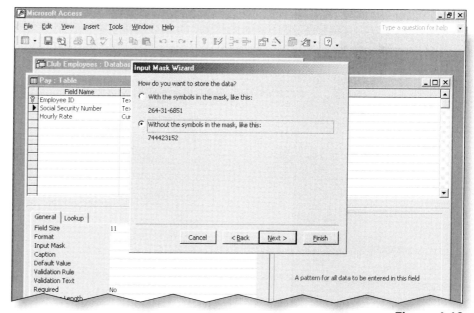

Figure 4.13

The Wizard now asks you how you want to store the data that is entered in this field. The default, storing the data without the hyphens, takes up less data storage space and is fine with you.

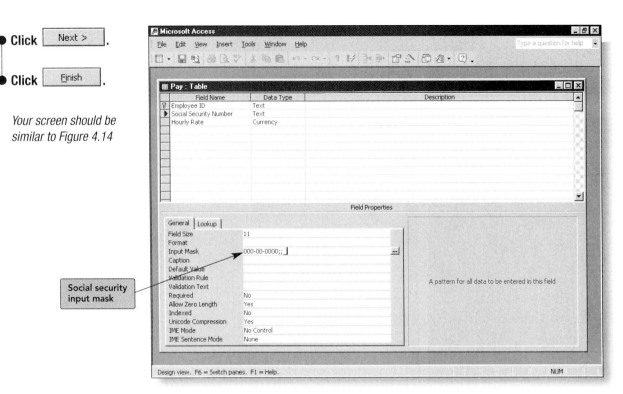

7 ● Click [Next >].

● Click [Einish].

Your screen should be similar to Figure 4.14

Figure 4.14

The input mask for the Social Security Number field is added to the General properties. The first part of the input mask, 000-00-0000, specifies a required number entry consisting of nine numbers. The hyphens are literal characters used to separate the parts of the entry. The first semicolon indicates the end of the mask definition. The second semicolon indicates the end of the second part of the input mask definition. Because there is nothing entered between the semicolons, this means that only the characters that are typed will be stored. Finally, the underline identifies the selected placeholder character.

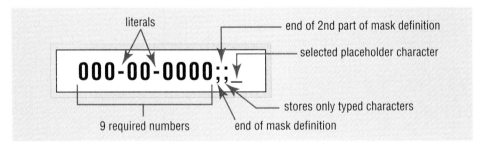

Creating a Lookup Field

Next you decide to change the current Hourly Rate field to a field that will make entering hourly pay rates easier, faster, and less prone to errors. The hourly pay rates at the club range from $7 to $14. In addition, if the employee is on salary, the field entry is the salary rather than an hourly pay rate. You want only the valid pay rates to be listed, so that anyone entering a new employee record in the Pay table will merely have to choose from this list to enter it as the rate for that employee. To do this, you will make the Hourly Rate field a lookup field.

concept 2

2 A **lookup field** provides a list of values from which the user can choose to make entering data into that field simpler. The lookup field can get the values from an existing table or a fixed set of values that are defined when the lookup field is created. A lookup field that uses another table as the source for values is called a **lookup list**, and one that uses fixed values is called a **value list**.

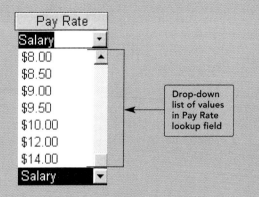

Drop-down list of values in Pay Rate lookup field

Lookup List Lookup Field

When the lookup field uses a table for the values it displays, an association is created between the two tables. Picking a value from the lookup list sets the foreign key value in the current record to the primary key value of the corresponding record in the related table. A **foreign key** is a field in one table that refers to the primary key field in another table and indicates how the tables are related. The field names of these two fields do not have to match, although their data types must be the same.

The related table displays but does not store the data in the record. The foreign key is stored but does not display. For this reason, any updates made to the data in the related table will be reflected in both the list and records in the table containing the lookup field. You must define a lookup list field from the table that will contain the foreign key and display the lookup list.

Value List Lookup Field

A lookup field that uses a fixed list of values looks the same as a lookup field that uses a table, except the fixed set of values is entered when the lookup field is created. A value list should be used only for values that will not change very often and do not need to be stored in a table. For example, a list for a Salutation field containing the abbreviations Mr., Mrs., or Ms. would be a good candidate for a value list. Choosing a value from a value list will store that value in the record—it does not create an association to a related table. For this reason, if you change any of the original values in the value list later, they will not be reflected in records added before this change was made.

You will use the Lookup Wizard to change the existing Hourly Rate field to a lookup field that uses fixed values. First you must change the field type to Text, because a lookup field cannot be created for a Currency data type.

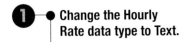

1 ● **Change the Hourly Rate data type to Text.**

● **Open the Data Type drop-down list and select Lookup Wizard.**

Additional Information

To create a new lookup field (as opposed to changing an existing field to a lookup field), you can access the Lookup Wizard in Design view by choosing Insert/Lookup Field. You can also create a new lookup field in Datasheet view by choosing Insert/Lookup Column.

Your screen should be similar to Figure 4.15

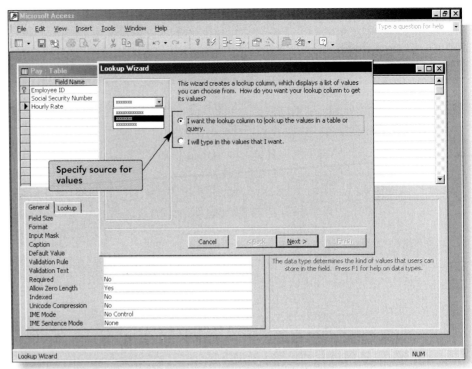

Figure 4.15

In the first Lookup Wizard dialog box, you specify the source for the values for the lookup field. You will enter your own values, the club's pay rates, for this field.

2 ● **Select: I will type in the values that I want.**

● **Click** Next > .

Your screen should be similar to Figure 4.16

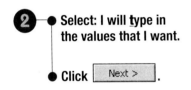

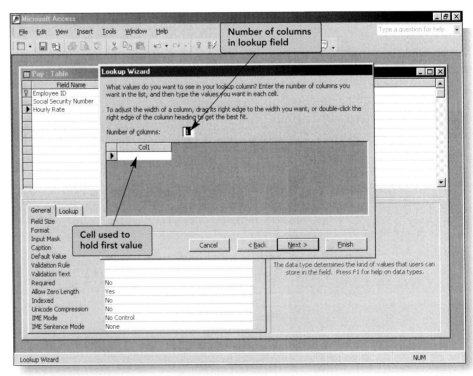

Figure 4.16

The next step in the Lookup Wizard is to enter the values you want listed in the lookup field. You can also add columns and adjust their widths to fit the values you enter, if necessary. You only need one column, and the current width is sufficient for the values you are going to enter.

3 ● **Click the entry box under Col1.**

● **Type $7.00.**

● **Press** Tab ⇆.

● **Enter the rest of the pay rates as follows, pressing** Tab ⇆ **to go from one cell to the next:**

$7.50
$8.00
$8.50
$9.00
$9.50
$10.00
$12.00
$14.00
Salary

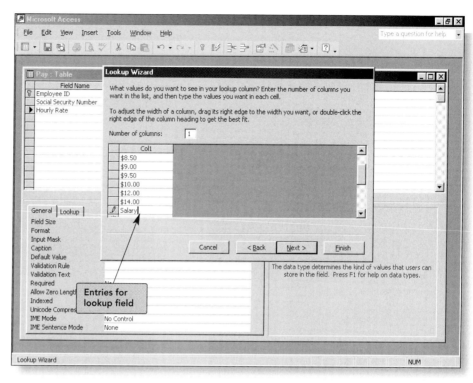

Figure 4.17

Additional Information

You can correct these entries the same way you do when entering data into any other field.

Your screen should be similar to Figure 4.17

After entering the field values, you can proceed to the next step in your lookup field creation and name the lookup field.

4 ● Click [Next >].

● Type **Pay Rate** in the text box.

● Click [Finish].

Your screen should be similar to Figure 4.18

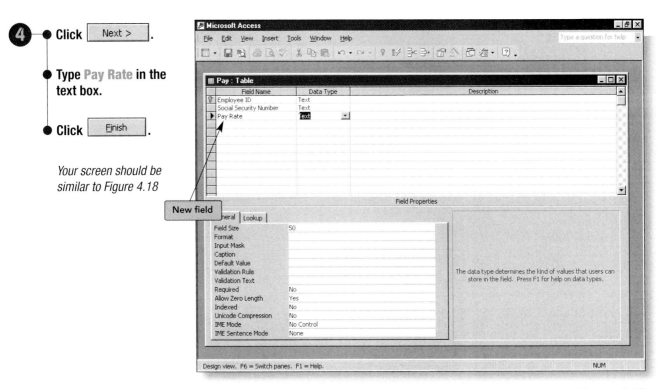

New field

Figure 4.18

The new Pay Rate lookup field has been added to the Pay table design. Next you will check the settings established for this field to see whether any changes are necessary.

5 ● Open the Lookup tab.

Your screen should be similar to Figure 4.19

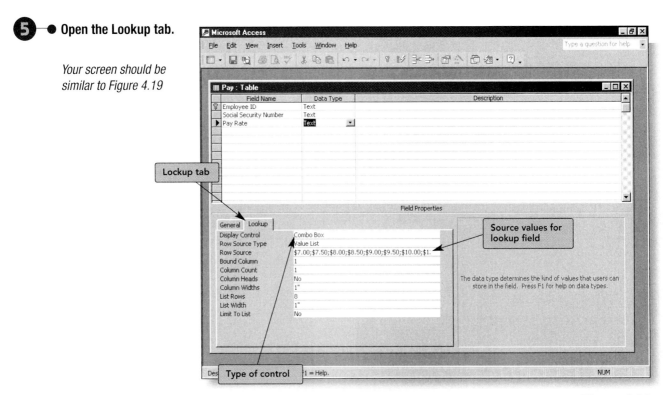

Lockup tab

Source values for lookup field

Type of control

Figure 4.19

The lookup list will display in a combo box (drop-down list) control on forms. It gets its list values from the value list containing the values you specified as the source. The other properties are set to the defaults for lookup fields. The only change you want to make is to restrict the data entry in that field to values in the lookup list. Then you will enter a sample employee pay record to test the table design.

6 ● **Change the Limit to List property to Yes.**

HAVING TROUBLE?
Select the property and click ▼ at the end of the box to open the drop-down list of options.

● **Save the table and switch to Datasheet view.**

● **Type 2151 in the Employee ID field and press** Tab ⇆.

● **Type 123456789 in the Social Security Number field and press** Tab ⇆.

● **Type 8.25 in the Pay Rate field and press** ←Enter.

Your screen should be similar to Figure 4.20

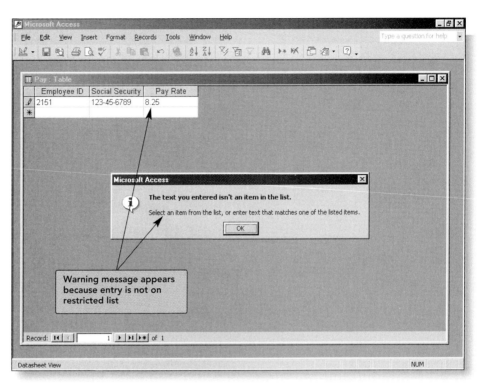

Warning message appears because entry is not on restricted list

Figure 4.20

A warning box advises you that the entry must match one of the listed items because you restricted the field entries in the Pay Rate field to the lookup values you specified.

7 ● Click [OK].

● **Select $9.50 from the list of values in the Pay Rate field.**

Clicking 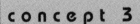 opens the list of values.

● **Press ⏎Enter.**

Your screen should be similar to Figure 4.21

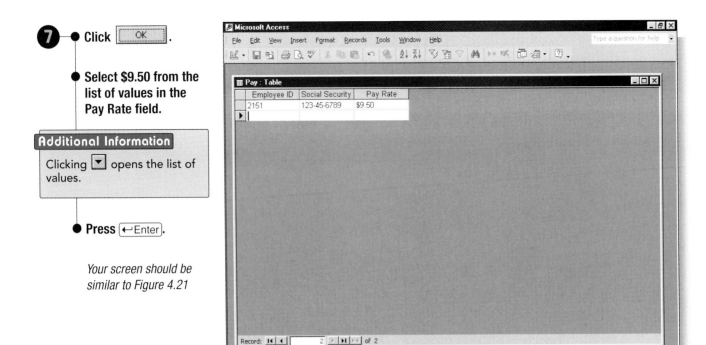

Figure 4.21

The Social Security input mask and the Pay Rate lookup field are working correctly. Now that you have finished designing and testing the Pay table, you are ready to add the real employee pay rate information to it.

Copying and Importing Data

The Employee ID information needed in the Pay table is the same information as in the Employees table. Rather than entering the same information again, you can copy it from that table to this one. The pay rate information is maintained by the Payroll department in an Excel workbook that you can import into this table as well.

concept 3

Copy and Import

3

Selections can be **copied** or duplicated to new locations in a database, between databases, or to other applications; or can be **imported** from another application and converted into a format that can be used in a table. Using these methods saves you time by not having to retype the same information. You can copy and import individual field entries, entire records, fields, con-

trols, and even database objects (such as entire tables) within and between Access databases as well as to and from other applications.

Additional Information

The Office Clipboard is available for use in any program, including non-Office programs that provides copy and cut capabilities, but you can paste only into Word, Excel, Access, PowerPoint, and Outlook.

Copying Data from Another Table

You will copy the information you need from the Employees table into the Pay table.

A selection that is copied duplicates the original, called the **source,** and pastes or inserts a duplicate at a new location, called the **destination.** When a selection is copied, the selection is stored in the Clipboard, also called the **System Clipboard,** a temporary Windows storage area in memory. The System Clipboard contents are then inserted at the new location specified. Office XP also includes an **Office Clipboard** that can store up to 24 items that have been cut or copied. This feature allows you to insert multiple items from various Office documents and paste all or part of the collection of items into another Office document.

First you will open the Office Clipboard task pane so you can see the copied items as they are added to the Office Clipboard.

1 ● Choose **Edit/Office Clipboard** to display the Clipboard task pane.

● If necessary, click [✂ Clear All] to remove any items currently stored in the Clipboard.

Your screen should be similar to Figure 4.22

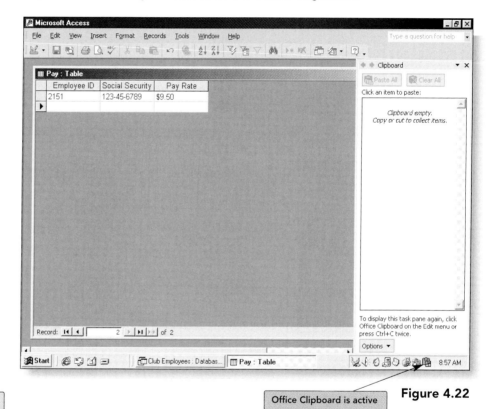

Office Clipboard is active

Figure 4.22

The 📋 icon appears in the taskbar when the Clipboard task pane is open in any Office application.

Next you will copy the Employee ID field column from the Employees table to the Clipboard.

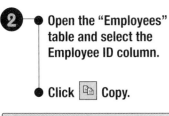

2 ● **Open the "Employees" table and select the Employee ID column.**

● **Click** 📋 **Copy.**

Another Method

The menu equivalent is Edit/Copy and the shortcut key is Ctrl + C. Copy is also available on the shortcut menu.

Your screen should be similar to Figure 4.23

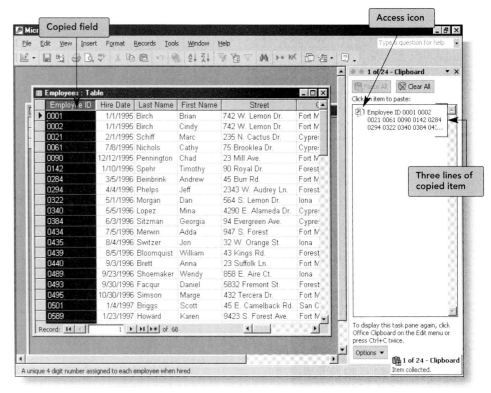

Figure 4.23

The Clipboard task pane displays an Access icon and up to three lines of the copied item's text. While looking at the Employee table, you think that in addition to the Employee ID you may also want to copy the Last Name field into a new field of the Pay table. Since you are currently viewing the table, you will copy the field now and paste it later.

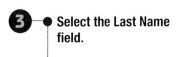

● **Select the Last Name field.**

● **Click** 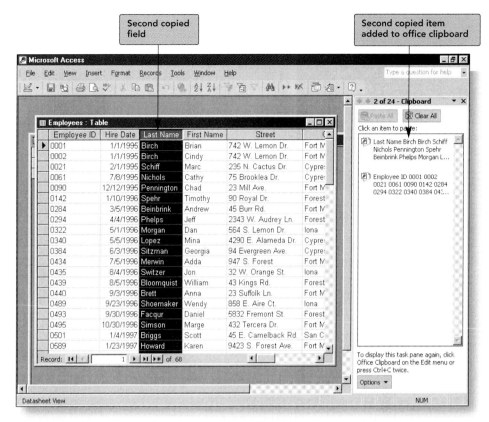 **Copy.**

Your screen should be similar to Figure 4.24

Figure 4.24

The Clipboard displays another Access icon and text for the second copied item. Items are added sequentially to the Office Clipboard as you copy them. Now you are ready to paste the items into the Pay table. You want to paste the Employee ID field first.

4 • **Close the "Employees" table.**

• **Switch to the "Pay" table and delete the sample record.**

• **Select the Employee ID column.**

• **Click the Employee ID item in the Office Clipboard task pane.**

• **Click** [Yes] **to confirm the Paste operation.**

Another Method

You can also click │ and select <u>P</u>aste from the item's menu. Additionally, you can use <u>E</u>dit/<u>P</u>aste or the shortcut key, [Ctrl] + V. Using this command, however, pastes the last copied item.

Your screen should be similar to Figure 4.25

Additional Information

The [Paste All] button inserts the contents of all copied items in the order in which they were added to the Office Clipboard.

5 • **Move to the Social Security Number field.**

• **Choose <u>I</u>nsert/<u>C</u>olumn.**

• **Select the new blank field column.**

• **Click the Last Name icon on the Clipboard task pane.**

• **Click** [Yes] **to confirm the operation.**

Your screen should be similar to Figure 4.26

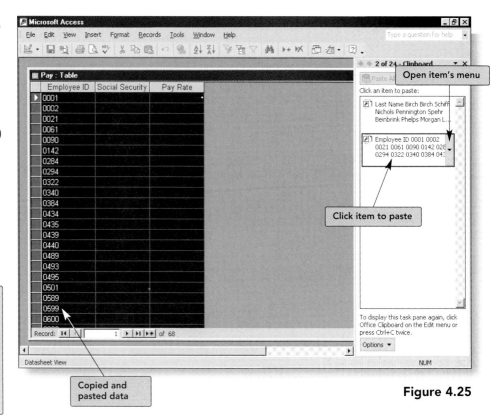

Copied and pasted data

Figure 4.25

The contents of the copied item are pasted into the selected field column. Next you want to insert the Last Name field information into a new field column in the Pay table.

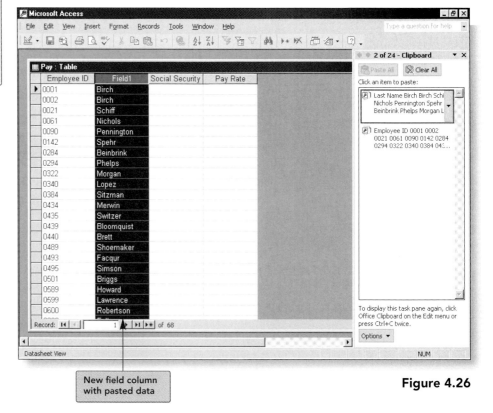

New field column with pasted data

Figure 4.26

Next you will name the new field column and then close the Office Clipboard task pane.

6 ● **Right-click the new field heading and choose Rename Column from the shortcut menu.**

● **Type Last Name in the column heading and press ←Enter.**

● **Click 🗙 Clear All and close the Clipboard task pane.**

Your screen should be similar to Figure 4.27

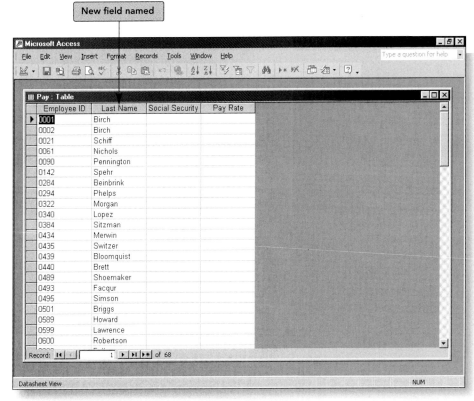

New field named

Figure 4.27

Importing Data from Another Application

You are now ready to enter the pay rate information. The club's Payroll department has provided you with an Excel workbook file that includes the employee ID number, social security number, and pay rate information for all employees in sorted order by employee number. After looking at the workbook, you decide it would be faster and more accurate to copy the information from the worksheet into the Pay table than it would be to enter it manually. To do this, you could open the workbook file in Excel and select and copy the data in the worksheet. Then you would paste the copied data into the appropriate location in the Pay table.

An alternative method is to import the entire worksheet contents into the database table. Using this method, you do not need to open the other application and select the information to be copied. However, the worksheet data must be in the same order as needed in the table (Employee ID, Social Security Number, and Pay Rate) and the table must be empty. You will delete the Last Name field and remove all records. Then you will import the worksheet data.

1 ● Choose **E**dit/Select **A**ll
Records.

● Click 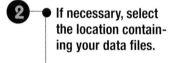 Delete
Record.

● Click [Yes] to
confirm the delete
operation.

● Select the Last Name
field.

● Choose **E**dit/Delete
Colu**m**n.

● Close the Pay table,
saving your changes.

● Choose **F**ile/**G**et
External Data/**I**mport.

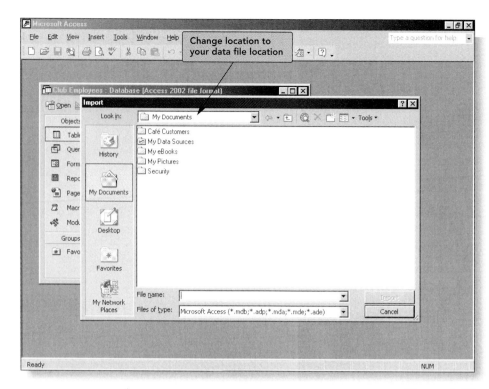

Figure 4.28

*Your screen should be
similar to Figure 4.28*

In the Import dialog box you specify the location, type, and name of the file
you want to import.

2 ● If necessary, select
the location contain-
ing your data files.

● From the Files of Type
drop-down list box,
select Microsoft Excel.

● Select the ac04_Pay
file.

● Click [Import].

*Your screen should be
similar to Figure 4.29*

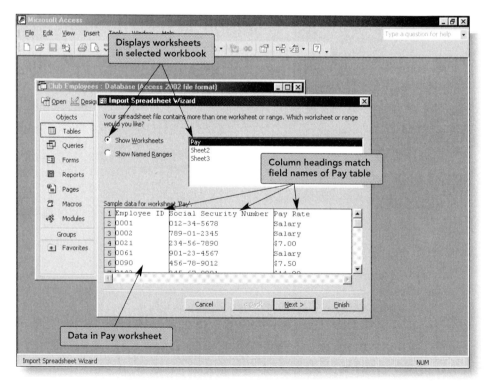

Figure 4.29

The Import Spreadsheet Wizard is started. From the first Wizard dialog box you need to select the worksheet or range to import. The default seletion, show worksheets, is correct for what you are doing.

3 • **If necessary, select Pay.**

• **Click** `Next >` **.**

Your screen should be similar to Figure 4.30

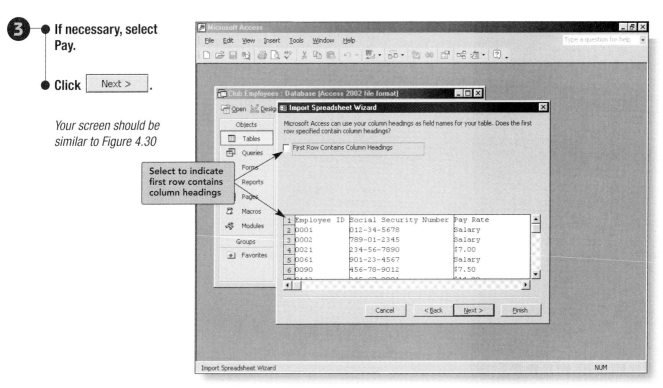

Figure 4.30

Next you specify whether to use the column headings in the worksheet as the field names. When importing to an existing table, the column headings in the imported file must match the column headings in the table, as they do here. Then you specify whether to save this data in a new table or an existing table. You want to save it in the existing Pay table.

4 • **Select First Row Contains Column Headings.**

• **Click** `Next >` **.**

• **Select In an Existing Table.**

• **Select "Pay" from the option's drop-down list.**

• **Click** `Next >` **.**

• **Click** `Finish` **.**

Your screen should be similar to Figure 4.31

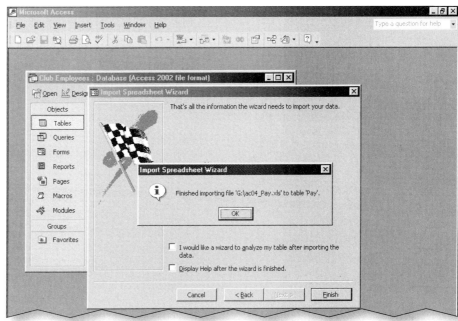

Figure 4.31

The message box informs you that the data was imported into the Pay table. Now you want to see the data in the table.

5 ● Click [OK].

● Open the "Pay" table.

Your screen should be similar to Figure 4.32

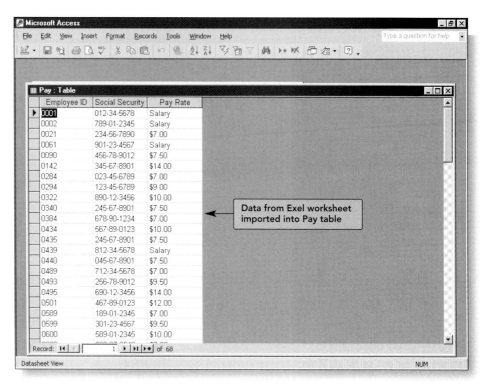

Data from Exel worksheet imported into Pay table

Figure 4.32

The pay data is complete for all records.

Making Fields Required

The final change you want to make to the Pay table is to require that data be entered into all fields. The Pay table includes only three fields, but each of these fields must be filled in for payroll purposes. To ensure that these fields are completed for each employee, you are going to apply the Required property to them.

concept 4

Required Property

4 The **Required property** specifies whether a value is required in a field. If the property is set to Yes for a field, you must enter a value in that field, and the value cannot be null (zero). If you set the Required property to Yes for a field in a table that already contains data, Access gives you the option of checking whether the field has a value in all existing records. The field must have a value in all instances in which data might be entered in the field—in the table itself as well as in forms, queries, reports, and any other datasheets based on the table.

You can set a Required property for any type of field except a field that has the AutoNumber data type assigned to it. A primary key field will not accept null values.

Because a primary key field will not accept null values by default, it automatically requires an entry. Therefore, you do not need to make the Employee ID field required.

1 ● Switch to Design view.

● Select the Social Security Number field.

● Change the Required field property to Yes.

● In a similar manner, change the Required property to Yes for the Pay Rate field.

Your screen should be similar to Figure 4.33

Required property set to Yes requires entry in field

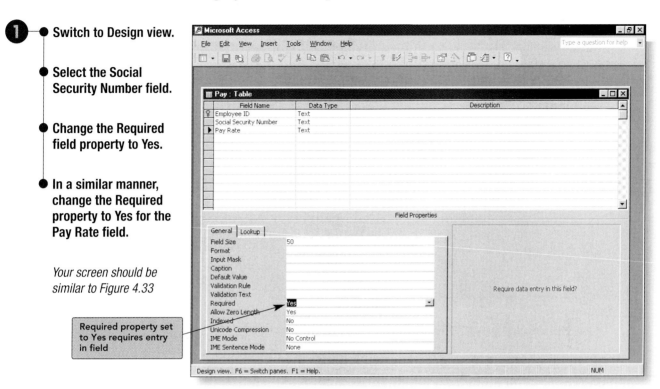

Figure 4.33

Next you will test this feature while adding your own record to the table.

2 ● Click 🖫 Save.

● Select No to skip testing for data integrity.

● Switch to Datasheet view.

● Move to a blank new record row.

● Enter your Employee ID number of 9999.

● Skip the Social Security Number field.

● Open the Pay Rate drop-down list and select $9.50.

● Press ←Enter.

Your screen should be similar to Figure 4.34

Required field missing data

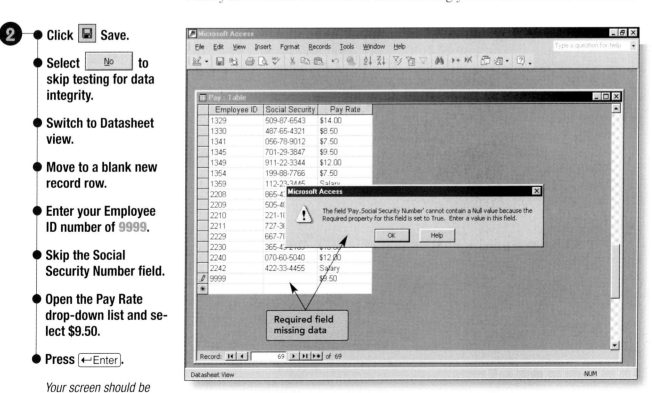

Figure 4.34

The displayed warning message informs you that the Social Security Number field is required and cannot contain a "null value"—in other words, it cannot be empty. You need to go back and enter data in this field.

3 ● Click [OK] to close the warning message box.

● Enter a fake social security number in the Social Security Number field.

● Press [←Enter] twice.

Your screen should be similar to Figure 4.35

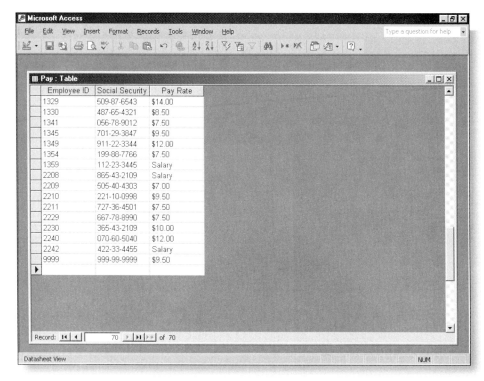

Figure 4.35

The record entry is complete. You are done with the Pay table design, and it contains your record. Before you proceed, you need to add your record to the rest of the tables in this database as well.

4 ● Close the "Pay" table.

● Beginning with the "Employees" table, add your information as the last record in each table of the database, using the following data where applicable:

ID: 9999
Hire Date: current date
Hours Worked for the week of June 28, 2002: 20
Location: Fort Myers
Job Title: Greeter

● Close all open tables.

Your screen should be similar to Figure 4.36

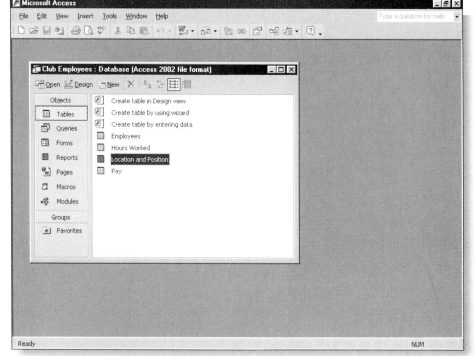

Figure 4.36

Using Calculations in Queries

The Club owners have asked you for a report showing the gross pay for all employees sorted by location and job title. As a basis for this report, you will create a query that uses all the tables in the Club Employees database and then add a calculated field to the query that calculates the weekly gross pay for each employee.

Creating a Multitable Query

You will use Design view to create the query. You want to query all four tables to obtain the information you need, but you are not going to add them to the query in the order they're listed.

Bold field name identifies primary entry field

1 Click ⊞ Queries from the Objects bar.

● Choose Create query in Design view.

● From the Show Table dialog box, add the Employees, Location and Position, Pay, and Hours Worked tables to the query design in that order.

● Close the Show Table dialog box.

● If necessary, maximize the Select Query window.

Your screen should be similar to Figure 4.37

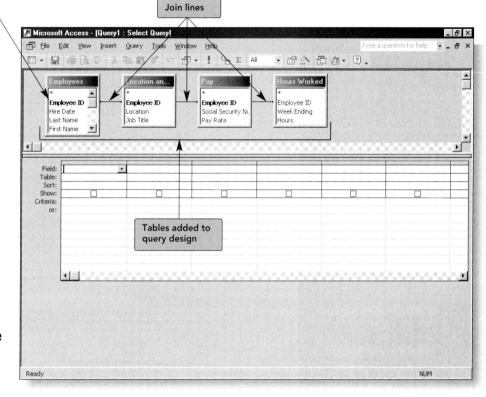

Figure 4.37

The tables are joined and displayed at the top of the design grid. Notice that the Employee ID field in the Hours Worked table is not bold. That is because bold is used to indicate primary key fields, and this field cannot be a primary key in this table because there are multiple entries with the same Employee ID numbers.

Next you will add the fields to be included in the query to the grid and sort them in the order requested by the club owners.

2 ● **Add the Last Name, First Name, Location, Job Title, Pay Rate, and Week Ending fields to the design grid in that order.**

Additional Information

Remember, to quickly add fields to a query, simply double-click on the field name.

● **Sort the Location and Job Title fields in ascending order.**

● **Run the query.**

Your screen should be similar to Figure 4.38

Last Name	First Name	Location	Job Title	Pay Rate	Week Ending
Robertson	Kirk	Cypress Lake	Aerobics Instructor	$10.00	6/28/2002
Facqur	Daniel	Cypress Lake	Aerobics Instructor	$9.50	6/14/2002
Facqur	Daniel	Cypress Lake	Aerobics Instructor	$9.50	6/28/2002
Thomas	Jennifer	Cypress Lake	Aerobics Instructor	$9.00	6/28/2002
Thomas	Jennifer	Cypress Lake	Aerobics Instructor	$9.00	6/14/2002
Robertson	Kirk	Cypress Lake	Aerobics Instructor	$10.00	6/14/2002
Walker	Aaron	Cypress Lake	Assistant Manager	$14.00	6/14/2002
Walker	Aaron	Cypress Lake	Assistant Manager	$14.00	6/28/2002
Ingles	Raya	Cypress Lake	Child Care Coordinator	$8.50	6/14/2002
Ingles	Raya	Cypress Lake	Child Care Coordinator	$8.50	6/28/2002
Schneider	Paul	Cypress Lake	Child Care Provider	$7.50	6/28/2002
Schneider	Paul	Cypress Lake	Child Care Provider	$7.50	6/14/2002
Rogondino	Pat	Cypress Lake	Child Care Provider	$7.50	6/28/2002
Rogondino	Pat	Cypress Lake	Child Care Provider	$7.50	6/14/2002
Switzer	Jon	Cypress Lake	Cleaning	$7.50	6/28/2002
Switzer	Jon	Cypress Lake	Cleaning	$7.50	6/14/2002
Sitzman	Georgia	Cypress Lake	Greeter	$7.00	6/14/2002
Sitzman	Georgia	Cypress Lake	Greeter	$7.00	6/28/2002
Talic	Elvis	Cypress Lake	Greeter	$7.50	6/28/2002
Falk	Nancy	Cypress Lake	Greeter	$7.00	6/14/2002
Falk	Nancy	Cypress Lake	Greeter	$7.00	6/28/2002
Talic	Elvis	Cypress Lake	Greeter	$7.50	6/14/2002
Ferguson	Robby	Cypress Lake	Manager	Salary	6/14/2002
Ferguson	Robby	Cypress Lake	Manager	Salary	6/28/2002
Briggs	Scott	Cypress Lake	Personal Trainer	$12.00	6/14/2002
Briggs	Scott	Cypress Lake	Personal Trainer	$12.00	6/28/2002

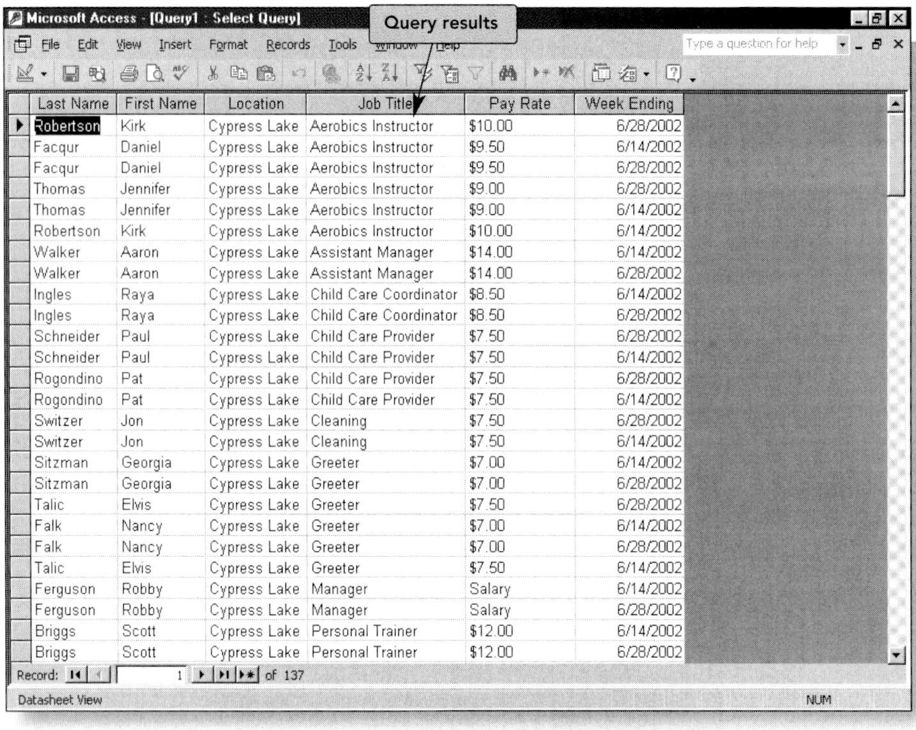

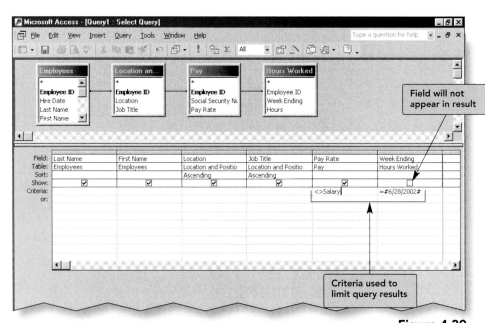

Figure 4.38

The query shows the selected fields for each record. Next you need to refine the query so it includes only employees who are paid hourly rates (not those on salary) for only the week ending 6/28/2002. Also, because the Club owners already know the report is for this date (which is what they requested), you will hide the Week Ending field so it will not show on the final report.

3 ● **Return to Query Design view.**

● **Enter the expression =6/28/2002 in the Week Ending Criteria cell.**

● **Clear the Show box for the Week Ending field.**

● **Enter <>Salary in the Pay Rate field Criteria cell.**

Your screen should be similar to Figure 4.39

Additional Information

The dates on your screen may display as two-digit years. This is a function of your system settings.

Figure 4.39

You are now ready to create a field to do the pay calculations for your report.

Adding a Calculated Field

To include the gross pay for the week ending 6/28/2002 in your report, you need to add a calculated field that will multiply each employee's hourly rate by the number of hours he or she worked that week.

concept 5

Calculated Field

5 A **calculated field** displays the results of a calculation in a query. You can perform a variety of calculations in queries. For example, you can calculate the sum of all inventory, the average salary for a department, or the highest sales figures among all sales personnel in the company. You can create your own calculation or use one of Access's seven predefined calculations called **functions**.

Function	What It Calculates
Sum	Totals values in a field for all records.
Average	Averages values in a field for all records.
Count	Counts number of values, excluding empty cells, in a field for all records.
Minimum	Finds lowest value in a field for all records.
Maximum	Finds highest value in a field for all records.
Standard Deviation	A measure of the dispersion of a frequency distribution.
Variance	Square of the standard deviation.

To create a calculated field, you enter an expression in the design grid that instructs Access to perform a calculation using the current field values. Then the calculated result is displayed in the calculated field column of the datasheet.

You are going to create a calculated field, named Gross Pay, which will multiply the value in the Hourly Rate field (located in the Pay Rate table) by the value in the Hours field (located in the Hours Worked table).

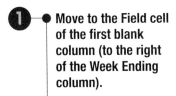

1 ● Move to the Field cell of the first blank column (to the right of the Week Ending column).

● Type **Gross Pay:**.

● Press `Spacebar`.

● Type **[Pay Rate]*[Hours]**.

Additional Information
Square brackets are used to designate field names in calculations.

● Press `↵Enter`.

HAVING TROUBLE?
If you made an error in your calculation entry, a message box will appear, advising you of the error. Close the message box and correct the error. A common error is to forget the colon following the field name.

● Increase the column width to fully display the expression.

Your screen should be similar to Figure 4.40

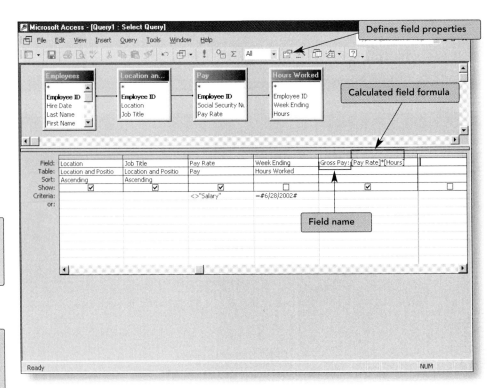

Figure 4.40

Before running the query, you want to change the new field's properties so it will display the calculated values as currency with two decimal places.

2 ● Select the new Gross Pay column.

● Click 🖼 Properties.

● From the Format drop-down list, select Currency.

● Close the Field Properties dialog box.

● Click ❗ Run.

Your screen should be similar to Figure 4.41

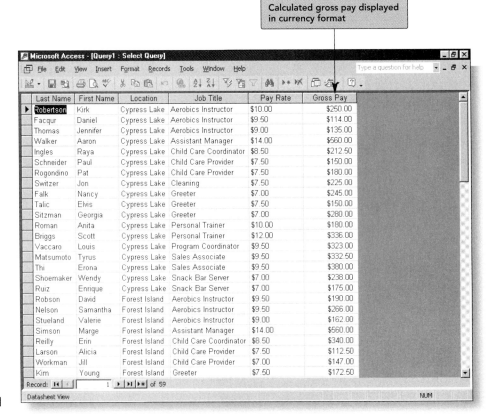

Figure 4.41

The query datasheet displays the gross pay for all employees except those on salary for the week ending 6/28/2002. Results are sorted by location and job title.

3 ● **Print a copy of the query datasheet for the club owners.**

● **Save this query as** Gross Pay 6/28/2002.

● **Close the query datasheet window.**

Creating a Crosstab Query

After seeing the gross pay datasheet, the Club owners are curious about the number of hours each employee is working. They have asked you for a simple datasheet that shows the average hours per employee for the last two weeks, excluding the employees on salary. To do this, you will create a crosstab query that will automatically summarize and calculate the data in the Hours query result.

concept 6

Crosstab Query

6 | A **crosstab query** summarizes table data and displays it in a tabular format. In a crosstab query, field values are calculated by sum, average, and count, and grouped along the left side and across the top of the datasheet in rows and columns. Being able to see table data grouped both horizontally and vertically is particularly helpful for comparing data in large tables where multiple records are entered one after another down the sheet.

First you will create a simple query to display only those records that do not contain 0 in the Hours Worked field.

1 ● Create a query using all the fields from the Hours Worked table. Set the Hours criteria to <>0.

● Run the query.

Your screen should be similar to Figure 4.42

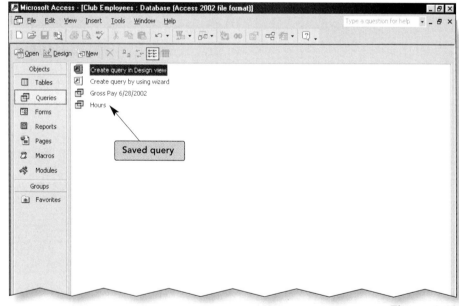

Figure 4.42

The query results show 117 records that contain entries in the Hours field.

2 ● Save the query as Hours and close the query.

Your screen should be similar to Figure 4.43

Saved query

Figure 4.43

Using the Crosstab Query Wizard

You will use the Crosstab Query Wizard to create a query called Hours Worked. The Wizard gives you step-by-step instructions on selecting fields for columns and rows, and for choosing the way you want the data summarized. Although you can select only one table for the original crosstab query, you can open the query in Query Design view and add more tables and fields if needed.

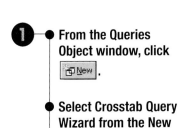

1 ● **From the Queries Object window, click** New .

● **Select Crosstab Query Wizard from the New Query dialog box.**

● **Click** OK .

Your screen should be similar to Figure 4.44

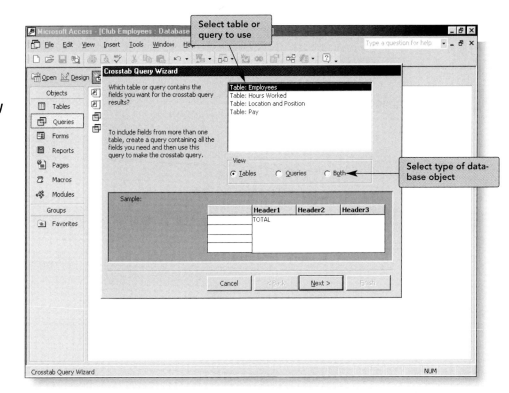

Figure 4.44

The first Crosstab Query Wizard dialog box asks you to select the tables or queries on which you want to base the crosstab query. Because Tables is the selected view, the names of all tables are displayed in the list box. You will use the Hours query.

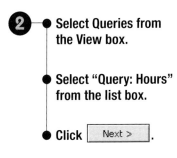

2 ● **Select Queries from the View box.**

● **Select "Query: Hours" from the list box.**

● **Click** Next > .

Your screen should be similar to Figure 4.45

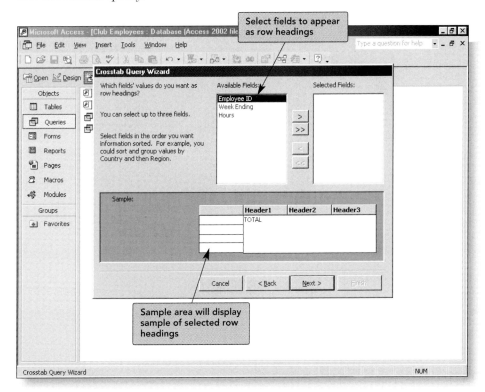

Figure 4.45

Next you are asked to select the field or fields that you want to use as row headings. These are the fields that will be displayed along the left side of your data sheet. The Sample area shows how your selections will look.

Add the Employee ID field to the Selected Fields list.

Click Next >.

Your screen should be similar to Figure 4.46

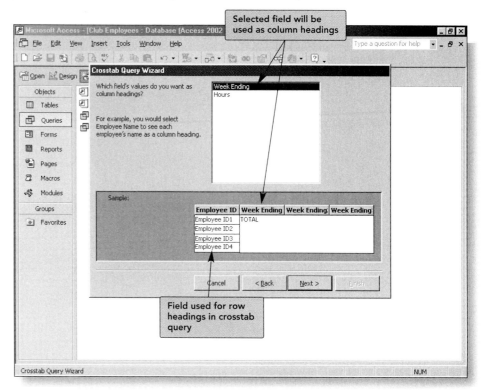

Figure 4.46

You are asked what fields are to be used as column headings (displayed along the top of the datasheet). You want to display the weeks in columns, so the current selection, Week Ending, is acceptable.

Click Next >.

Your screen should be similar to Figure 4.47

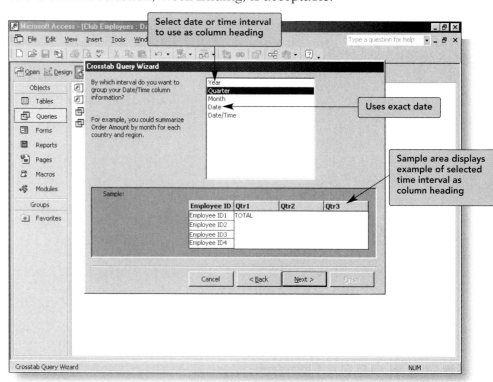

Figure 4.47

Since you selected a date field for the column headings, the Wizard asks you how you want the dates displayed: by year, by quarter, by month, by exact date, or by date and time. Because the table contains only two dates, you will use the exact date as the column heading.

5 ● **Select Date.**

● **Click** [Next >].

Your screen should be similar to Figure 4.48

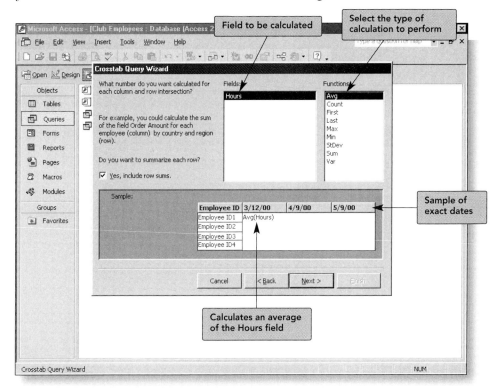

Figure 4.48

The remaining field, Hours, will be the one that is calculated. Since the Club owners asked to see an average number of hours for the last two weeks, the current selection is acceptable.

6 ● **Click** [Next >].

Your screen should be similar to Figure 4.49

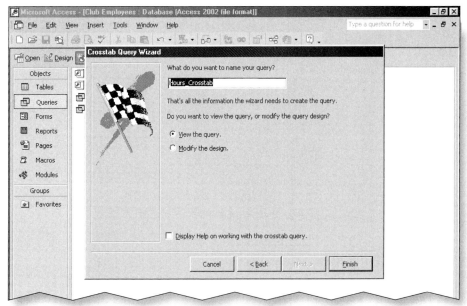

Figure 4.49

The final Wizard screen asks you what you want to name this query, and whether you want to view it right away or go into Design view so you can modify it. You like what the Wizard has used for the name of this query, and you decide to view the query first to determine whether it will need any modifications.

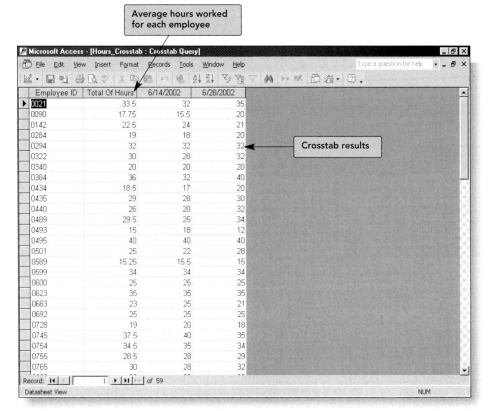

7 ● **Click** [Finish] .

Your screen should be similar to Figure 4.50

Figure 4.50

The Hours crosstab query automatically calculated the average number of hours per employee per week, which is what the Club owners have asked for. However, there are a few things about the query design that you do not like.

Refining the Query Design

First of all, you would like the columns to be in date order, with the average column last. Also, the Total Of Hours column name does not make it clear that this is an average of the hours worked, not the sum. You will move the columns and rename the column name.

1

- Switch to Design view.

- Replace "Total Of Hours" in the fourth Field cell with *Average Hours*.

- Switch to Datasheet view.

- Move the Average Hours column to the right of the 6/28/2002 column.

- If necessary, expand the Average Hours column to fully display the field name.

Your screen should be similar to Figure 4.51

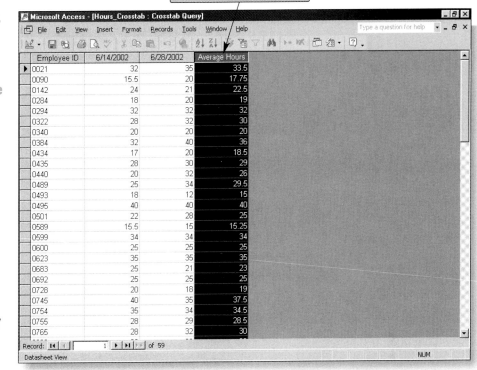

Column moved and column heading is more discriptive

Figure 4.51

The crosstab query is now easier to understand.

2

- Print a copy of the crosstab query for the Club owners.

- Save and close the crosstab query.

Defining Table Relationships

The first maintenance task you want to complete is to define permanent relationships between the tables in the Club Employees database.

concept 7

Relationship

7 A **relationship** establishes the association between common fields in two tables. The related fields must be of the same data type and contain the same kind of information, but can have different field names. The exception to this rule occurs when the primary key field in one of the tables is the AutoNumber type, which can be related to another AutoNumber field or to a Number field, as long as the Field Size property is the same for both. This is also the case when both fields are AutoNumber or Number—they always have to be the same field size in order to be related.

There are three types of relationships that can be established between tables: **one-to-one, one-to-many**, and **many-to-many**. Each of these is defined in the following table.

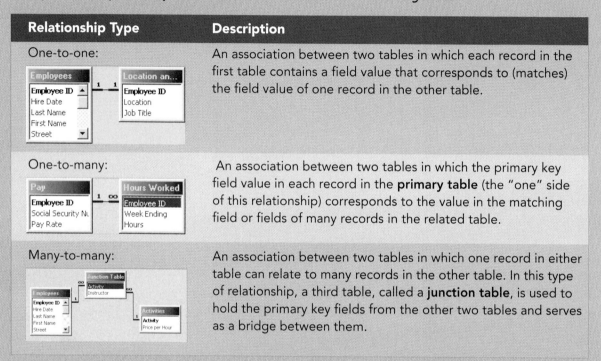

Relationship Type	Description
One-to-one:	An association between two tables in which each record in the first table contains a field value that corresponds to (matches) the field value of one record in the other table.
One-to-many:	An association between two tables in which the primary key field value in each record in the **primary table** (the "one" side of this relationship) corresponds to the value in the matching field or fields of many records in the related table.
Many-to-many:	An association between two tables in which one record in either table can relate to many records in the other table. In this type of relationship, a third table, called a **junction table**, is used to hold the primary key fields from the other two tables and serves as a bridge between them.

Once relationships are established, rules can be enforced, called the rules of **referential integrity**, to ensure that relationships between tables are valid and that related data is not accidentally changed or deleted. The rules ensure that a record in a primary table cannot be deleted if matching records exist in a related table, and a primary key value cannot be changed in the primary table if that record has related records.

The Relationships window is used to create and edit relationships. Before you can define relationships all tables must be closed.

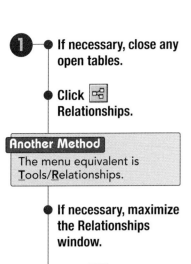

1 • If necessary, close any open tables.

• Click 🔲 Relationships.

Another Method

The menu equivalent is Tools/Relationships.

• If necessary, maximize the Relationships window.

• Click 🔲 Show Table to open the Show Table dialog box.

Another Method

The menu equivalent is Relationships/Show Table.

Your screen should be similar to Figure 4.52

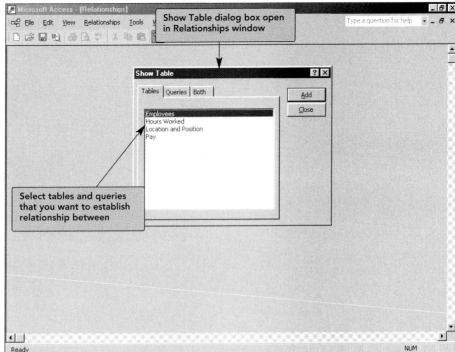

Figure 4.52

The Show Table dialog box is used to specify the tables and queries for which you want to define permanent relationships.

Additional Information

You can also use the Show Table dialog box to add more tables and queries to relationships that are already defined.

2 • Add the four tables to the Relationships window in the following order: Employees, Location and Position, Pay, and Hours Worked.

• Close the Show Table dialog box.

Your screen should be similar to Figure 4.53

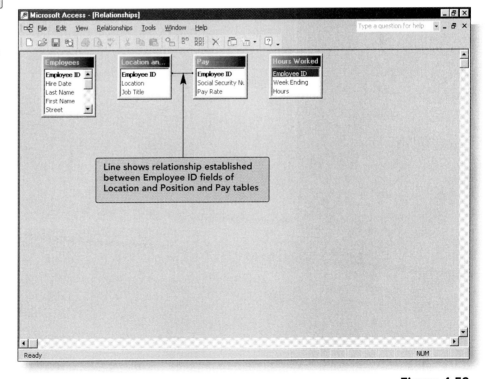

Figure 4.53

The Relationships window displays the selected tables. The four tables will be related on the Employee ID field. The line between the Employee ID fields of the Location and Position table and the Pay table shows the relationship that was established between those tables when creating the subdatasheet. You need to establish relationships between the other tables on the Employee ID field.

Establishing a One-to-One Relationship

You will first establish a one-to-one relationship between the Employees and the Location and Position tables in the Club Employees database. To do this, you drag the field that you want to relate from one table to the next.

1 ● Drag the Employee ID field from the Employees table onto the Employee ID field in the Location and Position table.

Your screen should be similar to Figure 4.54

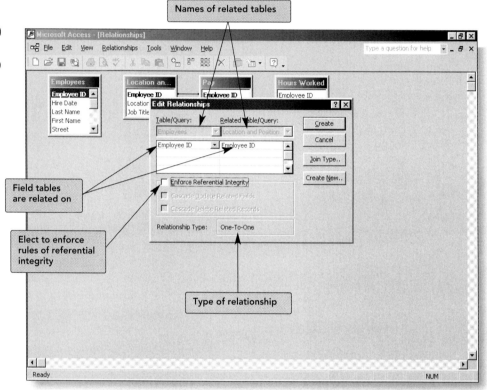

Figure 4.54

Additional Information

You also use the Edit Relationships dialog box to enforce referential integrity. You will learn how to do this shortly.

The Edit Relationships dialog box shows the names of the tables and their related field names. Notice that the Relationship Type box automatically displays "One To One." This is because each record in the Employees table has only one matching record in the Location and Position table.

2 ● Click [Create].

Your screen should be similar to Figure 4.55

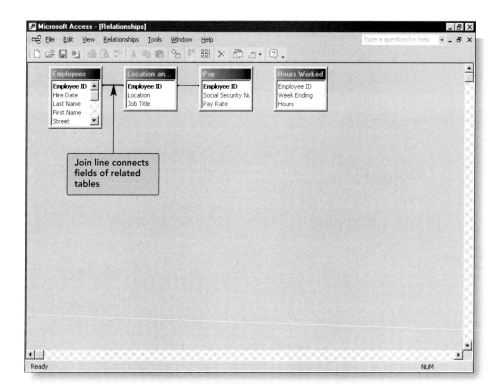

Join line connects fields of related tables

Figure 4.55

The related tables now have a join line connecting them.

Establishing a One-to-Many Relationship

The Hours Worked table includes multiple records for each employee (one record for the hours worked each week). Therefore, the relationship you establish between this table and the Pay table will be one-to-many.

1 ● Drag the Employee ID field from the Pay table onto the Employee ID field in the Hours Worked table.

Your screen should be similar to Figure 4.56

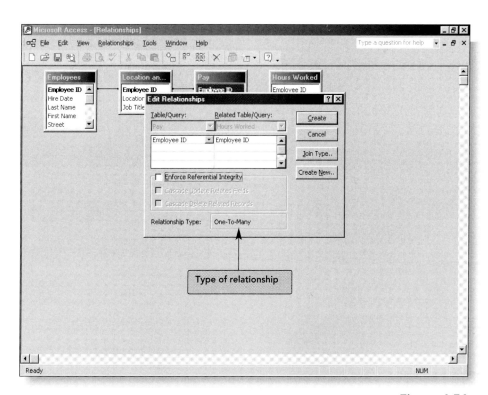

Type of relationship

Figure 4.56

"One-To-Many" is automatically displayed as the Relationship Type at the bottom of the Edit Relationships dialog box, because although there can be only one record in the Pay table for each Employee ID, the Hours Worked table can have many records that match it (with the same Employee ID).

Click Create **.**

Your screen should be similar to Figure 4.57

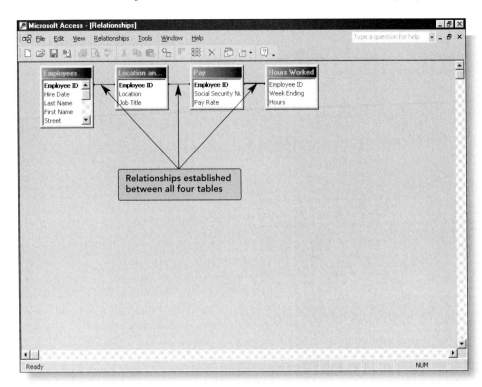

Figure 4.57

The tables in your database are now all related.

Enforcing Referential Integrity

Now that relationships exist among the tables, an erroneous change to a record in one of these tables could adversely affect its relationship with the others. You want to prevent this from happening by enforcing referential integrity for the tables.

1 • **Right-click the join line between the Employees and the Location and Position tables.**

• **Select Edit Relationship from the shortcut menu.**

Your screen should be similar to Figure 4.58

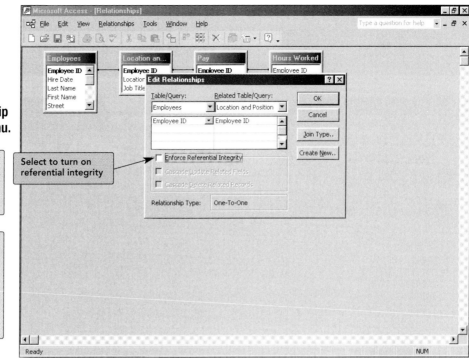

Select to turn on referential integrity

Figure 4.58

The Edit Relationships dialog box shows the tables and their current relationship.

2 • **Select Enforce Referential Integrity.**

• **Click** OK .

Your screen should be similar to Figure 4.59

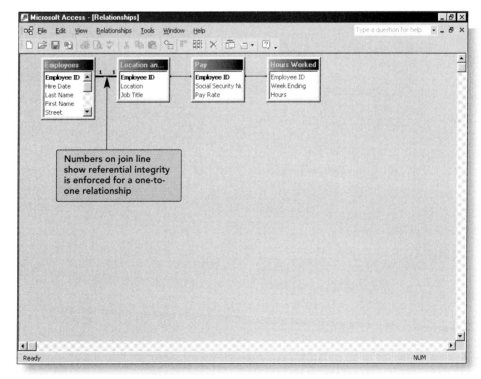

Numbers on join line show referential integrity is enforced for a one-to-one relationship

Figure 4.59

The number 1 next to each table above the join line indicates that referential integrity is enforced for a one-to-one relationship between these tables. You will now enforce referential integrity between the remaining tables.

3 ● **Enforce referential integrity between the Location and Position table and the Pay table.**

● **Enforce referential integrity between the Pay and the Hours Worked tables.**

Your screen should be similar to Figure 4.60

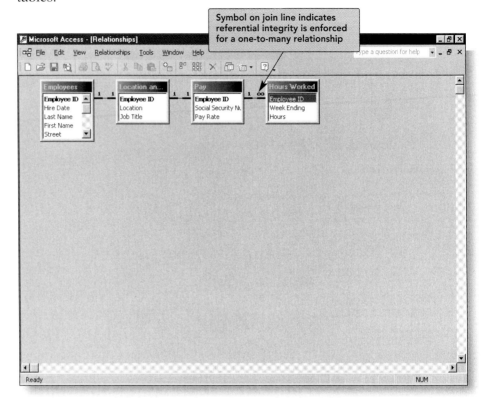

Symbol on join line indicates referential integrity is enforced for a one-to-many relationship

Figure 4.60

Notice that the join line between the Pay and Hours Worked tables displays a ∞ symbol on the right, which indicates "many." In this case, the referential integrity is being enforced for a one-to-many relationship.

Once referential integrity has been set, a warning message is automatically displayed if one of the rules is broken, and you are not allowed to complete the action you are trying to do.

Printing a Relationships Report

Before exiting the Relationships window, you decide to print a report that shows the current relationships between the tables in your database.

1 ● **Choose File/Print Relationships.**

Your screen should be similar to Figure 4.61

Preview of the Relationships report →

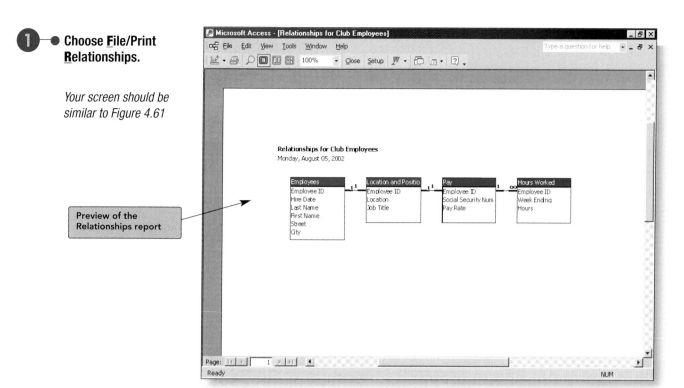

Figure 4.61

A preview of how the report will look when printed is displayed on the screen. The database name and creation date are automatically used as the report header. You can print this report as well as save it for future reference.

2 ● **Print the report.**

● **Save the report as** Database Relationships.

● **Close the report preview window.**

● **Close the Relationships window.**

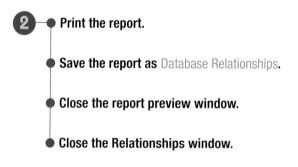

Additional Information

The relationships are automatically saved.

Using Subdatasheets

When relationships are established between tables, subdatasheets are automatically created.

Subdatasheet

8 A **subdatasheet** is a data table nested in another data table that contains data related or joined to the table where it resides. A subdatasheet allows you to easily view and edit related data. Subdatasheets are created automatically whenever relationships are established between tables. However, they can also be created manually using **I**nsert/**S**ubdatasheet.

Using this method creates a relationship between tables if one does not already exist. When creating subdatasheets manually, the source of the subdatasheet can be a table or query, and the related or joined data can be viewed and edited in the master table, a query, a form, or a subform. The **master table** is the table that holds the subdatasheet.

You will open the Employees table to see the subdatasheet that was added to it.

1 ● **Open the "Employees" table.**

Your screen should be similar to Figure 4.62

Expand indicators

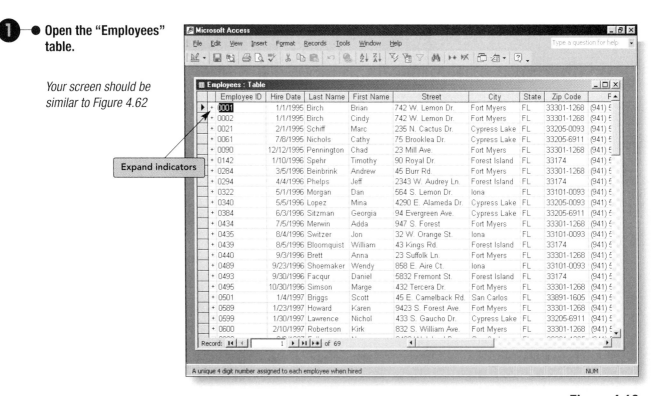

Figure 4.62

The Employee table displays expand indicators (+) at the beginning of each row. This signifies that there is a subdatasheet linked to the records in this table. The Employees table is the master table and the subdatasheet is the Location and Position table to which the Employees table has an established relationship.

You can display the individual subdatasheet record that is linked to a master table record by clicking the expand indicator for each record row, or you can display the entire subdatasheet at once. You will expand all the subdatasheet records.

2 ● **Choose Format/**
Subdatasheet/Expand
All.

Your screen should be
similar to Figure 4.63

Expanded
subdatasheet

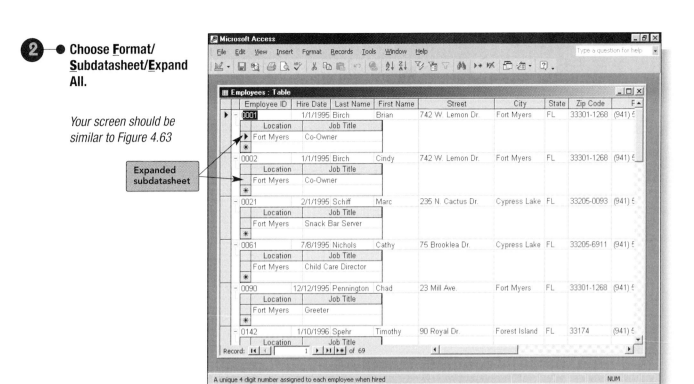

Figure 4.63

The Location and Position subdatasheet is displayed with its records positioned under each related record in the Employees table. You decide you do not need the subdatasheets that have been created as they may be confusing to others using the database. You will remove them.

3 ● **Choose Format/**
Subdatasheet/Remove.

Your screen should be
similar to Figure 4.64

Subdatasheet
removed

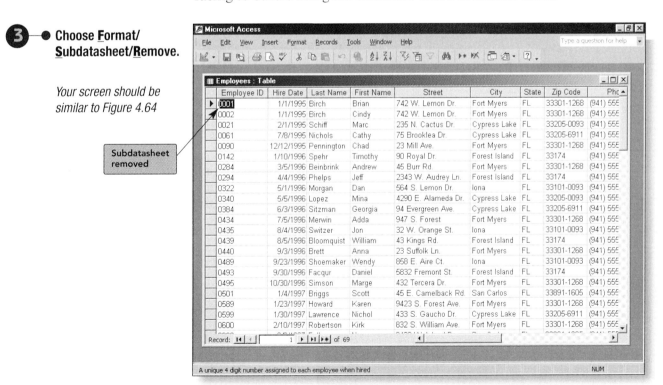

Figure 4.64

The Employees table is returned to its original display format, without the subdatasheet.

④ ● In the same manner, remove the sub-datasheets from the "Location and Position" and "Pay" tables.

● Close all open tables.

Your screen should be similar to Figure 4.65

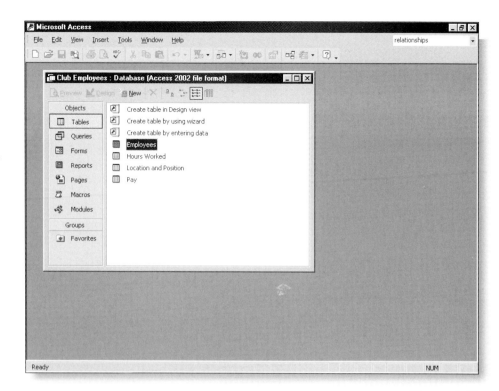

Figure 4.65

Backing Up and Restoring a Database

It is very important that you perform periodic backups of your database files. This ensures that you do not lose too much work if there is a power outage or a system failure. If a database file is lost or corrupted for some reason, you can easily restore the latest file you backed up. It will not include any changes you have made to the file since it was last backed up, but it is better than not having any file at all.

A **backup** operation saves a copy of the database or other type of file to a storage medium other than the computer's hard disk. Backups can be performed using the Windows Explorer, My Computer, Microsoft Backup, the MS-DOS Copy command, or other backup software. Database files can be backed up to any storage medium, such as a tape drive, zip cartridge, or CD. You can also back up files to a floppy disk, but keep in mind that the storage space on this type of disk is limited, and you may have to use backup software that will allow you to span several disks to copy your files onto them.

To back up a database file using Windows Explorer or My Computer, you simply insert the storage medium and drag the file you want to back up onto the medium's folder. To use another backup program, follow the instructions provided with that program.

It is a good idea to label the storage medium with the name of the file or files that it contains, the date the backup was done, and the word "Backup."

A **restore** operation copies a backup file from the storage medium back onto the computer's hard drive. You should use the same method to restore the file that you used to back it up (such as Windows Explorer, My Computer, Microsoft Backup, or other backup software). If you used the MS-DOS Copy command, you would use the Restore command to restore the backup copy.

In the same way you performed a backup operation with Windows Explorer or My Computer, you can restore a backup file by dragging it from the storage medium's directory to the database folder (or other folder where you want it to reside). However, keep in mind that if there is an existing file in the database folder with the same name as the backup copy file name, restoring the backup copy may replace the existing database file. If you want to save the existing file, rename it before you copy the backup file.

Since you only have one database to back up at this time, and it is already on a floppy disk, you will not perform any backup or restore operations at this time. However, you should make it a habit of backing up your files once you begin creating your own databases.

Before exiting, you will compact and repair the database.

1 ● Choose **T**ools/**D**atabase Utilities/**C**ompact and Repair Database.

● Close the database and exit Access.

concept summary

LAB 4

Working with Multiple Tables

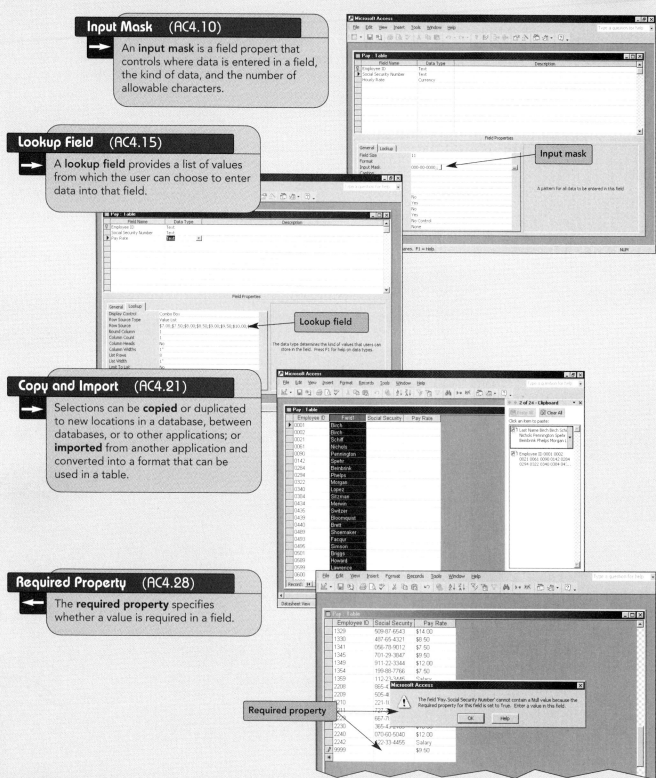

Input Mask   (AC4.10)

An **input mask** is a field propert that controls where data is entered in a field, the kind of data, and the number of allowable characters.

Lookup Field   (AC4.15)

A **lookup field** provides a list of values from which the user can choose to enter data into that field.

Copy and Import   (AC4.21)

Selections can be **copied** or duplicated to new locations in a database, between databases, or to other applications; or **imported** from another application and converted into a format that can be used in a table.

Required Property   (AC4.28)

The **required property** specifies whether a value is required in a field.

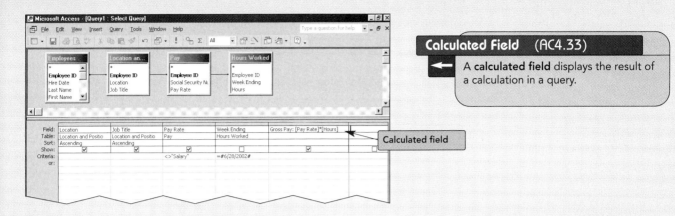

Calculated Field (AC4.33)

A **calculated field** displays the result of a calculation in a query.

Calculated field

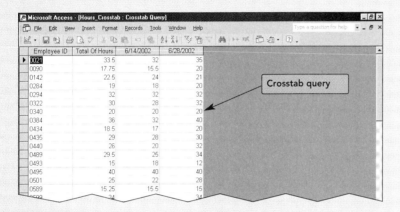

Crosstab Query (AC4.35)

A **crosstab query** summarizes table data and displays it in a tabular format.

Crosstab query

Relationship

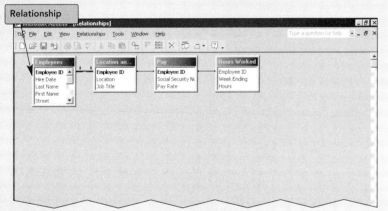

Relationship (AC4.47)

A **relationship** establishes the association between common fields in two tables.

Subdatasheet

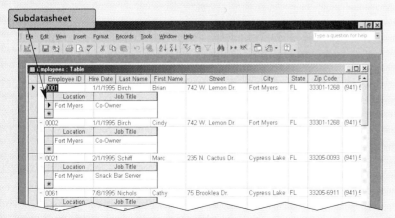

Subdatasheet (AC4.50)

A **subdatasheet** is a data table that is nested in another data table and that contains data related or joined to the table where it resides.

key terms

backup   AC4.52

calculated field   AC4.33

copy   AC4.20

crosstab query   AC4.35

destination   AC4.21

foreign key   AC4.15

function   AC4.33

import   AC4.20

input mask   AC4.10

junction table   AC4.42

literal characters   AC4.10

lookup field   AC4.15

lookup list   AC4.15

many-to-many   AC4.42

mask characters   AC4.10

master table   AC4.50

Office Clipboard   AC4.21

one-to-many   AC4.42

one-to-one   AC4.42

primary table   AC4.42

referential integrity   AC4.42

relationship   AC4.42

required property   AC4.28

restore   AC4.53

source   AC4.21

subdatasheet   AC4.50

System Clipboard   AC4.21

value list   AC4.15

mous skills

The Microsoft Office User Specialist (MOUS) certification program is designed to measure your proficiency in performing basic tasks using the Office XP applications. Getting certified demonstrates that you have the skills and provides a valuable industry credential for employment. After completing this lab, you have learned the following Microsoft Office User Specialist skills:

Skill	Description	Page
Creating and Modifying Tables	Add a predefined input mask to a field Create lookup fields	AC4.9 AC4.14
Creating and Modifying Queries	Add calculated fields to queries	AC4.33
Defining Relationships	Create one-to-many relationships Enforce referential integrity	AC4.45 AC4.46
Integrating with Other Applications	Import data to Access	AC4.25

command summary

Command	Shortcut	Button	Action
File/**G**et External Data/**I**mport			Brings data in from another file
File/Print **R**elationships			Creates a report that shows relationships in current database
Edit/**C**opy	Ctrl + C		Copies selected text to Clipboard
Edit/Office Clip**b**oard			Displays Office Clipboard task pane
Edit/**P**aste	Ctrl + V		Pastes text from Clipboard to current location
Edit/Delete Colu**m**n			Removes selected column from table
Insert/**L**ookup Field			Creates a lookup field with specified values from which to choose
Insert/**L**ookup Column			Creates a lookup column with specified values from which to choose
Insert/**S**ubdatasheet			Inserts a subdatasheet with values from a related table or query into current datasheet
F**o**rmat/**S**ubdatasheet/**E**xpand All			Shows entire subdatasheet that is embedded in current datasheet
F**o**rmat/**S**ubdatasheet/**R**emove			Removes subdatasheet that is embedded in current datasheet
Relationships/Show **T**able			Displays a dialog box for adding tables and queries to Relationships window
Relationships/Edit **R**elationship			Used to change existing relationships or create new relationships in current database and to enforce referential integrity
Tools/**R**elationships			Used to view and define permanent relationships between tables

Terminology

screen identification

In the following Access screen, several items are identified by letters. Enter the correct term for each item in the spaces provided.

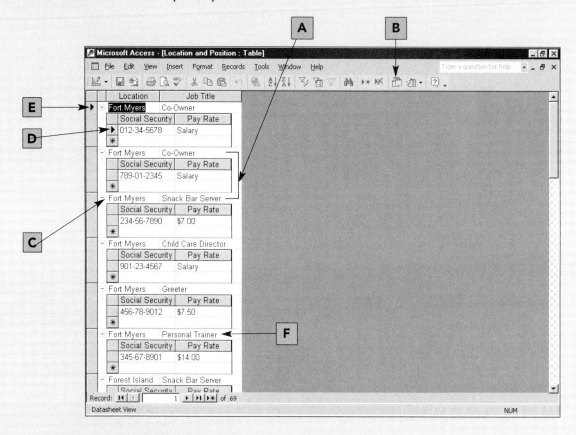

A. _____

B. _____

C. _____

D. _____

E. _____

F. _____

matching

Match the numbered item with the correct lettered description.

1. import   _____   **a.** summarizes table data and displays it in tabular format

2. junction table   _____   **b.** copies a backup file from the storage medium back onto a hard drive

3. value list   _____   **c.** displays the results of a calculation in a query

4. foreign key   _____   **d.** set of rules used to ensure that relationships between tables are valid

5. input mask   _____   **e.** holds the primary key fields between two tables

6. calculated field   _____   **f.** controls how data is entered in a field of a table, query, or form

7. restore operation   _____   **g.** field that refers to the primary key in another table and indicates a relationship between the two

8. crosstab query   _____   **h.** lookup field that used fixed values

9. referential integrity   _____   **i.** to retrieve data that is saved in another fomat and insert it into an Access table

10. required property   _____   **j.** specifies whether a value is required in a field

multiple choice

Circle the letter of the correct response.

1. Lookup field values are
   a. obtained from another table
   b. entered when the field is created
   c. obtained from the current table
   d. any of the above

2. A(n)_____provides a list of values from which the user can choose to make entering data into that field simpler.
   a. foreign key
   b. lookup field
   c. lookup list
   d. value list

3. A field whose Required property is set to Yes cannot contain a(n) _____ value.
   a. alphanumeric
   b. null
   c. existing
   d. any of the above

4. A(n)_____displays the results of a calculation in a query.
   a. key field
   b. expression
   c. number
   d. calculated field

5. The _____ are one or more fields in the embedded subdatasheet that will be linked to master fields in the master table.
   a. child fields
   b. key fields
   c. master fields
   d. lookup fields

6. A(n) _____ establishes the association between common fields in two tables.
   a. input mask
   b. source list
   c. child field
   d. relationship

7. The _____ is the table that holds the subdatasheet.
   a. master table
   b. main table
   c. relationship table
   d. subdatasheet table

8. One-to-many, many-to-many, and one-to-one are different types of _____.
   a. queries
   b. relationships
   c. filters
   d. reports

9. The _____ specifies whether a value is required in a field.
   a. lookup field
   b. calculated field
   c. Required property
   d. none of the above

10. The _____ mask character signifies that an entry, if made, must be a letter.
    a. #
    b. /
    c. ?
    d. !

true/false

Circle the correct answer to the following statements.

1. Once you have entered a value in a lookup field, you can go back and change it.	True	False
2. Once referential integrity is set, you cannot change the relationship between tables.	True	False
3. A Required property can be set for any type of field.	True	False
4. When inserting a subdatasheet, child and master fields must have the same name.	True	False
5. A primary key will not accept null values.	True	False
6. You can select multiple tables in the Crosstab Query Wizard.	True	False
7. The variance function measures the dispersion of a frequency distribution.	True	False
8. Fields in different tables must have the same name in order to be related.	True	False
9. The Table Wizard lets you select fields from multiple sample tables.	True	False
10. Values for a lookup field in one table can be obtained from values in another table.	True	False

Concepts

fill-in

Complete the following statements by filling in the blanks with the correct terms.

1. When referential integrity is enforced, a _____ value cannot be changed in the primary table if that record has related records.

2. Setting the _____ property for a field defines whether or not you must enter a value in the field.

3. A _____ _____ provides a list of values from which you can select to enter data in a field.

4. Data that is _____ from another application is converted into a format that can be used in a table.

5. Use a _____ to summarize table data.

6. The _____function finds the lowest value in a field for all records.

7. A _____ establishes an association between tables.

8. A backup operation places a copy of the selected file onto _____.

9. A _____ is a data table nested in another data table that contains data related or joined to the table where it resides.

10. An input mask format consists of _____ and _____ characters.

discussion questions

1. Discuss the differences between using the Table Wizard and the Design view for creating new data tables. When would you use one as opposed to the other?

2. Discuss the purpose of a crosstab query. When would it be better to use this type of query instead of a simple query?

3. Discuss how input masks and lookup fields can help data entry. To what types of field data could you apply input masks? For what types of data could you create lookup fields?

4. Discuss the purpose of table relationships. When and why should you enforce referential integrity among related tables? Are there any situations where this would be a hindrance rather than a help?

Hands-On Exercises

step-by-step

Adventure Travel Tours Client Database

★ 1. As the database administrator for Adventure Travel Tours, you have created a database that includes tables of clients and travel tour agents. Personnel has requested that these tables be integrated to provide a look at which clients are currently assigned an agent. They would also like to see the client membership by office and the number of return clientele. Your completed subdatasheet table and crosstab query are shown here.

a. In Windows re-name the ac04_ATT Clients & Agents file Clients & Agents. Open the "Clients" table. This table already has one lookup field, the Office Location, but you want to add another lookup field for identifying the clients who are as-signed agents.

Clients   9/6/2001

Client ID	First Name	Last Name	Address	City	State	Zip Code	Phone	Office	Agents
98542	Carl	Pederson	505 S. Tiller Ave.	Littleton	CO	80120	(303) 555-6333	Denver	
98564	Scott	Berco	707 Bryon Dr.	Sheridan	CO	80110	(303) 555-6789	Denver	
98565	Miguel	Wersal	318 2nd St.	Arvada	CO	80003	(303) 555-7200	Denver	
98594	Denise	Navarro	341 Grandview Ct.	Glendale	CO	80246	(303) 555-6328	Denver	
98633	Teddy	Wrightsell	99 Oasis St.	Denver	CO	80201	(303) 555-5775	Denver	
98643	Bryan	Neubart	34 Marigold Ln.	Littleton	CO	80129	(303) 555-3273	Denver	
98654	Jeremy	Odonnell	227 E. Oasis St.	Denver	CO	80218	(303) 555-7227	Denver	
98711	Mary	Olson	233 Marigold St.	Sheridan	CO	80110	(303) 555-5533	Denver	
98733	Anna	Armstrong	45 First St.	Littleton	CO	80120	(303) 555-0293	Lakewood	
98734	Beatrice	Antall	212 Maple Ave.	Littleton	CO	80129	(303) 555-2967	Denver	Cook
98745	Ron	Richardson	992 S. Chapel Ave.	Denver	CO	80201	(303) 555-7224	Denver	
98754	Diane	Hummell	727 E. 5th St.	Denver	CO	80221	(303) 555-6116	Denver	
98773	Vivian	Ossian	837 E. Holly Ln.	Littleton	CO	80129	(303) 555-3113	Denver	
98809	Rudolph	Zeh	405 Seaside Ct.	Arvada	CO	80002	(303) 555-2121	Denver	
98884	Tracy	Paffumi	102 W. Holly Ave.	Glendale	CO	80246	(303) 555-5863	Denver	
98889	Charles	Olm	1221 N. First St.	Denver	CO	80201	(303) 555-4774	Denver	
99847	Mark	Hallstrom	742 Ferry Rd.	Littleton	CO	80120	(303) 555-3383	Denver	Milligan
99856	Edsel	Wolff	424 N. Main St.	Littleton	CO	80120	(303) 555-3930	Lakewood	Merrick
99999	Student	Name	89 Any St.	Denver	CO	80225	(303) 555-4498	Denver	Sims

b. Switch to Design view and insert a new field named **Agents** below the Office Location field. Use the Lookup Wizard to specify that you want to look up values from another table. Select the Agents table as the table you want to use, and select the Last Name and Office Location fields as the fields whose values you want to use. Accept the column widths as they are displayed and the default to hide the key column. Label the lookup col-umn **Travel Agents**. Save the table.

Clients_Crosstab   9/6/2001

Agents	Total Of Client ID	Denver	Glendale	Lakewood
	134	94	26	14
Cook	4	4		
Howe	3	3		
Lii	1			1
Merrick	2			2
Milligan	3	3		
Nichols	2		2	
Quigley	1		1	
Sims	1	1		

c. Switch to Datasheet view. Sort the table in ascending order on Last Name. Locate the following client records and assign the agents as listed below. Adjust the Agents column width to fit the displayed data when you are finished with your selections.

Client	Agent
Beatrice Antall	Cook
Arved Chew	Milligan
Dennis Dalta	Cook
Monica Epp	Nichols
Lydia Fischer	Howe
Katherine Gryder	Cook
Mark Hallstrom	Milligan
Norma Jones	Quigley
James Lewis	Cook
Trent Maltos	Howe
Ahmed Momen	Howe
Yvonne Naffin	Merrick
Steve Sharp	Lii
Joseph Trimble	Milligan
Kim Vinton	Nichols
Edsel Wolff	Merrick

d. Add a new record with **99999** as the Client ID and your first and last names. Enter a fictional address and phone number. Select an office location from the lookup list and select an agent from that location.

e. If needed, best fit the column widths in the table. Sort the table on Client ID. Preview the table. Change the orientation of the table to landscape and then print page 5. Save and close the table.

f. Open the "Agents" table. Expand the subdatasheet so you can see all the client records that are related to each agent record. Remove the subdatasheet.

g. Personnel has requested a datasheet that shows the clients and agents at the different locations. To produce this datasheet, create a new query using the Crosstab Query Wizard. Select Clients as the table on which you want to base the query, Travel Agents as the row heading, Office as the column heading, and Client ID as the field you want calculated with the Count function. Accept the default query name (Clients_Crosstab). Run the query. Adjust the width of the columns to fit and print the crosstab query results in portrait orientation.

h. Close the query and the database, saving the changes.

Animal Rescue Foundation Foster Family Database

★★ **2.** The Animal Rescue Foundation database has made life much easier for the directors of this charity organization. The three tables it contains—Animals, Fosters, and Adopters—have helped them keep track of the animals that come into and are adopted out of their shelter, as well as the individuals who provide foster care or adopt these animals. They would like you to create a new query to show how long the animals that are still being boarded at Animal Angels have been there, which you will accomplish with a calculated field. Your completed Relationship Report and Boarded Animals query are shown here.

a. Use Windows to rename the file AC04_ARF file ARF Fosters.

b. Click 🖼 Relationships and add the Animals, Fosters, and Adopters tables, in that order.

c. Create a relationship between the Animals and Fosters tables, using the ID # field as the common field. Create another relationship between the Animals and Adopters tables, once again using the ID # as the common field. Print a Relationships report. Save the report using the name **Relationships for ARF**, and then close the report. Close the Relationships window, saving the changes.

d. Open the "Fosters" table. Change the Foster Last Name and Foster First Name fields in the first record to your first and last name. Expand the subdatasheet. Remove the subdatasheet. Change the page layout to landscape and print the first page of the table. Save and close the table.

e. Create a query in Design view. Add the Animals table to the design. Add the ID #, Type, Name, Status, and Boarded Date fields to the grid, in that order. You want only the records for animals that are still being boarded to be included in this query, so specify the criteria in the Status field as **B** (for Boarded). Because the status of "boarded" will be assumed in this query, the Status field does not need to be displayed, and you can deselect its Show option.

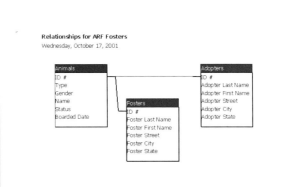

f. In the first blank Field column, enter the following equation to calculate the number of days an animal has been boarded at Animal Angels:

Days Boarded:
DateDiff('d',[Boarded Date],[Date])

g. Make sure the Show box is checked for the calculated field and then run the query. When you are asked to enter a parameter for the Date, enter **03/01/03**.

h. Adjust the column widths as necessary to view all displayed data. Change the name of the pet with the ID# of 045 to display your name. Print the query in portrait orientation.

i. Save the query as Boarded Animals and close it.

j. Close the ARF Fosters database.

Simply Beautiful Client Query

★ **3.** Maria Dell, the owner of Simply Beautiful, is quite pleased with the Clients table that you created in the spa's database. She would now like you to create two additional tables: one that contains data about the various spa packages and their costs and another that lists which clients have purchased which package. She would also like you to run a query that shows the spa packages purchased by clients and the total amount spent. When you are finished, you will have the query results shown here.

To create the tables and query, follow these steps:

a. Open the ac02_Simply Beautiful database file that you worked on in Step-by-Step Exercise 1 in Lab 3. (If this file is not

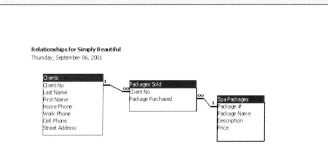

Client Purchases   10/17/2001

Last Name	1	2	4	5	6	7	Total Purchases
Chen				$100.00			$100.00
Finch	$350.00						$350.00
Franklin				$100.00			$100.00
Griffith					$75.00		$75.00
Grimes					$75.00		$75.00
Huye						$75.00	$75.00
Johnson					$75.00		$75.00
Kane	$350.00						$350.00
Lawry			$125.00				$125.00
Linderson					$75.00		$75.00
Marcellus						$75.00	$75.00
Marchand	$350.00						$350.00
Miller					$75.00		$75.00
Mitchell			$125.00				$125.00
Name	$350.00						$350.00
Pickett				$100.00			$100.00
Price			$125.00				$125.00
Riley	$350.00						$350.00
Townsend		$250.00					$250.00
Tran				$100.00			$100.00
Williams	$350.00						$350.00

Page 1

available, use ac04_Simply Beautiful.) In Windows rename the file Simply Beautiful. Open the "Clients" table and enter your first and last name for Client ID 100-24 (if it is not already entered). Close the Clients table.

b. Use the Table Wizard to create a new table using the following fields from the Products sample table. Rename the fields as shown.

Sample Table Field to Add	Rename Field
ProductID	Package #
ProductName	Package Name
ProductDescription	Description
UnitPrice	Price

c. Name the table **Spa Packages**, and let Access assign the primary key. Do not assign a relationship between this new table and the existing Clients table. Accept the default to begin entering records right away (without altering the table design) and finish the Wizard.

d. Enter the following records (do not worry about entering a Package #—it is an AutoNumber field):

Package Name	Description	Price
Day Dream	Deep-Tissue Massage, Aromatherapy, Body Wrap, Facial, Sauna	$350.00
Relaxation	Deep-Tissue Massage, Facial, Sauna	$275.00
Pampered Purification	Aromatherapy, Facial	$200.00
	Body Wrap, Sauna	$150.00
Inner Beauty	Deep-Tissue Massage	$125.00
Scent-Sational	Aromatherapy	$100.00
Angel Face	Facial	$75.00
Soaking Soother	Sauna	$75.00

e. Adjust the column widths to fit the data. Then save and close the table.

f. Create another table in Design view. Name the first field **Client #** and assign it a Data Type of Text and a Field Size of **6**.

g. Make the second field a lookup field that uses the Package # and Package Name field from the Spa Packages table. Accept the default Hide Key Column selection and the displayed column width. Name the lookup column **Package Purchased**, finish the Wizard, and save the table as Packages Sold. If you receive a message asking you whether you want to assign a primary key, do not do so (you will be entering multiple records for each client and package, so they will not be unique).

h. Switch to Datasheet view. Use the Office Clipboard to copy the Client No column from the Clients table to the Packages Sold table.

i. Select a spa package for each client (assign the Day Dream package to your record). Adjust the column widths as necessary and close the Packages Sold table.

j. Close the Clients table, if it is still open.

k. Create a relationship between the Clients and Packages Sold tables based on the Client No field, and enforce referential integrity. Create a relationship between the Package Purchased field in the Packages Sold table and the Package # field in the Spa Packages table, enforcing referential integrity. Print and save the Relationships report with the default file name; then save and close the Relationships window.

l. Create a new query in Design view and include all three tables. Add the Last Name, Package Purchased, and Price fields to the query design grid. Save the query as Package Revenue.

m. Use the Crosstab Query Wizard to create a crosstab query based on the Package Revenue query. Select Last Name as the row heading, Package Purchased as the column heading, and Price as the field you want calculated with the SUM function. Name the crosstab query Client Purchases.

n. Adjust the column widths. Rename the Total of Price field **Total Purchases**. Move the Total Purchases field to the last position in the crosstab query result.

o. Apply formatting of your choice to the datasheet. Print the crosstab query result in landscape orientation. Close and save the query.

p. Close the Simply Beautiful database.

Downtown Internet Cafe Inventory Database Improvements

★ ★
★

4. The database you created for the Downtown Internet Cafe contains a table with information about the cafe's inventory and vendors. You have used this table to design a vendor information form, as well as to create queries and reports on items that need to be ordered. The cafe's owner, Evan, has asked you to create another table that lists the costs of the inventory items, the quantity on hand and on order, as well as the vendors who carry these items. Evan would also like you to add a field to the existing To Be Ordered query that will calculate the cost of each order using values from both of the Cafe Purchases database tables. When you are finished, you will have a new database table and a query printout that looks similar to those shown here.

a. Rename the ac04_Cafe Purchases database Cafe Purchases. Open the "Inventory" table. Change the last inventory item #9999 to your name as the contact. Close the table.

b. Use the Table Wizard to create a new table based on the Sample Table called Products. Add the following fields from the sample table to your new table field list and rename them to match the corresponding Inventory table fields, as follows:

	Inventory Prices			10/17/2001
Item #	**Description**	**Vendor Name**	**Category**	**Unit Price**
1100	Coffee filters	Restaurant Supply	Paper Supplies	$115.00
1101	Stirrers	Restaurant Supply	Paper Supplies	$85.00
1102	Napkins	Restaurant Supply	Paper Supplies	$75.00
1104	Cups–small	Restaurant Supply	Paper Supplies	$115.00
1105	Cups–medium	Restaurant Supply	Paper Supplies	$125.00
1106	Cups–large	Restaurant Supply	Paper Supplies	$135.00
1108	Sugar	Restaurant Supply	Condiments	$95.00
1109	Sugar substitute	Restaurant Supply	Condiments	$95.00
1110	Powdered cream	Restaurant Supply	Condiments	$95.00
1720	Decaf Viennese	Pure Processing	Beverages	$75.00
1721	Decaf Sumatra	Pure Processing	Beverages	$75.00
1722	Decaf Guatamala	Pure Processing	Beverages	$75.00
1723	Decaf Columbian	Pure Processing	Beverages	$75.00
1724	Decaf Dark	Pure Processing	Beverages	$75.00
2575	Coffee mints	Tasty Delights	Condiments	$65.00
2900	Brochures	Pro Printing	Paper Supplies	$500.00
2924	Coffee mugs	Central Ceramics	Other	$375.00
3520	Columbian coffee	Quality Coffee	Beverages	$65.00
3521	Kenya coffee	Quality Coffee	Beverages	$65.00
3522	Guatamala coffee	Quality Coffee	Beverages	$65.00
3523	Java coffee	Quality Coffee	Beverages	$75.00
3524	Arabian coffee	Quality Coffee	Beverages	$65.00
3525	Sumatra coffee	Quality Coffee	Beverages	$75.00
3526	Ethiopian coffee	Quality Coffee	Beverages	$75.00
3527	Kona coffee	Quality Coffee	Beverages	$115.00
3528	Espresso Roast	Quality Coffee	Beverages	$75.00
3529	Italian Roast	Quality Coffee	Beverages	$65.00
3530	French Roast	Quality Coffee	Beverages	$65.00
7920	Morning blend tea	Better Beverages, Inc.	Beverages	$55.00
7921	Orange Pekoe tea	Better Beverages, Inc.	Beverages	$55.00
7922	Earl Grey tea	Better Beverages, Inc.	Beverages	$55.00
7926	Darjeeling tea	Better Beverages, Inc.	Beverages	$55.00
9999	Scones	Best Bakery	Baked Goods	$1.75

		To Be Ordered				10/17/2001
Vendor Name	**Contact**	**Phone**	**Description**	**# On Hand**	**Order Amount**	**Order Cost**
Best Bakery	Student Name	(909)555-5599	Scones	16	8	14
Better Beverages, Inc.	Mae Yung	(415) 555-1122	Earl Grey tea	17	7	385
Better Beverages, Inc.	Mae Yung	(415) 555-1122	Orange Pekoe tea	21	3	165
Central Ceramics	Dan O'Dell	(602) 555-1924	Coffee mugs	12	12	4500
Pure Processing	Nancy Young	(650) 555-5689	Decaf Columbian	13	11	825
Pure Processing	Nancy Young	(650) 555-5689	Decaf Dark	15	9	675
Quality Coffee	Fred Wilmington	(206) 555-9090	Sumatra coffee	14	10	750
Quality Coffee	Fred Wilmington	(206) 555-9090	Columbian coffee	19	5	325
Quality Coffee	Fred Wilmington	(206) 555-9090	Java coffee	16	8	600
Quality Coffee	Fred Wilmington	(206) 555-9090	Kona coffee	15	9	1035
Quality Coffee	Fred Wilmington	(206) 555-9090	Espresso Roast	10	14	1050
Quality Coffee	Fred Wilmington	(206) 555-9090	Italian Roast	20	4	260
Quality Coffee	Fred Wilmington	(206) 555-9090	French Roast	13	11	715
Quality Coffee	Fred Wilmington	(206) 555-9090	Guatamala coffee	23	1	65
Restaurant Supply	Manny Smith	(602) 555-0037	Coffee filters	15	9	1035
Restaurant Supply	Manny Smith	(602) 555-0037	Cups–large	12	12	1620

Page 1

Sample Table Field to Add	Rename Field
ProductID	Item #
ProductDescription	Description
SupplierID	Vendor Name
UnitPrice	Unit Price

c. Name the table **Inventory Prices**. Let Access assign the primary key. Do not assign a relationship between this new table and the existing Inventory table. Specify that you want to modify the table design, and then finish the Wizard.

d. Change the properties of the first three fields as follows so they match the corresponding fields in the Inventory table.

Field	Data Type	Description	Field Size
Item #	Text	A unique 4-digit product number	4
Description	Text	Name of product	50
Vendor Name	Text	Name of supplier	50

e. You decide to add a field that will identify the category of the item, such as coffee, tea, condiments, and so on. Rather than requiring the users of this database table to memorize each category name and enter it consistently, you are going to create a lookup field from which they can choose the appropriate category when entering new item records. To do this, insert a lookup field named Category above the Unit Price row. In the Lookup Wizard, specify that you want to type in your own lookup values and then enter the following names in the lookup column list and adjust the column width to fit the entries when you're through:

Beverages
Condiments
Baked Goods
Paper Supplies
Other

f. Name the lookup column **Category** and finish the Wizard.

g. Save the table design and switch to Datasheet view.

h. You can now copy the existing item numbers, descriptions, and vendor names from the Inventory table to the Inventory Prices table. Open the Office Clipboard and then open the Inventory table, and use the Clipboard to copy the Item #, Description, and Vendor Name columns from this table to the corresponding columns in the Inventory Prices table. Close the Office Clipboard and adjust the column widths in the Inventory Prices table to fit the displayed field data.

i. Select the appropriate category for each table record. Copy the unit price information from ac04_Prices workbook to the Unit Price field for each record in the table. When you are finished, adjust these two columns to fit the data you entered. Format the table to display blue text and gridlines. Apply a font of your choice.

j. Save and print the table in portrait orientation. Close this table as well as the Inventory table (if it is still open).

k. You are now ready to update the To Be Ordered query to include costs. Open the "To Be Ordered" query and add the Inventory Prices table to the query. Do not show the Special Order column.

l. Next you need to add a new field that will calculate the number of items that need to be ordered, based on the fact that Evan likes to keep an inventory of 24 units of every item on hand. In the blank field cell to the right of the Phone column, type the following: Order Amount: 24-[# On Hand].

m. The next calculation you want to perform is one that will multiply the # To Order value by the Unit Price. Add the Unit Price field from the Inventory Prices table to the blank field cell to the right of the Order Amount calculated field. In the next blank field cell enter: Order Cost: [Order Amount]*[Unit Price]. Set the format property to Currency.

n. Run the query. Adjust the column widths to fit the displayed data. Change the page orientation to landscape and print the query. Then save the query as Inventory Order Costs and close it.

o. Close the database.

EduSoft Product Database

★ ★ 5. The database you created for EduSoft Company currently contains a table that lists the educational software titles produced by the company as well as the subject of each package and the designer who is responsible for developing it. You have created several queries and reports based on this table, which has helped the marketing and development managers immensely. After hearing about the success of this database, the sales manager requested that you add tables that

Software Sales 9/6/2001

Order ID	Software Package	Date Sold	Quantity
00200	Write It II	6/5/2002	4
00200	Read It II	6/5/2002	4
00200	Spell It II	6/5/2002	4
00356	Musicalities	6/10/2002	1
87342	Any Body	6/15/2002	3
00223	Seeing Stars	6/16/2002	2
07554	Web Wise	6/18/2002	3
07554	Type It	6/18/2002	3
07554	Find It III	6/18/2002	3
65340	Say It	6/20/2002	10
65340	Write It III	6/20/2002	10
65340	Try It III	6/20/2002	10
24321	Read It II	6/22/2002	1
06532	Rain or Shine	6/24/2002	3
65342	Spell It	6/26/2002	15
SN999	Try It III	7/6/2002	1

Software Package	Price	Developer	Total Packages Sold	Total Sales
Say It	$75.99	Catherine Willis	10	$759.90
Spell It	$45.00	Catherine Willis	15	$675.00
Spell It II	$45.00	Catherine Willis	4	$180.00
Type It	$24.99	Catherine Willis	3	$74.97
Read It II	$69.99	Catherine Willis	1	$69.99
Read It II	$69.99	Catherine Willis	4	$279.96
Write It II	$45.00	Catherine Willis	4	$180.00
Write It III	$45.00	Catherine Willis	10	$450.00
Try It III	$75.00	Maggie O'Grady	1	$75.00
Try It III	$75.00	Maggie O'Grady	10	$750.00
Seeing Stars	$119.95	Maggie O'Grady	2	$239.90
Rain or Shine	$69.99	Maggie O'Grady	3	$209.97
Any Body	$55.00	Maggie O'Grady	3	$165.00
Find It III	$84.99	Juana Jimenez	3	$254.97
Musicalities	$119.99	Ben Hadden	1	$119.99
Web Wise	$55.00	Student Name	3	$165.00

contain data about packages that have been purchased so that queries can be run that show how the packages are selling and what the total monthly, quarterly, and annual purchase amounts are. You decide to start this process by creating a simple order table with product name, order date, and quantity purchased data. Then by adding a unit cost field to the existing Software Development table, you can use both tables to run a query that calculates the total sales per package to date. When you are finished, you will have a new database table and a query printout that looks similar to those shown here.

a. Rename the ac04_EduSoft database EduSoft Titles. Open the "Software" table. Enter your name as the Developer in the last record, and then save and close the table.

b. Use the Table Wizard to create a new table with the following fields from the Order Details Sample Table:

OrderID
ProductID
DateSold
Quantity

c. Name the table Software Sales, and let Access assign the primary key. Do not assign a relationship between this new table and the existing Software Development table. Specify that you want to modify the table design, and then finish the Wizard.

d. Change the Data Type of the OrderID field from AutoNumber to Text and change its Field Size to 5. Because multiple records will be entered for some orders (for multiple software packages purchased on the same order), each record will not necessarily have a unique OrderID, so you also need to remove the primary key from this field.

e. Test the DateSold input mask by selecting the Short Date mask in the Input Mask Wizard and entering numbers both with and without punctuation and of correct and incorrect lengths in the Try It box. Accept the rest of the input mask defaults and exit the Wizard.

f. Delete the ProductID field and insert a lookup field in its place. Specify that you want to use values from another table, select Software as the table you want to use as the source of these values, and select Product Code and Title as the fields containing the values. Accept the default Hide Key Column selection and the displayed column width. Name the lookup column Software Package, finish the Wizard, and save the table when prompted to do so.

g. Make all fields required.

h. Save the table design and switch to Datasheet view.

i. Enter an order number of 00200, select the Write It II software package, and enter a DateSold of 06/05/2002 and a quantity of 4. Since this order was for a school's third grade computer lab, there were two more software packages purchased on the same order. Therefore, you need to enter two more records with the same order number: one for 4 Read It II packages and another for 4 Spell It II packages. Enter the same DateSold date for both.

j. Enter 15 more orders, some with multiple software packages purchased under the same order and on the same date and others purchased as a single order. Use varying quantities for each order. When you are finished, adjust the column widths to fit the displayed data.

k. Add a final record with your first and last initials followed by 999 as the Order ID and today's date as the DateSold. You can select whatever software package and quantity you like. Print and close the table.

l. You are now ready to add a field to the Software table that will contain the cost of each software package. Open this table and switch to Design view. Add a field called **Price** with a Data Type of Currency. Save the design changes and switch back to Datasheet view. Enter prices for each of the software packages that were ordered thus far (the ones you selected in the Software Sales table, which you can see by expanding the subdatasheet). Close the table when you are finished.

m. Although you have not finished entering all the software package prices or orders, you decide to see whether you can use the combined table data to produce the sales-to-date query that the sales manager requested. Use the Simple Query Wizard to create a new query. Include the Software Package and Quantity fields from the Software Sales table, and the Developer and Price fields from the Software table. Select Summary as the type of query you would like to create and in the Summary Options box, select the Sum option for the Quantity field. Name the query Software Package Sales. Specify that you want to modify the query design and finish the Wizard.

n. In the query's Design view, change the Sum of Quantity: Quantity calculated field name to **Total Packages Sold: Quantity**. Then in the blank field column to the right, enter another calculated field: **Total Sales: [Quantity]*[Price]**. Assign the Currency property to the new field. Run the query.

o. Adjust the column widths to fit the displayed data. Apply formatting of your choice and then print the query.

p. Save and close the query. Close the database.

on your own

Associated Dental Tables

★ **1.** As database manager for the Associated Dental office, you have been maintaining a database that tracks the patient identification information. The bookkeeper has recently requested that you add a table to this table that will track patient payment information. Open the database you updated in On Your Own Exercise 3 of Lab 2 (Patient Information) and use the Table Wizard to create a new table. Select the Payments sample table and add the CustomerID, PaymentAmount, and PaymentDate fields, as well as any other payment method fields you want to include in your new table. Rename the CustomerID field to match the field name that you use for patient identification numbers in your existing patient information table (such as Patient ID). Name the table as desired. Change the Data Type of the Patient ID field from AutoNumber to Text, and remove the primary key from it so you can enter more than one record for each patient in this table (which you will do each time they make a payment). Copy the patient IDs from the patient identification table to this new table and enter at least one payment record for each. Print and close the table. Then insert this new table as a subdatasheet in the patient identification table. Print one page of the table with the subdatasheet displayed.

Lewis & Lewis Query

★★ **2.** The Lewis & Lewis database you created in On Your Own Exercise 2 of Lab 3 (Lewis Personnel) has alleviated the paperwork in personnel and helped keep track of employee information. Lewis & Lewis employs consultants to maintain their networks. To make the database even more effective, your manager has requested that the consultant information be included in the database. Use the Table Wizard to create a table that includes the fields listed in the Time Billed sample table. Use all the sample fields except the CustomerID field. Rename the EmployeeID field **Consultant ID**.

Create a lookup field for the HourlyRate field with values of your choice. Use an input mask to control the entry of the BillingDate field. Enter data for 15 consultants in the new table. Use a crosstab query to calculate the number of hours per consultant per week. Print the query results. Back up and close the database.

WriteOn! Database

★★ 3.   WriteOn! distributes writing supplies to many different stationery stores. They would like you to create a database to keep track of the products (writing paper, envelopes, notepads, and so on) they have in stock. Design a relational database named WriteOn! using the Table Wizard that includes the following two tables:

- Products: Product reference code, supplier ID, description, selling price, wholesale price, and quantity on hand for each product.
- Suppliers: Supplier ID, supplier name, street address, city, state, zip code, and reorder quantity for each product supplier.

Create input masks for the product reference code and supplier zip code fields. Create a lookup field for the reorder quantity. Enter at least 20 records into each table. Establish a relationship between the tables using the supplier ID fields. Query the database for products with a quantity on hand of less than 5. Print the query.

JK Enterprise Database Expansion

★★ 4.   You are continuing to work on a database for JK Enterprises. This database currently includes only one table, which contains expense report data. You want to add two more tables to the database: one that contains department information (such as the department name or number, manager name, and employees in each department), and another that contains expense information (such as project numbers and expense categories like travel or research). Open the database that you updated in On Your Own Exercise 3 of Lab 3 (JK Enterprises) and create the two new tables using sample tables from the Table Wizard or in Design view. Use input masks and lookup fields where applicable (such as the project number or expense categories field). Enter records into both tables, copying existing data from one table to another where possible. When the tables are completed, establish relationships between them (if they have not already been established due to the type of data manipulation you have done on them), and print a relationship report. Then use these tables to create a query that calculates the expense amounts by department.

Little League Database

★★ 5.   You have been hired as an intern by the Tri-Country Little League. They currently maintain a player database in Excel, but they would like to use Access to organize the equipment inventory and the coaches information. Import the Excel file ac04_Little League and save the database as Little League. Use the Table Wizard to create a new table named Coaches for the coaches information. Use the Mailing List sample table and include the fields FirstName, LastName, Title, OrganizationName, HomePhone, and EmailAddress. Change the field name OrganizationName to TeamName. Create a lookup field for the Title field using the values Coach, Assistant Coach, Manager, and Team Parent. Make the TeamName field a required property. The Little League would like to have a report that includes the complete rosters for each team. Use a crosstab query to create a report that includes the players information and the coaches information. Establish a relationship between the players table and the coaches table on the common field, Team. Print the relationship report. Back up and save the database.

on the web

Custom Tees

You have been hired by an entrepreneur who sells custom-design T-shirts online. She would like you to create a relational database named Custom Tees to help her keep track of the items she has for sale. Do some research on the Web about independent fashion retailers, then plan and create a relational database with appropriate tables. Enter at least 20 records into each of your tables. Create a crosstab query from your database. Print the crosstab query results. Create a relationship report for your database. Print the relationship report.

Creating Custom Forms

objectives

After completing this lab, you will know how to:

1.	Create a multiple-table form.
2.	Enhance a form's appearance.
3.	Change fonts and add colors.
4.	Create and use a subform.
5.	Create and use calculated controls.
6.	Use the Expression Builder.
7.	Add command buttons to a form.
8.	Create page headers and footers.
9.	Delete a form.

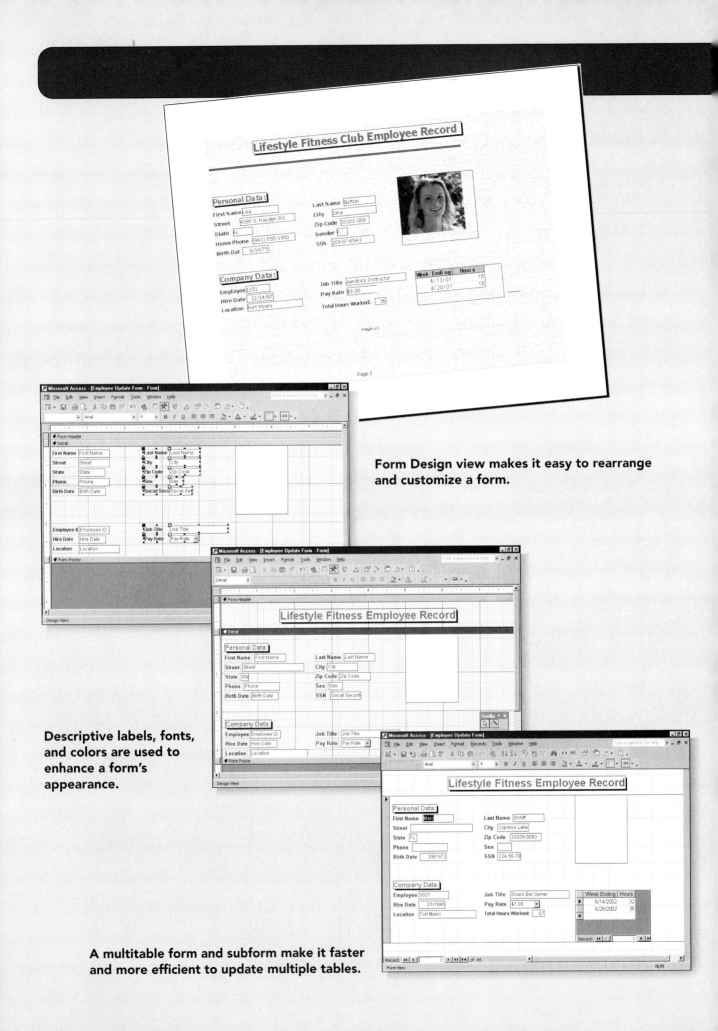

Form Design view makes it easy to rearrange and customize a form.

Descriptive labels, fonts, and colors are used to enhance a form's appearance.

A multitable form and subform make it faster and more efficient to update multiple tables.

1

2

3

4

5

6

Lifestyle Fitness Club

Now that all your data tables for the Lifestyle Fitness Club personnel records are complete, the owners would like you to create some tools that will make updating and viewing table data easier and more efficient. For example, they would like a form that will automatically update the Employees, Location and Position, Pay, and Hours Worked tables, rather than requiring each of these tables to be updated separately.

To do this, you will create a main

form that includes the employee data and add a subform to display the hours worked by each employee. The new form will also have a field that calculates the total number of hours the employee has worked.

When you are finished with the form, you will create command buttons and macros that will enable other database users to add new records and print forms at the click of a button. The completed form is shown on the previous page.

© Corbis

Concept Overview

The following concepts will be introduced in this lab:

1.	**Alignment and Spacing**	The position of controls on a form can be adjusted so that they are evenly aligned and so that the spacing between controls is the same.
2.	**Font**	A font, also commonly referred to as a typeface, is a set of charcters with a specific design.
3.	**Subform**	A subform is a form that is embedded in another form and is used to show data from another table or query.
4.	**Calculated Control**	A calculated control is used to display data that is calculated from a field in a table or query or from another control in the form.
5.	**Expression Builder**	The Expression Builder helps you select the type of function to use and the identifiers for the expression in database forms, reports, and queries.
6.	**Command Button**	A command button executes one or more actions on a form.

Creating a Form for Multiple Tables

You have been using several tables of employee information that need to be updated each time any of the information changes in an existing record. The Employee Data form you created earlier can update the records only in the Employees table. You want to create a form that will update the Employees, Pay, and Location and Position tables.

Using an AutoForm

You want to create a columnar form like you did when creating the Employee Data Form. In addition to the Form Wizard, Access includes an AutoForm feature that helps you quickly create many different types of forms. You will try out this feature to create the form you need.

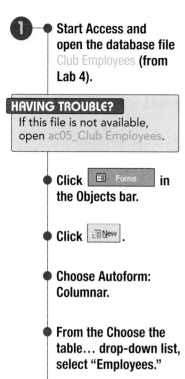

1 ● **Start Access and open the database file** Club Employees **(from Lab 4).**

HAVING TROUBLE?
If this file is not available, open ac05_Club Employees.

● **Click** 🗐 Forms **in the Objects bar.**

● **Click** 🗐 New **.**

● **Choose Autoform: Columnar.**

● **From the Choose the table... drop-down list, select "Employees."**

● **Click** OK **.**

Another Method
The menu equivalent is Insert/ Form/Autoform: Columnar.

Your screen should be similar to Figure 5.1

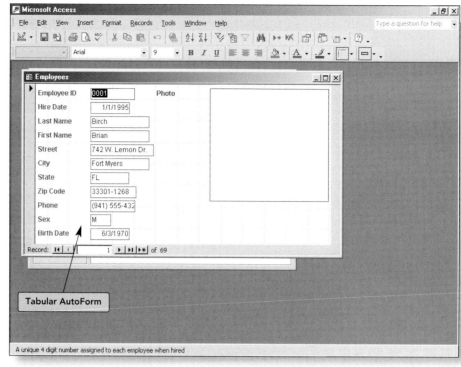

Figure 5.1

The AutoForm Wizard creates a tabular form using all the fields from the selected table. Because AutoForm applies the last used autoformat to the form, your form may appear in a different design. Now you would like to add fields from the Pay and Location and Position tables to the form. However, unlike a query in which you can add additional tables to the query in design view, in a form, once the **record source,** the underlying table or query on which the form is based, has been specified, you cannot add additional sources.

Instead, you could first create a query using the three tables as the record source and then use AutoForm to create the form based on the query. However, it is probably just as easy to use the Form Wizard.

Creating a Multiple-Table Form

The form will include fields from three of the employee tables: Employees, Location and Position, and Pay. This will provide one central location for entering and updating the Club employee records.

1 ● Close the Form window without saving the form.

● Double-click Create form by using wizard.

● Add the following fields from the "Employees" table to the form in the following order: First Name, Last Name, Street, City, State, Zip Code, Phone, Sex, Birth Date, Employee ID, Hire Date, Photo.

● Select the "Location and Position" table from the Tables/ Queries drop-down list and add its fields in the following order: Location, Job Title.

● Select the "Pay" table and add its fields in the following order: Pay Rate, Social Security Number.

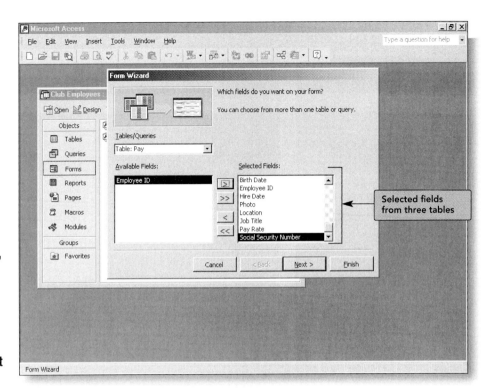

Figure 5.2

HAVING TROUBLE?

If you selected fields in the incorrect order, remove the fields that are out of order and reenter them in the correct order. If a field is missing, move to the field above where you want the new field inserted and add it.

Your screen should be similar to Figure 5.2

The order you selected the fields is the order in which they will display on the form. Now that you have selected all the fields from the tables that you want on the form, you can go on to select the layout and style of the form.

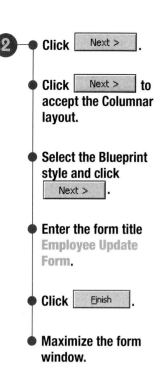

2
- Click Next >.

- Click Next > to accept the Columnar layout.

- Select the Blueprint style and click Next >.

- Enter the form title **Employee Update Form**.

- Click Finish.

- Maximize the form window.

Your screen should be similar to Figure 5.3

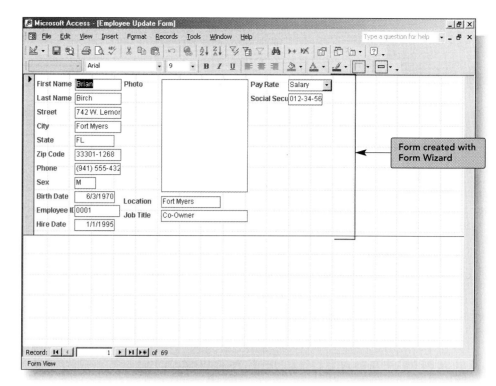

Figure 5.3

The Form window displays the form in the selected style and layout. Each field from the different tables is displayed in the form. You will modify the form's appearance later, but first you want to test the form's ability to update the associated tables.

Automatic Updating Across Tables

You will use your new form to make several changes to your record, and see the effect this has on the related tables.

1
- Move to the last record and if necessary change the employee name to your own. Change the data in the following fields:

Hire Date: Current Date

Location: Cypress Lake

Pay Rate: $12.00

Your screen should be similar to Figure 5.4

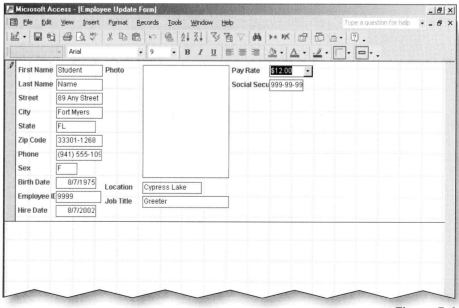

Figure 5.4

The form now reflects all the changes you want to make to your record, but because you have never used a multitable form, you want to make sure the tables themselves have been updated accordingly.

2 ● Close the form.

● To confirm that the changes were made to the tables, open the "Employees", "Location and Position", and "Pay" tables, go to the last record, and verify the changes.

Your screen should be similar to Figure 5.5

All three tables updated using the form

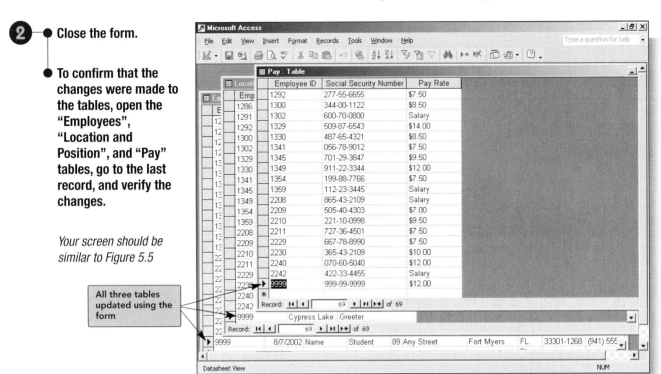

Figure 5.5

As you can see, using a single customized form to update records in all three tables simultaneously is a great time-saving feature. Next you will re-size the fields so all the data is displayed and do some other cosmetic changes to the form to improve its appearance.

Customizing the Form Layout

Now that you have created a form for updating multiple employee tables at once, you want to make it easy to use as far as its layout, or the way the fields are displayed and arranged on the form, as well. First of all, you would like the data entries to be completely displayed in each field. You would also like to make it more appealing to the eye by dividing it into sections and adding some different colors and font styles. The form layout you want to create is shown here.

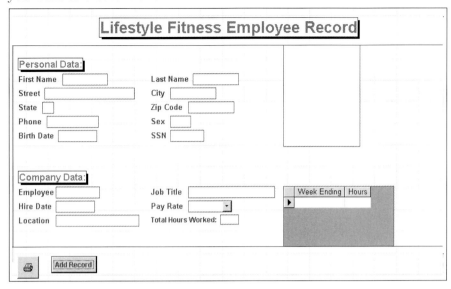

You will make all these changes in Form Design view.

① ● Open the "Employee Update Form."

● If necessary, maximize the form window.

● Click 🖾 ▾ Design View.

Another Method
The menu equivalent is View/Design View.

Your screen should be similar to Figure 5.6

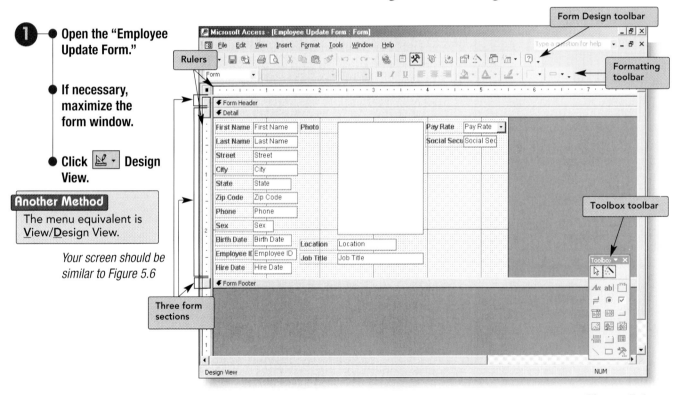

Figure 5.6

The Employee Update Form is displayed in the Form Design view window.

Working in Form Design View

Form Design view, like Report Design view, is used to create and modify the structure of a form. In this view, horizontal and vertical rulers are displayed to help you correctly place items in the Form Design window.

The Form Design window is divided into three sections: Form Header, Detail, and Form Footer. The contents of each section appear below the horizontal bar containing the name. The purpose of each of these sections is described in the following table.

Section	Description
Form Header	An optional section that you can include to display information such as the form title, instructions, or graphics. The contents of a form header appear at the top of the screen or, if you print the form, at the top of the first page. Form headers are not visible in Datasheet view, and do not scroll as you scroll through records.
Detail	The area where the table data is displayed.
Form Footer	Another optional section that can include notes, instructions, or grand totals. Form footers appear at the bottom of the screen or, if printed, at the end of the last page. Like form headers, form footers do not display in Datasheet view.

Form Design view also automatically displays three toolbars: Form Design, Formatting, and Toolbox. The **Form Design toolbar** contains the standard buttons as well as buttons that are specific to the Form Design view window, identified below.

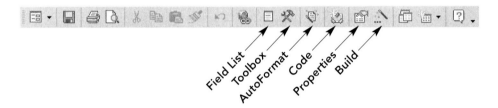

The **Formatting toolbar** contains buttons (identified below) that allow you to make text enhancements.

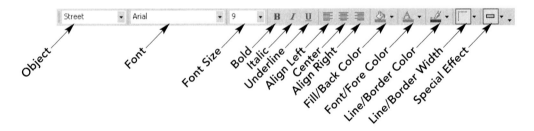

The **Toolbox toolbar** contains buttons (identified below) that are used to add and modify controls. The 🛠 Toolbox button on the Form Design toolbar is used to open the Toolbox toolbar.

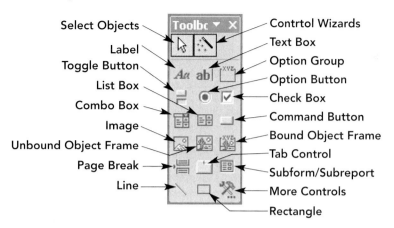

In addition, the Field List may be displayed. It displays a list of all the fields in the record source and can be used to add other fields to the form. The ▣ Field List button on the Form Design toolbar is used to open and close this list.

Before you work on the form's design, you want to make sure the tools you need are displayed. Because all the fields are already displayed on the form, you can close the Field List box if it is open.

1
- **If necessary, click 🛠 Toolbox on the Form Design toolbar to display the Toolbox toolbar.**

- **If necessary, click ▣ Field List on the Form Design toolbar to hide the Field List.**

Your screen should be similar to Figure 5.7

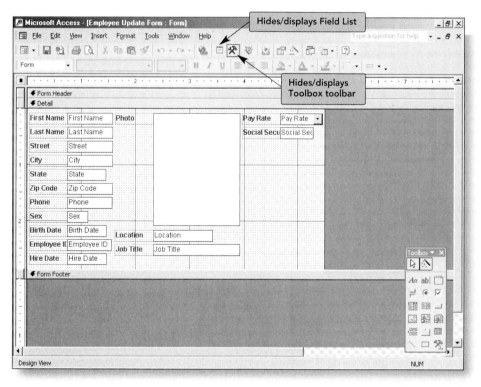

Figure 5.7

You are now ready to make some design changes to your form. The first design change you want to make is to rearrange the fields on the form by moving the form controls.

Rearranging Fields

HAVING TROUBLE?
See Concept 8 in Lab 3 to review the Controls feature.

Many of the controls on the form are compound controls, where the label control is displayed on the left and the text control is on the right in each set of controls. When you select a label control, its associated text control is also selected and the two controls will act as one when manipulated.

You want to separate the form fields into two sections: personal data and company data. There is not a lot of room to maneuver on this form, so you are going to move the company data fields out of the way so you can work on the top part of the form, the personal data area, first. The form will expand in size as you drag beyond its current edge.

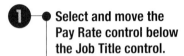

1 • Select and move the Pay Rate control below the Job Title control.

HAVING TROUBLE?
The mouse pointer must be 🖐 in order to move controls.

• Select and move Employee ID, Hire Date, Location, Job Title, and Pay Rate controls to the right side of the form (see Figure 5.8).

HAVING TROUBLE?
Remember to hold down the ⇧Shift key while selecting controls to select more than one. To deselect controls that are currently selected, click in any blank area of the form.

• Move the Social Security Number control below the Birth Date control.

• Deselect the control.

Your screen should be similar to Figure 5.8

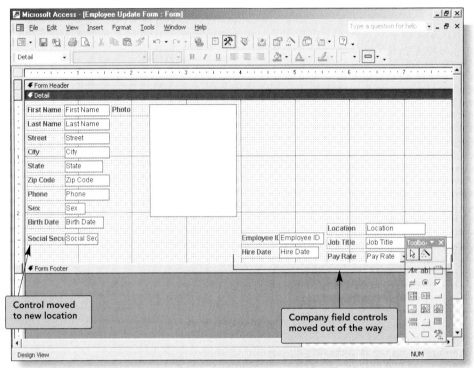

Figure 5.8

You now have some room at the top of the form to start arranging the personal data fields. On the first line of the form, you decide you want the employee's first and last names and picture. You also decide that, because it will be obvious what the photo is, you don't really need the Photo label, so you will remove it before moving the picture box.

2
- Select the Photo label control (not the text control, which in this case is the picture box).

- Press Delete.

- Select the Photo text control and move it to align the left edge of the box with the 5-inch mark on the horizontal ruler.

- Select the Last Name text and label controls and move them to the right of the First Name controls, as shown in Figure 5.9.

Your screen should be similar to Figure 5.9

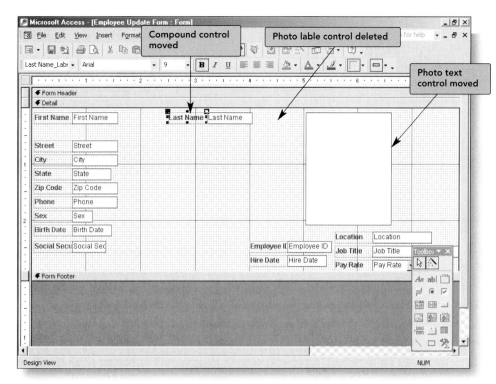

Figure 5.9

You have finished the first row of the form and are ready to move the rest of the personal data controls up to the personal data section.

3
- Select and move the following controls under the First and Last Name controls to create two columns (see Figure 5.10):

Street	City
State	Zip Code
Phone	Sex
Birth Date	Social Security Number

HAVING TROUBLE?
Do not be concerned if your controls are not evenly aligned with the left edge of the form or on the lines. You will learn how to adjust the alignment and spacing shortly.

Your screen should be similar to Figure 5.10

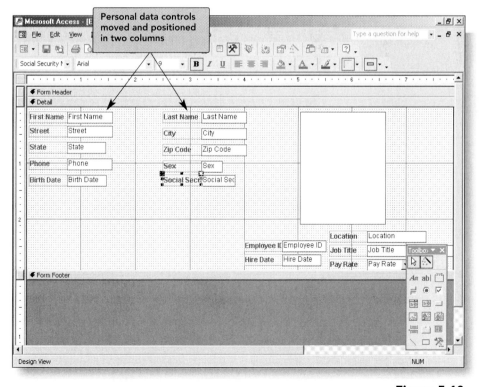

Figure 5.10

Next you will rearrange the fields you want to appear at the bottom of the form, in the company data section.

4 **Select and move the following controls beginning slightly below the 2-inch position on the vertical ruler:**

Employee ID   Job Title

Hire Date   Pay Rate

Location

Your screen should be similar to Figure 5.11

Company data controls moved and positioned

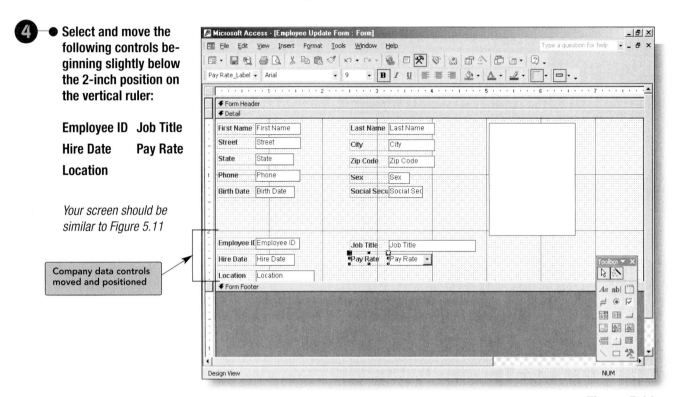

Figure 5.11

Positioning Controls

With all the moving around, the form controls are probably not positioned exactly on the form as you want them to be. To precisely position controls you can adjust their alignment and spacing.

concept 1

1 The position of controls on a form can be adjusted so that they are evenly aligned and so that the spacing between controls is the same. Controls can be **aligned** or positioned relative to other controls, in the following ways:

Alignment	Effect
Left	The left edges of the selected controls are evenly aligned with the left edge of the leftmost control.
Right	The right edges of the selected controls are evenly aligned with the right edge of the rightmost control.
Top	The top edges of the selected controls are evenly aligned with the top edge of the highest control.
Bottom	The bottom edges of the selected controls are evenly aligned with the bottom edge of the lowest control.

The **spacing**, or distance between controls, can be adjusted horizontally or vertically in the following ways:

Spacing	Effect
Equal	The space between selected controls is made equal by changing the space of the middle controls without changing the location of the outside controls.
Increase or Decrease	The spacing is increased or decreased by increments. In horizontal spacing, the leftmost control does not move; in vertical spacing, the highest control does not move.

Additional Information

If a control is selected in a group that you do not want selected, you can deselect individual controls by holding down ⇧Shift and clicking the control.

To align controls, you first select several controls that are in the same row or column. Another way to select a group of adjacent controls is to drag a selection box around the controls. To select the controls using this method, click ▧ in the Toolbox, point to a blank area above the first control, and click and drag a rectangle over the controls you want to select. The ▧ Toolbox button is the default button and is always selected if no other Toolbox button is in use.

① ● **Point to a blank area above the First Name control, click and drag until a box surrounds the eight controls on the left side of the form, and then release the mouse button.**

Additional Information

The box does not need to fully enclose the fields. A field that is partially in the box will still be selected.

● **Choose Format/Align/Left.**

● **Select the seven controls in the second column of the form (excluding the photo box) and left-align them.**

Additional Information

When aligning controls, you select only controls that are in the same row or column.

Your screen should be similar to Figure 5.12

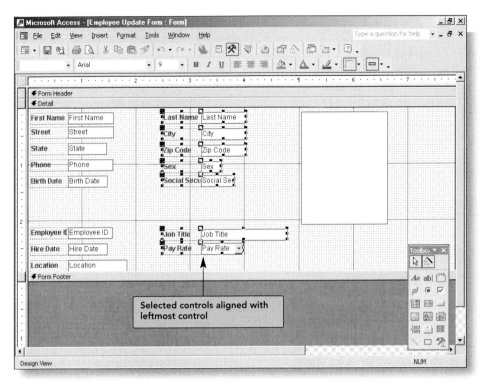

Figure 5.12

The controls in the selected groups all shifted to the left and are aligned with the control that was farthest left in the selection.

You now want to adjust the spacing between all the controls in the upper section of the form so that there is an even amount of vertical space between each control. This vertical spacing can be adjusted between controls in any group of three or more selected controls. The top and bottom controls do not change locations; only the middle controls in the selection are adjusted to equalize the spacing.

2

- Align the tops of the First Name and Last Name controls.

- Align the bottoms of the Birth Date and Social Security Number controls.

- Select the 5 controls in the top-left column.

- Choose Format/Vertical Spacing/ Make Equal.

- In a similar manner, make the vertical spacing between the controls in the top-right and bottom-left columns equal (exclude the Photo box).

- If necessary, adjust the alignment of the Job Title and Pay Rate controls appropriately.

- Deselect the controls.

Your screen should be similar to Figure 5.13

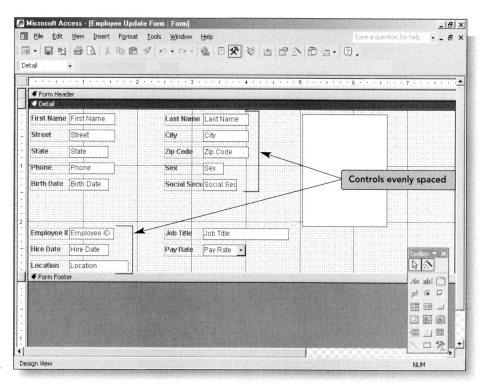

Figure 5.13

The vertical space between controls is adjusted to make the vertical spacing between the selected controls equal.

Adding Label Controls

Next you will add a label control in the form header to display the form title. In addition, you want to add two subheads within the form to identify the personal data and company data areas. The Toolbox buttons let you add text, arrows, boxes, and other design elements to a form. To add the control to the form header, you first need to expand the space in the Form Header area.

1 • **Point to the top of the Detail section bar.**

• **When the mouse pointer is a ✛, drag the Detail section bar down approximately .5 inch on the vertical ruler.**

Your screen should be similar to Figure 5.14

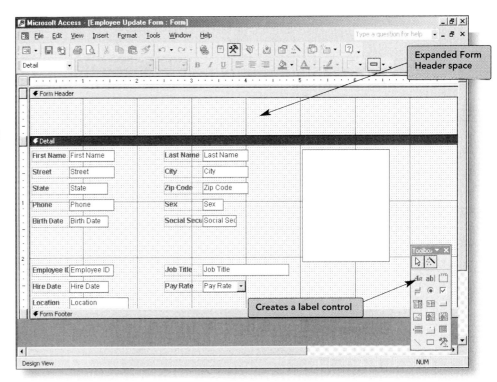

Figure 5.14

The 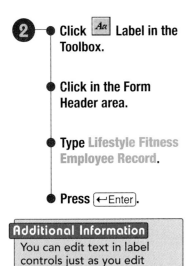 Label button on the Toolbox is used to add a label control to a form. The mouse pointer changes to ⁺A when this feature is in use. You indicate where you want the control to appear by clicking on the location in the window. Then an insertion point is displayed indicating that you can begin typing the descriptive label.

2 • **Click** *Aa* **Label in the Toolbox.**

• **Click in the Form Header area.**

• **Type Lifestyle Fitness Employee Record.**

• **Press ←Enter.**

Additional Information
You can edit text in label controls just as you edit other text.

Your screen should be similar to Figure 5.15

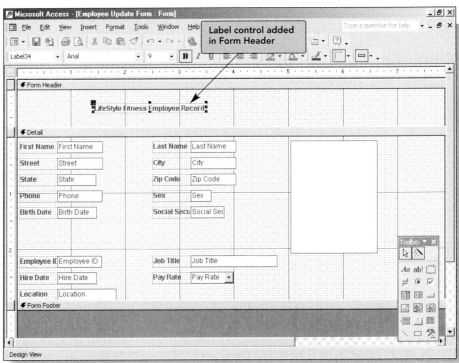

Figure 5.15

The text entry feature is turned off. The form title appears in a label control box and can be sized and moved like any other control. Now you will add two more label controls for the subheads in the Detail section.

3

- Select all the controls except the photo box control in the top section of the Detail area and move the controls down so the top row begins at the .5-inch mark on the vertical ruler.

- Select the five controls in the lower section and move them down to begin at the 2.5-inch mark on the vertical ruler.

- Add a label control containing the text Personal Data: in the space above the First Name control in the Detail section.

- In a similar manner, enter the subhead Company Data: in the space above the Employee ID control.

- Align the two subhead label controls along the left edge.

Your screen should be similar to Figure 5.16

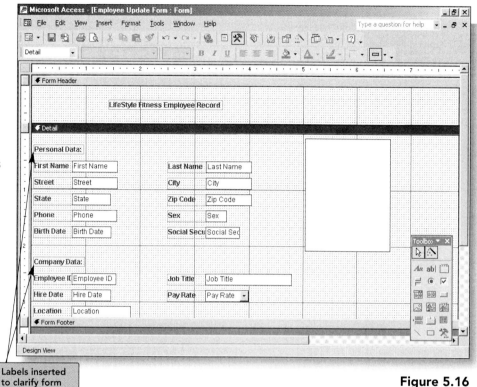

Labels inserted to clarify form

Figure 5.16

The two sections of the form are clearly identified.

Changing Fonts

Although the form contains everything you want on it now, all the text looks the same. To make the form more attractive, you decide to change some of the font settings.

Font

2   A **font**, also commonly referred to as a **typeface**, is a set of characters with a specific design. The designs have names such as Times New Roman and Courier. Using fonts as a design element can add interest to your forms and give users visual cues to help users find information quickly.

There are two basic types of fonts, serif and sans serif. **Serif** fonts have a flair at the base of each letter that visually leads the reader to the next letter. Two common serif fonts are Roman and Times New Roman. Serif fonts generally are used for text in paragraphs. **Sans serif** fonts do not have a flair at the base of each letter. Arial and Helvetica are two common sans serif fonts. Because sans serif fonts have a clean look, they are often used for headings.

Each font has one or more sizes. **Font size** is the height and width of the character and is commonly measured in **points**, abbreviated pt. One point equals about 1/72 inch, and text in most documents is 10 pt or 12 pt.

Several common fonts in different sizes are shown in the following table.

Font Name	Font Type	Font Size
Arial	Sans serif	This is 10 pt. This is 16 pt.
Courier New	Serif	This is 10 pt. This is 16 pt.
Times New Roman	Serif	This is 10 pt. This is 16 pt.

Although you must apply font changes to entire controls rather than changing individual characters or words, you can apply multiple font changes to a table, form, or report by selecting and changing fonts for individual controls. You should be careful, however, not to combine too many different fonts and colors. Also, avoid using fancy fonts that might make it difficult to read the screen or are distracting to use for long periods of time.

The first text enhancement you want to make is to increase the font size of the text controls in the Detail section of the form. Larger fonts make it easier to read the data that is displayed in the form.

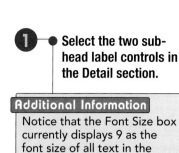

1
● Select the two sub-
head label controls in
the Detail section.

Additional Information
Notice that the Font Size box
currently displays 9 as the
font size of all text in the
selected controls.

● Click `9 ▾` **Font Size**
and select 12 from the
drop-down list.

*Your screen should be
similar to Figure 5.17*

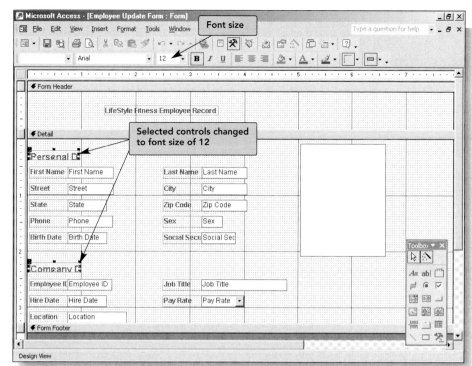

Figure 5.17

Now the labels are too large to be fully displayed in their control box. You
can size the control to fully display the label by dragging on the sizing handles, or you can automatically size the control to fit the contents. You want
to do the latter.

2
● Choose F**o**rmat/**S**ize/To **F**it.

The labels are now fully displayed in the control boxes. Next you want to
increase the size of the text controls in the Detail section to 10 points.

3 ● Select the 15 text controls in the Detail section and increase the font size to 10 points.

● Size the controls to fit.

Your screen should be similar to Figure 5.18

Selected controls font size increased to 10 points and sized to fit

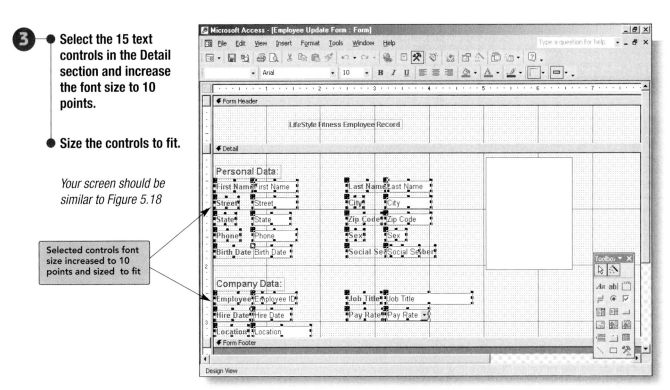

Figure 5.18

Finally, you will increase the size of the form title.

Label control font size increased to 20 points and sized to fit control box

4 ● Select the label control in the Form Header section and change the font size to 20.

● Size the control to fit.

● Position the control over the top of the form as in Figure 5.19.

Your screen should be similar to Figure 5.19

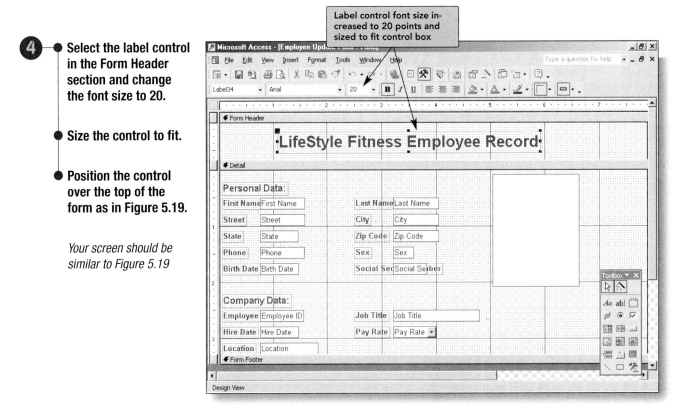

Figure 5.19

The final text enhancement you want to make is to add some color to the form.

Adding Color and Shadows

You can make controls more noticeable by adding color to their background, text, or borders. In addition, you can use special effects such as shadows to enhance the control border. You will make the text in the Form Header label red and add a shadow box to the control.

1
● Open the [A▾] Font/ Fore Color list and select ▓ Red from the color palette.

● Open the [▭▾] Special Effects drop-down list and select ▭ Shadowed.

● Add the same color and shadow effect to the form subheads.

● If necessary, adjust the spacing between the subhead controls and the first text control.

Additional Information
You can quickly apply the last used font color and shadow effect selection by clicking the corresponding button without opening the drop-down menu.

Your screen should be similar to Figure 5.20

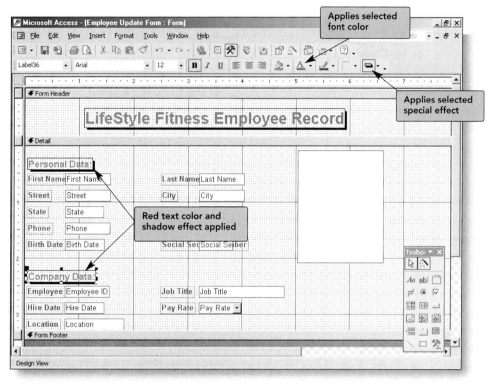

Figure 5.20

The color and shadow settings have been applied to the form title and subheads. To see how the actual form will look to users on the data-entry screen, you will switch back to Form view.

2 ● Click 🔲 ▾ Form View.

Your screen should be similar to Figure 5.21

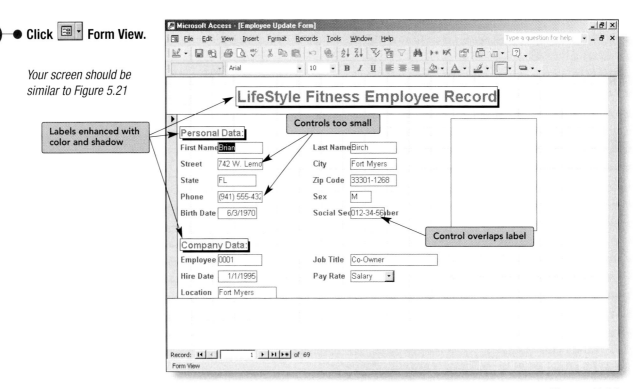

Figure 5.21

The layout and design changes greatly enhance the appearance of the form. However, now you can also see that the Street, Phone, and Social Security Number text box controls are not wide enough to display the data in the fields. You also notice that some of the text box controls are separated by too much space from the label controls, whereas others overlap the text box control.

Resizing Controls

After viewing several records in your form, you see that some of the fields need to be resized in order to display all the data. Additionally, there are some spacing problems between the labels and the data. To correct these problems, you will return to Form Design view and increase the size of some of the label controls and adjust the spacing between compound controls.

1 ● Switch back to Form
    Design view.

  ● Increase the size of
    the Street, Phone, and
    Location text box
    controls.

  ● Select the State text
    box control and
    reduce the size of
    the label box to two
    characters.

  ● Point to the move
    handle of the State
    text box control.

  ● When the mouse
    pointer is a 🖐, drag
    the control closer to
    the State label control.

  ● In a similar manner,
    adjust the size and
    spacing of all other
    controls as needed
    except the Social
    Security Number
    control.

*Your screen should be
similar to Figure 5.22*

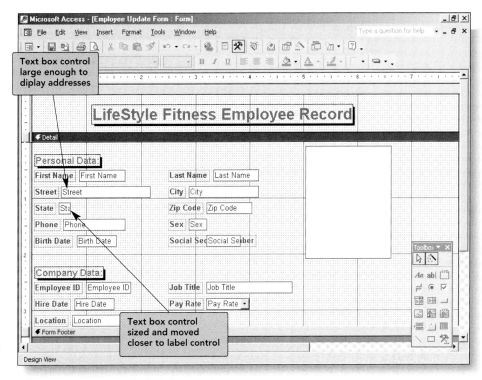

Figure 5.22

Changing the Label Caption

The Social Security Number field does not show all the entered data, and
the field label does not fully display either. Rather than having to extend
both the label and the field controls, you decide to abbreviate the label.

1 ● Double-click the
    Social Security
    Number label control.

Another Method

The menu equivalent is
View/Properties and the
shortcuts are F4 and 🖻.

*Your screen should be
similar to Figure 5.23*

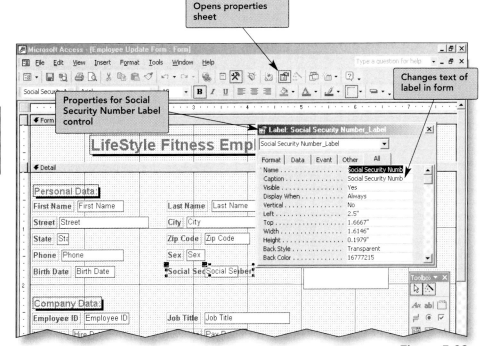

Figure 5.23

Each control has property settings that affect how the control looks and acts. Just as you do in the Design view of a table or report, you set form control properties in the Properties box.

The Label properties sheet window is used to change the way a label control is displayed on the screen. The Name is the actual field name, which is the way the field is identified in all related tables. You do not want to change this. You do, however, want to change the Caption, or the way the field is labeled on the form.

2

● **Replace the current Caption with SSN.**

● **Close the Label properties sheet.**

● **Appropriately size and adjust the spacing between the text box and label controls of the Social Security Number control.**

Your screen should be similar to Figure 5.24

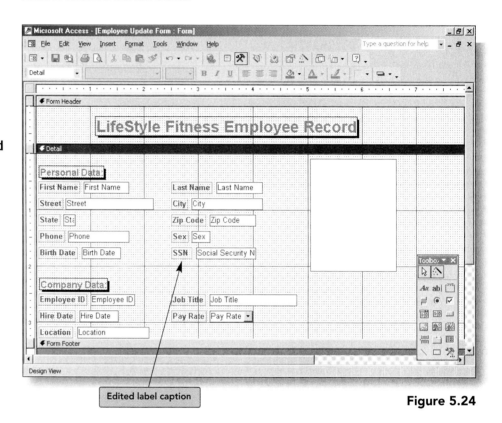

Edited label caption

Figure 5.24

You have adjusted all the controls and are ready to see how your form looks now. You also need to check the record that includes an employee photo to make sure it displays correctly.

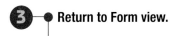

3
- Return to Form view.
- Display record 35.

HAVING TROUBLE?
To go directly to this record, type the number in the record number box and press [←Enter].

Your screen should be similar to Figure 5.25

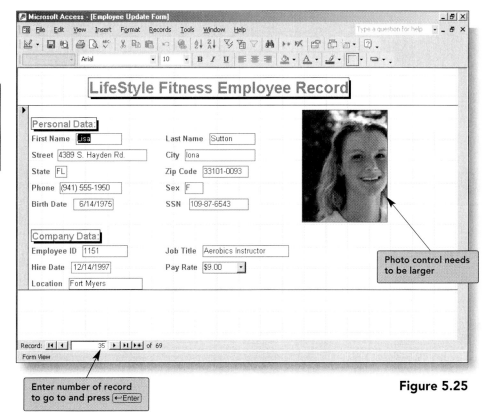

Enter number of record to go to and press [←Enter]

Figure 5.25

You can see that the photo control needs to be larger to fully display the picture.

4
- Return to Form Design view.
- Size the photo box control to 2 by 2 inches.
- Return to Form view and display record 35 again.

Your screen should be similar to Figure 5.26

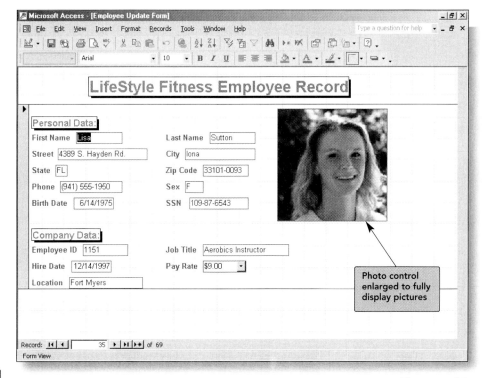

Figure 5.26

HAVING TROUBLE?
If necessary, return to Design view and readjust the photo control as needed until it displays as in Figure 5.26.

The picture is now fully displayed. You are done with your basic form design, and you can proceed to make further enhancements to it, the first of which will be to add a subform.

Using Subforms

The appearance of the form is much improved. However, as you are thinking about the use of the form, you realize that the form does not include the Hours Worked table data. You will add this table as a subform to the current form.

concept 3

Subform

3 A **subform** is a form that is embedded in another form and is used to show data from another table or query. The form that contains the subform is called the **main form**, and the form/subform combination may be referred to as a **hierarchical form**, a **master/detail form**, or a **parent/child form**.

A main form can have multiple subforms. In addition, a subform can contain another subform. Subforms can be embedded within subforms, up to ten levels deep. For example, you could have a main form that displays sales reps, a subform that displays products, another subform that displays product orders, and another subform that displays order details.

Subforms are particularly useful to show data from tables that have a one-to-many relationship. For example, the main form could show the sales representative data (the "one" side of the relationship) and the subform could show all the products the sales representative is responsible for selling (the "many" side of the relationship).

Creating a Subform

When creating a subform, there must be a pre-existing relationship between the main form and subform. This relationship has already been established when you specified table relationships for the database. Therefore, you are ready to add the subform to the main form. You will use the Control Wizards tool to assist in the process of creating the subform. Control Wizards are available for several of the controls you may want to create. Depending upon the control you select, the related Control Wizard is automatically started.

1 ● **Switch to Form Design view.**

● **If necessary, click** 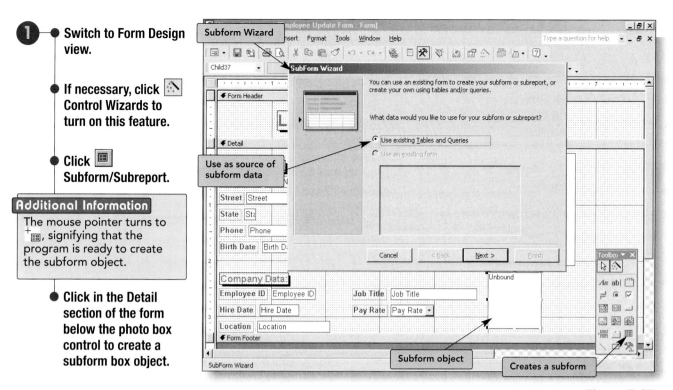 **Control Wizards to turn on this feature.**

● **Click** ⊞ **Subform/Subreport.**

Additional Information

The mouse pointer turns to ⁺⊞, signifying that the program is ready to create the subform object.

● **Click in the Detail section of the form below the photo box control to create a subform box object.**

Your screen should be similar to Figure 5.27

Figure 5.27

Because you selected the Subform control button, the SubForm Wizard is automatically activated. In the first SubForm Wizard dialog box appears in which you specify the source of data for the subform. You will use an existing table.

2 ● **If necessary, select Use existing Tables and Queries.**

● **Click** Next > .

Your screen should be similar to Figure 5.28

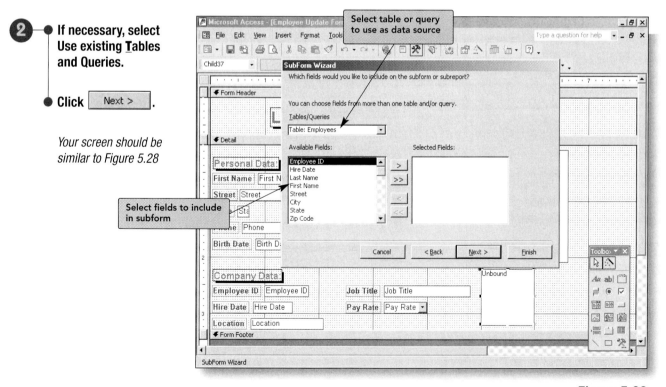

Figure 5.28

In the second Wizard dialog box, you specify the table to use as the data source and the fields from the selected table to display in the form.

3 • Select the "Hours Worked" table from the **T**ables/Queries drop-down menu.

• Add the Week Ending and Hours fields to the Selected Fields list.

• Click  .

Your screen should be similar to Figure 5.29

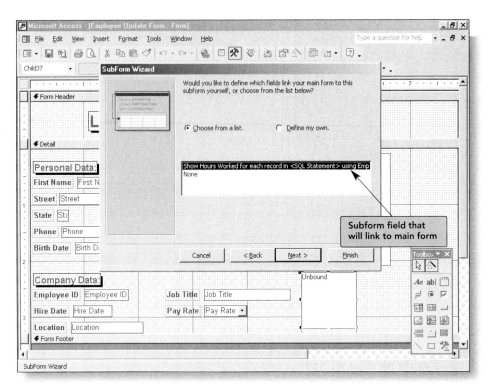

Figure 5.29

In the next Wizard screen, you are asked to specify the field in the subform that will link it to the main form. The list box correctly suggests using the Employee ID field.

4 • Click Next > .

Your screen should be similar to Figure 5.30

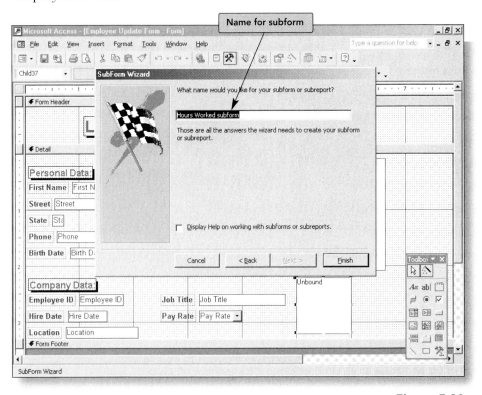

Figure 5.30

The final Wizard screen asks you to name the subform. You decide to accept the default name.

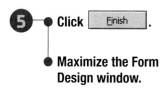

5 • **Click** [Finish].

• **Maximize the Form Design window.**

Your screen should be similar to Figure 5.31

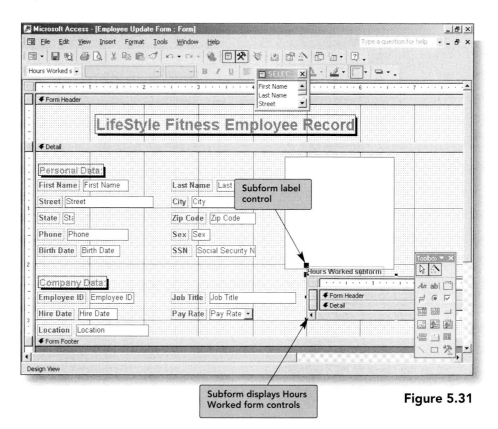

Figure 5.31

The subform displays the Hours Worked form controls.

Modifying a Subform

The form is now difficult to read with the added subform controls. You will get rid of unnecessary controls and readjust the layout a bit.

1 ● **If necessary, close the Field List box and move the Toolbox up so that it does not cover the subform.**

● **Select and delete the subform label control.**

● **Select and expand the subform object until the Form Footer bar is visible.**

HAVING TROUBLE?
Do not be concerned if you cover other controls at this point. You will resize the subform again later.

● **Size and position the Hours and Week Ending labels and text controls as in Figure 5.32.**

● **Scroll the window to fully display the subform.**

● **Reduce the size of the subform to just large enough to display the controls.**

Your screen should be similar to Figure 5.32

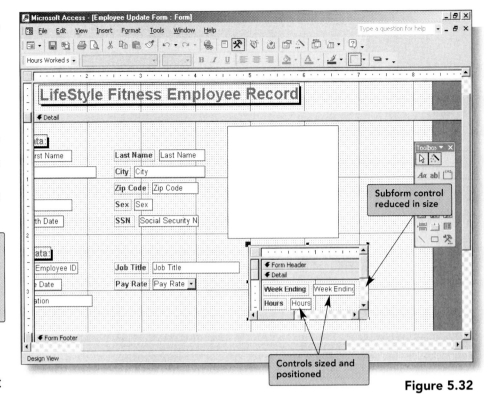

Figure 5.32

Now you want to see how your changes will look in the form.

2

● Switch to Form view.

● Best fit the Hours and Week Ending columns just as you would in a standard table.

Additional Information

You do not need to go into Design view to make this kind of change. However, if you want to make any changes to the subform design, such as increasing or decreasing the width of the subform border, you must do this is Design view.

● Using the scroll bar in the Form window, scroll two records forward to see a record with hours in the subform.

Your screen should be similar to Figure 5.33

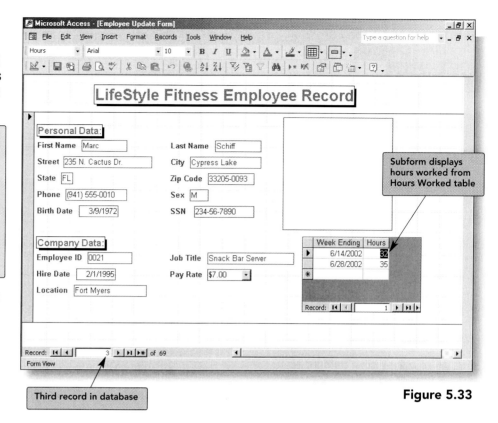

Figure 5.33

The first two employees' records did not display hours worked in the subform because they are paid on salary. The third record shows the hours worked for both weeks recorded in the table for that record.

To see how data is entered in a subform, you will add hours for a new week in your record.

3

● Display your record in the form and enter last Friday's date in a new row of the Week Ending field and 35 in the Hours field.

● Save the form.

Your screen should be similar to Figure 5.34

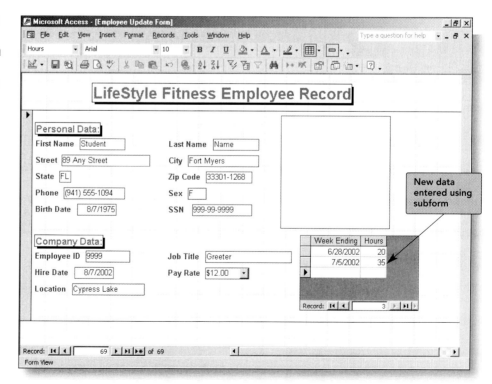

Figure 5.34

You have finished designing the basic form and subform. Next you will add some controls to make the data entry and tracking even easier.

Using Calculated Controls

Rather than having to add the hours manually for each employee each week to get the total number of hours worked, you can add a calculated control that will calculate the total hours worked for each employee.

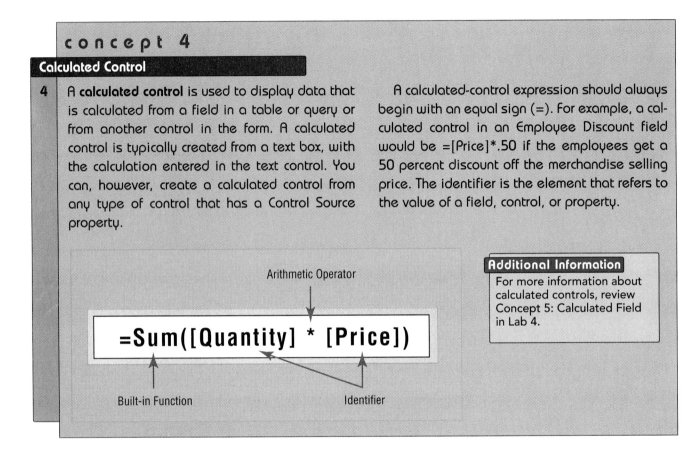

concept 4

Calculated Control

4 A **calculated control** is used to display data that is calculated from a field in a table or query or from another control in the form. A calculated control is typically created from a text box, with the calculation entered in the text control. You can, however, create a calculated control from any type of control that has a Control Source property.

A calculated-control expression should always begin with an equal sign (=). For example, a calculated control in an Employee Discount field would be =[Price]*.50 if the employees get a 50 percent discount off the merchandise selling price. The identifier is the element that refers to the value of a field, control, or property.

Arithmetic Operator

=Sum([Quantity] * [Price])

Built-in Function

Identifier

Additional Information

For more information about calculated controls, review Concept 5: Calculated Field in Lab 4.

Creating a Calculated Control

You need to add the calculated control to the subform. Because it calculates a subtotal, it is entered in the Form Footer area of the subform.

1 ● **Switch to Design view.**

● **Select the subform object and scroll the object to see the Form Footer bar.**

● **Drag down on the bottom of the Form Footer bar of the subform to expand this section.**

● **Click** 🔲 **Textbox.**

● **Click in the Form Footer area of the subform to add the text box control.**

Your screen should be similar to Figure 5.35

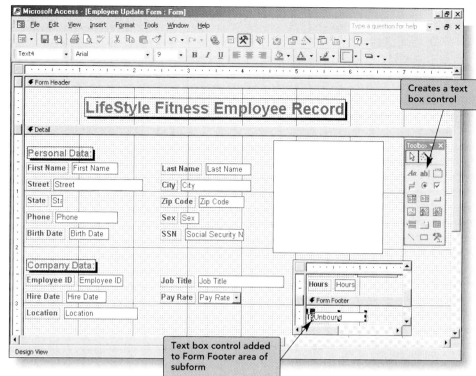

Figure 5.35

Text and label controls for a new text box have been added to the form. The label control caption, "Unbound," signifies the type of control it is. You decide to change this caption to something more specific to the data that this field will contain.

2 ● **Adjust the size and position of the controls so they do not overlap.**

● **Change the label control caption to** Total**.**

Your screen should be similar to Figure 5.36

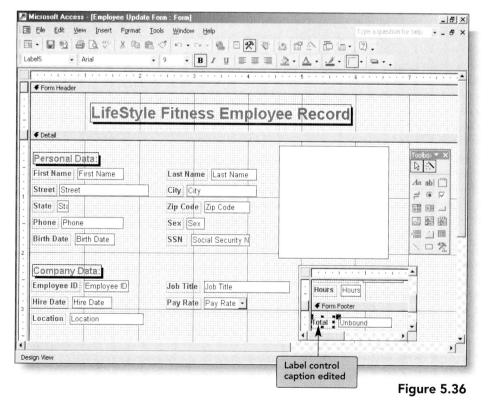

Figure 5.36

Next you will set the properties of the text control.

Setting Text Box Properties

Just like label controls, text box controls consist of properties that control how they look and behave. You need to modify the control to calculate a total.

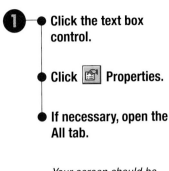

- Click the text box control.

- Click 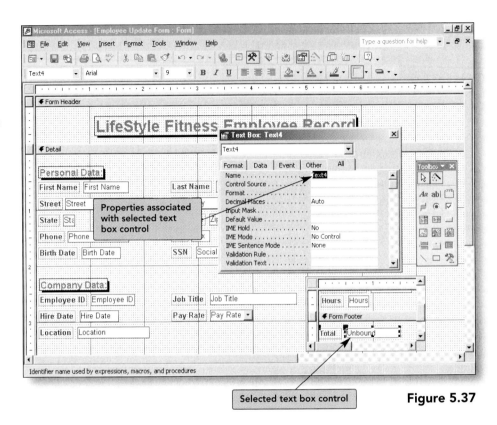 Properties.

- If necessary, open the All tab.

Your screen should be similar to Figure 5.37

Figure 5.37

The All tab of the Properties sheet for the Text Box control lists the default property settings associated with the selected control. The name "Text4" displayed in the Name text box is the default name assigned to the text control. Each text control is named Text followed by a number that identifies the order in which it was added to the form. This was the fourth text control added to the subform. Again, you decide to rename this control to something more specific to this field.

2 ● **Type** Total **in the Name field.**

Your screen should be similar to Figure 5.38

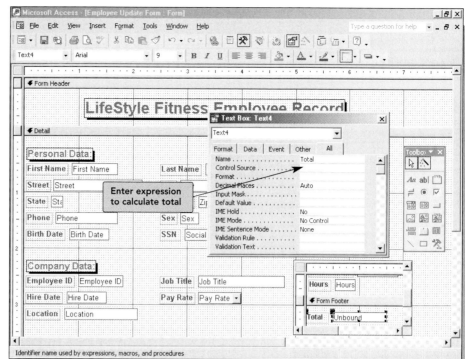

Figure 5.38

You are now ready to enter the calculation you want this field to perform.

Using the Expression Builder

HAVING TROUBLE?

Refer to Lab 2 Concept 3 Validity Checks for a discussion of expressions.

You enter the calculation you want the control to perform in the Control Source text box by either typing the expression directly in the box or by using the Expression Builder feature. You will use the Expression Builder to create an expression that will add the values in the Hours field and display the total.

concept 5

Expression Builder

5 | The **Expression Builder** helps you select the type of function to use and the identifiers for the expression in database forms, reports, and queries. The Expression Builder is made up of three main sections, which are described in the following table.

Section	Description
Expression box	Used to build the expression. To build an expression, you select elements from the other two sections and paste them in this box. You can also type parts of the expression directly in the box.
Operator buttons	A toolbar of commonly used operators for the selected expression element. The four types of operators are: mathematical, comparison, logical, and reference. Clicking one of these buttons adds it to the expression (in the expression box) at the current insertion point.
Expression elements	This section consists of three list boxes. The left box contains folders that list the objects (tables, queries, forms, and reports) in the database that is currently open, built-in and user-defined functions, constants (values that do not change, such as a specific number or text), operators, and common expressions. The middle box lists specific elements or element categories for the folder that is selected in the left box. For example, if Built-In Functions is selected in the left box, this box lists the categories of available functions. The right box lists the values (if any) for the elements selected in the left and middle boxes; for example, all Built-In Functions (the selected item in the left box) in the Date/Time category (the selected category in the middle box).

You access the Expression Builder from the Control Source text box.

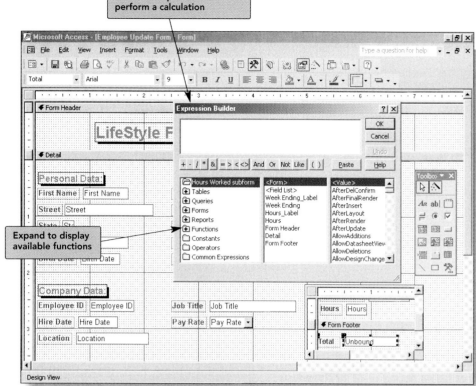

> Expression Builder helps you enter the expression to perform a calculation

1 ● **Click in the Control Source text box and click [...] to open the Expression Builder.**

Your screen should be similar to Figure 5.39

> Expand to display available functions

Figure 5.39

In the Expression Builder dialog box, you begin building your expression by specifying the type of operation you want to perform. You want to use the built-in Sum function to calculate a total. To access the built-in functions, you need to expand the Functions folder. The ⊞ button signifies that the folder contains subfolders that are not currently displayed. Clicking this button expands the folder so you can see the subfolders. Alternatively, a ⊟ button signifies that the folder is fully expanded. You click this button to collapse the folder so the subfolders are once again hidden.

2 ● Double-click the ⊞ button next to Functions in the left list box.

● Select Built-In Functions to open the folder.

● Scroll down the right list box of functions and double-click Sum.

Your screen should be similar to Figure 5.40

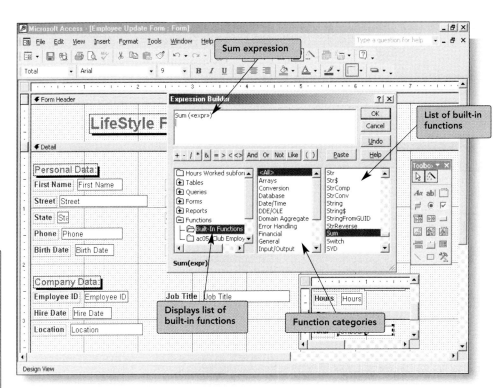

Figure 5.40

The expression box shows the selected function. Next you need to replace the text in the parentheses (<expr>, the expression placeholder) with the identifier to use. In this case, the identifier is the Hours field.

3 ● **Select <expr> in the expression box.**

● **Open the Hours Worked subform folder in the left list box.**

● **Double-click Hours in the middle list box.**

Your screen should be similar to Figure 5.41

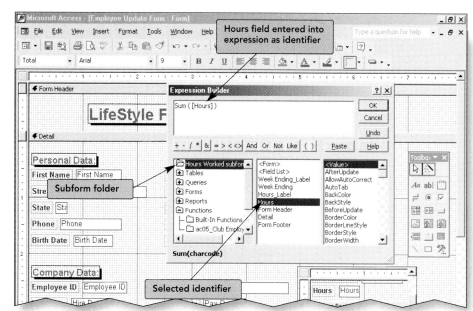

Figure 5.41

The expression box displays the selected identifier that will be used by the Sum function. Your expression is now complete and you can return to the form design.

4 ● **Click** [OK] .

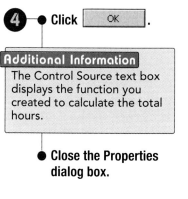

Additional Information

The Control Source text box displays the function you created to calculate the total hours.

● **Close the Properties dialog box.**

Your screen should be similar to Figure 5.42

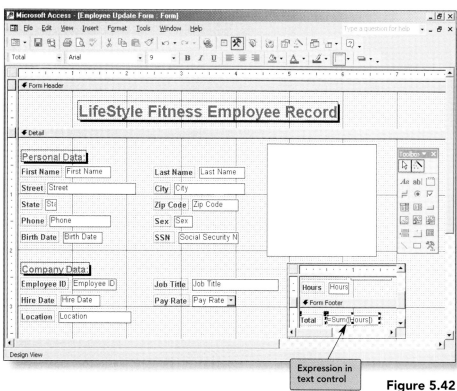

Figure 5.42

The text control displays the expression. Because the calculated control is entered in the subform, it will calculate the sum for the record information displayed in the subform only.

5 Switch to Form view.

● Save the changes you have made to the form.

Your screen should be similar to Figure 5.43

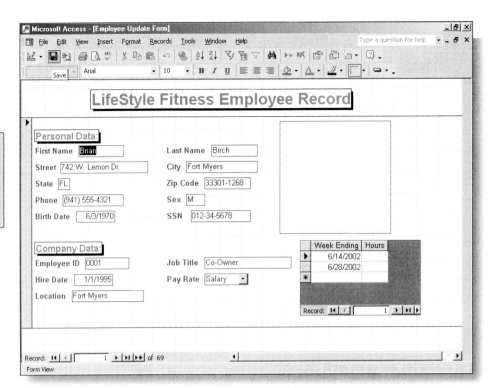

Figure 5.43

Because the Total control is entered in the Form Footer section of the subform it is not displayed in the form.

Adding a Control Reference

To display the total hours, you need to add a second calculated control in the main form that references the calculated control in the subform. This is called a **control reference**. You add a control reference in the same way you do a calculated control, by creating the text and label controls and setting the control properties. The difference is that the expression you build for this control references another control.

1 • Switch to Design view.

• Click 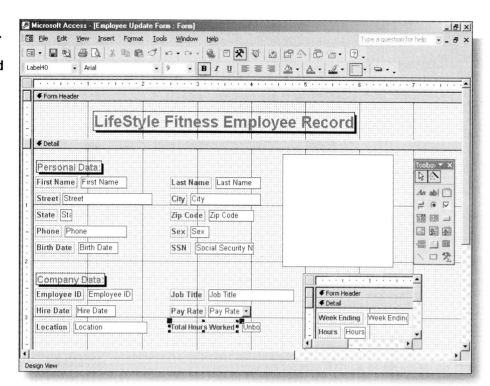 Text Box and click in the blank space under the Pay Rate field in the main form to add the text box control.

• Change the label control caption to Total Hours Worked.

• Change the Name for the text box control field to Total Hours.

• Size and position the control as in Figure 5.44.

Your screen should be similar to Figure 5.44

Figure 5.44

Next you need to enter the expression to display the calculated total hours from the subform. The expression is equal to the calculated total hours value.

2
- Select the text box control and display its properties.
- Click [...] in the Control Source text box to open the Expression Builder.
- Click the [=] Operator button to enter the type of calculation you want to perform.
- Double-click the [+] button next to Employee Update Form in the left list box of expression elements.
- Click the Hours Worked subform to open its folder.
- Double-click Total in the middle list box to specify the control in the subform that you want this control to reference.

Your screen should be similar to Figure 5.45

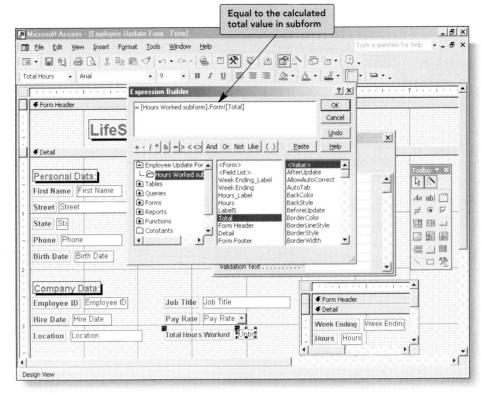

Figure 5.45

The expression references (is equal to) the control in the subform that calculates the total value.

3
- Click [OK].
- Close the Properties dialog box.

Your screen should be similar to Figure 5.46

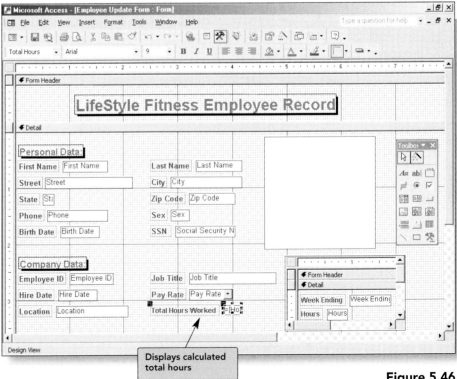

Figure 5.46

The controls are now set up to calculate and display the total hours worked.

The calculated controls you added to the form contain the required expressions, but you still need to do some minor layout adjustments so they are easier to see and use.

4 ● **Adjust the placement of the subform to top-align with the other controls in the Company Data section.**

● **Save the form changes and switch to Form view.**

● **Display record 3 in the form.**

HAVING TROUBLE?

If necessary, return to Design view and adjust the size of the subform and text box control to fully display the data.

Your screen should be similar to Figure 5.47

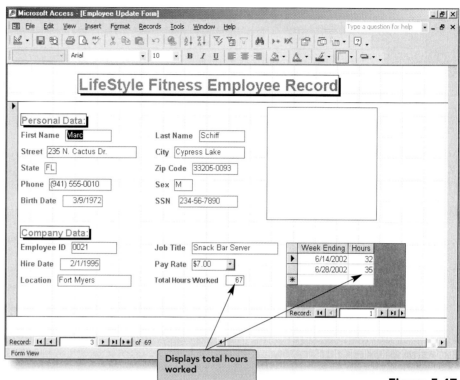

Figure 5.47

The calculated control in the main form displays the calculated value from the calculated field for that record from the subform.

Testing the Calculated Control

As the Hours table is updated, the total hours will be updated to reflect the change. To test this, you will add another pay week to your record.

- **1** ● Display your record.

  ● Enter the current date for the Week Ending date and 25 for the hours worked.

  ● Press ←Enter to complete the hours worked entry.

  Your screen should be similar to Figure 5.48

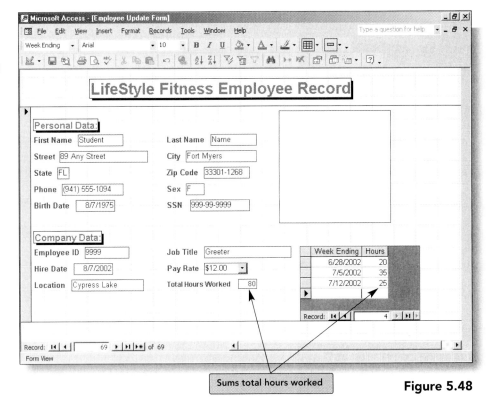

Sums total hours worked

Figure 5.48

The total hours worked reflects the total for the three weeks of hours recorded.

Using Command Buttons

You want to make it easier to print the form and to move to a new blank record. To do this, you decide to add some command buttons to the form.

concept 6

Command Button

6 A **command button** executes one or more actions on a form. For example, you can create command buttons that perform actions within a form, such as moving from record to record and adding, copying, saving, printing, and deleting a record. You can also create a command button that opens another form.

You can create a command button on your own by typing the instructions to be performed in the Properties dialog box, or you can select from over 30 types of predefined procedures to create a command button using the Command Button Wizard.

Creating Command Buttons

You will use the Command Button Wizard to add two command buttons to your form: one that prints the current record and another that displays a blank form. You will place them in the Form Footer section, which is a typical location for command buttons or other instructions on using a form. This way they do not appear at the bottom of every record when you print the form; however, they are visible when viewing each form.

1 ● **Switch to Form Design view.**

● **Expand the Form Footer section to make room for the button.**

● **Click** ▭ **Command Button.**

HAVING TROUBLE?
To use the Command Button Wizard, the 🔲 Control Wizard must be activated (the button must be pressed in). If it is not, click the 🔲 button to activate it.

Additional Information
The mouse pointer changes to ⁺□ after you select ▭, signifying that the program is ready to create the button.

● **Click along the left margin in the Form Footer section to add the command button at that location.**

Your screen should be similar to Figure 5.49

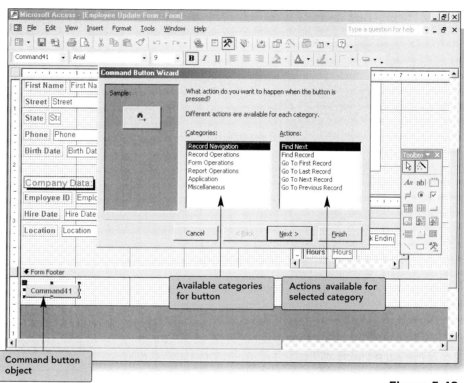

Figure 5.49

The Command Button Wizard dialog box displays a list of six predefined categories and their asscoiated actions that can be assigned to the button. The Record Navigation category is selected and displays six record navigation actions that can be assigned to a button. The action you will use to print the current record is in the Record Operations category. However, before selecting the command button category and action, you will take a look at the actions available in all categories.

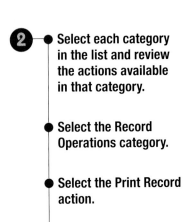

2 ● Select each category in the list and review the actions available in that category.

● Select the Record Operations category.

● Select the Print Record action.

● Click [Next >].

Your screen should be similar to Figure 5.50

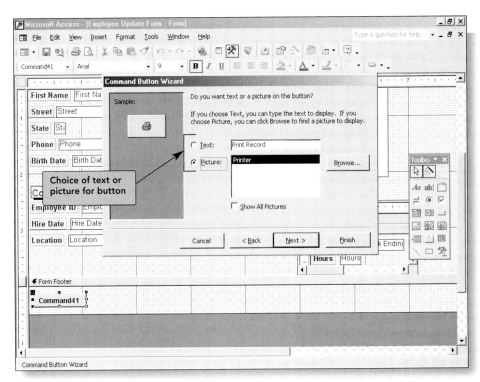

Figure 5.50

The second Wizard box gives you a choice of displaying a picture or text on the command button. You will use the default picture of a printer to indicate the action it will perform.

3 ● If necessary, select the **P**icture option.

● Click [Next >].

Your screen should be similar to Figure 5.51

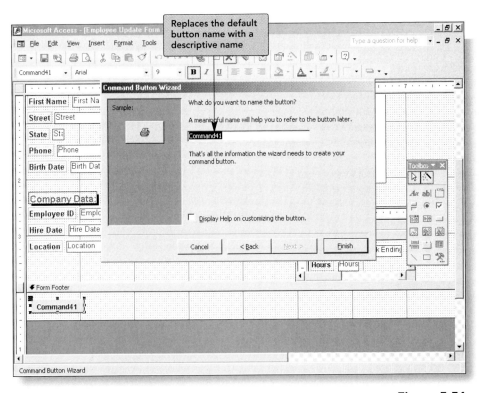

Figure 5.51

The final Wizard screen asks you what you want to name the button.

4 • Type **Print**.

• Click **Finish**.

Your screen should be similar to Figure 5.52

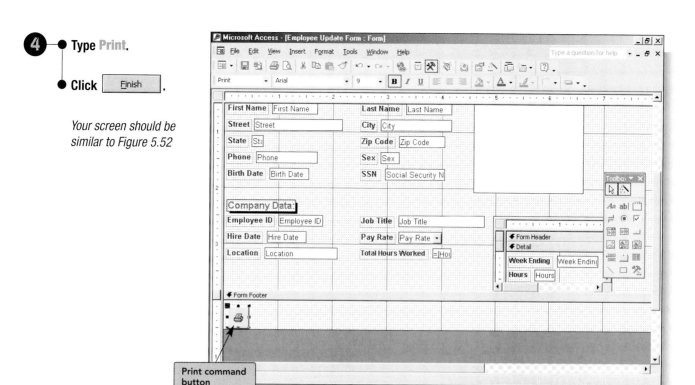

Print command button

Figure 5.52

The Print button is now ready to use. The second button you want to add is to display a blank new record for adding a new employee to the database.

5 • Click ⊟ **Command Button**.

• Place the button to the right of the Print button.

• From the Record Operations category, select Add New Record.

• Click **Next >**.

• Select Text to display text on the button, and use the default text suggestion.

• Click **Next >**.

• Name the button **New Record**.

• Click **Finish**.

• If necessary, adjust the position of the button.

Your screen should be similar to Figure 5.53

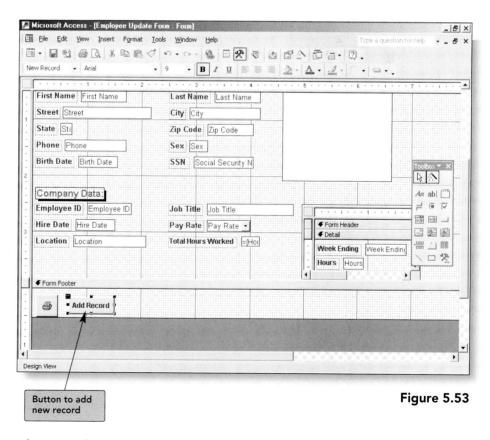

Button to add new record

Figure 5.53

The second command button has been added to the form.

Using a Command Button

Next you will test the New Record button. (You will use the Print button shortly when you print the form.)

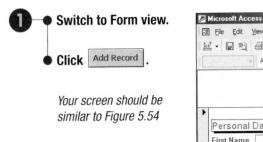

Switch to Form view.

Click Add Record.

Your screen should be similar to Figure 5.54

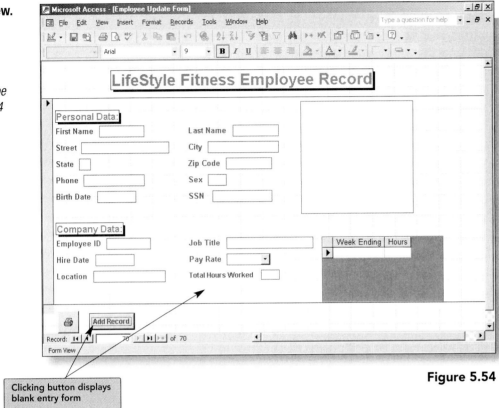

Figure 5.54

Clicking button displays blank entry form

A blank form is displayed and ready for entry of a new record, which confirms that the New Record button works.

Creating Page Headers and Footers

The final changes to the form that you want to make are changes that will affect the printed form. You want the form to be printed with a thick borderline at the top and the page number at the bottom of every page.

Adding the Page Header and Footer Sections

First you need to add a Page Header and Page Footer section to the form. Unlike form headers and footers, which print only on the first and last page of a form, page headers and footers print on every page.

Additional Information
You can only add a header and footer as a pair.

Your screen should be similar to Figure 5.55

Page Header section opened

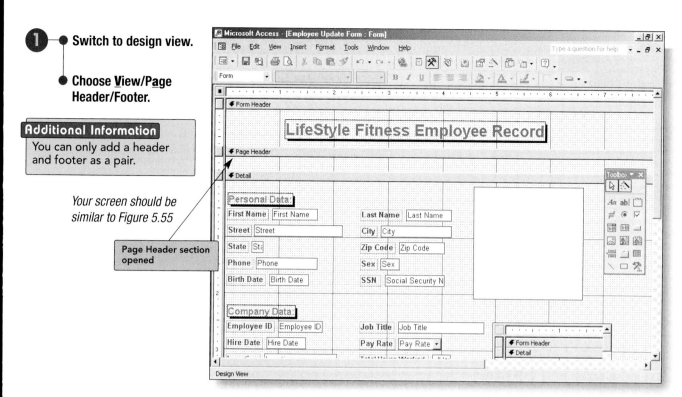

Figure 5.55

Page Header and Page Footer sections are added to the form. You can now adjust the size of these sections and add controls and objects to them just as you can in the other form sections.

Creating a Border Line

In the Page Header, you will create a border line that will appear at the top of every record when the form is printed.

① ● **Click ▭ Rectangle in the Toolbox.**

● **Click and drag to draw a thin rectangle from the left edge of the Page Header section to the 7.5-inch position.**

● **Click ◈▾ Fill/Back Color and select red.**

Your screen should be similar to Figure 5.56

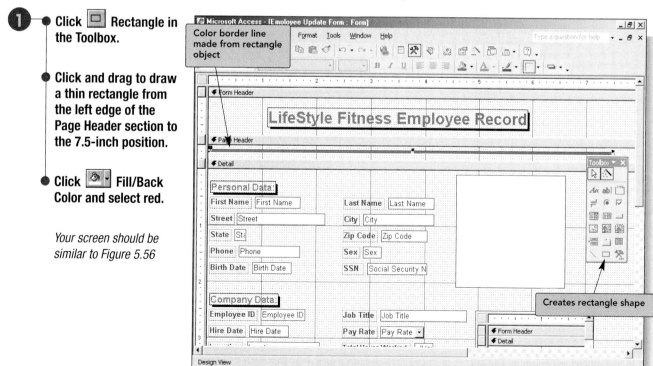

Figure 5.56

Inserting Page Numbers

Next you will add the page number in the Page Footer section.

1 ● **Choose Insert/Page Numbers.**

Your screen should be similar to Figure 5.57

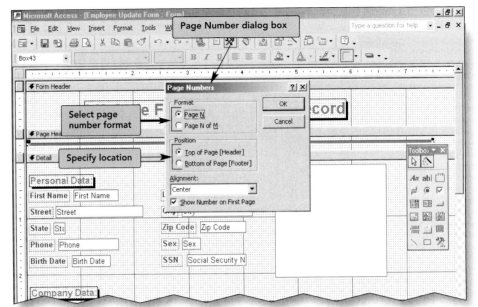

Figure 5.57

The Page Numbers dialog box lets you insert page numbers in your form in either the header or footer in the format "Page N" (which would print out as "Page 2" on the second page) or "Page N of M" (which would print out as "Page 2 of 5" on the second page). You can also choose the alignment of the page number (centered, left, or right) and whether you want the page number printed on the first page or not. You want the single page number centered in the footer and printed on the first and all pages.

2 ● **Select the following options (if they are not already selected): Page N, Bottom of Page [Footer], Alignment/Center, and Show number on First Page.**

● **Click** OK **.**

● **Scroll to the bottom of the form to see the Page Footer section.**

● **Save the form.**

● **If prompted, click** Yes **to save the objects.**

Your screen should be similar to Figure 5.58

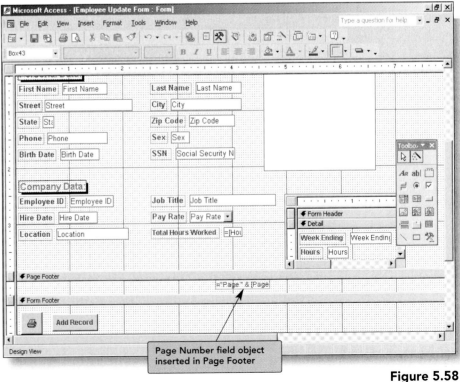

Figure 5.58

Your customized form has been designed and tested, and you are ready to print, save, and close it.

Previewing and Printing a Form

You decide to print one record to show the club owners. Before printing, you will preview how it will appear.

 Click 🔍 Print Preview.

Your screen should be similar to Figure 5.59

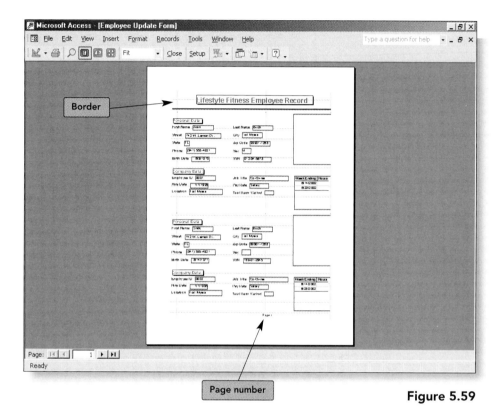

Figure 5.59

The border and page number appear in the page header and footer as you specified. However, because the form is too wide, it will not all fit on the page. To fix this, you will change the orientation of the printout.

2
- Click Setup .

- Open the Page tab and select **L**andscape.

- Click OK .

Your screen should be similar to Figure 5.60

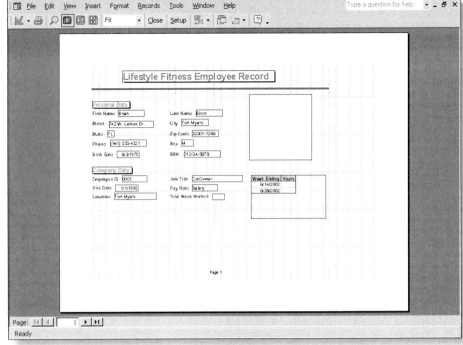

Figure 5.60

The form is displayed in landscape orientation. Now you will print your record.

3
- Close the preview window and display Form view.

- Display your record in the form.

- Print your record using the Print command button.

- Close the form, saving the changes.

Your screen should be similar to Figure 5.61

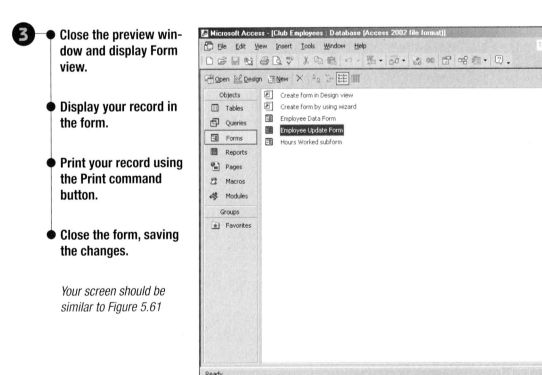

Figure 5.61

Deleting a Form

Now that you have a customized form that will update multiple tables in the database, you no longer need the original form you created to update the Employee table. You can easily delete this form from the database, just as you can all types of database objects.

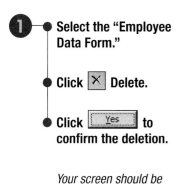

Select the "Employee Data Form."

Click ☒ **Delete.**

Click **Yes** **to confirm the deletion.**

Your screen should be similar to Figure 5.62

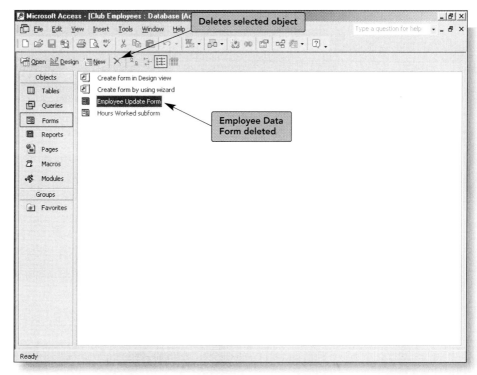

Figure 5.62

The Employee Data Form file has been deleted and is no longer listed in the Forms objects list.

As a final maintenance task, you will compact and repair the database before you close it.

Compact and repair the database.

Close the database.

LAB 5
Creating Custom Forms

Alignment and Spacing (AC5.15)

The position of controls on a form can be adjusted so that they are evenly aligned and so that the spacing between controls is the same.

Alignment and Spacing

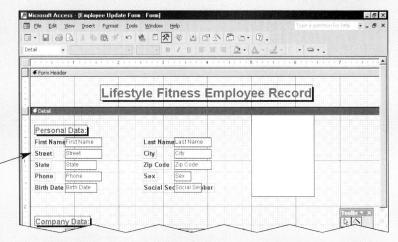

Font (AC5.20)

A **font**, also commonly referred to as a typeface, is a set of characters with a specific design.

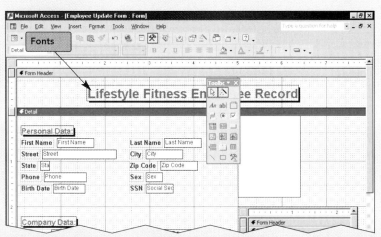

Subform (AC5.28)

A **subform** is a form that is embedded in another form and is used to show data from another table or query.

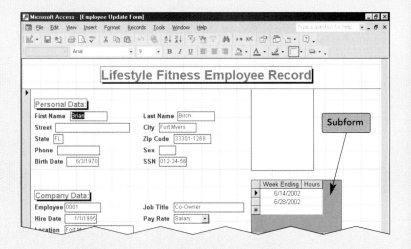

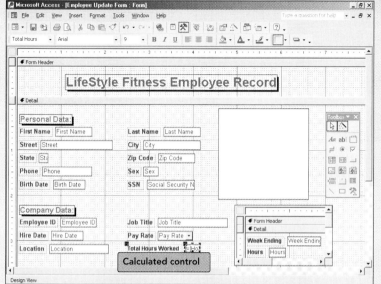

Calculated Control (AC5.34)

A **calculated control** is used to display data that is calculated from a field in a table or query or from another control in the form.

Expression Builder (AC5.38)

The **Expression Builder** helps you select the type of function to use and the identifiers for the expression in database forms, reports, and queries.

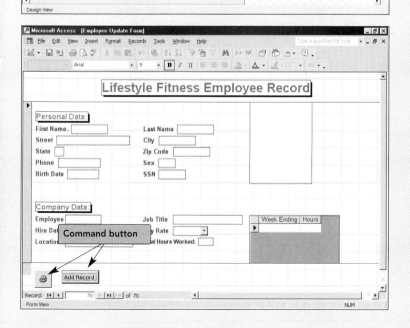

Command Button (AC5.46)

A **command button** executes one or more actions in a form.

LAB 5

Creating Custom Forms

key terms

align   AC5.15

calculated control   AC5.34

command button   AC5.46

control reference   AC5.42

Expression Builder   AC5.38

font   AC5.20

font size   AC5.20

Form Design toolbar   AC5.10

Formatting toolbar   AC5.10

hierarchical form   AC5.28

main form   AC5.28

master/detail form   AC5.28

parent/child form   AC5.28

point   AC5.20

record source   AC5.5

san serif   AC5.20

serif   AC5.20

spacing   AC5.15

subform   AC5.28

Toolbox toolbar   AC5.11

typeface   AC5.20

mous skills

The Microsoft Office User Specialist (MOUS) certification program is designed to measure your proficiency in performing basic tasks using the Office XP applications. Getting certified demonstrates that you have the skills and provides a valuable industry credential for employment. After completing this lab, you have learned the following Microsoft Office User Specialist skills:

Skill	Description	Page
Creating and Modifying Forms	Create and display forms	AC5.25, AC5.36
	Modify form properties	AC5.4

command summary

Command	Shortcut	Button	Action
View/**P**roperties	F4	🖼	Displays properties associated with selected item
View/**Pa**ge Header/Footer			Adds or removes Page Header and Footer sections in a form
Insert/**F**orm/Autoform: Columnar		New	Creates a columnar form using all the fields from the selected table or query
Insert/Page N**u**mbers			Displays the page number in page header or footer of the printed form
F**o**rmat/**A**lign/**L**eft			Aligns left edges of selected controls
F**o**rmat/**S**ize/To **F**it			Automatically resizes selected control to fit its contents
F**o**rmat/**V**ertical Spacing/ Make **E**qual			Equalizes vertical space between selected controls

Terminology

screen identification

In the following screen, several items are identified by letters. Enter the correct term for each item in the spaces provided.

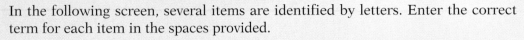

A. _____

B. _____

C. _____

D. _____

E. _____

F. _____

G. _____

matching

Match the numbered item with the correct lettered description.

1. typeface   _____   **a.** adds a label to a subform

2. subform   _____   **b.** form/subform combination

3.   _____   **c.** the underlying table or query on which a form is based

4. command button   _____   **d.** the area where the table data is displayed

5. identifier   _____   **e.** refers to the value of a field, control, or property

6. hierarchical form   _____   **f.** form imbedded within another form

7.   _____   **g.** displays the result of an expression in a form

8. calculated form   _____   **h.** the design and shape of characters

9. Detail   _____   **i.** displays data calculated from a field

10. record source   _____   **j.** executes one or more actions on a form

multiple choice

Circle the letter of the correct response.

1. Controls can be _____ relative to other controls in the following ways: left, right, top, and bottom.
   a. moved
   b. arranged
   c. aligned
   d. spaced

2. A calculated-control expression must begin with _____.
   a. =
   b. /
   c. '
   d. +

3. The primary form in a form/subform relationship is called the _____.
   a. hierarchical form
   b. source form
   c. main form
   d. destination form

4. To select more than one control on a form, hold down the _____ key while you click the control.
   a. ⇧ Shift
   b. Tab ⇆
   c. Alt
   d. ↵ Enter

5. The _____ toolbar contains buttons used to add and modify controls.
   a. Formatting
   b. Toolbox
   c. Form Design
   d. Form View

6. A form/subform combination is also called a _____.
  a. hierarchical form
  b. master/detail form
  c. parent/child form
  d. all of the above

7. The area on a form that contains the table data is called the _____ section.
  a. Detail
  b. Main
  c. Table
  d. Format

8. _____appear at the top of the screen or, if you print the form, at the top of the first page.
  a. Form headers
  b. Form footers
  c. Page headers
  d. Page footers

9. The _____ button must be activated in order to use the Command Button Wizard.
  a.
  b.
  c.
  d.

10. A calculated control displays data that is calculated from a _____.
  a. table
  b. query
  c. form
  d. none of the above

true/false

Circle the correct answer to the following questions.

1. You can create your own command buttons by writing an event procedure.	True	False
2. Form footers appear at the end of the last page when printed.	True	False
3. There are four types of operators: mathematical, comparison, logical, and reference.	True	False
4. You can embed a subform within a subform.	True	False
5. Page headers and footers print only on the first and last page of a form.	True	False
6. Subforms can be used to show data from tables or queries that have a one-to-many relationship.	True	False
7. To select both a text control and its associated label control, you click the label control.	True	False
8. You can create a calculated control from any type of control that has a Control Source property.	True	False
9. A calculated-control expression should always begin with an equal sign (=).	True	False
10. The identifier is the element that refers to the value of a field, control, or property.	True	False

Concepts

fill-in

Complete the following statements by filling in the blanks with the correct terms.

1. A _____ is the design and shape of characters.

2. The _____ spacing can be adjusted between any group of three or more selected controls.

3. _____ can be used to show data from tables or queries that have a one-to-many relationship.

4. You can create a _____ that opens another form.

5. The _____ displays a list of all the fields in the record source.

6. The form that contains the subform is called the _____ and the form/subform combination is called the _____.

7. A command button is created from _____ that you write yourself or select in the Command Button Wizard.

8. The _____ is the element that refers to the value of a field, control, or property.

9. Controls can be made more noticeable by adding _____ to their background, text, or borders.

10. A _____ control refers to two controls that act as one.

discussion questions

1. Discuss how multiple-form tables are used. When would it be more appropriate to use a subform as opposed to a multiple-form table?

2. Discuss the way a form's appearance can be enhanced. Why would you use these enhancements? What drawbacks are there to using too many enhancements?

3. Discuss the purpose of a calculated control. Give examples of the types of form fields where this feature would be most useful.

4. Discuss how command buttons can be used. What are some form functions that can be automated with a command button?

Hands-On Exercises

step-by-step

Adventure Travel Tours Client Form

★ **1.** You have set up a Client database for Adventure Travel Tours, with tables that contain data on the clients and travel agents at each office location. Next you need to create a form that will make entering data into these tables easier. As you did when you inserted the Clients table within the Agents table as a subdatasheet, you want the form to display the agent data and the records of the clients assigned to them. To do this, you will create a travel agents form with a clients subform. You are also going to customize this form by including different font sizes and colors as well as a form header and footer to make it more attractive. When you are finished, your form will look similar to the form shown here.

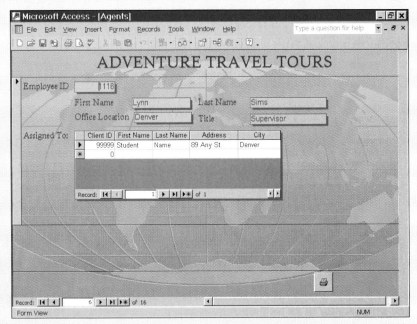

    a. Open the Clients & Agents database (which you worked on in Step-by-Step Exercise 1 of Lab 4).

    b. Use the Form Wizard to create a new form using all of the fields in the Agents table as well as all of the fields in the Clients table (in that order). Specify that you want to view the data with the Agents table as the main form and the Clients table as the subform. Use the Datasheet layout for the subform. Use the International style. Keep the form and subform names as Agents and Clients, and specify that you want to modify the form's design. Finish the Wizard.

    c. Move the First Name and Last Name controls to the same line and to the right of the Employee ID control. Move the Office Location and Title controls as the second line. Adjust the size, alignment, and spacing of the controls. Allow about .5-inch spacing between lines.

    d. Change the Clients label to **Assigned To:** and move the label and subform up so they are about .5 inch from the line above it.

    e. Change the font size of all labels and text in the main form to 14 points. Size the controls to fit. Do not allow the form size to extend beyond 6.5 inches.

f. Add a label in the Form Header section for the form title that reads **ADVENTURE TRAVEL TOURS**. Change the font size to 24. Size the label to fit, and center it at the top of the form. Apply a font color, border weight and color, background color, and special effect of your choice.

g. Display the Page Header and Footer sections. In the Page Header section, add a label that reads **Travel Agent Assignments**. Increase the font size to 18. Size the label to fit and center it on the form. Change the font and font color to one of your choice.

h. In the Page Footer area, insert an automatic page number control.

i. In the Form Footer, add a Print Record command button.

j. In Form view adjust the column widths in the subform so the entire contents are displayed. (You will need to scroll the form horizontally to access all the columns.) Change the agent assignment for Beatrice Antell from Cook to Sheridan and for Catherine Gryder from Cook to Vasquez.

k. Display the agent you selected for your record and print the form for your record only.

l. Save and close the form. Compact and repair the database. Close the database.

Animal Rescue Foundation Animal Tracking Form

★ ★ **2.** The director of the Animal Rescue Foundation likes the way the Fosters and Adopters tables show the corresponding animal data from the Animals table; however, he has asked if you can create a form that can be used to track the animal, foster care, and adoption data in one place to make it easier to view and update this information. To do this, you will create a main animal data form with two subforms for the foster and adoption data. Your completed form will look similar to that shown here.

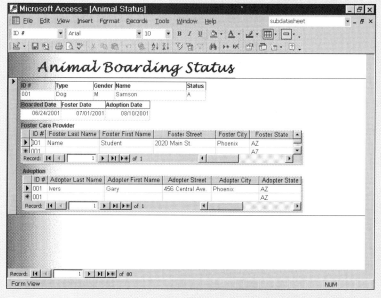

a. Open the ARF Fosters database (which you last worked on in Step-by-Step Exercise 2 of Lab 4).

b. Use the Form Wizard to create a new form and add all of the fields from the Animals table. Use the Justified layout and Blends style. Name the form **Animal Status** and open it in Design view.

c. Move the Boarded Date control boxes to the second line, to the left of the Foster Date and Adoption Date control boxes. (Hint: You will have to move the Foster Date and Adoption Date control boxes first to make room for the Boarded Date box.) Realign the control boxes as necessary after you have completed the move. Change the sizes of the three Date text control boxes so they are the same size (approximately 1 inch).

d. Increase the size of the Detail section and insert a subform at the bottom. Use the Fosters table and all of its fields as the source of the subform. Accept the default link option and name the subform **Foster Care Provider**.

e. Repeat the previous step to create another subform using the Adopters table and all of its fields. Name the subform Adoption. Adjust the size of both subforms to ¾ inch high by 5½ inches wide.

f. In the Form Header section, add a form title that reads **Animal Boarding Status** in a 22-point font of your choice. Assign a font color, border, background color, and special effect of your choice. Resize and center the title as necessary.

g. Add a 12-point label that reads **Created by [your name]** in the Page Header section. Center it below the title. Apply the same formats as the title. Add an automatic page numbering control in the Page Footer section.

h. In Form view adjust the column widths in the subforms so each column's contents are displayed.

i. Add a command button to print the current form (in the Form Operations category). Print the form for ID# 001 in portrait orientation.

j. Save and close the form. Compact and repair the database. Close the database.

Simply Beautiful Spa Form

★★ **3.** After reviewing the tables that you created for the Simply Beautiful spa, Maria Dell, the owner, has asked you to create a form that will enable users of the database to update information about the spa packages as well as about the clients who have purchased each package. This request will require you to create a multiple-table form using fields from all three tables in the Simply Beautiful database. She would also like this new form to enable users to access the existing Client Information form quickly so they can update it when necessary. You will provide this access with a command button that links the two forms. The completed form will look similar to the form shown here.

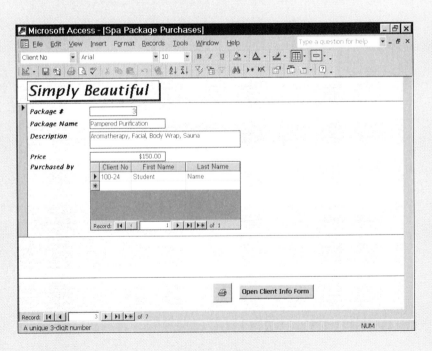

a. Open the Simply Beautiful database file (which you last worked on in Step-by-Step Exercise 3 of Lab 4).

b. Use the Form Wizard to create a new form using all fields from the Spa Packages table; the Client No, First Name, and Last Name fields from the Clients table; and the Package Purchased field from the Packages Sold table. Specify that you want to view the data by Spa Packages. Use the Datasheet layout for the subform and the Sumi Painting style. Name the form Spa Package Purchases and the subform Purchased by. Open the form in Form view.

c. Because the Package Name is already displayed on the main form, and the only clients that will display on a package's record will be the ones who purchased that package, you do not need the Package Name column to appear in the subform as well. Switch to Design view. Decrease the width of the subform the same as the Package Description text control box (approximately 4.5 on the horizontal ruler).

d. In Form view, adjust the column widths to display the Client No, First Name, and Last Name fields only.

e. Add the title Simply Beautiful in the Form Header section. Apply a font type, font size, color, background, border, and special effect as desired. Adjust its size to display the entire title.

f. Add a command button in the Form Footer section to open the Client Information form and show all the records. Specify that you want text to appear on the button and enter Open Client Info Form as the button label. Name the button Client Info Form. Resize the button as necessary. Add a second command button to print the current record.

g. Display the Page Header and Footer sections. In the Page Header, add a label that reads Spa Package Purchases. Assign a font size of 14 and a color, border, background color, and special effect of your choice. Resize and center the title as necessary

h. In the Page Footer, insert an automatic page number control.

i. Return to Form view and try out the Open Client Info Form command button. Close the Client Info Form to return to the Spa Package Purchases form. Change the package purchased for your record from Day Dream to Pampered Purification.

j. Print the form for the Pampered Purification package in portrait orientation. Save and close the form.

k. Compact and repair the database. Close the Simply Beautiful database.

Downtown Internet Cafe Form

★★ **4.** The database you created for the Downtown Internet Cafe contains two tables: one with data
★ regarding the cafe's inventory and vendors, and another with inventory item costs and order
information. To make it as easy as possible to review and update all of this data, the owner of the
cafe would like you to create a form that combines both tables. He would also like you to include
the same order calculations on this form as in the To Be Ordered query you created previously.
The completed multitable form will look similar to the form shown here.

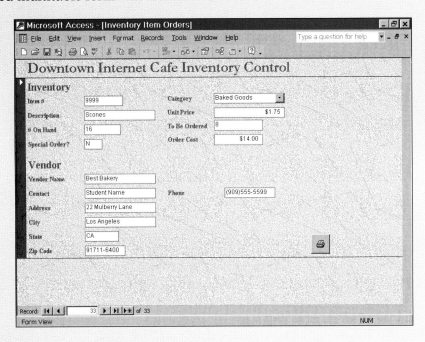

a. Open the Cafe Purchases database (which you last worked on in Step-by-Step Exercise 4 of
Lab 4).

b. Establish a one-to-one relationship between the Inventory and Inventory Prices tables.

c. Use the Form Wizard to create a multiple-table form with all of the fields from the Inventory
table and the Category and Unit Price fields from the Inventory Prices table. Use the
Columnar format and a style of your choice. Name the form Inventory Item Orders. Open the form
in Design view.

d. Divide the form into two sections: the top part for information pertaining to the inventory
items and costs and the bottom part for vendor information. Begin by expanding the Detail
section, moving controls, and adding "Inventory" and "Vendor" labels above each of the
sections.

e. Insert a calculated control in the Inventory section with the caption To Be Ordered. Use the
Expression Builder to calculate the number of items to be ordered by subtracting the # On
Hand from 24 (the amount of stock the owner likes to keep on hand). (Hint: Begin with an
equal sign, followed by the calculation.) Name the text box Control Order. Adjust the size and
placement of the new control. Save the form so the new calculated control will be available for
the next calculation. Display the form in Form view to check that your calculated field works
correctly.

f. Insert another calculated control next to the first with the label **Order Cost** and a calculation that multiplies the number of items to be ordered by the unit price. Name the text box **Control Cost**. Apply the Currency format property to the new calculated control. Adjust the size and placement of the new control.

g. Position, align, vertically space, and size all controls appropriately. Add an appropriate form header. Add a border line below the Vendor field controls to help visually separate the inventory items. Add other enhancements of your choice to the form.

h. Include a command button to print the current record.

i. Switch to Form view and locate the record with your name as the vendor contact. Select and print that record.

j. Save and close the form. Compact and repair the database. Close the database.

EduSoft Order Form

★ **5.** You are still working on the EduSoft Company's database. The database currently contains two
★ tables, Software and Software Sales, which you want to combine into one easy-to-use form. The owners have also requested that you include a calculation that shows the total sales to date as you did in the query you created previously. The completed form is shown here.

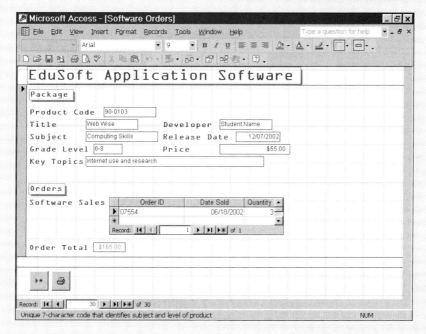

a. Open the EduSoft Titles database (which you last worked on in Step-by-Step Exercise 5 of Lab 4).

b. Create a multiple-table form with all of the fields from the Software table and the Order ID, DateSold, and Quantity fields from the Software Sales table. View the data by Software, use the Datasheet format, and select a style of your choice. Name the form **Software Orders** and open it in Form view.

c. The Key Topics text field is too short, the Price text field is too long, and the subform is too large and too close to the main form. Switch to Design view and fix these problems.

e. Insert a calculated control on the main form, below the subform, that multiplies the subform's total packages sold calculation by the package price. Name the label and text controls Order Total. Apply the Currency format property to the new calculated control.

f. Divide the form into two sections by moving all controls down, adding a label above the product information called Package Details, and one above the package order information called Orders. Add the title EduSoft Application Software to the Form header. Resize the controls as necessary and enhance the form as desired. (See the figure at the beginning of this exercise for reference.)

g. Insert a command button in the Form Footer section that will add a new record to the form. Insert another command button to print the current record.

h. Add automatic page numbers in the Page Footer section.

i. Switch to Form view and display the record with your name as the developer. If this record does not have any orders associated with it, add some. Select and print the record and then save and close the form. Compact and repair the database. Close the database.

on your own

Associated Dental Form

★ 1. You want to enhance the database you developed for Associated Dental by creating a form that combines both of its tables. This way, anyone (including you) who has to access or update a patient's contact, insurance, or payment information can do so in one central location. Open the Patient Information database you updated in On Your Own Exercise 1 of Lab 4 and use the Form Wizard to create a multiple-table form. Reformat the form to divide it into patient contact information and patient billing information. Add a form header with the company name, a page header with the form name, a form footer with Created by [your name], and a page footer with automatic page numbering. Print the first page of the form and then save and close it.

WriteOn! Data Entry Form

★ ★ 2. The WriteOn! database you created in On Your Own Exercise 3 in Lab 4 needs a data entry form. Create a form that can be used to enter all the data into the underlying tables. Use subform(s) where necessary. Add a calculated control to total the number of prints you have from different suppliers. Use the features you learned in these tutorials to enhance the appearance of the form. Create command buttons to print the form and any others that enhance the use of the form. Enter your name as one of the suppliers and print the form that displays your name.

Lewis & Lewis Data Entry Form

★ ★ 3. The database you have created for Lewis & Lewis has eased the workload in the personnel department. In order to facilitate data entry in the employee and consultant table, you have been asked to create a new form. Use the Lewis Personnel database you updated in On Your Own Exercise 2 of Lab 4. Create a multiple-table form that includes the information from both the employee and the consultant tables. Enhance the form's appearance using the techniques you learned in this lab. Add a command button to print the new form. Add your name to the page header. Use the new command button to print the form.

JK Enterprises Form

★ **4.** As database manager for JK Enterprises, you have created a database (JK Enterprises) that includes
★ expense report, department, and expense type/category data—all in separate tables (On Your Own
Exercise 4 in Lab 4). To make it more efficient you want to be able to update these tables using a
single form. Create a form from the expense report table and add the department and expense
type/category tables as subforms. Include a calculated control that displays the total expense
amount on each expense report. Reformat the form as desired. Include your name in the Form
Footer and automatic page numbers in the Page Footer. Print one page of this form and then save
and close it.

Tri-County Little League Form

★ **5.** The database you created for the Tri-County Little League in On Your Own Exercise 5 in Lab 4 has
★ been a successful upgrade for the league. They would like to use the database to keep an inventory
of the league equipment and track the equipment distribution. Create a multiple-table form
named **Team Rosters** that includes the data from the players and coaches tables. Then add a
subform to display the equipment allocation for each team. The league hands out a catcher's mitt,
a catcher's chest protector, a catcher's mask, six bats, and a case (12) of baseballs to each team.
Four teams have received a pitching machine in addition to the standard equipment. Enhance the
table's appearance using the skills you learned in the lab. Add a command button to the form to
print the form and one that will open the equipment form. Include your name and the current
date in the Page Footer. Print the first record in the table in Form view. Back up and save the
database.

on the web

Custom Tees Data Entry Form

The owner of the online custom T-shirt site has asked you to do some additional work on the Custom Tees
database you created in the On the Web exercise of Lab 4 to make entering data more efficient. Create a
data entry form for the tables in the database. Use subform(s) where necessary. Add a calculated control
for an appropriate field in the database. Use the features you learned in this lab to enhance the
appearance of the form. Create command buttons to print the form and any others that enhance the use
of the form. Enter your name as one of the designers or customers and print the form that displays your
name.

Creating Custom Reports, Macros, and Switchboards

LAB 6

objectives

After completing this lab, you will know how to:

1.	Group report records.
2.	Calculate group totals.
3.	Customize a report's layout.
4.	Enhance a report's appearance.
5.	Add a calculated control to a report.
6.	Create mailing labels using the Label Wizard.
7.	Create macros to automate database tasks.
8.	Create a switchboard to navigate a database.
9.	Secure a database with password protection.
10.	Use a Database Wizard.

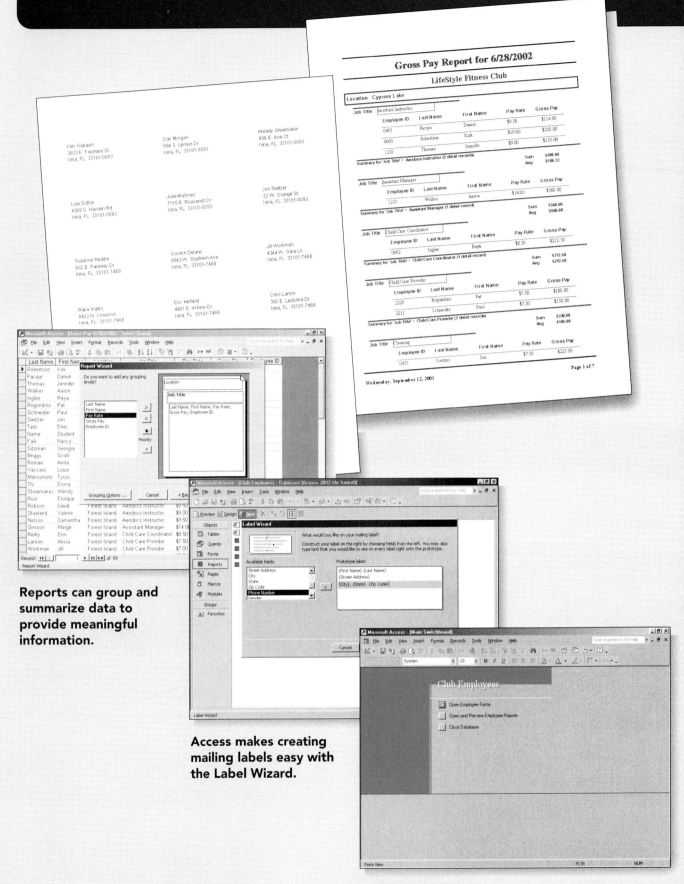

Reports can group and summarize data to provide meaningful information.

Access makes creating mailing labels easy with the Label Wizard.

Switchboards help users quickly navigate through objects in a database.

Lifestyle Fitness Club

The owners of the Lifestyle Fitness Club are impressed with your ability to use Access to locate and analyze the employee data. You have used the program to automate the updates and changes that occur to the employee tables and to quickly find answers to many different types of queries. Thus far, you have created simple reports from these queries that are quite acceptable for many informal uses.

Next, the Club owners would like you to create a more formal status report to be distributed to managers and accountants at the various Club locations. This report will group and summarize the payroll data in an organized and attractive manner, as shown in the report on the previous page.

You have also been asked to use the employee database to create mailing labels. A sample page of the labels you will create is shown on the previous page.

Finally, the owners would like you to develop macros and a switchboard system that will help the users of the employee database to quickly navigate through its forms and reports, to work with them as necessary, and then close the database when finished.

© Corbis

1	**Grouping Records** Records in a report can be grouped into categories to allow you to better analyze the data.
2	**Group Calculation** If you group data in your report, you can perform group calculations on values, such as a group total, an average, a minimum value, and a maximum value.
3	**Macro** A macro automates common database tasks, such as opening and printing tables, forms, and reports.
4	**Switchboard** A switchboard is an Access form that contains command buttons for performing a variety of actions in a database, such as viewing forms and reports, running macros, opening other switchboards, and exiting the application.

Creating a Grouped Report

The first report you want to create will display the employees' gross pay grouped by location and job title.

Planning the Report

You have sketched out the report to look like the one shown below.

```
Gross Pay Report for xx/xx/xx


Location:          XXXXXX
Job Title:         XXXXXX
Employee ID        Last Name       First Name      Gross Pay
XXXX               XXXXXX          XXXXXX          $XXXX.XX
XXXX               XXXXXX          XXXXXX          $XXXX.XX


Sum by Location                                    $XXXX.XX
Avg by Location                                    $XXXX.XX
Sum by Job Title:                                  $XXXX.XX
Avg by Job Title                                   $XXXX.XX
```

Running and Modifying the Associated Query

To create this report, you will use the Gross Pay 6/28/02 query that you already created (in Lab 4). It is usually helpful to run the query first to remind you of the data that the query gathers.

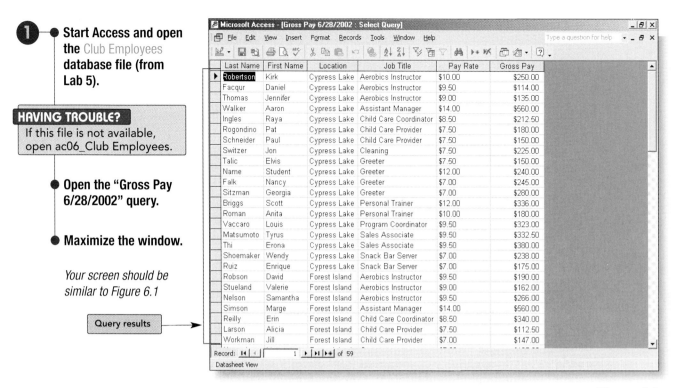

Figure 6.1

The query datasheet displays the Last Name, First Name, Location, Job Title, Pay Rate, and Gross Pay fields. In addition, you need the report to display the Employee ID field. To include this field in the report, you need to add it to the query design grid.

Opens new database object

Field added to query

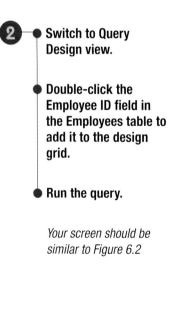

② ● **Switch to Query Design view.**

● **Double-click the Employee ID field in the Employees table to add it to the design grid.**

● **Run the query.**

Your screen should be similar to Figure 6.2

Figure 6.2

Now you are ready to create a report using the data from the query.

Using the New Object Button to Create a Report

Rather than switching to the Report tab of the Database window and choosing New, you can use the 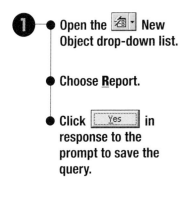 New Object button to create a new object of any type.

1 ● Open the 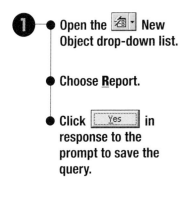 New Object drop-down list.

● Choose **R**eport.

● Click Yes in response to the prompt to save the query.

Your screen should be similar to Figure 6.3

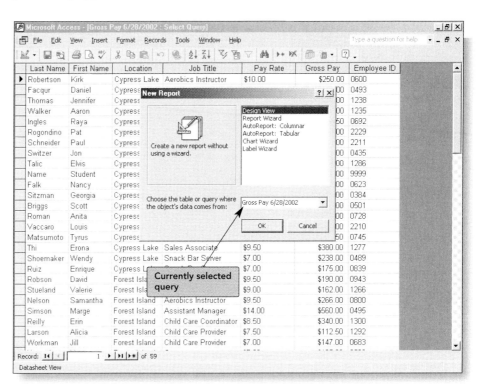

Figure 6.3

The New Report dialog box correctly displays the name of the selected query as the object on which the report will be based.

Using the Report Wizard to Create a Grouped Report

You will use the Report Wizard to create the grouped report. You can start this Wizard from the New Report dialog box.

1 ● Select Report Wizard.

● Click [OK].

Your screen should be similar to Figure 6.4

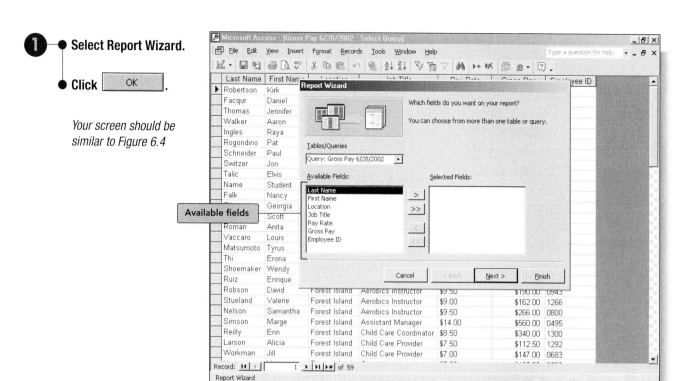

Available fields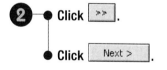

Figure 6.4

The Available Fields list box displays the fields that are included in the design grid in the Gross Pay 6/28/2002 query. You want to include all the fields in the report.

2 ● Click [>>].

● Click [Next >].

Your screen should be similar to Figure 6.5

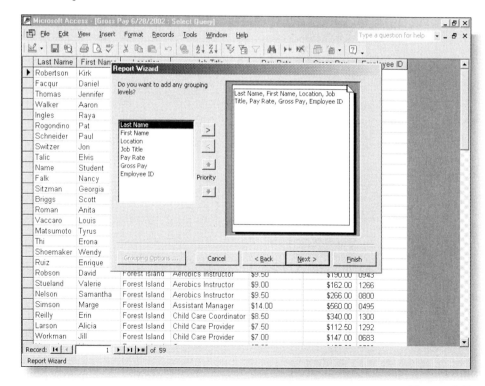

Figure 6.5

In the next dialog box, you need to select the fields on which you want to group the report.

concept 1

Grouping Records

1   Records in a report can be **grouped** by categories to allow you to better analyze the data. It is often helpful to group records and calculate totals for the entire group. For example, it might be useful for a store manager to group payroll records by department. Then, rather than getting a long list of pay for individual employees, the manager could get a report showing total payroll for each department. A mail-order company might group orders by date of purchase, then by item number to see detailed sales information.

In Access you can create a report that will automatically group records based on fields you choose to group by. You can group by as many as ten fields in any one report.

Groups should be created based on priority from the largest to the smallest.

You decide that you want to group the records by location and then by job title to make it easier for the Club owners to assess the staffing and workload and pinpoint any problem areas.

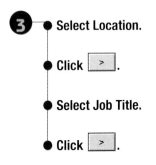

- ● **Select Location.**
- ● **Click** `>` **.**
- ● **Select Job Title.**
- ● **Click** `>` **.**

Your screen should be similar to Figure 6.6

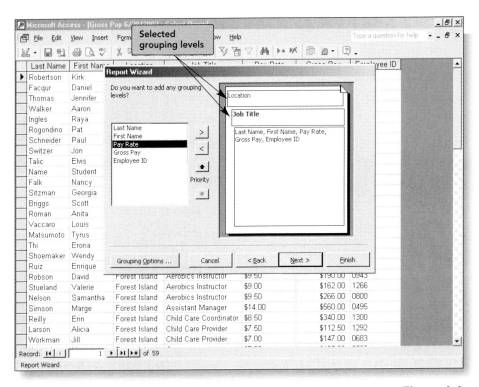

Figure 6.6

The report will group the data first by location and then by job title within the location.

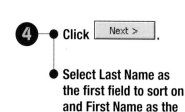

4 ● Click [Next >].

● **Select Last Name as the first field to sort on and First Name as the second field to sort on.**

Additional Information
Data is sorted by field within specified groups.

Your screen should be similar to Figure 6.7

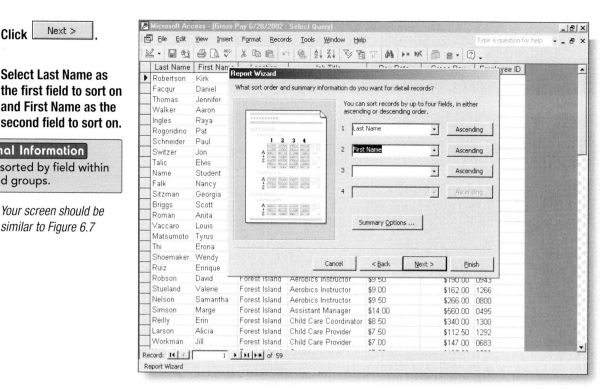

Figure 6.7

Because you have specified groups, you can also include calculations to summarize the grouped data.

5 ● Click [Summary Options ...].

Your screen should be similar to Figure 6.8

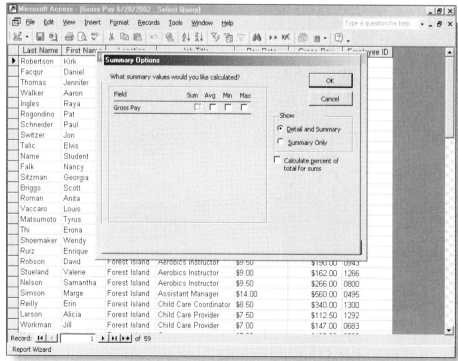

Figure 6.8

This Wizard screen asks you to choose the type of calculation you want to use to summarize the grouped data on your report.

concept 2

2 If you group data in your report, you can perform one or more of the following **group calculations** on values: Sum (adds all values by group), Avg (calculates the average value for the group), Min (calculates the lowest value for the group), and Max (calculates the highest value for the group).

You can select multiple calculations to complete different analyses of the data. For example, a mail-order company might calculate the sum of different products sold on each day of the month and the average sale for each day. You can also calculate the percent of total for the sums. For example, the mail-order company might want to know what percentage of total sales were made on a specific product for September 15.

You can further customize the report to display both detailed information and the summary information, or just the summary information while hiding the details about the individual items.

You would like the report to display a total and average for each location and job title.

6 ● Select Sum.

● Select Avg.

Your screen should be similar to Figure 6.9

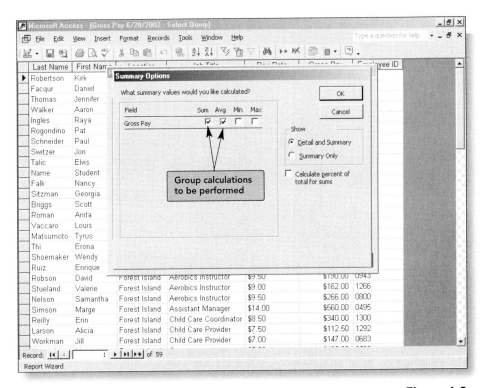

Figure 6.9

The report will display a total and average for the gross pay field for each group.

7 • Click [OK].

• Click [Next >].

Your screen should be similar to Figure 6.10

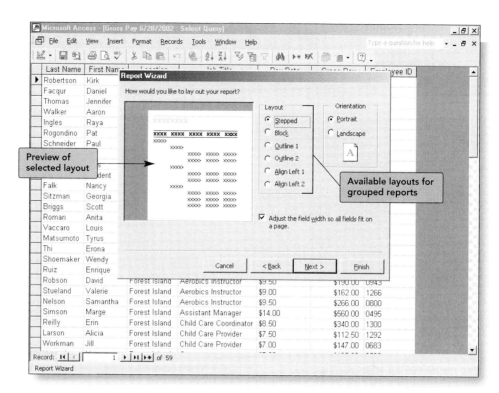

Labels in figure:
- Preview of selected layout
- Available layouts for grouped reports

Figure 6.10

In this dialog box you are asked to select from six different layout options for a grouped report.

8 • Select each layout option and look at the sample previews.

• Select Outline 2.

• Click [Next >].

Your screen should be similar to Figure 6.11

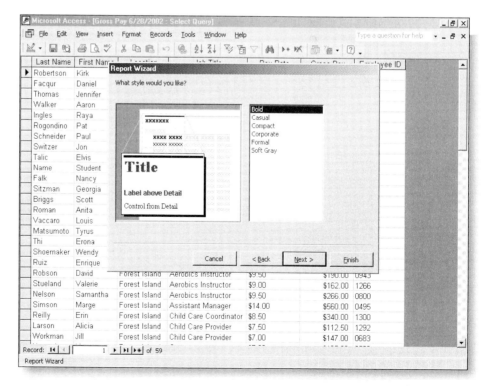

Figure 6.11

The next Wizard screen asks you to select a style for your report. You will use the Bold style.

9 ● Select the report style of Bold.

● Click **Next >**.

Your screen should be similar to Figure 6.12

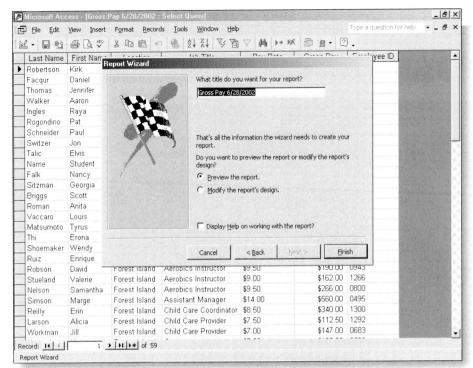

Figure 6.12

The final Wizard screen asks you to name your report.

10 ● Enter the report title of **Gross Pay Report for 6/28/2002**.

● Click **Finish**.

Your screen should be similar to Figure 6.13

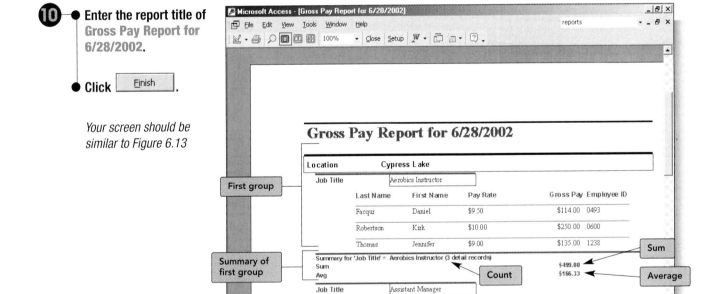

Figure 6.13

The data in the report is grouped by location and job title, and the records are alphabetized by last name within groups. The information for the Cypress Lake club is the first location group, and Aerobics Instructor is the first job title group within that location group. In addition, each location group displays a count of employees and the sum and average values for that job title.

Checking the Summary Calculations

You want to see how the Location summary calculations and the grand total calculations are included on the report. To do this, you will display a page in the middle of the report and then the last page.

1 ● **Display page 3 and look at the summary information at the end of the Cypress Lake group and the beginning of the Forest Island group.**

Your screen should be similar to Figure 6.14

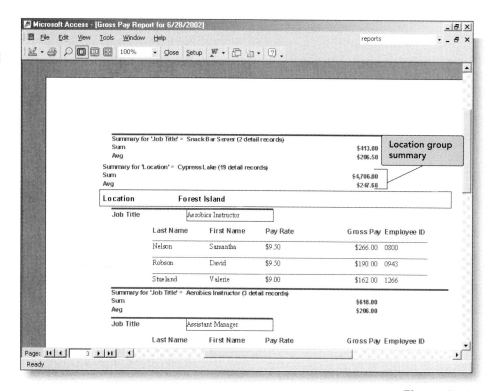

Figure 6.14

The summary information for Cypress Lake appears before the Forest Island group head. It includes a count value, and the total and average gross pay values for the club location.

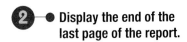

2 ● Display the end of the last page of the report.

Your screen should be similar to Figure 6.15

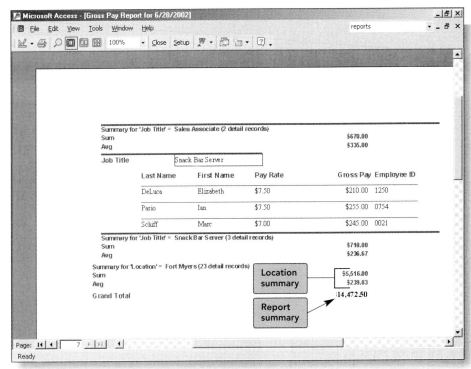

Figure 6.15

A grand total value for all clubs appears at the end of the report.

3 ● Display the top of page 1 again.

The report has all the data you requested, but you are not completely pleased with the way the report looks. You would like to move some things around to improve the report's appearance.

Customizing the Report Layout

As you looked through the report, you saw several changes you wanted to make. The first change is to rearrange the order of the fields in the report and to size the fields appropriately. In addition, you want to make the location group head more noticeable, to change the display of the date in the footer to exclude the day of the week, and to center the title over the report. As you recall from your previous work with reports, these changes are made in Report Design view.

● **If necessary, close the Field List.**

Your screen should be similar to Figure 6.16

Group Header sections

Detail section

Group Footer sections

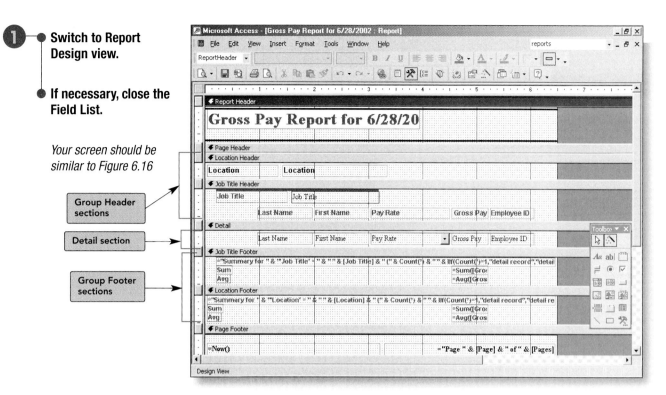

Figure 6.16

Notice that the Report Design view is slightly different for grouped reports than for the nongrouped reports you created previously. Besides the standard Report Header, Page Header, Detail, Page Footer, and Report Footer sections, there are also sections called Location Header and Job Title Header as well as Location Footer and Job Title Footer sections. These are called **Group Header and Footer sections**, and they display group identification information on the report each time the group changes. Notice that the Job Title section displays the label control for each field column, while the Detail section contains the text box controls. You will first move and resize several of the report controls.

Resizing and Rearranging Controls

First you will change the size of the report title, Location and Job Title labels.

1 • Increase the size of the report title to fully display the date.

• Resize the Location and Job Title label controls to fit their contents.

• Move the Location and Job Title text box controls closer to their Label controls.

Your screen should be similar to Figure 6.17

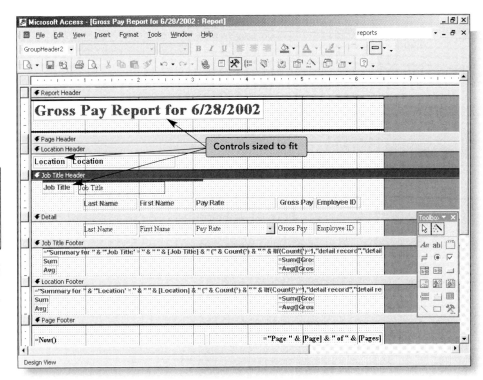

Figure 6.17

Next you will move several of the controls so the report layout is easier to read. Many of the same features you used in Form design are available in Report design.

2 • Select the Employee ID controls and move them to the 1-inch position.

• Decrease the size of the Pay Rate controls.

• Position the ten controls so they are evenly spaced between the 1-inch and 6-inch positions as shown in Figure 6.18.

• Save the changes you have made to the report.

Your screen should be similar to Figure 6.18

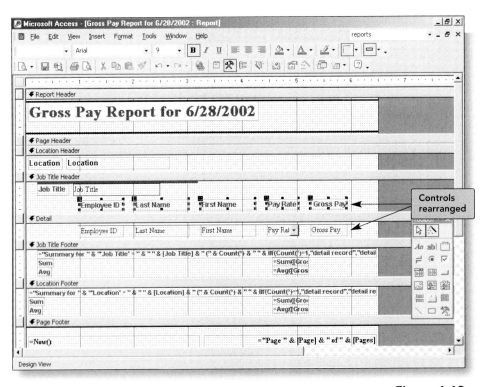

Figure 6.18

Before making more changes, you want to preview how these changes look first.

3 • Click 🔍 Preview.

Your screen should be similar to Figure 6.19

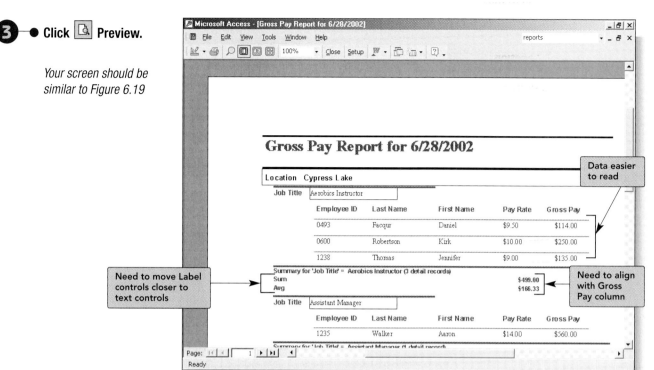

Figure 6.19

The rearrangement and resizing of the Detail fields makes the data in the report much easier to read. Next you want to align the summary data with the gross pay field column data.

4 • Return to Design view.

• Right-align the five Gross Pay text controls in the Job Title Footer, Location Footer, and Report Footer sections with the Gross Pay column in the Detail section.

• Move the five Gross Pay summary label controls to the left of their corresponding text controls.

Additional Information
Align the right border of the controls.

Your screen should be similar to Figure 6.20

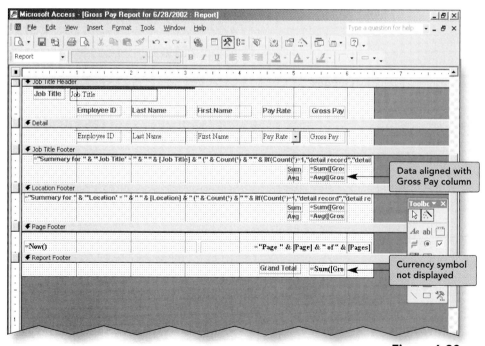

Figure 6.20

Again, you want to check how your changes look in the report preview.

5 ● Click  Preview.

● Display the last page
  of the report.

*Your screen should be
similar to Figure 6.21*

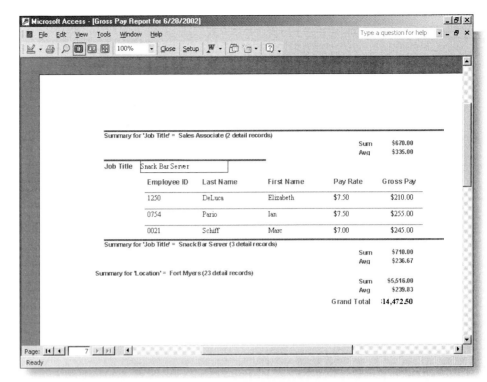

Figure 6.21

These changes make the report data much more organized. However, the
Grand total text control needs to be larger to display the currency symbol.

In addition, there are several other cosmetic changes you want to make
to the report to enhance its appearance.

Changing Text Alignment and Font and Fill Colors

First, you want the report title to stand out more. You decide to move the
title so it is centered horizontally over the report and vertically within the
Report Header section. You also want to center it within the control and
change its fill color.

1 ● Close the preview window.

● Select the report title control in the Report Header section.

● Move the title until the left border of the control aligns with the 1.25-inch ruler mark and the control is centered vertically in the Report Header section (see Figure 6.21).

● Select a color of your choice from the 🖎 ▾ Fill/Back Color palette.

● Click ☰ Center to center the label within the control.

Your screen should be similar to Figure 6.22

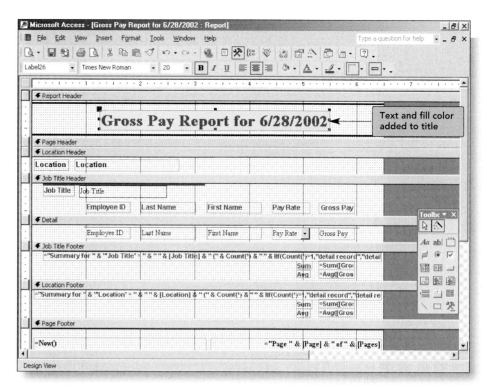

Figure 6.22

To make the location stand out more, you decide to change the color of the city name.

2 ● Select the Location text box control in the Location Header section.

Additional Information
Even though this is a compound control, you need to select the control individually to apply font color changes to it.

● Select a blue font color from the 🗛 ▾ Font/Fore Color palette.

● Save the report.

● Click 🔍 Preview.

Your screen should be similar to Figure 6.23

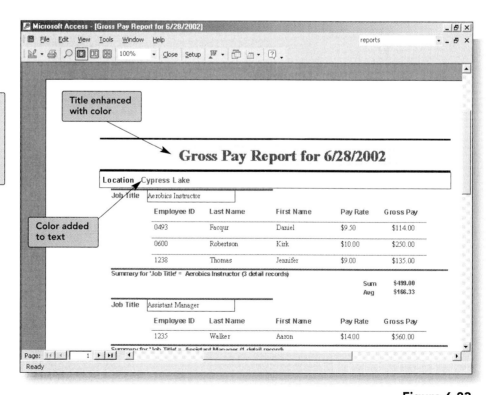

Figure 6.23

Working with Lines and Borders

Although the color text helps identify the location better, you think it would stand out even more if the rectangle surrounding the heading was in the same color. You also want to try out a heavier line weight.

1
● **Close the preview window.**

● **Click on the rectangle in the Location Header section to select it.**

● **Click** 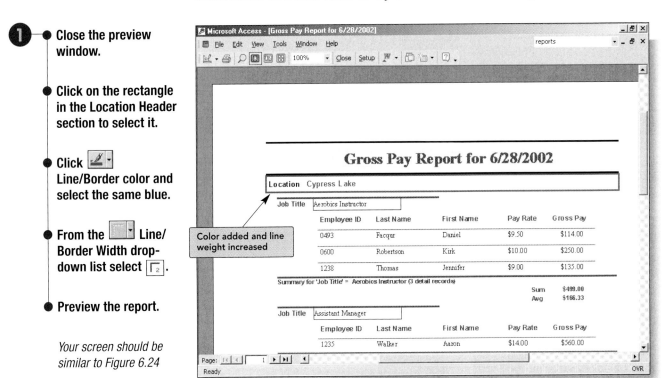 **Line/Border color and select the same blue.**

● **From the** ⬚ **Line/ Border Width drop-down list select** ▭ .

● **Preview the report.**

Your screen should be similar to Figure 6.24

Figure 6.24

You like how the color rectangle looks and also want to add a colored rectangle around the location subtotal information to make it easier to identify. You will insert a rectangle around the controls by drawing it and then adding color to it.

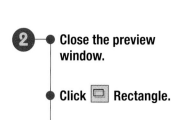

2 Close the preview window.

● Click 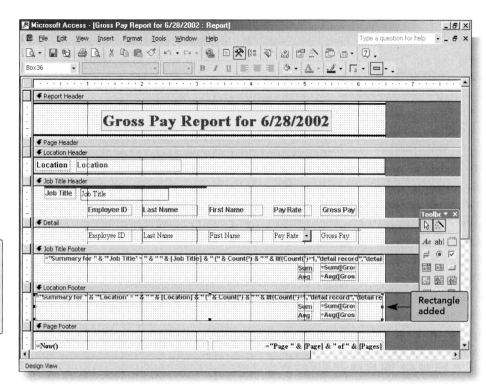 Rectangle.

● In the Location Footer section, drag to create a rectangle the full width of the report to enclose the Sum and Avg controls.

Additional Information

Do not extend the line beyond the 6.5-inch ruler position or the report will be too wide to fit on a single page when printed.

● Apply the same blue color to the rectangle.

Your screen should be similar to Figure 6.25

Figure 6.25

The default line weight of 1 is used. You think a single heavy line below the Grand Total values would also look good.

3 ● Click 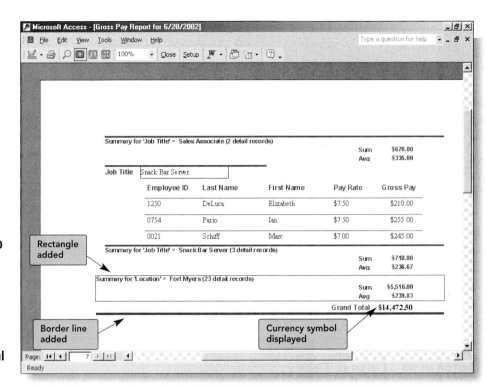 Line.

● From the [2 ▾] Line/ Border Width drop-down list select ◺.

● Click on the space along the left margin below the Grand Total controls in the Report Footer section and drag to the 6.5-inch position on the ruler to create the border line.

● Apply the same blue color to the line.

● Enlarge the Grand total text control to display the currency symbol.

● Save the report.

● Preview the last page of the report.

Your screen should be similar to Figure 6.26

Figure 6.26

The borders and colors enhance the report's appearance quite a bit. Now it is easy to see that the total gross pay for this period is $14,472.50.

Adding a Page Header

You would like the name of the Club to appear on every page of the report, so you will add it to the Page Header section. Unlike a report header, which prints only on the first page of a report, a page header will print at the top of every page. You want the page header to display the name of the Club using the same formats as the main title.

1
- Close the Preview window.
- Increase the size of the Page Header section to .5 inch.
- Click 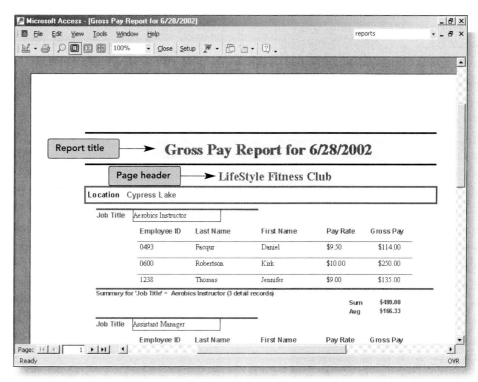 Label and click inside the Page Header section to place the label control.
- Type LIFESTYLE FITNESS CLUB and press ←Enter.
- Change the font to Times New Roman with a font size of 16.
- Size the label control to fit the contents.
- Center the label within the control.
- Apply the same background fill as in the report title to the control.
- Move the label control so it is centered horizontally and vertically in the Page Header section.
- Save the report.
- Switch to Print Preview.

Your screen should be similar to Figure 6.27

Figure 6.27

The report title appears centered and with the background color you selected, and the Club name is displayed under it.

Changing the Record Source

You also want to create the same report for the 6/14/2002 pay period. After a report is created, you can simply change the record source to display data from a different data source. First you need to create the query for the new source to display the information for this pay period. You will do this by revising the 6/28/2002 query.

1 ● **Open the "Gross Pay 6/28/2002" query.**

● **In Query Design view, change the Week Ending Criteria to 6/14/2002.**

● **Run the query and save it as Gross Pay 6/14/2002.**

Your screen should be similar to Figure 6.28

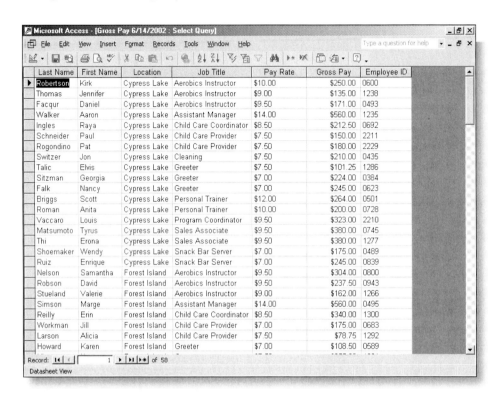

Figure 6.28

Now you are ready to create the new report by changing the record source. To do this you modify the report properties. A quick way to access the report properties is by clicking the Report Selector box located at the intersection of the rulers in the upper left corner of the Report Design window.

2 ● Close the query and
display the Report
Design window.

● Double click
Report Selector.

● Open the All tab.

Another Method

When no other objects in the
report are selected, you can
use <u>V</u>iew/<u>P</u>roperties or the
shortcuts F4 or 🖺 to open
the Report Properties dialog
box.

*Your screen should be
similar to Figure 6.29*

Figure 6.29

The All tab of the properties sheet for the report properties displays a list of
all properties associated with the report. The Record Source property identifies the Gross Pay 6/28/2002 query as the current source. You want to
change this to the new query. You will also change the report caption to reflect the change in the source. The caption appears in the title bar when the
report is previewed. Then you will save the new report and preview it.

3

- **Change the Record Source to** Gross Pay 6/14/2002.

- **Change the Report Caption to** Gross Pay 6/14/2002.

- **Close the Report Properties box.**

- **Change the date in the report title to** 6/14/2002.

- **Save the report as** Gross Pay for 6/14/2002.

- **Preview all pages of the new report.**

- **Display the Grand total on the last page.**

Your screen should be similar to Figure 6.30

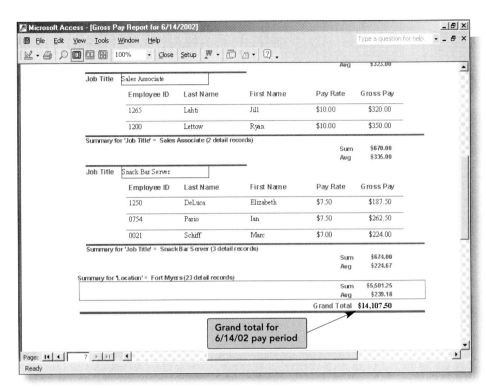

Figure 6.30

The report displays the information from the Gross Pay 6/14/2002 query. The total gross pay for this period was $14,107.50 as compared to the total gross pay of $14,472.50 for the 6/28/2002 period.

After seeing the two reports, the Club owners have asked that the second-period report include the total gross pay for the month of June. To provide this information, you will add a calculated control to the end of the 6/28/2002 report.

Using Calculated Controls in a Report

A calculated control works the same way in a report as it does in a form - you enter an expression into it that calculates values from other controls in the report or its underlying table or query, or from another report and it displays the results of that expression.

Creating a Text Box Control

Because you want the calculated control to display the monthly gross pay at the end of the 6/28/2002 report, you will add a text box control below the Grand Total field in the Report Footer section of the report. Just as in a form, text box controls are used to display data from a record source like the controls in the Detail section do, or to display any other data.

1 ●
- **Open and display the Gross Pay for the 6/28/2002 report in Design view.**

- **Increase the size of the Report Footer section by dragging the bottom border of the report down.**

- **Click** 🔲 **Text Box and place the new control under the Grand Total label control.**

- **Change the label caption to** June Gross Pay.

- **Size the label to fit.**

- **Move the new text controls so they are aligned with the Grand Total controls above them.**

Your screen should be similar to Figure 6.31

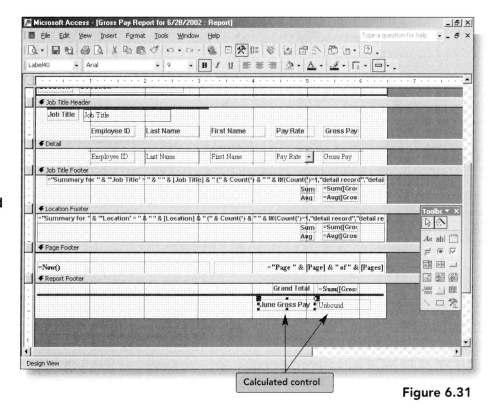

Calculated control

Figure 6.31

The calculation you will enter in this control will report the total gross pay for the month by adding the total gross pay for this pay period to the total gross pay for the previous period.

Summing Across Reports

As you did when adding calculated controls to your customized form, you will use the Expression Builder to help you enter the monthly gross pay calculation you want to include in the report. The expression will add the Gross Pay data from this report to the Total Gross Pay data in the new Gross Pay 6/14/2002 report.

1
- **Open the Properties dialog box for the June Gross Pay text control.**

- **Type** June Total **in the Name field.**

- **Click in the Control Source text box and click** ... **to open the Expression Builder.**

- **Enter the following calculation:** =[Gross Pay Grand Total Sum]+Reports![Gross Pay Report for 6/14/2002]![Gross Pay Grand Total Sum].

Additional Information

You can type some or all of the calculation directly in the expression box, or build the calculation by selecting the appropriate operator buttons and/or expression elements, or use a combination of both methods.

HAVING TROUBLE?

If you need help entering the calculation, review the section "Using the Expression Builder" in Lab 5.

- **Click**  .

- **Close the Properties dialog box.**

Your screen should be similar to Figure 6.32

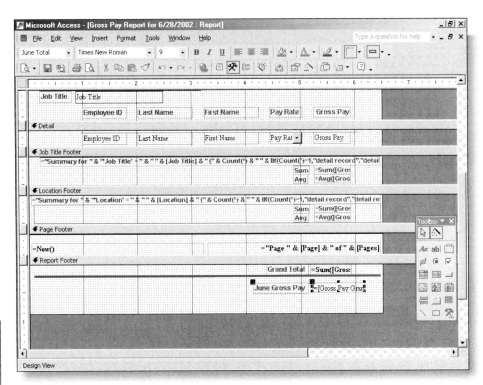

Figure 6.32

You have entered the calculated control and you can now check to see if and how it works in the report. The report to which the expression refers must be open in order for the value to be calculated.

2 ● **Switch to Print Preview.**

● **Display the Grand Total and June Grand Totals in the last page of the report.**

Your screen should be similar to Figure 6.33

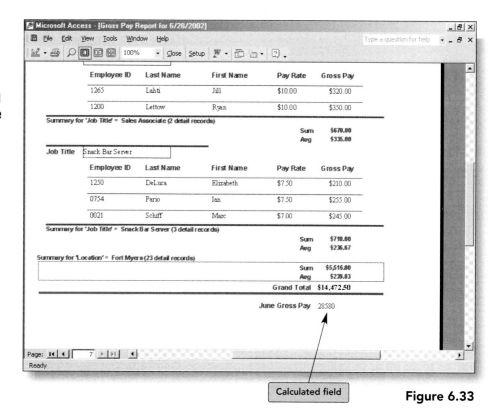

Calculated field

Figure 6.33

It looks like the calculated control has calculated the June gross pay value just fine. However, it is not displayed as currency. You would like to fix that, and also adjust the size and color so the calculated data matches the rest of the report layout.

● Display Report Design view.

● Display the Properties box for the June Gross Pay text control.

● Change the Format property to Currency and close the Properties box.

● Bold the text control.

● Apropriately size and align the June Gross Pay label and text box controls.

● Add two 3-point-weight blue lines below the June Gross Pay controls.

● Preview the last page of the report again.

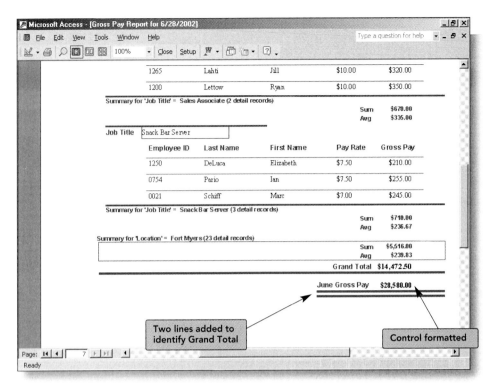

Figure 6.34

Your screen should be similar to Figure 6.34

You are now ready to print the report.

Printing a Grouped Report

Before you print your new grouped report, you want to preview it and make sure there are no further changes you need to make to it.

1 ● **Display page 1.**

● **Click** ▦ **Two Pages to change the preview to display two pages.**

● **Scroll through the entire report.**

● **If necessary, return to Design view to correct the size and placement of any controls, then preview the report again.**

Your screen should be similar to Figure 6.35

Displays 2 pages

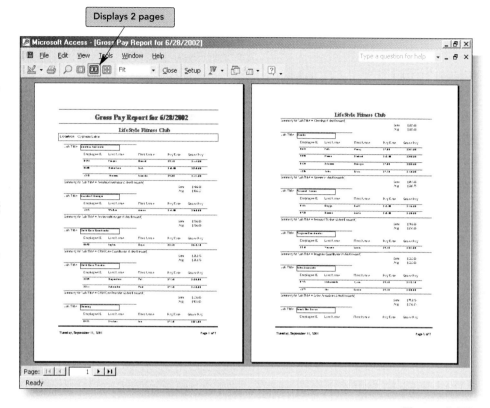

Figure 6.35

You are satisfied with the way the report looks, so you will print and then close it.

2 ● **Print pages 1, 2, and 7 of the report.**

● **Close both reports, saving any changes.**

Creating Mailing Labels

The final report that the Club owners have requested is one that will print mailing labels for every employee. A sample of a mailing label appears below:

Brian Birch
742 W. Lemon Dr.
Fort Myers, FL 33301-1268

Using the Label Wizard

You will use the **Label Wizard** to create the Club employee mailing labels.

1 • Click  and select Label Wizard from the New Report dialog box.

• Select Employees from the Choose the table... drop-down list.

• Click <u>OK</u>.

Your screen should be similar to Figure 6.36

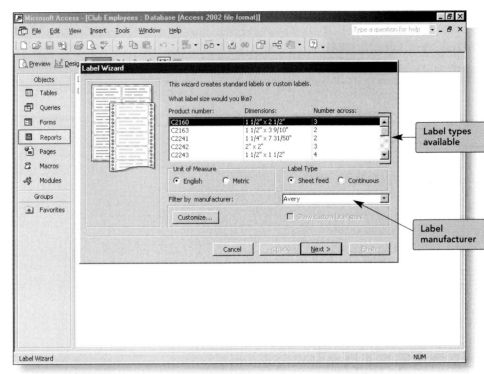

Figure 6.36

In the first Label Wizard dialog box, you specify the type of label you want to create. You can either use a predefined label or create a custom label. The Lifestyle Fitness Club uses predesigned mailing labels made by Avery, number C2160. These labels appear three across the width of the paper.

2 • If necessary, select English as the Unit of Measure.

• Select Avery from the Filter by Manufacturer drop-down list.

• Select C2160 under the Product number.

• Click <u>Next ></u>.

Your screen should be similar to Figure 6.37

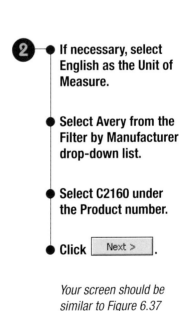

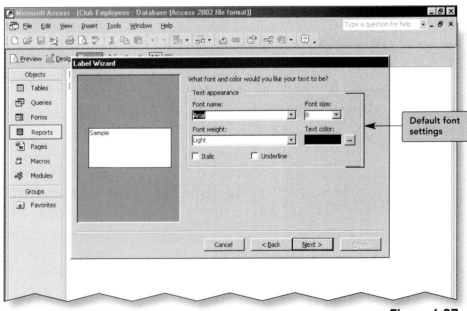

Figure 6.37

In this dialog box, you specify the font and text color settings for the labels. The default font is Arial and the default font size is 8. Because the Label Wizard remembers previous selections, your font size may be different.

3 ● **If necessary, change the font size to 9.**

● **Click** Next > .

Your screen should be similar to Figure 6.38

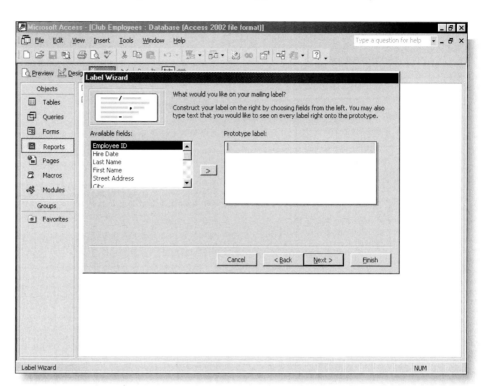

Figure 6.38

Just as with other reports, you select the fields from the table to include in the labels. Unlike other reports, however, as you select the fields, you also design the label layout in the Prototype Label box. You may type any additional text, such as punctuation or a holiday message, directly onto the prototype.

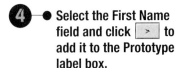

4 ● Select the First Name field and click ⟩ to add it to the Prototype label box.

Another Method

You can also double-click a field name to add it to the label prototype.

Your screen should be similar to Figure 6.39

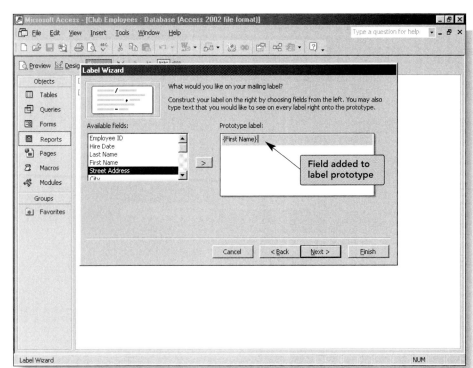

Figure 6.39

The First Name field is displayed in the Prototype label box. You want the last name to be on the same line as the first name, separated from the first name by a space. The address will then be entered on the next line.

5 ● Press Spacebar.

● Add the Last Name field to the label prototype.

● Press ←Enter.

● Add the Street field to the prototype and press ←Enter.

● Add the City followed by a comma and a space, the State followed by two spaces, and the Zip Code.

Your screen should be similar to Figure 6.40

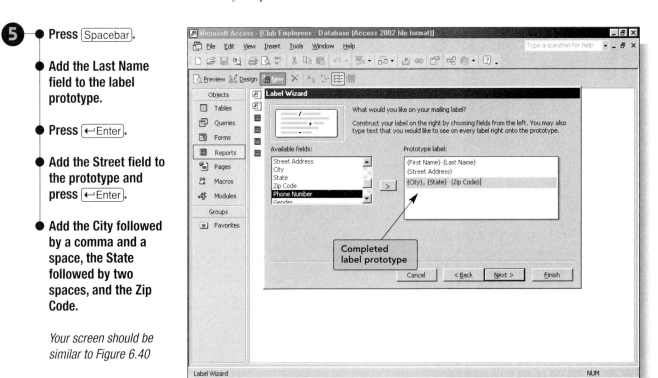

Figure 6.40

You are finished designing the label prototype and are ready to proceed with the label creation.

 Click Next > .

*Your screen should be
similar to Figure 6.41*

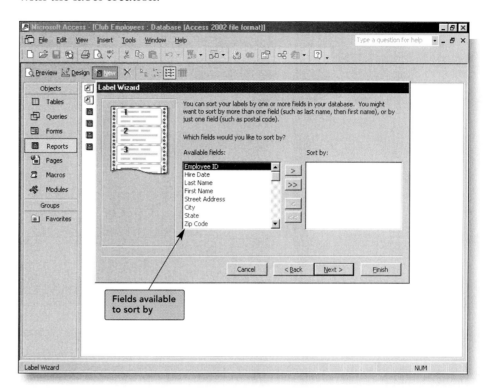

Fields available
to sort by

Figure 6.41

In this dialog box you can specify a field on which to sort the labels. You want to take advantage of postal discounts resulting from mailings that are sorted by zip code. Then you will name, finish, and preview the report.

7

● **Add the Zip Code field to the Sort By list box.**

● **Click** Next > .

● **Enter** Employee Mailing Labels **as the label report name.**

● **Click** Finish .

● **Maximize the Print Preview window.**

Your screen should be similar to Figure 6.42

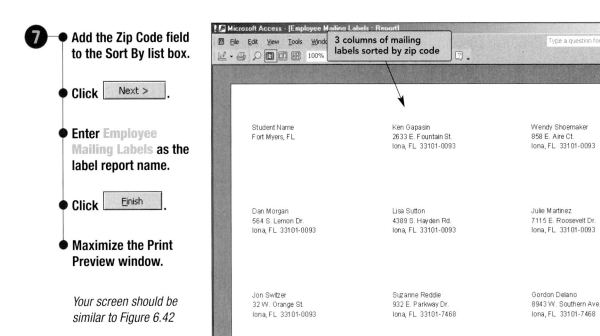

Figure 6.42

Three columns of mailing labels appear across the width of the page. The placement of the labels on the page corresponds to the C2160 Avery labels you selected using the Label Wizard. The labels are also sorted by zip code, from left to right across the rows, then down the page from top to bottom.

Printing Mailing Labels

You will print one page of the mailing labels on standard printer paper just to see what they look like. For an actual Club employee mailing, you would print them on Avery C2160 labels (the type of label you specified in the Label Wizard).

1

● **Print the page of labels that displays your name.**

● **Close the mailing labels report.**

Using Macros

By now, you have created database tables, forms, and reports that contain various types of data about the Lifestyle Fitness Club employees. You want to make it as easy as possible for users of this database to access the objects they need and view or print them as necessary, so you decide to incorporate several macros in the database.

3 A **macro** automates common database tasks, such as opening and printing tables, forms, and reports. To create a macro, you enter a series of actions that you want Access to perform. An **action** is a self-contained instruction that can be combined with other actions to automate tasks. In addition, you specify the arguments associated with the action. An **argument** provides additional information on how the action is to be carried out.

Once a macro is created, you can run it from the Macros section of the Database window. You can also attach a macro to a command button on a form or create a custom menu command or toolbar button that will execute the macro.

When a macro is run, Access starts at the beginning of the macro and performs all the specified actions in order until it reaches the end of the macro or, if the macro is part of a group of macros, the next macro in the group.

Creating a Macro

The first macro you want to create is one that will automate the most common action someone entering Club employee data will have to take—opening the Employee Update Form and maximizing its view window.

1 • Click [2 Macros] on the Objects bar.

• Click [2 New].

• If necessary, maximize the window.

Your screen should be similar to Figure 6.43

Macro Design window is empty because the macro does not contain any actions yet

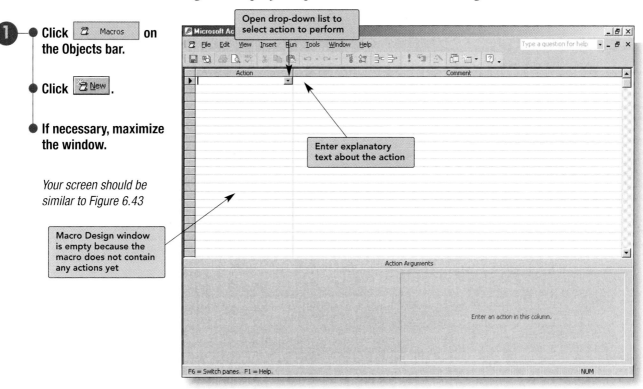

Figure 6.43

The Macro Design view window is used to specify the action you want the macro to perform. Because you have not defined the macro actions yet, the table is blank. To create a new macro, you select the actions you want it to perform from the pull-down list in the Action column and enter any explanatory information you want to include about each action (such as its purpose) in the Comment column. You enter any arguments associated with the selected action (such as the name of the form the macro will open) in the bottom portion of the Macro window.

The first action you want this macro to take is to open the Employee Update Form.

2
- Open the Action column drop-down menu.

- Scroll the Action list and select OpenForm.

- Type **Open Employee Update Form** in the Comment column of the same row.

Your screen should be similar to Figure 6.44

Arguments associated with current action

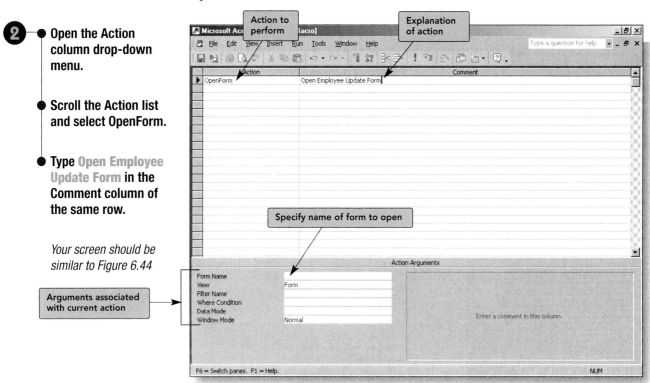

Figure 6.44

Two arguments for the selected action are already displayed in the Action Arguments section of the window. For this action, you also need to specify the name of the form you want to open in the Form Name argument field.

3
- Click in the Form Name field.

Additional Information
When a field is selected, a description of how to use it is displayed in the message box in the lower right corner of the screen.

- Open the Form Name drop-down menu and select "Employee Update Form" from the list.

Your screen should be similar to Figure 6.45

Form will open in Form view

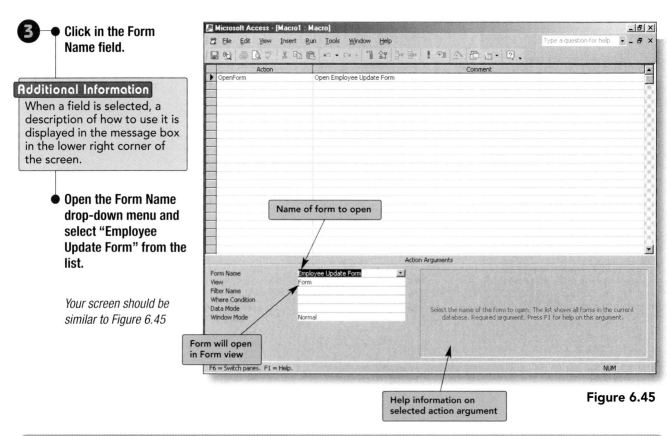

Figure 6.45

The last action you want this macro to perform is to maximize the table window. This action does not have any arguments. Then you will save the macro.

4 • In the second row of the Action column, select Maximize from the drop-down list.

• Type **Maximize window** in the Comment column.

• Click 🖫 Save.

• Enter **Open Employee Update Form** as the name for this macro.

• Click [OK].

Your screen should be similar to Figure 6.46

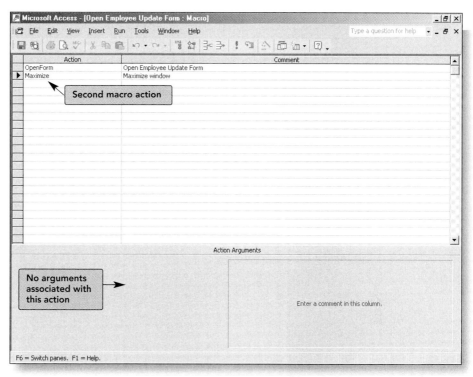

Figure 6.46

Running a Macro

Now you want to run the macro to see how it works.

5 • Close the Macro window.

• With the "Open Employee Update Form" macro selected, click [⚡ Run].

Another Method
The menu equivalent is Tools/Macro/Run Macro

Your screen should be similar to Figure 6.47

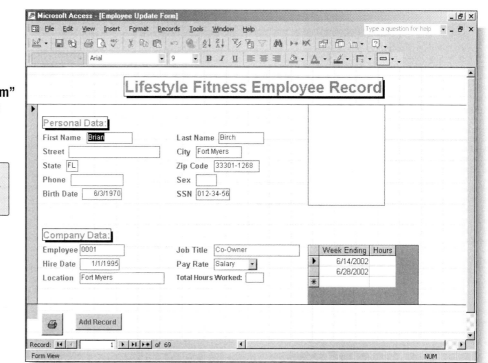

Figure 6.47

The Employee Update Form is opened in Form view and maximized.

Next you will create a macro to preview the form. Since the only difference between the macros is the specification for the action, you can just copy and then edit the macro.

Copying and Editing Macros

You will use Copy and Paste to copy the first macro you created, and then change the actions and arguments to correspond with what you want this macro to do.

1 ● Close the form.

● With the macro object name selected, click 🔁 Copy.

● Click 📋 Paste.

● Enter the macro name **Preview Employee Update Form**.

● Click [OK].

Your screen should be similar to Figure 6.48

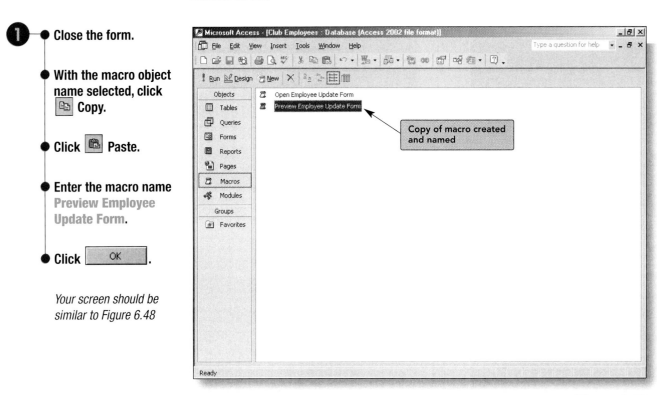

Figure 6.48

The copy of the macro now needs to be edited.

2 ● Click  Design view.

● Change the first comment line to **Preview Employee Update Form**.

● Change the View argument setting to **Print Preview**.

Your screen should be similar to Figure 6.49

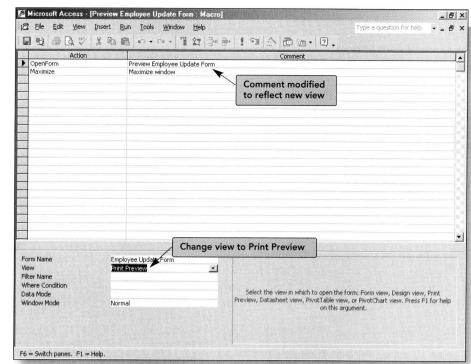

Figure 6.49

The second macro to preview the form is all set up and ready to try out.

3 ● Close and save the macro.

● Run the new macro to test it.

Your screen should be similar to Figure 6.50

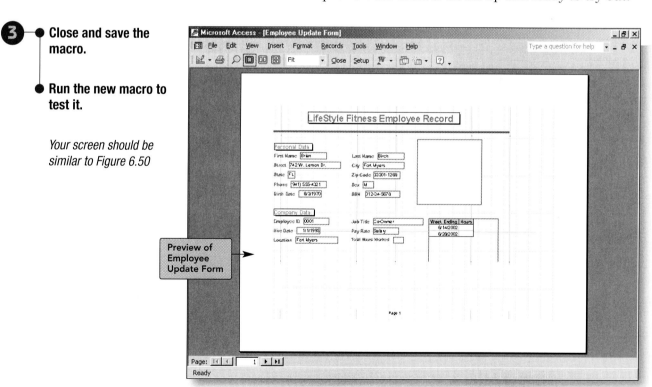

Figure 6.50

The macro automatically opens the Employee Update Form in preview mode. This will be handy when you or someone else just wants to preview and print the form, without making any changes.

Finally, you will create a third macro that will automatically print the mailing labels, without the user even having to open the report. Because this macro is slightly different from the other two, you will create it from scratch (rather than copying and editing an existing macro).

4
● Click ☒ to close the Employee Update Form.

● Click 🔂 New.

● Select OpenReport as the first action.

● Type **Print Employee Mailing Labels** as the first comment.

● From the Report Name argument field, select "Employee Mailing Labels."

● Save the macro as **Print Employee Mailing Labels**.

Your screen should be similar to Figure 6.51

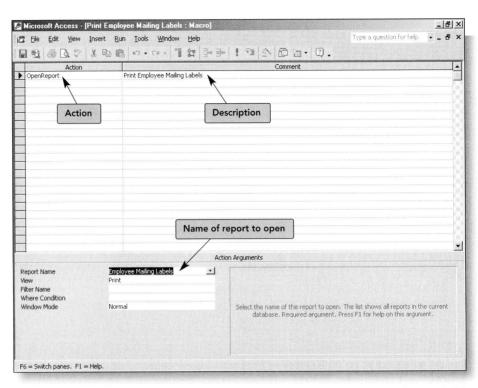

Figure 6.51

You will not test this macro as it will automatically print a copy of the entire Employee Mailing Labels Report.

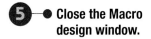

5 ● **Close the Macro design window.**

Your screen should be similar to Figure 6.52

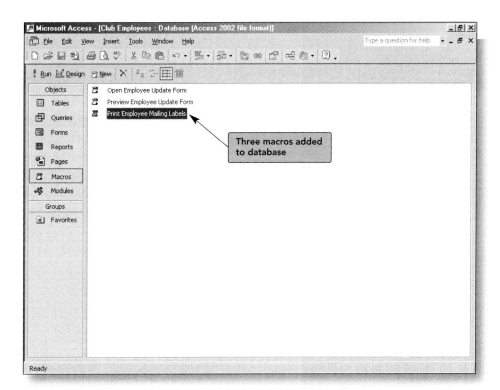

Three macros added to database

Figure 6.52

Users of this database can now open and preview the update form and print mailing labels by running the appropriate macros from the Macro section of the Objects bar.

Using a Switchboard

You want to provide the users of the Club Employees database with a way to easily navigate through the database objects, selecting what they want from one central "menu." You will do this by creating a switchboard of easy-to-use commands.

concept 4

4 A **switchboard** is a form that contains command buttons for performing a variety of actions in a database, such as viewing forms and reports, running macros, opening other switchboards, and exiting the application.

Each switchboard is called a **switchboard page**. You use the **Switchboard Manager** to create and modify switchboard pages. When you first use the Switchboard Manager, a Main Switchboard page is automatically created. You can put all the command buttons on this one page, or you can create individual switchboard pages that divide the command buttons by category and then use the Main Switchboard to access these pages. For example, you could create a switchboard page called View Tables that contains buttons for opening the tables in the database, and then place a View Tables button on the Main Switchboard that would take you to this page. You could use View Forms and View Reports switchboard pages in the same way.

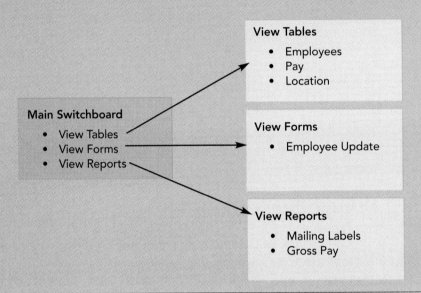

You decide to create separate switchboard pages for your table, form, and report macros and then add buttons to the Main Switchboard for each page. This will enable the database user to select the desired category and switch to the page that contains the items for that category.

Creating Switchboard Pages with the Switchboard Manager

To begin creating switchboard pages, you need to open the Switchboard Manager.

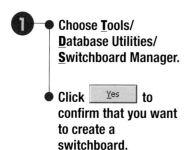

1 • Choose **T**ools/
Database Utilities/
Switchboard Manager.

• Click [Yes] to
confirm that you want
to create a
switchboard.

*Your screen should be
similar to Figure 6.53*

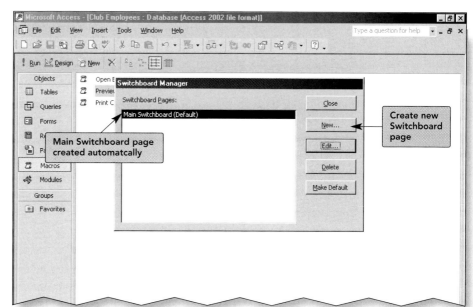

Create new
Switchboard
page

Main Switchboard page
created automatcally

Figure 6.53

The Switchboard Manager is opened with a Main Switchboard page
created automatically. You will edit this switchboard page to contain the
buttons for the individual switchboard pages shortly. First you will create
two new pages; one for forms and the other for reports.

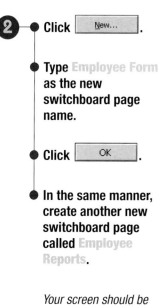

2 • Click [New...].

• Type Employee Form
as the new
switchboard page
name.

• Click [OK].

• In the same manner,
create another new
switchboard page
called Employee
Reports.

*Your screen should be
similar to Figure 6.54*

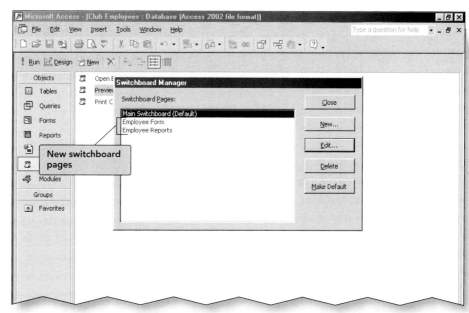

New switchboard
pages

Figure 6.54

The new switchboard pages are displayed in the Switchboard Manager dialog box. Next you will add the command buttons you want each switchboard page to contain.

Adding and Editing Switchboard Items

The first page you will work on is the Employee Form switchboard. You will add three new items to this switchboard page.

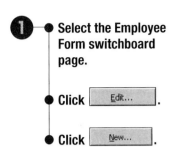

- Select the **Employee Form** switchboard page.

- Click 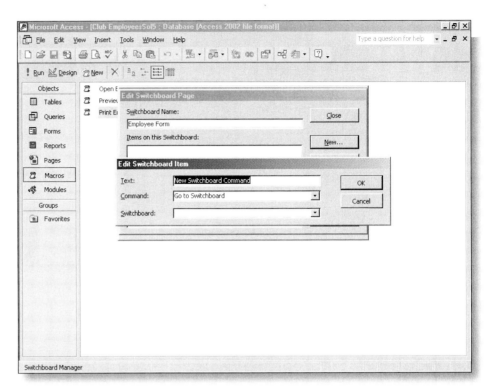 Edit...

- Click New....

Your screen should be similar to Figure 6.55

Figure 6.55

You use the Edit Switchboard Item dialog box to name your new item and select the action you want it to perform, or to change the name or action of an existing switchboard item. Because you already created macros to open and preview the Employee Update Form you will use these as the items in your switchboard. This way, when the user selects one of these items, the corresponding macro will be executed automatically.

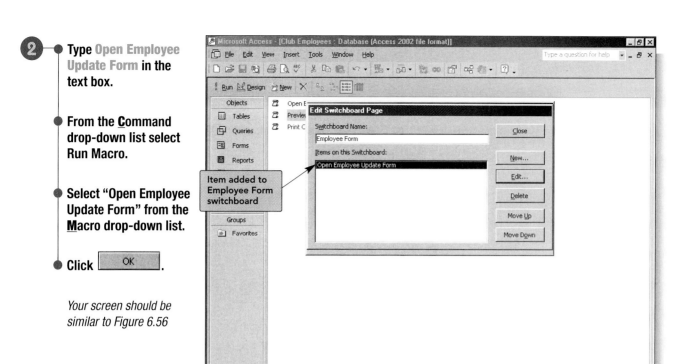

2 ● Type **Open Employee Update Form** in the text box.

● From the **C**ommand drop-down list select Run Macro.

● Select "Open Employee Update Form" from the **M**acro drop-down list.

● Click [OK].

Your screen should be similar to Figure 6.56

Figure 6.56

You have created your first switchboard item. Next you will add the Preview Employee Update Form macro as a second item on this switchboard page.

3 ● Repeat the same procedure to create a second item to preview the Employee Update Form using the appropriate macro.

Your screen should be similar to Figure 6.57

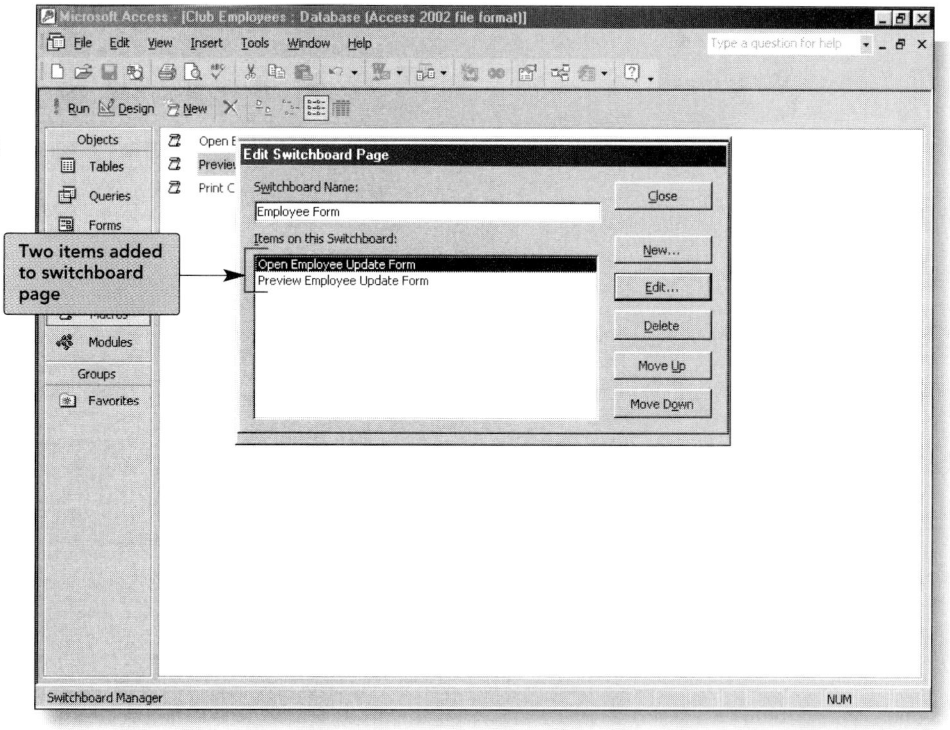

Figure 6.57

The switchboard page now contains two items that will run the macros. You also want to include an item that will allow the user to return to the Main Switchboard from this switchboard page.

4 ● Click [New...].

● Name the switchboard item **Return to Main Switchboard**.

● Leave the default **C**ommand selection, Go To Switchboard, as is.

● From the **S**witchboard drop-down list select Main Switchboard.

● Click [OK].

Your screen should be similar to Figure 6.58

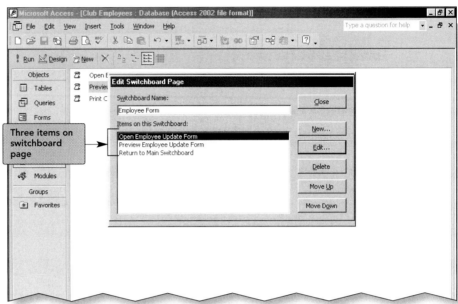

Figure 6.58

You are done adding items to the Employee Form switchboard page.

Next you will add items to the Employee Reports switchboard page. First you will add the report macros as you did on the previous switchboard page.

5 ● Click [Close] to close the Edit Switchboard Page dialog box.

● Select the Employee Reports switchboard page.

● Click [Edit...].

● Click [New...] and name the switchboard item **Print Employee Mailing Labels**.

● From the **C**ommand drop-down list select Run Macro.

● From the **M**acro drop-down list select "Print Club Employees Mailing Labels."

● Click [OK].

Your screen should be similar to Figure 6.59

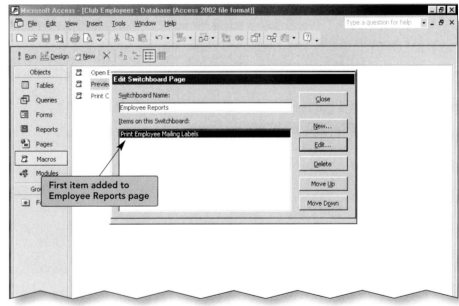

Figure 6.59

In addition you want the users to be able to open the address labels report from this page. This item does not have a macro associated with it.

6

- Click [New...].

- Name the switchboard item Open Employee Mailing Labels.

- From the **C**ommand drop-down list select Open Report.

- From the Report drop-down list select "Employee Mailing Labels."

- Click [OK].

- Add a last item to the Employee Reports page that will return to the Main Switchboard.

Your screen should be similar to Figure 6.60

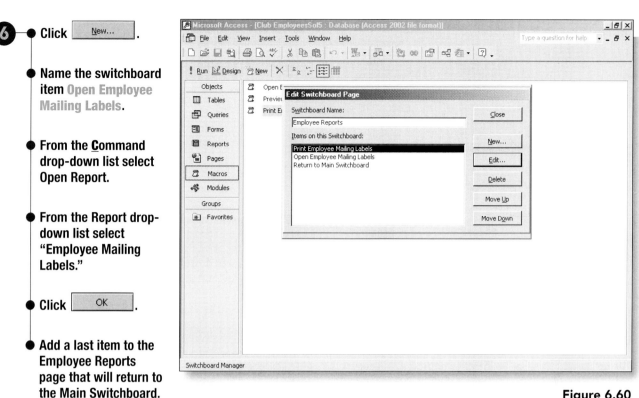

Figure 6.60

You are now ready to add items to the Main Switchboard that will allow users to switch to the pages you just created.

Adding Items to the Main Switchboard

You add items to the Main Switchboard in the same way you do other switchboard pages. The first two items you want to add are command buttons that will open the Employee Form and Employee Reports switchboard pages.

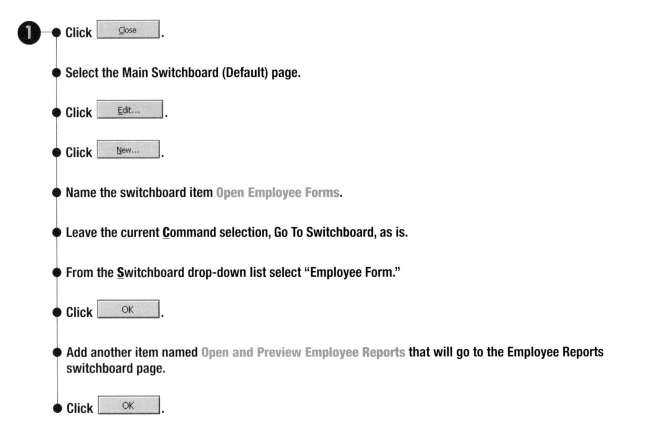

1 ● Click [Close].

● Select the Main Switchboard (Default) page.

● Click [Edit...].

● Click [New...].

● Name the switchboard item Open Employee Forms.

● Leave the current **C**ommand selection, Go To Switchboard, as is.

● From the **S**witchboard drop-down list select "Employee Form."

● Click [OK].

● Add another item named Open and Preview Employee Reports that will go to the Employee Reports switchboard page.

● Click [OK].

Additional Information

You can rearrange the order of items on a switchboard using the [Move Up] and [Move Down] buttons.

There are now two items on the Main Switchboard. You want to add a final item to this switchboard that will close the switchboard and the database.

2 ● Click New....

● Name the switchboard item Close Database.

● From the Command drop-down list select Exit Application.

● Click OK.

● Click Close to close the Edit Switchboard Page dialog box.

● Click Close to exit the Switchboard Manager.

● Click ▦ Tables on the Objects bar.

Your screen should be similar to Figure 6.61

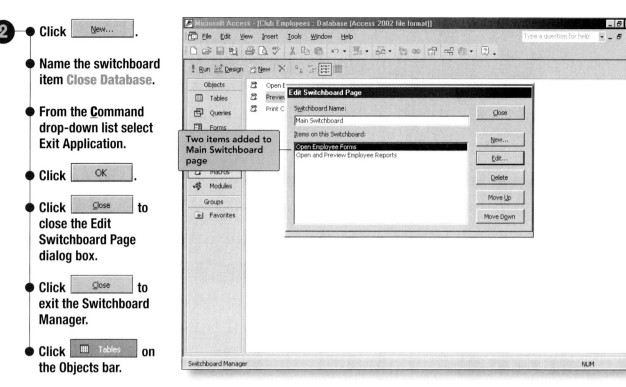

Figure 6.61

You have created a Main Switchboard that will enable users to access the forms and reports in the database from one central location and then close the database when they are through. In addition, a **Switchboard Items table** was automatically created that includes all the items on the Main Switchboard.

3 ● Open the "Switchboard Items" table.

Your screen should be similar to Figure 6.62

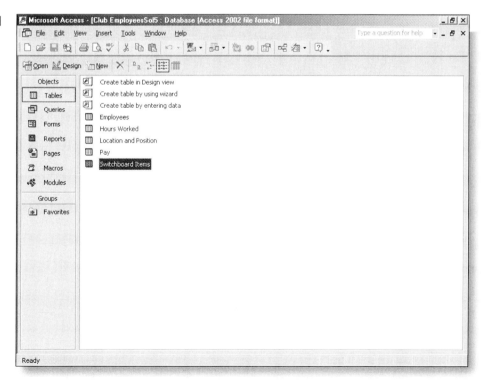

Figure 6.62

The table provides a summary of the items, commands and arguments included in each switchboard page. Because the actual Switchboard pages are forms, they are accessed from the Forms object.

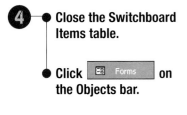

4 ● **Close the Switchboard Items table.**

● **Click** **on the Objects bar.**

Your screen should be similar to Figure 6.63

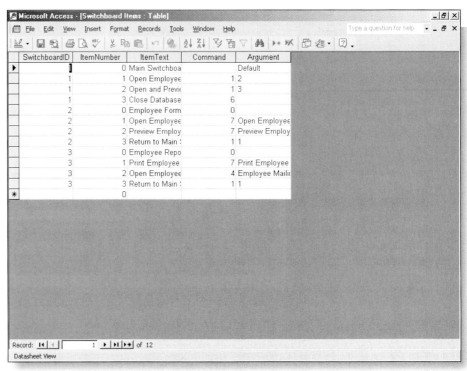

Figure 6.63

Using the Switchboard

To try out the new switchboard, you will use it to view the database items and close the database.

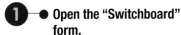

1 ● Open the "Switchboard" form.

Your screen should be similar to Figure 6.64

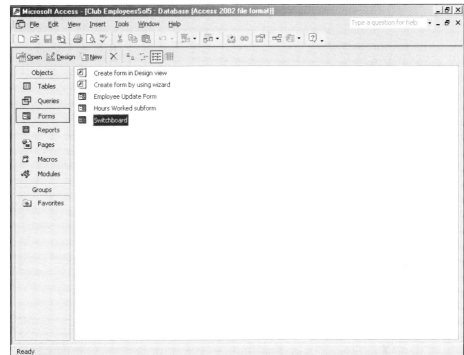

Figure 6.64

The Main Switchboard is displayed with buttons for all the items in it.

2 ● Click the Open Employee Forms button.

Your screen should be similar to Figure 6.65

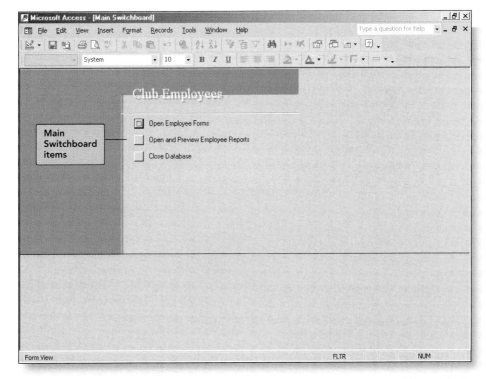

Figure 6.65

The Employee Form switchboard is displayed with buttons to the Employee Update Form and a final button to return to the Main Switchboard. When the user clicks one of the buttons, the corresponding macro will be executed. The user can then work with this form as usual (changing the form design; adding, editing, and deleting records; printing the form; and so on) and close the form when finished to return to the switchboard.

3 ● **Click the Open Employee Update Form button to try it out, and then close the form to return to the switchboard.**

● **Click the Return to Main Switchboard button.**

● **Try out the other buttons on the Main Switchboard and corresponding switchboard pages as desired. (Do not use the Print Employee Mailing Labels or Close Database buttons.)**

● **Return to the Main Switchboard when finished.**

Your screen should be similar to Figure 6.66

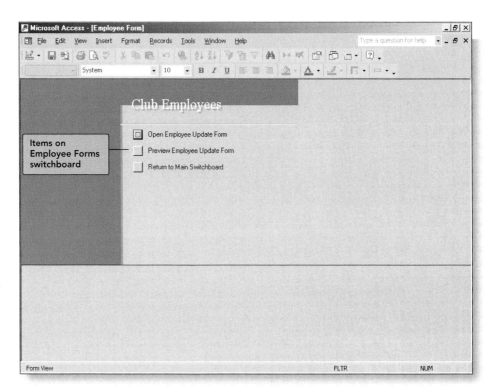

Figure 6.66

Automatically Displaying the Switchboard on Startup

The final adjustment to the switchboard you want to make is to have the Main Switchboard page open automatically when the database is opened rather than the Database window. Access allows you to customize how a database looks and acts when opened.

1 ● **Choose Tools/Startup.**

● **From the Display Form/Page drop-down menu select Switchboard.**

● **Click Display Database Window to clear the checkmark.**

Your screen should be similar to Figure 6.67

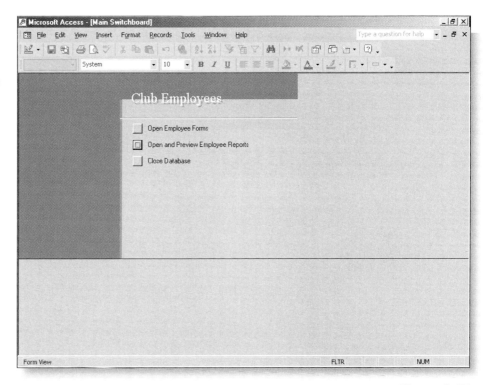

Figure 6.67

The Main Switchboard page will now display automatically when the database is opened, and the Database Window will not display.

2 ● **Click .**

● **Click the Close Database button on the Main Switchboard.**

The Club Employees database is closed.

Securing a Database

Because much of the information in the Club Employee database is confidential in nature, you want to prevent unauthorized users from opening the database. To do this, you can restrict access to the database by requiring that a password be entered in order to open the database. You can also set the database to **exclusive** access. This means that others in a multiuser environment cannot open the database while you are accessing it. Alternatively, you can set it to **multiuser** access, which allows multiple users to access and modify the database at the same time.

First you will change the mode of use to exclusive; then you will add a password to protect the database.

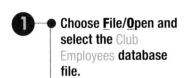

1 ● Choose **F**ile/**O**pen and select the Club Employees **database file.**

● From the ⬚ Open ▾ drop-down menu, select Open Exclusi**v**e.

Additional Information
You need to set the database to exclusive mode each time you open the file.

● Choose **T**ools/Securit**y**/Set **D**atabase Password.

Your screen should be similar to Figure 6.68

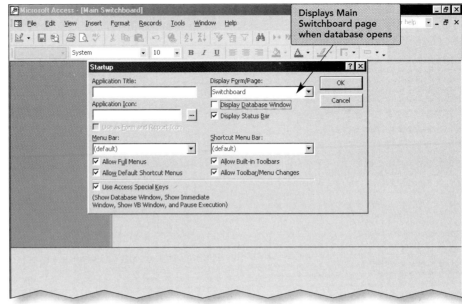

Figure 6.68

The database opens with the Main Switchboard window open automatically.

Additional Information
You can remove a password by opening the Database in Exclusive use and choosing **T**ools/Securit**y**/Unset **D**atabase Password.

You enter your password in the Password box and then confirm the password by entering it again in the Verify box. Because passwords are case sensitive, you must enter it using exactly the same capitalization each time. As you enter the password, asterisks are displayed instead of the characters you type to further ensure the privacy of your password.

2 ● Enter and then verify your first name as the password for the database file.

● Click ⬚ OK ⬚.

● Compact and repair the database file.

● Close the database and reopen it by entering your password in the Password Required dialog box.

● Close the database.

Your screen should be similar to Figure 6.69

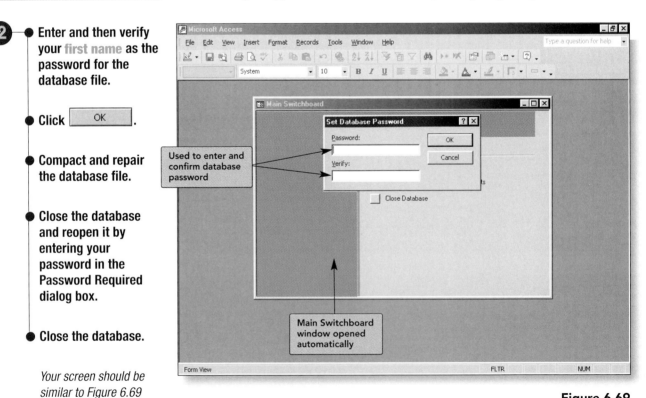

Figure 6.69

Using Database Wizards

You have created, edited, and used tables, queries, forms, reports, macros, and switchboards while creating the Club Employees database. You created many of the objects from scratch or with the help of one of the Access Wizards. In addition to the Wizards you have used, Access includes 10 Database Wizards that you can use to help create complete databases for different types of applications. To see the Database Wizards that are available.

Additional Information

More templates are available on the Microsoft Web site by clicking 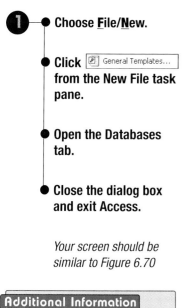 Templates on Microsoft.com .

1 ● Choose **F**ile/**N**ew.

● Click 🗐 General Templates... from the New File task pane.

● Open the Databases tab.

● Close the dialog box and exit Access.

Your screen should be similar to Figure 6.70

Additional Information

Try out a Database Wizard by completing the Access Project on page AC6.74.

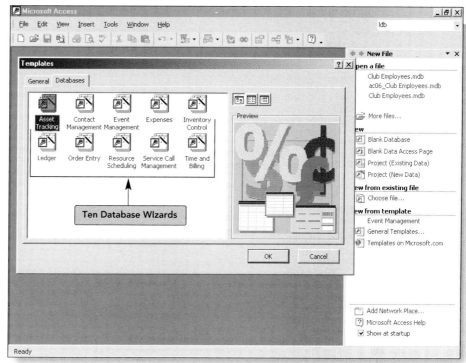

Figure 6.70

Each of the Wizards creates a database that is specifically designed for the selected type of application. They include predesigned tables, forms, reports, macros, and switchboards. You can then refine the database to meet your needs. Using the Database Wizards gives you a head start on creating many common types of databases.

Creating Custom Reports, Macros, and Switchboards

Grouping Records (AC6.8)

Records in a report can be **grouped** into categories to allow you to better analyze the data.

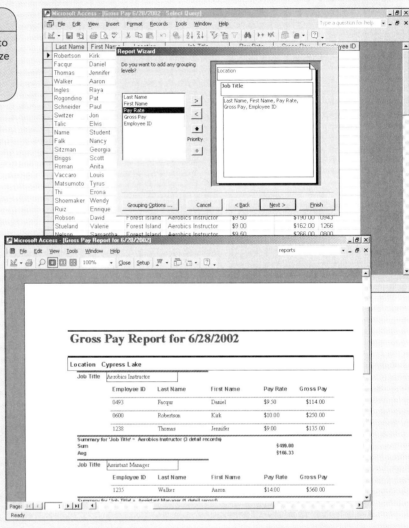

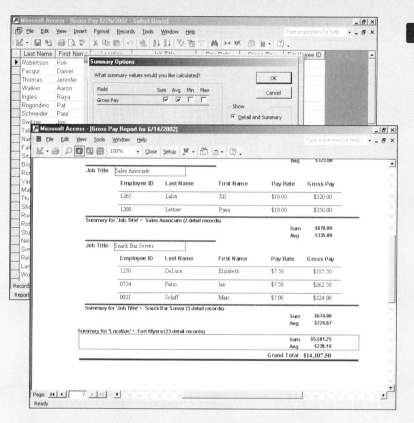

Group Calculations (AC6.10)

If you group data in your report, you can perform **group calculations** on values, such as a group total, an average, a minimum value, and a maximum value.

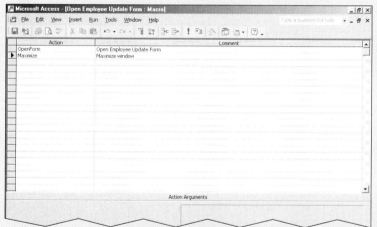

Macro (AC6.37)

A **macro** automates common Access database tasks, such as opening and printing tables, forms, and reports.

Switchboard (AC6.44)

A **switchboard** is an Access form that contains command buttons for performing a variety of actions in a database, such as viewing forms and reports, running macros, opening other switchboards, and exiting the application.

LAB 6

Creating Custom Reports, Macros, and Switchboards

key terms

action   AC6.37
argument   AC6.37
exclusive   AC6.55
group   AC6.8
group calculation   AC6.10
Group Header and
Footer section   AC6.15

macro   AC6.37
multiuser   AC6.55
switchboard   AC6.44
Switchboard Items table   AC6.51
Switchboard Manager   AC6.44
Switchboard page   AC6.44

mous skills

The Microsoft Office User Specialist (MOUS) certification program is designed to measure your proficiency in performing basic tasks using the Office XP applications. Getting certified demonstrates that you have the skills and provides a valuable industry credential for employment. After completing this lab, you have learned the following Microsoft Office User Specialist skills:

Skill	Description	Page
Creating and Using Databases	Creating databases using the Database Wizard	AC6.57
Producing Reports	Create and format reports	AC6.6
	Add calculated controls to reports	AC6.27
	Preview and print reports	AC6.31

command summary

Command	Shortcut	Button	Action
File/**O**pen/<database> Open Exclus**iv**e			Restricts use of database to a single user at one time
Tools/**D**atabase Utilities/ **S**witchboard Manager			Opens Switchboard Manager for creating and editing switchboards
Tools/Securit**y**/ Set **D**atabase Password			Requires entry of password to open database
Tools/Securit**y**/Unset **D**atabase Password			Removes password protection from database
Tools/Start**u**p			Customizes how the database looks and acts when opened
Tools/**M**acro/Run **M**acro			Executes the selected macro commands

Terminology

screen identification

In the following screen, several items are identified by letters. Enter the correct term for each item in the spaces provided.

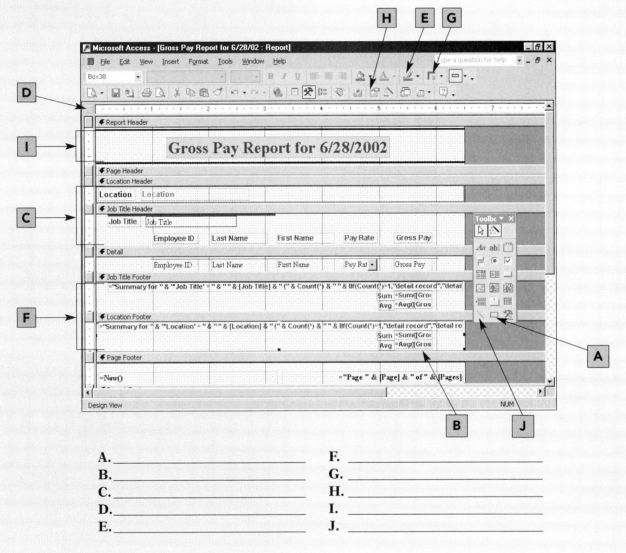

A. _____	F. _____
B. _____	G. _____
C. _____	H. _____
D. _____	I. _____
E. _____	J. _____

matching

Match the item on the left with the correct description on the right.

1. grouped   _____ **a.** provide additional information on how the action is to be carried out

2. switchboard   _____ **b.** self-contained instruction that when combined with others automates tasks

3. group calculations   _____ **c.** calculates the average value for the group

4. exclusive access   _____ **d.** adds all values by group

5. Avg   _____ **e.** data organized on a common attribute

6. arguments   _____ **f.** prevents users in multiuser environment from opening the database while you are accessing it

7. Sum   _____ **g.** refers to the name of each switchboard in a database

8. actions   _____ **h.** allows multiple users to access and modify the same database at the same time

9. multiuser access   _____ **i.** reports grouped on one or more fields can have calculation based on these groups

10. switchboard page   _____ **j.** form that contains command buttons

multiple choice

Circle the letter of the correct answer to the following statements.

1. A(n)_____database allows several users to access and modify the database at the same time.
   a. group
   b. multiuser
   c. exclusive
   d. calculated control

2. _____provide additional information on how an action is to be carried out.
   a. Command buttons
   b. Arguments
   c. Actions
   d. Macros

3. You use the _____to create and modify switchboard pages.
   a. Switchboard Manager
   b. adapter
   c. Switchboard Items table
   d. Switchboard Viewer

4. The _____ section in a grouped report displays the label control for each field column.
   a. Detail
   b. Group
   c. Header
   d. Footer

5. Sum, Avg, Min, and Max are called _____.
   a. macros
   b. calculated controls
   c. group calculations
   d. actions

6. A report can be grouped by as many as _____ fields.
   a. 3
   b. 5
   c. 10
   d. 15

7. Some macro actions require additional information called _____.
   a. parameters
   b. arguments
   c. options
   d. comments

8. A control's _____ affect how the control looks and acts.
   a. control settings
   b. property settings
   c. property attributes
   d. control attributes

9. The report page header prints at the top of _____.
   a. each group
   b. each page
   c. the first page only
   d. the last page only

10. A calculation in a report is entered in a _____.
    a. calculation control
    b. rectangle control
    c. label control
    d. text box control

true/false

Circle the correct answer to the following statements.

1.	You must select one of the predefined labels in the Label Wizard to create a label prototype for a report.	True	False
2.	A grouped report always displays both detailed information and the summary information.	True	False
3.	A password is used to prevent multiple users from accessing a database file at the same time.	True	False
4.	You must enter a comment for every macro action that you select.	True	False
5.	You can group by up to ten fields in any one report.	True	False
6.	A calculated control automatically displays the result of an expression in Number format.	True	False
7.	The Group Header section contains information that changes every time the group changes.	True	False
8.	Groups should be created based on priority from largest to smallest.	True	False
9.	A macro can be created to automate database tasks.	True	False
10.	A switchboard can be used to execute macros.	True	False

Concepts

fill-in

Complete the following statements by filling in the blanks with the correct terms.

1. A(n)_____is an Access form that contains command buttons for performing a variety of actions in a database.

2. _____ should be created based on priority from the largest to the smallest.

3. You can edit a switchboard in the _____ _____ or the _____ _____.

4. _____ can be added to the design of a report to display a calculated value.

5. Changing the _____ on which a report is based displays data from a different source in the report.

6. When you first use the _____, a Main Switchboard page is automatically created.

7. Records can be _____ by categories to allow better analysis of data.

8. To create a macro, you enter a series of _____ that you want Access to perform.

9. You can restrict access to a database with a password or by making it _____.

10. A form that contains command buttons for performing a variety of actions in a database is called a _____.

discussion questions

1. Discuss how grouping records in a report makes the report more meaningful.

2. Discuss how group calculations can be used in a report. Give examples of the kinds of information that could benefit from summary data.

3. Discuss how calculated controls can be used in a report. What types of calculations could you perform?

4. Discuss how macros and switchboards can help automate database operations. Give examples of some operations that could be automated with these tools.

Hands-On Exercises

step-by-step

Adventure Travel Tours Client Mailing Labels

★ **1.** The database that you created for Adventure Travel Tours contains the client and agent tables and forms the manager requested. Now you have been asked to use this data to create some reports. The first report they requested is one that groups the agents by location and lists the clients assigned to each agent. They would also like you to create mailing labels for the clients so they can use them to send out promotional materials. When you are finished, your grouped report and mailing label report will be similar to those shown here.

Agent and Client List

Created by Student Name

Office Location	Denver

Employee ID	112
Name	Mary Cook
Title	Agent
Total Client Count	6

Last Name	First Name
Datla	Dennis
Donato	Richard
Lewis	James
Priest	Mike
Seal	Jerry
Tobler	Greg

Employee ID	113
Name	Rachel Howe
Title	Agent
Total Client Count	13

Last Name	First Name
Fischer	Lydia
Jones	Cortina
Lucas	Lorena
Maltos	Trent
McCless	Ernest
Miller	Cindy
Mombeau	Erik
Momen	Ahmed

Thursday, October 18, 2001

Troy Muller
595 W. Evergreen Dr.
Arvada, CO 80002

Nellie Hesse
111 Chestnut Ave.
Arvada, CO 80002

Jhashkar Makineni
409 Seaside Ct.
Arvada, CO 80002

Ahmed Momen
973 Josephine Ave.
Arvada, CO 80002

David Khalsa
1023 Oak Dr.
Arvada, CO 80002

Gerald Crabill
605 Trenton Way
Arvada, CO 80002

Chris Wohltman
910 N. Lewis Ave.
Arvada, CO 80002

Katherine Gryder
386 E. 5th St.
Arvada, CO 80002

Rudolph Zeh
405 Seaside Ct.
Arvada, CO 80002

Hans Scherer
1134 Jackson Ave
Arvada, CO 80003

Gustavo Shams
211 Forest Ave.
Arvada, CO 80003

Lydia Fischer
395 Colfax St.
Arvada, CO 80003

Jennifer Davner
1932 Evergreen Dr.
Arvada, CO 80003

Miguel Wersal
318 2nd St.
Arvada, CO 80003

Richard Donato
1256 Sheridan Rd.
Arvada, CO 80004

Kathy Weiss
678 S. University
Arvada, CO 80004

Keith Jones
598 Trenton Way
Arvada, CO 80004

Marylou Chrys
297 Byron Dr.
Arvada, CO 80004

a. Open the Clients & Agents database (which you last updated in Step-by-Step Exercise 1 of Lab 5).

b. Use the Report Wizard to create a new report. Add the Office Location, Employee ID, FirstName, LastName, and Title fields (in that order) from the Agents table, and then add the Client ID, First Name, and Last Name fields from the Clients table. View the data by Agents and group the report by Office Location and Title. Sort the Client records by Last Name and then by First Name. Use the Align Left 2 layout in Portrait orientation. Use the Compact style and enter the report name, Agent and Client List.

c. Switch to Report Design view and make the following changes:
- Change the OfficeLocation label caption to Office Location.
- Change the First Name label caption to Name. Size the control to fit. Move the text control closer to the label control.
- Delete the Last Name label control. Move the Last Name text control up to the same line and next to the First Name text control.

d. Below the agent name in the Employee ID Header section, add a conrol to count the number of clients assigned to each agent. Change the control caption to Client Count. Size the controls appropriately. In the Report Footer, add another calculated control to display the total number of clients. Change the control caption to Total Client Count.

e. Open the Clients table and assign agents from the appropriate locations to each of the clients that does not yet have an Agent assignment. Preview the report.

f. Apply font color, fill color, line, and border colors to the report as you like. Adjust the formatting as required.

g. Expand the Page Header section and add a label that reads Created by your name. Format the label as necessary.

h. Print the first and last pages of the report. Save and close it.

i. To create the mailing labels start the Label Wizard and use the Clients table. Use the Agipa 119715 labels. (Hint: If you do not see these labels in the product list, check the Unit of Measure and make sure English is selected.) Increase the font size to 10 and the weight to Normal. Create a prototype by adding the name and address fields in the order they would normally appear in an address, including spacing and punctuation where necessary. Sort the labels by zip code, and name the report Client Mailing Labels.

j. Print the first page of labels and then close the report.

k. Close the database.

Animal Rescue Foundation Grouped Report and Mailing Labels

★★ **2.** You have finished creating the tables and forms for the Animal Rescue Foundation database, and you have asked the directors if there is anything in particular they would like to see. In response, they have asked for a report of the current status of all animals. They would also like to be able to quickly create mailing labels from the foster care and adopter table so they can use them to send thank you notes and other correspondence. When you are finished, your customized grouped report and mailing label reports should be similar to those shown here.

Animal Status

Created by Student Name

Status	A
Type	Cat
Quantity	23

Name	Boarded Date	Foster Date	Adoption Date	Adopter La...
Fluffy	01/09/2002	01/25/2001	02/12/2002	Samuals
Cally	08/03/2002	08/17/2002	09/30/2002	Castillo
Boris	07/11/2002		07/21/2002	Herrera
Coal	06/26/2002	07/03/2002	08/04/2002	Falano
	05/14/2002	05/20/2002	06/01/2002	Watson
Pinky	05/01/2002		05/20/2002	Lewis
	04/12/2002		04/22/2002	Herrington
Puddy	03/23/2002	04/18/2002	05/15/2002	Wendale
Sky	08/29/2002		09/11/2002	Klinger
	01/21/2002	02/04/2002	04/05/2002	Richards
	11/14/2001		12/24/2001	Richards
	12/06/2001	12/23/2001	01/07/2001	Smalley
Muffin	10/23/2001	10/25/2001	11/08/2001	Granger
Bruiser	09/10/2001		09/20/2001	Falk
	08/20/2001	09/01/2001	10/15/2001	Fadaro
Sylvester	07/18/2001	07/30/2001	09/01/2001	Ehmann
	07/01/2001		07/15/2001	Dodd
Tabby	06/15/2001	06/20/2001	07/01/2001	Candelari
Mew	02/17/2002		03/01/2002	Smith
	10/30/2002		11/30/2002	Snider
	11/15/2002	12/03/2002	01/07/2003	Ehmann
Tom	09/15/2001		09/23/2001	Fulton

10/19/2001

Mailing labels:

Timothy Spehr 800 Maple Dr. Phoenix, AZ 82891-1605	Jane Fadaro 79 S. Central Ave. Phoenix, AZ 82891-1605	Scott Samuals 90 First Ave. Phoenix, AZ 82891-1605
Kurt Ehmann 7867 Forest Ave. Phoenix, AZ 82891-1605	Scott Briggs 45 E. Camelback Rd. Phoenix, AZ 82891-1605	Laurie Lewis 801 Alpha Dr. Phoenix, AZ 82891-1605
James Watson 4232 Tiller Ave. Phoenix, AZ 82891-1605	Daniel Klinger 289 E. Heather Ave. Phoenix, AZ 82891-1605	Student Name 456 Central Ave. Phoenix, AZ 82891-1605
Kurt Ehmann 7867 Forest Ave. Phoenix, AZ 82891-1605	Michael Granger 12 E. 7th St. Phoenix, AZ 82891-1605	Fran Smithson 899 First Ave. Phoenix, AZ 82891-1605
Jane Fadaro 79 S. Central Ave. Phoenix, AZ 82891-1605	Toni Steverson 76 Thomas Rd. Phoenix, AZ 82891-1605	Kimberly Young 1212 S. Central Ave. Phoenix, AZ 82891-1605
Jose Artis 358 Maple Dr. Chandler, AZ 83174-2311	Tom Marvin 67 Birch Lane Chandler, AZ 83174-2311	James Kennedy 5 E. Highland Rd. Chandler, AZ 83174-2311

a. Open the database named ARF Fosters (which you last worked on in Step-by-Step Exercise 2 of Lab 5).

b. Use the Query Wizard to create a new query. From the Animals table add the Status, Type, Name, Boarded Date, Foster Date, and Adoption Date fields. Then select the Adopters table and add the Adopter Last Name field. Name the query **Animal Status**.

c. Use the Report wizard to create a report using all the fields from the Animal Status query. Group the report by Status and then by Type. Do not select any sort fields for this report. Use the Align Left 1 layout in Portrait orientation. Use the Bold style and name the report **Animal Status**.

After looking at the report preview, you see that it needs several layout changes, such as a larger font size for the boarded, foster, and adopter data, as well as increased space between categories so it is easier to read.

d. Switch to Report Design view and make the following changes:

- Move the 10 label and text controls in the Type Header and Detail sections to begin at the .25-inch position and end at the 6.25-inch position. Space and align the controls on the line appropriately (see the figure at the beginning of this exercise). Increase the font size of the controls to 10 and left-justified. Size the label controls to fit.
- Increase the font size of the Status and Type controls to 12. Size and position the controls appropriately.

e. Below the Status controls in the Status Header section, add a control to count the number of animals in each status category. Change the control caption to Number. Size the controls appropriately. In the Report Footer, add another calculated control to display the total number of animals. Change the control caption to Total Number.

f. Change the control property of the Now date control in the Page Footer so it displays in Short Date format.

g. In the Report Header section add a label in 12 point that reads Created by your name. Position the label box as you like.

h. Make any other layout changes you like. Print the first and last pages of the report. Save and close it.

i. You are now ready to create the two mailing label reports that were requested. Use the Label Wizard to create each report, one with name and address fields from the Fosters table and the other with name and address fields from the Adopters table. Use the Avery 3110 label and create a standard mailing label prototype for each. Sort the labels by zip code, and name the first report Foster Care Mailing Labels and the second report Adopters Mailing Labels.

j. In Label Design view, change the font to Times New Roman and 12 point for both label reports. Print the page of labels in the Adopters report that contains your name. Save and close both reports.

k. Close the database.

Simply Beautiful Database Reports

★ ★ **3.** Maria Dell, the owner of the Simply Beautiful spa, is quite pleased with how the database you created for her has automated what used to be quite time-consuming manual record-keeping tasks. She
is particularly pleased with how the data can be used to track the sales of massage packages offered
at the spa. Her most recent request is for a report that shows the spa packages that were purchased
and by whom, as well as the sales total for each package and the total income generated from these
sales. The report will include group calculations as well as a calculated control that will generate the
grand total. The completed grouped report is shown here.

a. Open the Simply Beautiful database file (which you last
worked on in Step-by-Step
Exercise 3 of Lab 5).

b. Use the Report Wizard to create a new report that contains
the Package #, Package Name,
and Description fields from
the Spa Packages table; the
Client No from the Packages
Sold table; and the First Name
and Last Name fields from the
Clients table. Specify that you
want to view the data by
Packages Sold and group the
report by Package Name. Do
not sort on any fields. Use the
Outline 1 layout and the
Casual style. Name the report
Spa Packages Sold.

c. Switch to Report Design view
and make the following
changes: (Refer to the figure
for an example of how the layout can be modified).

- Delete the Package # controls and the Description
label control.
- Move the Description text
control to the right of the
Package name controls.

- Adjust the sizes and position of the Package Name and Description controls.
- Change the color of the Package Name controls to violet.
- Size and reposition the three client controls appropriately. Left-align the text controls.

d. In the Page Footer change the format property of the date control to Short Date.

e. You are now going to add a calculated control to count the number of packages sold. Expand
the Report Footer section and insert a text box control. Change the label caption to Total
Packages Sold, and resize the box to fit the contents. Access the Unbound text control's property settings and use the Expression Builder to create a Count expression that will calculate
the number of packages sold. (Hint: You can use any of the fields in the Detail section of the
report as the Count expression to produce the desired results.)

f. Apply a font size of 12, violet font color, and shadowed special effect for emphasis to the Total Packages Sold labels and text controls. Size and position the Total Packages Sold controls appropriately.

g. Make further enhancements to the report layout as desired (text color, font size and style, special effects). Print the report. Then save and close it.

h. Close the database.

EduSoft Reports and Security

★ ★ **4.** As database manager for the EduSoft Company, you get many requests for reports on software ti-
★   tles, development, sales, and so on from the company's department heads and marketing personnel. For example, you just received a request from the product sales manager to create a report that is grouped by software package number, summarizes the sales of each package, and includes a calculated total of all packages sold. The completed report will look similar to that shown here. There has also been some concern about unauthorized use of the database, so you are going to assign a password that will be given out upon management approval only.

a. Open the EduSoft Titles database (which you last worked on in Step-by-Step Exercise 5 of Lab 5).

b. Create a new report using the Report Wizard and all fields from the "Software Package Sales" query. Group the report by Software Package. Do not select any sort fields. Select the Sum for the Total Packages Sold and Total Sales fields in the Summary Options. Select the layout and style of your choice. Name the report Software Package Sales.

c. In Report Design view make the following changes:
- Change the Total Packages Sold label to # Sold.
- Resize the control boxes for this field as well as any others that are too large or too small.
- Position the Detail text controls and their corresponding label controls appropriately.
- Delete everything in the Software Package Footer and close the Footer space.
- Resize and position the control boxes in the Report Footer so they are in line with their corresponding Detail controls.
- Format the Grand Total controls as you like to make them stand out more.

d. Change the date format in the Page Footer to Short Date. Make any other layout and format changes you wish. Print, save, and close the report.

Software Package Sales

Software Package	Price	Developer	# Sold	Total Sales
15-0101				
	$75.99	Catherine Willis	10	$759.90
15-0201				
	$45.00	Catherine Willis	15	$675.00
15-0202				
	$45.00	Catherine Willis	4	$180.00
15-0301				
	$24.99	Catherine Willis	3	$74.97
15-0502				
	$69.99	Catherine Willis	1	$69.99
	$69.99	Catherine Willis	4	$279.96
15-0602				
	$45.00	Catherine Willis	4	$180.00
15-0603				
	$45.00	Catherine Willis	10	$450.00
24-0103				
	$75.00	Maggie O'Grady	1	$75.00
	$75.00	Maggie O'Grady	10	$750.00
24-0202				
	$119.95	Maggie O'Grady	2	$239.90
24-0302				
	$69.99	Maggie O'Grady	3	$209.97
24-0303				
	$55.00	Maggie O'Grady	3	$165.00
63-0103				
	$84.99	Juana Jimenez	3	$254.97
80-0101				
	$119.99	Ben Hadden	1	$119.99
90-0103				
	$55.00	Student Name	3	$165.00
		Grand Total	77	$4,649.65

9/13/2001   Page 1 of 1

e. Create macros that will open and maximize the tables, forms, and reports in this database. Test the macros after you create them.

f. Create a switchboard page for each object category (tables, forms, etc.) and create a switchboard item that will run each macro in that category. Also include an item on each page that will return to the Main Switchboard page. Edit the Main Switchboard page to include items that will access the other switchboard pages as well as a final item that will close the Main Switchboard and current database. Change the database startup options so the Main Switchboard page is displayed automatically when you open this database.

g. Display the Switchboard Items table. Best fit the columns. Add your name in the Item Text field of the first row. Print the table.

h. Test each switchboard, ending with the Main Switchboard button that closes the database.

i. Reopen the database in exclusive mode and secure the database by assigning a password to it. Close and save the database.

Downtown Internet Cafe Macros and Reports

★★ 5. Evan, the owner of the Downtown Internet Cafe, is finding the database and its tables, forms,
★ queries, and reports that you created quite useful for keeping track of inventory items and order details. In fact, he would like you to create another report that groups orders by vendor, includes product pricing information, and calculates the order costs. You have also been thinking about automating the database even further by creating macros to access its various tables, forms, and so on, as well as a switchboard to centralize the database operations, which you will do after creating the grouped report. Your completed report will be similar to the one shown here.

a. Open the Cafe Purchases database (which you last worked on in Step-by-Step Exercise 4 of Lab 5).

b. Open the "Inventory Order Costs" query. In Query Design view, hide the # On Hand field. (You will not need it for the report.) Run and save the query.

c. Create a new report object from the Query window using the Report Wizard. Add all fields from this query to the report. Group the report by Vendor Name. Do not select any sort fields. Open the Summary Options and select the Sum option for the Order Cost field. Select the layout and style of your choice. Name the report Stock Orders.

d. Switch to Report Design view and make the following changes:
   ■ Change the Order Amount label to Quantity.

Stock Orders

Vendor Name	Description	Contact	Phone	Quantity	Order Cost
S & S Bakery	Scones	Student Name	(909) 555-5599	8	$14.00
			Total Vendor Order		$14.00
Water Beverages, Inc	Earl Grey tea	Mae Yung	(415) 555-1122	7	$385.00
	Orange Pekoe tea	Mae Yung	(415) 555-1122	3	$165.00
			Total Vendor Order		$550.00
Crystal Ceramics	Coffee mugs	Dan O'Dell	(602) 555-1924	12	$4,500.00
			Total Vendor Order		$4,500.00
Pure Processing	Decaf Colombian	Nancy Young	(650) 555-5689	11	$825.00
	Decaf Dark	Nancy Young	(650) 555-5689	9	$675.00
			Total Vendor Order		$1,500.00
Tasty Coffee	Sumatra coffee	Fred Wilmington	(206) 555-9090	10	$750.00
	Colombian coffee	Fred Wilmington	(206) 555-9090	5	$325.00
	Java coffee	Fred Wilmington	(206) 555-9090	8	$600.00
	Kona coffee	Fred Wilmington	(206) 555-9090	9	$1,035.00
	Espresso Roast	Fred Wilmington	(206) 555-9090	14	$1,050.00
	Italian Roast	Fred Wilmington	(206) 555-9090	4	$260.00
	French Roast	Fred Wilmington	(206) 555-9090	11	$715.00
	Guatamala coffee	Fred Wilmington	(206) 555-9090	1	$65.00
			Total Vendor Order		$4,800.00
Restaurant Supply	Coffee filters	Manny Smith	(602) 555-0037	9	$1,035.00
	Cups-large	Manny Smith	(602) 555-0037	12	$1,620.00
			Total Vendor Order		$2,655.00
			Grand Total:		$14,019.00

Wednesday, October 24, 2001   Page 1 of 1

- Fix the size, position, and spacing of all controls in the report so that all data is fully displayed.
- In the Vendor Name Footer, delete the Summary for Vendor Name control. Change the Sum label control to **Total Vendor Order** and move it adjacent to the Sum text control. Add text and fill colors to the controls.
- In the Report Footer, move the Grand Total label control adjacent to the text control.
- Add emphasis to the Grand Total controls by enlarging the font size and applying the same text and fill color as the Vendor summary controls. Size the controls to fit.
- Add other enhancements of your choice to the report.

e. Print, save, and close the report.

f. Create macros that will open and maximize the tables, form, and reports in this database. Test the macros after you create them.

g. Create a switchboard page for each object category (tables, forms, etc.) and create a switchboard item that will run each macro in that category. Also, include an item on each page that will return to the Main Switchboard page. Edit the Main Switchboard page to include items that will access the other switchboard pages as well as a final item that will close the Main Switchboard and current database. Change the database startup options so the Main Switchboard page is displayed automatically when you open this database.

h. Display the Switchboard Items table. Best fit the columns. Add your name in the first row in the Item text field. Print the table.

i. Test each switchboard, ending with the Main Switchboard button that closes the database.

on your own

Lewis & Lewis Mailing Labels

★ 1. The Personnel director at Lewis & Lewis has requested mailing labels in order to distribute information on the company's holiday food drive. Use the Lewis Personnel database you worked on in On Your Own Exercise 3 of Lab 5 to create the desired mailing labels. Create a query that can be used to create mailing labels. Create mailing labels for both employees and consultants. Print the mailing label report.

WriteOn! Query and Mailing Labels

★ 2. The WriteOn! database you worked on in On Your Own Exercise 2 in Lab 5 would be more useful if it also contained a table with contact information for the suppliers. Create a new table that uses the Supplier ID as the key field and address and phone information of each supplier. Enter data into the table. Create a query that can be used to create mailing labels. Create mailing labels for the suppliers. Print the mailing label report.

Associated Dental Reports and Mailing Labels

★★ 3. Part of your job at Associated Dental is to maintain the patient database. You just received a request for a report that groups records by dentist and includes the contact and billing information for the patients assigned to each dentist. You also need to create patient mailing labels for appointment reminders. Open the Patient Information database you updated in On Your Own Exercise 1 of Lab 5 and use the Report Wizard to create a report that includes the dentist name field; the patient name, address, and phone fields; and patient billing fields from the appropriate tables. Group the report by dentist name and sort it by patient last and first names. Make any changes necessary to the report layout to make it easier to read or enhance its appearance. Add a Report Header with the dental office name and a Report Footer with **Created by your name**. Print the first page of the report and then save and close it. Create the mailing label report using the Label Wizard and the patient contact information table. Print the first page of labels and close the report.

JK Enterprise Reports

★★ 4. Your job in the accounting department of JK Enterprises includes updating employee expense
★ records as well as generating reports based on these records. You have recently received a request from the CFO for a report grouped by department that calculates the total expenses for each department and the grand total of expenses incurred to date. Open the JK Enterprises database that you updated in On Your Own Exercise 4 of Lab 5 and the expense query you created earlier. Create a report based on this query that is grouped by department and includes a summary showing the expense totals. Format the report as necessary and/or desired and then print, save, and close the report. Create macros that will open the various tables, forms, queries, and reports in the database. Also, create a switchboard that contains these macros as well as a button to close the database. Change the database startup options to automatically display the Main Switchboard when the database is opened. Finally, secure the database with a password.

Tri-County Little League Reports

★★ 5. The Tri-County Little League is preparing for the upcoming season and would like to use their new
★ database to distribute registration forms to returning players and advertise the league in the local neighborhoods. The Little League chair has requested several reports the administrators will use to advertise the upcoming season. She would like you to provide her with a report that groups addresses by team. She would also like to know the average age of the players by team. Using the Little League database you worked on in On Your Own Exercise 5 of Lab 5, perform group calculations to determine the mean age by team. Add macros to print the reports and open the Players table. Use the Switchboard Manager to create switchboard pages for each of the items you have created thus far. Create mailing labels for the returning players. Print the first page of labels. Secure the database with exclusive access to prevent corruption of the rosters. Complete and save the database.

on the web

Custom Tees Reports

The owner of the online custom T-shirt Web site is happy with the form you created (Custom Tees in the On the Web exercise of Lab 5). Next you have been asked to create a report that groups the T-shirt styles by category. If necessary, add a field to the appropriate table that contains categories for different T-shirt styles (such as monograms, logos, characters, designs, etc.). Create a query with appropriate fields from the database to show the T-shirts in each category. Create a report based on this query that is grouped by category. Reformat the report as necessary and then print and save the report. Create a switchboard that contains options to open, print, and preview the objects in the database. Set the switchboard to open automatically and password-protect the database.

Decorator's Resource Gallery

Olivia Mba is the Customer Service Department Manager at Decorator's Resource Gallery. She has asked you to create a database that employees and sales people can use to enter and maintain customer orders. You will use the Order Entry Database Wizard to create a database that manages customer order information.

1. Use the Order Entry Database Wizard to create the database named DRG Orders Database. Make the following selections from the Wizard dialog box.
   - Add the Notes field to the Customer Information table and add the Home Phone field to the Employees table.
   - Select the Ricepaper style for screen displays.
   - Select the Formal style for the printed reports.
   - Title the database Decorator's Resource Gallery Order Entry. Include a picture on the printed report using the file ac06_Sofa.

2. Enter the information below into the My Company Information form. When you are finished, close the form.

Company	Decorator's Resource Gallery
Address	1328 Mason St.
City	Helena
State	MT
Postal Code	59601
Country Region	US
Phone Number	(406) 555-SOFA
Fax Number	(406) 555-7632

3. Use the switchboard to enter Employee and Product information. (Hint: Use the Enter/View Other Information button.)
   - Enter your name and three additional employee records.
   - Enter the following information into the Products form.

Products	
Product Name	Unit Price
Chelsea Sofa	$1,195.00
Savannah Armoire	$2,495.00
Newport Console	$495.00
Dalton Desk	$2,595.00
Susser Hutch	$3,995.00

   - Decorator's Resource Gallery has an in-house shipping and delivery department. Open the Shipping Methods form and enter In-House.

4. Use the switchboard to view the Orders by Customer form. Enter the following information into the Orders by Customer form.

First Name	Dobrenz
Last Name	Aafedt
Billing Address	8903 Pleasant Valley Dr.
City	Helena
State/Province	MT
Postal Code	59601
Country/Region	US
Phone Number	(406) 555-9212
Notes	Customer would like care and handling information from the manufacturer.
Employee	Your Name
Product	Dalton Desk
Quantity	1
Shipping Method	In-House
Payment Method	Check
Payment Amount	$1,300.00

   e. Enter nine additional Customer Information records. Include notes on the customer's order in at least three records.

   f. Mr. Aafedt has called and requested an additional item. Add a new order to his record.

   g. Print the Sales by Employee report. Save and close the database.

Using Advanced Presentation Features

Objectives

After completing this lab, you will know how to:

1.	Create a new presentation from existing slides.
2.	Create a numbered list.
3.	Use Format Painter.
4.	Create a custom background.
5.	Change the design template.
6.	Modify graphics.
7.	Zoom slides.
8.	Change the stacking order of objects.
9.	Wrap text in an object.
10.	Group, ungroup, and align objects.
11.	Create and modify a chart.
12.	Create and modify an organization chart.
13.	Export an outline to Word.
14.	E-mail a presentation.
15.	Rehearse timings.
16.	Prepare overheads or 35mm slides.

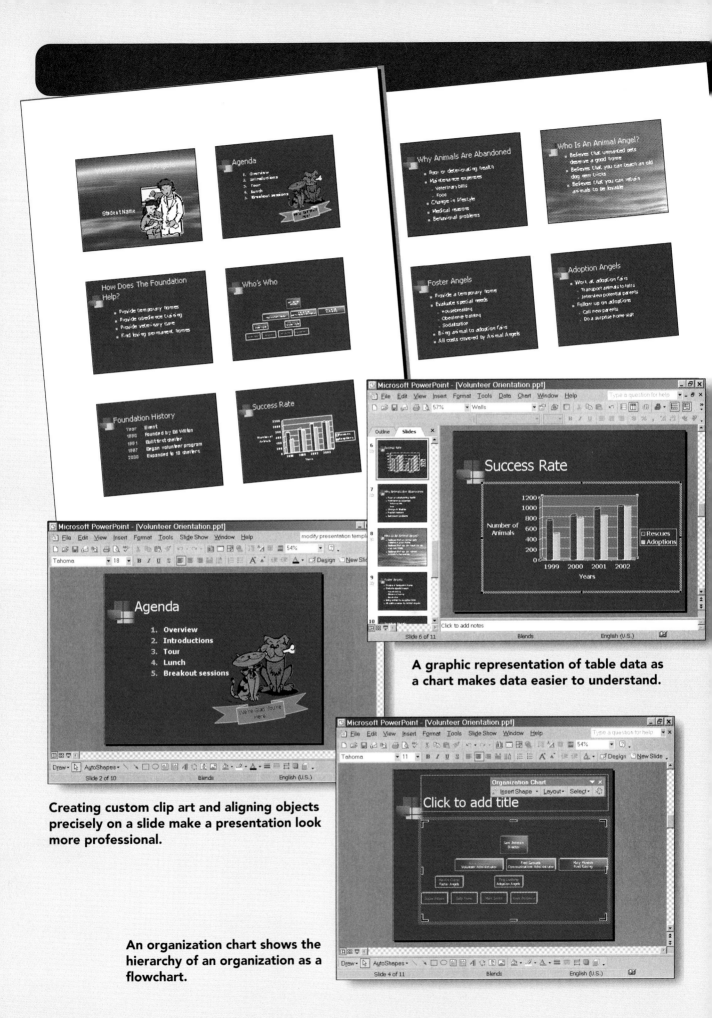

A graphic representation of table data as a chart makes data easier to understand.

Creating custom clip art and aligning objects precisely on a slide make a presentation look more professional.

An organization chart shows the hierarchy of an organization as a flowchart.

Angels Rescue Foundation

The volunteer recruitment presentation you created for the Animal Rescue Foundation was a huge success. Now the agency director has asked you to create a presentation to use during new volunteer orientation programs. To create this presentation, you will modify and expand the recruitment presentation. This will include creating a new slide that presents an overview of the orientation, and another slide showing the organization of the agency. In addition, you plan to make the presentation more interesting by adding customized clip art and a custom background.

To help with these enhancements, PowerPoint 2002 includes several tools, such as graphs and organization charts, that are designed to help present data. You will also use several Drawing tool features to help present clip art more professionally. Several slides from the completed presentation are shown here.

© Corbis

Concept Overview

1	**Group**	A group is two or more objects that are treated as a single object.
2	**Stacking Order**	Stacking order refers to the order in which objects are inserted in the different layers of a slide. As each object is added to the slide, it is added to the top layer.
3	**Object Alignment**	Object alignment refers to the position of objects relative to each other by their left, right, top, or bottom edges; or horizontally by their centers or vertically by their middles; or in relation to the entire slide.
4	**Chart**	A chart is a visual representation of numeric data that is used to help an audience grasp the impact of your data more quickly.
5	**Collecting and Pasting**	Collecting and pasting is the capability of the program to store multiple copied items in the Office Clipboard and then paste one or more of the items into another location or document.
6	**Organization Chart**	An organization chart is a map of a group, which usually includes people, but can include any items that have a hierarchical relationship.

Creating a New Presentation from Existing Slides

You worked very hard developing the content and layout for the volunteer recruitment presentation. Now you need to create a new presentation to be used during the volunteer orientation meeting. Much of the material in the volunteer recruitment presentation can also be used in the volunteer orientation presentation. To make the task of creating the new presentation easier, you will use the existing presentation, modify it to fit your needs, and save it as a new presentation. You have already made a few changes to the presentation. You changed the design of the presentation and removed a few slides that you will not need in the orientation presentation.

1

- **Start PowerPoint.**

- **Open the file**
  pp03_Recruitment.

- **If necessary, switch to Normal view.**

- **Change the title of slide 1 to Welcome Animal Angels.**

- **Replace Student Name on slide 1 with your name.**

- **Look at each of the slides to see the changes that have been made.**

- **Delete slide 10.**

Your screen should be similar to Figure 3.1

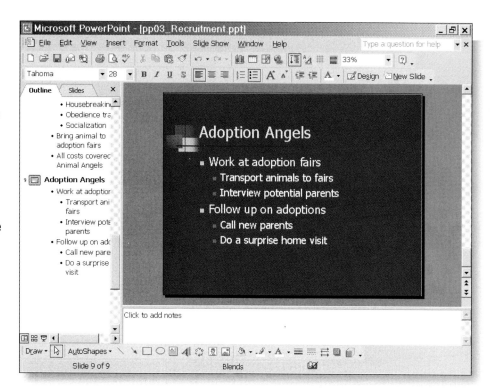

Figure 3.1

Copying Slides from Another Presentation

Now you want to replace the ending slide you just deleted with a slide from another presentation you have been working on. To do this, you will copy the slide from the other presentation into the volunteer orientation presentation.

1 Open the file
pp03_Animal Angels3.

● Select slide 1 in the
Outline tab.

● Click 🗐 Copy.

● Close the pp03_Animal
Angels3 presentation.

● If necessary, click on
slide 9.

● Click 📋 Paste.

*Your screen should be
similar to Figure 3.2*

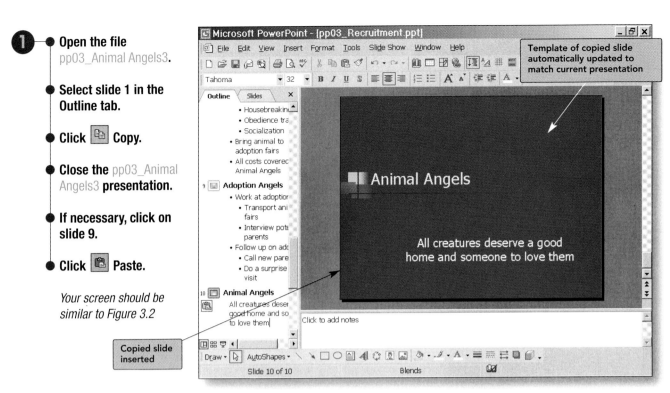

Figure 3.2

The copied slide is inserted into the presentation after the current slide. In addition, the slide template of the copied slide automatically updated to match that of the current presentation.

Saving the New Presentation

Before you make any additional changes, you will save the file as a new presentation.

1 ● Modify the title of slide
10 to Thank You For
Joining Animal
Angels.

● Reduce the size of the
title placeholder to
display the entire vol-
unteer group name on
the second line.

● Save the revised pres-
entation as Volunteer
Orientation.

*Your screen should be
similar to Figure 3.3*

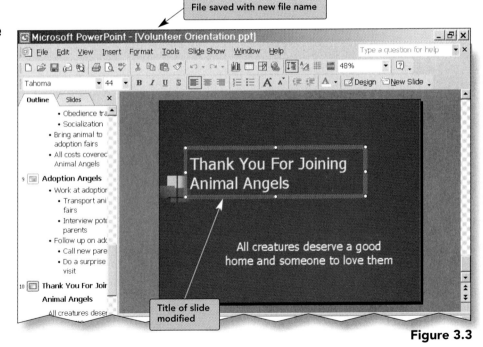

Figure 3.3

By modifying an existing presentation and saving it as a new presentation, you have saved a lot of time in the creation of your new presentation.

Enhancing the New Presentation

Now that the basic presentation is assembled, you want to make some enhancements, such as adding an agenda slide, changing the color of text on a few slides, and adding some more content.

Creating a Numbered List

First you want to change the second slide, which shows the topics of discussion, to a slide showing the agenda for the orientation. Since the agenda shows a sequential order of events, you want to use a numbered list rather than bullets.

1 ● **Change the title of slide 2 to Agenda.**

● **Select the six bulleted items.**

● **Type the text for the following five bulleted items:**
   Overview
   Introductions
   Tour
   Lunch
   Breakout sessions

● **Select the five bulleted items on slide 2 in the Outline tab.**

● **Click ▤ Numbering.**

Your screen should be similar to Figure 3.4

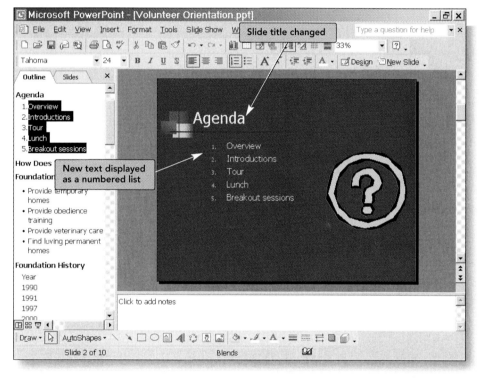

Figure 3.4

Another Method

You can also change a bulleted list into a numbered list by typing. To do this, press [Backspace] to remove the bullet at the beginning of the line, type 1, A, a, I, or i followed by a period or closing parenthesis, type the text, and then press [←Enter] to start a new line. The next line is automatically numbered using the same style.

The bullets have been replaced with numbers, indicating a sequential order of events.

You would also like to change the size of the numbers so they will stand out more on the slide.

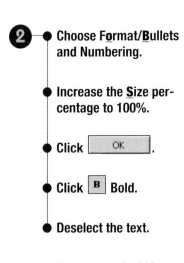

2 ● Choose F**o**rmat/**B**ullets and Numbering.

● Increase the **S**ize percentage to 100%.

● Click [OK].

● Click **B** Bold.

● Deselect the text.

Your screen should be similar to Figure 3.5

Additional Information

The Numbered tab of the Bullets and Numbering dialog box also allows you to select from several other numbering styles as well as specify a starting number.

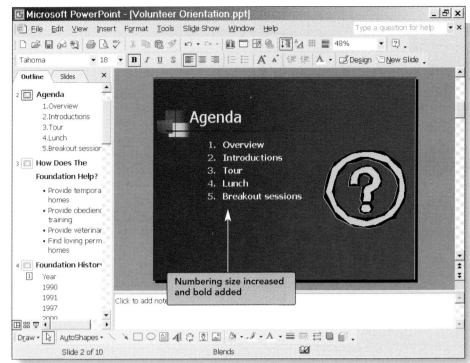

Figure 3.5

The numbers have changed to the size you selected and now stand out more from the text.

Using Format Painter

You decide that slide 4, which shows the history of the Animal Rescue Foundation, could benefit from the addition of a little more color. To help you quickly apply the same formats to multiple selections, you will use the Format Painter tool. This feature applies the formats associated with the current selection to new selections. If the selection is a paragraph, the formatting is applied to entire paragraphs. If the selection is a character, it is applied to a word or selection you specify.

- Display slide 4.

- Select the word "Year" in the slide.

- Change the font to Arial, bold, and the font color to gold.

- Double-click 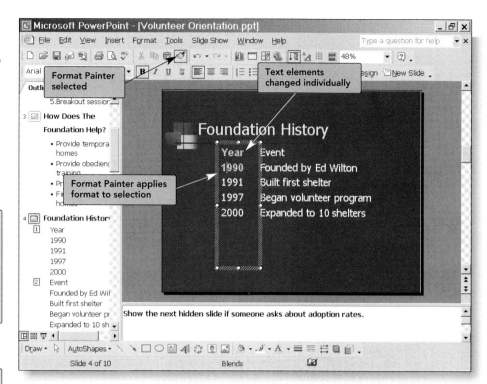 Format Painter.

Additional Information

Single-clicking 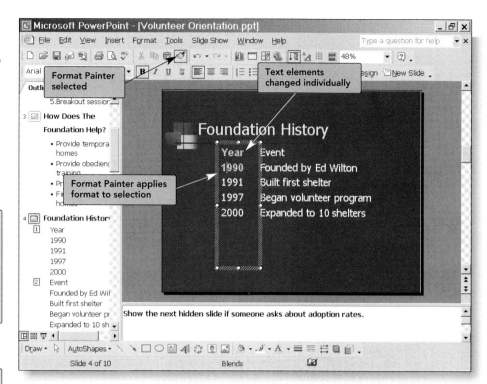 Format Painter applies the format to one selection, whereas double-clicking allows you to apply the format multiple times.

- Click 1990.

Additional Information

When this feature is on, the mouse pointer appears as 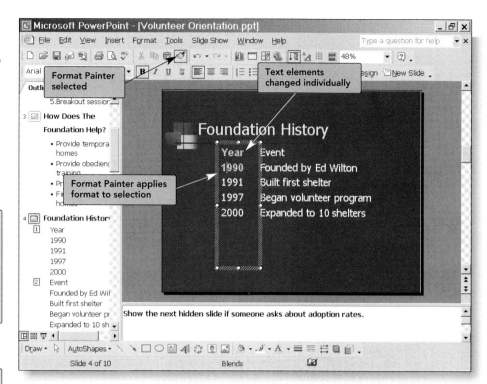.

Your screen should be similar to Figure 3.6

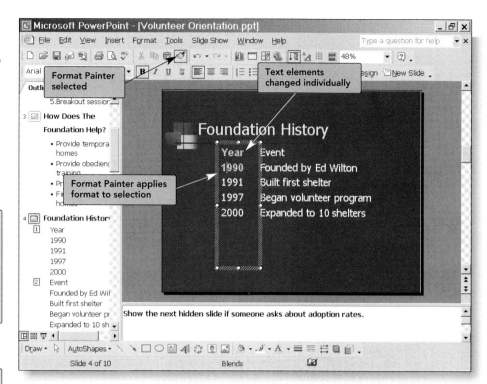

Figure 3.6

The text automatically changed to the same font settings associated with the selection when you turned on Format Painter. In one single click, you quickly applied three formats.

2

- Use Format Painter to format the remaining three years.

- Click 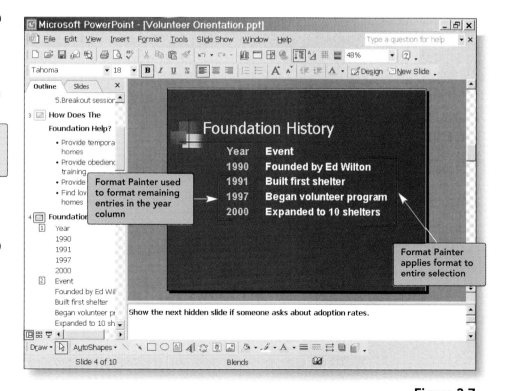 Format Painter to turn off the feature.

Another Method

You can also press [Esc] to turn off the Format Painter.

- Change "Event" to Arial and bold.

- Use Format Painter to change all the event text to match the heading.

- Turn off Format Painter.

- Deselect the text.

Your screen should be similar to Figure 3.7

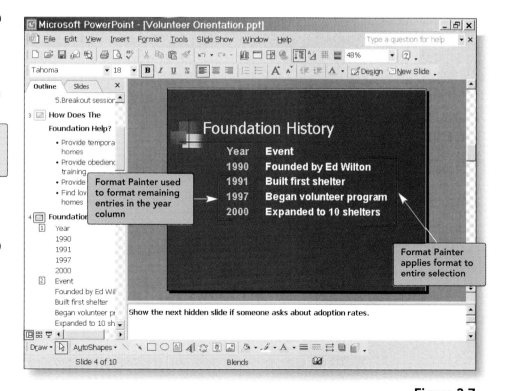

Figure 3.7

Modifying the Design Template

Although you like the template design you selected for this presentation, you think the presentation would benefit by adding a little variety. To do this, you decide to change the appearance of several of the slides by changing the slide background and using a different design template.

Creating a Custom Background

The content of slide 7 is all text, so you want to add a more interesting background. You have a scanned image of a photo of a sunset that you think would look good.

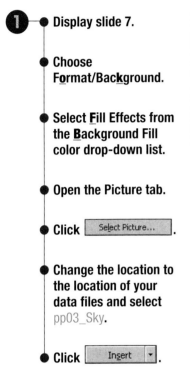

1. ● **Display slide 7.**

● **Choose**
Format/Bac**k**ground.

● **Select Fill Effects from**
the Background Fill
color drop-down list.

● **Open the Picture tab.**

● **Click** Select Picture... .

● **Change the location to**
the location of your
data files and select
pp03_Sky.

● **Click** Insert .

Your screen should be
similar to Figure 3.8

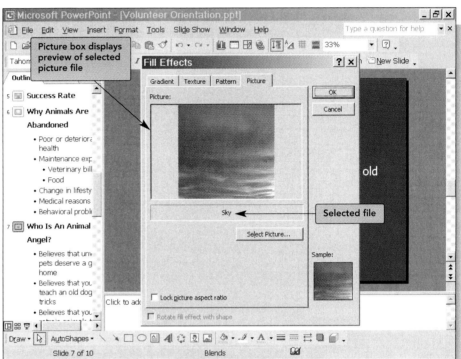

Figure 3.8

The Sky picture is displayed in the Picture box so you can see how it will look on the slide.

2

- Click [OK].

- Click [Apply].

Additional Information

Clicking [Apply to All] applies the selected background to all slides in the presentation.

- Change to Slide Sorter view.

- Save the presentation.

Your screen should be similar to Figure 3.9

Additional Information

To remove a background effect, choose [Automatic] from the Background dialog box.

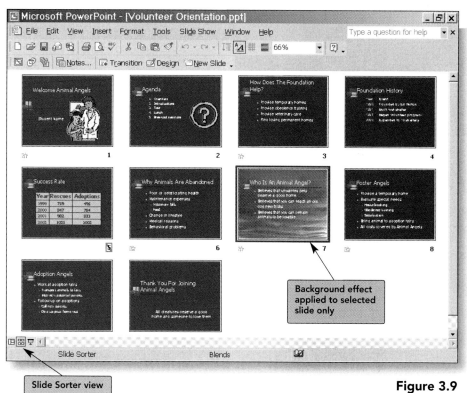

Figure 3.9

Applying a Design Template to Selected Slides

Next you want to change the design template for the first and last slides in the presentation to another template. Design templates can be applied to selected slides as well as to an entire presentation.

1

- Select slides 1 and 10.

- Display the Slide Design task pane.

- From the Shortcut menu of any template design, select Show Large Previews.

- Locate the Clouds design and select Apply to Selected Slides from the shortcut menu.

Your screen should be similar to Figure 3.10

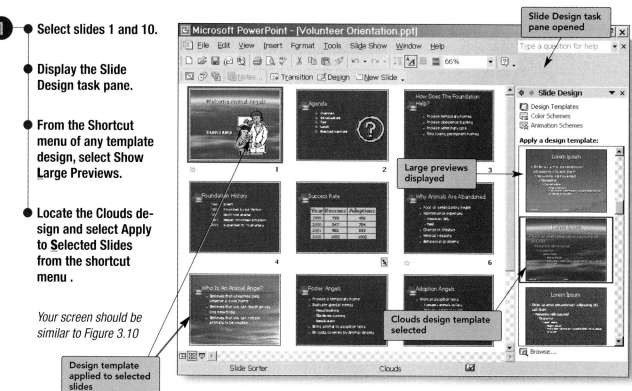

Figure 3.10

Customizing Graphics

You want to replace the question mark clip art on the Agenda slide with a graphic of a cat and a dog. You were unable to find a graphic of a cat and dog together that you liked, so you decide to create a custom graphic from two separate graphics. You will do this by opening and modifying the graphics individually, then grouping them into one object.

concept 1

Group

1 A **group** is two or more objects that are treated as a single object. Many clip art pictures are composed of several different elements that are grouped together. This allows you to easily move, re-size, flip, or rotate all pieces of the group as a single unit. Features or **attributes**, such as line or fill color, associated with all objects in the group can also be changed at one time.

Sometimes you may want to ungroup the parts of an object so that the individual parts can be manipulated independently. Other times you may want to combine several objects to create your own graphic object that better suits your needs.

Ungrouped

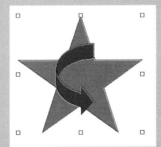

Grouped

First you need to delete the existing clip art and placeholder. Then you will insert, position, and modify the new picture.

The presentation now inlcudes two design templates. After applying a second design template to the presentation, a new set of slide masters is created. In order to make changes throughout your presentation you must make design changes to both pairs of masters.

1 **Double-click on slide 2.**

Delete the question mark graphic.

Press Delete **to delete the clip art placeholder.**

Insert the graphic file pp03_Cat Smiling.

Your screen should be similar to Figure 3.11

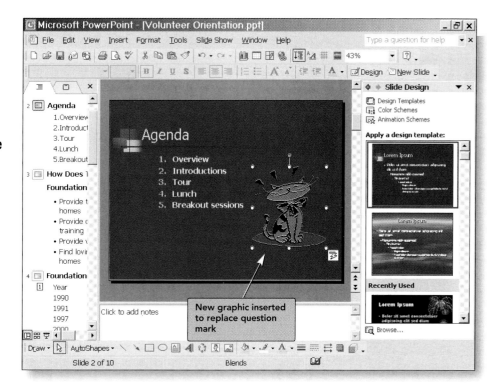

Figure 3.11

The cat graphic is made up of several elements grouped together.

Zooming the Slide

To make complex graphics easier to work with, you can turn off the display of panes and increase the magnification of the slide. In Normal view the slide is sized by default to fit within the pane and is about 60 percent of full (100 percent) size. You can increase the onscreen display size up to four times normal display (400 percent) or reduce the size to 33 percent. Changing the Zoom percentage only affects the onscreen display of the slide; it does not change the actual font or object sizes.

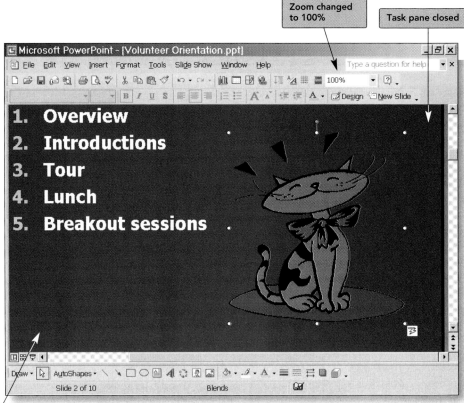

Zoom changed to 100%

Task pane closed

1
- Close the Tabs pane and the Slide Design task pane.

- Open the 60% Zoom drop-down menu (on the Standard toolbar).

- Choose 100%.

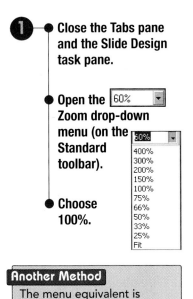

Another Method

The menu equivalent is View/Zoom.

Your screen should be similar to Figure 3.12

Entire slide cannot be displayed in the window

Figure 3.12

The slide display is increased to 100 percent, and the entire slide is now too large to fully display in the window. The graphic is much larger, and as you make changes to the graphic, you will be able to more easily select different parts of the object.

You want to modify the graphic first by coloring one of the triangles above the cat. You can customize graphics by adding and deleting pieces of the graphic, changing the fill and line colors, and otherwise editing the graphic using features on the Drawing toolbar. However, to do this, the graphic must be a drawing object.

Converting Graphics to Drawing Objects

Because this is an imported graphic (it was not originally created within the program using the Drawing features), it first needs to be converted to a drawing object that can be manipulated using features included within PowerPoint.

1 ● **Right-click on the graphic and choose Edit Picture.**

● **Click** [Yes] **to convert the graphic to a Microsoft Office drawing object.**

● **Click on one of the black triangles to select it.**

Your screen should be similar to Figure 3.13

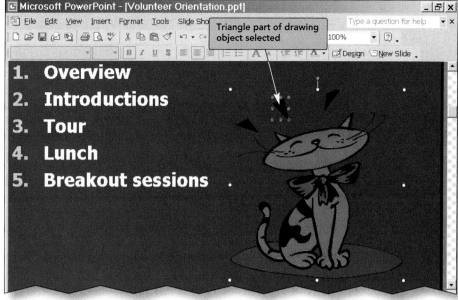

Figure 3.13

Once a graphic has been converted to a drawing object, the individual parts can be selected and edited just as you would an individual drawing object that you created using the Drawing features. For example, you can change the fill color of the selected triangle.

2 ● **Open the** [🎨 ▾] **Fill Color drop-down list and select any color from the palette.**

Your screen should be similar to Figure 3.14

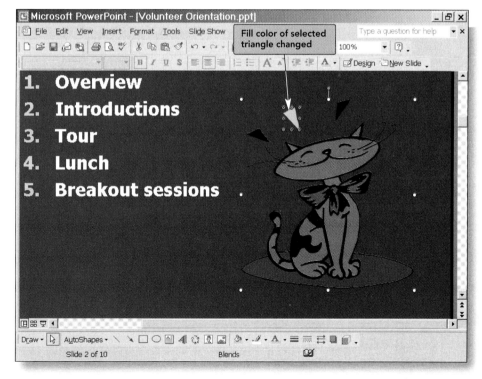

Figure 3.14

The color of the selected object within the selected graphic object has changed to the color you specified.

Ungrouping an Object

You decide you do not like the triangles and you want to delete them. To delete an individual object from a graphic, you must first ungroup the object.

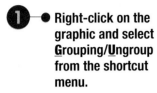

Right-click on the graphic and select Grouping/Ungroup from the shortcut menu.

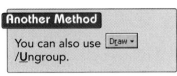

Another Method

You can also use Draw ▾ /Ungroup.

Your screen should be similar to Figure 3.15

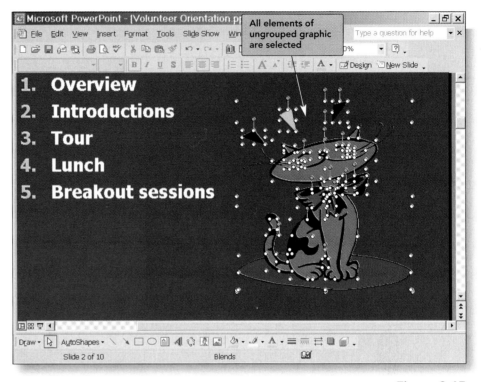

Figure 3.15

The graphic has been ungrouped and all the elements in the graphic are selected.

Deleting a Graphic Element

You first need to deselect all the elements, and then select only the elements in the graphic object you want to delete. Clicking outside the selected object will deselect all elements. Then to select a specific object, you can click anywhere on a filled object or click on the border of an unfilled object.

1 ● Click anywhere outside the graphic to
deselect all the
elements.

● Click on a triangle to
select the object.

● Press Delete.

● In the same manner,
delete the other two
triangles.

Additional Information
Select multiple objects by
holding down Ctrl while
clicking on each object.

*Your screen should be
similar to Figure 3.16*

Additional Information
This graphic was made by
starting with a black outline
of the entire image filled with
black, and then overlaying
colored pieces to construct
the cat. Because of this
construction, certain areas of
the graphic can't be deleted.

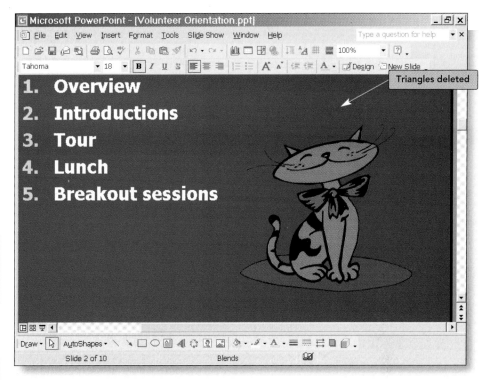

Figure 3.16

The three triangles are deleted.

Recoloring Objects

Next you will change the color of the cat's bow tie to coordinate with the
slide background.

1 ● Select the five red
parts of the bow tie.

HAVING TROUBLE?
Carefully point to the red
color when selecting the
objects. If you accidentally
select and format the wrong
area, click ↺ ▾ Undo and try
again.

● Open 🎨 ▾ Fill Color
and select a bright
pink color.

● If necessary, select
any other parts of the
bow tie that you may
have missed and
change the color to
the same color.

*Your screen should be
similar to Figure 3.17*

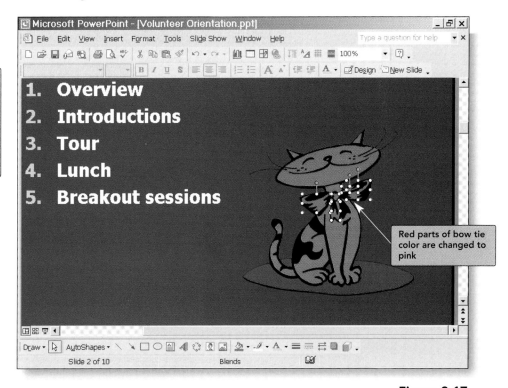

Figure 3.17

Regrouping the Graphic

You think the graphic looks a lot better now. Next you will add the graphic of the dog to the slide and combine it with the cat graphic. You will regroup the parts of the cat graphic again and then insert the picture of the dog.

1 ● **Click on the cat to select the cat graphic.**

● **Choose Grouping/Regroup from the shortcut menu.**

● **Open the 100% ▾ Zoom drop-down menu and choose Fit.**

● **Insert the picture pp03_Dog Smiling.**

Your screen should be similar to Figure 3.18

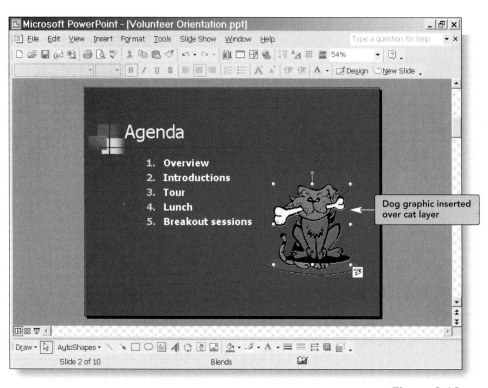

Figure 3.18

Changing the Stacking Order

The dog graphic was inserted in the slide overlaping the cat graphic. This is because as each new object is added to a slide, it is added to a separate drawing layer that stacks on top of the previous layer.

Stacking Order

2 **Stacking order** refers to the order in which objects are inserted in the different layers of a slide. As each object is added to the slide, it is added to the top layer. Adding objects to separate layers allows each object to be positioned precisely on the page, including in front of or behind other objects. As objects are added to a slide, they may overlap. You can move objects up or down within a stack using the Order button on the Drawing toolbar.

Triangle is on top of stack **Triangle is sent to the back** **Square is brought to the front**

Sometimes it is easy to lose an object behind another. If this happens, you can press [Tab↹] to cycle forward or [⇧Shift] + [Tab↹] to cycle backward through the stacked objects until the one you want is selected.

You want to move the dog object to be alongside the cat. You also want to increase the size of the dog.

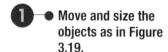

1 **Move and size the objects as in Figure 3.19.**

Your screen should be similar to Figure 3.19

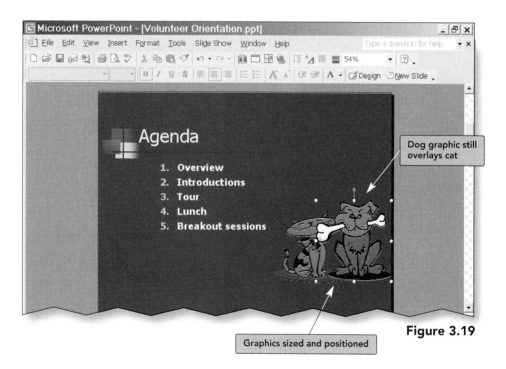

Figure 3.19

Did you notice when you moved the cat object, that all the objects in the group were identified and moved as a group? In contrast, when you moved and sized the dog object, because it has not been converted to a drawing object yet, separate parts were not identified as it was manipulated.

Now you want to see if the graphic would look better if the dog object were behind the cat. To change the order of these two objects, you will send the dog object to the back of the stack.

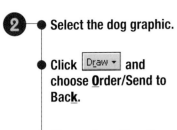

Select the dog graphic.

Click Draw ▾ and choose **O**rder/Send to Bac**k**.

Size and position the graphics as in Figure 3.20.

Additional Information

The Bring **F**orward and Send **B**ackward options move the object forward or backward in the stack one layer at a time.

Your screen should be similar to Figure 3.20

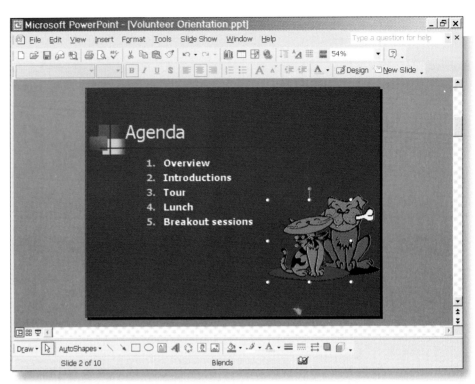

Figure 3.20

The dog is now behind the cat and the graphic looks much better because the bone does not cover the cat's face.

Grouping Objects

Now you want to combine the two graphics into one by grouping them, and then you will size them appropriately on the slide.

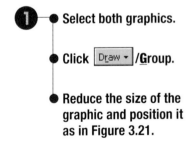

Select both graphics.

Click Draw ▾ /**G**roup.

Reduce the size of the graphic and position it as in Figure 3.21.

Your screen should be similar to Figure 3.21

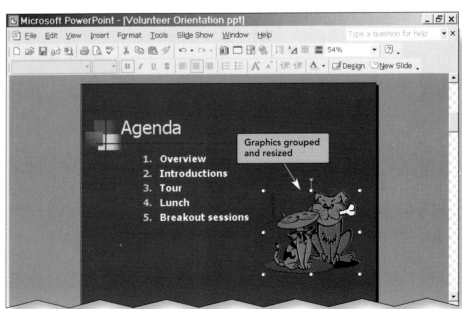

Figure 3.21

The two graphics now appear unified. Because the objects are grouped, they size and move as a single object.

Wrapping Text in an Object

Below the pet graphic, you decide to add a banner that welcomes the volunteers.

1 ● Create a Curved Down Ribbon AutoShape banner and display it below the graphic as shown in Figure 3.22.

● Change the fill color to the same color as the cat's bow tie.

● Right-click on the object and choose Add Te**x**t from the shortcut menu.

● Type We're Glad You're Here!

● Click outside the AutoShape to turn off text editing.

Your screen should be similar to Figure 3.22

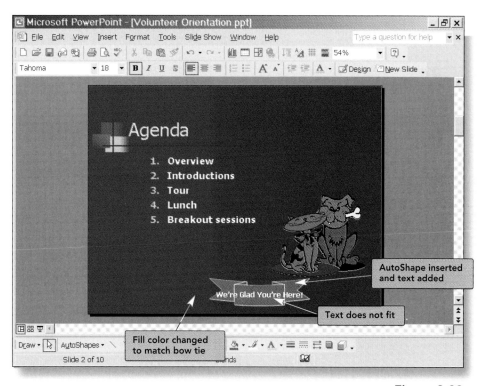

Figure 3.22

Notice that the text does not fit inside the center of the graphic. Although you could manually increase the size of the banner to fit the text, you would rather wrap the text in the AutoShape and then resize the banner to fit the text.

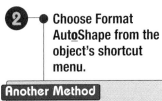

2 ● Choose Format **Auto**Shape from the object's shortcut menu.

Another Method
The menu equivalent is F**o**rmat/Aut**o**Shape.

● Open the Text Box tab.

● Select **W**ord wrap text in AutoShape.

● Select Resize AutoShape to **f**it text.

● Click ⬚ OK ⬚.

Your screen should be similar to Figure 3.23

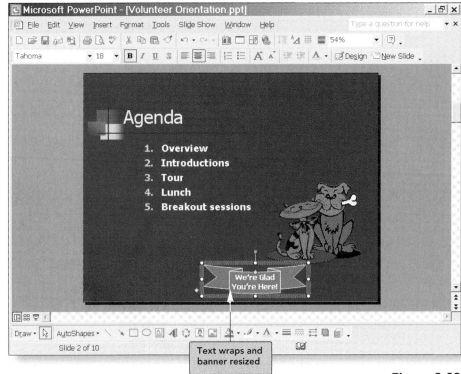

Figure 3.23

The text wraps to a second line and the size of the AutoShape has adjusted to fully display the two lines of text. You will change the text color and adjust the size and placement of the banner.

3 ● Select the text in the banner and change the font color to black.

● Size, position, and rotate the AutoShape as shown in Figure 3.24.

HAVING TROUBLE?
Use the rotate handle to rotate the banner.

Your screen should be similar to Figure 3.24

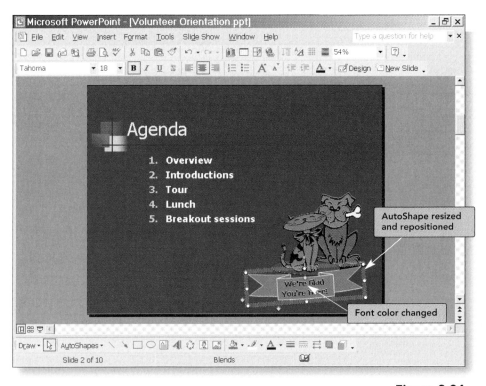

Figure 3.24

Aligning Objects

Next you want to center the banner below the graphic. Although you can position objects on your slides visually by dragging to the approximate location, you can make your slides appear more professional by using the tools in PowerPoint to precisely align and position objects.

concept 3

Object Alignment

3 **Object alignment** refers to the position of objects relative to each other by their left, right, top, or bottom edges; or horizontally by their centers or vertically by their middles; or in relation to the entire slide. There are several methods for aligning objects. You can align objects to a **grid**, an invisible series of lines that form small squares on the slide. By default, whenever you move, resize, or draw an object, the object's corners "snap" to the nearest intersection of the grid. Using the grid helps align objects more accurately. You can also snap an object to other shapes so that new objects align themselves with the pre-existing shapes. The grid lines run through the vertical and horizontal edges of other shapes, and the new shape aligns with the closest intersection of that grid.

Another way to align an object is to use a guide. A **guide** is a line, either vertical or horizontal, that you position on the slide. When an object is close to the guide, the object's center or corner (whichever is closer) snaps to the guide.

A third way to align objects is to other objects. For example, you can align the centers or the left edges of two objects. Using this method allows you to precisely align the edges or tops of selected shapes. At least two objects must be selected to align them.

   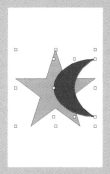 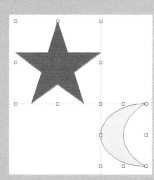

Center aligned   **Left aligned**   **Right aligned**   **Middle aligned**   **Aligned to guides**

Objects can also be aligned relative to the slide as a whole, such as to the top or side of a slide. Objects can further be arranged or distributed so that they are an equal distance from each other vertically, horizontally, or in relation to the entire slide. You must have at least three objects selected to distribute them.

Additional Information
Use **V**iew/Gri**d** and Guide to display grid lines and guides.

You will align the centers of the two objects and then group them into one object.

1 ● Select both the banner and the pet graphic.

● Click **Draw ▾** and choose **Align** or **Distribute/Align Center.**

HAVING TROUBLE?
Make sure the Relative to **S**lide option is not selected. If it is, using Align Center will align the object with the center of the slide, not the other object.

● Group the two objects together.

● Size and position the graphic as in Figure 3.25.

● Click on the slide to deselect the grouped object.

● Save the presentation.

Your screen should be similar to Figure 3.25

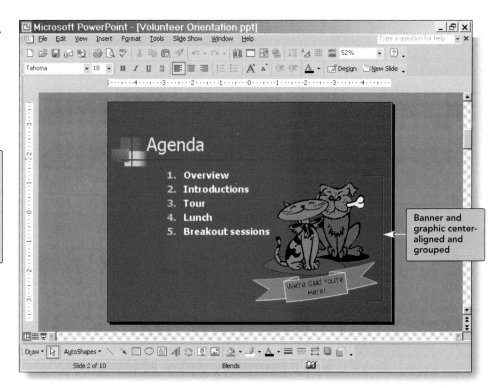

Figure 3.25

Creating a Chart Slide

The next change you want to make is to show the adoption success rate data in slide 5 as a chart rather than a table.

concept 4

Charts

4 A **chart**, also called a graph, is a visual representation of numeric data. When you are presenting data to an audience, they will grasp the impact of your data more quickly if you present it as a chart. PowerPoint 2002 includes a separate program, Microsoft Graph, designed to help you create 14 types of charts with many different formats for each type.

Each type of chart represents the data differently and has a different purpose. It is important to select the type of chart that will provide the right emphasis to support your presentations. The basic chart types are described below.

Type of Chart	Description
Area	Shows the relative importance of a value over time by emphasizing the area under the curve created by each data series.
Bar	Displays categories vertically and values horizontally, placing more emphasis on comparisons and less on time. Stacked-bar charts show the relationship of individual items to a whole by stacking bars on top of one another.
Column	Similar to a bar chart, except categories are organized horizontally and values vertically. Shows data changes over time or comparison among items.
Line	Shows changes in data over time, emphasizing time and rate of change rather than the amount of change.
Pie	Shows the relationship of each value in a data series to the series as a whole. Each slice of the pie represents a single value in a data series.

Most charts are made up of several basic parts as identified and described below.

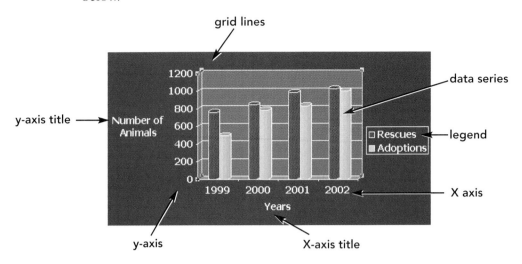

Part	Description
X axis	The bottom boundary of the chart, also called the **category axis**, is used to label the data being charted; the label may be, for example, a point in time or a category.
Y axis	The left boundary of the chart, also called the **value axis**, is a numbered scale whose numbers are determined by the data used in the chart. Each line or bar in a chart represents a data value. In pie charts there are no axes. Instead, the data that is charted is displayed as slices in a circle or pie.
Data Series	Each group of related data that is plotted in a chart.
Legend	A box containing a brief description identifying the patterns or colors assigned to the data series in a chart.
Titles	Descriptive text used to explain the contents of the chart.

You will create the chart in a new slide following the slide containing the table of data on success rates. PowerPoint includes a special slide layout for charts that includes a placeholder that opens the Graph application.

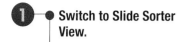 • **Switch to Slide Sorter View.**

• **Insert a new slide in Title and Chart slide layout after slide 5.**

Another Method
You can also use Insert/Chart or click 📊 to add a chart object to a slide.

• **Double-click on slide 6.**

• **Choose View/Normal (Restore Panes).**

• **If necessary, display the Outline tab and size the pane appropriately.**

Your screen should be similar to Figure 3.26

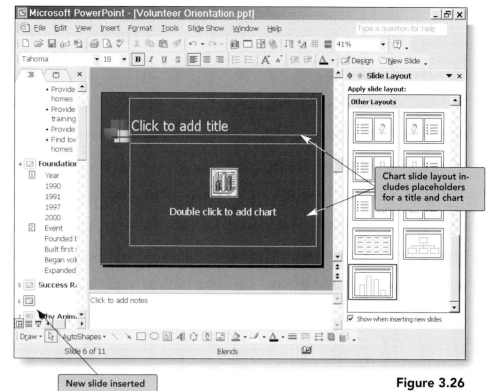

Figure 3.26

Copying Data

The chart slide layout includes a placeholder for the title and another placeholder for the chart. When you double-click on the chart placeholder, the Microsoft Graph application will open and you will be asked to enter the data you want to chart. Because this data is already contained in the table in slide 5, you will copy the data from the table into the chart. You will also copy the title text from slide 5 into the chart slide. You could copy and paste the selections one after the other, or you can use the Office Clipboard to collect multiple items and paste them as needed.

concept 5

Collecting and Pasting

5 **Collecting and pasting** is the capability of the program to store multiple copied items in the Office Clipboard and then paste one or more of the items into another location or document. For example, you could copy a chart from Excel and a paragraph from Word, then switch to PowerPoint and copy the two stored items into a slide in one easy step. This saves you from having to switch back and forth between documents and applications multiple times.

The Office Clipboard and the System Clipboard are similar, but separate, features. The major difference is that the Office Clipboard can hold up to 24 items, whereas the System Clipboard holds only a single item. The last item you copy to the Office Clipboard is al-

ways copied to the System Clipboard. When you use the Office Clipboard, you can select from the items stored to paste in any order.

The Office Clipboard is available in all Office XP applications, and is accessed through the Clipboard task pane. Once the Clipboard task pane is opened, it is available for use in any program, including non-Office programs. In some programs where the Cut, Copy, and Paste commands are not available, or in non-Office programs, the Clipboard task pane is not visible but it is still operational. You can copy from any program that provides copy and cut capabilities, but you can only paste into Word, Excel, Access, PowerPoint, and Outlook.

First you will copy the slide title text from slide 5 to the Office Clipboard.

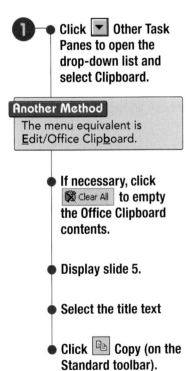

1 ● Click ▼ **Other Task Panes to open the drop-down list and select Clipboard.**

Another Method
The menu equivalent is Edit/Office Clipboard.

● **If necessary, click** 🗙 Clear All **to empty the Office Clipboard contents.**

● **Display slide 5.**

● **Select the title text**

● **Click** 📋 **Copy (on the Standard toolbar).**

Your screen should be similar to Figure 3.27

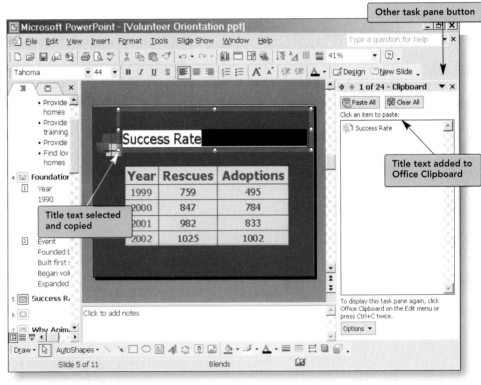

Figure 3.27

The Clipboard task pane displays a PowerPoint icon representing the copied item and the first few lines of the copied selection. Next you will copy the contents of the table into the Office Clipboard. As items are copied, they are added sequentially to the Office Clipboard with the last copied item at the top of the list.

2
● **Drag to select the entire contents of the table.**

● **Click 🗎 Copy.**

● **If necessary, close the Tables and Borders toolbar.**

Your screen should be similar to Figure 3.28

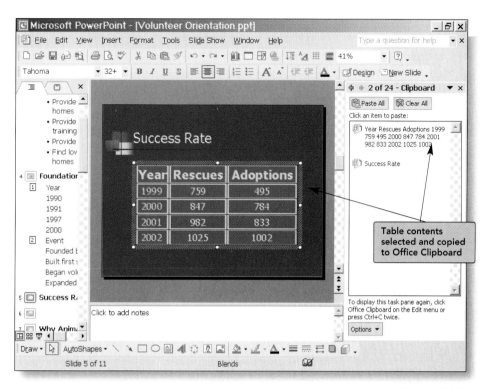

Figure 3.28

The Office Clipboard now contains two PowerPoint document icons, one for each copied item.

The 🗎 Office Clipboard icon appears in the system taskbar to show that the Clipboard | 🗎 **1 of 24 - Clipboard** | is active. It also briefly displays a ScreenTip indicating that 1 out of a possible 24 items was collected as the selection is copied.

Specifying the Chart Data

Now you are ready to start the Microsoft Graph application and use the table data to create the chart.

1 ● **Display slide 6.**

● **Close the Tabs pane.**

● **Double-click** [icon] **in the placeholder.**

Your screen should be similar to Figure 3.29

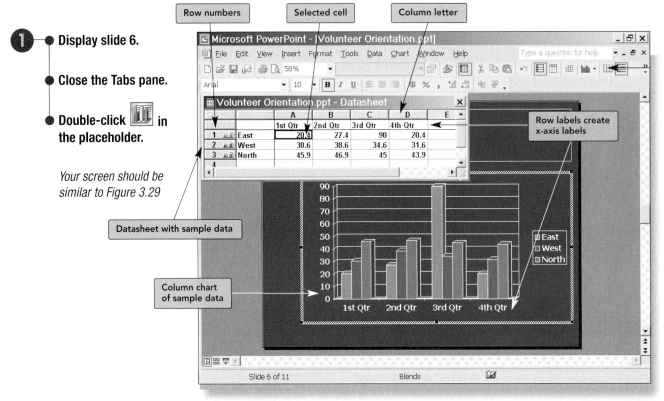

Figure 3.29

The Graph program is activated and a datasheet containing sample data is displayed in the Datasheet window. A column chart using the sample data from the datasheet is displayed in the slide. The **datasheet** is a table consisting of rows and columns. As in a table, the intersection of a row and column creates a **cell** in which text or data is entered. Notice that the datasheet displays the column letters A through E and row numbers 1 through 4. Each cell has a unique name consisting of a column letter followed by a row number. For example, cell A1 is the intersection of column A and row 1. The cell that is surrounded by the border is the selected cell and is the cell you can work in.

In addition to displaying sample data, the datasheet also contains placeholders for the column labels, which are used as the legend in the chart, and for the row labels, which are used as X-axis labels.

You need to replace the sample data in the datasheet with the data you copied from slide 5. Unfortunately, because the Graph application is running, the Clipboard task pane is not displayed. However, because the table data was the last item copied to the Clipboard, you can simply click [icon] Paste in the Standard toolbar to insert the last copied item from the System Clipboard into the datasheet.

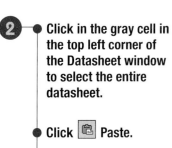

2 ● Click in the gray cell in the top left corner of the Datasheet window to select the entire datasheet.

● Click 📋 Paste.

● Click OK in response to the advisory dialog box.

Your screen should be similar to Figure 3.30

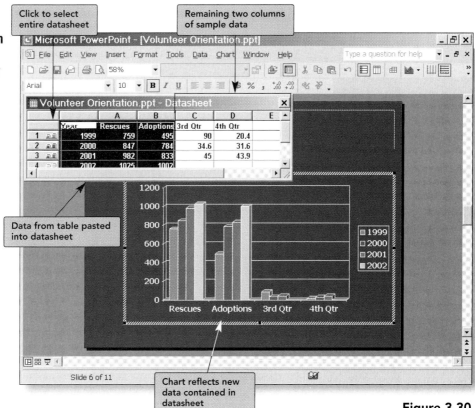

Figure 3.30

The datasheet is updated and displays the data from the table. The chart also reflects the change in data. Finally, you need to remove the remaining two columns of sample data.

3 ● Drag over the column letters C and D to select both columns.

● Press Delete.

Your screen should be similar to Figure 3.31

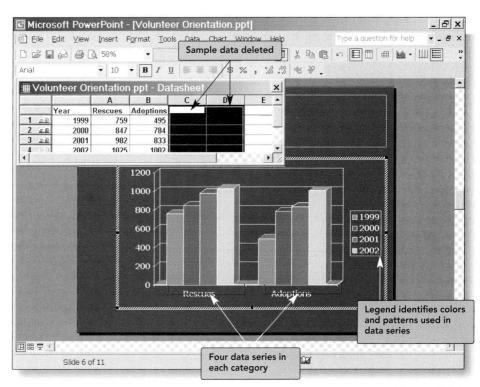

Figure 3.31

Each data series has a unique color or pattern assigned to it so that you can identify the different series. The legend identifies the color or pattern associated with each data series. As you can see, the values and text in the chart are directly linked to the datasheet, and any changes you make in the datasheet are automatically reflected in the chart.

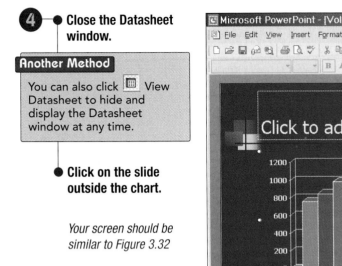

4 ● **Close the Datasheet window.**

Another Method

You can also click 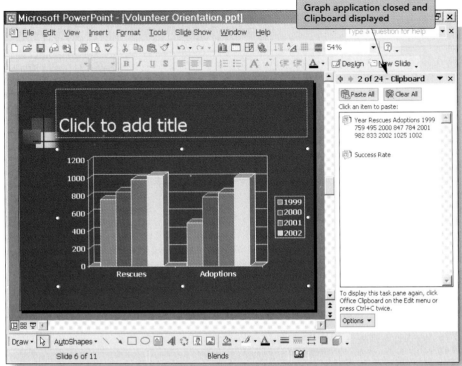 View Datasheet to hide and display the Datasheet window at any time.

● **Click on the slide outside the chart.**

Your screen should be similar to Figure 3.32

Figure 3.32

The Graph application is closed, and because the PowerPoint application is active again, the Office Clipboard task pane is displayed. Before modifying the chart, you will copy the title from the Office Clipboard into the slide.

5 ● **Click** in the chart title placeholder.

● **Click** on the Success Rate icon in the Office Clipboard task pane.

● **Click** 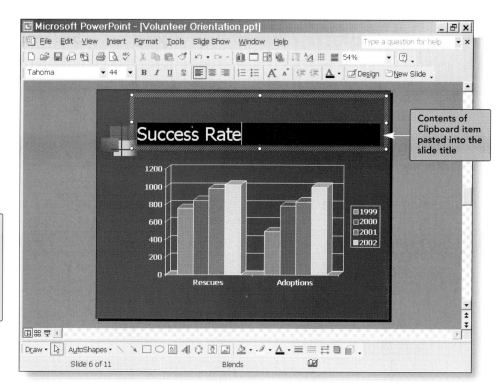 **Clear All** to clear the contents of the Office Clipboard.

Additional Information

The Office Clipboard Paste All option inserts the contents of all copied items in the order in which they were added to the Office Clipboard.

● **Close** the Office Clipboard task pane.

Your screen should be similar to Figure 3.33

Figure 3.33

The contents of the first copied item are pasted into the title of the slide.

Modifying Chart Data

As you look at the chart, you decide you want to change it so that the data is displayed based on the columns of data (years), not the rows of data (Rescue and Adoption categories), which is the default. To modify the chart, you need to activate the Graph application again. Then you can use the features on the Graph menu and toolbar to edit the chart.

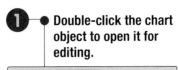

① ● **Double-click the chart object to open it for editing.**

Another Method

You can also use Chart Object/Edit from the chart objects shortcut menu.

● **Click** **By Column.**

Another Method

The menu equivalent is Data/Series in Columns.

Your screen should be similar to Figure 3.34

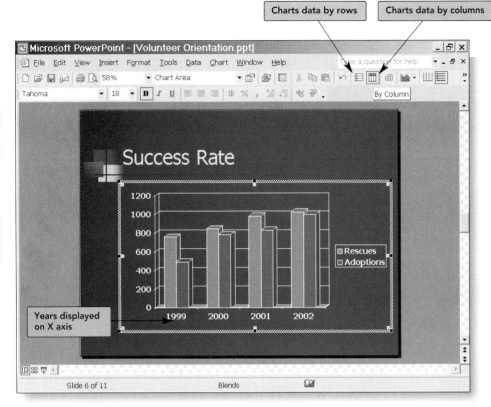

Figure 3.34

The years are now displayed along the X axis. The chart now shows the increasing success rate for adoptions and rescues over time more clearly.

Adding Axis Titles

Next you want to add labels along the axes to clarify the information in the chart.

① ● **Choose Chart/Chart Options.**

● **If necessary, open the Titles tab.**

Your screen should be similar to Figure 3.35

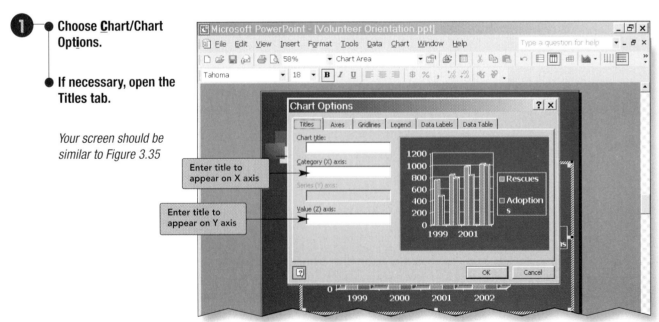

Figure 3.35

The Chart Options dialog box is used to add features to a chart, including titles, legends, and gridlines, that make it easier to understand the data in the chart. You will add titles along the two axis lines.

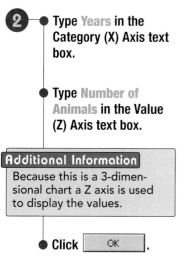

2 ● Type Years in the Category (X) Axis text box.

● Type Number of Animals in the Value (Z) Axis text box.

Additional Information

Because this is a 3-dimensional chart a Z axis is used to display the values.

● Click [OK].

Your screen should be similar to Figure 3.36

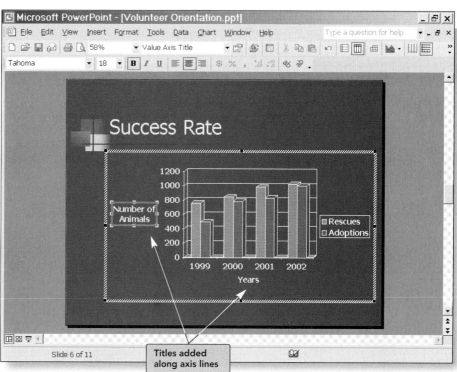

Figure 3.36

The labels you entered appear along the appropriate axis.

Changing Chart Formats

Next you want to change the color and appearance of the data series to give them more visual interest.

1 ● **Click on any one of the Adoptions columns to select all the columns for that data series.**

● **Click 🗐 Format Data Series.**

Another Method

The menu equivalent is Format/Selected Data Series, and the keyboard equivalent is Ctrl + 1. You can also double-click the chart element or choose Format Data Series from the Shortcut menu.

● **If necessary, open the Patterns tab.**

Your screen should be similar to Figure 3.37

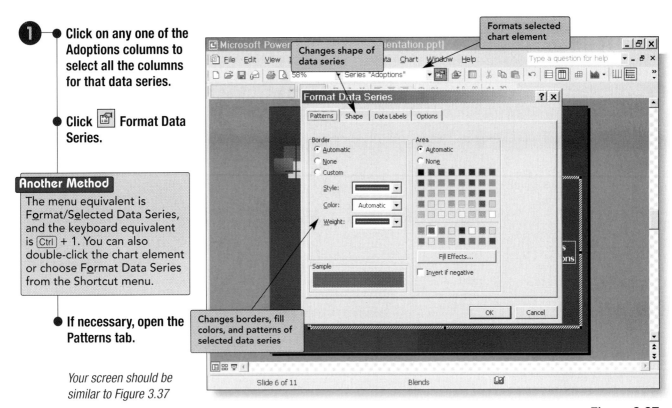

Figure 3.37

The Format Data Series dialog box is used to modify the appearance of the selected data series. The default chart colors are colors associated with the presentation design template. You want to change the color and shape of the bars. From the Patterns tab, you can select different borders and fill colors and patterns. The Shape tab is used to select different chart series shapes. You will change the color to gold and the shape to a cylinder.

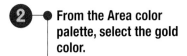

2 ● From the Area color palette, select the gold color.

● Open the Shape tab.

● Select the cylinder shape, 4.

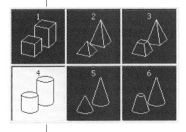

● Click [OK].

● Deselect the data series.

Your screen should be similar to Figure 3.38

Additional Information

You can also change other elements of the chart, such as the background and text color, gridlines, and scale.

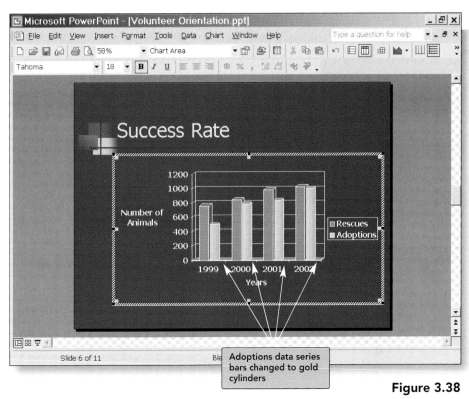

Figure 3.38

The four Adoptions data series bars have changed to a gold cylinder shape.

3 ● Change the Rescues data series in the same way, using plum as the color and the same cylinder shape.

Your screen should be similar to Figure 3.39

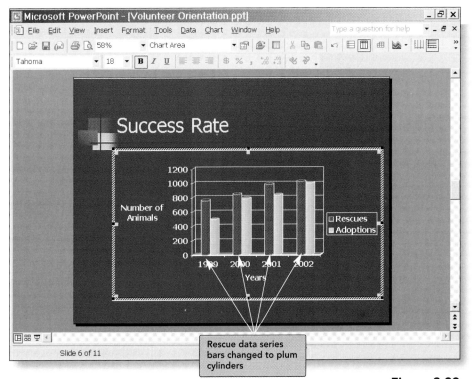

Figure 3.39

Next you want to add color to the chart walls.

4 ● **Double-click on the background behind the data series.**

● **Select a blue color from the area color palette.**

● **Click** OK .

Your screen should be similar to Figure 3.40

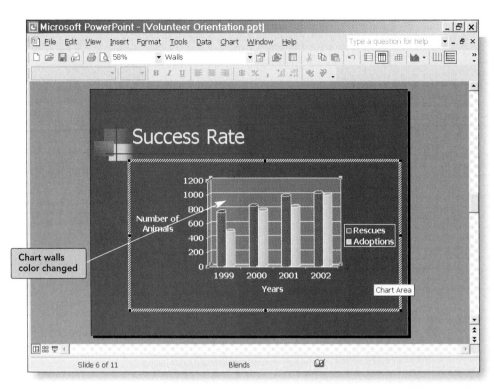

Figure 3.40

The chart is now much more attractive and more meaningful. Now that the success rate is represented in a chart, you decide to delete the slide containing the same information in table layout.

5 ● **Click outside the chart to close the Graph application.**

● **Switch to Slide Sorter view.**

● **Delete slide 5.**

● **Save the presentation.**

Your screen should be similar to Figure 3.41

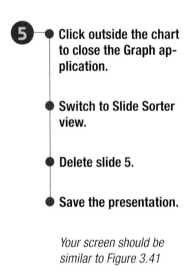

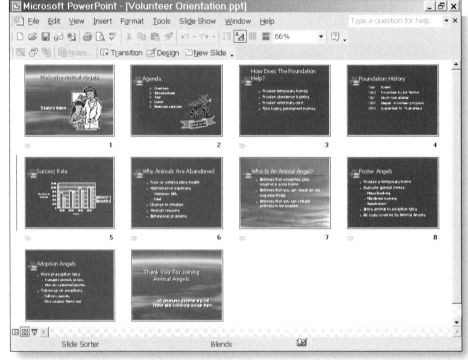

Figure 3.41

Creating an Organization Chart

To provide the volunteers with an overview of the structure of the Animal Rescue Foundation organization, you want to include an organization chart in the presentation.

concept 4

Organization Charts

4 An **organization chart** is a map of a group, which usually includes people, but can include any items that have a hierarchical relationship. A **hierarchy** shows ranking, such as reporting structures within a department in a business. PowerPoint 2002 includes a separate application called Microsoft Organization Chart that is designed to help you quickly create organization charts.

There are several different styles of organization charts from which you can choose, depending on how you would like to display the hierarchy and how much room you have on your slide. A basic organization chart is shown below. All organization charts consist of different levels that represent the hierarchy. The top-most box in the organization chart is at level 1. All boxes that report directly to it are at level 2. Those boxes reporting to a level 2 box are at level 3, and so forth. An organization chart can have up to 50 levels.

The **manager box** is the top-level box of a group. **Subordinate boxes** report to the manager box. **Co-worker boxes** are boxes that have the same manager. Co-workers form a group. A **group** consists of all the boxes reporting to the same manager, excluding assistant boxes. **Assistant boxes** represent administrative or managerial assistants to a manager. A **branch** is a box and all the boxes that report to it. A **level** is all the boxes at the same level regardless of the boxes each reports to.

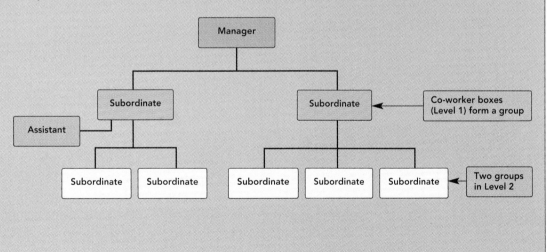

You will add a new slide following slide 3 to display the organization chart. Just as when creating a chart, there is a special slide layout for organization charts that includes a placeholder that opens the Organization Chart application.

1 • **Insert a new slide after slide 3 using the Title and Diagram or Organization Chart slide layout.**

• **Close the Slide Layout task pane.**

• **Double-click slide 4.**

• **Double-click 🔲 in the organization chart placeholder.**

• **Double-click 🔲 Organization Chart in the Diagram Gallery dialog box.**

Your screen should be similar to Figure 3.42

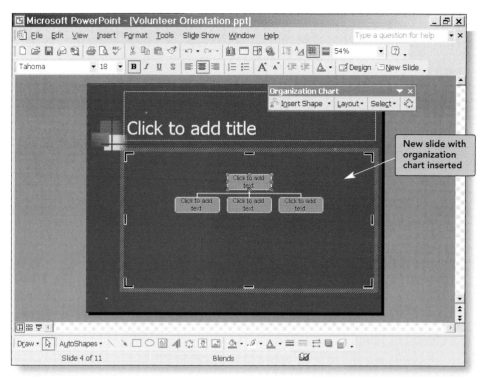

New slide with organization chart inserted

Figure 3.42

The Organization Chart toolbar contains the commands and tools to create and edit the organization chart.

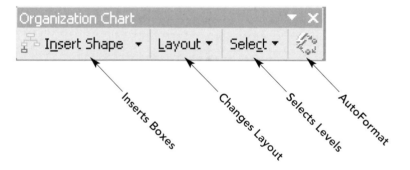

When you create a new organization chart, a chart containing four boxes (the default) is displayed. To enter information into the box, you type over the field labels. The top box in the organization chart is already selected. You will enter the name of the director of the Animal Rescue Foundation in the top-level box. You will also increase the zoom to make it easier to see the text in the boxes.

2 ● **Increase the zoom to 75%.**

● **Type** Sam Johnson.

● **Press** [←Enter].

● **Type** Director.

● **Click on the organization chart background.**

Your screen should be similar to Figure 3.43

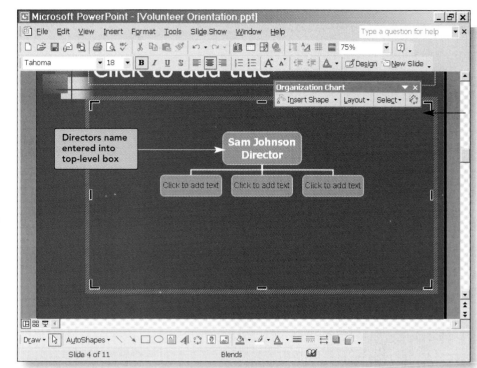

Figure 3.43

The box and font size will change to accommodate whatever you type in the boxes.

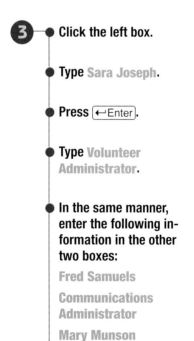

3 ● **Click the left box.**

● **Type** Sara Joseph.

● **Press** [←Enter].

● **Type** Volunteer Administrator.

● **In the same manner, enter the following information in the other two boxes:**

Fred Samuels

Communications Administrator

Mary Munson

Fund Raising

● **Click on the chart background.**

Your screen should be similar to Figure 3.44

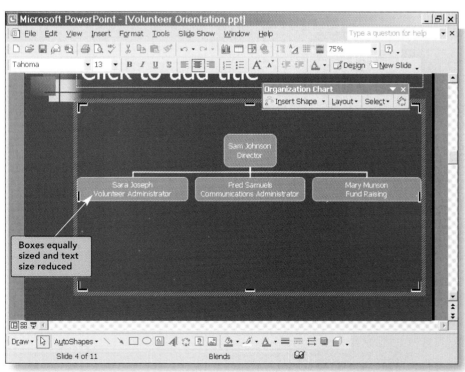

Figure 3.44

The subordinate boxes were equally sized to the size needed to display the largest amount of text and the font size was reduced.

Adding Boxes

Since this orientation is for volunteers, you are going to expand only the Volunteer Administrator section of the organization chart. To add a box, you first select the type of box to add and then select the box to link it to. You will add two subordinate boxes for the two people who report directly to Sara Joseph.

1 ● Click the box for Sara Joseph.

● Open the [Insert Shape ▾] drop-down menu and select **S**ubordinate.

● Click the new subordinate box.

● Type Martin Crane.

● Press ◄┘Enter.

● Type Foster Angels.

● Click on the chart background.

Your screen should be similar to Figure 3.45

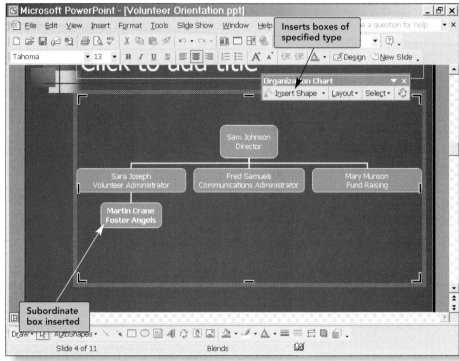

Figure 3.45

The new box appears in the same color background as the existing boxes. Next you will add a co-worker box next to Martin Crane.

2 ● **Click on Martin Crane's box.**

● **Open the**  **drop-down menu and select Coworker.**

● **Click the new co-worker box.**

● **Type Peg Ludwig.**

● **Press ←Enter.**

● **Type Adoption Angels.**

● **Click on the chart background.**

Your screen should be similar to Figure 3.46

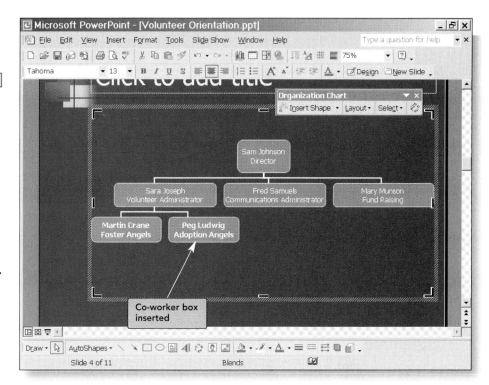

Figure 3.46

Enhancing the Organization Chart

To make the organization chart more interesting, you decide to change the appearance of the boxes, text, and lines. You could select each element individually and make changes, but PowerPoint includes an AutoFormat option that provides prepackaged styles.

1 ● **Click AutoFormat.**

Your screen should be similar to Figure 3.47

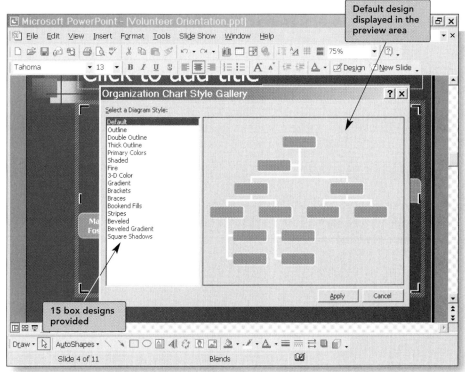

Figure 3.47

From the Organization Chart Style Gallery dialog box, you can select 15 different box designs. The selected design, Default, is displayed in the preview area.

2

- **Select several diagram styles and preview the samples.**

- **Choose Square Shadows.**

- **Click** Apply **.**

Your screen should be similar to Figure 3.48

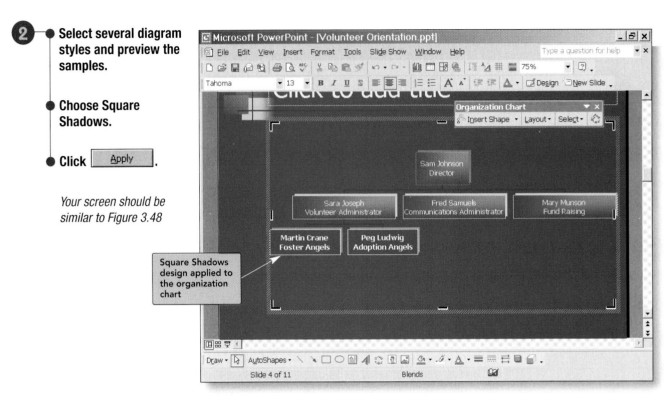

Square Shadows design applied to the organization chart

Figure 3.48

The final enhancement is to make the Volunteer section of the organization chart stand out, so you decide to color and bold the names in the boxes.

3

- **Click on Sara Joseph's box to select it and drag to select her name.**

- **Click** B **Bold.**

- **Click** A **Font Color and select bright pink.**

- **Use Format Painter to apply the same formats to the names in the two boxes below Sara Joseph.**

- **Click on the chart background.**

Your screen should be similar to Figure 3.49

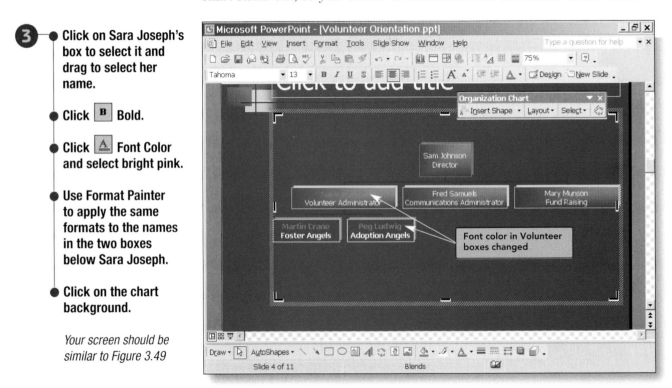

Font color in Volunteer boxes changed

Figure 3.49

Changing the Layout

You also decide to add to the chart the names of the volunteer assistants who work for the coordinators.

1 ● **Add two subordinate boxes under Martin Crane and enter the names Susan Allison and Maria Garcia.**

Additional Information

Clicking [Insert Shape ▾] will insert the default shape of subordinate.

● **In a similar manner, under Peg Ludwig add two subordinate boxes and enter the names Jamul Johnson and Kaye Benjamin.**

● **Change the font color to bright pink in the new boxes.**

Your screen should be similar to Figure 3.50

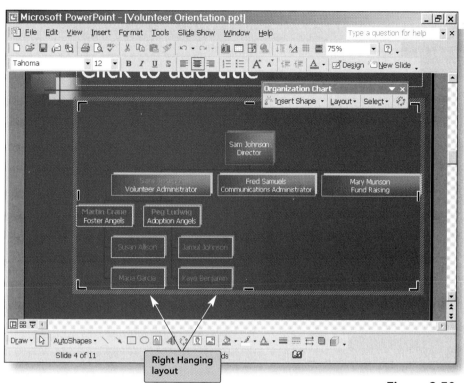

Figure 3.50

PowerPoint automatically adds the new subordinate boxes in a Right Hanging layout. You want to change the arrangement of the boxes. You can change the arrangement of the entire organization chart or only selected levels. You will rearrange the co-worker boxes to appear in the Standard layout to match the rest of the chart. To change a level, select the level above the level whose layout you want to change.

2 • Click the box for Martin Crane.

• Open the Layout ▾ drop-down menu and choose **S**tandard.

• In a similar manner, change the layout for the boxes beneath Peg Ludwig.

• Click on the slide background.

• Return the zoom to Fit.

Your screen should be similar to Figure 3.51

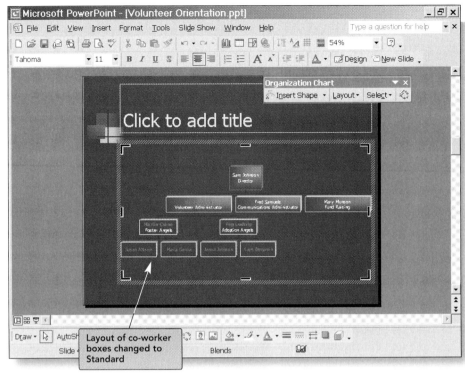

Figure 3.51

Additional Information
You can click on the chart to reopen the Organization Chart application to further modify the chart at any time.

The last step is to add the title.

3 • Type Who's Who as the slide title.

• Save the presentation.

• Choose **V**iew/**N**ormal (Restore Panes).

Your screen should be similar to Figure 3.52

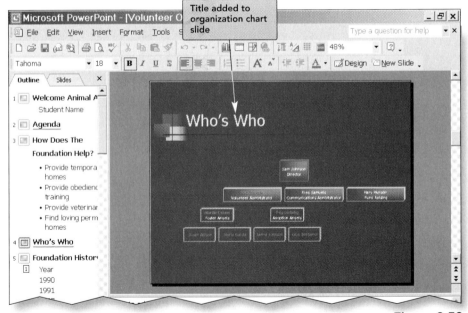

Figure 3.52

4 ● To see how all the changes you have made to the presentation look, run the presentation beginning with slide 1.

● Print the presentation as handouts, six per page.

Your handouts will be similar to those shown here

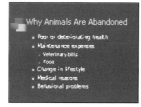

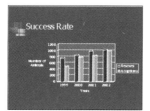

Become an Animal Angel   1

Exporting a Presentation Outline to Word

Now that the presentation is nearly complete, you need to send a copy of the text portion of the presentation to the director for approval. To do this quickly, you can save the text of the presentation to a text file.

Choose File/Send to/Microsoft Word.

Your screen should be similar to Figure 3.53

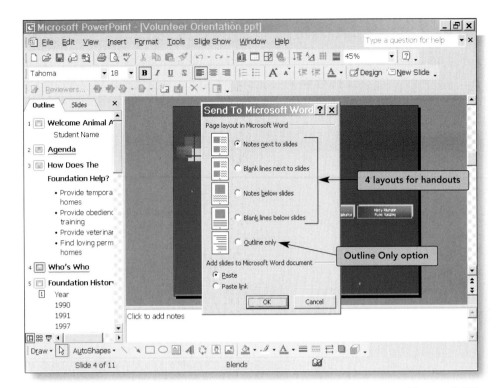

Figure 3.53

From the dialog box, you can select from four layouts for handouts, or you can create a document containing the outline only. If you choose a handout layout, you can also choose to include the slides in the handouts or just provide links to the slides. You want to create a Word document of just the outline of the presentation.

Select Outline Only.

Click OK **.**

Your screen should be similar to Figure 3.54

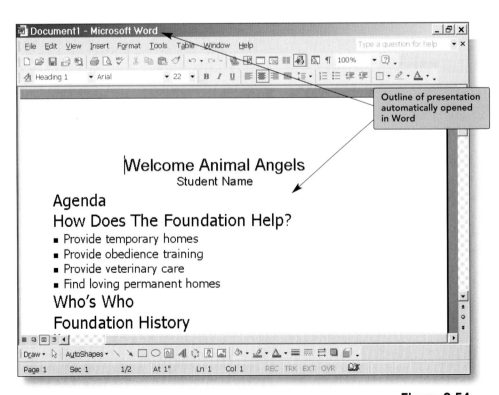

Figure 3.54

Word opens and displays the outline for the presentation. The document is saved as an .rtf (Rich Text Format) document type so that various types of word processing applications can open it.

3 ● Scroll through the document to review the outline.

● Save the document as Orientation Outline **with a Word document (.doc) file type.**

● Print the outline and exit Word.

E-mailing a Presentation

The director has asked you to send a copy of the presentation for review by e-mail. To do this, you will send the presentation as an attachment to an e-mail message. An **attachment** is a copy of a file that is included with an e-mail message. The attached file can then be opened by the recipient using the application in which it was created.

1 ● **Click** [image] **E-mail (as Attachment).**

HAVING TROUBLE?
If you do not have an e-mail program installed, the [image] button is not displayed and you will need to skip this section.

● **If necessary, click** [OK] **in the Choose Profile dialog box.**

Another Method
The menu equivalent is **F**ile/Se**n**d to/Mail Re**c**ipient (as Attachment).

Your screen should look similar to Figure 3.55

HAVING TROUBLE?
If your default e-mail program is other than Outlook Express, your e-mail window will look slightly different.

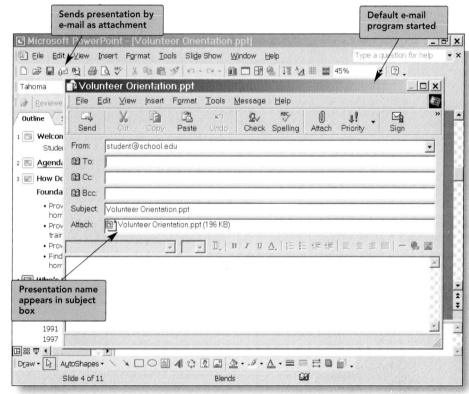

Figure 3.55

The default e-mail program on your system is started, and a new message window is displayed.

Additional Information

To send an e-mail message to multiple recipients, separate the e-mail addresses with semicolons.

You need to specify the recipient's e-mail address, the e-mail address of anyone you want to send a courtesy copy of this message to (CC:), and the subject and body of the message. You can use the toolbar buttons to select recipient names from your e-mail address book, attach a file to the message, set the message priority (high, normal, or low priority), include a follow-up message flag, and set other e-mail options. The file name of the presentation appears in the Subject box and in the Attach box by default.

2 ● Enter the e-mail address of the person you want to send the message to in the To box.

Additional Information

Your instructor will provide the e-mail address to use. For example, if you have a personal e-mail address, your instructor may want you to use it for this exercise.

● Enter the following in the message text area:
Attached is the presentation I have been working on for the new volunteer orientation meeting. Please give me your suggestions.

● Press ←Enter twice and type your name.

Your screen should look similar to Figure 3.56

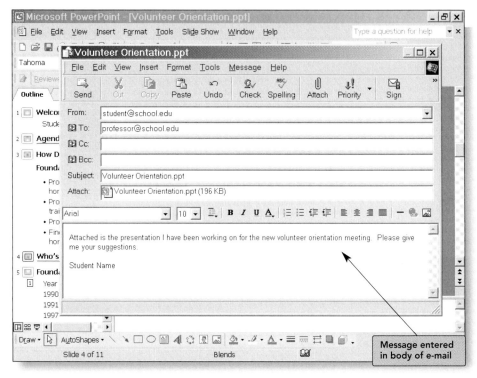

Figure 3.56

You are now ready to send the e-mail message. If you have an Internet connection, you could click [Send] to send the e-mail message. Instead, you will save it to be sent at a later time.

3 ● Choose **File/Save As** and save the message as Volunteer Presentation.

● Close the e-mail window.

HAVING TROUBLE?

If you do not have an Internet connection established, you will not be able to send this message. Click ⊠ to close the connection message.

When the message is sent, the recipient can open the attachment and view the presentation using PowerPoint.

Delivering Presentations

Typically presentations are delivered by connecting a computer to a projector to display the slides on a large screen. Before delivering a presentation, it is important to rehearse it so that you are well prepared and at ease with both the equipment and the materials. It is best to rehearse in a setting as close as possible to the real situation with a small audience who will give you honest feedback. Since most presentations are allotted a set amount of time, as part of the rehearsal you may also want to keep track of the time spent on each slide and the total time of the presenation.

Rehearsing Timing

To help with this aspect of the presentation, PowerPoint includes a timing feature that records the length of time spent on each slide and the total presentation time while you are rehearsing. If the presentation runs either too long or too short, you can quickly see which slides you are spending too much or too little time on and adjust the presentation accordingly.

1 ● **Choose Slide Show/Rehearse Timings.**

Your screen should be similar to Figure 3.57

Figure 3.57

The Rehearsal toolbar appears and starts a clock to time your delivery. The ➡ button advances to the next step in the show and the ❙❙ will pause the timing. You can also return to the previous slide to repeat the rehearsal and apply new timings to the slide using the ↰ button on the toolbar.

Normally you would read your narration aloud while you rehearse the timing. For this exercise, think about what you would say for each slide. The toolbar will record the time for each slide. When you reach the end of the presentation, a message box displays the total time for the presentation.

2 ● **Advance through the slide show as you would during the actual presentation.**

● **Click** Yes **to keep the slide timings.**

Your screen should be similar to Figure 3.58

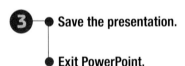

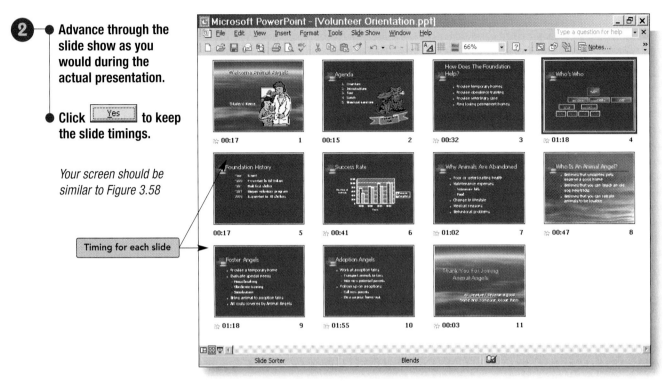

Figure 3.58

The presentation is displayed in Slide Sorter view, showing the timing for each slide. Now that you can see the individual timings, you can easily see where you are spending too little or too much time.

Once the slide show includes preset timings for each slide, you can use the timings to advance the slides automatically for you during the presentation. To turn on this feature use Sli**d**e Show/**S**et Up Show and select the Use Timings option to advance slides.

3 ● **Save the presentation.**

● **Exit PowerPoint.**

Preparing Overheads and 35mm Slides

If you are unsure of the availability of a data projector, you may want to convert the presentation to overheads or 35mm slides. To create overheads, you print your presentation as black-and-white or color transparencies. Put the transparencies into the printer instead of paper. Be sure to order the type of transparency that is appropriate for your printer.

You can also transform your electronic slides to 35mm slides by contacting a local service bureau. Follow their instructions for sending the presentation.

concept summary

LAB 3

Using Advanced Presentation Features

Group   (PP3.12)

A **group** is two or more objects that are treated as a single object.

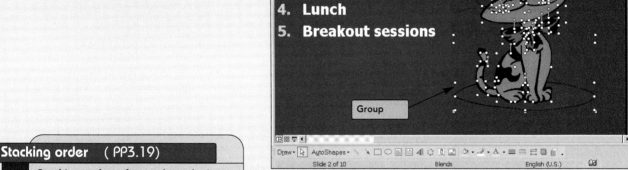

Group

Stacking order   (PP3.19)

Stacking order refers to the order in which objects are inserted in the different layers of a slide. As each object is added to the slide, it is added to the top layer.

Stacking order

Agenda

1. Overview
2. Introductions
3. Tour
4. Lunch
5. Breakout sessions

Object Alignment   (PP3.23)

Object alignment refers to the position of objects relative to each other by their left, right, top, or bottom edges; or horizontally by their centers or vertically by their middles; or in relation to the entire slide.

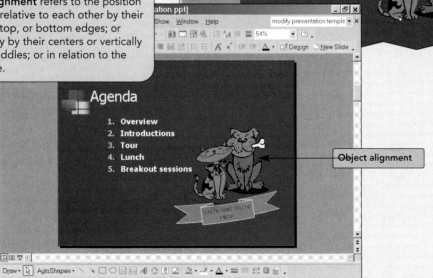

Agenda

1. Overview
2. Introductions
3. Tour
4. Lunch
5. Breakout sessions

Object alignment

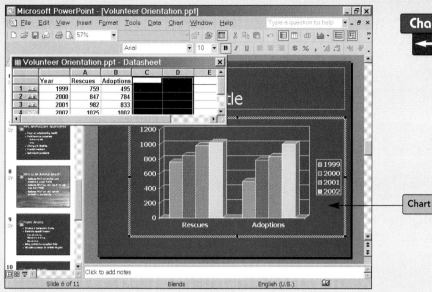

Chart (PP3.25)

A **chart** is a visual representation of numeric data that is used to help an audience grasp the impact of your data more quickly.

Chart

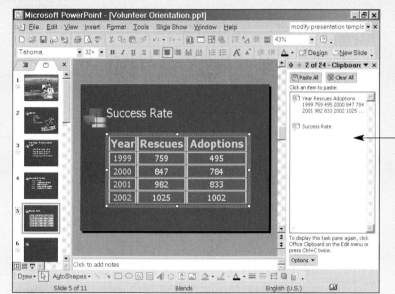

Collecting and Pasting (PP3.28)

Collecting and pasting is the capability of the program to store multiple copied items in the Office Clipboard and then paste one or more of the items into another location or document.

Collecting and Pasting

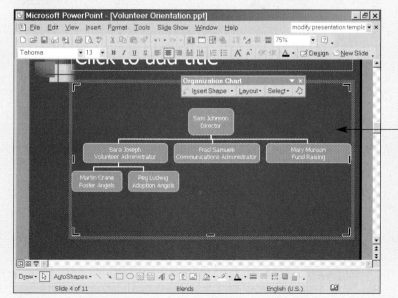

Organization Chart (PP3.39)

An **organization chart** is a map of a group, which usually includes people, but can include any items that have a hierarchical relationship.

Organization chart

lab review

LAB 3
Using Advanced Presentation Features

key terms

assistant box   PP3.39

attachment   PP3.49

attribute   PP3.12

branch   PP3.39

category axis   PP3.26

cell   PP3.30

chart   PP3.25

collecting and pasting   PP3.28

co-worker box   PP3.39

data series   PP3.32

datasheet   PP3.30

grid   PP3.23

group   PP3.12, PP3.39

guide   PP3.23

hierarchy   PP3.39

legend   PP3.26

level   PP3.39

manager box   PP3.39

object alignment   PP3.23

organization chart   PP3.39

stacking order   PP3.19

subordinate box   PP3.39

titles   PP3.26

value axis   PP3.26

X axis   PP3.26

Y axis   PP3.26

mous skills

The Microsoft Office User Specialist (MOUS) certification program is designed to measure your proficiency in performing basic tasks using the Office XP applications. Getting certified demonstrates that you have the skills and provides a valuable industry credential for employment. After completing this lab, you have learned the following Microsoft Office User Specialist skills:

Skill	Description	Page
Creating Presentations	Add slides to and delete slides from presentations	PP3.5, PP3.6, PP3.27, PP3.40
Inserting and Modifying Text	Insert, format, and modify text	PP3.7, PP3.9
Inserting and Modifying Visual Elements	Add tables, charts, clip art, and bitmap images to slides	PP3.13, PP3.24, PP3.39
	Customize slide backgrounds	PP3.10
Modifying Presentation Formats	Apply formats to presentations	PP3.8, PP3.11
	Rehearse timing	PP3.51
	Modify slide layout	PP3.3
Working with Data from Other Sources	Export a presentation as an outline	PP3.48
Managing and Preparing Presentations	Deliver presentations	PP3.51

www.mhhe.com/oleary

command summary

Command	Shortcut	Button	Action
File/Sen**d** To/Microsoft **W**ord			Exports text of presentation to Word
File/Sen**d** To/Mail Re**c**ipient (as Attachment)		☐	Sends presentation or selected slide as an e-mail attachment
Edit/Office Clip**b**oard			Opens Clipboard task pane
View/Gr**i**d and Guides			Displays guidelines that help align objects
View/**Z**oom		`100% ▾`	Changes size of onscreen display of slide
Insert/C**h**art			Adds a chart object to a slide
F**o**rmat/**B**ullets and Numbering		☰ ☰	Creates bulleted or numbered lists
F**o**rmat/**B**ackground			Applies colors, patterns, or pictures to a slide background
F**o**rmat/Aut**o**Shape			Changes characteristics of an AutoShape
Sli**d**e Show/**R**ehearse timings			Starts slide show and sets timings for slide
`Draw ▾`/**G**roup			Groups objects together
`Draw ▾`/**U**ngroup			Ungroups objects
`Draw ▾`/**O**rder/Send to Bac**k**			Sends object to bottom of stack
`Draw ▾`/Gr**i**d and Guides			Aligns objects to grid or guides
`Draw ▾`/**A**lign or Distribute			Aligns or distributes objects
Chart Datasheet			
F**o**rmat/**Se**lected Data Series	Ctrl + 1		Applies patterns, shapes, and other to formats selected data series
Data/Series in **C**olumns			Arranges chart based on columns in Datasheet window
Chart/Chart **O**ptions			Adds and modifies chart options such as titles, legends, and gridlines
Organization Chart			
`Insert Shape ▾`/**S**ubordinate			Adds a box below selected box
`Insert Shape ▾`/**C**oworker			Adds a box at same level as selected box
`Layout ▾`/**St**andard			Applies standard layout to selected boxes
		🖌	Applies selected design to boxes of organization chart

Terminology

screen identification

In the following PowerPoint screen, several items are identified by letters.
Enter the correct term for each item in the spaces that follow.

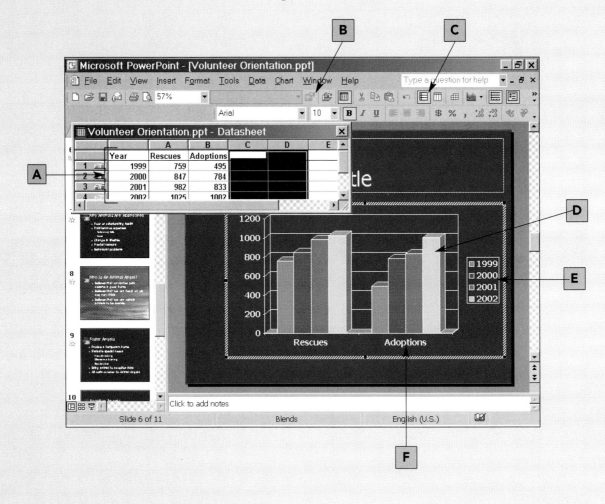

A. _____   D. _____

B. _____   E. _____

C. _____   F. _____

Match the numbered item with the correct lettered description.

1.   _____   **a.** two or more objects treated as a single object

2. datasheet   _____   **b.** table consisting of rows and columns

3. value axis   _____   **c.** group of related data plotted in the chart

4. hierarchy   _____   **d.** file copied along with an e-mail message

5. data series   _____   **e.** line that snaps an object to position on a slide

6. attachment   _____   **f.** shows ranking within a department

7. cell   _____   **g.** applies multiple formats to the selected text

8.   _____   **h.** intersection of a row and column

9. guide   _____   **i.** used to convert text to a numbered list

10. group   _____   **j.** scale whose numbers are determined by the data used in the chart

Circle the letter of the correct response to the questions below.

1. The _____ allows the user to apply new formats to selected text.
   a. Format Design
   b. Apply Design
   c. Design Painter
   d. Format Painter

2. Many clip art images are made up of multiple parts that are _____ together.
   a. applied
   b. grouped
   c. ungrouped
   d. arranged

3. _____ means to position objects relative to each other by their left, right, top, or bottom edges.
   a. Stacking
   b. Grouping
   c. Object alignment
   d. Branch

4. A(n) _____ is a vertical or horizontal line that helps align objects on a slide.
   a. grid
   b. guide
   c. align gauge
   d. form gauge

5. The intersection of a row and column creates a(n) _____ in which text or data is entered.
   a. grid
   b. legend
   c. axis
   d. cell

6. The table used to create a chart in PowerPoint is called a _____.
   a. database
   b. worksheet
   c. datasheet
   d. chart form

7. The _____ is the top-level box of a group.
   a. co-worker box
   b. manager box
   c. subordinate box
   d. branch

8. PowerPoint documents can be _____ to Microsoft Word.
   a. imported
   b. exported
   c. extracted
   d. moved

9. When more than one line of text is displayed in an AutoShape, the _____ option must be selected.
   a. word-wrap
   b. multi-line
   c. continue next
   d. resize

10. _____ is the capability of a program to store multiple copied items in the Office Clipboard and then paste one or more of the items into another location or document.
   a. Collecting and pasting
   b. Grouping
   c. Stacking
   d. Attaching

true/false

Circle the correct answer to the following statements.

1.	A presentation can be edited in Outline and Slide Sorter views.	True	False
2.	You can copy information to the Office Clipboard from any program that provides copy and cut capabilities, but you can only paste from it into Word, Excel, Access, PowerPoint, and Outlook.	True	False
3.	You cannot work in a selected cell.	True	False
4.	You must have at least three objects selected to distribute them.	True	False
5.	.bmp, .jpg, .gif, and .png file types can be converted to drawing objects and ungrouped.	True	False
6.	A grid is a line that is used to position objects on a slide.	True	False
7.	A scanned picture can be used as a background for a slide.	True	False
8.	You cannot overlap objects as they are added to a slide.	True	False
9.	The entire lower level of an organization chart can be selected and modified without affecting the upper levels.	True	False
10.	The Office Clipboard and the System Clipboard both hold multiple objects.	True	False

Concepts

fill-in

Complete the following statements by filling in the blanks with the correct terms.

1. A(n) _____ is a box and all the boxes that report to it.

2. To work with separate parts of a graphic, you must _____ the elements.

3. The _____ ensures that as each object is added to the slide, it is added to the top layer.

4. _____ have the same manager.

5. A(n) _____ presentation can be opened and viewed from an e-mail.

6. When an object is close to the _____, the center or corner snaps to the line.

7. Changing the _____ percentage only affects the onscreen display of the slide; it does not change the actual font or object size.

8. A(n) _____ can include any items that have a hierarchical relationship.

9. When the Format Painter is used to apply formatting on a(n) _____, it is applied to a word or selection you specify.

10. A(n) _____ chart emphasizes the area under the curve.

discussion questions

1. Discuss the advantages of grouping and ungrouping objects. Give examples of when you would need to ungroup an object and when you would want to group objects.

2. Discuss the differences between the System Clipboard and the Office Clipboard. What advantages does the Office Clipboard provide for collecting and pasting?

3. Discuss how organization charts are created and used. Give two examples of other hierarchical relationships that could be represented by an organization chart.

Hands-On Exercises

rating system

★ Easy

★★ Moderate

★★★ Difficult

step-by-step

Employee Morale Presentation

★ 1. Chirag Shah works in the personnel department of a manufacturing company. Chirag has recently been studying the ways that employee morale can affect production levels and employee job satisfaction. Chirag has been asked to hold a meeting with department managers to suggest methods that can be used to improve employee morale. He has already started a PowerPoint presentation to accompany his talk, but still needs to make several changes and enhancements to the presentation. Several slides of the completed presentation are shown here.

   a. Start PowerPoint and open the presentation pp03_Employee Motivation. Replace the Student Name placeholder with your name. Switch to Slide sorter view.

   b. Return to Normal view. Insert the clip art graphic pp03_Motivation on slide 2. Size and place the clip art to the right of the text. Ungroup the clip art and remove the tan background from behind the man. Change the tie and shirt to brighter green colors. Regroup the clip art.

   c. Convert the five demoted bullets on slide 3 to a numbered list. Add color to the numbers.

   d. Demote the last three bullets on slide 5. Add a callout AutoShape containing the words You're doing a good job, Thanks! Bold the text in the AutoShape. Position the AutoShape appropriately on the slide.

   e. Insert the clip art of pp03_Money on slide 7. Size and place the clip art to the right of the text. Ungroup the clip art and change the green color of the money to a darker green. Regroup the clip art.

f. Save the presentation as Employee Motivation2. Print the presentation as handouts, six slides per page.

g. Export the presentation outline to Word. Save the Word document as Motivation Outline using the Word document file type (.doc). Print the outline.

Water Safety Presentation

★ **2.** The Arizona division of the Red Cross has hired you to help them create a presentation to inform Maricopa County residents about the importance of water safety. The presentation is partially completed, and you have been asked to enhance it so that it can be used at an upcoming meeting. Several slides of the completed presentation are shown here.

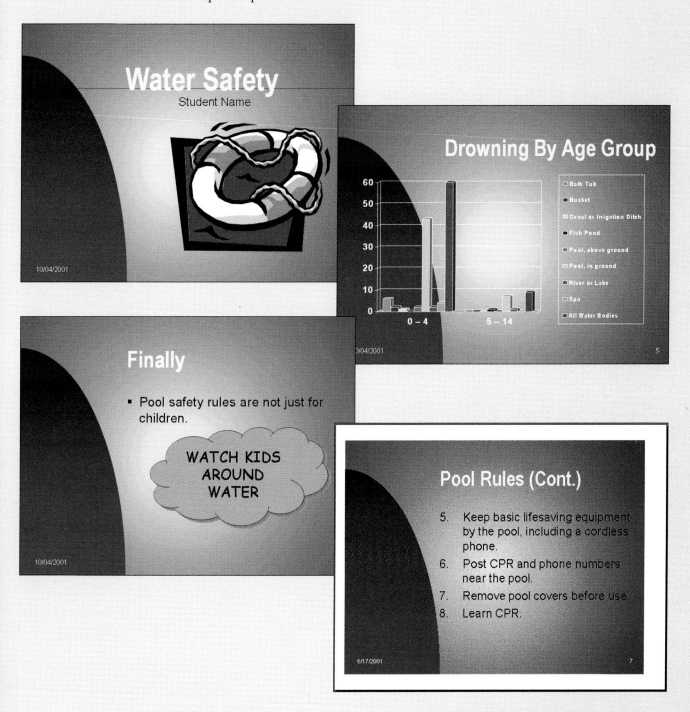

a. Start PowerPoint and open the pp03_Water Safety presentation. Enter your name on the first slide in place of Student Name.

b. Use the pp03_Gradblu2 file as a background fill effect for all the slides.

c. Use the slide master to change the text color of bulleted items to black. Change the font color of the text styles to black.

d. Insert the clip art pp03_Water on the first slide. Appropriately size and position the clip art. Modify the clip art by changing the background to blue.

e. Insert the clip art pp03_Pool on the second slide. Appropriately size and position the clip art. Add a blue border line around the graphic.

f. On slide 4 enhance the column headings by applying fill and text colors, increasing the row height, and vertically and horizontally centering the labels. Bold all the text in the table.

g. Insert a Title Chart slide after slide 4. Copy the slide title and data (exclude the Total column and row) from slide 4. Paste the data into the chart datasheet on slide 5. Delete the data in columns C, D, and E of the datasheet. Make the chart as large as possible and enhance it using the Microsoft Graph features. Paste the slide title you copied into the title for the chart slide.

h. The pool rules have a duplicated slide. Delete slide 6. Apply a numbered list to the pool rules on slides 6 and 7. Set the numbering on slide 7 to begin at 5.

i. Create an AutoShape of your choice on the last slide. Add the text WATCH KIDS AROUND WATER in the AutoShape. Word wrap and resize the AutoShape to fit the text.

j. Change the fill color to complement the slide. Increase the text size and bold the text. Resize the AutoShape if needed.

k. Save the presentation as Water Safety2. E-mail the presentation to your instructor. Print the presentation with six slides per page.

Emergency Driving Statistics

★ ★ **3.** Your presentation on Emergency Driving has really turned out well (Practice Exercise 3 of Lab 2). You have recently finished a survey project for the department of public safety on the causes of accidents. It is no surprise to you that blowouts are a significant cause of accidents in your area. You think this new data will fit nicely into the presentation as a chart. Several slides of the completed presentation are shown here.

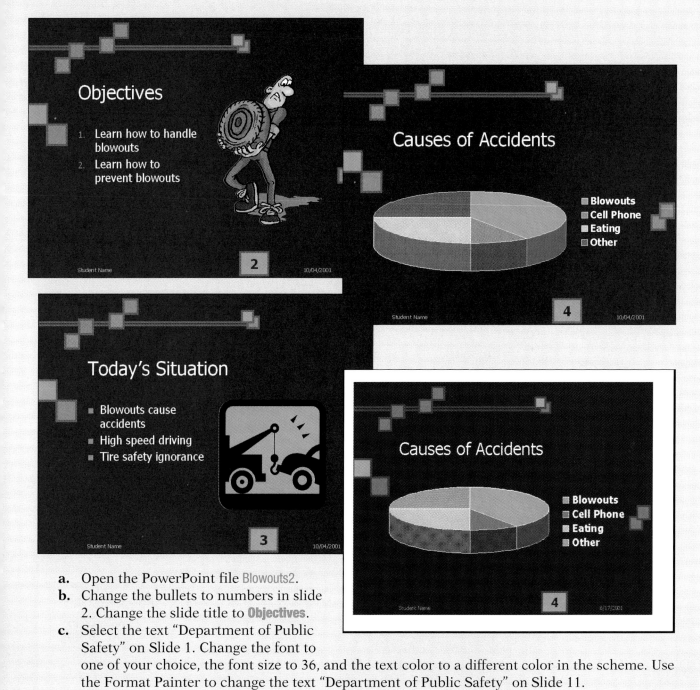

a. Open the PowerPoint file Blowouts2.

b. Change the bullets to numbers in slide 2. Change the slide title to Objectives.

c. Select the text "Department of Public Safety" on Slide 1. Change the font to one of your choice, the font size to 36, and the text color to a different color in the scheme. Use the Format Painter to change the text "Department of Public Safety" on Slide 11.

d. Select and ungroup the image of the tow truck on slide 3. Change the white background and wheels to a color of your choice. Regroup the image.

e. Insert a new Title and Chart slide after slide 3. Title the slide **Causes of Accidents**. Insert a 3-D pie chart and enter the following data into the datasheet:

Blowouts	Cell Phone	Eating	Other
40	10	25	25

f. Change the colors of the Eating slice and the Other slice by selecting the slice and double-clicking. Remove the border lines around the chart and the legend. Size the chart to fit the slide.

g. Delete the clip art on slide 2 and insert the image pp03_Spare Tire. Adjust the image appropriately.

h. Save your completed presentation as Blowouts3. Print the presentation with six slides per page.

Market Analysis Presentation

★ ★ **4.** You are working on a market analysis presentation for a presentation at the upcoming board of directors meeting for the Sports Company. You need to modify the presentation by including a chart of the sales and a marketing plan. Several slides of the completed presentation are shown here.

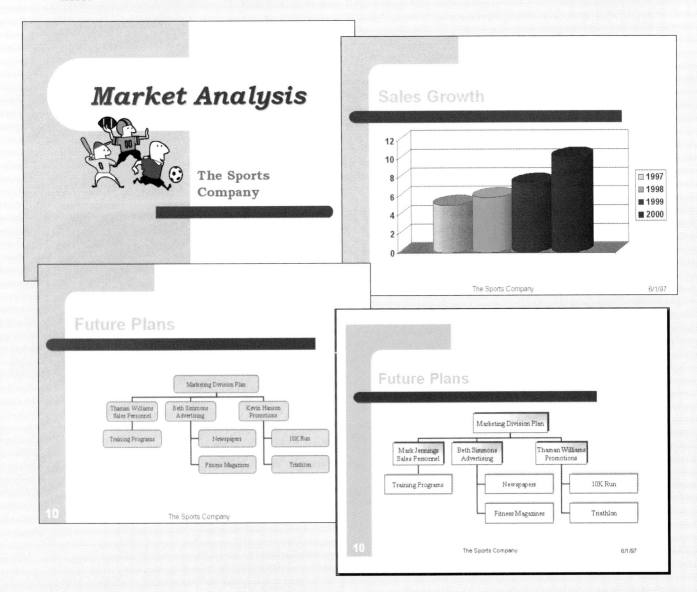

a. Start PowerPoint and open the file pp03_Final Marketing Presentation. Delete the graphic from slide 1. Insert the files pp03_Baseball Man, pp03_Football Man, and pp03_Basketball Man. Group and size the objects as shown.

b. Remove the blue box from behind the graphic on slide 2, and reposition and size the graphic appropriately.

c. Insert a new slide after slide 5 using the Title and Chart layout. Copy the entire contents of the table on slide 5 and paste it into the chart datasheet. Delete the extra sample data from the datasheet.

d. Enhance the appearance of the chart by changing the colors of the columns. Change the bars to cylinders. Add other enhancements of your choice.

e. Copy the title from slide 5 into the title placeholder on slide 6. Delete slide 5.

f. Insert a new slide after slide 9 using the organization chart layout. Title the slide Future Plans. Enter Marketing Division Plan in the top-level box. Enter the following information into the other chart boxes:

   Thaman Williams, Sales Personnel (second level)
   Beth Simmons, Advertising (second level)
   Kevin Hanson, Promotions (second level)
   Training Programs (third level under Thaman Williams)
   Newspapers (third level under Beth Simmons)
   Fitness Magazines (third level under Beth Simmons)
   10K Run (third level under Kevin Hanson)
   Triathlon (third level under chart style)

g. Export the outline to Word. Save the Word document as Sports Company Outline. Print the outline.

h. Save the presentation as Sports Company Presentation. Print the presentation with six slides per page.

Nutrition and Exercise Presentation

★★ **5.** Annette Ramirez is the new Lifestyle Fitness Club nutritionist. She would like to use the
★ presentation on exercise currently in use by the club to discuss the benefits of a nutrition plan.
She has asked you to modify the current presentation to include some nutrition information.
Several slides of the completed presentation are shown here.

a. Start PowerPoint and open the file
pp03_Exercise for Clients.

b. Apply the Profile design template to the
entire presentation. Remove the background image from all slides.

c. Change the title on slide 1 to **Fitness and
Nutrition**. Change the font and size of the
title. Reposition the text appropriately.

d. Change the title on slide 2 to **What
Exercise and Nutrition Can Do for You**. Add a
level 1 bullet, **Exercise**, above the existing
bullets. Demote the two original bullets
to level 2. Insert a new level 1 bullet,
Nutrition, and two new level 2 bullets,
Healthy Choices and **Tips**, below the existing bullets.

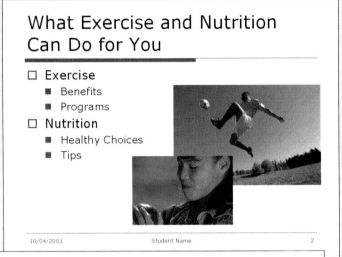

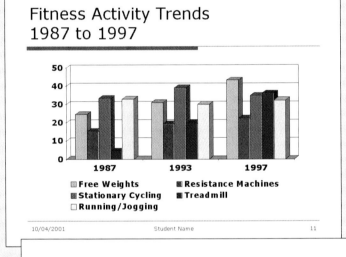

e. Insert the file pp03_Exercise on Slide 2. Group the graphics as shown in the example.

f. Change the appearance of the table on slide 9 by using text colors, adjusting row heights, and vertically and horizontally centering the labels. Jazzercise has been changed to Spinning, adjust the entries accordingly.

g. Check all slides and adjust the text and graphics as needed throughout.

h. Open the Excel file pp03_Fitness Trends. Using the Office Clipboard, copy the two title lines and then copy the worksheet data. Exit Excel. Insert a new slide after slide 10 using the chart layout. Paste the worksheet data into the chart datasheet. Paste the title from Excel into the slide title placeholder. Size the title text appropriately. Move the legend below the chart. Delete the border line around the legend. Modify the chart using the features you learned in the tutorial.

i. On the last slide delete the text box. Create an AutoShape in a shape of your choice and add the text **Make it part of your life!** Word wrap and size the AutoShape text. Change the fill color to match the colors on the slide. Adjust the text size and color as appropriate.

j. Save the presentation as Fitness and Nutrition. Export the outline to Word. Save the Word file as Fitness and Nutrition Outline. Print the outline. Print the presentation with six slides per page.

Bicycle Safety Presentation

★ **1.** A local law enforcement officer who is also a member of the PTA saw your presentation on bike safety (Lab 2, On Your Own 2). The officer has asked you to give a presentation to other officers who have been recruited to work with school children on bike safety. Using your file Better Bike Safety2, modify your presentation for the officers. Include appropriate clip art, and group and ungroup the clip art as needed. Use an AutoShape to highlight a welcome message on the second slide. Save your updated presentation as DPS Bike Safety. E-mail the presentation to your instructor or print the presentation with six slides per page.

Family Reunion Presentation

★ ★ **2.** Your family is holding a reunion in Las Vegas this year. They have heard all about your new computer skills, and one of your aunts has requested you put on a presentation following the welcome dinner. Using the skills you have learned so far, create a presentation that includes an organization chart for your family tree, photos you have scanned, family anecdotes, and graphics. Save your presentation as Family Reunion and print it with six slides per page. Consider e-mailing your completed work to a family member.

Credit Counseling Presentation

★ ★ **3.** As part of your job as Program Director at Debt Counseling USA, you have been asked to create a presentation for the new customer seminar. Use the data provided in pp03_Credit Debt to create a presentation on steps to eliminate or cut back on credit card debt. Use the skills you have learned in the lab to include a pie chart of average monthly expenses, and a numbered list of steps to creating a budget, and modify the clip art in the file. Format the slides as you like. Save your presentation as Credit Debt Presentation. Print the slides.

Updating Travel Italy Presentation

★ ★ **4.** Your fellow Getaway Travel Club members are really excited about the upcoming summer trip to Italy. Your presentation to the club officers on the costs associated with adding Rome and Venice to your itinerary went very well (Lab 2, On Your Own 3). They have asked you to show your presentation to the entire club and put the changes up to a vote. You decide that the data you included in the first presentation would be easier to understand and more convincing if it were presented in chart form. Using your file Travel Italy, modify the presentation for the whole group. Create charts for the costs you researched in the previous exercise. Update your information on the key tourist attractions with better graphics. Save your updated presentation as Travel Italy2. Export the presentation to Word as an outline and print the slides.

Placement Service Orientation

★ ★ **5.** Part of your job at the Lee Placement Services agency is to process new-hire paperwork and complete employee orientation. You have been asked to update the presentation you did on your company's services in Lab 1, On Your Own 4. Using the file Placement Services, update the presentation to explain the company's benefit package and include an organizational chart. It should show how contract employees report to the Human Resources contract manager, while full-time employees report to the Human Resources internal manager. All managers report to the owner. Enter your name as a header. Save the presentation as Lee Orientation and print the final presentation with six slides per page.

Computer Virus Presentation

Your computer survey class requires you to do a research project on computer viruses. Do some research on the Web to learn more about viruses. Create a PowerPoint presentation that includes the features you have learned. Search the Web for appropriate clip art images that you can group or ungroup as necessary to enhance your slides. If appropriate data is available, create a chart that displays the increase in viruses reported over the last five years. Include your name and the current date in a footer on the slides. Save your presentation as Computer Viruses. Export the slides to Word as an outline. Print the outline and six slides per page handouts.

Creating a Presentation for a Kiosk and the Web

LAB 4

objectives

After completing this lab, you will know how to:

1.	Create a presentation by importing an outline.
2.	Insert slides from another presentation.
3.	Create a complex table.
4.	Add animated graphics.
5.	Create and modify a WordArt object.
6.	Add sound and movies.
7.	Set up a presentation for a kiosk.
8.	Save a presentation with Pack and Go.
9.	Create custom shows.
10.	Create an agenda slide.
11.	Add hyperlinks and action buttons.
12.	Publish a presentation on the Web.

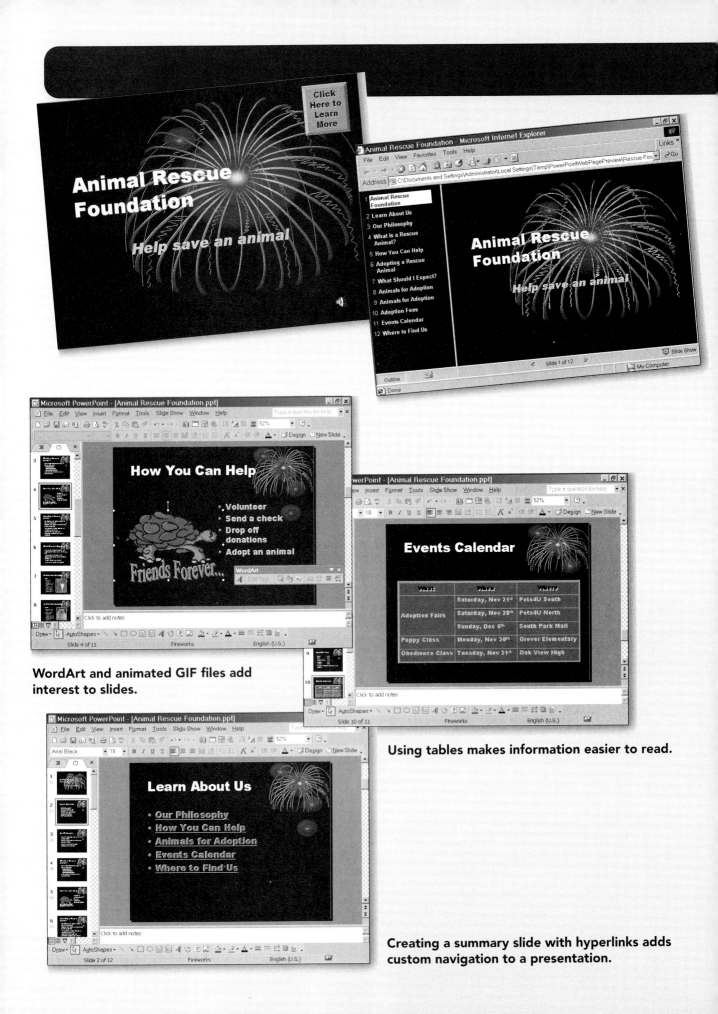

WordArt and animated GIF files add interest to slides.

Using tables makes information easier to read.

Creating a summary slide with hyperlinks adds custom navigation to a presentation.

Animal Rescue Foundation

The director of the Animal Rescue Foundation has asked you to create a presentation promoting the organization that will run on a kiosk in the local shopping mall. This presentation needs to capture the attention of passers-by in a very busy area. Two ways to capture attention are to add animation and sound. You will add several different animation and sound features to your presentation, along with music that will play throughout the entire presentation. At the end, the presentation will loop back to the first slide and continue playing.

You also want to publish this presentation on the Animal Rescue Foundation's Web site. PowerPoint 2002 will automatically convert a presentation to a format that runs on the Web. Since you want to give the viewer a means to navigate through the presentation, you will add navigation buttons that go forward and back through the slides. You will also add a home page that contains links to key slides in the presentation. The completed self-running presentation and Web page are shown on the facing page.

© Corbis

Creating a Presentation from Multiple Sources

Often, as you are developing a presentation, you will have information from a variety of sources, such as text from a Word document or slides from other presentations. You can easily incorporate this information into a presentation without having to recreate it again.

Importing a Word Outline

Additional Information

Text created in other word processing programs can also be used to create a new presentation. The text files that PowerPoint can import are Word (.doc), Rich Text Format (.rtf), plain text format (.txt), or HTML (.htm) files.

You started developing the content for the promotional presentation by creating an outline in Word. Additionally, you have another document that contains information about specific animals that are available for adoption. You will use the information from both of these documents to quickly create the new presentation.

1 ● Start PowerPoint.

*Your screen should be
similar to Figure 4.1*

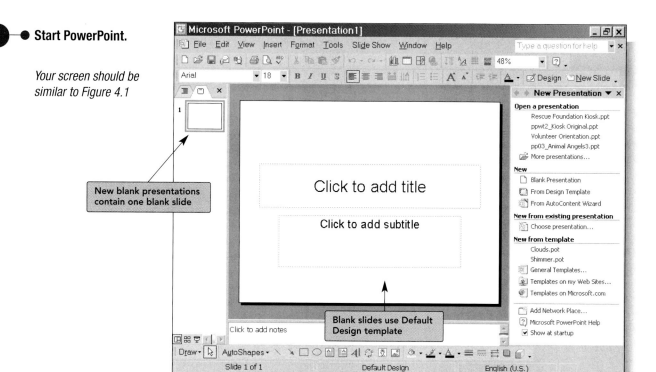

Figure 4.1

Additional Information

In Word, if you apply Outline Numbering styles to the outlined text, save the file as a Rich Text Format (.rtf) file before importing it to PowerPoint. This removes the Numbering style so that outline numbers do not appear on the slides, but maintains the heading styles.

A blank new presentation consisting of a single slide in the Default Design template is displayed. You will add slides containing the text for the presentation by importing the outline you created in Word. For best results, the document you want to import should be formatted using heading styles so PowerPoint can easily convert the file content to slides. PowerPoint uses the heading levels to determine the slide title and levels for the slide body text. If heading levels are not available, PowerPoint determines these features from the paragraph indentations.

As you created the outline in Outline view in Word, heading styles were automatically applied. Now all you have to do is import the outline into PowerPoint.

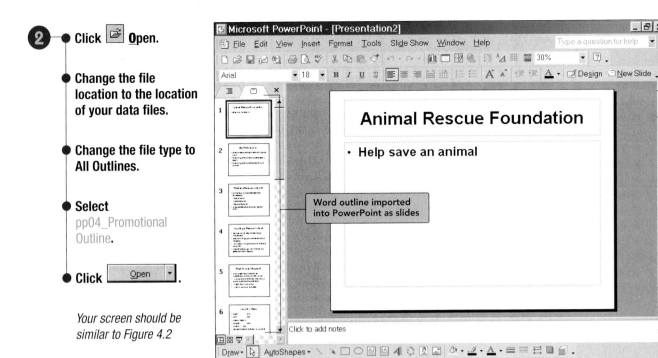

Figure 4.02

The outline text is imported into the blank presentation and inserted as separate slides. Each level 1 heading appears as an individual slide title. Text formatted as a level 2 heading is a main body text point, a level 3 heading is a second-level body text point, and so on.

Creating a Presentation from a Design Template

As you look at the default template design, you see that it will take a lot of time to add design features to the presentation. Rather than add the text from the second Word document about the animals available for adoption to this presentation, you will create another new presentation from a design template. Then you will incorporate the slides from the default presentation into the new presentation.

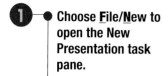

1 ● Choose **File/New** to open the New Presentation task pane.

Additional Information

Clicking ☐ New on the Standard toolbar opens a blank new presentation in the Default Design template and the Slide Layout task pane.

● Click [☐ From Design Template].

● If necessary, select **Show Large Previews** from the thumbnails shortcut menu.

● Apply the Fireworks template.

Your screen should be similar to Figure 4.3

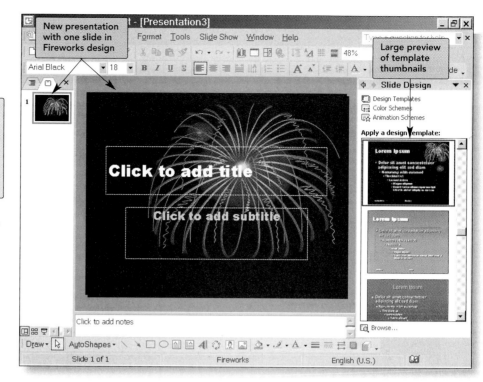

Figure 4.3

Additional Information

Each unnamed presentation you open during a session is assigned a number.

A new presentation (Presentation3) consisting of one slide in the Fireworks design is displayed. Next you will copy the slides from Presentation2 into this presentation.

2 ● Switch to Presentation 2.

● Change to Slide Sorter view.

● Select all slides.

● Click 📋 Copy.

● Close Presentation2 without saving it.

● Click 📋 Paste.

Your screen should be similar to Figure 4.4

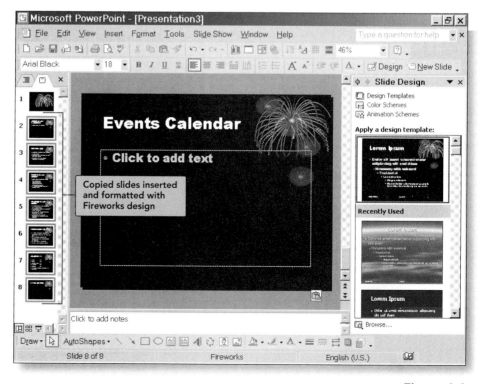

Figure 4.4

The copied slides are inserted into the new presentation and are formatted using the Fireworks template design.

Inserting Slides from an Outline

Now you want to add the information about the animals available for adoption.

- Move to slide 6.

- Choose Insert/Slides from Outline.

- Change to your data file location.

- Select pp04_Animals for Adoption.

- Click [Insert].

- Split the text between two slides.

Your screen should be similar to Figure 4.5

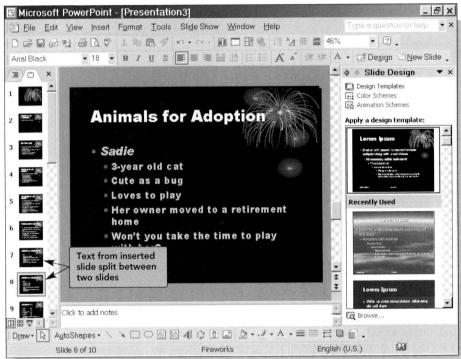

Figure 4.5

Slides 7 and 8 now contain the information about the animals currently available for adoption.

Inserting Slides from Another Presentation

Next you want to add two more slides to the presentation. To save time, you will insert slides that have already been created in another presentation into your current presentation. First you will add a slide after slide 4.

Display slide 4.

Choose Insert/Slides from Files.

Open the Find Presentation tab, if necessary.

Your screen should be similar to Figure 4.6

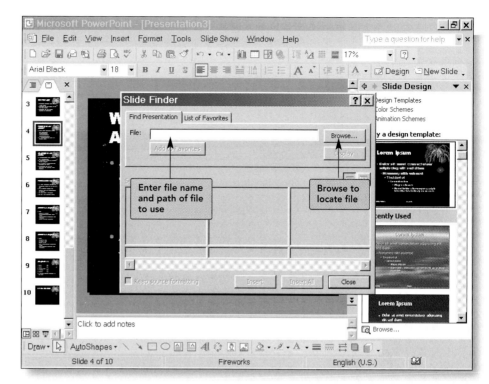

Figure 4.6

The Slide Finder dialog box is used to locate the presentation file containing the slides you want to copy into your current presentation. You can enter the file name and path directly in the File text box, or use the Browse... button to locate and select the file just as you would when opening an existing presentation.

Click Browse...

Change the Look In location to the location of your data files.

Select pp04_Foundation Introduction.

Click Open.

Your screen should be similar to Figure 4.7

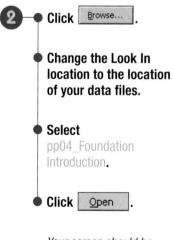

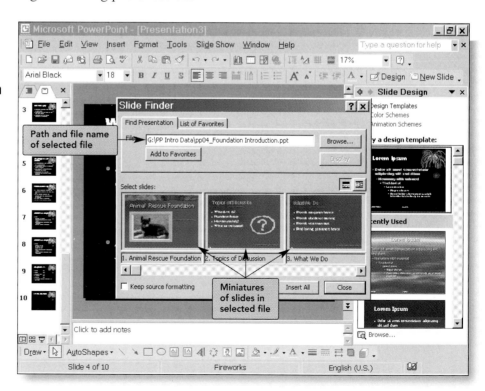

Figure 4.7

The path and file name of the selected file are displayed in the File text box. In addition, miniatures of the slides in the presentation are displayed in the Select Slides area. You can view the slides in two different formats: horizontal or list. Horizontal format displays a miniature of each slide side by side with the slide title below each slide. This is the default view. List format displays the titles of all slides in the presentation in a list and a preview of the selected slide.

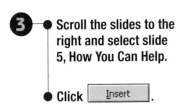

Additional Information

Click 🖾 to switch to horizontal format and 🖽 to switch to list format.

3 ● **Scroll the slides to the right and select slide 5, How You Can Help.**

● **Click** Insert .

Your screen should be similar to Figure 4.8

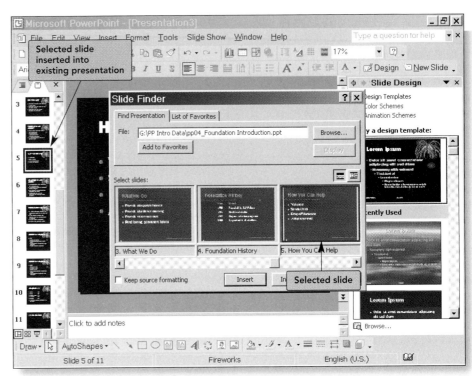

Figure 4.8

The selected slide from the Foundation Introduction presentation file is inserted into the new presentation and the template design is applied to the slide. Next you will insert the last slide from the Foundation Introduction presentation as the ending slide (12) of the new presentation.

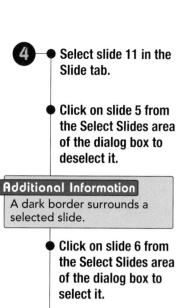

4 ● Select slide 11 in the Slide tab.

● Click on slide 5 from the Select Slides area of the dialog box to deselect it.

Additional Information
A dark border surrounds a selected slide.

● Click on slide 6 from the Select Slides area of the dialog box to select it.

● Click ___Insert___ .

● Click ___Close___ .

Your screen should be similar to Figure 4.9

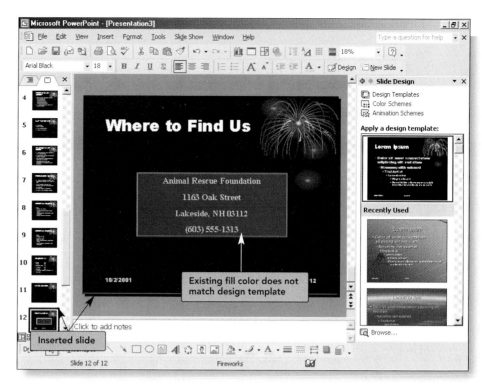

Figure 4.9

Now that all the slides you need have been added to the presentation, you need to make a few design adjustments. First you need to change the fill color of the text box to coordinate with the template colors.

5 ● Select the text box and change the fill color to the dark rose color from the slide color palette.

Your screen should be similar to Figure 4.10

Figure 4.10

Make the following changes to the slides specified.

6

- Delete slide 1.

- Change the slide layout of slide 1 to Title Slide.

- Apply the Title, Text, and Content slide layout to slide 7.

- Insert the picture file pp04_Jake from your data files on slide 7.

- Appropriately size and position the picture.

- Add a 6 pt dark gold border around the picture.

HAVING TROUBLE?

Use the ▤ Line Style and ✐ Line Color on the Drawing toolbar.

Your screen should be similar to Figure 4.11

Figure 4.11

The addition of the graphic adds much more impact to the slide.

7

- Repeat the same steps to add the picture file pp04_Sadie from your data files to slide 8.

- Run the slide show from the beginning to see how all the changes you have made so far look.

- Save the presentation as Animal Rescue Foundation.

Creating a Complex Table

Next you want to add a calendar of events in a table format. The table will display the type, date, and location of the event. Your completed table will be similar to the one shown below.

What	When	Where
	Saturday, Nov 21st	Pets4U South
Adoption Fairs	Saturday, Nov 28th	Pets4U North
	Sunday, Dec 6th	South Park Mall
Puppy Class	Monday, Nov 30th	Grover Elementary
Obedience Class	Tuesday, Nov 31st	Oak View High

PowerPoint includes several different methods that you can use to create tables. One method is to apply the Table slide layout to a slide. You used this method to create a simple table in Lab 2. Another method uses the Insert/Table command or the 🔲 Insert Table button to create a simple table consisting of the same number of rows and columns. Finally, Draw Table can be used to create any type of table, but is most useful for creating complex tables that contain cells of different heights or a varying number of columns per row. You will use the Draw Table feature to create this table.

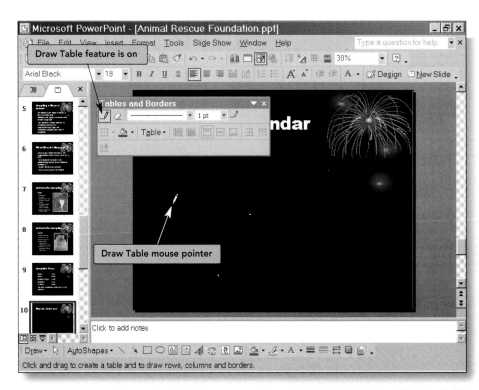

1 • **Display slide 10, Events Calendar.**

• **Apply the Title Only slide layout.**

• **Close the Slide Layout task pane.**

• **Click 🔳 Tables and Borders.**

Your screen should be similar to Figure 4.12

Figure 4.12

The Tables and Borders toolbar appears, and the mouse pointer changes to a ✎ pen when positioned on the slide. This indicates the Draw Table feature is on.

Using Draw Table to create a table is similar to the way you would use a pen to draw a table. First you define the outer table boundary by dragging diagonally to the size you want. Then you drag to create the column and row lines. A dotted line appears to show the boundary or lines you are creating as you drag. When creating row or column lines, drag from the beginning boundary to the end to extend the line the distance you want.

When creating a table using this feature, it is also helpful to display the ruler so you can more accurately draw the table lines.

You will use Draw Table to create the table boundary and columns and rows. As you do, refer to Figure 4.13 for guidance.

2 ● Choose **View/Ruler** to display the ruler.

● Drag downward and to the right to create an outer table boundary of approximately 3.5 inches by 7.5 inches.

● Add two vertical column lines at positions 2.5 and 5.5 on the ruler.

● Draw five horizontal lines to create the rows as shown in Figure 4.13. (Lines 2 and 3 begin at the end of the first column.)

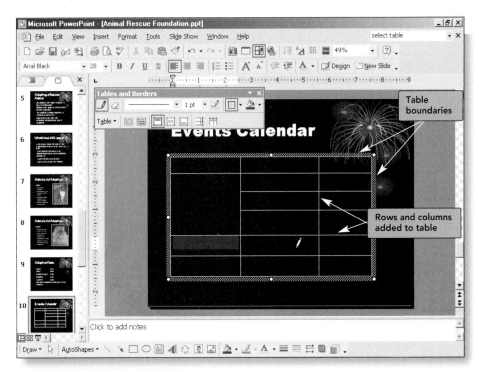

HAVING TROUBLE?
If you make an error, click ⟲ Undo or click ⟲ Eraser and click the line.

Your screen should be similar to Figure 4.13

Figure 4.13

Do not be concerned if your table is not exactly like that in Figure 4.13. You will adjust the table lines shortly.

Entering Data

Now you are ready to enter the information into the table. As you enter the text, the cells will automatically increase in size to accommodate the entries and the text will wrap in the cells.

1 ● Click  Draw Table to turn off the Draw Table feature.

Another Method
Typing in any cell will also turn off Draw Table.

● Enter the data shown at right.

Additional Information
You can copy and edit similar table entries to save time.

Additional Information
The "st" and "th" following the date will automatically change to superscript as soon as you enter a space after the word.

Your screen should be similar to Figure 4.14

	Col A	Col B	Col C
Row 1	What	When	Where
Row 2	Adoption Fairs	Saturday, Nov 21st	Pets4U South
Row 3		Saturday, Nov 28th	Pets4U North
Row 4		Sunday, Dec 6th	South Park Mall
Row 5	Puppy Class	Monday, Nov 30th	Grover Elementary
Row 6	Obedience Class	Tuesday, Dec 1st	Oak View High

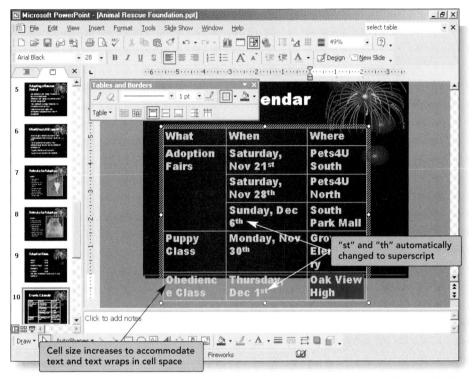

Figure 4.14

Because the table size has increased to accommodate the information in the table, it is too large to fit on the slide. You will fix this by making the font size of the text in the table smaller.

Additional Information

Many commands for working with tables are available by clicking [Table ▾] on the Tables and Borders toolbar.

Enhancing the Table

Next you need to adjust the size of the text, size the columns and rows appropriately, and add other enhancements to the table. As you continue to modify the table, the contents of many cells can be selected and changed at the same time. The following table describes how to select different areas of a table.

Area to Select	Procedure
Cell	Drag across the contents of the cell.
Row	Drag across the row Use [Table ▾]/Select Row.
Column	Drag down the column Use [Table ▾]/Select Column.
Multiple cells, rows, or columns	Drag through the cells, rows, or columns Select the first cell, row, or column, and hold down [⇧Shift] while clicking on another cell, row, or column.
Contents of next cell	Press [Tab⇄].
Contents of previous cell	Press [⇧Shift] + [Tab⇄].
Entire table	Drag through all the cells Use [Table ▾]/Select Table Click the cross-hatched table border.

Additional Information

A dotted table border indicates the entire table and all its contents are selected.

First you will reduce the size of the text. You could do this by selecting a point size from the [28 ▾] drop down list. Another way, however, is to decrease the size by units.

- Select the entire table.
- Click 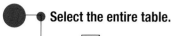. Decrease Font Size twice.

HAVING TROUBLE?
Clicking [A] increases the fonts size by units.

Your screen should be similar to Figure 4.15

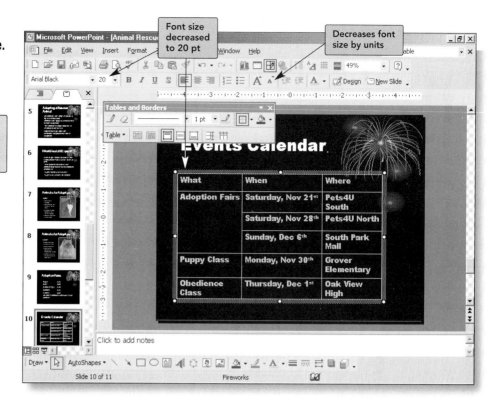

Figure 4.15

The font size has quickly been reduced by two units and at 20 points the table now fits in the slide. Next, you will adjust the column widths so that the cell contents will display on a single line.

- Point to the right border of column A and drag to increase or decrease the column width until the information in the What column just fits on a single line.

- In the same manner, adjust the When and Where column widths as needed to display the cell contents on a single line.

HAVING TROUBLE?
You may need to increase the size of the entire table to display the cell contents on a single line.

- Position the table as in Figure 4.16.

Your screen should be similar to Figure 4.16

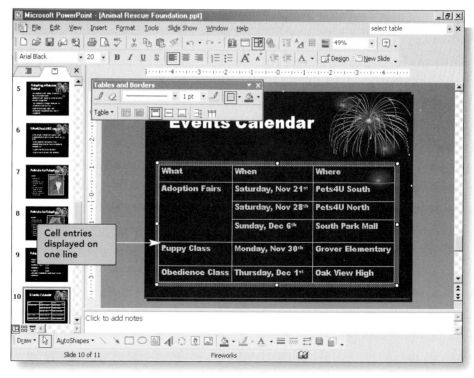

Figure 4.16

You also want to adjust the heights of the rows so they are all the same and center the text in several cells.

3 ● Select the table.

● Click ⊞ Distribute Rows Evenly in the Tables and Borders toolbar.

● Click 🔳 Center and 🔲 Center Row Vertically to change the orientation of the text in row 1 to centered horizontally and vertically.

● Click 🔲 to center vertically the text "Adoption Fairs" in row 2 of column A.

Your screen should be similar to Figure 4.17

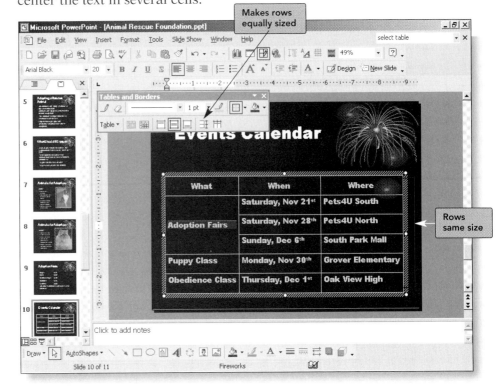

Figure 4.17

Next you will add some color to the table.

4 ● Select the entire table and apply a fill color of your choice to the selection.

● Select row 1 and change the text to an appropriate color, bold, and shadowed.

Your screen should be similar to Figure 4.18

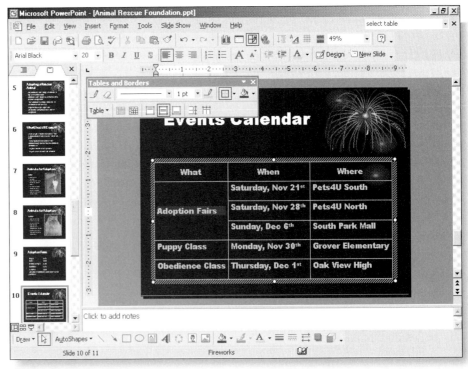

Figure 4.18

The final enhancement is to make the table border wider and a different color.

5 ● Select the entire table.

● Choose 6 pt from the [1 pt ▼] Border Width drop-down list.

● Choose a color from the [✎] Border Color drop-down list.

● Click [▦] Outside Borders.

Another Method

You can also use the Format/Table command or [Table ▼] / Borders and Fill to add, change, and remove borders and fills.

● Turn off Draw Table and click outside the table to deselect it.

● Close the Tables and Borders toolbar.

● Turn off the display of the ruler.

● Save the presentation.

Figure 4.19

Your screen should be similar to Figure 4.19

The table displays the information in an attractive and easy-to-read manner.

Adding Interest to the Presentation

Although you like the look of the Fireworks template, you feel it is rather static for a kiosk presentation and want to add some action to the presentation. You will do this by adding an animated graphic to a slide.

concept 1

Animated GIF

1 An **animated GIF** file is a type of graphic file that has motion. It consists of a series of GIF (Graphic Interchange Format) images that are displayed in rapid succession to produce an animated effect. They are commonly used on Web pages and can also be incorporated into PowerPoint presentations.

When an animated GIF file is inserted into a PowerPoint slide, it does not display action until you run the presentation. If you save the presentation as a Web page and view it in a browser, the animated GIF files run as soon as you view the page containing the graphic.

You cannot modify an animated graphic image using the features in the Picture toolbar. If you want to make changes to the graphic, such as changing the fill color or border, you need to use an animated GIF editing program.

Additionally, you want to add graphic text to the slide to further enhance the slide.

Adding Animated Graphics

You want to enhance the How You Can Help slide by adding an animated graphic that will really capture the attention of viewers.

1
- Display slide 4 in Normal view.

- Apply the Title, Content, and Text slide layout to the slide.

- Click 🖾 Insert Picture.

- Specify your data file location and select pp04_Turtle.

- Click [Insert ▾].

Additional Information
The Microsoft Clips Online Web site includes many animated graphics in the Motion category.

- Size and position the graphic as shown in Figure 4.20.

Your screen should be similar to Figure 4.20

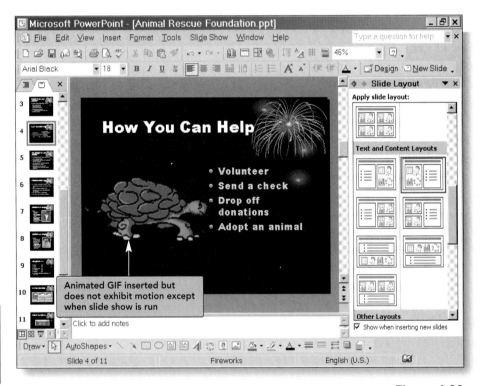

Figure 4.20

The turtle graphic will not exhibit motion until you run the slide show.

2 ● Display the slide in Slide Show to see the animation.

● Press [Esc] to stop the slide show.

Creating a WordArt Object

To add further interest to the slide, you will add the phrase "Friends Forever" below the turtle. To make this phrase unique and more interesting, you will enter it using the WordArt feature.

concept 2

WordArt

2 The **WordArt** feature is used to enhance slides by changing the shape of text, adding 3-D effects, and changing the alignment of text on a line. You can also rotate, flip, and skew WordArt text. The text that is added to a slide using WordArt is a graphic object that can be edited, sized, or moved to any location on the slide.

Use WordArt to add a special touch to your presentations, but limit its use to a single element on a slide. You want the WordArt to capture the viewer's attention. Here are some examples of WordArt.

You will create a WordArt object for the text to appear below the turtle.

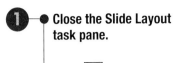

1
- **Close the Slide Layout task pane.**

- **Click** 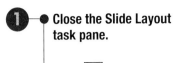 **Insert WordArt.**

Your screen should be similar to Figure 4.21

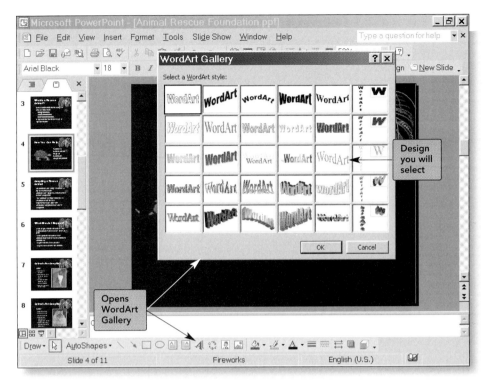

Figure 4.21

The first step is to select one of the 30 styles or designs of WordArt from the WordArt Gallery dialog box. These styles are just a starting point. As you will see, you can alter the appearance of the style by selecting a different color, shape, and special effect.

2
- **Select** WordArt **(fifth column, third row).**

- **Click** OK.

Your screen should be similar to Figure 4.22

Figure 4.22

Next, in the Edit WordArt Text dialog box, you need to enter the text you want displayed using the selected WordArt design.

3

- **Type Friends Forever.**

- **From the** `36 ▾` **drop-down list, increase the font size to 44.**

- **Click** `OK`.

- **Move the WordArt object to the position shown in Figure 4.23.**

Your screen should be similar to Figure 4.23

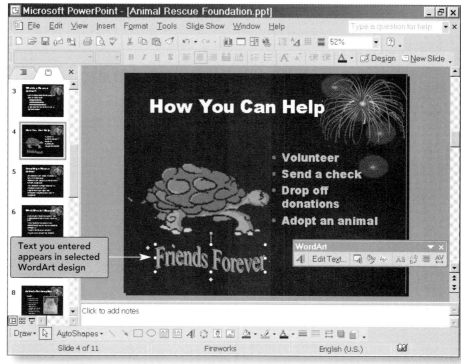

Figure 4.23

Now the text you entered is displayed in the selected WordArt style on the slide. The handles surrounding the WordArt object indicate that it is selected. Whenever a WordArt object is selected, the WordArt toolbar is displayed. The WordArt toolbar buttons (identified below) are used to modify the WordArt.

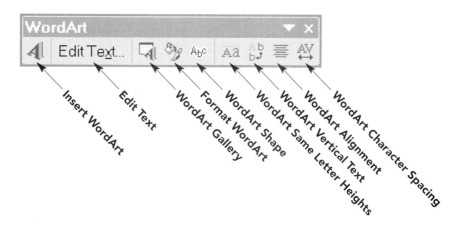

Editing WordArt Text

As you look at the WordArt, you decide that you want to add three ellipses following the text to lead the reader to the next slide. The text can be entirely changed or simply edited, as you will do.

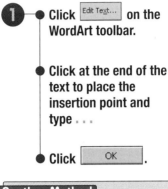

1 ● Click `Edit Text...` on the WordArt toolbar.

● Click at the end of the text to place the insertion point and type . . .

● Click `OK`.

Another Method

You can also double-click the WordArt object to edit the text.

Your screen should be similar to Figure 4.24

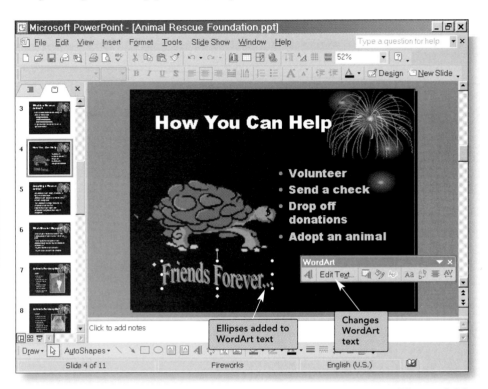

Figure 4.24

The change you made to the text in the Edit WordArt Text dialog box appears in the WordArt object.

Enhancing a WordArt Object

Now you want to change the appearance of the WordArt object to make it more interesting. First you will change the shape of the object.

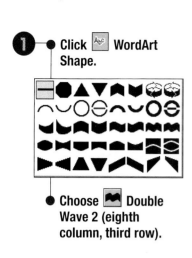

1 ● Click  WordArt Shape.

● Choose ⌇ Double Wave 2 (eighth column, third row).

Your screen should be similar to Figure 4.25

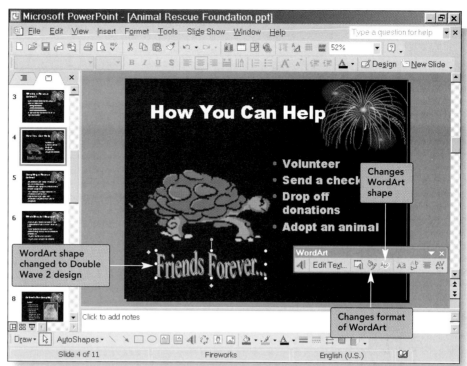

Figure 4.25

Next you want to change the color of the WordArt characters so they match the color scheme of the design template.

2 ● Click ⚒ Format WordArt.

● Open the Colors and Lines tab.

Your screen should be similar to Figure 4.26

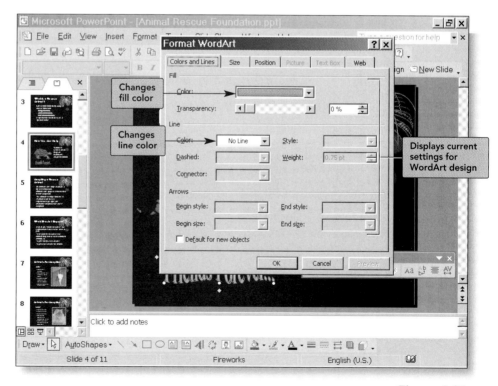

Figure 4.26

The Format WordArt dialog box shows the color and line settings for the selected WordArt design style. You want to change the colors so they fit more with the color scheme of the design template.

3 ● Open the Fill **C**olor drop-down list box.

● Select the orange color of the slide color scheme from the color palette.

● Open the Line C**o**lor drop-down list.

● Select the same color from the color palette.

● Click ` OK `.

Your screen should be similar to Figure 4.27

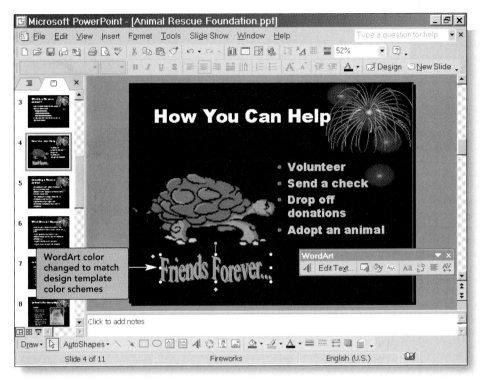

WordArt color changed to match design template color schemes

Figure 4.27

The selected fill color is used to fill the object, and the line color is applied to the outline surrounding the WordArt shape. The last changes you want to make are to increase the size of the WordArt object and to slant the text to the right. You also want to rotate the object to appear at an angle across the lower corner of the slide.

4 ● Drag the sizing handles to increase the WordArt object size to that shown in Figure 4.28.

● Move the rotate handle ⟳ slightly to the left to slant the text to the right.

HAVING TROUBLE?
Drag the green rotate handle to rotate the object.

● Position the object as in Figure 4.28.

● Group the two objects.

Your screen should be similar to Figure 4.28

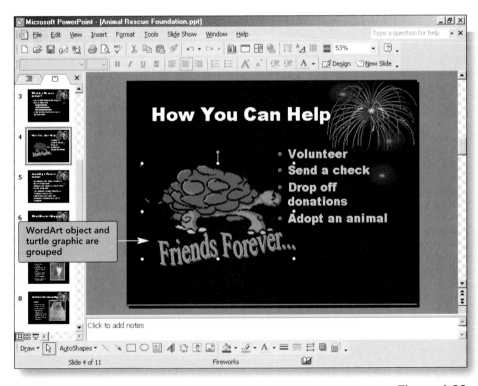

WordArt object and turtle graphic are grouped

Figure 4.28

Now that you are finished enhancing the WordArt object, you want to see how it will look full screen.

5 ● Click 🖵 Slide Show.

● Press Esc and click outside the WordArt object to deselect it.

● If necessary, close the WordArt toolbar.

● Save the presentation.

Setting Up the Presentation for a Kiosk

A presentation that is designed to run unattended on a kiosk has several special requirements. Because there is no one available while the slide show is running to clarify content and answer questions, you could record a narration to accompany the presentation. However, you feel the presentation content is both clear and complete and you decide to simply include background music to attract attention and to make the presentation more enjoyable as it runs. Next, you need to add slide transitions and to specify how long to display a slide before advancing to the next slide. Finally, you need to set up the presentation to be self-running.

Additional Information

When recording a voice narration, you need a sound card and a microphone. Use Slide Show/Record Narration. The slide show runs while you speak into the microphone. Once the slide show is complete, you can choose to save the timings along with the narration.

Adding Sound and Movies

Now that the content of the slides is complete, you want to add some background sound to the presentation as it is playing on the kiosk. There are several ways to add sound to a presentation. You can add discreet sounds that play when you click on an icon or automatically when the slide displays. You can play music from a file or a CD that runs continuously throughout the presentation. You can record a narration for your presentation; this, however, will override any other sounds you have programmed into it. You can also incorporate movie clips into a presentation.

concept 3

Sound and Movie Files

3 Almost all PCs today are equipped with multimedia capabilities, which means they can play the most commonly used sound and movie files. This table lists the most common sound and movie file types.

Format	File Extension
Waveform-audio	.wav
Musical Instrument Digital Interface	.mid
Video for Windows	.avi
Moving Picture	.mpeg
Quick Time for Windows	.mov

WAV files are typically used for sounds, and MIDI files are typically used for music. Most sound cards are capable of playing MIDI files, but because they were developed for synthesizers, you will not hear the true sound quality through a PC sound card.

AVI files do not require any special hardware or software to run, but they produce the lowest quality video. Both MPEG and MOV files produce better quality video, but both require special software, and MPEG requires special hardware.

When you choose to run a presentation on the Web, choose file types that are most commonly used. If you cannot control the computer on which your presentation will run, limit your audio to WAV files and your video to AVI files.

Additional Information

To play a CD, use Insert/Movies and Sounds/Play CD Audio Track.

For your kiosk, you want music to play continuously while the presentation runs. You could play tracks from a CD if the PC in the kiosk had a CD-ROM drive. However, to be safe, you decide to use a short sound clip of classical music.

1
- Display slide 1.
- Choose **I**nsert/Mo**v**ies and Sounds/So**u**nd from File.
- Change to your data file location.
- Select pp04_Canon.

> **Additional Information**
> The Windows Media folder contains many short sound files.

- Click [OK].
- Click [Yes] to confirm that you want the sound to play automatically.
- Move the sound icon  to the lower right corner of the slide.

Your screen should be similar to Figure 4.29

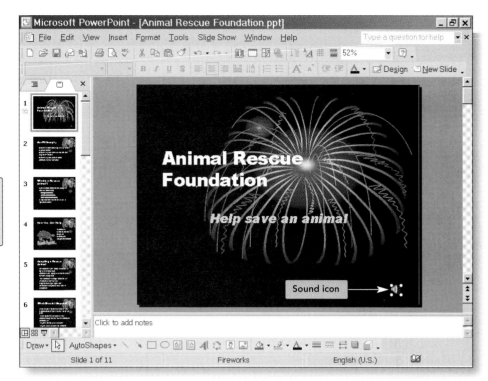

Figure 4.29

Now that you have added the music, you need to program how to play it during the slide show. You want the music to play continuously while the slide show runs.

2
- Choose Sli**d**e Show/Cus**t**om Animation.
- Open the pp04_Canon drop-down list in the Custom Animation task pane.
- Select **E**ffect Options.
- If necessary, open the Effect tab.

Your screen should be similar to Figure 4.30

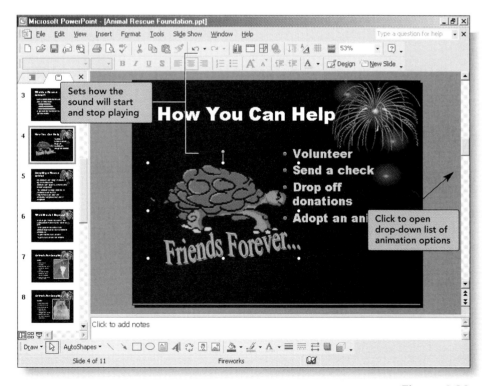

Figure 4.30

For each object on a slide, you can assign effects such as animation to the media element and control the order and timing. You want the music to start playing from the beginning of the presentation and to stop after the last slide (11).

3 ● Under Stop Playing, click A_fter and enter **11** in the text box.

● Click [OK] .

● Run the slide show from the beginning.

HAVING TROUBLE?
You need speakers and a sound card on your system to hear the sound.

The music played continuously as you moved from slide to slide and stopped at the end of the presentation.

Another Method
You can also preview the sound in Normal view by double-clicking the sound icon.

Adding Slide Transitions

You also want the slide show to display different transition effects as it runs and to automatically advance to the next slide after a set time has elapsed.

1 ● Switch to Slide Sorter view.

● Select all the slides.

● Click 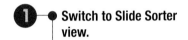 Transition .

● Choose Random Transition at Medium speed as the effect.

● Select Automatically after.

● Change the timing to advance the slides automatically every 7 seconds.

Additional Information
Leaving the On Mouse Click option selected allows the user to advance to the next slide before the 7 seconds are up.

● Click [Apply to All Slides] .

Your screen should be similar to Figure 4.31

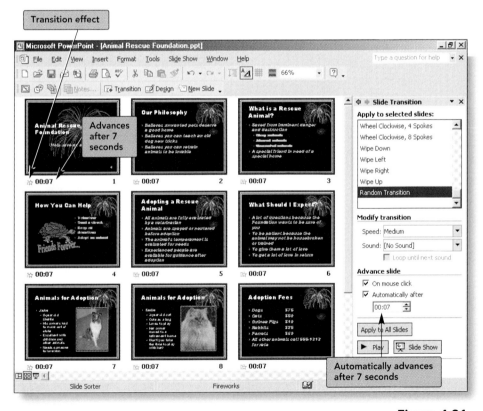

Figure 4.31

Making the Presentation Self-Running

Now you will make the slide show self-running so that it will restart automatically when it has finished.

1 ● **Close the Slide Transition task pane.**

● **Choose Slide Show/Set Up Show.**

Your screen should be similar to Figure 4.32

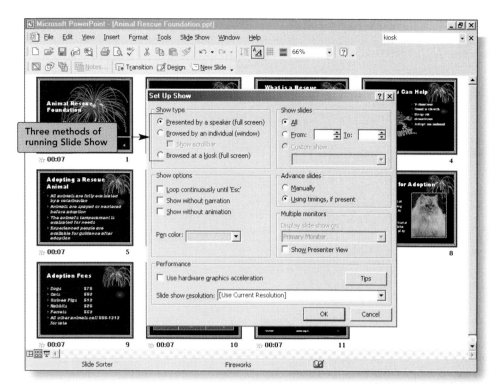

Figure 4.32

The Set Up Show dialog box allows you to choose from three ways of running a show. The first option, Presented by a Speaker, is the default and most frequently used style. As you have seen, this method requires that a speaker run the presentation. The second option, Browsed by an Individual, is used when one person views the presentation in a small window over an intranet (a network within an organization) or on a Web page. The third option, Browsed at a Kiosk, is the option you will use to create a self-running presentation that is displayed full screen. You can run the entire presentation or selected slides. The presentation will automatically play at full screen and restarts automatically.

2 ● **Select Browsed at a kiosk (full screen).**

● **Click** [OK].

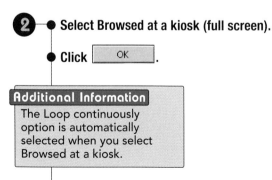

Additional Information

The Loop continuously option is automatically selected when you select Browsed at a kiosk.

● **Run the slide show from the beginning and press [Esc] to end it after it loops to the beginning again.**

● **Adjust the timing if the show is too fast or slow.**

● **Save the presentation again.**

Using Pack and Go

Now that the presentation is complete, you need to ship it out to the mall directors to install on their kiosks. The best way to do this is to use the Pack and Go Wizard, which packs all the files and fonts in your presentation together onto a disk. And if you are not sure if PowerPoint is installed on the computer running your show, you can include the PowerPoint Viewer, which is software that will run your show.

1 ● Choose File/Pack and Go.

Your screen should be similar to Figure 4.33

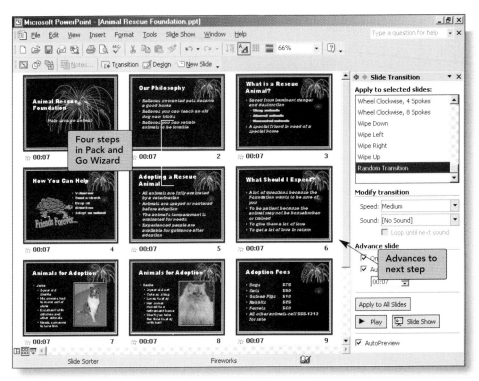

Figure 4.33

The opening Wizard dialog box shows the four steps you will complete. You will move to the first step.

2 ● **Click** Next > .

Your screen should be similar to Figure 4.34

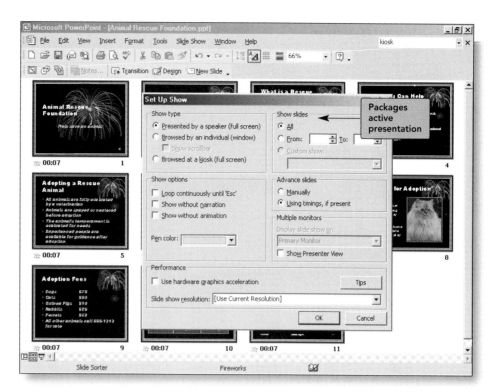

Figure 4.34

In the second Pack and Go Wizard dialog box, you are asked to select the presentation you want to pack. You can select the active presentation, which is the one you are working on, or select a presentation from your disk.

3 ● **If necessary, select Active presentation.**

● **Click** Next > .

Your screen should be similar to Figure 4.35

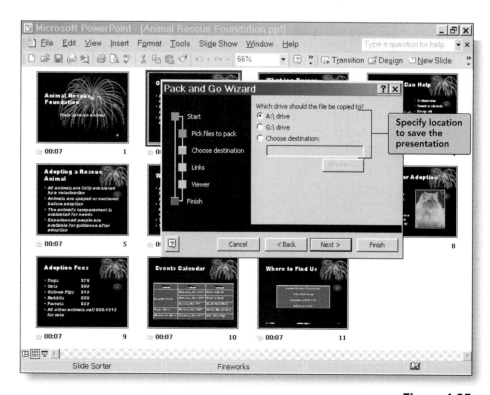

Figure 4.35

From the third Pack and Go dialog box, you select the location where you want to pack the presentation. The external drives on your system are listed as options because Pack and Go is most commonly used to copy to a floppy disk. You can also choose a destination on your hard disk or a network location.

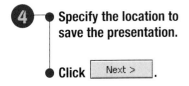

Specify the location to save the presentation.

● **Click** Next > .

Your screen should be similar to Figure 4.36

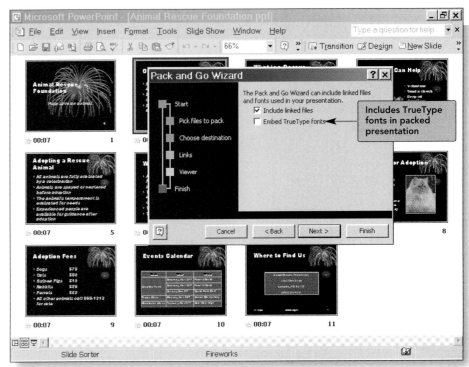

Figure 4.36

Additional Information
True Type Fonts are scalable fonts that appear on screen exactly as they will appear when printed.

In the fourth Pack and Go Wizard dialog box, you can include any linked files or TrueType fonts. Including linked files copies the specified files to the disk so they can be opened on the destination computer. Embedding TrueType fonts ensures that the text will display correctly even if the font is not installed on the destination computer. Since this presentation does not include linked files, you do not need that option checked.

Additional Information

You could leave the Include Linked Files option selected even if the presentation does not include linked files.

● **Select Embed TrueType fonts.**

● **Click** Next >.

Your screen should be similar to Figure 4.37

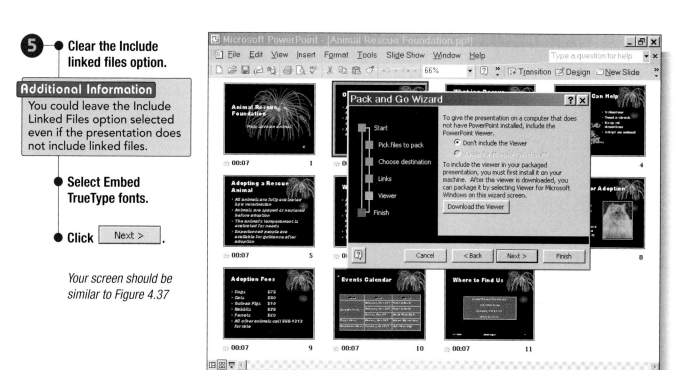

Figure 4.37

The fifth Pack and Go Wizard dialog box asks if you want to include the PowerPoint Viewer. If you are not sure if PowerPoint is installed on the destination computer, select this option. In this case, however, all the locations that will be running the presentation already have the PowerPoint Viewer installed.

6 ● **If necessary, select Don't include the viewer.**

● **Click** Next >.

Your screen should be similar to Figure 4.38

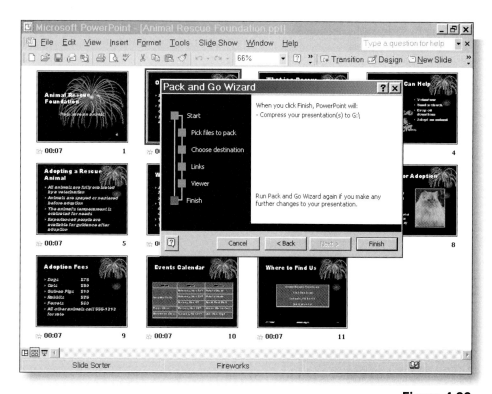

Figure 4.38

You have entered all the information PowerPoint needs to pack your presentation.

 **7** ● **Click** Finish .

After a few moments the process is completed, and the presentation is stored at the disk location specified. The presentation is stored as PRES0.PPZ on the disk. In addition, another file, PNGSETUP.EXE, is automatically included in the same location. To unpack the presentation, use Windows Explorer to go to the location containing the packed presentation. Then double-click PNGSETUP.EXE and specify the destination location where you want the presentation copied. It can then be run using PowerPoint or the Viewer.

Setting Up the Presentation for Browsing

The Animal Rescue Foundation main shelter has a computer in the lobby that they want to use to show this same presentation. Rather than have the presentation loop continuously, you want to change it to a presentation that can be run by an individual using mouse control. This gives viewers the ability to control the slide show and go back to review a slide immediately or go forward more quickly to see other slides. To add this capability, you will create several custom shows and add hyperlinks and navigation controls to the presentation.

Creating Custom Shows

First you will group some slides into custom shows.

concept 4

Custom Show

4 A **custom show** is a presentation that runs within a presentation. For example, you may have one presentation that you need to give to two different groups. The overview slides are the same for both groups, but there are a few slides that are specific to each group. Rather than create two separate presentations, you can include all the slides in your main presentation and then group the specific slides into two custom shows that run after the overview slides. While you are running the slide show, you can jump to the specific custom show that you created for that audience.

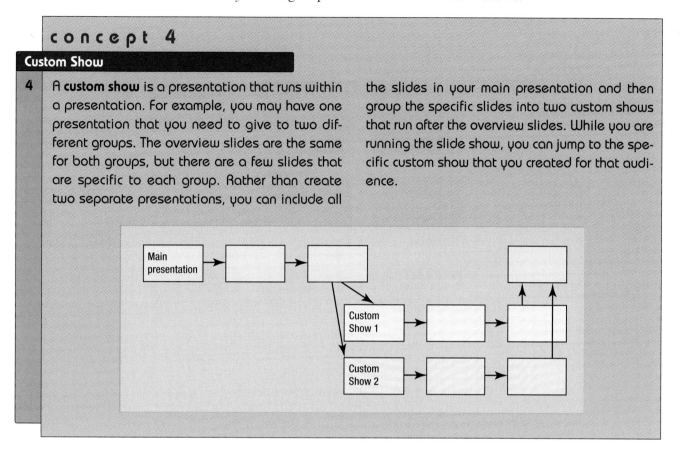

You are going to create two custom shows within your presentation. One custom show will run the slides that describe adopting rescue animals. The other custom show will run the slides that describe the animals that are available for adoption.

1 ● **Choose Slide Show/Custom Sho<u>w</u>s.**

● Click New....

Your screen should be similar to Figure 4.39

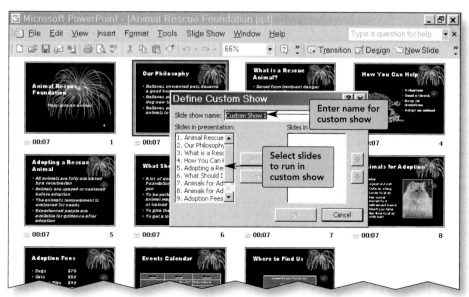

Figure 4.39

In the Define Custom Show dialog box, you name the custom show and select the slides that will run within the show. All the slides in a custom show must also be in the main presentation.

2 ● **In the Slide Show Name text box, type About Adoption.**

● **In the Slides in Presentation list box, select slides 3, 5, 6, and 9.**

HAVING TROUBLE?

To select multiple slides, hold down Ctrl while you click on the slides you want to include.

● **Click** Add >> .

Your screen should be similar to Figure 4.40

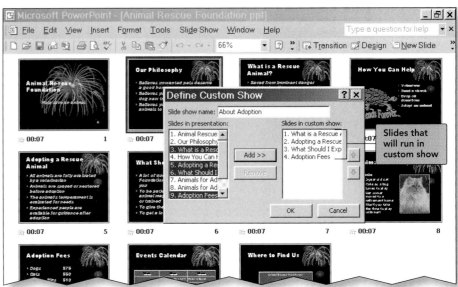

Figure 4.40

Next you want to make slide 2 in the custom show, slide 1. To change the order of the slides in the custom show, select a slide in the Slides in Custom Show list box, and then click one of the arrows to move the slide up or down the list. This will not change the order of the slides in the main presentation.

3 ● **Select slide 2 from the Slides in Custom Show list box.**

● **Click** ⬆ .

● **Click** OK .

● **Create another custom show titled Animals for Adoption that runs slides 7, 8, and 11.**

Your screen should be similar to Figure 4.41

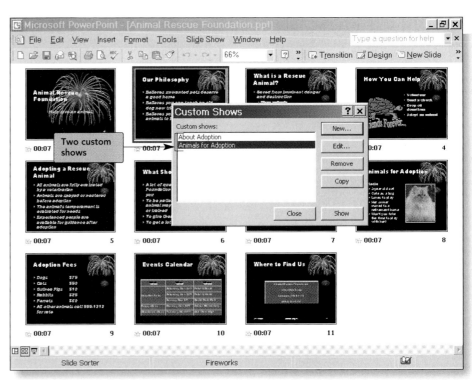

Figure 4.41

The name of the second custom show is added to the dialog box. Now you will see how the About Adoption custom show runs.

4 ● **Select About Adoption from the Custom Show list box.**

● **Click** 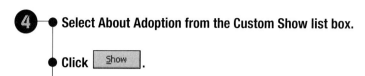 **Show .**

● **View the four slides and press** Esc **to end the custom show.**

The custom show plays in a continual loop and does not play the sound. The sound only plays if you start the presentation from slide 1.

Creating an Agenda Slide

Now that you have created the custom shows, you will create an agenda slide to use as a starting point for the entire presentation. An **agenda slide** contains a list of items or main topics from the presentation. Viewers can then make a selection from the list, and the presentation will jump directly to the slide containing the selected topic or a custom presentation will automatically run. When the custom show is finished, the presentation returns to the agenda slide.

To create an agenda slide, you first create a summary slide consisting of a bulleted list of agenda items. A summary slide is created automatically from slides in the presentation whose titles you want to appear as agenda items.

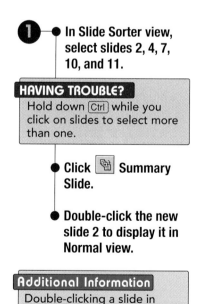

1 ● **In Slide Sorter view, select slides 2, 4, 7, 10, and 11.**

HAVING TROUBLE?
Hold down Ctrl while you click on slides to select more than one.

● **Click** 📄 **Summary Slide.**

● **Double-click the new slide 2 to display it in Normal view.**

Additional Information
Double-clicking a slide in Slide Sorter view displays the slide in the last used view.

Your screen should be similar to Figure 4.42

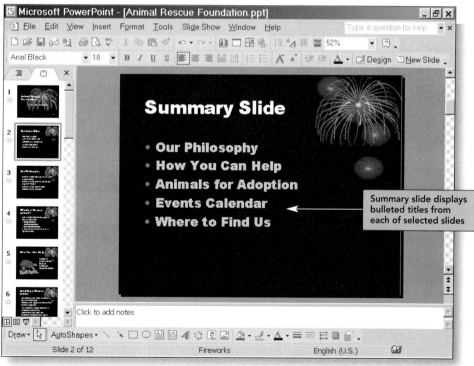

Figure 4.42

A new slide titled Summary Slide appears as slide 2. The summary slide is always inserted in front of the slide containing the first selected item. The slide contains bulleted titles from each of the selected slides.

Adding Hyperlinks

The next step in creating an agenda slide is to create a hyperlink from each bulleted item to its corresponding slide or custom show.

concept 5

Hyperlink

5 **Hyperlinks** provide a quick way to jump to other slides, custom shows, presentations, objects, e-mail addresses, or Web pages. You can assign the hyperlink to text or to any object, including pictures, tables, clip art, and graphs. You can jump to sites on your own system or network as well as to sites on the Internet and the Web. The user jumps to the referenced location by clicking on the hyperlink.

In addition, PowerPoint includes special objects called **action buttons** that can be inserted in a presentation and assigned a hyperlink. Action buttons consist of shapes, such as right- and left-facing arrows, that are used to navigate through a presentation. They are designed specifically for self-running presentations and presentations that run on a company network or the Web.

1 ● Select the first bulleted item.

● Choose Sli<u>d</u>e Show/<u>A</u>ction Settings.

● If necessary, open the Mouse Click tab.

Your screen should be similar to Figure 4.43

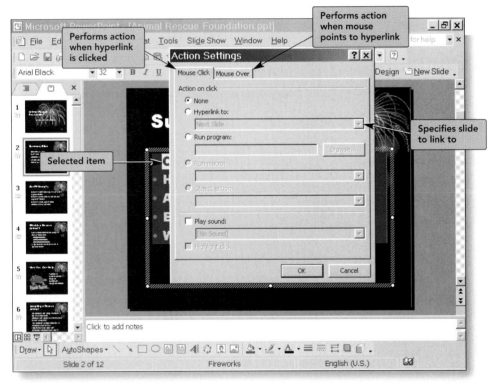

Figure 4.43

The two tabs in the Action Settings dialog box allow you to specify the action that is needed to activate the hyperlink. Mouse Click performs an action when the viewer clicks the hyperlink, and Mouse Over performs the action when the mouse pointer rests or passes over the hyperlink. Within each tab you specify the type of action you want to perform: jump to another location using a hyperlink, play a sound, or run a program or macro. Generally, it is best to use Mouse Click for hyperlinks so that you do not accidentally go to a location because you passed the mouse pointer over the hyperlink. Mouse Over is commonly used to play sounds or to highlight an object.

The first bulleted item will be a hyperlink to the next slide in the presentation. This is the default hyperlink selection.

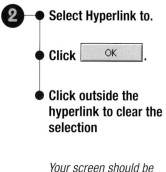

● **Select Hyperlink to.**

● **Click** OK **.**

● **Click outside the hyperlink to clear the selection**

Your screen should be similar to Figure 4.44

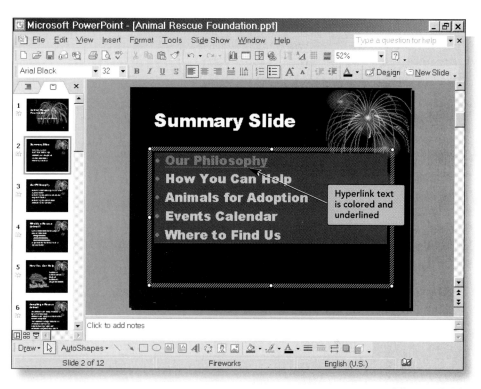

Figure 4.44

The hyperlink text appears underlined and in color. The color of the hyperlink text is determined by the presentation's color scheme.

The second bulleted item will be a hyperlink to the About Adoption custom show. You want the custom show to run and then return to the slide containing the hyperlink.

3 • Select the text in the second bulleted item.

• Choose Sli**d**e Show/**A**ction Settings.

• Select Hyperlink to.

• From the Hyperlink To drop-down list, select Custom Show.

HAVING TROUBLE?
Scroll the list box for the full list of options.

Your screen should be similar to Figure 4.45

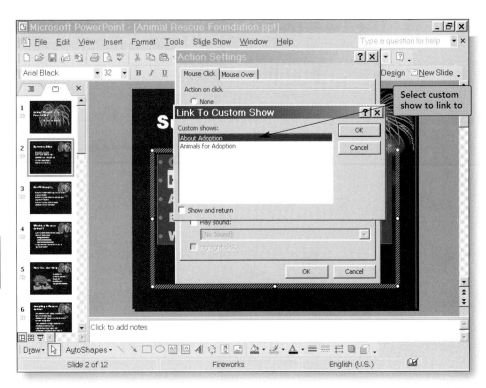

Figure 4.45

From the Link To Custom Show dialog box, you select the custom show you want to create a hyperlink to.

4 • Select About Adoption from the Custom Show dialog box.

• Select the Show and Return option.

• Click 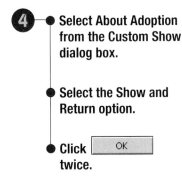 twice.

Your screen should be similar to Figure 4.46

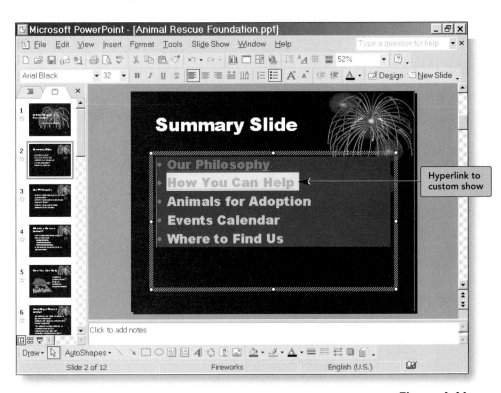

Figure 4.46

When the second bulleted item is selected, it will start the custom show. Now you need to add links for the remaining three items. The third bulleted item will be a hyperlink to the custom show named Animals for Adoption. The fourth and fifth will be to slides of the same name.

5 ● Link the third bulleted item to the Animals for Adoption custom show, selecting the Show and return option.

● To link the fourth item, select Slide as the Hyperlink To option and select slide 11.

● To link the fifth item, select Slide as the Hyperlink To option and select slide 12.

● Change the title of the agenda slide to Learn About Us.

● Click outside the title to deselect it.

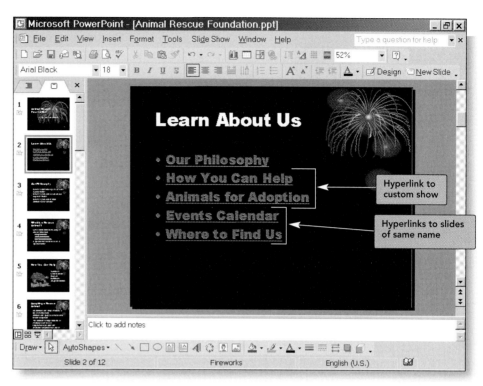

Figure 4.47

Another Method

You can also use Insert/Hyperlink or  to create and edit hyperlinks.

Your screen should be similar to Figure 4.47

Using Hyperlinks

Next you want to try out one of the hyperlinks to see how they work. To activate the hyperlinks, you need to run the slide show.

1 ● Run the slide show beginning with slide 2.

HAVING TROUBLE?

To run the slide show starting from the current slide, click 🖳. Using Slide Show/View Show or F5 begins the presentation at slide 1.

● Click on the Animals for Adoption hyperlink.

Additional Information

The mouse pointer shape changes to a 🖑 when pointing to a hyperlink.

Your screen should be similar to Figure 4.48

First slide in custom show

Figure 4.48

The slide show jumps to the first slide of the custom show and begins running the custom show.

2 ● When the custom show loops again to the first slide, press Esc to end the custom show and display the agenda slide.

● Press Esc to end the slide show presentation.

● Save the presentation as Rescue Foundation Self Running.

Additional Information

The color of a selected hyperlink is different from those that have not been selected. This color change identifies those links that have already been viewed.

Adding Action Buttons

To help the viewer navigate through the presentation, you decide to add action buttons to the slides. Action buttons perform their associated action when you click on them or pass the mouse over them.

You have decided to have the first slide display continuously until the viewer clicks on a button to start the presentation. Once in the presentation, each slide will have a home button that will take the viewer back to the agenda slide, a forward button that will go to the next slide, and a backward button that will return to the previous slide.

1 • Display slide 1 in
Normal view.

• Choose Sli**d**e
Show/Ac**t**ion Buttons.

• Click ☐ Custom
(first column, first
row).

• In the upper right
corner of the slide,
drag to create a button
that is approximately 1
inch by 1 inch.

• In the Mouse Click tab
of the Action Settings
dialog box, hyperlink
the button to the next
slide.

• Click OK.

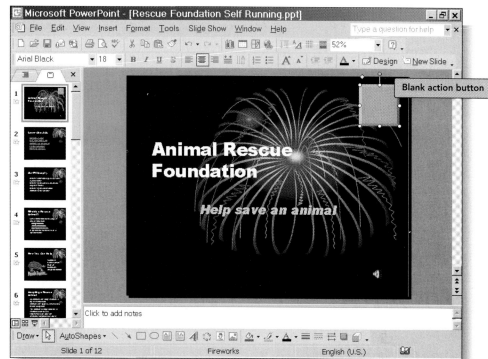

Figure 4.49

*Your screen should be
similar to Figure 4.49*

Next you need to add text to the button that contains the instructions for
the viewer. You add button text just as you add text to a text box.

2 ● Right-click on the button and choose Add Te**x**t from the shortcut menu.

● Type Click Here to Learn More.

● Right-click on the button and choose Format Aut**o**Shape.

● Open the Text Box tab.

● Select **W**ord wrap text in AutoShape.

● Select Resize AutoShape to **f**it text.

● Click OK .

● Change the text color to black and the font size to 16.

● Click outside the action button to deselect it.

Your screen should be similar to Figure 4.50

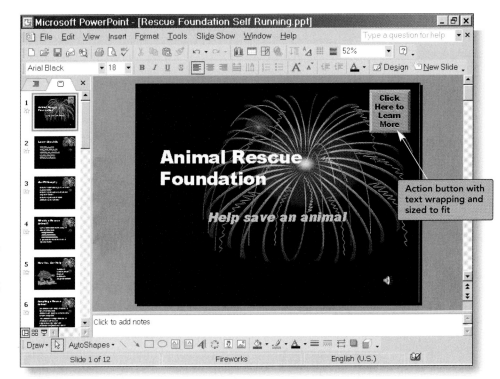

Figure 4.50

You will follow the same procedure to add three other buttons to the slides: forward, backward, and home. These buttons are predesigned, and contain icons that represent the action they perform. Therefore, you do not need to add text to the button. Since you want these buttons to appear on all slides other than title slides, you will add them to the Slide Master.

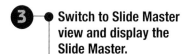 **Switch to Slide Master view and display the Slide Master.**

HAVING TROUBLE?
In Slide Master view, two slides appear in the Slide tab. Be sure to modify the Slide Master and not the Title Master.

● **Delete the three footer object boxes.**

● **Choose Slide Show/Action Buttons.**

● **Click** 🏠 **Home (second column, first row).**

● **Click in the lower right of the footer area to create a default size button.**

● **Add a hyperlink to slide 2, the agenda slide.**

● **Click** OK **twice.**

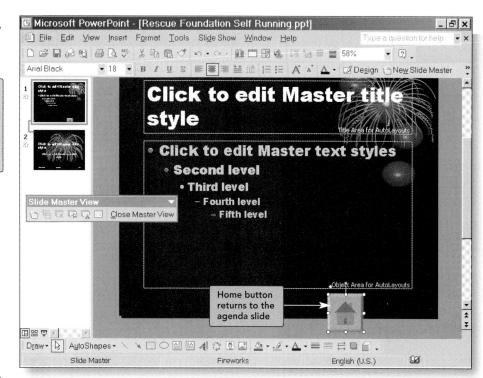

Figure 4.51

Your screen should be similar to Figure 4.51

Now you want to reduce the size of the button by about half. In addition to changing the size of an object by dragging to an approximate size, you can change the size by entering an exact measurement for the objectís height and width or by entering a percentage value to increase or decrease the object from its original size. Since you want to make the object about half its original size, you will reduce it by 50 percent.

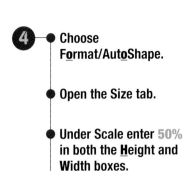

4 ● Choose Format/AutoShape.

● Open the Size tab.

● Under Scale enter 50% in both the **H**eight and **W**idth boxes.

● Click OK .

● Move the button to the location shown in Figure 4.52.

Additional Information
If the slide miniature is displayed, you can see how the button looks on the current slide.

Your screen should be similar to Figure 4.52

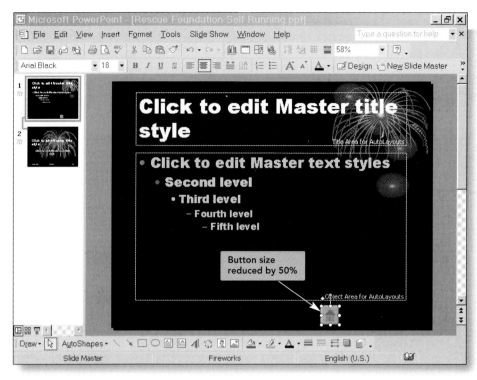

Figure 4.52

Now you will add the forward and back buttons.

5 ● To the right of the home button, add a default size ◁ Back or Previous button that hyperlinks to the previous slide.

● To the right of the back button, add a default size ▷ Forward or Next button that hyperlinks to the next slide.

● Select the two new buttons and reduce their size by 50 percent.

HAVING TROUBLE?
Hold down ⟨⇧Shift⟩ while clicking each button to select multiple objects.

Your screen should be similar to Figure 4.53

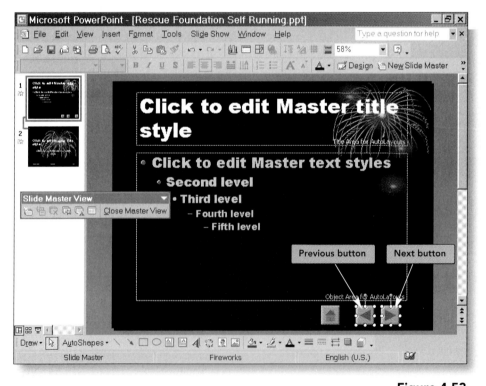

Figure 4.53

Finally, you want to position and align the three buttons.

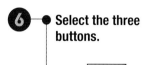

Select the three buttons.

Click `Draw ▾` **and choose** **A**lign or Distribute/Align **T**op.

Click `Draw ▾` **and choose** **A**lign or Distribute/Distribute **H**orizontally.

Additional Information
There must be at least three objects selected to align and distribute objects.

Your screen should be similar to Figure 4.54

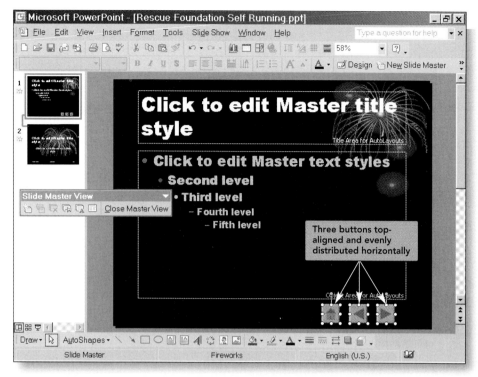

Figure 4.54

Additional Information
The outside controls do not move; only the middle control moves to equalize the spacing.

The three buttons are evenly aligned with the top of the buttons and are an equal distance apart horizontally. Because the buttons were added to the slide master, they will appear in the same location on each slide in the presentation. You want to check the slides to make sure the buttons do not interfere with any of the text or graphics on the slides.

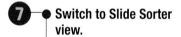

Switch to Slide Sorter view.

Make any necessary adjustments to objects on the slides so they do not overlap the buttons.

Your screen should be similar to Figure 4.55

Figure 4.55

Using Action Buttons

Now you are ready to run the revised presentation using the buttons. First you will turn off the features that make the presentation run continuously and change the music to play longer while the presentation is running.

1 • **In Slide Sorter view, select all slides.**

• **Open the Slide Transition task pane.**

• **Clear the Automatically After option.**

• **Click** `Apply to All Slides` **.**

• **In Normal view, select the sound object on slide 1.**

• **Open the Custom Animation task pane.**

> **Additional Information**
>
> Click ▼ Other Task Panes and select the task pane you want to display.

• **Open the pp04_Canon drop-down list and select Effect Options.**

• **Increase the number of slides to stop playing after to 25.**

• **Click** `OK` **.**

• **Run the slide show beginning at slide 1 and practice using the buttons.**

Your screen should be similar to Figure 4.56

Figure 4.56

2 • **When you are done running the presentation, save the presentation again.**

Publishing a Presentation on the Web

Finally, you want to save the presentation for publishing on the World Wide Web (WWW). To publish a presentation, you save a copy of the presentation in Hypertext Markup Language (HTML) format.

concept 6

Hypertext Markup Language

6 All Web pages are written using a programming language called **Hypertext Markup Language (HTML)**. HTML commands control how the information on a page, such as font colors and size, is displayed. HTML also allows users to click on highlighted text or images and jump to other locations on the same page, to other pages in the same site, or to other sites and locations on the Web altogether.

HTML commands are interpreted by the browser software program you are using to access the WWW. A **browser** is a program that connects you to remote computers and displays the Web pages you request. The computer that stores the Web pages and sends them to a browser when requested is called the **server**.

To publish your presentation on the Web, you need to remove a few features that you added. For example, sound files typically make a Web page difficult to load. In addition, when you save the file as a Web page, you will lose any custom show capabilities, so you must replace the hyperlinks on the agenda slide. Also, you need to remove the transitions.

1 ● Delete the sound icon and button from slide 1.

● Remove the transition from all slides.

● Change the hyperlink on slide 2 for How You Can Help to link to slide 4.

● Change the Animals for Adoption hyperlink to link to slide 8.

● Close the task pane.

● Display slide 1.

Your screen should be similar to Figure 4.57

Figure 4.57

Now that the presentation is ready for Web delivery, you can save it as a Web page. You will save it to a folder and include a page title. A page title is the name that will appear in the title bar of the browser when the page is displayed.

2 ● **Choose File/Save as Web Page.**

● **Specify the location to save the file.**

● **Click** 🗁 **Create New Folder.**

● **Enter the folder name** Rescue Foundation Web.

● **Click** OK .

● **Enter the file name** Rescue Foundation Web.

● **Click** Change Title... .

Your screen should be similar to Figure 4.58

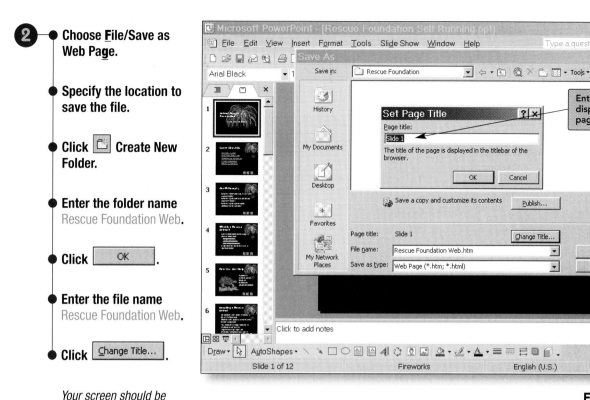

Figure 4.58

3 ● **In the Page title text box, type** Animal Rescue Foundation.

● **Click** OK .

● **Click** Save .

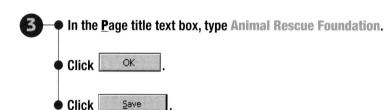

Additional Information
The file type is automatically set to Web page.

The file is converted to an HTML document and saved in the folder you created. In addition, another folder was automatically created that contains all the elements on the page, such as images and hyperlinks. By default, the name of the supporting folder is the name of the Web page plus an underscore (_), a period, and the word "files." In this case, the supporting folder name is Rescue Foundation Web_.files. All supporting files, such as those for bullets, graphics, and background, are contained in the supporting folder. Any graphics that were added to the page that were not already JPEG or GIF files are converted to that format. When you move your files to a server, you need to include the HTML file and the associated supporting folder that contains all the elements on the page. If you do not, the page will not display correctly.

Now, you want to see the Web page that was created.

4 ● Choose **F**ile/We**b** Page Preview.

● If necessary, maximize the browser window.

Your screen should be similar to Figure 4.59

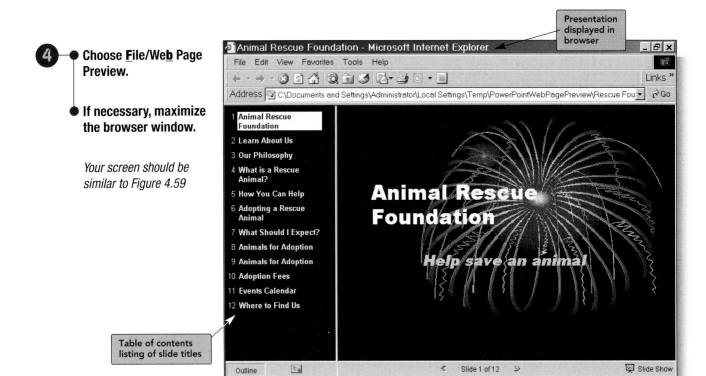

Table of contents listing of slide titles

Figure 4.59

The browser on your system is loaded offline, and the page you created is displayed in the browser window. The left side of the window displays a table of contents listing consisting of the slide titles. Clicking on a title will display the associated slide on the right side. To navigate through the presentation, you can use the table of contents list, the action buttons, or the agenda slide hyperlinks.

5 • Try out the various methods of navigation in the presentation.

• When you are finished, click ☒ Close to exit the browser.

• Preview slides 2, 5, and 11 as handouts, three per page.

• Include a header on the handout that displays the current date and your name.

Your screen should be similar to Figure 4.60.

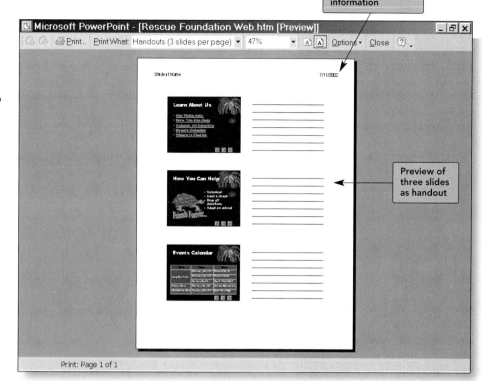

Click to add header information

Preview of three slides as handout

Figure 4.60

6 • Print the handout.

• Save the Web page again.

• Exit PowerPoint.

LAB **4**

Creating a Presentation for a Kiosk and the Web

Animated GIF (PP4.20)

An **animated GIF** file is a type of graphic file that has motion.

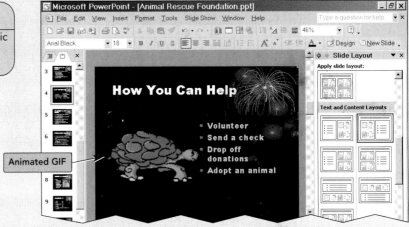

WordArt (PP4.21)

The **WordArt** feature is used to enhance slides by changing the shape of text, adding 3-D effects, and changing the alignment of text on a line.

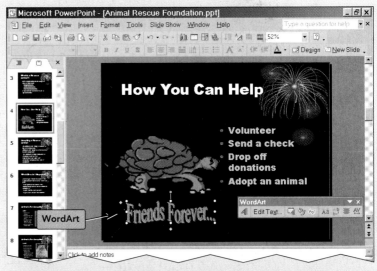

Sound and Movie Files (PP4.28)

Almost all PCs today are equipped with multimedia capabilities, which means they can play the most commonly used **sound and movie files**.

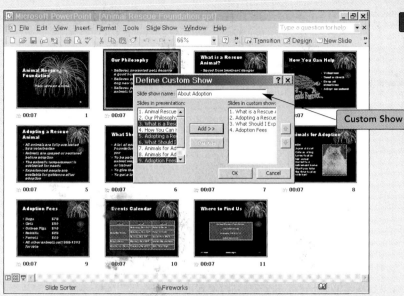

Custom Show (PP4.37)

A **custom show** is a presentation that runs within a presentation.

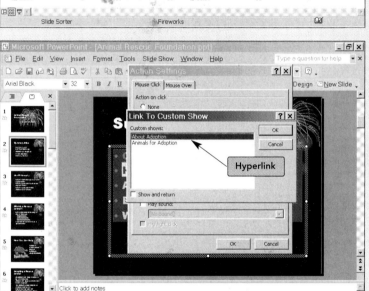

Hyperlink (PP4.40)

Hyperlinks provide a quick way to jump to other slides, custom shows, presentations, objects, e-mail addresses, or Web pages.

Hypertext Markup Language (PP4.51)

All Web pages are written using a programming language called **Hypertext Markup Language** (HTML). HTML commands control how the information on a page, such as font colors and size, is displayed.

key terms

action button   PP4.40

agenda slide   PP4.39

animated GIF   PP4.20

browser   PP4.49

custom show   PP4.37

hyperlink   PP4.40

Hypertext Markup Language
(HTML)   PP4.51

server   PP4.51

WordArt   PP4.21

mous skills

The Microsoft Office User Specialist (MOUS) certification program is designed to measure your proficiency in performing basic tasks using the Office XP applications. Getting certified demonstrates that you have the skills and provides a valuable industry credential for employment. After completing this lab, you have learned the following Microsoft Office User Specialist skills:

Skill	Description	Page
Creating Presentations	Create presentations (manually and using automated tools)	PP4.5, PP4.6
	Add slides to and delete slides from presentations	PP4.8
Inserting and Modifying Text	Import text from Word	PP4.4
Inserting and Modifying Visual Elements	Add tables, charts, clip art, and bitmap images to slides	PP4.12
	Add OfficeArt elements to slides	PP4.21
	Apply custom formats to tables	PP4.16
Modifying Presentation Formats	Apply slide transitions	PP4.30
	Modify slide layout	PP4.12
	Add links to a presentation	PP4.40
Working with Data from Other Sources	Add sound and video to slides	PP4.27
Managing and Delivering Presentations	Set up slide shows	PP4.31, PP4.37
	Deliver presentations	PP4.37, PP4.50, PP4.54
	Manage files and folders for presentations	PP4.53
	Work with embedded fonts	PP4.34
	Publish presentations to the Web	PP4.51
	Use Pack and Go	PP4.32

Command	Button	Action
File/Save as Web Page		Publishes presentation on Web
File/Web Page Preview		Displays presentation in browser
File/Pack and Go		Puts all files needed for presentation into one file for use on other machines
Insert/Slides from Files		Inserts selected slides from another presentation
Insert/Slides from Outline		Creates slides from outline text
Insert/Movies and Sounds/ Sound from File		Inserts sound or movie files into selected slide
Insert/Movies and Sounds/ Play CD Audio Track		Plays a CD
Insert/Hyperlink	🔲	Creates a hyperlink
Format/AutoShape/Size		Changes size and scale of selected AutoShape
Slide Show/Set Up Show		Sets up presentation to run for specific situations
Slide Show/Record Narration		Records narration to accompany presentation
Slide Show/Custom Shows		Creates presentations within a presentation
Slide Show/Action Buttons		Adds navigation buttons to a slide
Slide Show/Action Settings		Specifies action that is needed to activate hyperlinks
Slide Show/Custom Animation		Adds motion and determines how sound is played

Terminology

screen identification

In the following PowerPoint screen, several items are identified by letters. Enter the correct term for each item in the spaces that follow.

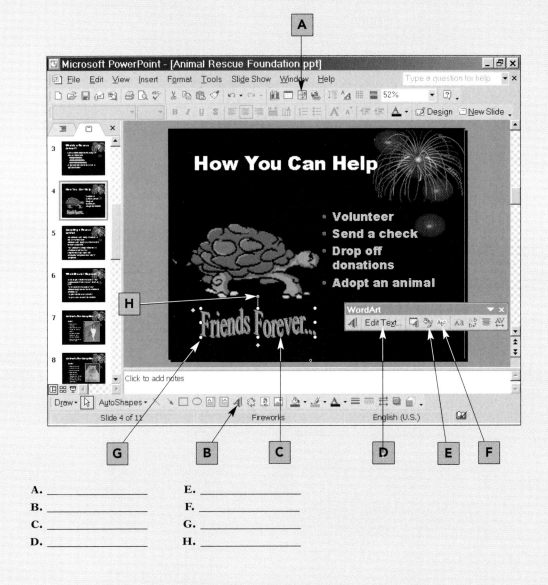

A. _____   E. _____

B. _____   F. _____

C. _____   G. _____

D. _____   H. _____

matching

Match the numbered item with the correct lettered description.

1. agenda slide _____ **a.** vertically centers cell contents

2. server _____ **b.** combination of multiple images that appear to move

3. .mpeg _____ **c.** creates a home action button

4. ▣ _____ **d.** file used to unpack a presentation

5. action buttons _____ **e.** moving picture file extension

6. ⌂ _____ **f.** contains a list of items or main topics from the presentation

7. custom show _____ **g.** computer that stores Web pages and sends them to a browser

8. hyperlink _____ **h.** shapes that are used to navigate through a presentation

9. Pngsetup.exe _____ **i.** allows user to jump to a new location in the presentation

10. animated GIF _____ **j.** presentation that runs within another presentation

multiple choice

Circle the letter of the correct response.

1. The feature that is used to enhance your presentation by changing the shape of text, adding 3-D effects, and changing the alignment of text is called _____.
   a. Art
   b. WordArt
   c. DrawShape
   d. WordWrap

2. A(n) _____ is a presentation that runs within a presentation.
   a. custom show
   b. moving picture
   c. hyperlink
   d. agenda slide

3. If you do not have control over what computer your presentation will run on, use _____ and _____ files for audio and video.
   a. WAV, MPEG
   b. MIDI, AVI
   c. WAV, AVI
   d. MIDI, MOV

4. The _____ feature is most useful for creating complex tables that contain cells of different heights or varying number of columns per row.
   a. Insert Table
   b. Draw Table
   c. Table slide layout
   d. Create Table

5. _____ control(s) how the information on a Web page is displayed.
   a. Formatting
   b. Browsers
   c. HTML commands
   d. Servers

6. The _____Wizard puts all the files and fonts for a presentation onto one disk.
   a. Compress and Go
   b. Pack and Take
   c. Pack and Go
   d. Compress and Take

7. A(n) _____ loops back to the beginning slide and allows users to select what parts of the presentation they want to view.
   a. special show
   b. continuous show
   c. custom show
   d. agenda show

8. _____ provide a quick way to jump to other slides or Web pages.
   a. Action buttons
   b. Text links
   c. Hyperlinks
   d. Hypertext commands

9. Pages on the Web are written using the _____ programming language.
   a. WWW
   b. HTML
   c. MPMC
   d. HMCL

10. A _____ is a program that displays Web pages.
   a. viewer
   b. browser
   c. server
   d. control

true/false

Check the correct answer to the following statements.

1. A presentation can be created from a Word outline document.	True	False
2. WordArt is used to enhance predrawn images.	True	False
3. Individual slides from one presentation can be inserted into another presentation.	True	False
4. Animated images only move when the slide show is run.	True	False
5. When a table is created in PowerPoint, it must have an equal number of columns and rows.	True	False
6. Movies can be inserted into a PowerPoint presentation.	True	False
7. When a presentation is run on a kiosk, it must have user interaction to repeat itself.	True	False
8. A unique show runs a presentation within a presentation.	True	False
9. An agenda slide can be linked to other slides in the presentation.	True	False
10. Action buttons can be added to the slide master and appear on all slides in the presentation.	True	False

Concepts

fill-in

Complete the following statements by filling in the blanks with the correct terms.

1. Text that is added to a slide using _____ is a graphic object that can be edited, sized, or moved to any location on the slide.

2. When a(n) _____ file is inserted into a PowerPoint slide, it does not display action until you run the presentation.

3. _____ files are typically used for sounds, and _____ files are typically used for music.

4. The programming language used on the Web is called _____.

5. _____ files do not require any special hardware but they produce the lowest quality video.

6. When a custom show is finished, the presentation returns to the _____.

7. A(n) _____ is a presentation within a presentation.

8. A(n) _____ slide is created from the titles of the selected slides.

9. _____ buttons can be added to a presentation to move to other slides in the presentation.

10. Pres0.ppz is a file name associated with a PowerPoint presentation that has been _____.

discussion questions

1. Discuss how animated GIF files can enhance a presentation. List three examples of when using an animated GIF file would be appropriate. List three examples of when animated GIF files may distract from a presentation.

2. Discuss how the Pack and Go Wizard is used. When would you want to use Pack and Go?

3. Discuss how action buttons and hyperlinks can be used in a presentation.

Hands-On Exercises

step-by-step

Water Safety Kiosk

★ **1.** The Red Cross liked your presentation on water safety, which you enhanced in Step-by-Step Exercise 2 in Lab 3, and would like you to make it into a presentation that will run at the local shopping mall. They would also like to show it on their Web site. Some of the completed slides are shown here.

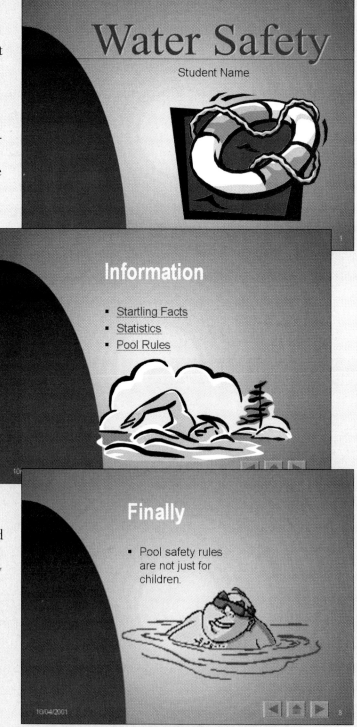

   a. Start PowerPoint and open the presentation Water Safety2.

   b. Remove the title on slide 1 and replace it with a WordArt object, of your choice, with the text Water Safety.

   c. Delete the AutoShape on slide 8 and insert the file pp04_Swimmer. Increase the size of the object to fill the slide.

   d. Delete the graphic on slide 2 and insert the file pp04_Lake. Increase the size of the object to fill the slide.

   e. On slide 2 change the title to Information.

   f. On slide 2 create Mouse Click hyperlinks from the three bulleted items to the appropriate slides. Link Statistics to slide 4.

   g. Add a home button to the slide master to return to the Information slide. Add forward and backward buttons. Size and position the three buttons appropriately. Check all slides and adjust as needed to display correctly.

   h. Set the slides to advance automatically after 10 seconds.

   i. Save the presentation as Water Presentation. Print the presentation with six slides per page.

   j. Turn off the auto advance feature and save the presentation as a Web page called Water Safety Web. View the Web page and run the presentation.

Emergency Driving Techniques Kiosk

★ **2.** To complete this problem, you must have completed Step-by-Step exercise 3 in Lab 3. The department of public safety outreach program on Emergency Driving Techniques has generated a large response from the community. Though the topic was originally intended to run only once, at the community meeting, the response has been such that the director has decided to install a kiosk to run the presentations in the lobby of your office building. You will prepare the presentation for the kiosk and make some final changes. Some of the completed slides are shown here.

   a. Start PowerPoint and open the file Blowouts3.

   b. Delete the graphic from slide 7 and insert the animated graphic pp04_Road Sign. Resize the graphic as shown in the example. Display the slide in Slide Show to see the animation.

   c. Delete the drawing object on slide 13. Insert the WordArt design in column 2 and row 3 of the Gallery with the text Drive Safely!. Position it where the drawing object was.

   d. Change the font of the WordArt text to one of your choice and the font size to 40 pt. Resize the object appropriately. Rotate the object slightly clockwise. Insert the file pp04_Alignment on slide 7. Size as shown in the example. View it in Slide Show.

   e. Switch to Slide Sorter view. Select all the slides and choose Random Transition at medium speed as the effect. Choose settings that will advance the slides automatically every 7 seconds.

   f. Make the slide show self-running. Run the Pack and Go Wizard and include the PowerPoint Viewer on the disk.

   g. Save your presentation as Blowouts4. Print the presentation with four slides per page.

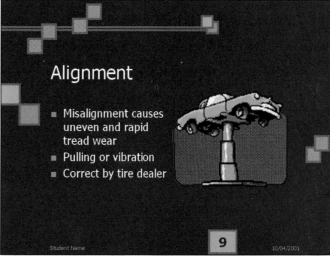

European Tour Kiosk

★ 3. The MBA office that you work in has a summer program in Toulouse, France. You have been asked to set up a kiosk presentation for display in the Student Union so those students thinking about going will have some more information. They also want to make it available on their Web site. Some of the completed slides are shown here.

a. Start PowerPoint and open the file pp04_Toulouse. Include your name on the title slide. Insert the graphic pp04_Countryside. Adjust slide layout as needed. Apply the same image to the background of slide 1.

b. Create two custom slide shows, one titled **Food** that displays slides 5 through 8, and another titled **Side Trips** that displays slides 9 and 10.

c. Apply the design template Slit. Change the font of the body text on all slides to a font of your choice. Edit the title in the Slide Master. Change font and font size to one of your choice.

d. Create a summary slide that includes slides 2 through 5, 9, and 11. Title the slide **Topics**.

e. Add Mouse Click hyperlinks from each item on the agenda slide to the appropriate slide or custom slide show (Jambon & Fromage links to the Food custom show). Select a different color for the hyperlink text.

f. Insert the graphic pp04_City Street on slide 2 and adjust the layout as required.

g. Add home, back, and forward action buttons to the slide master. The home button should return to the agenda slide. Size and position the buttons appropriately. Select a different color for the buttons. Reposition any text or graphics in the presentation as needed.

h. Set the slides to advance automatically after 10 seconds with slow transition. Set the presentation to run on a kiosk as a continuous loop.

i. Insert an audio of your choice to run while the presentation runs.

j. Insert the file pp04_Restaurant on slide 8 and adjust the slide as needed. Replace the clip art of the train on slide 11 with the file pp04_Train.

k. Insert a Custom Action Button with the text. Click to begin slide 1. It should proceed to the next slide. Change the color to match the design.

l. Run the slide show and test all the hyperlinks. Edit any slides as necessary.

m. Save the presentation as Toulouse Kiosk. Print the presentation with six slides per page.

n. Turn off the automatic advance setting and remove the audio. Redo the two hyperlinks that linked to custom shows to link to the appropriate slides. Save the presentation as a Web page called Toulouse Web. Preview the Web page and run the presentation.

Fitness Web Page

★ **4.** The Lifestyle Fitness Club would like you to create several new pages for their Web site. The outline containing the text for the pages has already been created. You will create a presentation using the information in this outline. Several slides of the completed presentation are shown here.

a. Create a new presentation using the Stream design template and Title and Text layout. Add slides to the presentation using the Word outline pp04_Fitness Outline.

b. Delete the blank first slide. Apply the Title slide layout to the first slide. Add your name as a subtitle on the title slide.

c. Change the slide layout of slide 2 to Text & Content. Insert pp04_Race. On slide 4 insert the file pp04_Woman. Size the picture appropriately and position as shown.

d. Use the numbered bullet style to consecutively number the tips on slides 5 and 6.

e. Insert a new slide at the end of the presentation. Use the Title Only layout. Title the slide Why People Go To Fitness Clubs.

f. Insert a table with 3 columns and 9 rows. Enter the following information. Include appropriate column headings and formatting.

Tone my body	41%	159
Lose weight	31%	119
Meet people	0%	1
Reduce stress	3%	12
Bulk up	11%	41
Stay active	13%	49
Avoid feeling guilty	2%	7
Get out of house	1%	2

g. Add home, back, and forward action buttons to the slide master. Change the fill color of the buttons to dark yellow. Appropriately size and position the buttons.

h. Save the presentation as Fitness Pages and as a Web page named Fitness Web Pages. Preview the presentation in Web Preview. Print the presentation with four slides per page.

Sports Company Kiosk and Web Page

★ ★
★
5. The Sports Company is expanding its advertising. They would like to have a kiosk presentation to send to their stores that features some special products in the stores. They would also like the presentation available on the Web. Several slides of the completed presentation are shown here.

a. Create a presentation using the Orbit design template and Title and Text layout. Add slides to the presentation by inserting the Word document file pp04_Sports Company Advertising Outline.

b. Delete the blank slide 1. Apply the Title slide layout to slide 1. Enter your name as a subtitle on the title slide. Insert the graphic pp04_Weight Lifter. Adjust the slide layout as needed.

c. Make two custom slide shows, one for Products and one for Services. The Products custom show should display slides 4, 5, and 6. The Services custom show should display slides 7 and 8.

d. Hyperlink the titles of the Products and Services slides to the appropriate custom show.

e. Insert the file pp04_Tennis Racquet in slide 6. Position the graphic to the right of the text. Size the picture appropriately.

f. Remove the main title and the placeholder on slide 1. Replace it with an appropriately sized and shaped WordArt that contains the same text. Change the color to match the presentation design.

g. Insert the graphic pp04_Mountain Bike on slide 4. Size and position the graphic. Adjust the layout as needed.

h. Insert the sound file pp04_Onestop on slide 1. Set the sound to play when the presentation starts and to play for all slides.

i. Add home, forward, and back action buttons to the slide master. Color, size, and position the buttons appropriately.

j. Insert the graphics pp04_Soccer, pp04_Football, pp04_Tennis, and pp04_Baseball in slide 2. Position the graphics and text as shown above.

k. Apply a random transition to all slides to advance automatically after 7 seconds. Set the slide show to run on a kiosk.

l. Save the presentation as Sports Company Kiosk. Run the presentation to test the hyperlinks. Print the presentation with six slides per page.

m. Remove the sound from the first slide. Remove the Products and Services hyperlinks. Add hyperlinks on the Products and Services slides for each bulleted item to the appropriate slide. Remove the transition settings and timings. Save the presentation as a Web presentation with the name Sports Company Web. Preview the presentation in Web Preview.

on your own

Better Bikes Company Kiosk

★ **1.** The response to your bike safety presentation (Lab 3, On Your Own 1) has been overwhelmingly positive. You decide that the information you have presented would make a good presentation to run on the kiosk in your safety equipment display. Create a new presentation by modifying the file DPS Bike Safety for use on a kiosk. Add the store name (Better Bikes Company) in a WordArt design of your choice. Include appropriate animation and clip art, slide transitions, preset timing, and sound that runs continuously with the slide show. Set up the show to be browsed at a kiosk and to automatically play at full screen and loop continuously. Save the presentation as Bike Safety Kiosk and print the presentation with six slides per page.

Carpooling Kiosk

★★ **2.** As cities surrounding Seattle get larger, rush hour traffic to the business district increases. You have been hired by the Washington Department of Transportation to create a presentation on the benefits of mass transit and carpooling for the lobby of their offices. Use the information in the file pp04_Mass Transit to create a presentation that will run on a kiosk giving people information on how mass transit use and carpooling will benefit their city. Use the features you learned in PowerPoint, including sound and animation. Include your name in a footer on all slides. Save the presentation as Mass Transit and print the presentation with six slides per page.

Getaway Travel Club Web Page

★★
★ **3.** The Getaway Travel Club unanimously adopted your proposal to amend the itinerary for the Italy Trip this summer. They have asked you to post the information on the Web. Create a Web-based presentation. Open the presentation Travel Italy2 (Lab 3, On Your Own 4) and create a custom show and an agenda slide with hyperlinks. Include action buttons, sound, animation, and WordArt. Include your name in the footer of all slides. Preview the presentation. Save the presentation as Travel Italy Web and print the presentation with six slides per page.

Lee Placement Services Employee Web Page

★★
★ **4.** The president of Lee Placement Services has recently visited the other branch offices. Several of the branch managers have suggested that the company provide a booklet for the new hires explaining the company benefits and organization. Instead of an informational booklet, she has decided that the information you have compiled in your previous presentations would be an excellent Web page. Modify the Lee Orientation file (Lab 3, On Your Own 5) for use on the Web. Create a custom show and an agenda slide with hyperlinks. Include action buttons, sound, animation, and WordArt with the company name (Lee Placement Services, Inc.). Save the file as Lee Orientation Web. Print the presentation.

MusicFirst Web Presentation

★ **5.** MusicFirst, a large retail chain of stores that sells CDs, concert clothing, and jewelry, would like you
★   to create a presentation featuring a new artist monthly. This presentation will run on the company
    home page. Spotlight your favorite musician and their latest release. Create a presentation with
    the features you have learned in PowerPoint. Include music and custom slide shows within the
    presentation. Include your name and the date in a footer on the slides. Save your file as MusicFirst
    Web and print the presentation with six slides per page.

on the web

Artist's Assembly Web Page

The Sedona Artist's Assembly provides a space for up-and-coming textile artists. Create a Web
presentation for the group with the features you have learned in PowerPoint. Research the Web or visit
a local gallery to locate items that can be spotlighted in the presentation. Include music and custom
slide shows within the presentation and add your name and the date in a footer on the slides. Preview
the presentation. Save the presentation as SAA Web and print the presentation with six slides per page.

Working Together 2: Linking and Document Collaboration

Case Study

Adventure Travel Company

The manager for Adventure Travel Tours has asked you to provide a monthly status report for the bookings for the four new tours. You maintain this information in an Excel worksheet and want to include the worksheet of the tour status in a memo each month. You will learn how to share information between applications while you create the memo.

You are also working on developing a brochure for the Mt. Everest tour. Writing documents, such as travel brochures and newsletters, is often not a solo effort. One person is typically responsible for assembling the document, but several people may be involved in writing and/or reviewing the text. You will learn about the collaboration features in Word 2002 that make it easy to work on a group project.

Linking an Excel worksheet to a Word document allows the Word document to be quickly updated when data in the worksheet changes.

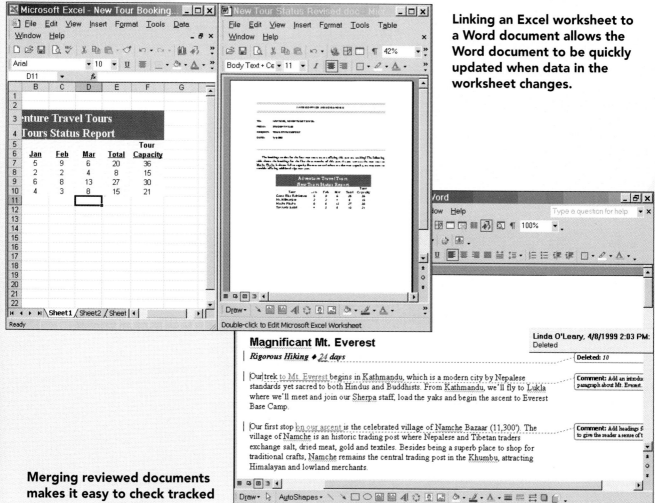

Merging reviewed documents makes it easy to check tracked changes and comments.

Sharing Information between Applications

All Microsoft Office applications have a common user interface such as similar commands and menu structures. In addition to these obvious features, the applications have been designed to work together, making it easy to share and exchange information between applications.

The memo to the manager about the new tour status has already been created using Word. However, you still need to add the Excel worksheet data to the memo.

1 ● **Start Word and open the file** wdwt2_New Tour Status.

● **In the memo header, replace "Student Name" with your name.**

● **Change the zoom to Page Width.**

● **Save the file as** New Tour Status Revised.

Your screen should be similar to Figure 1

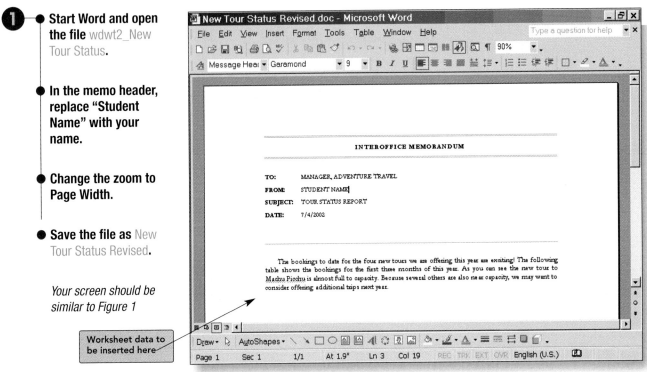

Worksheet data to be inserted here

Figure 1

Linking an Excel Worksheet

You will insert the worksheet data below the paragraph. To insert the information from the Excel workbook file into the Word memo you need to open the workbook file and copy the worksheet range.

1 ● **Start Excel and open the workbook file** wdwt2_New Tour Bookings.xls.

● **Save the file as** New Tour Bookings Linked.

● **Tile the two open windows vertically.**

HAVING TROUBLE?

Select Tile Windows Vertically from the Taskbar shortcut menu.

● **Select the worksheet range A3 through F10.**

● **Click** 🖺 **Copy to copy the selected range to the System Clipboard.**

● **Switch to the Word document window and move to the blank space below the paragraph.**

Your screen should be similar to Figure 2

Additional Information

Using 🖺 inserts the worksheet in Word as a table that can be manipulated within Word.

Another Method

You can also insert an object as an embedded object, which stores the entire source file in the document in which it was inserted. Opening the embedded object opens the program in which it was created.

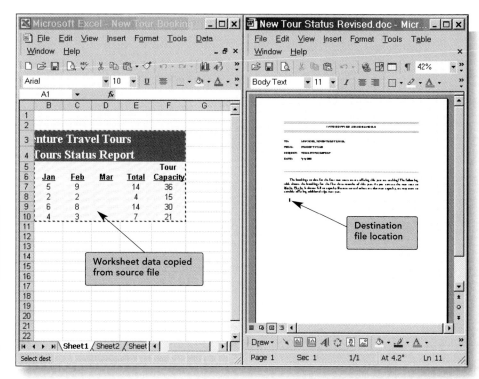

Worksheet data copied from source file

Destination file location

Figure 2

You will insert the worksheet into the memo as a linked object. A **linked object** is information created in one application that is inserted into a document created by another application while maintaining a link between the files. When an object is linked, the data is stored in the **source file** (the document it was created in). A graphic representation or picture of the data is displayed in the destination file (the document in which the object is inserted). A connection between the information in the **destination file** to the source file is established by the creation of a link. The link contains references to the location of the source file and the selection within the document that is linked to the destination file.

When changes are made in the source file that affect the linked object, the changes are automatically reflected in the destination file when it is opened. This is called a **live link**. When you create linked objects, the date and time on your machine should be accurate. This is because the program refers to the date of the source file to determine whether updates are needed when you open the destination file.

You will make the worksheet a linked object, so it will be automatically updated when you update the data in the worksheet.

2 ● **Choose E̲dit/Paste Special.**

● **Select Paste Li̲nk.**

Your screen should be similar to Figure 3

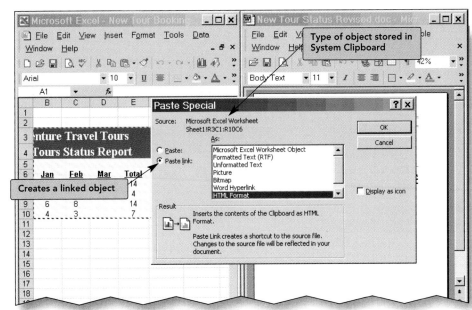

Figure 3

The Paste Special dialog box displays in the Source area the type of object contained in the Clipboard and its location. From the As list box, you select the type of format in which you want the object inserted into the destination file. The Result area describes the effect of your selections. In this case, you want to insert the object as an Excel Worksheet object, and a link will be created to the worksheet in the source file. Selecting the Display as Icon option changes the display of the object from a picture to an icon. Then to open or edit the object, you would double-click the icon. You need to change the type of format only.

3 ● **Select Microsoft Excel Worksheet Object.**

● **Click OK.**

● **Select the worksheet object and center it below the paragraph.**

Your screen should be similar to Figure 4.

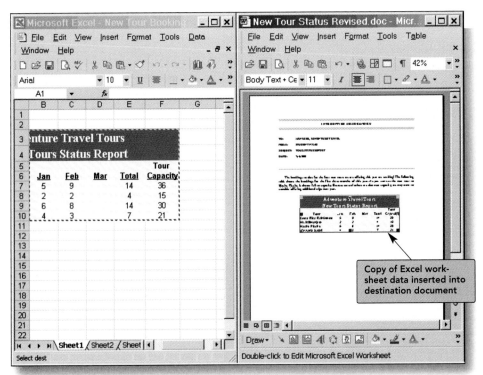

Figure 4

Updating a Linked Object

While preparing the memo, you received the tour booking for March and will enter this information into the worksheet. To make these changes, you need to switch back to Excel. Double-clicking on a linked object quickly switches to the open source file. If the source file is not open, it opens the file for you. If the application is not open, it both opens the application and the source file.

Another Method

The menu equivalent is Edit/Linked **O**bject.

1 ● **Switch to the Excel window.**

● **Enter the values for March in the cells specified.**

D7   6
D8   4
D9   13
D10 8

● **Press** ⏎Enter.

Your screen should be similar to Figure 5

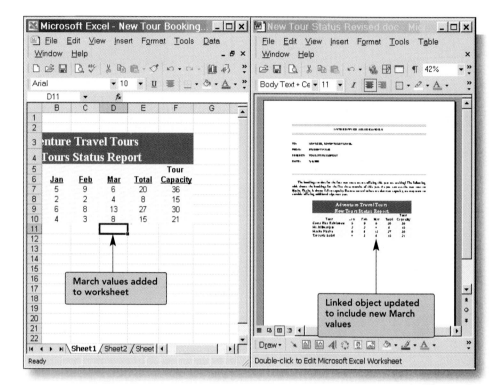

Figure 5

The worksheet in the memo reflects the changes in data. This is because any changes you make to the worksheet in Excel will be automatically reflected in the linked worksheet in the Word document.

2 ● **Undo the tiled windows.**

● **Exit Excel, saving the worksheet file.**

● **Print the memo.**

● **Close and save the Word document.**

Linking documents is a very handy feature, particularly in documents whose information is updated frequently. If you include a linked object in a document that you are giving to another person, make sure the user has access to the source file and application. Otherwise the links will not operate correctly.

Using Collaboration Features

Your second project is to review a document that a co-worker wrote for the new brochure being developed on the Africa Safari tour. You want to enter your suggested changes in the document and return it to the author. Word 2002 offers several features that make collaboration on documents easy and efficient.

Tracking Changes to a Document

To show the author what changes you are suggesting, you will use the Track Changes feature. When this feature is turned on, each insertion, deletion, or formatting change that is made to a document is identified or tracked.

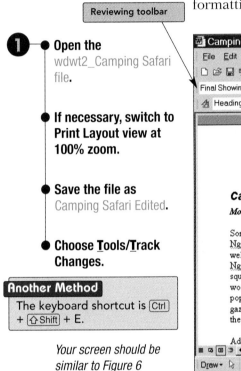

1 ● **Open the** wdwt2_Camping Safari **file.**

● **If necessary, switch to Print Layout view at 100% zoom.**

● **Save the file as** Camping Safari Edited.

● **Choose Tools/Track Changes.**

Another Method
The keyboard shortcut is Ctrl + ⇧Shift + E.

Your screen should be similar to Figure 6

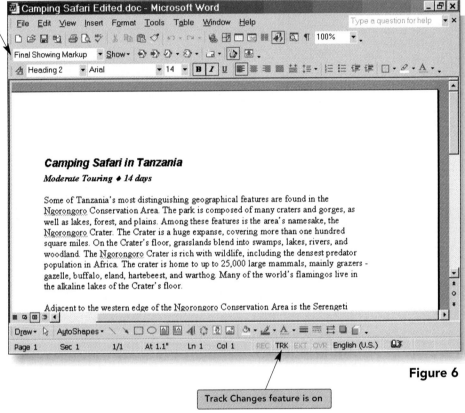

Figure 6

When Track Changes is enabled, "TRK" appears in the status bar and the Reviewing toolbar shown below is displayed. Now, any changes you make to the document will be marked to show the **tracked changes.**

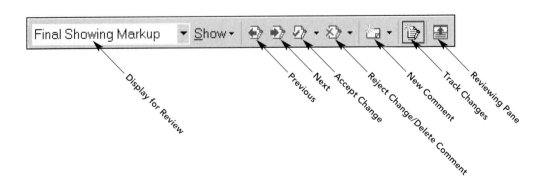

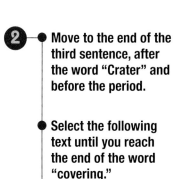

2
- Move to the end of the third sentence, after the word "Crater" and before the period.

- Select the following text until you reach the end of the word "covering."

- Press Delete.

- Type **, which covers.**

Your screen should be similar to Figure 7

HAVING TROUBLE?
If revision marks are not displayed, choose <u>V</u>iew/Mar<u>k</u>up to turn on this feature.

Additional Information
The balloons appear only in Print Layout and Web Layout views.

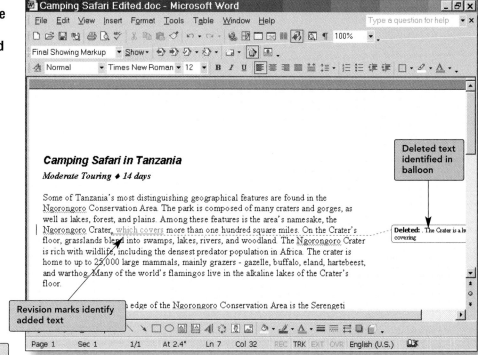

Figure 7

Different **markup** elements are used to identify the changes. The inserted text is identified with a red underline called a **revision mark** that indicates an insertion was made. The text you deleted is displayed in a **balloon** in the right margin. Dotted lines connect the balloons to the text that was changed.

The next change you want to make is to change the word "Crater" to all lowercase characters when it appears by itself.

3
- Highlight the "C" in the word "Crater" in the next sentence.

- Type a lowercase **c**.

- Make the same change to the word "Crater" in the last sentence of this paragraph.

- Point to any revision mark.

Your screen should be similar to Figure 8

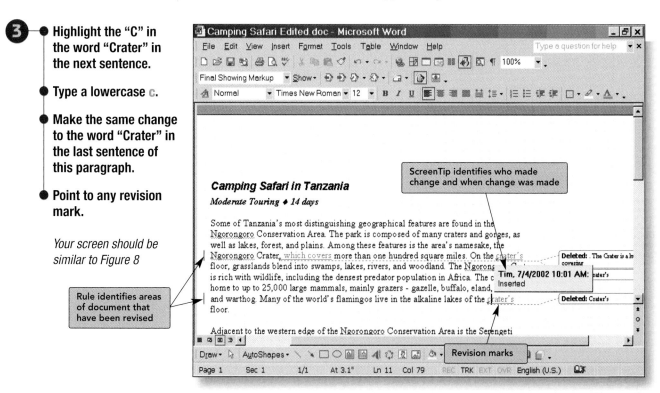

Figure 8

The change is identified with a revision mark and the deletion appears in the balloon. Pointing to a revision mark displays a ScreenTip with information about who made the change and when the change was made. The lines of the document that have been changed are identified with a vertical rule along the outside margin. The different markup elements help preserve the layout of the document while changes are being tracked.

Adding Comments

You want to add a comment before you send the document to the author. A **comment** is a note that can be added to a document without changing the document text. You will add a comment suggesting that there should be more information about the activities and camping experiences that will be encountered on the safari.

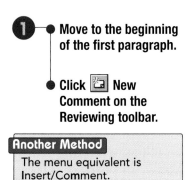

1 ● **Move to the beginning of the first paragraph.**

● **Click** 🔳 **New Comment on the Reviewing toolbar.**

Another Method

The menu equivalent is Insert/Comment.

Your screen should be similar to Figure 9

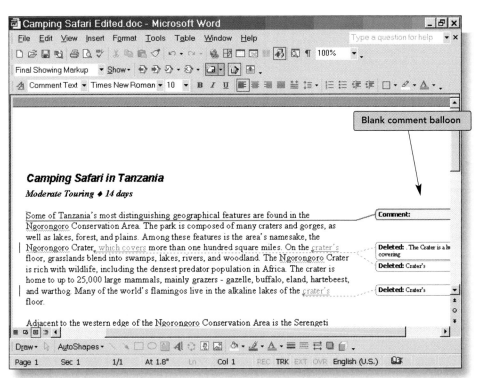

Figure 9

Another Method

You can also click 🔲 to display the Reviewing pane where you can type a comment. To close the Reviewing pane, click 🔲 again.

A blank **comment balloon** is displayed in the margin and a line connects it to the location where you inserted the comment. Next you need to add the text of the comment.

2

● Type **Please add more information about the activities and camping experiences on this tour.**

● Click 🖺 to turn off Track Changes.

Your screen should be similar to Figure 10

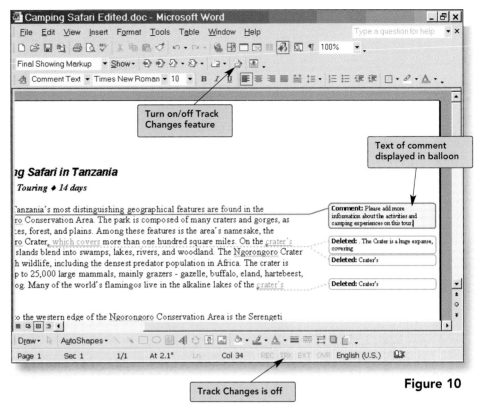

Turn on/off Track Changes feature

Text of comment displayed in balloon

...ng Safari in Tanzania

...Touring ♦ 14 days

...anzania's most distinguishing geographical features are found in the
...ro Conservation Area. The park is composed of many craters and gorges, as
...es, forest, and plains. Among these features is the area's namesake, the
...ro Crater, which covers more than one hundred square miles. On the crater's
...slands blend into swamps, lakes, rivers, and woodland. The Ngorongoro Crater
...h wildlife, including the densest predator population in Africa. The crater is
...p to 25,000 large mammals, mainly grazers - gazelle, buffalo, eland, hartebeest,
...og. Many of the world's flamingos live in the alkaline lakes of the crater's

...to the western edge of the Ngorongoro Conservation Area is the Serengeti

Comment: Please add more information about the activities and camping experiences on this tour.

Deleted: . The Crater is a huge expanse, covering

Deleted: Crater's

Deleted: Crater's

Page 1   Sec 1   1/1   At 2.1"   Ln   Col 34   REC TRK EXT OVR English (U.S.)

Track Changes is off

Figure 10

Another Method

You can also record comments using 🖺 New Comment/**V**oice Comment. You must have sound capabilities and a microphone to record and listen to recorded comments.

Now, any further changes you make will not be tracked.

Adding Text Animation

You only reviewed the first few paragraphs and want to indicate where you stopped in the document. A clever way of marking the document is with animated text.

1

● Move to the blank line after the first paragraph.

● Type **I stopped reviewing here.**

● Select the text and apply a font color of your choice.

● Choose **Format/Font/Text Effects.**

Your screen should be similar to Figure 11

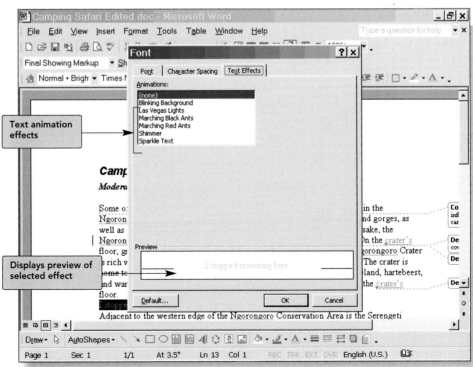

Text animation effects

Displays preview of selected effect

Font

Font | Character Spacing | Text Effects

Animations:

(none)
Blinking Background
Las Vegas Lights
Marching Black Ants
Marching Red Ants
Shimmer
Sparkle Text

Preview

I stopped reviewing here.

Default...   OK   Cancel

Page 1   Sec 1   1/1   At 3.5"   Ln 13   Col 1   REC TRK EXT OVR English (U.S.)

Figure 11

The available effects are listed in the Animations list box, and a sample of the animation effect associated with the selected text appears in the Preview area. Since no effect has been applied yet, the text is not animated.

2 ● Select each effect to preview how it will appear.

● Select Las Vegas Lights.

● Click [OK].

● Deselect the text.

● Save the document.

Your screen should be similar to Figure 12

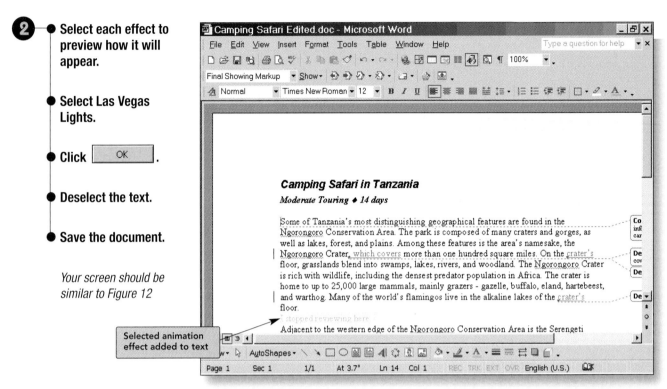

Selected animation effect added to text

Figure 12

The text will blink when viewing the document, but the animation effect will not print.

Sending a Document via E-mail

Additional Information
Using File/Send To/Mail Recipient (for Review) inserts the active document into the body of the e-mail message, where it can be edited by the recipient directly in the e-mail message and returned.

Next you will return the edited document to the author. The most efficient way is via e-mail with the document as an attachment. An **attachment** is a file that is sent with the e-mail message but is not part of the e-mail text. You open the attachment with the application in which it was created.

Note: Skip this section if you do not have Microsoft Outlook installed on your system.

❶ ● Choose **F**ile/Sen**d** To/M**a**il Recipient (as Attachment).

● Maximize the e-mail window.

Your screen should be similar to Figure 13

File name of attachment

Message area

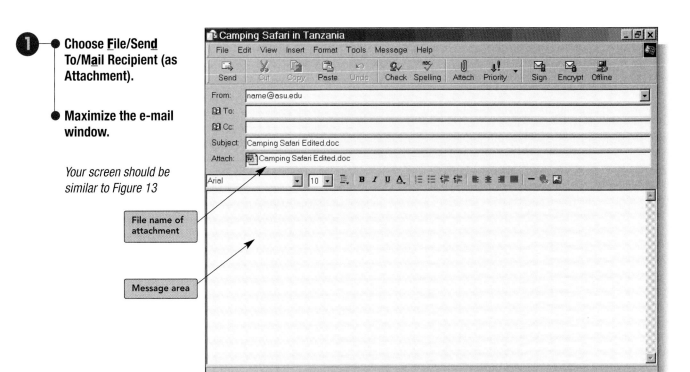

Figure 13

An e-mail window is displayed in which you can address your e-mail message. Notice that the Subject and the Attach fields show the filename of the attached document. The extension indicates the application in which the file will open, which is helpful to know.

Sends message

❷ ● In the To field, type your e-mail address.

● In the message area, type: **Please consider these comments to your attached document.**

Your screen should be similar to Figure 14

Body of e-mail message

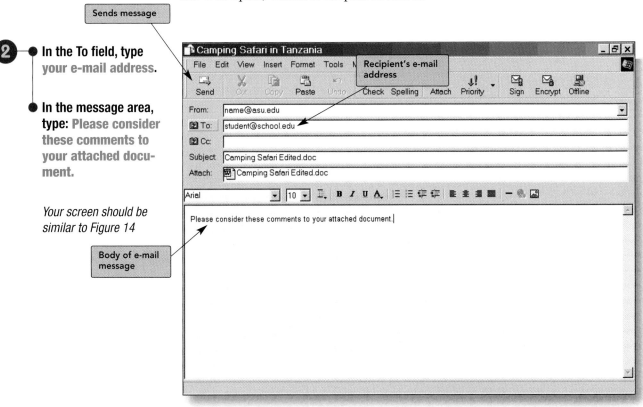

Figure 14

Now you are ready to send the message. If you have access the Internet, you could click [icon] to send the e-mail message. Instead, you will save it to be sent at a later time.

3 ● **Choose File/Save As and save the message as** Safari e-mail**.**

● **Click** [X] **to close the e-mail window.**

● **Close the Reviewing toolbar.**

● **Close the Word document.**

Reviewing Documents

While checking your e-mail for new messages, you see that two co-workers have returned a document you snet to them to review with their comments and tracked changes. You have downloaded the attachments and saved them as files on your system. Now you want to review the suggested changes.

Comparing and Merging Documents

When you receive multiple reviewer comments for the same document, the easiest way to review them is to merge the documents together. You will open the first reviewed document.

1 ● **Open** wdwt2_Everest Changes 2**.**

● **If necessary, switch to Print Layout view.**

● **Scroll the document to see the changes.**

Your screen should be similar to Figure 15

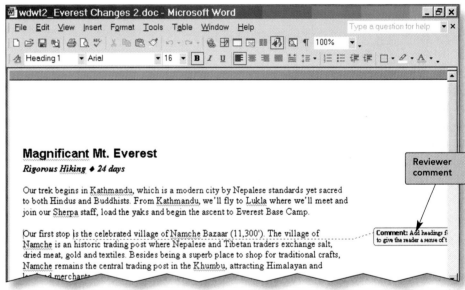

Figure 15

This reviewer only inserted one comment. To make sure that the reviewer did not change the document without using the Track Changes option, you will compare this document to the original using the Legal Blackline option. When you use Legal Blackline, Word compares the documents and creates a third document showing what changed between the two. The documents being compared are not changed.

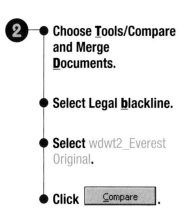

2 • Choose **T**ools/Compare and Merge **D**ocuments.

• Select Legal **b**lackline.

• **Select** wdwt2_Everest Original.

• **Click** [Compare].

Your screen should be similar to Figure 16

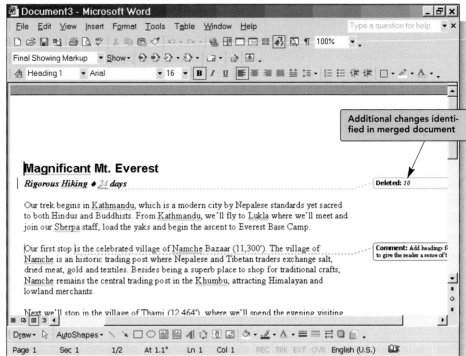

Figure 16

A new document is created showing the differences in the reviewed document from the original document. The next step is to merge this new document with the other reviewer's document so you can review all the changes together.

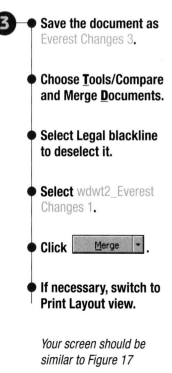

3 • Save the document as Everest Changes 3.

• Choose **T**ools/Compare and Merge **D**ocuments.

• Select Legal blackline to deselect it.

• **Select** wdwt2_Everest Changes 1.

• **Click** [Merge ▾].

• If necessary, switch to Print Layout view.

Your screen should be similar to Figure 17

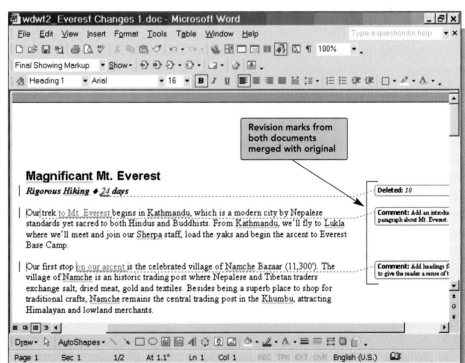

Figure 17

The revision marks and comments from both documents are now combined with the wdwt2_Everest Changes 1 document. Word automatically assigns unique colors to the comments and tracked changes made by the first eight reviewers who revise a document. You would like to see who the reviewers are.

4 • **Point to the first balloon.**

Another Method

You can also select **R**eviewers from the Show ▾ drop-down menu on the Reviewing toolbar.

Your screen should be similar to Figure 18

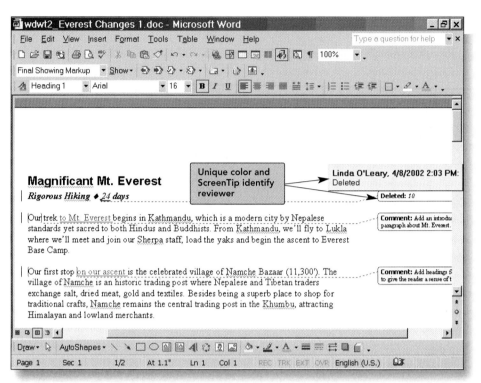

Figure 18

A ScreenTip displays the reviewer's name and the date of the change.

Accepting or Rejecting Changes to a Document

Before you begin to review the individual changes, you want to view the document in several different ways. The different views are described below.

Option	Effect
Final Showing Markup	Displays the final document with the insertions underlined and the deletions indicated in the revision balloons.
Final	Displays how the document would appear if you accepted all the changes.
Original Showing Markup	Displays the original document with the deletions underlined and the insertions indicated in the revision balloons.
Original	Displays the original unchanged document so you can see how the document would look if you rejected all the changes.

You want to see how the document would look if you accepted all changes.

1 ● **If necessary, display the Reviewing toolbar.**

● **From the** [Final Showing Markup ▼] **Display for Review drop-down list select Final.**

Your screen should be similar to Figure 19

Selected view of merged document

Document with all changes incorporated

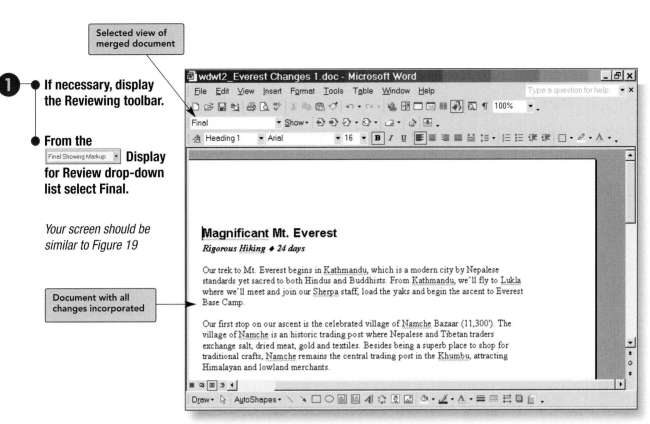

Figure 19

The document appears as it would look if you accepted all changes and ignored all the comments. Next you want to see the original document before the changes were made.

2 ● **From the** [Final ▼] **Display for Review drop-down list select Original.**

Your screen should be similar to Figure 20

Displays original document

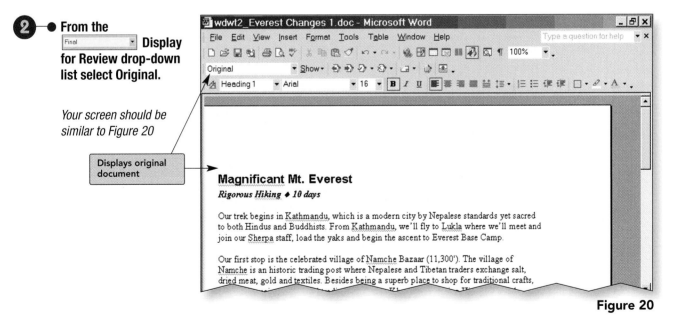

Figure 20

The original document appears without the suggested changes. You can quickly switch between the document views to check the changes. You want to display the final document with markups and review each change individually.

3 • From the [Original ▼] **Display for Review drop-down list select Final Showing Markup.**

• Click 🔲 **Reviewing Pane.**

• Click 🔷 **Next.**

Additional Information

Clicking 🔷 moves to the previous change or comment.

Your screen should be similar to Figure 21

Reviewing Pane

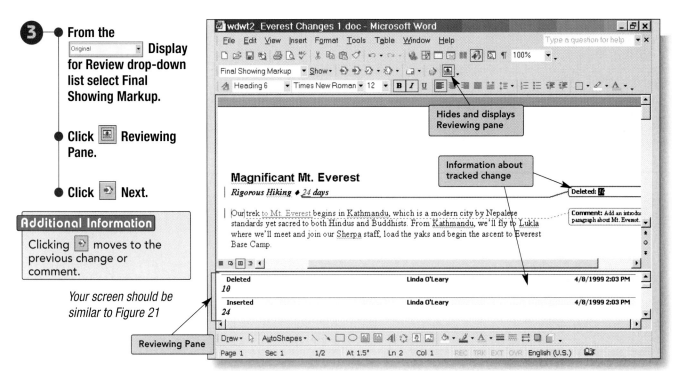

Figure 21

Additional Information

Often Word cannot display the complete text of a change or comment in a balloon, and it is necessary to view the comments in the Reviewing Pane.

The Reviewing Pane is displayed at the bottom of the document window and the information about the first change is displayed. The first tracked change to delete the number 10 is highlighted. Since this tour is 24 days in length, you want to accept the change.

4 • Click 🔷 **Accept Change.**

Your screen should be similar to Figure 22

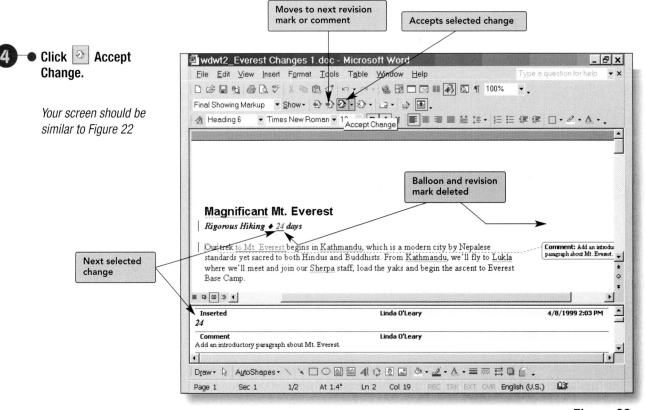

Figure 22

The number 10 is deleted along with the revision mark and the balloon. The next suggested change, to insert the number 24, is highlighted. Again, this is correct and you want to accept the change.

5 ● Click ⬜ Accept Change.

Your screen should be similar to Figure 23

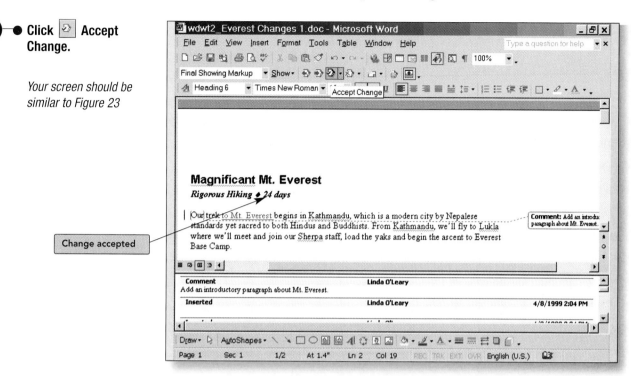

Change accepted

Figure 23

The number 24 is added to the document and the revision mark is removed. The next change is a comment. You will address the comments after you review the changes. For now you will bypass the comment, go to the next change, and accept the insertion of the words "to Mt. Everest."

6 ● Click ⬜ Next 3 times.

● Click ⬜ Accept Change.

Your screen should be similar to Figure 24

Accepted inserted text

Next change

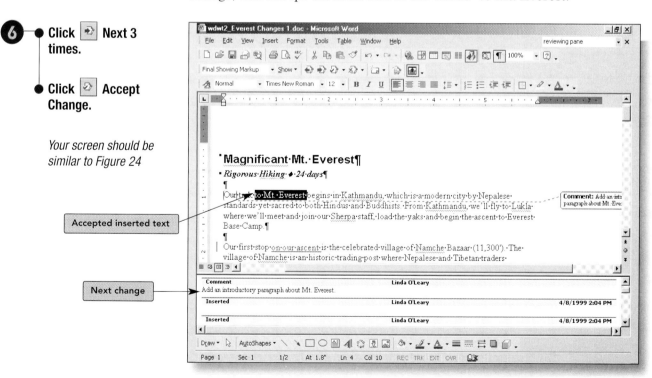

Figure 24

The next change is to insert "on our ascent". You feel this change is unnecessary and you will reject it.

7 Click ▶ Next.

Click ◇ Reject Change.

HAVING TROUBLE?

You can use ↶▾ to undo the last acceptance or rejection of a tracked change.

Your screen should be similar to Figure 25

Rejects change

Change rejected and text removed

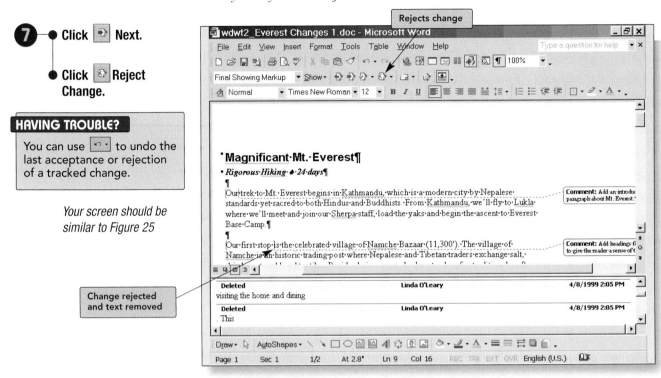

Figure 25

The rest of the changes in the document are acceptable. You will accept all the remaining changes and then look at the comments.

8 From the ◇ **Accept Change** drop-down list select Accept All **Changes in Document.**

Your screen should be similar to Figure 26

All remaining changes accepted

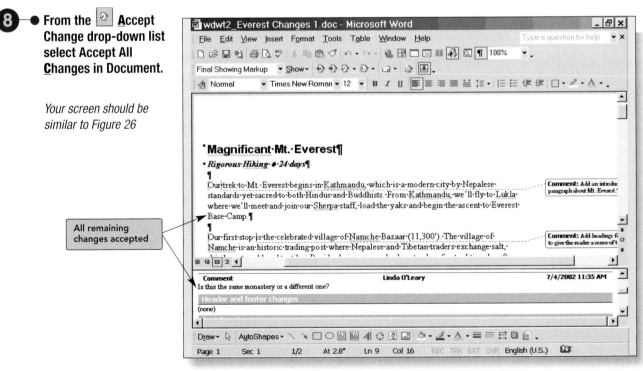

Figure 26

Now, the only review item left is the comments.

Reviewing Comments

In the first comment, the reviewer wants you to add an introductory paragraph about Mt. Everest. This sounds like a good suggestion. In fact, you already have a paragraph you had written and saved in a separate file that you can add to the document that will take care of this.

1 ● **Move to the beginning of the first paragraph.**

● **Insert the file** wdwt2_Everest Paragraph.

● **Right-click on the comment balloon.**

● **Choose Delete Comment from the shortcut menu.**

Your screen should be similar to Figure 27

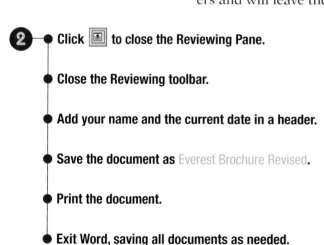

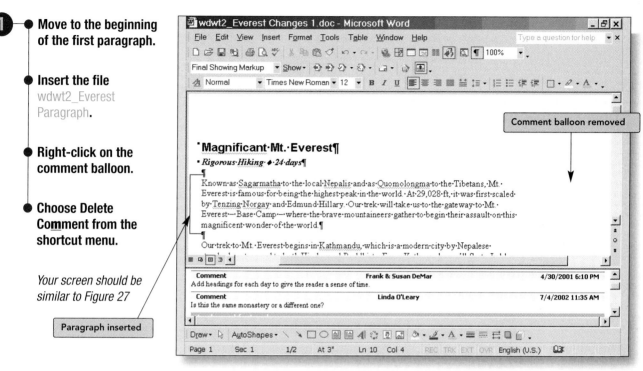

Figure 27

You feel the remaining comments require some discussion with the reviewers and will leave them in the document for now.

2 ● **Click** 🔲 **to close the Reviewing Pane.**

● **Close the Reviewing toolbar.**

● **Add your name and the current date in a header.**

● **Save the document as** Everest Brochure Revised.

● **Print the document.**

● **Exit Word, saving all documents as needed.**

Collaborating Online

In addition to collaboration through the exchange of documents and accepting and rejecting tracked changes, there are two other ways that you can collaborate with many reviewers at once. The first way is to hold an online meeting using the Microsoft NetMeeting feature. Each person you invite to the online meeting must also be running NetMeeting to receive your invitation.

In an online meeting, you are in control of the collaboration. Each person in the meeting can add comments to the document in real time, if you give them access. When you turn on collaboration, each person in the online meeting can take turns editing the document. The person whose turn it is to edit the document is the only one whose mouse will operate, and their initials will appear next to the mouse pointer.

The second way to collaborate is by using the Web Discussions feature, which needs to be set up by a system administrator. It enables you and other people to insert comments into the same document at the same time. This makes your job as document author much easier. You can see all the comments made by the reviewers, and they can too. Thus, if there is a discrepancy with the comment, the reviewers can discuss it among themselves.

lab review

Working Together 2: Linking and Document Collaboration

key terms

attachment   WDWT2.10

balloon   WDWT2.7

comment   WDWT2.8

comment balloon   WDWT2.8

destination file   WDWT2.3

linked object   WDWT2.3

live link   WDWT2.3

markup   WDWT2.7

revision marks   WDWT2.7

source file   WDWT2.3

mous skills

The Microsoft Office User Specialist (MOUS) certification program is designed to measure your proficiency in performing basic tasks using the Office XP applications. Getting certified demonstrates that you have the skills and provides a valuable industry credential for employment. After completing this lab, you have learned the following Microsoft Office User Specialist skills:

Skill	Description	Page
Workgroup Collaboration	Compare and merge documents	WDWT2.12
	Insert, view, and edit comments	WDWT2.8, WDWT2.16, WDWT2.19

command summary

Command	Shortcut Keys	Button	Action
Word			
File/Sen**d** To/M**a**il Recipient (as Attachment)		🖼	Sends the document as an e-mail attachment
File/Sen**d** To/M**a**il Re**c**ipient (for Review)			Sends the document as part of body of e-mail message
Edit/Paste **S**pecial/Paste L**i**nk			Pastes contents of Clipboard as a linked object
Edit/Linked **O**bject			Edits selected linked object
View/M**a**rkup			Displays/hides markup elements
Insert/Co**m**ment		🖼	Adds a note to the document
F**o**rmat/**F**ont/**T**ext Effects			Adds animation to selected text
Tools/**T**rack Changes	Ctrl + ⇧Shift + E		Marks changes to document
Tools/Compare and Merge **D**ocuments			Combines documents and identifies differences
Reviewing Toolbar			
		Final Showing Markup ▾	Displays merged document in different views
		🖼	Accepts highlighted change
		🖼	Rejects highlighted change or deletes selected comment
		🖼	Inserts a new comment
		🖼	Displays or hides Reviewing pane
E-mail Window			
File/Save **A**s			Saves e-mail message to name and location specified
File/**S**end		Send	Sends e-mail message to recipient

Hands-On Exercises

rating system

★ Easy

★★ Moderate

★★★ Difficult

step-by-step

Payroll Department Memo

★ **1.** Karen works for a large hotel chain in the payroll department. She has recently created a new time sheet to be used to track hours worked and wants to send a memo informing department managers of the new procedure. She also wants to include a copy of the time sheet from Excel in the memo. The completed memo is shown below.

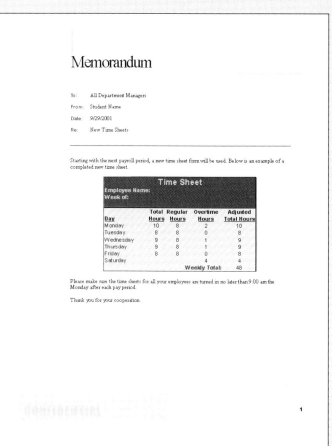

a. Start Word and open the document wdwt2_Time Sheet Memo.

b. In the memo header, replace the From placeholder with your name.

c. Start Excel and open the workbook file wdwt2_Time Sheet.xls. Link the range containing the time sheet to below the first paragraph in the Word memo. Center the time sheet in the memo.

d. You still need to complete the sample by entering the hours worked on Saturday. In the excel Worksheet, enter 4 as the Saturday hours worked.

f. Save the Excel workbook as Time Sheet. Exit Excel.

g. Save the Word document as Time Sheet Linked. Preview and print the document.

New Customer Memo

★ ★ **2.** You work for The Sports Company, a sporting goods retail store, as an Associate Manager. The credit card department has sent you a draft of a letter to be sent to new credit card customers and has asked for your input. You will use the Track Changes feature to indicate your revisions. The letter with the revision marks will look like that shown below.

  a. Start Word and open the document wdwt2_Credit Card Letter.

  b. Turn on Track Changes while editing the document.

  c. Make the following changes to the document:

■ Add **Sports Company** following the word "new" (second sentence of first paragraph).

■ Begin a new paragraph with the sentence "It will identify you..." (last sentence, second paragraph).

■ Change the text "It will identify" to **Your new credit card identifies**.

■ Insert the contents of the file wdwt2_Credit Card Paragraph below the third paragraph.

■ Highlight the second paragraph and add the comment: **Change to itemized list**.

■ Replace the placeholder in the closing with your name.

  d. Turn off Track Changes.

  e. Save the revised letter as Credit Card Letter Revised and print the letter.

Updating Adventure Travel Tours' Web site

★ **3.** You have been working on the content of the FAQ page for the Adventure Travel Tours Web site and have sent it out for review to several co-workers for input. You recently received one of the reviews back and want to update the document with the suggested changes. The revised FAQ document is shown here.

a. Open the file wdwt2_Draft FAQs.

b. Turn on the tracking feature to accept/reject changes and respond to each suggested change as you think appropriate.

c. In response to the comment about the minimum numbers of participants, add the following: **Our minimum is usually 6, but varies by trip.** Delete the comment.

d. In response to the comment to change the note to an answer, add an appropriate question heading and revise the note accordingly. Format the question heading like the others. Delete the comment.

e. Turn off the Track Changes feature.

f. Add your name and the current date to the header.

g. Save the file as FAQs Revised.

Student Name
Date

Answers to Frequently Asked Questions

How long have you been in business?
For over 15 years, Adventure Travel Tours has been offering adventures to the most intriguing destinations in the world.

What kind of trips are offered?
We have adventures that range from easy get-aways to challenging treks. We explore the world on foot, by kayak or raft, bicycle, 4-wheel drive, cruise ship or a combination of these vehicles! If you are a novice, we can teach you to kayak, or to safely summit a mountain.

How do I know what each trip is like?
This Web site provides full details of each trip. If you still have questions, call us at 1-800-555-3344, or email us at AdventureTraveler@AdventureTravelTours.com. We would be happy to discuss our adventure trips with you!

What is your maximum group size?
We keep our groups small - usually less than 16 participants. Our minimum is usually 6, but it varies by the trip.

What if I am traveling alone?
About half of our trip participants are individuals traveling alone. We also have people traveling with a friend, a spouse, or their entire family! We get single men as well as single women traveling with ATTours. It is a safe, convenient way to experience a new part of the world.

How are accommodations handled if I am a single traveler?
Prices are based on double occupancy. If you are traveling alone, and wish to share accommodations, we will assign a roommate if one is available. If you request single accommodations, or if a roommate cannot be found, you are requested to pay the single supplement. Single rooms are limited, and are based on availability.

Can I be comfortable doing adventure travel?
Adventure travel and physical comfort can go hand-in-hand. Join us for a hike through the Black Forest and you will sleep in charming inns and dine in many fine restaurants. If you prefer mountaineering, these amenities will, of course, be unavailable. But our camping trip arrangements are and comfortable. For example, our African safari trips provide spacious sleeping tents, a dining tent and a shower tent. Hot water is available, and a full camp staff takes care of all the chores!

Who are your guides?
Our skilled guides are skilled in their field (mountain climbing, sea kayaking, cycle touring, etc.). Besides running and leading our own trips, we hire local experts to lead our trips. These men and women know their homeland intimately, and are enthusiastic and accommodating. They "show you the ropes" and encourage you every step of the way!

What's the food like?
On hotel and inn-based trips we dine in local restaurants and have the pleasure of experiencing a variety of local cuisine. We eat equally well on our camping trips, which feature an abundance of fresh and delicious food. On high altitude climbing trips a combination of fresh food and freeze-dried is used. All water used for cooking and drinking is purified by filter or it is boiled.

Case Study

The Downtown Internet Café

The first project you are working on is to send Evan a copy of the Customers2 workbook to look at and make changes to as needed. You will send it to him for review by e-mail. When it is returned to you, you will review the suggested changes and update the workbook with the necessary changes.

The second project you are working on is to check the inventory on hand of certain items. If some items are overstocked, you plan to run a special on them. This information is maintained in an Access database table. You plan to import the table into Excel to quickly analyze the inventory numbers.

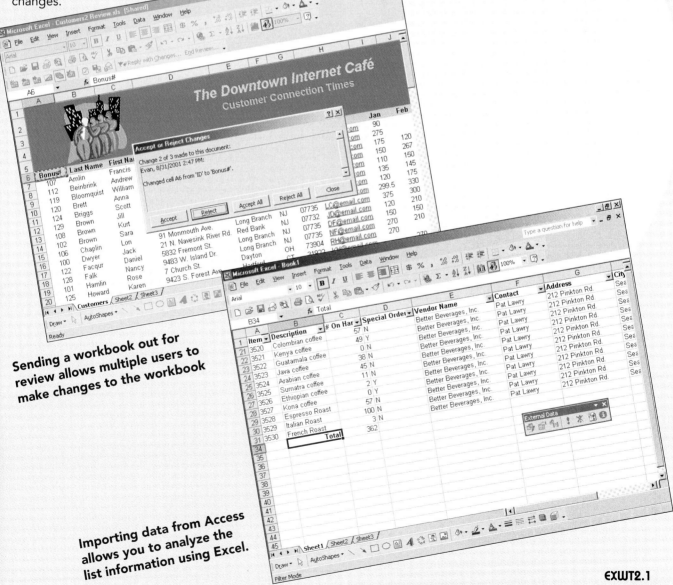

Sending a workbook out for review allows multiple users to make changes to the workbook

Importing data from Access allows you to analyze the list information using Excel.

Reviewing a Workbook

Microsoft Office XP makes it easy to work with others to develop and use workbooks. You can send a workbook or other document for review so that the recipients can add comments and make changes to it. As the reviewed documents are sent back to you, you can combine them with your original copy of the document, and then use the reviewing tools to accept or reject the changes.

Sending the Workbook for Review

Note: You will need the Customers2 file you saved at the end of Lab 6.

Now you will send the Customers2 workbook to Evan via e-mail to review.

1 ● **Open the workbook file** Customers2 **from your Café Customers folder.**

● **Choose File/Send to/Mail Recipient (for Review).**

Your screen should be similar to Figure 1

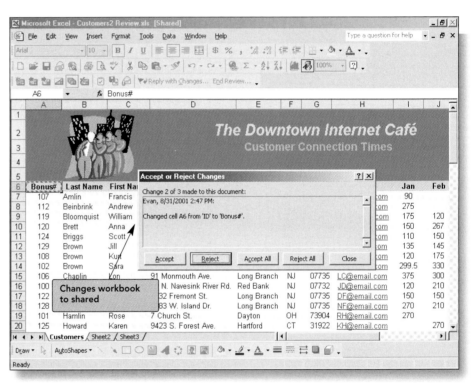

Figure 1

An informational message is displayed notifying you that the workbook status needs to be changed to shared in order to track reviewers' comments. Initially, a workbook's status is **exclusive,** which allows only one user the capability to edit the workbook at one time. A **shared workbook** allows multiple users to make changes to the workbook at the same time.

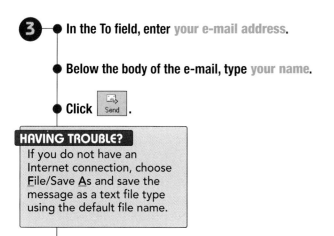

② ● Click [Yes].

● **Save the workbook as** Customers2 Review **in the Café Customers folder.**

● **Click** [Save].

Your screen should be similar to Figure 2

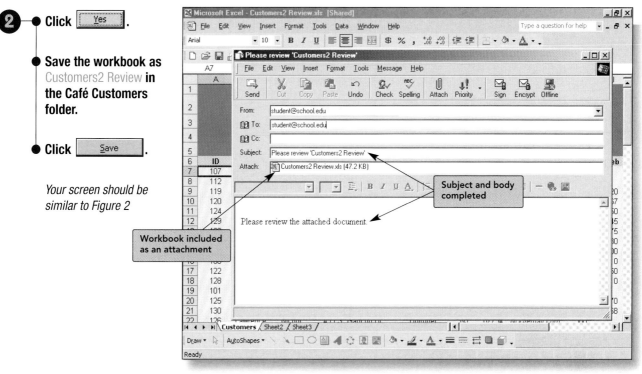

Figure 2

The new e-mail message window is displayed. Because the command to send the workbook by e-mail was to send it for review, the subject and body of the message already include appropriate information. The workbook is included as an attachment to the e-mail message.

③ ● **In the To field, enter** your e-mail address.

● **Below the body of the e-mail, type** your name.

● **Click** [Send].

> **HAVING TROUBLE?**
> If you do not have an Internet connection, choose File/Save As and save the message as a text file type using the default file name.

● **Close the workbook.**

Combining Reviewed Workbooks

A short while later, while checking your e-mail for new messages, you see that Evan has returned the workbook with his changes. You have downloaded the attachment and saved it using a different file name to the same folder. Now you want to review the suggested changes.

When you receive reviewers' comments, the easiest way to review them is to merge the reviewed copy with the original.

1 ● **Open the file**
exwt2_Customers2 Original.

● **Choose Tools/Compare and Merge Workbooks.**

● **Select** exwt2_Customers2 Review.

● **Click** [OK].

Your screen should be similar to Figure 3

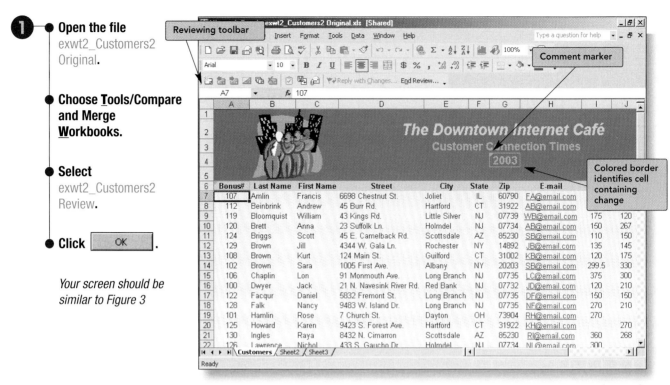

Figure 3

The changes from Evan's reviewed workbook are combined with and displayed in the original worksheet. The Reviewing toolbar is automatically displayed.

Viewing Changes

The changes that are made in a shared workbook are maintained in a separate **History worksheet**. The **change history** is also displayed directly on the worksheet using onscreen highlighting. Cells that contain changes are identified with a colored border and comment marker. The change history includes information about who made the change, the date of the change, and the data that were changed.

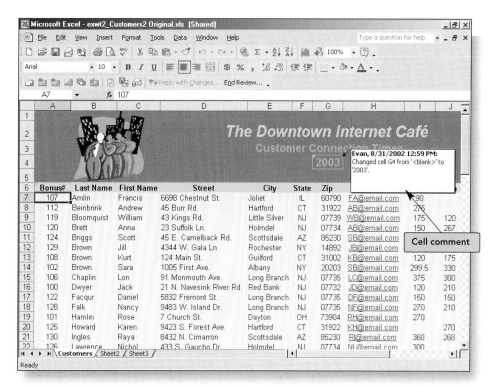

Figure 4

Cell comments containing the change history for that cell are automatically
added to the worksheet whenever the reviewer makes a change. In this
case, Evan changed the column label from ID to Bonus #. Next, you will
look at the History worksheet of all changes.

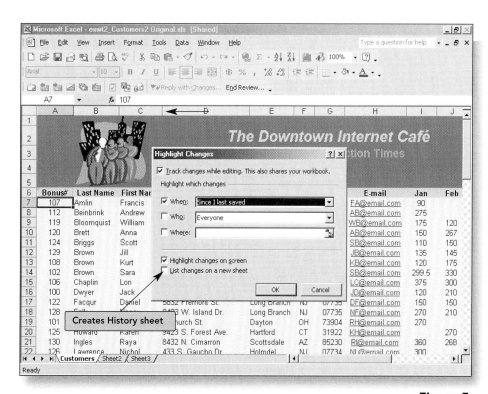

Figure 5

From the When check box, you can enter a date to specify an interval of elapsed time or to review all changes that have not been reviewed yet. The Who check box is used to specify that you want to review changes made by specific persons and the Where check box is used to specify that you want to see changes made to a specific range of cells.

3 ● If necessary, select the When check box.

● Select All from the When drop-down list.

● If necessary, clear the Who and Where check boxes.

● Select List changes on a new sheet.

● Click [OK].

Your screen should be similar to Figure 6

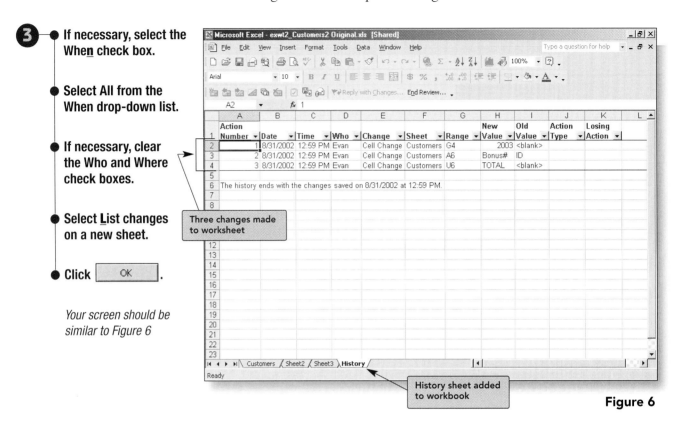

Figure 6

A temporary History sheet has been inserted in the workbook and opened. You can quickly see that Evan made three changes to the worksheet. You can also use the filter arrows next to the column labels to isolate specific changes. Using the History sheet is particularly useful when there are many reviewers and a lot of changes to track.

Reviewing Changes

You want to review the changes in the worksheet one by one and make a decision as to whether to accept or reject each change.

Additional Information

The following types of changes are not tracked: sheet names, insert and delete worksheets, all cell formatting, hide/unhide rows and columns, and add/edit cell comments.

1 ● Switch to the Customers sheet.

● Choose **T**ools/**T**rack Changes/**A**ccept or Reject Changes

Your screen should be similar to Figure 7

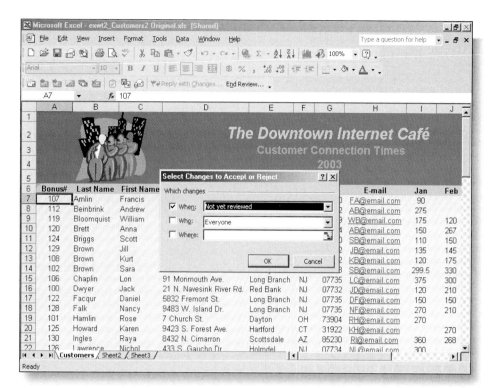

Figure 7

Again, you specify the When, Who, and Where settings. You want to review all changes made by everyone in the entire worksheet.

2 ● Click [OK].

Your screen should be similar to Figure 8

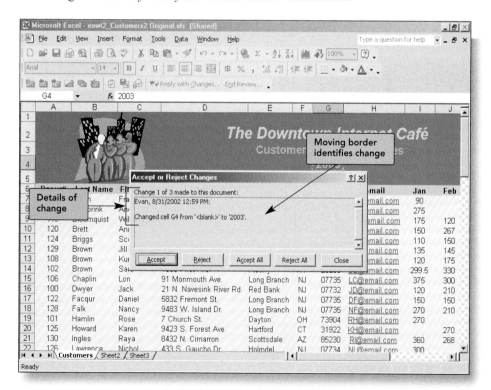

Figure 8

The first change that was made is the addition of the date in cell G4. The change is identified with a moving border. Because Evan entered the wrong date, you will reject it.

3 • Click **Reject** .

*Your screen should be
similar to Figure 9*

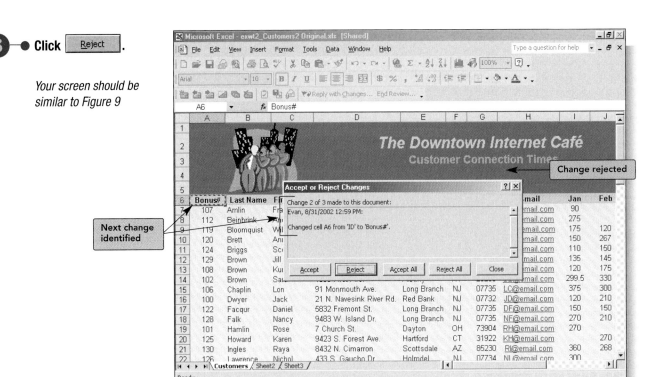

Figure 9

The change is deleted and the next change is identified. You will accept this change.

4 • Click **Accept** .

HAVING TROUBLE?
If necessary, move the dialog box to see the identified change.

*Your screen should be
similar to Figure 10*

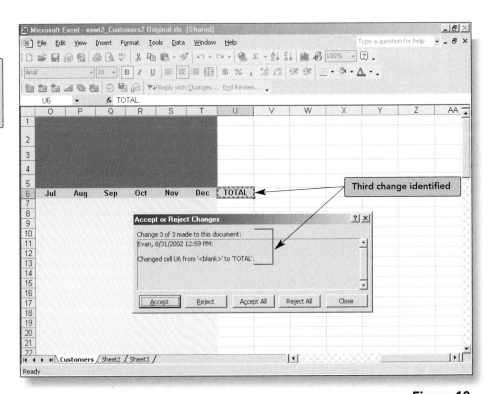

Figure 10

No change is made because the change was already included in the worksheet when the files were merged. The last change is identified. Again you will accept this change.

5 • Click [Accept].

• **Save the workbook as** Customers2 Final **to the Customers folder.**

Your screen should be similar to Figure 11

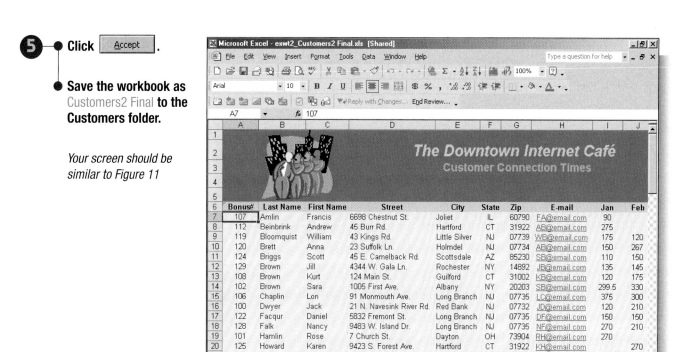

Figure 11

The History sheet was removed when you started the process of reviewing changes. To see how the History worksheet has been updated to reflect your decisions, you need to recreate the worksheet.

6 • Choose **Tools/Track Changes/Highlight Changes.**

• Choose **List changes on a new sheet.**

• Click [OK].

• Scroll the window to the right.

Your screen should be similar to Figure 12

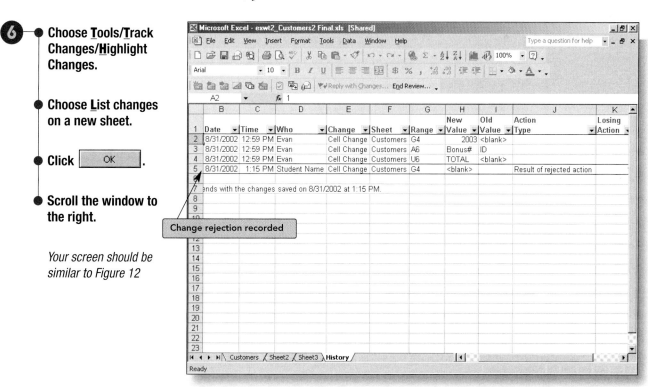

Change rejection recorded

Figure 12

The History worksheet has recorded the rejection action in the Action Type column for cell G4. Accepted actions are not noted, as they were already incorporated into the worksheet when it was merged.

Ending the Review

To complete the worksheet, you will enter the correct date in G4 and format the TOTAL column.

1 ● **Switch to the Customers sheet.**

● **Enter** 2002 **in cell G4.**

● **Copy the format from T1 to U1:U5.**

● **Copy the format from T7 to U7:U59.**

● **Click anywhere to deselect the column.**

Your screen should be similar to Figure 13

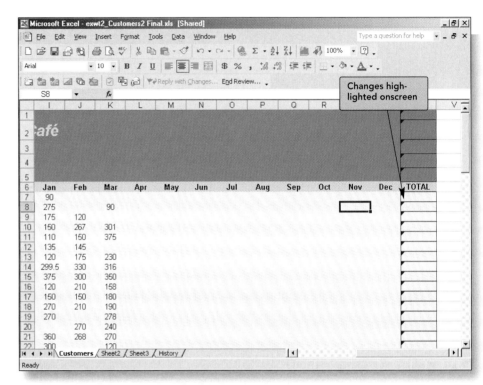

Figure 13

Because the track changes feature is still on for the workbook, your changes are identified onscreen.

Now that you have reviewed all the comments, you want to end the review process.

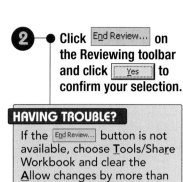

② ● Click [End Review...] on the Reviewing toolbar and click [Yes] to confirm your selection.

HAVING TROUBLE?

If the [End Review...] button is not available, choose **T**ools/**Sha**re Workbook and clear the **A**llow changes by more than one user in the Editing tab.

● Click [Yes] to clear the change history and remove the shared status.

● Click [Yes] to confirm your selection.

● Press [Ctrl] + [Home].

Your screen should be similar to Figure 14

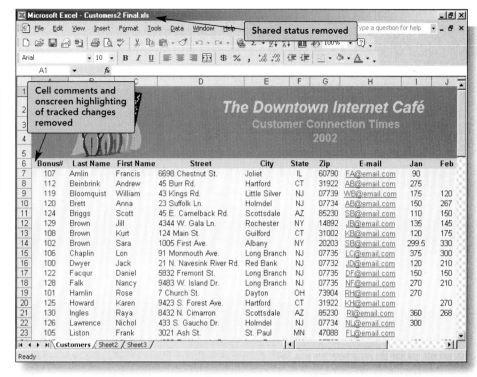

Figure 14

The onscreen highlighting of tracked changes is removed. When the review process is over, you cannot combine any more reviewed workbooks with your original workbook.

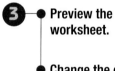

● Preview the worksheet.

● Change the orientation to landscape.

● Set the print area as A1:K39.

● Print the worksheet using the print area settings.

● If necessary, close the Reviewing toolbar.

● Save and close the workbook file.

Your printed output should be similar to that shown here.

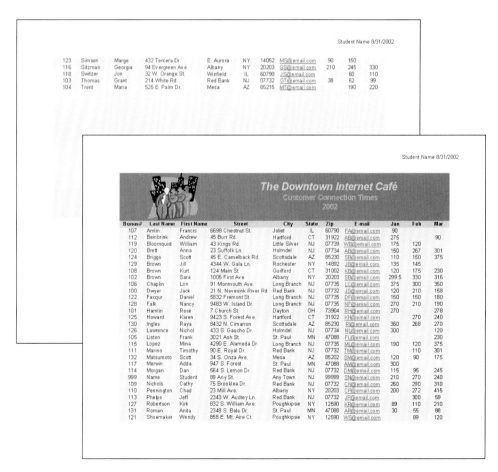

Importing Data

The other project you are working on is to check the inventory on hand of certain items. If some items are overstocked, you plan to run a special on them. This information is maintained in an Access database table. You will import the table into Excel to quickly analyze the inventory numbers.

Importing Access Table Data to Excel

Additional Information

Exporting saves data in another format so that it can be used in an application other than the application in which it was created.

Importing converts external data that have been saved in another format into a format that can be used by the application. **External data** is data that are stored outside the application, in this case Excel, such as a database or text file.

You want to import the data from the Vendors table of the Café Supplies Access database to an Excel workbook so that you can perform additional mathematical analysis on the data.

1 ● **Click** ☐ **New.**

● **Choose D**ata/Import External **D**ata/Import **D**ata

● **Select** exwt2_Café Supplies.mdb **from your data file location.**

● **Click** Open ▾.

● **Select the Vendors table from the Select Table dialog box.**

● **Click** OK .

Your screen should be similar to Figure 15

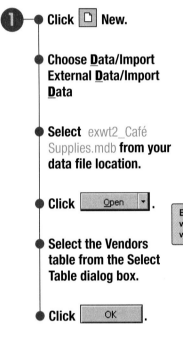

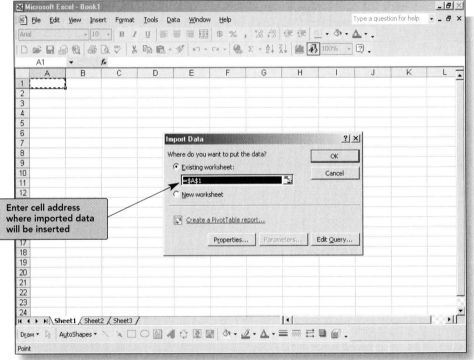

Enter cell address where imported data will be inserted

Figure 15

Next, you need to specify where you want the data inserted. The default selection, cell A1, in the worksheet is appropriate. When specifying the location, be careful to select an area that is empty below and to the right of the selected cell so that data you want to keep are not overwritten.

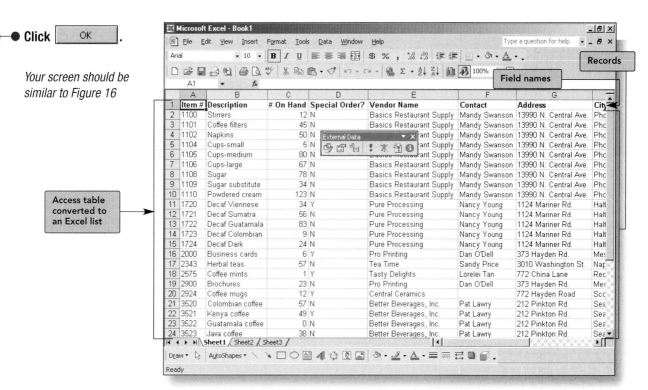

2 — ● Click OK .

Your screen should be similar to Figure 16

Access table converted to an Excel list

Figure 16

The database table is converted to an Excel list with the field names in the first row of the worksheet and the records beginning in row 2. The column heads and column widths are formatted as they appeared in the Access table.

Analyzing the List

Now the data can be manipulated using Excel commands and features. You want to find out how much coffee is on hand to determine what coffee specials to offer next week.

1 ● Choose
Data/Filter/AutoFilter.

● From the Vendor Name
field select Better
Beverages, Inc.

● Calculate the total
coffee on hand in cell
C34.

● Enter, bold, and right-
align the label Total
in cell B34.

*Your screen should be
similar to Figure 17*

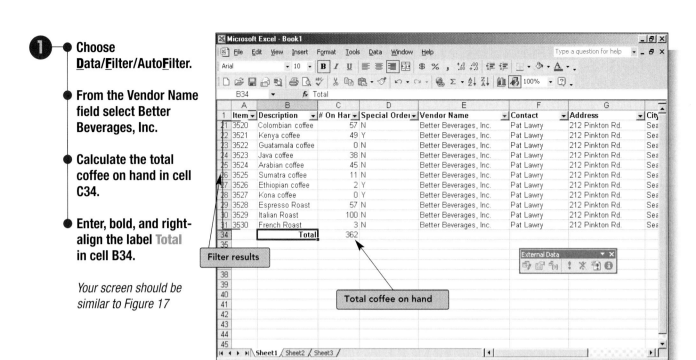

Figure 17

You can now easily see that the Italian Roast coffee quantity on hand is very
high and decide to offer a special on that item. At the same time, you need
to order several coffees whose quantity is very low. You will print out the filtered list for Evan to confirm your ordering decisions.

2 ● Select the range A1:C34.

● Specify this range as the selection to print and then preview the worksheet.

● Center the worksheet horizontally.

● Enter your name and the current date right-aligned on separate lines in a custom header.

● Print the worksheet.

Your printed output should be similar to that shown here.

Student Name
8/31/02

Item #	Description	# On Hand
3520	Colombian coffee	57
3521	Kenya coffee	49
3522	Guatamala coffee	0
3523	Java coffee	38
3524	Arabian coffee	45
3525	Sumatra coffee	11
3526	Ethiopian coffee	2
3527	Kona coffee	0
3528	Espresso Roast	57
3529	Italian Roast	100
3530	French Roast	3
	Total	362

Now that you have the information you need, you will remove the filter and save the workbook.

3
- **Remove the filter.**
- **Close the External Data toolbar.**
- **Save the worksheet as** Café Supplies**.**
- **Exit Excel.**

Working Together 2: Reviewing a Workbook and Importing Access Data

key terms

change history   EXWT2.4

exclusive   EXWT2.2

export   EXWT2.12

external data   EXWT2.12

History worksheet   EXWT2.4

import   EXWT2.12

shared workbook   EXWT2.2

command summary

Command	Action
File/Send to/Mail Recipient (for Review)	Sends the active workbook as an attachment to an e-mail message and sets up the file for review
Data/Import External Data/Import Data	Imports data from an external source into a worksheet
Tools/Share Workbook/Allow changes by more than one user	Changes workbook status to shared or exclusive
Tools/Track Changes/Accept or Reject Changes	Sequentially moves to each tracked change and lets you decide to accept or reject each
Tools/Track Changes/Highlight Changes/List changes on a new sheet	Displays a separate History sheet of all tracked changes
Tools/Compare and Merge Workbooks	Combines workbooks sent to review

Hands-On Exercises

step by step

rating system

★ Easy

★★ Moderate

★★★ Difficult

★ **1.** You have completed the analysis of projected donations for the next year for the Animal Rescue Foundation. Now you want to send the workbook to Mary Munson, the Fund Raising Administrator, for review and comments. The revised analysis is shown here.

    a. Start Excel and open the workbook file ARF Analysis (from Lab 4, exercise 5).

    b. Send the workbook by e-mail for review to a classmate with the file name of ARF Analysis Review. In the body of the e-mail, ask your classmate to make the changes shown below to the workbook and to use the Reply with Changes option to send the workbook back to you.

Student Name   9/04/02

Animal Rescue Foundation
Analysis and Projections

	2001 Income	5% Increase	10% Increase	10% Decrease	5% Decrease	Current Scenario
Annual Memberships	$54,834	$57,576	$60,317	$49,351	$52,092	$54,834
Phone Solicitation	$6,400	$6,720	$7,040	$5,760	$6,080	6,400
Corporate Donations	$45,000	$47,250	$49,500	$40,500	$42,750	45,000
Raffle Tickets	$2,894	$3,039	$3,183	$2,605	$2,749	2,894
Pet Shows	$16,000	$16,800	$17,600	$14,400	$15,200	16,000
Other	$24,000	$25,200	$26,400	$21,600	$22,800	24,000
Total	$149,128	$156,584	$164,041	$134,215	$141,672	$149,128

Sheet	Cell	Change
Spring/Summer	D3	Current year
	D3	Current year
Fall/Winter	C10	5000
Analysis	A3	Add [Current year] – [Next year] to the subtitle

    c. When you receive the reply, save the reviewed workbook as ARF Analysis Review2. Merge the reviewed and original workbooks.

    d. Track the changes and accept all changes except the change to cell C10.

    e. Save the workbook as ARF Analysis2 and print the Analysis worksheet.

★★ **2.** After developing the worksheet to show the effects of a change in sales from –5 to 10 percent for Adventure Travel Tours, you want the manager to review it. You will send it to the manager by e-mail and then respond to the changes. The revised Adventure Travel Sales worksheet will be similar to the one shown here.

Adventure Travel Tours
Packages Sold
in 2002

	Jan-Mar	Apr-Jun	Jul-Sept	Sept-Dec	Total
Lower 48	2568	1502	899	610	5579
Alaska/Hawaii	1520	510	1115	799	3944
Europe	1444	1223	1988	1250	5905
Orient	1824	786	1452	478	4540
Other	987	875	1276	625	3763
Total	8343	4896	6730	3762	23731

Increase Percentage   0.03

Packages Needed in 2003

	Jan-Mar	Apr-Jun	Jul-Sept	Sept-Dec	Total
Lower 48	2645	1547	926	628	5746
Alaska/Hawaii	1566	525	1148	823	4062
Europe	1487	1260	2048	1288	6082
Orient	1879	810	1496	492	4676
Other	1017	901	1314	644	3876
Total	8593	5043	6932	3875	24443

a. Start Excel and open the workbook file ATT Sales2 (from Lab 5, exercise 5).

b. Unprotect the worksheet.

c. Send the workbook by e-mail for review to a classmate with the file name of ATT Sales Review. In the body of the e-mail, ask your classmate to make the changes shown below to the workbook and to use the Reply with Changes option to send the workbook back to you.

Cell	Change
C3	in 2002
E8	1250
E10	725
A15	Packages Needed in 2003

d. When you receive the reply, save the reviewed workbook as ATT Sales Review2. Merge the reviewed and original workbooks.

e. Track the changes and accept all changes except the change to cell E10. Create a History sheet.

f. Change the value in E10 to 625.

g. Save the workbook as ATT Sales3 and print the worksheet and History sheet.

★ **3.** Alice works at the Decorator's Resource Gallery. An invoice for a garden themed office has arrived. The decorator has requested the prints all be by the same artist. Alice believes Bassett prints will be ideal. She needs to find out the number of prints by Basset in stock. To do this, she plans to use the information in the Access Gallery Database file and analyze it using Excel.

a. Open a blank workbook in Excel.

b. Import the Vendor table from the exwt2_Decorator's Resource Gallery file.

c. Filter the list to display the artist Bassett only.

d. Total the Quantity column. Include a label for the total value. Add the title **Decorator's Resource Gallery: Artist Inventory** above the data. Apply formatting of your choice.

e. Print the filtered list. Include your name and the date in a header.

f. Remove the filter and save the workbook as Artist Inventory.

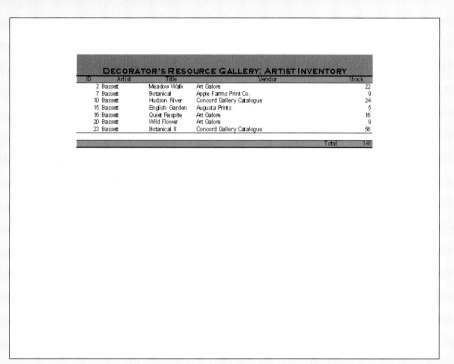

DECORATOR'S RESOURCE GALLERY: ARTIST INVENTORY				
ID	Artist	Title	Vendor	Stock
2	Bassett	Meadow Walk	Art Galore	22
7	Bassett	Botanical	Apple Farms Print Co.	9
10	Bassett	Hudson River	Concord Gallery Catalogue	24
15	Bassett	English Garden	Augusta Prints	5
16	Bassett	Quiet Respite	Art Galore	16
20	Bassett	Wild Flower	Art Galore	9
23	Bassett	Botanical II	Concord Gallery Catalogue	56
			Total	141

Working Together 2: Exporting and Creating Data Access Pages

Case Study

The Lifestyle Fitness Club accountants have reviewed the 6/28/2002 Gross Pay query you created and would like to do some further data manipulation on it. However, they are more used to working in Excel and would like you to export the Access query so it can be opened in Excel.

The Club has also just established an intranet to share internal information among employees who are authorized to use it, such as the Club managers. The owners would like you to create a data access page containing the Club employee data so it can be viewed online and discussed during the next management meeting.

Note: This lab assumes that you already know how to use Excel and that you have completed all of the previous Access labs.

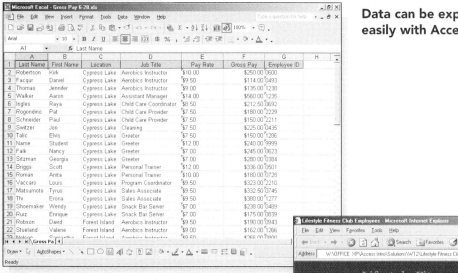

Data can be exported and imported easily with Access.

Database objects can be quickly converted to Web pages.

Exporting Access Data

The club accountants would like to further analyze the data in the Gross Pay 6/28/2002 query using Excel. You will export the query datasheet to an Excel workbook for them to use.

Exporting saves Access data in another format so it can be used in an application other than Access. Importing, as you have learned, retrieves data that has been saved in another format into an Access table. Access can import and export data in the following formats:

- Text files (.asc, .txt, .csv, .tab) — These include delimited text and fixed-width text. **Delimited text** is a file containing values separated by commas, tabs, semicolons, or other characters as in the following example: 3/2/98 0:00:00,/"Reddie","Suzanne". **Fixed-width text** is a file containing values arranged so that each field has a certain width, as in the following example: 3/2/98 0:00:00 Reddie Suzanne.

- Rich text format (.rtf) — This file format retains all the format settings, such as font, alignment, and number formatting for column heads and data, as shown below:

Hire Date	Last Name	First Name
9/23/96	Shoemaker	Wendy
8/4/96	Switzer	Jon
3/2/98	Reddie	Suzanne

- Microsoft Excel 3, 4, 5–7, and 97–2002

- Microsoft Exchange, all versions

- Lotus 1-2-3 WK1, WK3, and WJ2

- dBase III, IV, and 5

- Paradox 3, 4, 5, and 7–8

- SQL tables, Microsoft Visual FoxPro, and data from other programs and databases that support ODBC (Open Database Connectivity)

- HTML version 1.0 in list format and versions 2.0 and 3.x in list or table format

- XML, all versions

When you import a file that has been saved in any of these formats, Access converts the information into Access database table format. Access files that are exported to any of these formats can be read and used by the applications that use these formats.

Exporting an Access Query to Excel

Rather than opening the Gross Pay 6/28/2002 query, you can simply select the query object name from the Queries tab and export it to an Excel file format. Because Excel does not allow slashes (/) in file and sheet names, you will rename the query before exporting it.

1 ● **Start Access and open the** Club Employees **database.**

HAVING TROUBLE?

If this file is not available, use ac06_Club Employees.

● **When prompted, enter the password to open the database (this should be your first name).**

● **Click** 🗔 **Database Window to display the Database window.**

● **Select the "Gross Pay 6/28/2002" query object.**

● **Choose Rena<u>m</u>e from object shortcut menu and replace the two / characters with hyphens.**

● **Press** ⟵Enter **to complete the rename.**

● **Choose <u>F</u>ile/<u>E</u>xport.**

Your screen should be similar to Figure 1

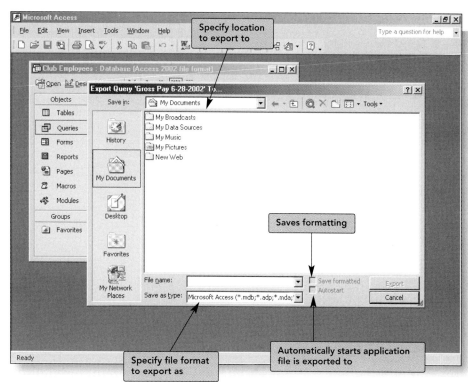

Figure 1

You use the Export Query dialog box to specify where and in what format you want to export the selected query. In addition, you can specify whether you want to include the original file formatting in the new file and whether you want to have the exported file automatically opened in the selected application. You will save the query in Excel 2002 file format, preserving the original table formats such as fonts and field widths. You will also have the Excel application start automatically and display the new file.

2 ● **Select the location to save the file.**

● **In the File name box, enter the file name Gross Pay 6-28.**

● **From the Save as type drop-down list box, select Microsoft Excel 97-2002.**

● **Select Save formatted.**

● **Select Autostart.**

● **Click [Export].**

Your screen should be similar to Figure 2

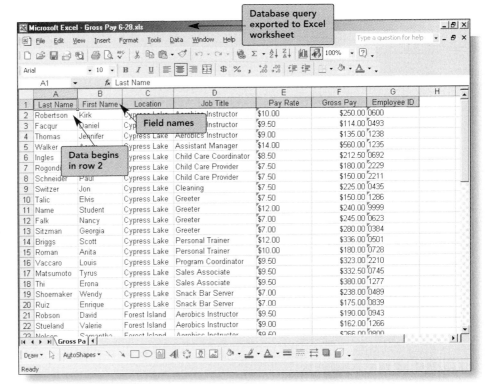

Figure 2

The database query is saved to an Excel file format, and Excel 2002 is started. The new workbook file is open with the information from the query displayed in it. The field names are placed in the first row of the worksheet, and the data begins in row 2. The column heads and column widths are formatted as they appeared in the query datasheet. Now the data can be manipulated using Excel commands and features. For example, it would be easy to calculate total and average values by departments.

3 If necessary, maximize the Excel worksheet window.

● Calculate a grand total of the Gross Pay column in cell F61.

● Enter the label TOTAL in cell E61.

● Bold the label and calculated gross pay total.

Your screen should be similar to Figure 3

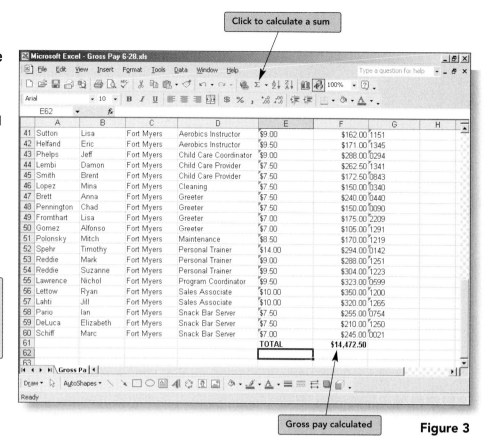

Click to calculate a sum

Gross pay calculated

Figure 3

The gross pay total is the same as the value calculated in the report.

4 ● Print the worksheet.

● Save the revised workbook.

● Exit Excel.

Putting Access Data Online

You have also been asked to put the employee data on the Club's **intranet** (an internal network set up by a company to share data online). To do this, you will create a **data access page**. This is a Web page created in Access that is connected to a database and that can be displayed and edited by the online viewer.

There are several methods you can use to create a data access page, depending on what you want it to contain and how you want it to be connected to the source data. You can use the Page Wizard to create a data access page with fields from multiple database objects (tables, forms, reports, and/or queries). The AutoPage feature will create a data access page with all fields from a single table, query, or view. In addition you can create a new data access page in Design view using existing table or query data, or convert an existing Web page into a data access page.

If you create a data access page when a database is open, Access creates a **shortcut** to the page and displays the shortcut in the Database window. If you create a page without opening a database, Access creates a **standalone page** (a page that does not have a shortcut to it from anywhere else).

Using the Page Wizard

Because you have been asked to include data from more than one table in the Web page, you will use the Page Wizard to create a data access page with multiple database objects and fields.

1
- **Click** [Pages] to open the Pages object.
- **Click** [New].
- **Select Page Wizard.**
- **Select "Employees" as the table on which to base the object data.**
- **Click** [OK].

Your screen should be similar to Figure 4

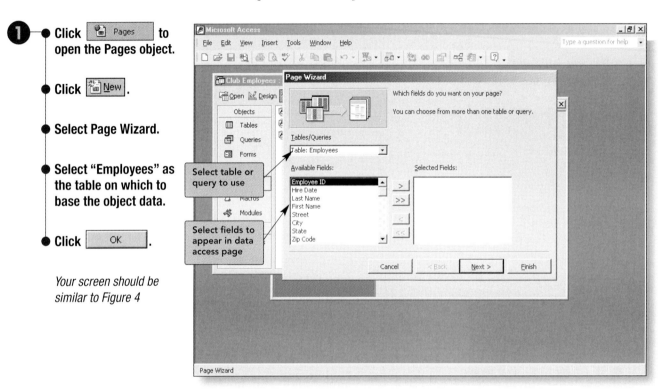

Figure 4

Next you select the fields you want to include on the data access page.

2 ● Add all fields except Birth Date from the Employees table, the Location and Job Title fields from the Location and Position table, and the Pay Rate field from the Pay table.

● Click [Next >].

Your screen should be similar to Figure 5

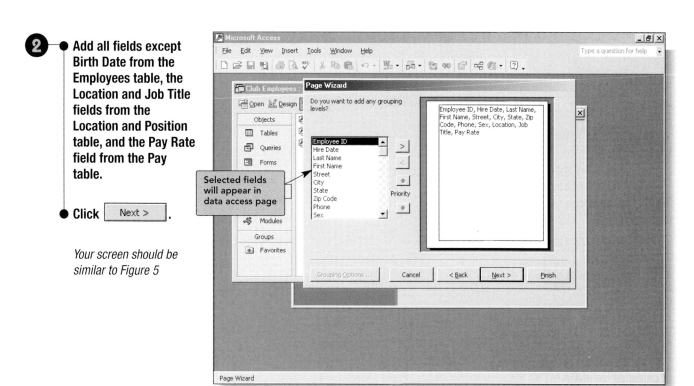

Selected fields will appear in data access page

Figure 5

Like some of the other Access Wizards you have worked with, you can select groupings and sort orders for a data access page. You are not sure how the Club owners are going to review this data in their meeting, so you decide not to do any specific field ordering at this time.

3 ● Click [Next >].

● Click [Next >].

Your screen should be similar to Figure 6

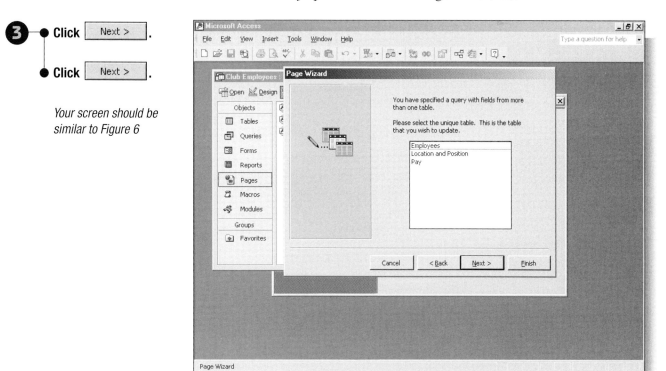

Figure 6

The next Wizard screen asks you to select the table with the data you will be updating. Because the Employees table contains the majority of the employee data, you decide to select this one as the primary table.

4 ● **Select "Employees"**
and click Next >.

● **Name the page**
Lifestyle Fitness Club
Employees.

● **Select** **O**pen the page.

● **Click** Finish.

● **Maximize the window.**

Your screen should be
similar to Figure 7

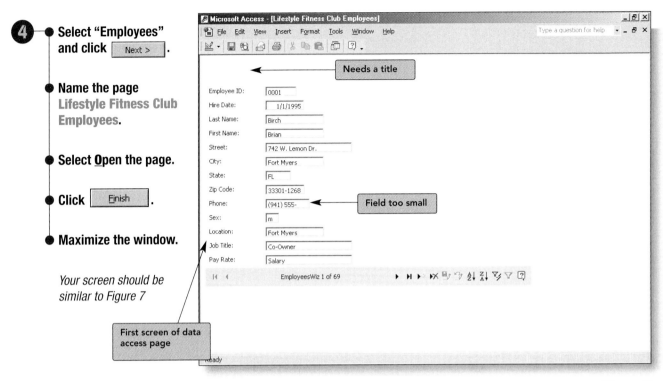

Figure 7

The first screen of the data access page is displayed in Page view. It is very similar to a form, but it is stored in a separate file in HTML format. **HTML,** which stands for **Hypertext Markup Language,** is a programming language used to create Web pages. HTML commands control the display of information on a page, such as font colors and size, and how an item will be processed when displayed in a browser. A **browser** is a program that connects you to remote computers and displays the Web pages you request.

Modifying a Data Access Page

You notice that the phone number is not completely displayed and there is no page title. Additionally, since the data access page will be displayed in a browser, you want to enhance the appearance of the page. As with other Access database objects, you use Design view to make changes to the layout of a data access page.

1 ● Click 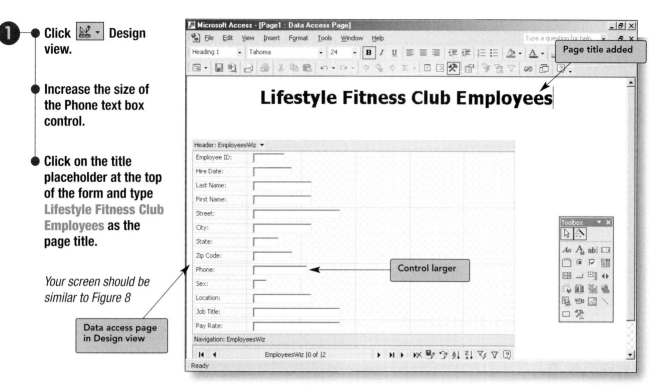 Design view.

● Increase the size of the Phone text box control.

● Click on the title placeholder at the top of the form and type **Lifestyle Fitness Club Employees** as the page title.

Your screen should be similar to Figure 8

Data access page in Design view

Figure 8

You can quickly enhance the appearance of the page by applying a theme to the page. A **theme** is a predesigned set of background color, designs, fonts, and other special effects.

2 ● Choose F**o**rmat/T**h**eme.

● Select Artsy from the Choose a **T**heme list.

Your screen should be similar to Figure 9

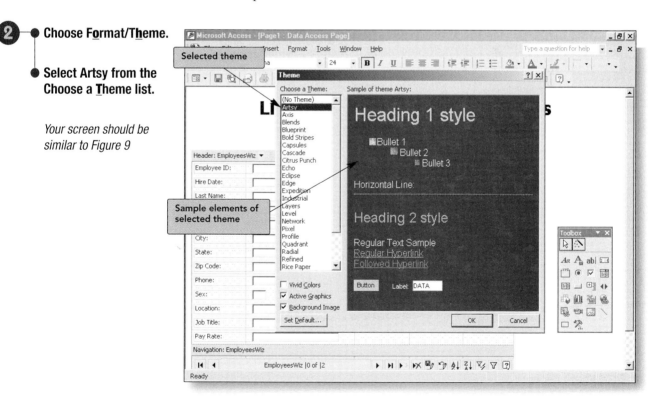

Figure 9

The Choose a Theme list displays the names of all the themes. The preview area displays a sample of the selected theme, showing the background design, bullet and horizontal line style, and character formats that will be applied to headings, normal text, and hyperlinks.

3 ● **Select several other themes to preview them.**

● **Select the Cascade theme.**

● **If necessary, select Vivid Colors.**

● **Click** OK **.**

Your screen should be similar to Figure 10

Cascade theme applied

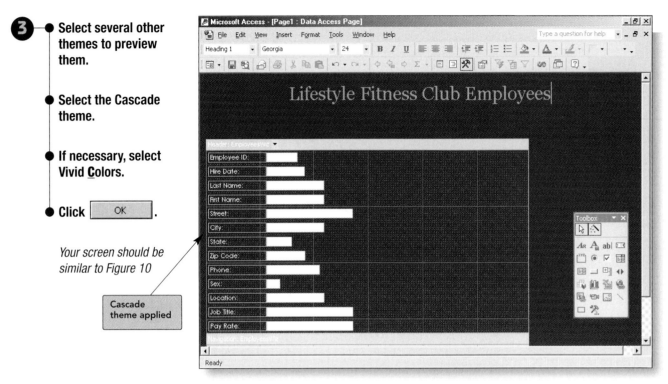

Figure 10

The formatting settings associated with the selected theme are applied to the page.

Previewing the Page

Now you want to see how the page will look in the browser.

Note: The following step assumes that you have Microsoft Internet Explorer 5.0 or later on your system. If this program is not available, skip to the next section, Adding Hyperlinks.

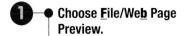

1 • Choose **F**ile/We**b** Page Preview.

• Click **Yes** in response to the prompt to save the file.

• Save the file to your location using the default file name.

• Click **OK** in response to the advisory message.

• Enter your database password (this should be your first name).

Your screen should be similar to Figure 11

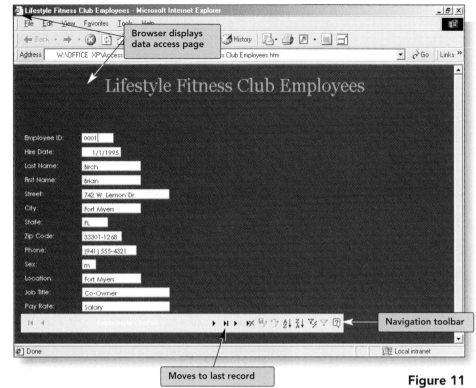

Figure 11

The Internet Explorer browser on your system is started and displays the data access page. Notice at the bottom of the page, a navigation toolbar displays buttons that can be used to move to records in the database as well as perform some basic manipulations to the database such as deletions, sorts, and filters.

2 • Click ▶| Last on the navigation bar to display your record.

• Print your record.

• Close the browser window.

Your screen should be similar to Figure 12

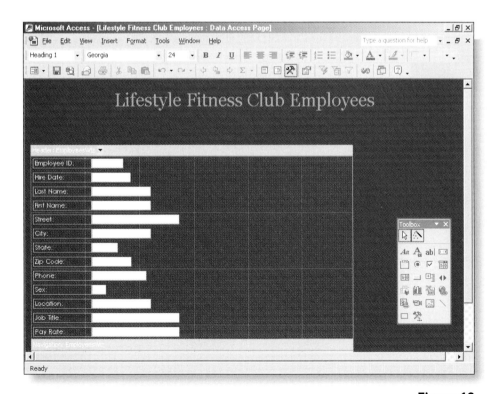

Figure 12

Adding Hyperlinks

You want to add a hyperlink in the data access page to the Gross Pay workbook you created. A **hyperlink**, when clicked on, allows the user to jump to another location in the same or different database table, form, report, or query; to a document in a different application; or to a Web page.

● Click  Hyperlink in the Toolbox.

● Click to the right of the Pay Rate field to place the hyperlink.

Another Method
The menu equivalent is Insert/Hyperlink and the keyboard shortcut is Ctrl + K.

Your screen should be similar to Figure 13

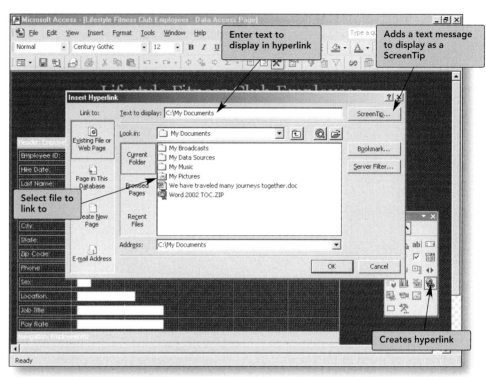

Figure 13

You use the Insert Hyperlink dialog box to specify the file to which you want the hyperlink to jump. You can also specify whether you want the hyperlink field to display the address of the linked file or a text message. You can also add a ScreenTip that will display whenever the mouse pointer rests on the hyperlink field. You want to link to the Excel Gross Pay 6-28 workbook file.

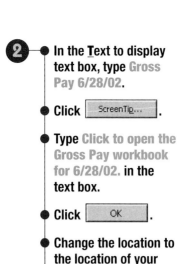

2
- In the **T**ext to display text box, type Gross Pay 6/28/02.
- Click ScreenTip....
- Type Click to open the Gross Pay workbook for 6/28/02. in the text box.
- Click OK.
- Change the location to the location of your files and select Gross Pay 6-28.xls.
- Click OK.
- Size the control to fit the text and position it as in Figure 14.

Your screen should be similar to Figure 14

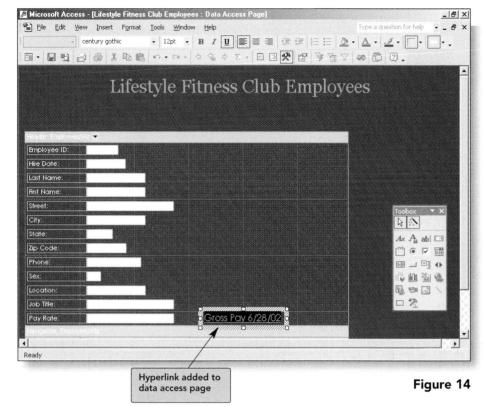

Hyperlink added to data access page

Figure 14

Now you're ready to test the hyperlink.

Note: If you do not have Internet Explorer, you will not be able to test the hyperlink.

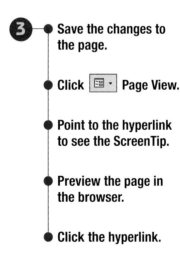

3
- Save the changes to the page.
- Click ▦ ▾ Page View.
- Point to the hyperlink to see the ScreenTip.
- Preview the page in the browser.
- Click the hyperlink.

Your screen should be similar to Figure 15

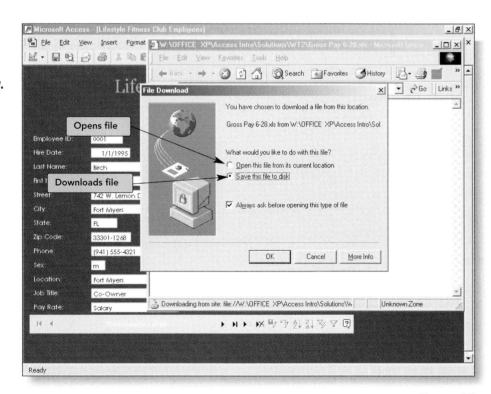

Opens file

Downloads file

Figure 15

You can download the referenced object in the hyperlink to your disk or open it. You want to open it to see the contents of the workbook.

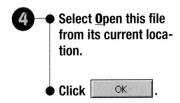

4 ● Select <u>O</u>pen this file from its current location.

● Click ⬚ OK ⬚ .

Your screen should be similar to Figure 16

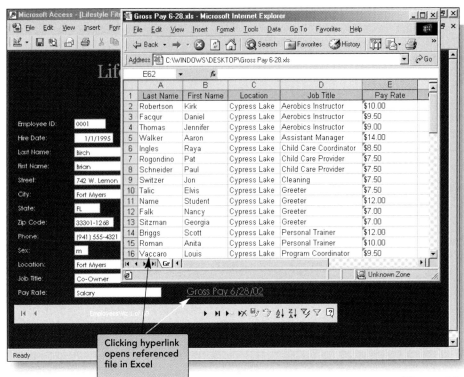

Figure 16

The Excel application is started and the workbook file is opened. Using a hyperlink makes it very easy to access other files from the data access page.

5 ● Exit Excel without saving changes to the workbook.

● Close the data access page.

Your screen should be similar to Figure 17

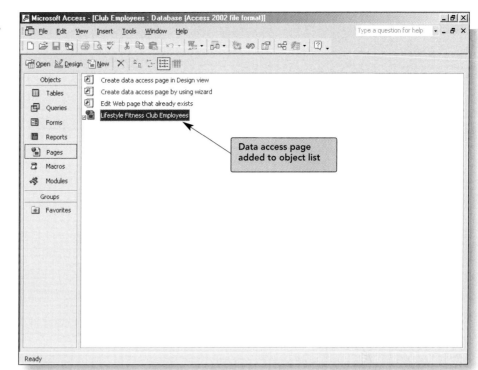

Data access page added to object list

Figure 17

The data access page has been added as a new object in the Pages objects list of the Club Employees database.

6 ● Exit Access.

lab review

key terms

browser   ACWT2.8

data access page   ACWT2.5

delimited text   ACWT2.2

export   ACWT2.2

fixed-width text   ACWT2.2

HTML (Hypertext Markup Language)   ACWT2.8

hyperlink   ACWT2.12

intranet   ACWT2.5

shortcut   ACWT2.6

standalone page   ACWT2.6

theme   ACWT2.9

mous certification guide

The Microsoft Office User Specialist (MOUS) certification program is designed to measure your proficiency in performing basic tasks using the Office XP applications. Getting certified demonstrates that you have the skills and provides a valuable industry credential for employment. After completing this lab, you have learned the following Microsoft Office User Specialist skills:

Skill	Description	Page
Integrating with Other Applications	Export data from Access	ACWT2.2
	Create a simple data access page	ACWT2.5

command summary

Command	Shortcut Keys	Button	Action
File/**E**xport			Saves Access data in another format so it can be used in another application
File/We**b** Page Preview			Previews data acccess page in browser window
Insert/Hyper**l**ink	Ctrl + K		Inserts a hyperlink
F**o**rmat/Th**e**me			Applies a predesigned theme to Web page

Hands-On Exercises

step-by-step

Exporting Cafe Inventory Prices

★ **1.** The Downtown Internet Cafe has just hired an accountant, and she would like to use the information in the Inventory Prices table to set up her own pricing spreadsheet in Excel. You are more than happy to provide this, and in addition you will export it to Excel for her. In return, she will send you the customer contact information sheet that she created in Excel so that you can import it into Access and use it as necessary. Your completed customers table is shown here.

a. Open the Cafe Purchases database.

b. Export the Inventory Prices table to an Excel 97-2002 file type. Save it with the file name Cafe Inventory Prices. Select Save formatted and Autostart.

c. In cell E36, enter a formula to calculate the average unit price. Add the label **Average Unit Price** in cell D36. Bold both entries. Enter your name in cell B36.

d. Print the worksheet. Save and close the workbook. Exit Excel.

Item #	Description	Vendor Name	Category	Unit Price
9999	Scones	Best Bakery	Baked Goods	$1.75
3524	Arabian coffee	Quality Coffee	Beverages	$65.00
1721	Decaf Sumatra	Pure Processing	Beverages	$75.00
1722	Decaf Guatamala	Pure Processing	Beverages	$75.00
1723	Decaf Colombian	Pure Processing	Beverages	$75.00
1724	Decaf Dark	Pure Processing	Beverages	$75.00
3521	Kenya coffee	Quality Coffee	Beverages	$65.00
1720	Decaf Viennese	Pure Processing	Beverages	$75.00
3523	Java coffee	Quality Coffee	Beverages	$75.00
3520	Columbian coffee	Quality Coffee	Beverages	$65.00
3525	Sumatra coffee	Quality Coffee	Beverages	$75.00
3526	Ethiopian coffee	Quality Coffee	Beverages	$75.00
3527	Kona coffee	Quality Coffee	Beverages	$115.00
3528	Espresso Roast	Quality Coffee	Beverages	$75.00
3529	Italian Roast	Quality Coffee	Beverages	$65.00
3530	French Roast	Quality Coffee	Beverages	$65.00
7920	Morning blend tea	Better Beverages, Inc.	Beverages	$55.00
7921	Orange Pekoe tea	Better Beverages, Inc.	Beverages	$55.00
7922	Earl Grey tea	Better Beverages, Inc.	Beverages	$55.00
7926	Darjeeling tea	Better Beverages, Inc.	Beverages	$55.00
3522	Guatamala coffee	Quality Coffee	Beverages	$65.00
1108	Sugar	Restaurant Supply	Condiments	$95.00
1109	Sugar substitute	Restaurant Supply	Condiments	$95.00
1110	Powdered cream	Restaurant Supply	Condiments	$95.00
2575	Coffee mints	Tasty Delights	Other	$65.00
2924	Coffee mugs	Central Ceramics	Other	$375.00
2900	Brochures	Pro Printing	Other	$500.00
1100	Coffee filters	Restaurant Supply	Paper Supplies	$115.00
1106	Cups-large	Restaurant Supply	Paper Supplies	$135.00
1105	Cups-medium	Restaurant Supply	Paper Supplies	$125.00
1104	Cups-small	Restaurant Supply	Paper Supplies	$115.00
1102	Napkins	Restaurant Supply	Paper Supplies	$75.00
1101	Stirrers	Restaurant Supply	Paper Supplies	$85.00

Student Name   Average Unit Price $ 102.40

Creating an Edusoft Data Access Page

★ ★ **2.** You have received a request from the Department at EduSoft Company for a copy of the Software Package Sales database query in Excel format so they can check it against their department's product order records. As a second project, you will create a data access page containing the requested data. When you are finished, you will have a data access page that looks like the page shown here.

a. Open EduSoft Titles database.

b. Export the Software Package Sales query to an Excel 97–2002 file type. Set up the file to Autostart and include formatting. Save it as EduSoft Sales.

c. Insert formulas to sum the Total Packages Sold and the Total Sales in row 19 below each column. Include a label **Total** in cell C19 and your name in cell A19. Apply the same format to the row as in the rest of the worksheet.

d. Print the worksheet. Save and close the workbook. Exit Excel.

e. Use the Page Wizard to create a data access page containing all fields from the Software table except Developer and Release Date. Select an ascending sort by grade level. Name the page EduSoft Software.

f. View the data access page. Add the title **EduSoft Software Packages**. Apply a theme of your choice.

g. Save the data access page as EduSoft Software.

h. Preview the page in Internet Explorer. Print the first screen and exit the browser. Exit Access.

Creating a Simply Beautiful Data Access Page

★ ★ **3.** Maria Dell, the owner of the Simply Beautiful spa, is very impressed with the Spa Packages
★ database table that you created. In fact, she would like you to save it as a Web page so she can use
it on the Web site she is having developed for the spa. Your completed data access page is shown
here.

a. Open the Simply Beautiful
database.

b. Create a data access page
containing the Spa
Packages table data.

c. View the page and make
cosmetic changes in
Design view, such as resizing the text controls and
adding a theme. Save the
page as **Spa Packages**.

d. Preview the page in the
browser. Print a page
screen and exit the
browser.

e. Close the Simply Beautiful
database.

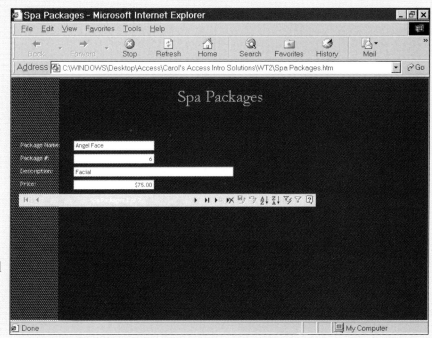

Working Together 2: Reviewing, Embedding, and Broadcasting a Presentation

Case Study

Animal Rescue Foundation

Now that the presentation to promote the Animal Rescue Foundation is nearly complete, you want to have several people review the presentation. To do this, you have sent copies of the presentation by e-mail to the agency director and several other administrators. You have asked them to add comments and make changes directly in the presentation and return it to you. When you receive the reviewed presentations back you will combine them with the original presentation and look at the comments and changes to determine which changes to make.

Once the kiosk presentation is finalized, you want to send a copy to the local shopping malls that provide a kiosk for use by local volunteer organizations. You decide to create a letter that contains the presentation embedded in it. You will then e-mail the letter to the shopping mall directors.

Finally, you want to see how you can distribute the presentation over the Web to audiences at different locations. To do this, you will look into broadcasting the presentation.

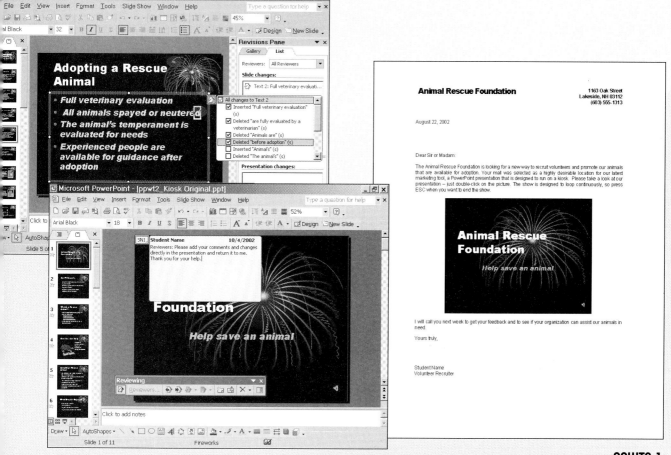

Reviewing a Presentation

Before sending the presentation to the shopping malls for use in the kiosks, you want to get feedback from several people in the organization first. You will do this by sending a copy of the presentation to each person for review. The review process consists of several steps: prepare the presentation to send to reviewers; send the presentation; receive the reviewed presentaions back; merge the reviewed presentations and respond to changes; and end the review.

Adding a Comment

Before you send the presentation for review, you want to add a comment to the reviewers. A **comment** is a remark that is displayed in a separate box and attached to a file.

1 ● **Start PowerPoint.**

● **Open the file**
ppwt2_Kiosk Original.

● **Display slide 1 in Normal view.**

● **Choose Insert/Comment.**

Your screen should be similar to Figure 1

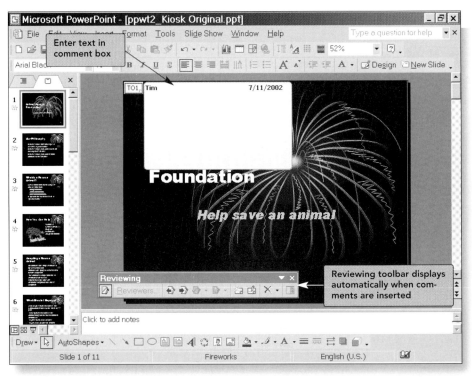

Figure 1

A comment box is displayed in which the text of the comment is entered. The name of the user inserting the comment appears on the first line followed by the system date. When you add a comment, the Reviewing toolbar automatically appears.

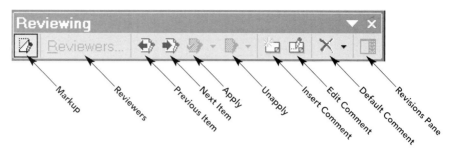

You will use the Reviewing toolbar shortly, when you review the comments sent back to you by the reviewers.

2 ● **Type the following comment text:**
Reviewers: Please add your comments and changes directly in the presentation and return it to me. Thank you for your help.

Your screen should be similar to Figure 2

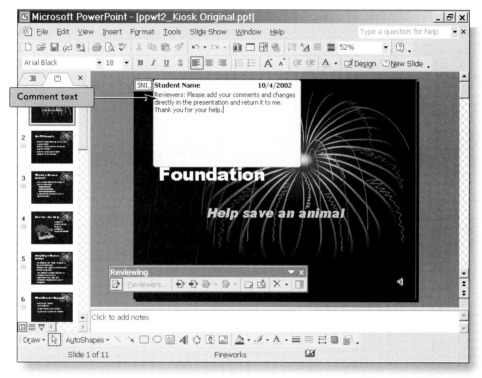

Figure 2

After entering comment text, clicking outside the comment closes it and displays an icon called a **comment marker** that indicates a comment has been added to the presentation. To see the comment text again, simply point to the marker.

3 ● Click outside the comment.

● Point to the comment marker.

Your screen should be similar to Figure 3

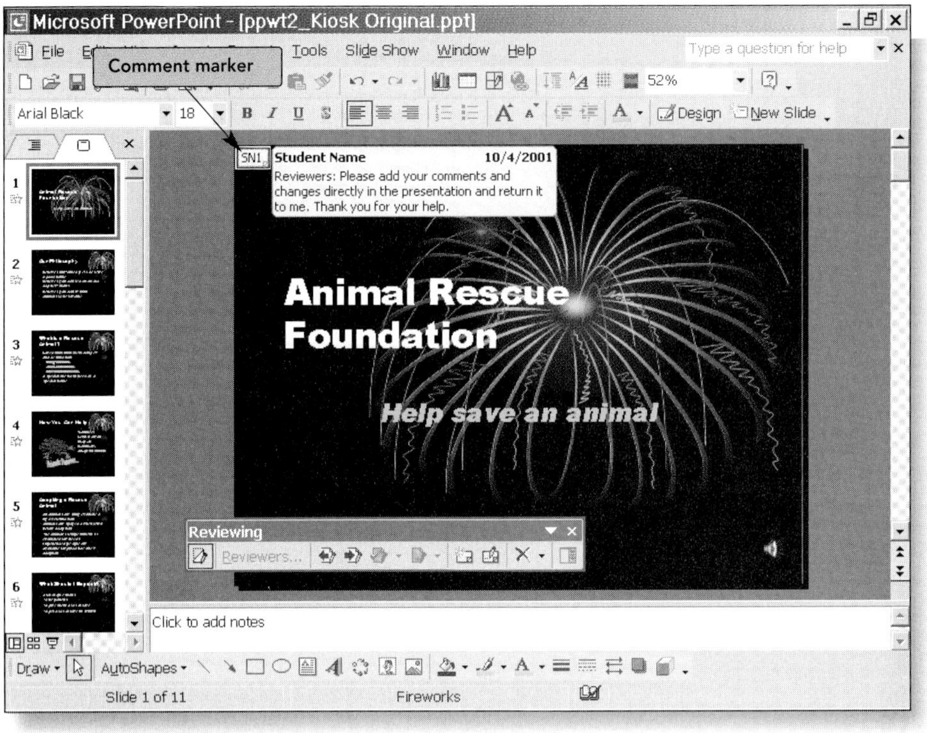

Additional Information

If you need to edit the comment, click 📝 Edit Comment on the Reviewing toolbar or double-click on the comment marker.

Figure 3

The comment is displayed in a balloon that is sized to fit the contents.

4 ● Save the presentation **as** Kiosk Review.

Sending the Presentation for Review

Now you will send the presentation to the director and another administrator via e-mail for review.

1 ● Choose **F**ile/**Sen**d to/**M**ail Recipient (for Review).

● In the To field, enter your e-mail address.

Your screen should be similar to Figure 4

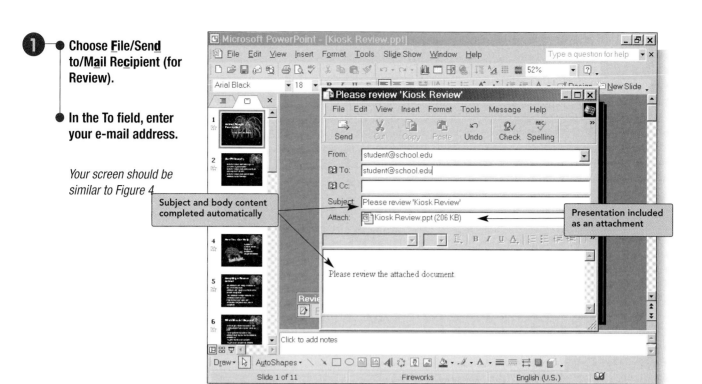

Figure 4

Because the command to send the presentation by e-mail was to send it for review, the subject and body of the message already include appropriate information. The presentation is included as an attachment to the e-mail message.

2 ● In the body of the e-mail, type the following message below the default message: **Please return your comments and changes to me by Friday. Thanks!**

● Press ⏎Enter twice and type your name.

Your screen should be similar to Figure 5

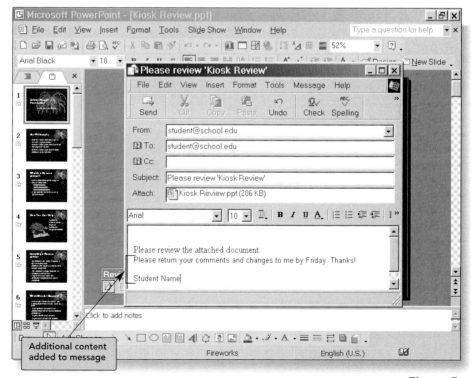

Figure 5

If you were connected to the Internet, you would send the message next. Instead, you will save the message as a text file.

3 ● Choose **F**ile/Save **A**s and save the message as a text file type using the default file name.

● Close the e-mail window.

Combining Reviewed Presentations

Additional Information

If all the reviewers are using Outlook, PowerPoint 2002 will prompt you to combine the reviewed presentations with the original when you double-click the attachment.

The next day while checking your e-mail for new messages, you see that both reviewers have returned the presentation with their comments and changes. You have downloaded the attachments and saved them as files on your system. Now you want to review the suggested changes.

When you receive multiple reviewers' comments, the easiest way to review them is to merge the reviewed presentations with the original.

1 ● Choose **T**ools/Com**p**are and Merge Presentations.

● Change to your data file location and select ppwt2_Kiosk Review[2] **and** ppwt2_Kiosk Review[3].

● Click Merge .

● If necessary, dock the Reviewing toolbar below the Formatting toolbar.

HAVING TROUBLE?

Hold down Ctrl while selecting multiple files.

Additional Information

When a presentation is sent for review, PowerPoint retains the name of the file but adds a number at the end in sequential order for each reviewer.

Your screen should be similar to Figure 6

HAVING TROUBLE?

If the Revisions task pane is not displayed, click ⊞ in the Reviewing toolbar.

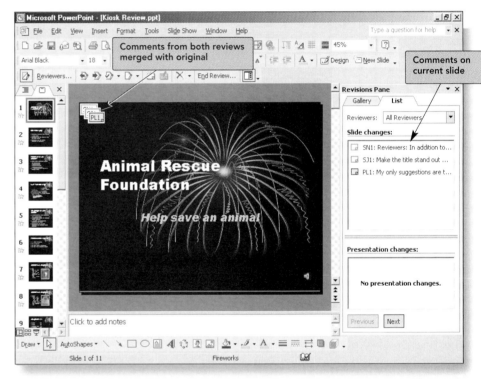

Figure 6

The changes and comments from both reviewed presentations are now included in the original presentation that was sent for review. The first slide has three comment markers in the upper left corner with the reviewer's initials and the number of the comment. Each reviewer's comments appear in a different color.

The Revisions task pane also opens to assist you in reviewing the comments and changes. The Revision pane displays the comments on the current slide. You want to see the names of the reviewers.

- **If necessary, open the List tab in the Revisions pane.**

- **Open the Reviewers drop-down list.**

Your screen should be similar to Figure 7

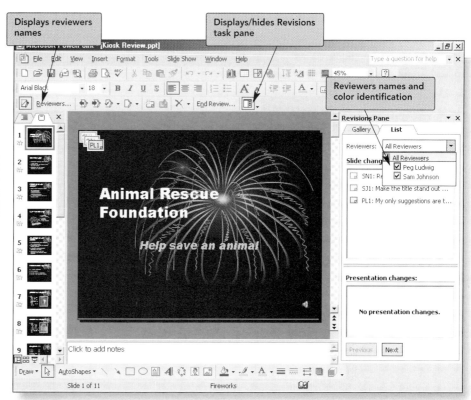

Figure 7

Deleting a Comment

The comment you added when you sent the presentation for review is the first comment listed in the Revisions task pane. You want to delete this comment before you begin to review the comments from the reviewers.

- **Click the first comment in the Slide changes list of the Revisions task pane.**

Your screen should be similar to Figure 8

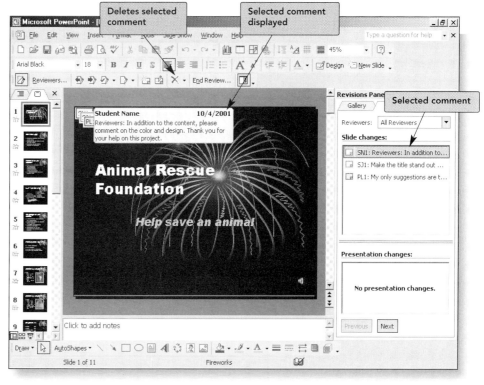

Figure 8

The comment box opens on the slide so you can delete the comment.

 **Click** ✕ ▾ **Delete Comment.**

Your screen should be similar to Figure 9

Figure 9

The comment is removed from the slide and the Revisions pane. You are now ready to start reviewing the comments and changes made by the reviewers.

Responding to Comments and Changes

You will use the Reviewing toolbar to navigate through the comments and changes made to the presentation by the reviewers.

1 ● Click  **Next Item on the Reviewing toolbar.**

Your screen should be similar to Figure 10

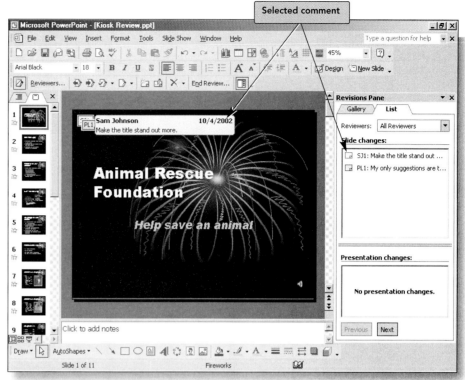

Figure 10

You think the suggestion in the first comment is a good idea. You decide to bold and make the title text larger.

2 ● Click ✕▾ **Delete Comment.**

● **Display the title master.**

HAVING TROUBLE?
Use View/Master/Slide Master.

● **Change the title text size to 54 pt and bold.**

● **Return to Normal view.**

● **Point to the comment.**

Your screen should be similar to Figure 11

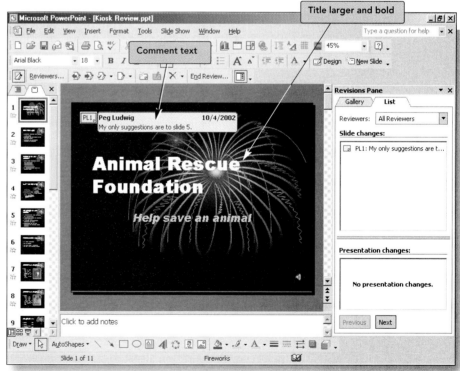

Figure 11

The title now stands out more. The last comment on this slide refers you to changes made to slide 5.

You decide to go to slide 5 next and look at the changes.

3 Click on slide 5 in the Slide tab.

Point to the comment.

Your screen should be similar to Figure 12

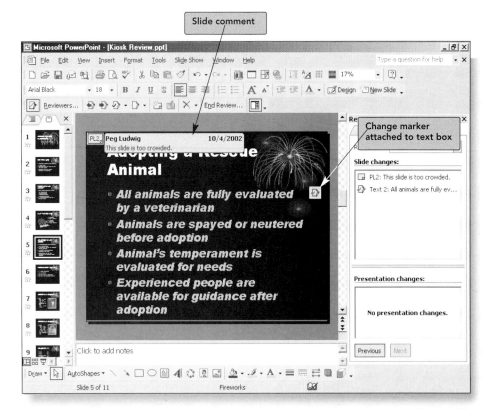

Figure 12

The comment on slide 5 notes that there is too much text on this slide. The slide also displays a **change marker** [⊡] attached to the text box indicating where a reviewer made changes to the presentation. You will delete the comment and look at the suggested changes.

4 ● Delete the comment.

● Click [□].

Your screen should be similar to Figure 13

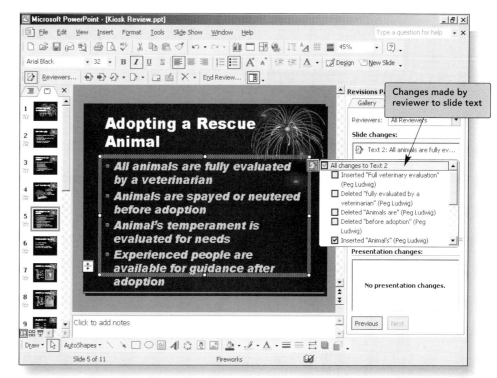

Figure 13

All the insertions and deletions that were made to the text are listed. Each item is preceded with a check box. Selecting the item will display the change in the slide.

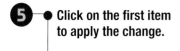

5 ● Click on the first item to apply the change.

Additional Information
The checkmark indicates that the change was added to the presentation.

● Point to the second item.

Your screen should be similar to Figure 14

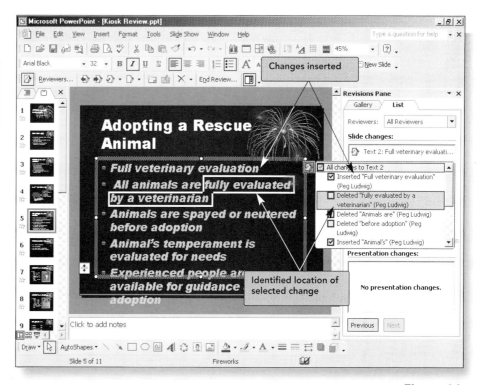

Figure 14

Additional Information
You can undo the change using [□] Unapply on the Reviewing toolbar or by clicking on the item to clear the checkmark.

The first change is inserted, and the change you are pointing to is circled in the text box to show you the area that will be affected if you accept this change.

As you look at the next few changes, they all look good to you and you decide to incorporate them into the presentation.

6 ● **Click on the second, third, and fourth items.**

Your screen should be similar to Figure 15

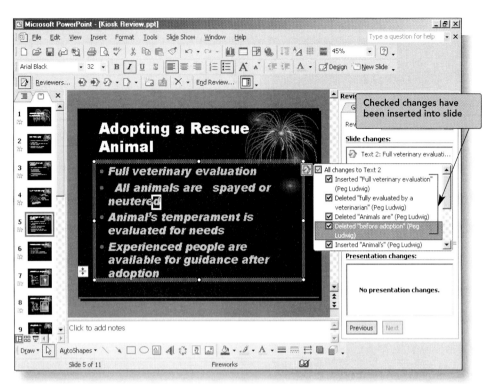

Checked changes have been inserted into slide

Figure 15

The three changes have been made in the slide. So far, you think all the changes look good and decide to just go ahead and apply all the changes to the slide.

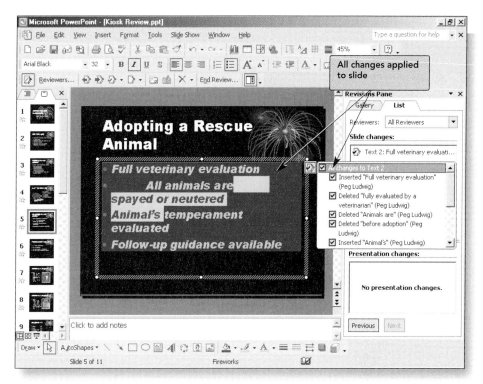

Figure 16

The changes look good, and you just need to make a few adjustments to the spacing.

8 ● **Click** ✕ ▾ **Delete to remove the change marker.**

● **Fix the spacing and alignment of the items in the slide.**

Your screen should be similar to Figure 17

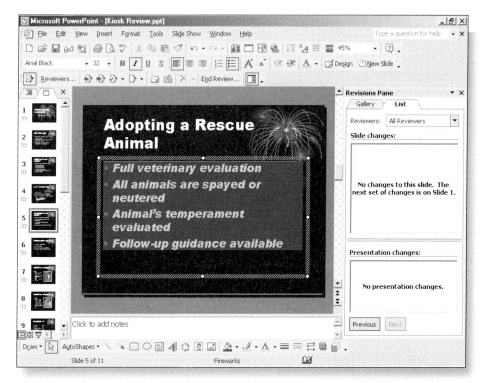

Figure 17

Now you want to see if you missed any comments in the previous slides and respond to them as needed.

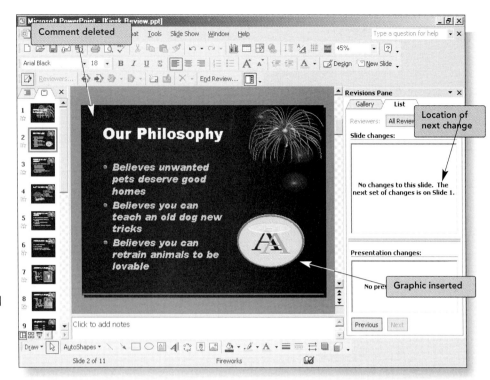

9 ● Click 🗗 Previous Item.

● Apply all the suggested text changes.

● Following the comment suggestion, insert the ppwt2_Halo graphic file on slide 2.

● Position and size the graphic and text appropriately.

● Click ✍ Set Transparent Color in the Picture toolbar and click on the white background of the graphic to make it transparent.

HAVING TROUBLE?
You may need to display and hide the Picture toolbar.

● Clear the selection.

● Delete the comment and change marker on slide 2.

Your screen should be similar to Figure 18

Figure 18

Next you will continue checking for more comments and making the suggested changes. Notice the Slide changes area of the Revisions Pane indicates the next changes are on slide 1.

10 ● Click 🖼️ **Previous Item.**

● **Delete the comment from slide 1.**

Your screen should be similar to Figure 19

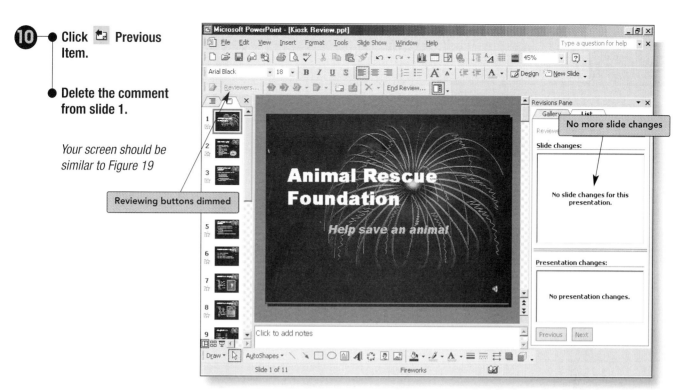

Figure 19

The Revisions Pane indicates there are no more changes or comments in the presentation, and the buttons on the Reviewing toolbar are dimmed.

Ending the Review

Another Method

To manually end the review, click End Review... on the Reviewing toolbar.

PowerPoint automatically ends the review process if you have applied the reviewer changes you want, deleted all change markers, and saved the presentation. When the review process is over, you cannot combine any more reviewed presentations with your original presentation. Since you do not plan to get any more reviews, you decide to save the file.

Save the presentation as Kiosk Final.

Your screen should be similar to Figure 20

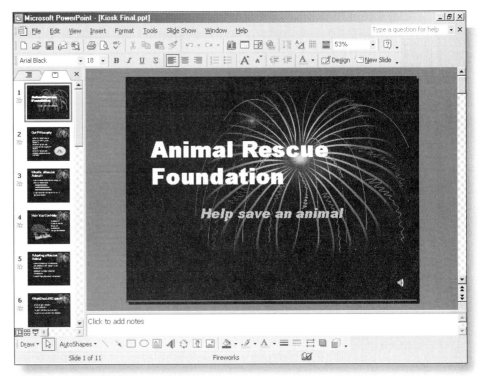

Figure 20

The review is ended and the task pane and Reviewing toolbar are automatically closed.

Collaborating Online

As suggested by the agency director, you looked into other methods you can use to get the presentation reviewed by other animal shelters and members of the Animal Protection Association.

There are two ways that you can collaborate with many reviewers at once. The first way is to hold an online meeting using the Microsoft NetMeeting feature. Each person you invite to the online meeting must also be running NetMeeting to receive your invitation. In an online meeting, you are in control of the collaboration. Each person in the meeting can add comments to the presentation in real time, if you give them access. When you turn on collaboration, each person in the online meeting can take turns editing the presentation. The person who is controlling the presentation is the only one whose mouse will operate, and that person's initials appear next to the mouse pointer.

The second way to collaborate is by using the Discussion feature, which needs to be set up by a system administrator. It enables you and other people to insert comments into the same document at the same time. This makes your job as document author much easier. You can see all the comments made by the reviewers, and they can too, which means if there is a question about a comment, the reviewers can discuss it among themselves.

Distributing the Presentation

The agency director is very pleased with the changes you made, and tells you to send out the presentation to the local malls. You have already created a letter to the mall directors and just need to insert the presentation file in the letter document file. Then you will send the letter as an e-mail attachment.

Embedding a Presentation

To insert the presentation in the letter, you will open the letter in Word and embed the PowerPoint presentation file in the document. An embedded object is inserted in a document and becomes part of that document, called the **destination document**. This means that you can modify it without affecting the **source document** where the original object resides.

① ● Start Word and, if necessary, maximize the application window.

● Open the file
ppwt2_Mall Letter.

Your screen should be similar to Figure 21

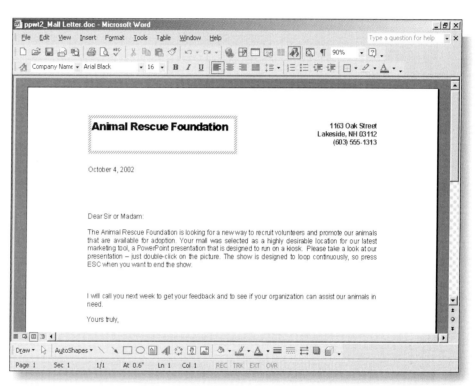

Figure 21

Now you want to embed the presentation. When you embed a PowerPoint presentation, the first slide of the presentation is displayed in the document. You want the embedded presentation to appear below the first paragraph of the letter.

2 ● **Move to the blank line below the first paragraph.**

● **Choose Insert/Object.**

● **Open the Create From File tab.**

● **Click** [Browse...] **.**

● **Change to your data file location and select** Kiosk Final.ppt**.**

● **Click** [Insert] **.**

● **Click** [OK] **.**

Your screen should be similar to Figure 22

Figure 22

The opening slide of the presentation is inserted as an embedded object in the letter. Before you send the letter, you want to run the slide show to make sure that it looks good and runs correctly. The directions to run the presentation from within the Word document file are included in the first paragraph of the letter.

3 ● **Double-click on the embedded object.**

> **Another Method**
> The menu equivalent is Edit/Presentation Object/Show, or you can choose Presentation Object/Show from the shortcut menu.

● **View the entire presentation and press** [Esc] **to end the show when it begins over again.**

Editing an Embedded Object

> **Additional Information**
> The source program must be installed on the viewer's system to edit the object.

As you viewed the presentation, you think that the last slide would look better if it included a graphic. You decide to add the Dog Wagging animated graphic to the slide. Rather than editing the PowerPoint presentation file and then reinserting it into the letter, you will make the changes directly to the object that is embedded in the letter. The source program, the program used to create the embedded object, is used to edit data in an embedded object.

1 ● **Choose Presentation**
Object/Edit from the
object's shortcut
menu.

Another Method
The menu equivalent is
Edit/Presentation
Object/Edit.

Your screen should be
similar to Figure 23

Presentation open
for editing

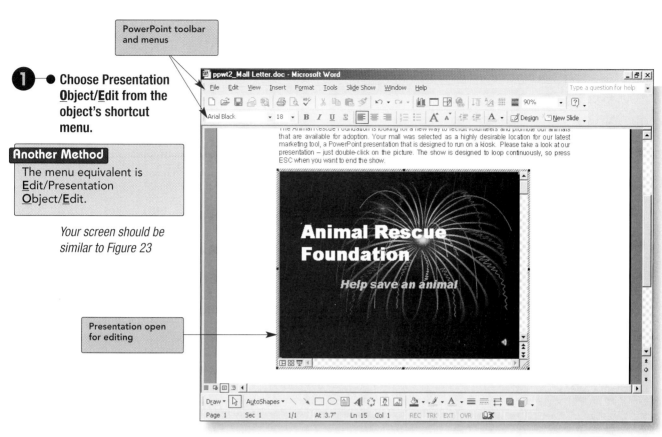

Figure 23

The presentation is open in an editing window, and the PowerPoint menus
and toolbars replace some of the menus and toolbars in the Word application window. The first slide of the embedded object is displayed in an editing window. Now you can use the PowerPoint commands to edit the object.

2 ● **Use the scroll bar to**
display the last slide.

● **Insert the graphic**
ppwt2_Dog Wagging.

● **Position and size the**
graphic and text box
as in Figure 24.

HAVING TROUBLE?
Use the rotate handle to
change the angle of the
graphic.

● **Click** 🖵 **to run the**
slide show.

● **Press** [Esc] **to end the**
show after seeing the
animated graphic.

Your screen should be
similar to Figure 24

Graphic inserted
in embedded
presentation

Runs slide show

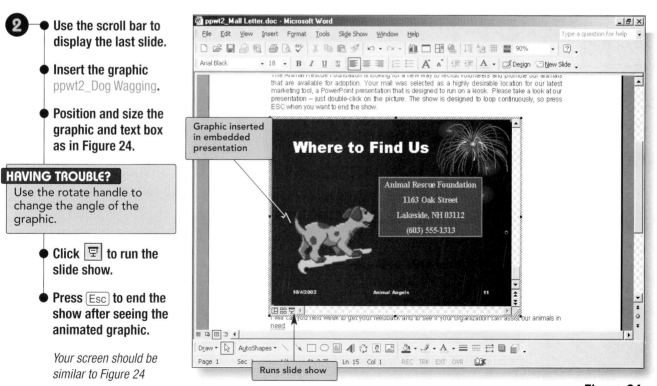

Figure 24

Now that the presentation is updated, you will close the source program.

3 • **Click outside the object to close the source application.**

• **Reduce the size of the embedded object and center it.**

• **Replace Student Name in the closing with your name**

• **Save the letter as** Kiosk Presentation Letter.

• **Preview and print the letter.**

• **Exit Word.**

Your printed letter should be similar to that shown here

Animal Rescue Foundation

1163 Oak Street
Lakeside, NH 03112
(603) 555-1313

August 22, 2002

Dear Sir or Madam:

The Animal Rescue Foundation is looking for a new way to recruit volunteers and promote our animals that are available for adoption. Your mall was selected as a highly desirable location for our latest marketing tool, a PowerPoint presentation that is designed to run on a kiosk. Please take a look at our presentation – just double-click on the picture. The show is designed to loop continuously, so press ESC when you want to end the show.

I will call you next week to get your feedback and to see if your organization can assist our animals in need.

Yours truly,

Student Name
Volunteer Recruiter

Next you will update the presentation in PowerPoint with the same change you made in the presentation in the Word document.

4 • **Display slide 11.**

• **Insert the** ppwt2_Dog Wagging **graphic in the slide.**

• **Position and size it as you did in the embedded presentation in the letter.**

• **Save the revised presentation.**

Now that the letter is complete, you want to send the letter via e-mail to the list of local malls. This is only one way to distribute your presentation. You could also just send an e-mail with the presentation as an attachment or you could send a diskette in the mail containing the presentation along with a letter of introduction. By embedding the presentation in the letter, you create both an e-mail distribution method and also a printed letter that contains the first slide in your presentation as a graphic.

Broadcasting a Presentation

Note: To complete this section, the Broadcast feature must be installed on your system.

Another way to distribute a presentation is to broadcast a presentation over the Web. **Broadcasting** makes it possible to deliver a presentation to an audience at different locations. The viewers can view the presentation live or on demand. The presentation is saved in HTML format on a server that is accessible to the audience and is displayed in a Web browser. Your system administrator must set up a server location where you can store the files to be shared by all the viewers. Outlook can be set up to schedule and automatically start the presentation at a specified time. If you are using other e-mail applications, a hyperlink appears in the body of the e-mail and the audience double-clicks on the hyperlink to start the broadcast.

Recording a Broadcast

You decide to try out this feature to see if you want to use it in the future by recording and saving a broadcast.

1 ● Choose Slide Show/Online Broadcast/Record and Save a Broadcast.

Your screen should be similar to Figure 25

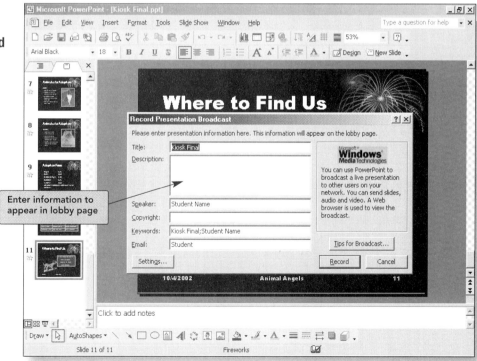

Figure 25

The first step is to enter information you want to appear on the **lobby page**. The lobby page is a page of information that is displayed in the viewer's browser before the broadcast starts. It includes information about the broadcast, including the title, subject, and host's name. It also displays a countdown to the starting time of the broadcast. The presentation file name automatically displays in the Title text box. You want to add a short description to appear on the lobby page when viewers receive the presentation.

2 • **In the Description text box type:** This presentation is designed to encourage people to help the Foundation by adopting an animal or volunteering.

• **Replace the name in the Speaker text box with your name.**

• **Click** Settings... .

Your screen should be similar to Figure 26

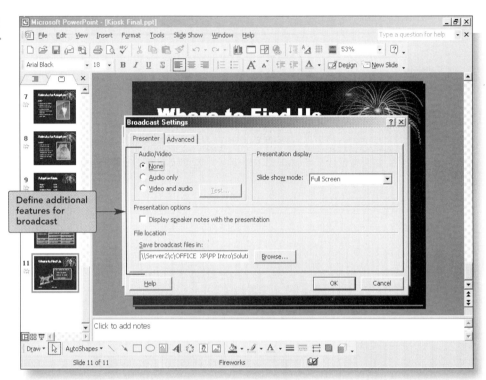

Figure 26

Next, in the Presenter tab, you define more features of the broadcast. You can send audio and video along with your presentation. Both of these types of files can slow down Web delivery, however, so you can turn them off if needed. You also need to specify the location where the broadcast files will be stored. If you are recording a broadcast, the location can be anywhere you want. However, when you actually schedule a broadcast, the location should be a server location that is accessible to the recipients. Once you have specified these items, you run the presentation to record it.

3 • If necessary, select
None.

• Specify the location
where you want to save
the broadcast files.

• Click [OK].

• Click [Record].

HAVING TROUBLE?
It may take several minutes
before [Start] is available.

• Click [Start].

*Your screen should be
similar to Figure 27*

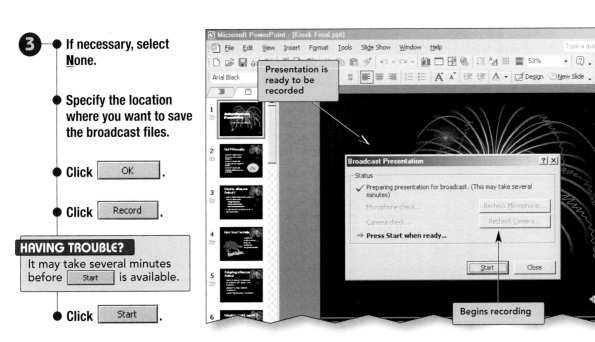

Figure 27

The slide show runs while it is being recorded. While it is running you
could also record your narration to accompany the broadcast.

4 • Run the presentation
to the end.

• Press [Esc] to end
recording.

*Your screen should be
similar to Figure 28*

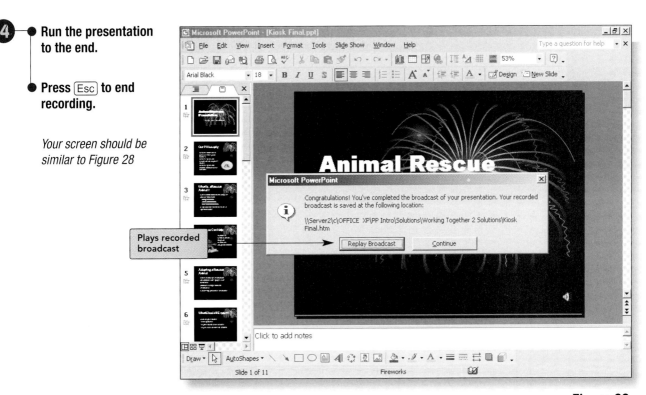

Figure 28

A congratulatory message appears indicating the slide show has successfully been recorded.

Playing the Broadcast

Next you will replay the broadcast to make sure it recorded correctly.

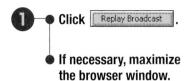

Click Replay Broadcast .

● **If necessary, maximize the browser window.**

Your screen should be similar to Figure 29

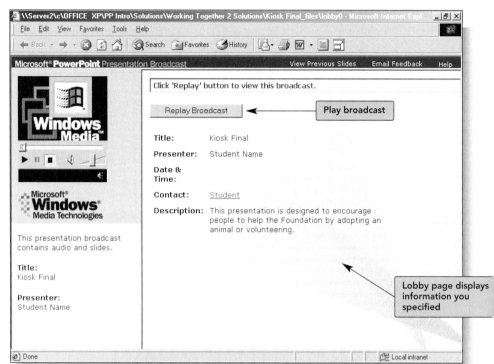

Figure 29

The lobby page with the information you entered is displayed in the browser window.

2 • Click  .

• When complete, close the browser window.

Your screen should be similar to Figure 30

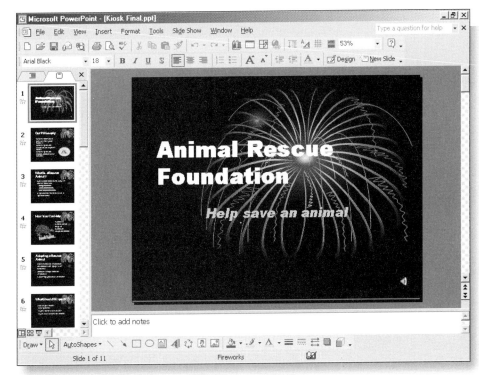

Figure 30

The PowerPoint window is displayed again.

The presentation is saved in HTML format. To make the recorded presentation available to others, a copy of it needs to be **published** or saved to a Web server. Then, you need to provide the link to the lobby page to users so they can access the presentation whenever they want. All the audience would need to view the presentation is a browser

When you schedule a live broadcast, the recipients of the invitation receive an e-mail message with the broadcast date and time. If they are using Outlook and accept the invitation, they will receive a reminder 15 minutes before the broadcast begins. The reminder contains a View This Netshow button, which they click to open the lobby page in their browser. The lobby page starts a countdown to the broadcast, and when the timer reaches zero, the presentation broadcast begins. Depending on the options the presenter selected, audience members might be able to chat with one another and send e-mail messages to the presenter.

Additional Information

Use File/Save as Web Page/Publish and specify the location of the Web server where the presentation will be stored.

3 • Close the presentation.

• Exit PowerPoint.

Working Together 2: Reviewing, Embedding, and Broadcasting a Presentation

key terms

broadcast   PPWT2.21

change marker   PPWT2.10

comment   PPWT2.2

comment marker   PPWT2.3

destination document
PPWT2.17

lobby page   PPWT2.22

publish   PPWT2.25

source document   PPWT2.17

mous skills

The Microsoft Office User Specialist (MOUS) certification program is designed to measure your proficiency in performing basic tasks using the Office XP applications. Getting certified demonstrates that you have the skills and provides a valuable industry credential for employment. After completing this lab, you have learned the following Microsoft Office User Specialist skills:

Skill	Description	Page
Workgroup Collaboration	Set up a review cycle	PPWT2.4
	Review presentation comments	PPWT2.8
	Schedule and deliver presentation broadcasts	PPWT2.21, PPWT2.25
	Publish presentations to the Web	PPWT2.25

command summary

Command	Action
File/**S**ave as Web page/**P**ublish	Saves presentation in HTML format to a Web server
File/**Sen**d to/**M**ail Re**ci**pient (for Review)	Sends presentation as an e-mail attachment and activates recipient's Reviewing toolbar
Insert/**Co**m**m**ent	Inserts a comment into presentation
Tools/**Com**p**a**re and Merge Presentation	Combines reviewed presentation with the original
Sli**d**e Show/**O**nline Broadcast/**R**ecord and Save a Broadcast	Records a presentation for online broadcast
Sli**d**e Show/**O**nline Broadcast/**S**chedule a Live Broadcast	Sets up a live broadcast
Word 2002	
Edit/Presentation **O**bject/S**h**ow	Runs embedded presentation as a slide show
Edit/Presentation **O**bject/**E**dit	Edits an embedded object
Insert/**O**bject/Create from **F**ile	Inserts the contents of a file into document

Hands-On Exercises

rating system

★ Easy

★★ Moderate

★★★ Difficult

step-by-step

Distributing the Water Safety Presentation

★★ **1.** Because the presentation you created on water safety (Step-by-Step Exercise 1, Lab 4) for the Red Cross had such a positive response, you have been asked to distribute it to other malls in the state. You will do this by embedding it in a Word document and sending it via e-mail. The completed letter is displayed here.

a. Start Word 2002 and open the ppwt2_Water Safety Letter file.

b. Insert the Water Presentation PowerPoint file you saved below the first paragraph. Reduce the size of the object and center it.

c. Edit the embedded presentation by inserting a new slide before the last slide of the presentation listing Red Cross locations—Flagstaff, Tucson, and Phoenix—and the toll-free number of 1-800-555-5555.

d. Replace the name in the closing with your name.

e. Save the document as Water Safety Letter.

f. E-mail the document to your instructor for review.

g. Print the letter.

h. Make the same changes to the Water Presentation PowerPoint file and save it as Water Presentation2.

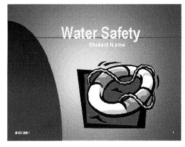

Water Safety Council

1900 24ᵀᴴ St.
Phoenix, AZ 85200
(602) 555-1000

August 22, 2002

Dear Sir or Madam:

The Water Safety Council along with your local Red Cross foundation is looking for a new way to promote awareness of water safety. Your mall was selected as a highly desirable location for our latest marketing tool, a PowerPoint presentation that is designed to run on a kiosk. Please take a look at our presentation – just double-click on the picture. The show is designed to loop continuously, so press ESC when you want to end the show.

I will call you next week to get your feedback and to see if you can assist by running the presentation in the mall kiosk during the summer months.

Yours truly,

Student Name

Promoting the Fitness Web Page

★★ **2.** The Lifestyle Fitness Club presentation you created for the Web (Step-by-Step Exercise 4, Lab 4) has received positive feedback from the members. You would like to provide the Web pages to affiliated clubs in other states to use on their Web sites. You decide to do this by embedding it in a Word document and sending it via e-mail. The completed letter is displayed here.

a. Start Word 2002 and create a letter to let the recipients know how to view the presentation.

b. Embed the Fitness and Nutrition PowerPoint file in the letter. Reduce the size of the object and center it.

c. Edit the embedded presentation to include comments about how the recipients can customize the presentation for their own use.

d. Insert your name in the closing of the letter.

e. Save the document as Fitness Presentation Letter. E-mail the document as an attachment to your instructor for review.

f. Print the letter.

Lifestyle Fitness Club   10 W. Monterrey Ave.
                                                   Fort Meyers, FL
                                                   (603) 555-1313

October 5, 2001

Dear Sir or Madam:

We recently developed a fitness and nutrition PowerPoint presentation for our members that we would like to share with your club. It has been very well received by our members.

The presentation can be easily converted to a Web page using PowerPoint and can be uploaded to your Web site for viewing by your members. Please take a look at our presentation—just double-click on the picture and click to advance through the slides or use the navigation buttons.

FITNESS AND NUTRITION

Presented by
Lifestyle Fitness

The presentation includes comments on how you can customize the slides for your use. Just delete the comments before converting it to a Web page. We hope you like the presentation and that your members will it enjoy it also.

Yours truly,

Student Name
Program Coordinator

Distributing the Sports Company Web Page

★★ **3.** The Sports Company's kiosk presentation has worked out well. The store manager would like you to send the presentation you created (Step-by-Step Exercise 5, Lab 4) to the store managers of the other stores in the state. The completed letter is shown here.

a. Start Word 2002 and create a letter that describes the presentation and how to access it.

b. Embed the Sports Company Kiosk presentation in the letter. Reduce the size of the embedded object and center it.

c. Edit the embedded presentation to include comments suggesting changes they might make to customize the presentation for their own use.

d. Insert your name in the closing of the letter.

e. Save the document as Sports Company Letter.

f. E-mail the document to your instructor for review.

g. Print the letter.

The Sports Company
10025 N. Park Blvd.
Glenwood Springs, CO
(602) 555-1212

October 5, 2001

Dear Store Managers:

We have recently developed a PowerPoint presentation that features many of the new products at the store. It is running on a kiosk at the front entrance of our store and has been well received by our customers. Please take a look at the presentation – just double-click on the picture. The show is designed to loop continuously, so press ESC when you want to end the show.

Feel free to use this presentation in your store.

Yours truly,

Student Name
The Sports Company

Word Command Summary

Command	Shortcut	Button	Action
File/**N**ew	Ctrl + N	🗋	Opens new document
File/**N**ew/General Templates/ Web Pages/Web Page Wizard			Creates a new Web site
File/**N**ew/GeneralTemplates/ Letters & Faxes/Mailing Label Wizard			Starts Mailing Label Wizard to create mailing labels
File/**O**pen	Ctrl + O	🖼	Opens existing document file
File/**C**lose	Ctrl + F4	✕	Closes document file
File/**S**ave	Ctrl + S	🖫	Saves document using same file name
File/Save **A**s			Saves document using a new file name, type and/or location
File/Save as Web Pa**g**e			Saves file as a Web page document
File/We**b** Page Preview			Previews Web page in browser window
File/Page Set**u**p			Changes layout of page including margins, paper size, and paper source
File/Page Set**u**p/**L**ayout/**V**ertical Alignment			Aligns text vertically on a page
File/Print Pre**v**iew		🔍	Displays document as it will appear when printed
File/**P**rint	Ctrl + P	🖨	Prints document using selected print settings
File/Sen**d** To/M**a**il Recipient (as Attachment)		📧	Sends the document as an e-mail attachment
File/Sen**d** To/M**a**il Re**c**ipient (for Review)			Sends the document as part of body of e-mail message
File/E**x**it	Alt + F4	✕	Exits Word program
Edit/**U**ndo	Ctrl + Z	↺ ▾	Restores last editing change
Edit/**R**edo	Ctrl + Y	↻ ▾	Restores last Undo or repeats last command or action
Edit/**R**epeat	Ctrl + Y		Repeats last action
Edit/Cu**t**	Ctrl + X	✂	Cuts selected text and copies it to Clipboard
Edit/**C**opy	Ctrl + C	📋	Copies selected text to Clipboard
Edit/Office Clip**b**oard			Activates Office Clipboard and displays the task pane

Command	Shortcut	Button	Action
Edit/**P**aste	Ctrl + V	📋	Pastes text from Clipboard
Edit/Paste **S**pecial/Paste Li**n**k			Pastes contents of Clipboard as a linked object
Edit/Select All	Ctrl + A		Selects all text in document
Edit/**F**ind	Ctrl + F		Locates specified text
Edit/**R**eplace	Ctrl + H		Locates and replaces specified text
Edit/Linked **O**bject			Edits selected linked object
Edit/**G**oTo	Ctrl + G		Moves to specified location
Edit/Chart **O**bject/**E**dit			Opens Chart object for editing
View/**N**ormal		▤	Displays document in Normal view
View/**W**eb Layout		▣	Shows document as it will appear when viewed in a Web browser
View/**P**rint Layout		▣	Shows how text and objects will appear on the printed page
View/**O**utline		▤	Shows structure of document
View/Tas**k** Pane			Displays or hides task pane
View/**T**oolbars			Displays or hides selected toolbar
View/**R**uler			Displays or hides horizontal ruler
View/**S**how Paragraph Marks			Displays or hides paragraph marks
View/**D**ocument Map		▧	Displays or hides Document Map pane.
View/**H**eader and Footer			Displays header and footer areas
View/**F**ootnotes			Hides or displays note pane
View/Mar**k**up			Displays/hides markup elements
View/**D**atasheet			Displays Datasheet table for Open Chart object
View/**Z**oom		100% ▾	Changes onscreen character size
View/**Z**oom/**P**age width			Fits display of document within right and left margins
View/**Z**oom/**W**hole Page			Displays entire page onscreen
View/**Z**oom/**M**any Pages			Displays two or more pages in document window
View/HTML Sour**c**e			Displays HTML source code
Insert/**B**reak/**P**age break	Ctrl + ↵Enter		Inserts hard page break
Insert/**B**reak/Con**t**inuous			Inserts a section break and starts next section on same page as current section
Insert/**B**reak/**N**ext Page			Inserts a section break and starts next section on a new page
Insert/Page Nu**m**bers			Specifies page number location
Insert/Date and **T**ime			Inserts current date or time, maintained by computer system, in selected format
Insert/**A**utoText			Enters predefined text
Insert/**A**utoText/AutoTe**x**t/ **S**how AutoComplete suggestions			Turns on AutoText feature

Command	Shortcut	Button	Action
Insert/Symbol			Inserts selected symbol
Insert/Comment		🗊	Adds a note to the document
Insert/Reference/Footnote	Alt + Ctrl + F		Inserts footnote reference at insertion point
Insert/Reference/Caption			Inserts caption at insertion point
Insert/Reference/Cross-reference			Inserts cross-reference at insertion point
Insert/Reference/Index and Tables/ Table of Contents			Inserts table of contents
Insert/Picture/Clip Art			Inserts selected clip art at insertion point
Insert/Picture/From File			Inserts selected picture into document
Insert/Picture/AutoShapes		AutoShapes ▾	Inserts selected AutoShape
Insert/Diagram		🔄	Inserts a diagram
Insert/Text Box		🖼	Inserts text box
Insert/Object/Microsoft Graph Chart			Creates a chart in the document
Insert/Hyperlink	Ctrl + K	🌐	Inserts hyperlink in Web page
Format/Font/Font/Font		Times New Roman ▾	Changes typeface
Format/Font/Font/Size		12 ▾	Changes type size
Format/Font/Font/Color		A	Changes type color
Format/Font/Font/Font Style/Italic	Ctrl + I	*I*	Makes selected text italic
Format/Font/Font/Font Style/Bold	Ctrl + B	**B**	Makes selected text bold
Format/Font/Font/ Underline style/Single	Ctrl + U	U	Underlines selected text
Format/Font/Text Effects			Adds animation to selected text
Format/Font/Character Spacing			Changes spacing between characters
Format/Paragraph/Indents and Spacing/Special/First Line			Indents first line of paragraph from left margin
Format/Paragraph/Indents and Spacing/Alignment/Left	Ctrl + L	≡	Aligns text to left margin
Format/Paragraph/Indents and Spacing/Alignment/Centered	Ctrl + E	≡	Centers text between left and right margins
Format/Paragraph/Indents and Spacing/Alignment/Right	Ctrl + R	≡	Aligns text to right margin
Format/Paragraph/Indents and Spacing/Alignment/Justified	Ctrl + J	≡	Aligns text equally between left and right margins
Format/Paragraph/Indents and Spacing/Alignment/Line Spacing			Changes amount of space between lines
Format/Theme			Applies a predesigned theme to Web page
Format/Style		Normal ▾	Applies selected style to paragraph or characters
Format/Picture/Layout/Wrapping style			Specifies how text will wrap around picture
Format/Bullets and Numbering		≣ ≣	Creates a bulleted or numbered list

Command	Shortcut	Button	Action
Fo**r**mat/**B**orders and Shading			Adds borders and shadings to selection
		⊡	Adds outside border
		⊤	Adds top border
		⊥	Adds bottom border
Fo**r**mat/**B**orders and Shading/ **H**orizontal Line			Adds graphic horizontal line to Web page
Fo**r**mat/Bac**k**ground/**F**ill Effects			Applies background color to selection
Fo**r**mat/T**h**eme			Applies a predesigned theme to Web page
Fo**r**mat/**C**olumns		☰	Specifies number, spacing, and size of columns
Fo**r**mat/**T**abs			Specifies types and positions of tab stops
Fo**r**mat/**D**rop Cap/**D**ropped			Changes character format as a dropped capital letter
Fo**r**mat/**S**tyles and Formatting		🅰	Opens Styles and Formatting task pane
Fo**r**mat/Re**v**eal Formatting			Opens Reveal Formatting task pane
Fo**r**mat/**W**ordArt/Size		✏	Sizes, rotates, and scales WordArt object
Fo**r**mat/**W**ordArt/Colors and Lines		✏	Applies fill and line color to WordArt object
Fo**r**mat/Text B**o**x/Layout		✏	Changes wrapping style and alignment of text box
Fo**r**mat/Te**x**t Direction/**O**rientation		‖↕	Changes direction of text in a table
Tools/**S**pelling and Grammar	F7	ᵃᵇᶜ✓	Starts Spelling and Grammar tool
Tools/**L**anguage/**T**hesaurus	Shift + F7		Starts Thesaurus tool
Tools/**T**rack Changes	Ctrl + ⇧Shift + E		Marks changes to document
Tools/**C**ompare and Merge **D**ocuments			Combines documents and identifies differences
Tools/**L**anguage/**H**yphenation			Specifies hyphenation settings
Tools/L**e**tters and Mailings/ **M**ail Merge Wizard			Starts Mail Merge Wizard
Tools/L**e**tters and Mailings/ Show Mail Merge **T**oolbar			Displays Mail Merge toolbar
Tools/L**e**tters and Mailings/ **E**nvelopes and Labels/**E**nvelopes			Creates and prints delivery and return address on envelopes
Tools/**A**utoCorrect Options/ **S**how AutoCorrect Options buttons			Displays or hides AutoCorrect options
Tools/**C**ustomize/**O**ptions/**S**how Standard and Formatting toolbars on two rows			Displays Standard and Formatting toolbars on two rows
Tools/**O**ptions/Edit/O**v**ertype mode	Ins	OVR	Switches between Insert and Overtype modes

Command	Shortcut	Button	Action
Tools/**O**ptions/View/**A**ll		¶	Displays or hides formatting marks
Tools/**O**ptions/View/ScreenTips			Turns off and on the display of screen tips
Tools/**O**ptions/View/**A**ll	Ctrl + Shift	¶	Displays or hides special characters
Tools/**O**ptions/Edit/**O**vertype mode		OVR	Switches between insert and overtype modes
Tools/**O**ptions/Spelling & Grammar			Changes settings associated with the Spelling and Grammar checking feature
T**a**ble/Draw Ta**b**le		⊞	Creates a table using Draw Table feature
T**a**ble/**I**nsert Table		▭	Inserts table at insertion point
T**a**ble/**I**nsert Columns			Inserts new columns in a table
T**a**ble/**I**nsert/Row **A**bove			Inserts a new row in table above the selected row
T**a**ble/Sele**c**t/**T**able			Selects entire table
T**a**ble/**M**erge Cells		⊞	Merges cells in a table
T**a**ble/Table Auto**F**ormat			Applies selected format to table
T**a**ble/Con**v**ert/Te**x**t to Table			Converts selected text to table format
T**a**ble/**S**ort			Rearranges items in a selection into sorted order
T**a**ble/F**o**rmula			Inserts a formula into a table
T**a**ble/Show **G**ridlines			Displays gridlines in a table
T**a**ble/Table Pr**o**perties/**T**able/**C**enter			Centers the selected table
T**a**ble/Table Pr**o**perties/**T**able/**O**ptiona/ Automatically resi**z**e to fit contents			Automatically resizes columns in the table to fit text or graphic
T**a**ble/Table Pr**o**perties/Col**u**mn			Adjusts width of selected columns
T**a**ble/**A**utofit/Distribute Rows Eve**n**ly		⊞	Evenly sizes selected rows
Help/Microsoft Word **H**elp		?	Opens Help window
Dr**a**w ▾ Or**d**er/Bring to Fron**t**			Brings object to front of stack
Dr**a**w ▾ **G**roup			Creates a group from selected objects
Dr**a**w ▾ **U**ngroup			Ungroups a grouped object
Dr**a**w ▾ Regr**o**up			Regroups an ungrouped object
Insert Shape/**S**ubordinate			Inserts a shape below the selected superior shape
Layout/**R**ight Hanging			Hangs subordinate shapes to right of superior shape
Layout/**E**xpand Organization Chart			Expands drawing canvas around organization chart
Checkbox		☑	Allows selection of more than one item
Drop-Down box		⊞	Displays available choices in a list
Textbox		abl	A box where you can enter one line of text

Command	Shortcut	Button	Action
Text Area			A box where you can enter more than one line of text
Reset			Clears entries in form
Submit			Submits data in form to specified location

Excel Command Summary

Command	Shortcut	Button	Action
File/Open <file name>	Ctrl + O	📂	Opens an existing workbook file
File/Close		✕	Closes open workbook file
File/Save <file name>	Ctrl + S	💾	Saves current file on disk using same file name
File/Save As <file name>			Saves current file on disk using a new file name
File/Save as Web Page			Creates a Web page from the entire active workbook or the current worksheet selection.
File/Web Page Preview			Displays the active workbook as a Web page in the browser without actually publishing it
File/Print Area/Set Print Area			Sets area of worksheet to be printed
File/Print Area/Clear Print Area			Clears print area
File/Send to/Mail Recipient			Sends the active document to the e-mail recipient.
File/Page Setup/Page/Landscape			Changes orientation to landscape
File/Page Setup/Header/Footer			Adds header and/or footer
File/Print Preview		🔍	Displays worksheet as it will appear when printed
File/Print	Ctrl + P	🖨	Prints a worksheet
File/Print/Entire Workbook			Prints all the sheets in a workbook
File/Properties			Displays information about and documents the workbook
File/Exit		✕	Exits Excel 2002
Edit/Undo	Ctrl + Z	↺ ▾	Undoes last editing or formatting change
Edit/Redo	Ctrl + Y	↻ ▾	Restores changes after using Undo
Edit/Copy	Ctrl + C	📋	Copies selected data to Clipboard
Edit/Paste	Ctrl + V	📋	Pastes selections stored in Clipboard
Edit/Paste Special			Inserts the object as an embedded object
Edit/Paste Special/Paste Link			Creates a link to the source document
Edit/Links			Modifies selected link
Edit/Linked Object/Edit Link			Modifies selected linked object
Edit/Fill			Fills selected cells with contents of source cell
Edit/Clear/Contents	Delete		Clears cell contents

Command	Shortcut	Button	Action
Edit/Clear/Comments		▣	Deletes comment in selected cell
Edit/Delete/Entire row			Deletes selected rows
Edit/Delete/Entire column			Deletes selected columns
Edit/Delete/Shift Cells Left			Deletes selected cells and shifts remaining cells to left
Edit/Delete/Shift Cells Up			Deletes selected cells and shifts remaining cells up
Edit/Move or Copy Sheet			Moves or copies selected sheet
Edit/Find	Ctrl + F		Searches selected cells for a specified value
Edit/Replace	Ctrl + H		Searches for a specified value and replaces it with another specified value
Edit/Delete Sheet			Deletes selected sheets from a workbook.
View/Toolbars			Displays or hides selected toolbar
View/Comments		▣	Displays all comments or hides all displayed comments
View/Zoom		100% ▾	Changes magnification of window
Insert/Cells/Shift Cells Right			Moves existing cells to the right when you insert new cells
Insert/Cells/Shift Cells Down			Moves existing cells down when you insert new cells
Insert/Copied Cells			Inserts row and copies text from Clipboard
Insert/Rows			Inserts a blank row
Insert/Columns			Inserts a blank column
Insert/Chart		▥	Inserts chart into worksheet
Insert/Function	⇧Shift + F3	ƒ*	Inserts a function
Insert/Name/Define			Assigns a name you specify to a cell or range of cells
Insert/Name/Paste			Places the selected cell or cell range name in the formula bar or lists names in the worksheet
Insert/Name/Create			Creates a range name using the text in cells
Insert/Comment		▣	Inserts a new comment in selected cell
Insert/Edit Comment		▣	Edits comment in selected cell
Insert/Object			Inserts an entire file as an embedded object.
Insert/Hyperlink	Ctrl + K		Inserts a new hyperlink or modifies the selected hyperlink
Insert/Hyperlink/Remove Link			Removes hyperlink settings from selected cell
Insert/Picture/From File			Inserts picture at insertion point from disk
Format/Cells/Number/Currency			Applies Currency format to selection
Format/Cells/Number/Accounting		$	Applies Accounting format to selection

Command	Shortcut	Button	Action
Format/Cells/Number/Date			Applies Date format to selection
Format/Cells/Number/Percent		%	Applies Percent format to selection
Format/Cells/Number/Decimal places		.00 / .0	Increases or decreases the number of decimal places associated with a number value
Format/Cells/Alignment/Horizontal/ Left (Indent)		≣	Left-aligns entry in cell space
Format/Cells/Alignment/Horizontal/ Center		≣	Center-aligns entry in cell space
Format/Cells/Alignment/Horizontal/ Right		≣	Right-aligns entry in cell space
Format/Cells/Alignment/Indent/1		譚	Indents cell entry one space
Format/Cells/Alignment/Horizontal/ Center Across Selection		國	Centers cell contents across selected cells
Format/Cells/Font			Changes font and attributes of cell contents
Format/Cells/Font/Font Style/Bold	Ctrl + B	B	Bolds selected text
Format/Cells/Font/Font Style/Italic	Ctrl + I	I	Italicizes selected text
Format/Cells/Font/Underline/Single	Ctrl + U	U	Underlines selected text
Format/Cells/Font/Color		A ·	Adds color to text
Format/Cells/Patterns/Color		◇ ·	Adds color to cell background
Format/Row/Height			Changes height of selected row
Format/Row/Hide			Hides selected rows or columns
Format/Row/Unhide			Displays rows and columns that were previously hidden
Format/AutoFormat			Applies selected table format
Format/Column/Width			Changes width of columns
Format/Column/AutoFit Selection			Changes column width to match widest cell entry
Format/Sheet/Rename			Renames sheet
Format/Style			Applies selected style to selection
Format/Style/Style name/Currency			Applies currency style to selection
Format/Style/Style name/Percent		%	Changes cell style to display percentage
Format/Selected Data Series/ Data Labels	Ctrl + 1		Inserts data labels into chart
Format/Selected Legend	Ctrl + 1	圁	Changes legend
Format/Selected Chart Title	Ctrl + 1	圕	Changes format of selected chart title
Format/Selected Data Series	Ctrl + 1	圕	Changes format of selected data series
Format/Selected Object		圕	Changes format of embedded objects
Chart/Chart Type		⬛ ·	Changes type of chart
Chart/Chart Options			Adds options to chart

Command	Shortcut	Button	Action
Chart/Location			Moves chart from worksheet to chart sheet
Tools/Share Workbook/Allow changes by more than one user			Changes workbook status to shared or exclusive
Tools/Track Changes/Accept or Reject Changes			Sequentially moves to each tracked change and lets you decide to accept or reject each
Tools/Track Changes/Highlight Changes/List changes on a new sheet			Displays a History sheet of all tracked changes
Tools/Compare and Merge Workbooks			Combines workbooks sent to review
Tools/Protection/Protect Sheet sheet's contents			Prevents unauthorized users from changing a
Tools/Scenarios			Creates and saves sets of data used to perform what-if analyses
Tools/Formula Auditing/ Show Auditing Toolbar			Displays auditing toolbar
Tools/Solver			Calculates a formula to achieve a given value by changing one of the variables that affects formulas.
Tools/Macro/Macros	Alt + F8		Runs, edits, or deletes selected macro
Tools/Macro/Record New Macro			Records a series of actions as a macro
Tools/Macro/Stop Recording			Stops the recording of a macro
Tools/Macro/Security			Sets security level associated with macros in a workbook
Tools/Spelling	F7	✓	Spell-checks worksheet
Tools/Goal Seek			Adjusts value in specified cell until a formula dependent on that cell reaches specified result
Tools/Formula Auditing/ Show Watch Window			Opens the Watch Window toolbar
Tools/AutoCorrect Options/ AutoFormat As You Type/Internet and network paths with hyperlinks			Turns on/off feature to automatically format Internet and network paths as hyperlinks
Data/Sort		↕	Arranges selected data alphabetically, numerically, or by date
Data/Filter/AutoFilter			Displays items based on selections in a list or database range
Data/Filter/Show All			Redisplays all records after a filter operation has been performed
Data/Form			Displays a data form dialog box for record entry and modification
Data/Table			Creates a data table based on specified input values and formulas
Data/Import External Data/Import Data			Imports data from an external source into a worksheet

Command	Shortcut	Button	Action
Window/**A**rrange			Arranges open windows side-by-side, vertically, horizontally, or tiled.
Visual Basic Editor			
File/**C**lose and Return			Closes the Visual Basic Editor window and returns to Microsoft Excel to the active Excel worksheet
Run/Run sub/Userform	F5		Runs macro
Window/Un**f**reeze Panes			Unfreezes window panes
Window/**F**reeze Panes			Freezes top and/or leftmost panes
Window/**S**plit			Divides window into four panes at active cell
Window/Remove **S**plit			Removes split bar from active worksheet

Access Command Summary

Command	Shortcut	Button	Action
File/New	Ctrl + N	[icon]	Opens New File task pane
File/Open	Ctrl + O	[icon]	Opens an existing database
File/Open/<database> Open Exclusive			Restricts use of database to a single user at one time
File/Get External Data/Import			Copies data from a file saved in another format into an Access database
File/Close		[X]	Closes open window
File/Save	Ctrl + S	[icon]	Saves database object
File/Export			Saves an Access database object in another file format so it can be used in a different application
File/Page Setup/		Setup	Sets page margins and page layout for printed output
File/Web Page Preview			Displays the data access page in the Internet Explorer browser
File/Print/Pages/From			Prints selected pages
File/Print Preview		[icon]	Displays file as it will appear when printed
File/Print	Ctrl + P	[icon]	Specifies print settings and prints current database object
File/Print Relationships			Creates a report that shows relationships in current database
File/Exit		[X]	Closes Access
Edit/Undo	Ctrl + Z	[icon]	Cancels last action
Edit/Cut	Ctrl + X	[icon] or [icon]	Removes selected item and copies it to the Clipboard
Edit/Copy	Ctrl + C	[icon]	Duplicates selected item and copies to the Clipboard
Edit/Office Clipboard			Displays Office Clipboard task pane
Edit/Paste	Ctrl + V	[icon]	Inserts copy of item in Clipboard
Edit/Select Record			Selects current record
Edit/Select All Records	Ctrl + A		Selects all controls on a form
Edit/Find	Ctrl + F	[icon]	Locates specified data

Command	Shortcut	Button	Action
Edit/Replace	Ctrl + H		Locates and replaces specified data
Edit/Delete Rows		⊟	Deletes selected field in Design view
Edit/Delete Column			Removes selected column
Edit/Primary Key		🔑	Defines a field as a primary key field
Edit/Clear Grid			Clears query grid
View/Design View		☑ ▾	Displays Design view
View/Datasheet View		▦ ▾	Displays table in Datasheet view
View/Form View			Displays a form in Form view
View/Properties	F4	🖆	Displays current properties for selected item
View/Page Header/Footer			Adds or removes Page Header and Footer sections in a form
View/Toolbars/Task Pane			Displays task pane
View/Zoom/%		Fit ▾	Displays previewed database object at specified percentage
Insert/Form/AutoForm: Columnar		New	Creates a columnar form using all fields from the selected table or query
Insert/Page Numbers			Inserts a page number text box in page header or footer of a form
Insert/Rows		⊟	Inserts a new field in table in Design view
Insert/Column			Inserts a new field in a table in Datasheet view
Insert/Object			Inserts an object into current field
Insert/Lookup Field			Creates a lookup field with specified values from which to choose
Insert/Lookup Column	Ctrl + K	🖳	Creates a lookup column with specified values from which to choose
Insert/Hyperlink			Inserts a hyperlink
Insert/Subdatasheet			Inserts a subdatasheet with values from a related table or query into current datasheet
Insert/Report			Creates a new report object
Filter/Apply Filter/Sort		▽	Applies filter to table
Query/Run		!	Displays query results in Query Datasheet view
Query/Show Table		🖫	Displays Show Table dialog box
Format/Column Width			Changes width of table columns in Datasheet view
Format/Column Width/Best Fit			Sizes selected columns to accommodate longest entry or column header
Format/Hide Columns			Hides columns
Format/Unhide Columns			Redisplays hidden columns
Format/Font/Size			Sets font size of selection

Command	Shortcut	Button	Action
Format/Align			Aligns edges of selected form controls: left, right, top, bottom, or to grid
Format/Size/To Fit			Automatically resizes selected control to fit its contents
Format/Vertical Spacing/Make Equal			Equalizes vertical space between selected controls
Format/Theme			Applies selected theme to data access page
Format/Subdatasheet/Expand All			Shows entire subdatasheet that is embedded in current datasheet
Format/Subdatasheet/Remove			Removes subdatasheet that is embedded in current datasheet
Records/Remove Filter/Sort			Displays all records in table
Records/Data Entry			Hides existing records and displays Data Entry window
Records/Sort/Sort Ascending		⏶⏷	Reorders records in ascending alphabetical order
View/Toolbox		⚒	Displays/Hides Toolbox
View/Zoom/%			Displays previewed document at specified percentage
View/Zoom/Fit to Window			Displays entire previewed document page
View/Pages			Displays specified number of pages of previewed document
Relationships/Show Table		⊞	Used to add tables and queries to Relationships window
Relationships/Edit Relationship			Used to change existing relationships or create new relationships in current database and to enforce referential integrity
Records/Filter/Filter by Form		⊞	Displays blank datasheet for entering criteria to display specific information
Records/Filter/Filter by Selection		▽⚡	Displays only records that contain a specific value
Records/Apply Filter/Sort		▽	Applies filter to table
Tools/Relationships		⊟	Used to view and define permanent relationships between tables
Tools/Database Utilities/ Switchboard Manager			Opens Switchboard Manager for creating and editing switchboards
Tools/Database Utilities/ Compact and Repair Database		⊞	Displays blank datasheet for entering criteria to display specific information
Tools/Database Utilities/ Switchboard Manager			Opens Switchboard Manager for creating and editing switchboards
Tools/Security/ Set Database Password			Requires entry of password to open database

Command	Shortcut	Button	Action
Tools/Securit**y**/Unset **D**atabase Password			Removes password protection from database
Tools/Start**u**p			Customizes how the database looks and acts when opened
Tools/**M**acro/Run **M**acro			Executes the selected macro commands
Window/Database			Displays selected window
		⬚	Displays Database window

PowerPoint Command Summary

Command	Shortcut	Button	Action
File/New	Ctrl + N	▯	Creates new presentation
File/Open	Ctrl + O	▱	Opens selected presentation
File/Close		✕	Closes presentation
File/Save	Ctrl + S	▮	Saves presentation
File/Save As			Saves presentation using new file name
File/Save as Web Page			Saves a presentation in HTML format
File/Save as Web Page/Publish			Saves a presentation to a Web server
File/Pack and Go			Puts all files needed for presentation into one file for use on other machines
File/Web Page Preview			Displays presentation in browser
File/Print Preview		▱	Displays a preview of selected output
File/Print	Ctrl + P	▤	Prints presentation using default print settings
File/Send To/Microsoft Word			Exports presentation text to Word
File/Send To/Mail Recipient (for Review)			Sends presentation or selected slide as an e-mail attachment and activates the recipient's Reviewing toolbar
File/Send to/Mail Recipient (as Attachment)			Sends presentation a selected slide as an e-mail attachment
File/Properties			Displays statistics and stores documentation about file
File/Exit		✕	Exits PowerPoint program
Edit/Undo	Ctrl + Z	↶ ▾	Undoes the last action
Edit/Office Clipboard			Opens Clipboard task pane
Edit/Paste Special			Inserts a selection as an embedded object
Edit/Paste Special/Paste Link			Inserts a selection as a linked object
Edit/Select All	Ctrl + A		Selects all slides in presentation, all text and graphics in active window, or all text in selected object
Edit/Delete Slide	Delete		Deletes selected slide
Edit/Find	Ctrl + F		Finds selected text
Edit/Replace	Ctrl + H		Replaces selected text

Command	Shortcut	Button	Action
Edit/Links			Changes settings associated with linked objects
Edit/Linked Object/Open			Opens the source application of the linked object
View/Normal		▦	Displays current slide in Normal view
View/Slide Sorter		▦	Switches to Slide Sorter view
View/Slide Show	F5	▦	Runs slide show
View/Notes Page			Displays notes pages
View/Master/Slide Master	⇧Shift + ▢		Displays the slide and title masters for the current presentation
View/Task Pane			Displays or hides task pane
View/Toolbars			Displays or hides toolbars
View/Ruler			Turns on/off display of the ruler
View/Header and Footer			Specifies information that appears as headers and footers on slides, notes, outlines, and handout pages
View/Zoom		100% ▾	Changes the size of onscreen display of slide
Insert/New Slide	Ctrl + M	▦	Inserts new slide
Insert/Duplicate Slide			Inserts duplicate of selected slide
Insert/Comment			Inserts a comment into presentation
Insert/Slides from Files			Inserts selected slides from another presentation
Insert/Slides from Outline			Creates slides from outline text
Insert/Picture/Clip Art		▦	Inserts selected clip art
Insert/Picture/From File			Inserts picture from file on disk
Insert/Picture/AutoShapes			Inserts an AutoShape object
Insert/Text box		▦	Adds a text box object
Insert/Movies and Sounds/ Sound from File			Inserts sound or movie files into selected slide
Insert/Movies and Sounds/ Play CD Audio Track			Adds a CD audio track to a PowerPoint slide
Insert/Chart			Adds a chart object to a slide
Format/Font/Font		Times New Roman ▾	Changes font typeface
Format/Font/Font Style/Bold	Alt + B	**B**	Adds bold effect to selection
Format/Font/Font Style/Italic	Alt + I	*I*	Adds italic effect to selection
Format/Font/Size		24 ▾	Changes font size
Format/Font/Color		A ▾	Adds color to selected text
Format/Bullets and Numbering		▦ ▦	Applies/removes selected bullet or numbering style
Format/Alignment/Align Left	Ctrl + L	▦	Left-aligns selection
Format/Alignment/Center	Ctrl + E	▦	Center-aligns selection
Format/Alignment/Align Right	Ctrl + R	▦	Right-aligns selection

Command	Shortcut	Button	Action
Format/**A**lignment/**J**ustify	Ctrl + J	▤	Justifies selection
Format/Slide **D**esign			Applies selected design template to one or all slides in a presentation
Format/Slide **L**ayout			Changes or creates a slide layout
Format/Bac**k**ground			Applies colors, patterns, or pictures to a slide background
Format/Aut**o**Shape			Changes characteristics of an AutoShape
Format/Aut**o**Shape/Size			Changes size and scale of selected AutoShape
Format/Se**l**ected Data Series			Applies patterns, shapes, and other formats to selected data series
Data/Series in **C**olumns			Arranges chart based on columns in Datasheet window
Chart/Chart **O**ptions			Adds and modifies chart options such as titles, legends, and gridlines
Tools/Com**p**are and Merge Presentations			Combines reviewed presentations with original
Tools/**S**pelling and Grammar	F7	ᵃᵇᶜ✓	Spell and grammar checks presentation
Tools/**O**ptions/Spelling and Style/Check Style			Checks presentation style
Sli**d**e Show/**S**et Up Show			Sets up presentation to run for specific situations
Sli**d**e Show/**R**ehearse Timings			
Sli**d**e Show/Record **N**arration			
Sli**d**e Show/Ac**t**ion Buttons			Adds navigation buttons to a slide
Sli**d**e Show/**A**ction Settings			Specifies action that is needed to activate hyperlinks
Slide Show/Animation Sc**h**emes		[No Effect ▾]	Adds predesigned builds to selected slides
Slide Show/Custo**m** Animation			Adds motion and determines how sound is played
Slide Show/Slide **T**ransition		▣	Adds transition effects
Slide Show /**H**ide Slide		▣	Hides selected slide
Sli**d**e Show/**C**ustom Shows			Creates presentations within a presentation
Sli**d**e Show/**O**nline Broadcast/Record and Save a Broadcast			Records a presentation for broadcast
Slide Show Shortcut Menu			
Go/By **T**itle	H		Displays hidden slide
Go/Slide **N**avigator			Moves to specified slide
Screen/**B**lack	B		Blacks out/redisplays screen
Screen/**E**rase	E		Erases freehand annotations
Pointer Options/**A**utomatic			Sets pointer to an arrow and hides after 15 seconds of non-use
Pointer Options/**P**en	Ctrl + P		Turns on freehand annotation

Command	Shortcut	Button	Action
Draw Menu Options			
`Draw ▾` /**G**roup			Groups objects together
`Draw ▾` /**U**ngroup			Ungroups objects
`Draw ▾` /Regr**o**up			Regroups pieces of a graphic
`Draw ▾` /**O**rder/Send to Bac**k**			Sends object to bottom of stack
`Draw ▾` /Gr**i**d and Guides			Aligns objects to grid or guides
`Draw ▾` /**A**lign or Distribute			Aligns or distributes objects
`Draw ▾` /**A**lign or Distribute/ Align **T**op			Aligns selected objects evenly with top edges
`Draw ▾` /**A**lign or Distribute/ Distribute **H**orizontally			Aligns selected objects evenly horizontally
Table Toolbar			
`Table ▾` /Bord**e**rs and Fill		`1 pt ▾` `✎` `▦`	Applies border and fill colors to cells in a table
`Table ▾` /Selec**t** Row			Selects a row of cells in a table
`Table ▾` /Select C**o**lumn			Selects a column of cells in a table
`Table ▾` /**S**elect Table			Selects all cells in a table
Organization Chart			
`Insert Shape ▾` /**S**ubordinate			Adds a box below selected box
`Insert Shape ▾` /**C**oworker			Adds a box at same level as selected box
`Layout ▾` /**S**tandard			Applies Standard layout to selected boxes

Word Glossary of Key Terms

absolute link   A link that identifies the file location of the destination file by its full address. Also called a fixed link.

active document   The document containing the insertion point and that will be affected by any changes you make.

active window   The window you can work in identified by a highlighted title bar, the insertion point, and scroll bars.

address file   The data source file used in a merge; it typically contains name and address data to be combined with the main document.

alignment   The positioning of paragraphs between the margins: left, right, centered, or justified.

antonym   A word with the opposite meaning.

attachment   A file that is sent along with an e-mail message, but is not part of the e-mail text.

author   The process of designing and creating a Web page.

authoring   The process of creating a Web page.

AutoComplete   A feature that recognizes commonly used words or phrases and can automatically complete them for you if chosen.

AutoCorrect   A feature that makes basic assumptions about the text you are typing and automatically corrects the entry.

AutoFormat   The feature that makes certain formatting changes automatically to your document.

automatic grammar check   The feature that advises you of incorrect grammar as you create and edit a document, and proposes possible corrections.

automatic spelling check   The feature that advises you of misspelled words as you create and edit a document, and proposes possible corrections.

AutoShape   A ready-made shape that is supplied with Word.

AutoText   A feature that provides commonly used words or phrases that you can select and quickly insert into a document.

background   A color or design applied behind the text on a Web page.

balloon   A box that displays markup elements such as comments and tracked changes in the margin of the document.

browser   A program that connects to remote computers and displays Web pages.

bulleted list   Displays items that logically fall out from a paragraph into a list, with items preceded by bullets.

caption   A title or explanation for a table, picture, or graph.

case sensitive   The capability to distinguish between uppercase and lowercase characters.

cell   The intersection of a column and row where data is entered in a table.

character formatting   Formatting features, such as bold and color, that affect the selected characters only.

Character style   A combination of any character formats that affect selected text.

chart   A visual representation of numeric data. Also called a graph.

clip art   A collection of graphics that is usually bundled with a software application.

collect and paste   The capability of the program to store multiple copied items in the Office Clipboard and then paste one or more of the items.

comment   A note that can be added to a document without changing the document text.

comment balloon   A balloon that displays the text of a comment.

controls   Graphic objects designed to automate the process of completing a form.

cross-reference   A reference in one part of a document to related information in another part.

cursor The blinking vertical bar that shows you where the next character you type will appear. Also called the insertion point.

custom dictionary A dictionary of terms you have entered that are not in the main dictionary of the Spelling Checker.

data field Each category of information in the data source.

data series Each group of related data that is plotted in the chart. Each data series has a unique color or pattern assigned to it so that you can identify the different series.

datasheet The data validation restrictions you place on a field.

data source The file that supplies the data in a mail merge.

default The initial Word document settings that can be changed to customize documents.

destination The location to which text is moved or copied.

destination file A document in which a linked object is inserted.

diagram A graphic object that can be used to illustrate concepts and to enhance documents.

Document Map Displays the headings in the document.

document window The area of the application window that displays the contents of the open document.

drag and drop A mouse procedure that moves or copies a selection to a new location.

drawing layer The layer above or below the text layer where floating objects are inserted.

drawing object A simple object consisting of shapes such as lines and boxes.

drop cap A large, uppercase character with the top part of the letter even with the line and the rest of the letter extending into the paragraph below it.

edit The process of changing and correcting existing text in a document.

embedded object An object, such as a picture graphic, that becomes part of the Word document and that can be opened and edited using the program in which it was created.

endnote A reference note displayed at the end of the document.

end-of-file marker The horizontal line that marks the end of a file.

field A placeholder code that instructs Word to insert information in a document.

field code The code containing the instructions about the type of information to insert in a field.

field name A name used to label each data field in the data source.

field results The results displayed in a field according to the instructions in the field code.

fixed link A link that identifies the file location of the destination by its full address. Also called an absolute link.

floating object A graphic object that is inserted into the drawing layer and which can be positioned anywhere on the page.

font A set of characters with a specific design. Also called a typeface.

font size The height and width of a character, commonly measured in points.

footer The line or several lines of text at the bottom of every page just below the bottom margin line.

footnote A reference note displayed at the bottom of the page on which the reference occurs.

form Collection of fields on a Web page that are used to get information or feedback from users.

format To enhance the appearance of the document to make it more readable or attractive.

Format Painter The feature that applies formats associated with the current selection to new selections.

formatting marks Symbols that are automatically inserted into a document as you enter and edit text and that control the appearance of the document.

Formatting toolbar The toolbar that contains buttons representing the most frequently used text-editing and text-layout features.

formula Table entry that does arithmetic calculations.

frame A division of a window that can be scrolled separately.

frames page The container for frames in a Web site. The frames page serves as the file name for the collection of frames. It is invisible to the user when viewing the Web site.

function A prewritten formula that performs a calculation automatically in a table.

global template The normal document template whose settings are available to all documents.

graphic   A non-text element in a document.

group   Two or more objects that are treated as a single object.

hard page break   A manually inserted page break that instructs Word to begin a new page regardless of the amount of text on the previous page.

header   The line or several lines of text at the top of each page just above the top margin line.

heading style   A style that is designed to identify different levels of headings in a document.

home page   The top-level or opening page to a site.

HTML (Hypertext Markup Language)   A programming language used to create Web pages.

hyperlink   A connection to locations in the current document, other documents, or Web pages. Clicking a hyperlink jumps to the specified location.

hyphenation   Inserts a hyphen (-) in long words that fall at the end of a line to split the word between lines.

hyphenation zone   An unmarked space along the right margin that controls the amount of white space in addition to the margin that is allowed at the end of a line.

inline object   An object that is inserted directly in the text at the position of the insertion point, becoming part of the paragraph.

Insert mode   Method of text entry in which new characters are inserted into existing text, which moves to the right to make space for the new characters; the text on the line is reformatted as necessary.

insertion point   The blinking vertical bar that shows you where the next character you type will appear on the line. Also called the cursor.

kerning   Adjusting the spacing between particular pairs of letters, depending on the font design.

landscape   Orientation in which text is printed across the length of page.

leader characters   Solid, dotted, or dashed lines that fill the blank space between tab stops.

legend   A box containing a brief description that identifies the patterns or colors assigned to the data series in a chart.

line spacing   The vertical space between lines of text.

linked object   Information created in a source file from one application and inserted into a destination file of another application while maintaining a link between files.

live link   A linked object that automatically reflects in the destination document any changes made in the source document when the destination document is opened.

Mail Merge   A feature that combines a text document with a data document or file containing names and addresses to produce a merged document or form letter.

main dictionary   The dictionary of terms that comes with Word 2002.

main document   The document that contains the basic form letter with merge fields in a merge operation.

markup   Elements used to identify changes made to a document when Track Changes is on.

menu   Method used to tell a program what you want it to do.

menu bar   A bar that displays the menu names that can be selected.

merge field   A field code that controls what information is used from the data source and where it is entered in the main document.

newsletter-style columns   The arrangement of text in a document so that it flows from the bottom of one column to the top of the next column.

Normal template   The document template that is opened when you start Word.

note pane   Lower portion of the window that displays footnotes.

note reference mark   A superscript number or character appearing in the document at the end of the material being referenced.

note separator   The horizontal line separating footnote text from main document text.

note text   The text in a footnote.

numbered list   Displays items that convey a sequence of events in a particular order, with items preceded by numbers or letters.

object   An item that can be sized, moved, and manipulated.

operator   Specifies the type of calculation to perform. The most common operators are + (add), – (subtract), * (multiply), and / (divide).

optional hyphen A hyphen that is inserted automatically when a word is broken between two lines because the full word did not fit.

outlined numbered list Displays items in multiple outline levels that show a hierarchical structure of the items in the list.

Overtype mode Method of text entry in which new text types over the existing characters.

page break Marks the point at which one page ends and another begins.

page margin The blank space around the edge of the page.

pane A split portion of the document window that can be scrolled independently.

paragraph formatting Formatting features, such as alignment, indentation, and line spacing, that affect an entire paragraph.

paragraph style A combination of any character formats and paragraph formats that affect all text in a paragraph.

picture An illustration such as a scanned photograph.

placeholder Text in a template that marks the space and provides instructions for the text that should be entered at that location.

point Measure used for height of type; one point equals 1/72 inch.

portrait Orientation of the page, in which text is printed across the width of the page.

protocol The rules that control how hardware and software on a network communicate.

record All the fields of data that are needed to complete the main document for one entity in a merge operation.

relative link Identifies the destination location in relation to the location of the HTML file.

revision marks Red underlines that identify where an insertion was made while Track Changes is on.

ruler The ruler located below the Formatting toolbar that shows the line length in inches.

sans serif font A font, such as Arial or Helvetica, that does not have a flair at the base of each letter.

scroll bar A window element located on the right or bottom window border that lets you display text that is not currently visible in the window. It contains scroll arrows and a scroll box.

section A division into which a document can be divided that can be formatted separately from the rest of the document.

section break Marks the point at which one section ends and another begins.

section cursor A colored highlight bar that appears over the selected command in a menu.

select To highlight text.

selection rectangle The rectangular outline around an object that indicates it is selected.

serif font A font, such as Times New Roman, that has a flair at the base of each letter.

shortcut menu A menu of the most common menu options that is displayed by right-clicking on the selected item.

sidebar An article set off from other articles or information that highlights an article next to it.

sizing handles Black squares around a selected object that can be used to size the object.

SmartTag A feature that recognizes data such as names, addresses, telephone numbers, dates, times, and places as a particular type. The recognized item can then be quickly added to a Microsoft Outlook feature.

soft page break A page break automatically inserted by Word to start a new page when the previous page has been filled with text or graphics.

soft space A space automatically entered by Word to align the text properly on a single line.

sort To arrange alphabetically or numerically in ascending or descending order.

source The location from which text is moved or copied.

source file The document that stores the data for the linked object.

source program The program in which an object was created.

Standard toolbar The toolbar that contains buttons for the most frequently used commands.

status bar A bar displayed at the bottom of the document window that advises you of the status of different program conditions and features as you use the program.

story Text that is contained in a single text box or linked text boxes.

style A set of formats that is assigned a name.

synonym A word with a similar meaning.

tab stop A marked location on the horizontal ruler that indicates how far to indent text when the [Tab⇆] key is pressed.

table Displays information in horizontal rows and vertical columns.

table reference The letter and number (for example, A1) that identify a cell in a table.

tag An HTML code embedded in a Web page document that supplies information about the page's structure.

target link Link that targets a heading or object on a page.

task pane A pane that provides quick access to features as you are using them.

template A document file that includes predefined settings that can be used as a pattern to create many common types of documents.

text box Container for text or graphics.

theme Predesigned Web page effects that can be applied to a Web page to enhance its appearance.

Thesaurus Word feature that provides synonyms and antonyms for words.

thumbnail A miniature representation of a picture.

toolbar A bar of buttons commonly displayed below the menu bar. The buttons are shortcuts for many of the most common menu commands.

tracked changes Insertions, deletions, and formatting changes that are made to a document while Track Changes is on.

TrueType A font that is automatically installed when you install Windows.

typeface A set of characters with a specific design. Also called a font.

Uniform Resource Locator (URL) a fixed file location that includes the full path to the location or address of the Web page.

wallpaper A background consisting of an image, pattern or texture.

Web page A document that uses HTML to display in a browser.

wizard A guided approach to creating special types of documents, such as Web sites, consisting of a series of dialog boxes in which you specify settings. The wizard creates a document based on your selections.

word wrap A feature that automatically determines where to end a line and wrap text to the next line based on the margin settings.

WordArt A supplementary application included with the Word program that is used to enhance a document by changing the shape of text, adding 3-D effects, and changing the alignment of text on a line.

Excel Glossary of Key Terms

3-D reference A reference to the same cell or range on multiple sheets in the same workbook.

3-D shape A line, AutoShape, or freeform drawing object that has a three-dimensional effect applied to it.

absolute reference A cell or range reference in a formula whose location remains the same (absolute) when copied. Indicated by a $ character entered before the column letter or row number or both.

active cell The cell displaying the cell selector that will be affected by the next entry or procedure.

active pane The pane that contains the cell selector.

active sheet A sheet that contains the cell selector and that will be affected by the next action.

active workbook The workbook that contains the cell selector and that will be affected by the next action.

adjacent range A rectangular block of adjoining cells.

adjustable cell In Solver, the cell or cells whose values will be changed in order to attain the value set in the target cell.

alignment The vertical or horizontal placement and orientation of an entry in a cell.

area chart A chart that shows trends by emphasizing the area under the curve.

argument The data used in a function on which the calculation is performed.

arrange windows The arrangement of multiple open workbook windows on the screen tiled, cascading, horizontally, or vertically.

AutoFill Feature that logically repeats and extends a series.

autoformat A built-in combination of formats that can be applied to a range.

automatic recalculation The recalculation of a formula within the worksheet whenever a value in a referenced cell in the formula changes.

browser A program that connects you to remote computers and displays the Web pages you request.

cascade The window arrangement that displays one workbook window on top of the other, cascading down from the top of the screen.

case sensitive The capability to distinguish between uppercase and lowercase characters.

category-axis Another name for the X-axis of a chart.

category-axis title A label that describes the X-axis.

category name Labels displayed along the X-axis in a chart to identify the data being plotted.

cell The space created by the intersection of a vertical column and a horizontal row.

cell selector The heavy border surrounding a cell in the worksheet that identifies the active cell.

change history Information in a shared workbook that is maintained about changes made to the worksheet.

chart A visual representation of data in a worksheet.

chart gridlines Lines extending from the axis lines across the plot area that make it easier to read and evaluate the chart data.

chart object One type of graphic object that is created using charting features included in Excel 2002. A chart object can be inserted into a worksheet or into a special chart sheet.

chart title Appears at the top of a chart and is used to describe the contents of the chart.

ClipArt A collection of graphics that is usually bundled with a software application.

column A vertical block of cells one cell wide in the worksheet.

column letters The border of letters across the top of the worksheet that identifies the columns in the worksheet.

column-oriented In a data table, the orientation of the data in a table down a column as opposed to across a row (row-oriented).

combination chart A chart type that includes mixed data markers, such as both columns and lines.

comment Notes attached to cells that can be used to help clarify the meaning of the data, provide documentation or ask a question.

constant A value that does not change unless you change it directly by typing in another entry.

control Graphic objects that are designed to automate the process of completing information in a worksheet.

copy area The cell or cells containing the data to be copied.

custom dictionary An additional dictionary you create to supplement the main dictionary.

criteria A set of limiting conditions that you want records to meet in order to be displayed.

data form A special form that makes it easy to enter records in a list.

data labels Labels for data points or bars that show the values being plotted on a chart.

data marker Represents a data series on a chart. It can be a symbol, color, or pattern, depending upon the type of chart.

data series The numbers to be charted.

data table A type of what-if analysis where one or more variables are changed to see the effect on the formula or formulas that include these variables.

database An organized collection of related information consisting of fields and records. Also called a list in Excel.

date numbers The integers assigned to the days from January 1, 1900, through December 31, 2099, that allow dates to be used in calculations.

dependent cell The cell that receives the linked data.

dependent workbook The workbook file that receives the linked data.

destination The cell or range of cells that receives the data from the copy area or source.

destination file A document in which a linked object is inserted.

destination document The workbook file in which a linked object is inserted.

digital signature An electronic encryption-based stamp of authentication.

discussion comments Comments that are attached to a document and stored on a discussion server so they can be read and responded to by multiple reviewers.

discussion server A computer that stores discussion text and information about the file being discussed.

drawing object Object consisting of shapes such as lines and boxes that can be created using features on the Drawing toolbar.

embed Information inserted into a destination file of another application that becomes part of this file but can be edited within the destination file using the server application.

embedded chart A chart that is inserted into another file.

embedded object Information inserted into a destination file of another application that becomes part of this file but can be edited within the destination file using the server application.

exclusive Workbook status that allows editing by only one user at a time.

explode To separate a wedge of a pie chart slightly from the other wedges in the pie.

export To save data in another format so that it can be used in an application other than the application in which it was created.

external data Data that is created in another application.

external reference formula A formula that creates a link between workbooks.

field A single category of data in a list, the values of which appear in a column of a worksheet.

field name A label used to identify the data stored in a field.

fill handle A small black square located in the lower-right corner of the selection that is used to create a series or copy to adjacent cells with a mouse.

filter A restriction placed on records in a database to temporarily isolate a subset of records.

Find and Replace Feature that quickly finds and automatically replaces specific information with new information.

font The typeface, type size, and style associated with a worksheet entry that can be selected to improve the appearance of the worksheet.

footer A line (or several lines) of text that appears at the bottom of each page just above the bottom margin.

form A formatted worksheet that is designed to be completed by filling in data in the blank spaces.

format Formats are settings that affect the display of entries in a worksheet.

Formatting toolbar A toolbar that contains buttons used to change the format of a worksheet.

formula An entry that performs a calculation.

Formula bar The bar near the top of the Excel window that displays the cell contents.

freeze To fix in place on the screen specified rows or columns or both when scrolling.

function A prewritten formula that performs certain types of calculations automatically.

Goal Seek Tool used to find the value needed in one cell to attain a result you want in another cell.

graphic A non-text element or object, such as a drawing or picture that can be added to a document.

group An object that contains other objects.

header A line (or several lines) of text that appears at the top of each page just below the top margin.

heading Row and column entries that are used to create the structure of the worksheet and describe other worksheet entries.

History worksheet A worksheet that displays the history of tracked changes in a worksheet.

horizontal The window arrangement that displays one open workbook window above the other.

HTML (Hypertext Markup Language) A programming language whose commands are interpreted by the browser software you are using and which controls how the information on a Web page is displayed,

hyperlink A special type of link that provides a shortcut or jump to another location in the same or different workbook, to a document in a different application, or to a document on a Web site.

IF function A function that checks to see if certain conditions are met and then takes action based upon the results of the check.

import To bring in external data for use in a worksheet.

input cell A cell in which a list of values is substituted to see the resulting effect on the related formulas. Input values can be listed down a column (column-oriented) or across a row (row-oriented).

landscape The orientation of the printed document so that it prints sideways across the length of the page.

legend A brief description of the symbols used in a chart that represent the data ranges.

line chart A chart that represents data as a set of points along a line.

link A relationship created between files that allows data in the destination file to be updated automatically when changes occur in the source file.

linked object Information created in a source file from one application and inserted into a destination file of another application while maintaining a link between files.

list An organized collection of related information consisting of fields and records. Also called a database.

list range The area of the worksheet containing the records in a list.

live link A linked object that automatically reflects in the destination document any changes made in the source document when the destination document is opened.

logical operator Symbols used in formulas that compare values in two or more cells.

macro A stored series of keystrokes and commands. When the macro is executed or run, the stored actions are performed automatically.

macro recorder A tool used to create a macro by recording a series of actions as macro statements as they are performed.

main dictionary The dictionary included with Office XP.

margins The blank space around the edge of the paper.

merged cell A cell made up of several selected cells combined into one.

minimal recalculation The recalculation of only the formulas in a worksheet that are affected by a change of data.

mixed reference A cell address that is part absolute and part relative.

multilevel sort A sort on more than one column or field.

name A description of a cell or range that can be used in place of cell or range references.

name box The area located on the left side of the formula bar that provides information about the selected item such as the reference of the active cell.

nested function A second argument in a function that is enclosed within its own set of parentheses.

nonadjacent range Cells or ranges that are not adjacent but are included in the same selection.

nper The argument in the PMT function that is the total number of payments.

number A cell entry that contains any of the digits 0 to 9 and any of the special characters + = ( ) , . / $ % ∑ =.

number formats Affect how numbers look onscreen and when printed.

object An element such as a text box that can be added to a workbook and that can be selected, sized, and moved. In Visual Basic, the *object* is the item that the statement will affect (such as a cell, cell range, worksheet, or workbook). The object is enclosed in parentheses and surrounded by quotes.

one-variable data table A data table can contain one or more formulas and each formula refers to one input cell.

operand A value on which a numeric formula performs a calculation.

operator Specifies the type of calculation to be performed.

order of precedence Order in which calculations are performed and can be overridden by the use of parentheses.

pane A division of the worksheet window, either horizontal or vertical, through which different areas of the worksheet can be viewed at the same time.

password A secret code that prevents unauthorized users from turning off protection.

paste area The cells or range of cells that receive the data from the copy area or source.

picture An illustration such as a scanned photograph.

pie chart A chart that compares parts to the whole. Each value in the data range is a wedge of the pie (circle).

plot area The area of the chart bounded by the axes.

portrait The orientation of the printed document so that it prints across the width of the page.

principal In the PMT function, the principal or *pv* argument is the amount of the loan.

print area A defined range that is saved with the worksheet and printed by default.

property In Visual Basic Editor, the property is the action you want to perform on the object. The property consists of reserved words that have special meaning and direct Excel to perform the specified action.

protection A worksheet feature that prevents users from making changes to data and formats.

pv The argument in the PMT function that is the amount of the loan. Also called the principal.

range A selection consisting of two or more cells in a worksheet.

range name A descriptive name assigned to a cell or range of cells.

rate In the PMT function, the rate argument is the interest rate of the loan.

record A row of a database or list consisting of a group of related fields.

reference The column letter and row number of a cell.

relative reference A cell or range reference that automatically adjusts to the new location in the worksheet when the formula is copied.

remark statement Descriptive statement lines in a macro that are not executed.

row A horizontal block of cells one cell high in the worksheet.

row numbers The border of numbers along the left side of the worksheet that identifies the rows in the worksheet.

row-oriented In a data table, the orientation of the data in a table across a row as opposed to down a column (column-oriented).

run To execute the commands stored in the macro.

sans serif font A font, such as Arial or Helvetica, that does not have a flair at the base of each letter.

scenario A named set of input values that you can substitute in a worksheet to see the effects of a possible alternative course of action.

selection handles Small boxes surrounding a selected object that are used to size the object.

selection rectangle Border around selected object indicating it can be sized or moved.

series formula A formula that links a chart object to the source worksheet.

serif font A font, such as Times New Roman, that has a flair at the base of each letter.

shared workbook A workbook that is set up for use by multiple people at the same time.

sheet reference Used in references to other worksheets and consists of the name of the sheet enclosed in quotes and is separated from the cell reference by an exclamation point.

sheet tab On the bottom of the workbook window, the tabs where the sheet names appear.

sizing handle Box used to size a selected object.

Solver A tool that is used to perform what-if analyses to determine the effect of changing values in two or more cells, called the adjustable cells, on another cell, called the target cell.

source The cell or range of cells containing the data you want to copy.

source file The document that stores the data for the linked object.

source cell The cell or range of cells containing the data you want to copy.

source document The document that stores the data for the linked object.

source workbook The workbook file that supplies linked data.

sort To rearrange the records in a list in ascending or descending alphabetical order.

spell-checking Feature that locates misspelled words and proposes corrections.

spreadsheet A rectangular grid of rows and columns used to enter data.

stack The order in which objects are added in layers to the worksheet.

stacked-column chart A chart that displays the data values as columns stacked upon each other.

standard toolbar A toolbar that contains buttons used to complete the most frequently used menu commands.

statement The types of information you enter into the Visual Basic Editor are called statements.

style A named combination of formats that can be applied to a selection.

Sub procedure In Visual Basic Editor, a Sub procedure begins with a statement that starts the macro and ends with one that closes the macro (an End Sub statement). Sub procedures can also include remarks about the macro (such as its name and purpose) and functions (such as returning values to the procedure).

syntax Rules of structure for entering all Visual Basic statements.

Tab scroll buttons Located to the left of the sheet tabs, they are used to scroll sheet tabs right or left.

target cell In Solver, the cell you set to the value that you want to be attained.

template A workbook file that contains predesigned worksheets that can be used as a pattern for creating other similar sheets in new workbooks. It has an .xlt file extension.

text A cell entry that contains text, numbers, or any other special characters.

text box A rectangular object in which you type text.

thumbnail Miniature images displayed in the Clip Organizer.

tiled A window arrangement in which open workbook windows are displayed one after the other in succession, across and down the screen.

title In a chart, descriptive text that explains the contents of the chart.

two-variable data table A data table that uses only one formula that refers to two different input cells, one column-oriented and one row-oriented. The purpose of this table is to show the resulting effect on the formula when the values in both of these cells are changed.

typeface The appearance and shape of characters. Some common typefaces are Roman and Courier.

value axis Y axis of a chart that usually contains numerical values.

value axis title A label that describes the values on the Y axis.

variable The resulting value of a formula that changes if the data it depends on changes.

vertical The window arrangement in which open workbook windows are displayed side by side.

Visual Basic Editor A programming application used to write and edit macros attached to Excel workbooks.

Web page A document that can be used on the World Wide Web (WWW) and is displayed in a browser.

Web discussion A review feature that allows users to attach comments to a file that can be read and responded to by all reviewers.

what-if analysis A technique used to evaluate what effect changing one or more values in formulas has on other values in the worksheet.

word wrap Feature that automatically determines when to begin the next line of text.

workbook The file in which you work and store sheets created in Excel 2002.

workbook window A window that displays an open workbook file.

worksheet Similar to a financial spreadsheet in that it is a rectangular grid of rows and columns used to enter data.

X-axis The bottom boundary line of a chart.

Y-axis The left boundary line of a chart.

Z-axis The left boundary line of a 3-D chart.

Access Glossary of Key Terms

action A self-contained instruction that can be combined with other actions to automate tasks.

action query A type of query used to make changes to multiple records in one operation.

align To position a control relative to other controls.

argument Provides additional information on how a macro is to be carried out.

AutoReport Wizard Creates a report, either tabular or columnar, based on a table or query, and adds all fields to the report.

backup Operation that saves a copy of the database or other type of file to a storage medium other than the computer's hard disk.

Best Fit A feature that automatically adjusts column width to fit the longest entry.

bound control A control that is linked to a field in an underlying table.

bound object A graphic object that is stored in a table and connected to a specific record and field.

browser A program that connects a user to remote computers and displays Web pages.

calculated control Control that displays data that is calculated from a field in a table or query or from another control in the form.

calculated field A field that displays the results of a calculation.

cell The space created by the intersection of a vertical column and a horizontal row.

character string A group of text characters.

child field A field in the embedded subdatasheet that will be linked to a master field in the master table.

clip art A collection of professionally drawn images that is usually included with a software program.

column selector bar In Query Design view, the thin gray bar just above the field name in the grid.

column width The size of a field column in Datasheet view. It controls the amount of data you can see on the screen.

command button User-created button that executes one or more actions on a form.

common field A field that is found in two or more tables. It must have the same data type and the same kind of information in each table, but may have different field names.

compact The database makes a copy of the file and rearranges how the file is stored on disk for optimal performance.

comparison operator A symbol used in expressions that allows you to make comparisons. The > (greater than) and < (less than) symbols are examples of comparison operators.

control An object in a form or report that displays information, performs actions, or enhances the design.

control reference A second calculated control in the main form that references the calculated control in the subform.

copy To duplicate a selection to another location.

criteria A set of limiting conditions.

criteria expression An expression that will select only the records that meet certain limiting criteria.

crosstab query A type of query that summarizes large amounts of data in an easy-to-read, row-and-column format.

current record The record, containing the insertion point, that will be affected by the next action.

data access page A Web page created in Access that is connected to a database and that can be displayed and edited by the online viewer.

database An organized collection of related information.

Database toolbar Toolbar that contains buttons that are used to perform basic database features.

datasheet Data from a table, form, or query that is displayed in row-and-column format.

Datasheet form A form layout that is similar to a table datasheet, in that information is displayed in rows and columns.

data type Attribute for a field that determines what type of data it can contain.

delimited text A file format that contains values separated by commas, tabs, semicolons, or other characters.

design grid The lower part of the Query Design window, which displays settings that are used to define the query.

destination The location where a copied selection is inserted.

destination file The document in which a linked object is inserted.

drawing object A simple graphic consisting of shapes such as lines and boxes that can be created using a drawing program such as Paint.

exclusive Type of database that prevents others in a multiuser environment from opening the database while you are accessing it.

expand indicator The + symbol in a datasheet that indicates a subdatasheet is available. Clicking the button expands the subdatasheet.

export To save Access data in another format so it can be used in another application.

expression A combination of operators, identifiers, and values that produce a result.

Expression Builder Access feature used to enter expressions in database forms, reports, and queries.

field A single category of data in a table, the values of which appear in a column of a datasheet.

Field List Displays a list of all the fields in the record source and can be used to add other fields to a form.

field name Label used to identify the data stored in a field.

field property An attribute of a field that affects its appearance or behavior.

field selector A small gray box or bar in datasheets and queries that can be clicked to select the entire column. The field selector usually contains the field names.

field size Field property that limits a text data type to a certain size or limits numeric data to values within a specific range.

filter A restriction placed on records in an open form or datasheet to temporarily isolate a subset of records.

Filter by Form A method that filters records based on multiple criteria that are entered into a blank datasheet.

Filter by Selection A type of filter that displays only records containing a specific value.

fixed-width text A file format that contains values arranged so that each field has a certain width.

fonts A set of characters with a specific design. Also called a typeface.

font size The height and width of the character, commonly measured in points.

foreign key A field in one table that refers to the primary key field in another table and indicates how the tables are related.

form A database object used primarily to display records onscreen to make it easier to enter and make changes to records.

Form Design toolbar: Contains the standard buttons as well as buttons that are specific to the Form Design view window.

Formatting toolbar In Form and Report Design views, contains buttons used to customize the appearance of the form or report.

function A predefined calculation provided by Access to calculate sum, average, etc.

graphic A non-text element or object, such as a drawing or picture, which can be added to a table.

group A way of organizing data on a common attribute. When data is grouped, calculations can be performed on all data in each group.

group calculation A calculation performed on the data in a group in a report.

Group Header and Footer section A section of Report Design that contains information on the groups.

hierarchical form A form/subform combination.

hyperlink Allows the user to jump to another location in the same or different database, table, form, or query; to a document in a different application; or to a Web page.

Hypertext Markup Language (HTML) A programming language used to create Web pages.

identifier A part of an expression that refers to the value of a field, a graphic object, or property.

import To retrieve data that has been saved in another format and insert it into an Access table.

input mask Used in fields and text boxes to format data and provide control over what values can be entered into a field.

intranet An internal network set up by a company to share data online.

join Creates a relationship between tables by linking common fields in multiple tables.

join line In the Query Design window, the line that joins the common fields between one or more table field lists.

junction table Holds the primary key fields from the other two tables in a many-to-many relationship.

landscape Printing orientation that prints across the length of the page.

linked object An object that is pasted into another application. The data is stored in the source document, and a graphic representation of the data is displayed in the destination document.

literal characters Characters in an input mask that display just as they appear.

live link A link in which, when the source document is edited, the changes are automatically reflected in the destination document.

lookup field Provides a list of values the user can choose from to enter data into that field.

lookup list A lookup field that uses another table as the source for values.

macro Automates common Access database tasks, such as opening and printing tables, forms, and reports.

main form The primary form that can have multiple subforms.

many-to-many An association between two tables in which one record in either table can relate to many records in the other table.

margin The blank space around the edge of a page.

mask character Characters in an input mask that define the characterstics of the input mask.

master/detail form A form/subform combination.

master field A field from the master table that is linked to a child field in the subdatasheet.

master table The table that holds the subdatasheet.

move handle The large box in the upper left corner of a selected control that is used to move the control.

multitable query A query that uses more than one table.

multiuser A type of database that allows multiple users to access and modify the database at the same time.

navigation buttons Used to move through records in Datasheet and Form views. Also available in the Print Preview window.

Navigation mode In Datasheet view, when the entire field is highlighted.

object A table, form, or report that can be selected and manipulated as a unit.

Office Clipboard An Office XP storage area in memory that can store up to 24 items.

one-to-many An association between two tables in which the primary key field value in each record in the primary table corresponds to the value in the matching field or fields of many records in the related table.

one-to-one An association between two tables in which each record in the first table contains a field value that corresponds to the field value of one record in the other table.

operator A symbol or word used to specify the type of calculation to perform in an expression.

orientation The direction the paper prints, either landscape or portrait.

parent/child form A form/subform combination.

picture An illustration such as a scanned photograph.

point Unit of measure for characters in a font; 1 point equals 1/72 inch.

portrait Printing orientation that prints the report across the width of a page.

primary key One or more fields in a table that uniquely identify a record.

primary table The "one" side of two related tables in a one-to-many relationship.

query Used to view data in different ways, to analyze data, and to change data.

query datasheet Where the result or answer to a query is displayed.

record A row of a table, consisting of a group of related fields.

record number indicator A small box that displays the current record number in the lower left corner of most views. The record number indicator is surrounded by the navigation buttons.

record selector Displayed to the left of the first column; it can be used to select an entire record in Datasheet view.

record source The underlying table or query on which a form or report is based.

referential integrity A set of rules used by Access to ensure that relationships between tables are valid and that related data is not accidentally changed or deleted.

relational database Database in which a relationship is created by having a common field in the tables. The common field lets you extract and combine data from multiple tables.

relationship The association between common fields in two tables.

report Printed output generated from queries or tables.

Required property Specifies whether a value is required in a field.

restore Operation that copies a backup file from the storage medium back onto the computer's hard disk.

row label In the design grid of Query Design view, identifies the type of information that can be entered in the row.

Sans serif Fonts that do not have a flair at the base of each letter.

serif Fonts with a flair at the base of each letter that visually leads the reader to the next letter.

Show box A box in the Show row of the design grid that, when checked, indicates that the field will be displayed in the query result.

sizing handles Small boxes surrounding a selected control that are used to size the control.

sort To temporarily reorder table records in the datasheet.

source The original selection that is copied.

source file The document in which a linked object is created.

spacing The distance between controls.

standalone page A data access page that does not have a shortcut to it from anywhere else.

subdatasheet A data table that is nested in another data table and that contains data related or joined to the table where it resides.

subform A form that is embedded in another form.

switchboard An Access form that contains command buttons for performing a variety of actions.

switchboard items table A table that is created automatically when a switchboard is created and includes all items on the Main Switchboard.

Switchboard Manager Access feature used to create and modify switchboard pages.

switchboard page Each switchboard in a database.

System Clipboard A temporary Windows storage area in memory.

table Consists of vertical columns and horizontal rows of information about a particular category of things.

tab order The order in which Access moves through a form or table when the T key is pressed.

tabular form A form layout in row-and-column format with records in rows and fields in columns.

task pane A separate, scrollable pane displaying shortcuts to frequently used features.

theme A predesigned set of background color, designs, fonts, and other special effects.

Toolbox toolbar Contains buttons that are used to add and modify controls.

typeface The design and shape of characters, such as Times Roman and Courier.

unbound control A control that is not connected to a field in an underlying table.

unbound object A graphic object that is associated with the table as a whole, not with a specific record, and does not change when you move from record to record.

Undo A feature used to cancel your last action.

validation rule An expression that defines the acceptable values in a validity check.

validation text Text that is displayed when a validation rule is violated.

validity check Process of checking to see whether data meets certain criteria.

value A part of an expression that is a number, date, or character string.

value list A lookup field that uses fixed values.

view One of several windows or formats that Access provides for working with and looking at data.

workspace The large area of the screen where different Access windows are displayed as you are using the program.

PowerPoint Glossary of Key Terms

action button   A special object that can be inserted into a presentation and assigned a hyperlink. Used in self-running presentations and presentations that work on a company network or the Web.

agenda slide   A slide that lists the agenda items or main topics of a presentation from which viewers can select.

alignment   Settings that allow you to change the horizontal placement of an entry in a placeholder or a table cell.

animated GIF   A type of graphic file that has motion.

animation   Effect that adds action to text and graphics so they move around on the screen.

animation scheme   A preset visual effect that can be added to slide text.

assistant box   In an organization chart, a box representing administrative or managerial assistants to a manager.

attachment   A file that is sent along with an e-mail message but is not part of the message.

attribute   Features associated with an object that can be isolated and changed one at a time.

AutoContent Wizard   A guided approach that helps you determine the content and organization of your presentation through a series of questions.

AutoCorrect   Feature that makes certain types of corrections automatically as you enter text.

AutoShape   A ready-made drawing project supplied with PowerPoint.

branch   In an organization chart, a box and all the boxes that report to it.

broadcast   A tool for collaboration that will display a presentation to a selected audience through your browser.

browser   A program that connects you to remote computers and displays the pages you request.

build   An effect that progressively displays bulleted items as the presentation proceeds.

category axis   The bottom boundary of the chart, which is used to label the data being charted. Also called the X axis.

cell   The intersection of a row and column in a table.

change marker   An icon that indicates a reviewer made a change to a slide.

character formatting   Formatting features that affect the selected characters only.

chart   A visual representation of numeric data. Also called a graph.

clip art   Professionally drawn images.

clips   Media files such as art, sound, animation and movies.

collecting and pasting   The capability of the program to store multiple copied items in the Office Clipboard and then paste one or any of the items.

comment   A remark that is displayed in a separate box and attached to a slide.

comment marker   An icon that indicates a comment is attached to a slide.

co-worker box   In an organization chart, a box having the same manager as another box. Co-workers form a group.

custom dictionary   A dictionary you can create to hold words you commonly use but that are not included in the dictionary that is supplied with the program.

custom show   A presentation that runs within a presentation.

data series Each group of related data that is plotted in the chart. Each data series has a unique color or pattern assigned to it so that you can identify the different series.

datasheet A table consisting of rows and columns that is used to enter the data that you want represented in a chart.

default Initial program settings.

demote To move a topic down one level in the outline hierarchy.

design template Professionally created slide design that can be applied to your presentation.

destination document The document where an embedded object is inserted.

destination file The document receiving the linked or embedded object.

drawing object An object consisting of shapes such as lines and boxes that can be created using the Drawing toolbar.

Drawing toolbar A toolbar that is used to add objects such as lines, circles, and boxes.

embedded object An object that is inserted into another application and becomes part of the document. It can be edited from within the document using the source program.

font A set of characters with a specific design.

font size The height and width of a character, commonly measured in points.

footer Text or graphics that appear on the bottom of each slide.

format To enhance the appearance of a slide to make it more readable or attractive.

Formatting toolbar A toolbar that contains buttons used to modify text.

graphics A nontext element, such as a chart, drawing, picture, or scanned photograph, in a slide.

grid An invisible series of lines that form small squares on the slide and that are used to position objects.

group Two or more objects that are treated as a single object. In an organization chart, all the boxes reporting to the same manager, excluding assistant boxes.

guide A line, either vertical or horizontal, that you position on the slide. When an object is close to the guide, the center or corner (whichever is closer) snaps to the guide.

hierarchy A visual representation that shows ranking, such as reporting structures within a department in a business.

hyperlink A connection to other slides, custom shows, presentations, objects, e-mail addresses, or Web pages. The user jumps to the referenced location by clicking on the hyperlink.

Hypertext Markup Language (HTML) The programming language used to write Web pages. If controls how information on the page, such as font colors and size, is displayed.

landscape Orientation of the printed output across the length of the paper.

layout A predefined slide organization that is used to control the placement of elements on a slide.

legend A box containing a brief description that identifies the patterns or colors assigned to the data series in a chart.

level All the boxes in an organization chart at the same level regardless of the boxes each reports to.

linked object An object that is created in a source file and linked to a destination file. Edits made to the source file are automatically reflected in the destination file.

live link A link that automatically updates the linked object whenever changes are made to it in the source file.

lobby page In a broadcast, the page that displays information about the broadcast including the title, subject, and host's name.

macro A stored sequence of actions.

main dictionary Dictionary that comes with the Office XP programs.

manager box In an organization chart, the top-level box of a group.

master A special slide on which the formatting of all slides in a presentation is defined.

move handle Used to move menu bars and toolbars to a new location.

notes page Printed output that shows a miniature of the slide and provides an area for speaker notes.

object An item on a slide that can be selected and modified.

object alignment To position objects relative to each other by their left, right, top, or bottom edges; or horizontally by their centers or vertically by their middles; or in relation to the entire slide.

Office Assistant   Used to get help on features specific to the Office application you are using.

organization chart   A map of a group, which usually includes people, but can include any items that have a hierarchical relationship.

Outlining toolbar   Displayed in Outline view, it is used to modify the presentation outline.

pane   In Normal view, the separate divisions of the window that allow you to work on all aspects of your presentation in one place.

paragraph formatting   Formatting features that affect entire paragraphs.

picture   An image such as a graphic illustration or a scanned photograph.

placeholder   Box that is designed to contain objects such as the slide title, bulleted text, charts, tables, and pictures.

point   A unit of type measurement. One point equals about 1/72 inch.

portrait   Orientation of the printed output across the width of the paper.

promote   To move a topic up one level in the outline hierarchy.

publish   To save a presentation in HTML format to a Web server.

rotate handle   The ◎ on the selection rectangle of a selected object that allows you to rotate the object in any direction.

sans serif   A font that does not have a flair at the base of each letter, such as Arial or Helvetica.

selection rectangle   Hashed border that surrounds a selected placeholder.

serif   A font that has a flair at the base of each letter, such as Roman or Times New Roman.

server   The computer that stores Web pages and sends them to a browser when requested.

sizing handles   Small boxes surrounding selected objects that are used to change the size of the object.

slide   An individual page of the presentation.

slide show   Used to practice or to present the presentation. It displays each slide in final form.

source document   The document from which an embedded object was attained.

source file   The file from which a linked or embedded object is obtained.

source program   The program used to create the linked or embedded object.

stacking order   The order in which objects are inserted in the different layers of a slide.

standard toolbar   A toolbar that contains buttons that give quick access to the most frequently used program features.

subordinate box   In an organization chart, a box reporting to a manager box.

table   An arrangement of horizontal rows and vertical columns.

template   A file that includes predefined settings that can be used as a pattern to create many common types of presentations.

text box   A container for text or graphics.

thumbnail   A miniature view of a slide.

titles   Descriptive text used to explain the content of a chart.

transition   An effect that controls how a slide moves off the screen and the next one appears.

typeface   A set of characters with a specific design

value axis   The left boundary of a chart, consisting of a numbered scale whose numbers are determined by the data used in the chart. Also called the Y axis.

view   A way of looking at the presentation.

WordArt   Used to enhance slide text by changing the shape of text, adding 3-D effects, and changing the alignment of text on a line.

workspace   The large area containing the slide where your presentations are displayed as you create and edit them.

X axis   The bottom boundary of the chart, which is used to label the data being charted. Also called the category axis.

Y axis   The left boundary of the chart, consisting of a numbered scale whose numbers are determined by the data used in the chart. Also called the value axis.

Data File List

Supplied/Used File	Created/Saved As
Lab 1	
	Flyer
wd01_Flyer2	Flyer3
wd01_Elephants (graphic)	
Step-by-Step	
1.	Dress Code
2.	Top Stresses
wd01_Stress (graphic)	
3.	Executive Style
wd01_Executive1 (graphic)	
wd01_Executive2 (graphic)	
4.	B&B Ad
wd01_Sunshine (graphic)	
5. wd01_Making Sushi	Making Sushi2
wd01_sushi (graphic)	
On Your Own	
1.	Career Report
2.	Reunion
3.	Lab Rules
4.	PomPom
5.	Cruise Flyer
On the Web	
1.	Writing Tips
Lab 2	
wd02_Tour Letter	Tour Letter2
wd02_ Flyer4	
Step-by-Step	
1. wd02_Cleaning Checklist	Cleaning Checklist2
2.	Career Fair
3. Making Sushi2 (from Lab 1, PE 5)	Making Sushi3
wd02_Rice	
4. wd02_Thank You Letter	Thank You Letter2
5. wd02_Coffee Flyer	Coffee Flyer2

Supplied/Used File	Created/Saved As
On Your Own	
1.	Internship Letter
2.	Insurance Comparison
3.	To Do List
4.	New Staff Memo
5.	For Sale Flyer
On the Web	
1.	Election Results
Lab 3	
wd03_Tour Research	Tour Research2
	Research Outline
wd03_Lions (graphic)	
wd03_Parrots (graphic)	
Step-by-Step	
1.	Workout
2. wd03_Internet	Internet2
3. wd03_Antique Shops	Antique Shops2
4. wd03_Cafe Flyer	Cafe Flyer2
wd03_coffee (graphic)	
wd03_Computer User (graphic)	
5. wd03_Scenic Drives	Scenic Drives2
wd03_Mountain (graphic)	
6. wd03_Water	Water2
wd03_Swimmer (graphic)	
On Your Own	
1. wd03_Alzheimer	Alzheimer2
2. wd03_Computer	Computer2
3.	Job Search
4.	Research
On the Web	
1.	Computer Virus
Working Together	
wdwt_Tour Flyer	New Tour Presentations
wdwt_Locations	Locations
Step-by-Step	
1. Locations (from WT Lab)	LosAngeles
wdwt1_LosAngeles	
2. Executive Style (from Lab 1, PE 3)	Executive Style
3. B&B Ad (from Lab 1, PE 4)	B&B
On Your Own	
1.	Web Design

Supplied/Used File	Created/Saved As
Lab 4	
wd04_Headline	Newsletter Headline
wd04_Tanzania Facts	
wd04_Be An Adventure Traveler	March Newsletter
wd04_Costa Rica Adventure	
wd04_Newsletter Articles	
Step-by-Step	
1. wd04_Fitness Club Headline	Fitness Headline2
wd04_Fitness Club	Fitness Club Newsletter
wd04_Exercise Bike	
wd04_Jogger	
2. wd04_Scenic Drives	Scenic Drives Newsletter
Newsletter Headline (from Lab 4)	
wd04_Road	
wd04_Canada	
wd04_MtDoug	
wd04_Huts	
3. wd04_Coffee	Internet Cafe Newsletter
wd04_Conversation	
wd04_Coffee Beans	
wd04_Coffee Cup	
4. wd04_Hikes	National Parks Newsletter
wd04_Park Headline	
wd04_Survival Skills	
wd04_Fire	
wd04_Shelter	
wd04_Signaling	
wd04_Food & Water	
wd04_First Aid	
5. wd04_Air Travel	Air Travel Newsletter
On Your Own	
1.	Activity Newsletter
2.	Power Plant Newsletter
3. wd04_Water	Water Newsletter
4.	PTA Newsletter
5.	Garden Newsletter
On The Web	
	My Newsletter
Lab 5	
wd05_Mountain	Tour Sales Memo
wd05_Tour Letter5	Client List

Supplied/Used File	Created/Saved As
	Tour Main Document
	Tour Merge Document
	Tour Mailing Labels
Step-by-Step	
1. wd05_Mountain	Yoga Memo
2.	Membership Memo
3. wd05_Video Tower Letter	Video Data Source
	Video Merge Document
4. wd05_Vet Letter	Vet Data Source
	Vet Merge Document
5. wd05_Cafe Bonus	Cafe Data Source
	Cafe Merge Document
On Your Own	
1.	Leisure Activities
2.	New Car Info
3.	Hand Washing
4.	Movie Data
5.	Frequent Flyer Letter
	Default
On The Web	
1.	Cover Letter and Resume
Lab 6	
wd06_ATT Home Page	Adventure Travel Tours Web Site
wd06_Tour List	
wd06_New Tours	
wd06_Construction	
wd06_Elephant Walking	
wd06_New Tours	
Step-by-Step	
1. wd06_Home Page Text	Home Page Text2
wd06_SCNewsletter	Sports Company Web Site
2. wd06_Pets Home Page	Animal Angels Web Site
wd06_Parrots	
wd06_Cat	
wd06_Puppies	
wd06_Lizard	
3. wd06_Patron	Downtown Internet Cafe Web Site
wd06_Laptop	
wd06_City	
wd06_Services	
wd06_Coffee Online	Cafe Home Page2

OFR1.4

Reference 1: Data File List

www.mhhe.com/oleary

Office XP

Supplied/Used File	Created/Saved As
4.	My Home Page
5. wd06_Virus Text Page	Virus Web Site
wd06_Virus	
wd06_Trojan Horses	

On Your Own

Supplied/Used File	Created/Saved As
1. My Home Page (from exercise 4)	(expansion of personal web site)
2.	My TV Site
3. Adventure Travel Web site (from Lab 6)	(expansion of Adventure Travel Tours Web Site)
wd06_Tour FAQs	
4.	Club Web Site
5.	(expansion of Animal Angels Web Site)

On The Web

Supplied/Used File	Created/Saved As
	Web Design

Working Together 2

Supplied/Used File	Created/Saved As
wdwt2_Camping Safari	Camping Safari Edited
wdwt2_New Tour Bookings.xls	New Tour Bookings Linked
wdwt2_New Tour Status	New Tour Status Revised
wdwt2_Everest Original	Everest Changes3
wdwt2_Everest Changes1	Everest Brochure Revised
wdwt2_Everest Changes2	Safari e-mail
wdwt2_Everest Paragraph	

Step-by-Step

Supplied/Used File	Created/Saved As
1. wdwt2_Time Sheet Memo	Time Sheet Linked
wdwt2_Time Sheet.xls	Time Sheet
2. wdwt2_Credit Card Letter	Credit Card Letter Revised
wdwt2_Credit Card Paragraph	
3. wdwt2_Draft FAQs	FAQs Revised

1 Excel Reference

Data File List

Supplied/Used file	Created/Saved As
Lab 1	
ex01_Forecast2	Forecast
ex01_Internet (graphic)	Forecast3
Step-by-Step	
1. ex01_Improvements	Park Improvements
2. ex01_New Positions	Jobs
3. ex01_Poverty Level	Poverty Level
ex01_Family (graphic)	
4. ex01_IT Salaries	IT Salaries
ex01_Disks (graphic)	
5. ex01_Springs Budget	Springs Projected Budget
On Your Own	
1.	Class Grades
2.	Personal Budget
3.	Weekly Sales
4.	Job Analysis
5.	Membership
On the Web	
1.	Spreadsheet Design
Lab 2	
ex02_Cafe Sales	Cafe Sales Charts
Step-by-Step	
1. ex02_Real Estate Prices	Real Estate Charts
2. ex02_Tiger Data	Tiger Charts
3. ex02_Birds	Bird Observations
4.	Youth Sport Charts

Supplied/Used file	Created/Saved As
5. ex02_Higher Education	Higher Education Charts
On Your Own	
1. ex02_Job Market	Seminar
2.	Grades
3.	Stocks
4.	Statistics
5.	Insurance
Lab 3	
ex03_First Quarter Forecast	Forecast4
ex03_Annual Forecast	Annual Forecast Revised
Step-by-Step	
1. ex03_Sandwich Shop	Sandwich Shop2
2. ex03_West Income Statement	West Income Statement2
3. ex03_Time Sheets	Time Sheets2
4. ex03_Grade Report	Grade Report2
5. ex03_Springs Forecast	Springs Forecast2
6. ex03_African Safari	African Safari2
On Your Own	
1. Personal Budget (from Lab 1)	Personal Budget2
2.	Art Expenses
3.	Stock Analysis
On the Web	
1.	My Business
Working Together	
exwt1_Sales Forecast Memo	Sales Forecast Memo Linked
Cafe Sales Charts (from Lab 2)	Cafe Sales Charts Linked
exwt1_Forecast Memo	Second Quarter Forecast
Annual Forecast Revised (from Lab 3)	
Practice Exercises	
1. exwt1_Rescue Memo	Rescue Memo Linked
exwt1_Contributions	Contributions2
2. exwt1_Tour Status Report	March Status Report
exwt1_Adventure Travel Monthly	Adventure Travel Monthly2

Supplied/Used file	Created/Saved As
3. exwt1_Hotel Memo	Hotel Memo2
exwt1_Hotel Data	
Lab 4	
ex04_Revised Annual Forecast	2002 Forecast
	Forecast Template.xlt
	2003 Forecast
Step-by-Step	
1. ex04_West Side Income	West Side Income.xlt
	West Side Income1
2. ex04_Travel Analysis	ATT Analysis Template
	ATT Revenue Analysis
	ATT Revenue Analysis2
3. ex04_Personal Budget	Personal Budget2
4. ex04_School GPA	GPA Analysis
5. ex04_ARF Contributions	ARF Analysis
On Your Own	
1.	LFC Revenue Analysis
2.	LocalNet Projections
3.	Spring Break Analysis
4.	Art Equipment Analysis
5.	Expansion Projections
On the Web	
1.	Stock Analysis
Lab 5	
ex05_Loan Analysis	Loan Analysis
ex05_Bonus Dollars	Loan Analyzer
	Bonus Dollars
	Monthly Bonus Form.xlt
Step-by-Step	
1. ex05_ARF Volunteers	ARF Bonus Awards
2. ex05_Grades	Gradebook
3. ex05_Electronics Analyzer	Electronics Analyzer
4. ex05_Currency Exchange	Currency Converter
5. ex05_ATT Sales	ATT Sales2

Supplied/Used file	Created/Saved As
On Your Own	
1.	Macros
2.	My 401K
3.	Furniture Loan Analysis
4.	Sports Company Credit Card
5.	Speeding Fines
On the Web	
1.	Computer Comparisons
Lab 6	
ex06_Customer List	Customer1
ex06_Customers2	Customers2
ex06_Bonus Dollars Web	March Bonus Dollars.htm
Step-by-Step	
1. ex06_Kodiak Database	Kodiak Database Update
2. ex06_Wilson Employees	Wilson Employee Rewards
3. ex06_LFC Database	LFC Analysis
4. ex06_ATT Client List	ATT Client List2
5. ex06_ARF Inventory	ARF Inventory2
	ARF Inventory Web
On Your Own	
1.	Statter's Suppliers
2.	Toy Inventory
3.	Summer Baseball League
4.	Cleaning Company Customers
5.	Budget Analysis
On the Web	
1. Stock Analysis	StockAnalysis.Web
Working Together 2	
Customers2 (from Lab 6)	Customers2 Review (in Cafe Customers folder)
exwt2_Customers2 Original	Customers2 Final (in Cafe Customers folder)
exwt2_Customers2 Review	
exwt2_Cafe Supplies.mdb	Café Supplies

Supplied/Used file	Created/Saved As
Step-by-Step	
1. ARF Analysis	ARF Analysis Review
	ARF Analysis Review2
	ARF Analysis2
2. ATT Sales2	ATT Sales Review
	ATT Sales Review2
	ATT Sales3
3. exwt2_Decorator's Resource Gallery	Artist Inventory

Access Reference 1

Data File List

Supplied/Used File	Created/Saved As
Lab 1	
ac01_Friend1 (graphic)	Lifestyle Fitness Employees: Employees (table)
Step-by-Step	
1.	Beautiful: Clients (table)
2.	Happenings: Advertisers (table)
3.	Supplies: Vendors (table)
4.	Adventure Travel: Travel Packages (table)
5. ac01_Whitedog (graphic)	Animal Rescue: Tracking (table)
On Your Own	
1.	Music Collection: CD Catalog (table)
2.	Lewis Personnel: Phone List (table)
3.	Patient Information: Patient Data (table)
4.	JK Enterprises: Expenses (table)
On the Web	
	Golden Oldies: Inventory (table)
Lab 2	
ac02_EmployeeRecords	Employee Data Form (form)
Step-by-Step	
1. ac02_Simply Beautiful	Client Info (form)
2. ac02_Happening Ads	Advertiser Information (form)
3. ac02_Cafe Supplies	Vendor Info (table)
4. ac02_Learning	EduSoft Titles (form)
5. ac02_AA	Angel's Animals (form)
On Your Own	
1. Adventure Travel (from Lab 1)	Packages (form)
2. JK Enterprises	JK Expenses (form)
3. Patient Information (from Lab 1)	Administration (form)
4. Lewis Personnel: Phone List	Human Resources (form)

Supplied/Used File	Created/Saved As
On the Web	
1. Golden Oldies (from Lab 1)	Collectibles (form)
Lab 3	
ac03_Personnel Records	Car Pool (query)
	3-year Service Awards (query)
	5-year Service Awards (query)
	Employee Address Report (report)
	Iona to Fort Meyers Car Pool Report (report)
Step-by-Step	
1. ac02_Simply Beautiful	
2. ac02_ Happening Ads	Bimonthly Advertisers (query)
3. ac02_ Cafe Supplies	Low Stock (query)
	Order Items (report)
4. ac02_ Learning	Old Math and Science (query)
	96-97 Math and Science Titles (report)
5. ac03_Angels	Adoptees (query)
	Animal Adoption Report (report)
On Your Own	
1. ac02_Learning	
2. Lewis Personnel (from Lab 2)	Home Address (query)
3. JK Enterprise (from Lab 2)	Pending (query)
	Pending Expenses (report)
4. ac03_Angels	Foster (query)
	Foster Angels (report)
On the Web	
Golden Oldies (from Lab 2)	Complete Products (query)
Working Together	
acw1_ServiceAwards	
ac03_Personnel Records	Service Awards Linked (document)
Step-by-Step	
1. ac02_Simply Beautiful	Beautiful 35+ Clients (document)
2. ac02_Cafe Supplies	Special Orders (query)
	Special Orders (document)
3. ac02_Learning	3+ Products (query)
Old Math and Science (query)	EduSoft 3+ (document)
Lab 4	**Database: Table**
ac04_Att	
ac04_Club Employees	Club Employees: Pay (table)
ac04_Pay.xls	Club Employees: Pay (table)
	Hours (query)
	Hours_Crosstab (query)
	Database Relationships (report)

Supplied/Used File	Created/Saved As
Step-by-Step	
1. ac04_Clients & Agents	Clients & Agents: Clients_Crosstab (query)
2. ac04_ARF	ARF Fosters: Boarded Animals (query)
3. ac04_Simply Beautiful	Simply Beautiful: Spa Packages (table) Package Revenue (query)
4. ac04_Cafe Purchases	Cafe Purchases: Inventory Prices (table) Inventory Order Costs (query)
5. ac04_EduSoft	EduSoft Titles: Software Sales (table) Software Package Sales (query)
On Your Own	
1. Associated Dental	Patients (table)
2. Lewis Personnel	
3. WriteOn!	Products (table) Suppliers (table)
4. JK Enterprises	
5. ac04_Little League	Little League: Coaches (table)
On the Web	
	Custom Tees
Lab 5	
Club Employees (from Lab 4)	Club Employees: Employee Update Form (form)
Step-by-Step	
1. Clients & Agents (from Lab 4)	Agents (form) Clients (subform)
2. ARF Fosters (from Lab 4)	Animal Status (form) Foster Care Provider (subform)
3. Simply Beautiful (from Lab 4)	Spa Package Purchases (form) Purchased by (subform)
4. Cafe Purchases (from Lab 4)	Inventory Item Orders (form)
5. EduSoft Titles (from Lab 4)	Software Orders (form)
On Your Own	
1. Associated Dental (from Lab 4)	
2. WriteOn! (from Lab 4)	
3. Lewis Personnel (from Lab 4)	
4. JK Enterprises (from Lab 4)	
5. Little League (from Lab 4)	
On the Web	
Custom Tees (from Lab 4)	

Supplied/Used File	Created/Saved As
Lab 6	
Club Employees (from Lab 5)	Gross Pay Report for 6/28/2002 (report)
	Gross Pay 6/14/2002 (query)
	Gross Pay for 6/14/2002 (report)
	Employee Mailing Labels (report)
	Open Employee Update Form (macro)
	Preview Employee Update Form (macro)
	Print Employee Mailing Labels (macro)
	Employee Form (switchboard page)
	Employee reports (macro)
	Return to Main Switchboard (switchboard page)
	Print Employee Mailing Labels (switchboard item)
	Open Employee Mailing Labels (switchboard item)
	Open Employee Forms (switchboard item)
	Open and Preview Employee Reports (switchboard item)
	Close Database (switchboard item)
Step-by-Step	
1. Clients & Agents (from Lab 5)	Agent and Client List (report)
	Client Mailing Labels (labels)
2. ARF Fosters (from Lab 5)	Animal Status (query)
	Animal Status (report)
	Foster Care Mailing Labels
	Adopters Mailing Labels
3. Simply Beautiful (from Lab 5)	Spa Packages Sold (report)
4. Edusoft Titles (from Lab 5)	Software Package Sales (report)
5. Cafe Purchases (from Lab 5)	Stock Orders
On Your Own	
1. Lewis Personnel (from Lab 5)	
2. WriteOn! (from Lab 5)	
3. Associated Dental (from Lab 5)	
4. JK Enterprises (from Lab 5)	
5. Little League (from Lab 5)	
On the Web	
Custom Tees (from Lab 5)	
Access Project	
ac06_Sofa	Decorator's Resource Gallery Order Entry: Sales by Employee (report)
Working Together 2	
Club Employees (from Lab 6)	Gross Pay 6-28.xls
	Lifestyle Fitness Club Employees.htm
Step-by-Step	
1. ac04_Cafe Purchases	Cafe Inventory Prices.xls
2. ac04_EduSoft	Software Package Sales.xls
	EduSoft Software.htm
3. ac04_Simply Beautiful	Spa Packages.htm

PowerPoint Reference 1

Data File List

Supplied/Used File	Created/Saved As
Lab 1	
	Volunteer
pp01_Volunteer1	Volunteer2
pp01_Puppy (graphic)	
Step-by-Step	
1. pp01_Balance	Balance1
pp01_Time (graphic)	
pp01_Traffic (graphic)	
pp01_QuestionMark (graphic)	
2. pp01_Resume	Resume1
pp01_Goals (graphic)	
pp01_Correspondence (graphic)	
3.	Blowouts
pp01_Tire (graphic)	
pp01_Wheel (graphic)	
pp01_Unprepared (graphic)	
pp01_Repair (graphic)	
4.	Coffee
pp01_CoffeeShop (graphic)	
pp01_CoffeeMug (graphic)	
pp01_Cup (graphic)	
5.	Workplace Issues
pp01_Ergonomics (graphic)	
pp01_PhysicalHealth (graphic)	
pp01_MentalHealth (graphic)	
pp01_Handshake (graphic)	
pp01_Board Meeting (graphic)	

Supplied/Used File	Created/Saved As
On Your Own	
1.	Better Bike Safety
pp01_BikeSafety (data)	
2.	Phone Etiquette
pp01_Memo (data)	
3.	Presentation Aids
pp01_VisualAids (data)	
4.	Placement Services
5.	Web Design
Lab 2	
pp02_Volunteer2	Volunteer3
pp02_QuestionMark (graphic)	
Step-by-Step	
1. Balance1	Balance2
2. pp02_ASU Presentation	ASU Presentation1
pp02_PalmWalk (graphic)	
pp02_StudentServices (graphic)	
pp02_Library (graphic)	
pp02_FineArts (graphic)	
3. Blowouts	Blowouts2
4. Coffee	Coffee Show
5. Workplace Issues (from Lab 1)	Workplace Issues2
pp02_Arrows (graphic)	
On Your Own	
1.	Interview Techniques
2. Better Bikes Safety (from Lab 1)	Better Bikes Safety2
3.	Travel Italy
4. Web Design (from Lab 1)	Web Design2
5.	Travel Favorites
Working Together	
Volunteer3 (from Lab 2)	Volunteer3 Linked
ppwt1_OrientationMeetings	
ppwt1_RescueData	Rescue Data Linked
Step-by-Step	
1. ppwt1_Blowout Signs	Blowouts3
Blowouts2	
2. ppwt1_CoffeePrices	Coffee Prices Linked
Coffee	Coffee Show Linked
3. Workplace Issues2 (from Lab 2)	Workplace Issues2 Linked
ppwt1_EnergyUse	EnergyUse Linked

Supplied/Used File	Created/Saved As
Lab 3	
pp03_Recruitment	Volunteer Orientation
pp03_Animal Angels3	Orientation Outline
pp03_Sky	Volunteer Presentation.eml
pp03_Cat Smiling	
pp03_Dog Smiling	
Step-by-Step	
1. pp03_Employee Motivation	Employee Motivation2
	Motivation Outline
pp03_Motivation (graphic)	
pp03_Money	
2. pp03_Water Safety	Water Safety2
pp03_Gradblu2 (graphic)	
pp03_Water (graphic)	
pp03_Pool (graphic)	
3. Blowouts2 (from Lab 2)	Blowouts3
pp03_Spare Tire (graphic)	
4. pp03_ Final Marketing Presentation	Sports Company Outline
pp03_Baseball Man (graphic)	Sports Company Presentation
pp03_Football Man (graphic)	
pp03_Basketball Man (graphic)	
5. pp03_Exercise for Clients	Fitness and Nutrition
pp03_ Fitness Trends	Fitness and Nutrition Outline
pp03_Exercise (graphic)	
On Your Own	
1. Better Bike Safety2 (from Lab 2)	DPS Bike Safety
2.	Family Reunion
3. pp03_Credit Debt	Credit Debt Presentation
4. Travel Italy (from Lab 2)	Travel Italy2
5. Placement Services (from Lab 1)	Lee Orientation
On the Web	
	Computer Viruses
Lab 4	
pp04_Promotional Outline	Animal Rescue Foundation
pp04_Animals for Adoption	Rescue Foundation Self Running
pp04_Foundation Introduction	
pp04_Turtle (graphic)	Rescue Foundation Web

Supplied/Used File	Created/Saved As
pp04_Jake (graphic)	
pp04_Sadie (graphic)	
pp04_Turtle (graphic)	
pp04_Canon (sound)	

Step-by-Step

Supplied/Used File	Created/Saved As
1. Water Safety2 (from Lab 3)	Water Presentation
pp04_swimmer (graphic)	Water Safety Web
pp04_Lake (graphic)	
2. Blowouts3 (from Lab 3)	Blowouts4
pp04_Road Sign (graphic)	
pp04_Alignment (graphic)	
3. pp04_Toulouse	Toulouse Kiosk
	Toulouse Web
pp04_Countryside (graphic)	
pp04_City Street (graphic)	
pp04_Restaurant (graphic)	
pp04_Train (graphic)	
4. pp04_Fitness Outline	Fitness Pages
	Fitness Web Pages
pp04_Race (graphic)	
pp04_Woman (graphic)	
5. pp04_Sports Company Advertising Outline	Sports Company Kiosk
pp04_Weight Lifter (graphic)	Sports Company Web
pp04_Tennis Racquet (graphic)	
pp04_Mountain Bike (graphic)	
pp04_Onestop (sound)	
pp04_Soccer (graphic)	
pp04_Football (graphic)	
pp04_Tennis (graphic)	
pp04_Baseball (graphic)	

On Your Own

Supplied/Used File	Created/Saved As
1. DPS Bike Safety (from Lab 3)	Bike Safety Kiosk
2. pp04_Mass Transit	Mass Transit
3. Travel Italy2 (from Lab 3)	Travel Italy Web
4. Lee Orientation (from Lab 3)	Lee Orientation Web
5.	MusicFirst Web

Supplied/Used File	Created/Saved As
On the Web	
	SAA Web
Working Together 2	
ppwt2_Kiosk Original	
ppwt2_Kiosk Review [2]	
ppwt2_Kiosk Review [3]	
ppwt2_Halo	Kiosk Final
ppwt2_Mall Letter	Kiosk Presentation Letter
Kiosk Final.ppt	
ppwt_Dog Wagging	Kiosk Final.htm Letter
Step-by-Step	
1. ppwt2_Water Safety Letter	Water Presentation2
Water Safety2 (from Lab 3)	Water Safety Letter
Water Presentation	
2. Fitness and Nutrition (from Lab 3)	Fitness Presentation Letter
3. Sports Company Kiosk	Sports Company Letter

Word Reference 2

MOUS Skills

Word Core Certification

Standardized Coding Number	Activity	Lab	Page	Lab Exercises	
				Step-by-Step	On Your Own
W2002-1	**Inserting and Modifying Text**				
W2002-1-1	Insert, modify, and move text and symbols	1	1.2,1.39	1,2,3,4,5	1,2,3,5
		2	2.12,2.14,2.20	1,3,4,5	2,5
		4	4.17	1,2,3,4,5	1,2,3,4,5
		6		1,2,3,4,5	1,2,3,4,5
W2002-1-2	Apply and modify text formats	1	1.46	1,2,3,4	1,2
		2	2.44	1,2,5	
W2002-1-3	Correct spelling and grammar usage	1	1.18,1.23	1,2,3,4,5	
		2	2.5,2.10	1,4	
W2002-1-4	Apply font and text effects	1	1.50	1,2,3,4,5	2
		2	2.41, 2.42	2,3,5	
W2002-1-5	Enter and format Date and Time	2	2.24	2,3,4	1
		5	5.8	1,2,3,4,5	1,2,3,4,5
W2002-1-6	Apply character styles	3	3.6	1,2,3,4,5	1,2,3,4
W2002-2	**Creating and Modifying Paragraphs**				
W2002-2-1	Modify paragraph formats	1	1.53	1,3,4,5	1,2,4
		2	2.28,2.31	1,2	
		4	4.30	1,2,3,4,5	1,2,3,4,5
W2002-2-2	Set and modify tabs	2	2.35	2,5	2,5
		4	4.30	2	
		5	5.40	1,2,3,4,5,	1,2,3,4,5
W2002-2-3	Apply bullet, outline, and numbering format to paragraphs	2	2.46	3,4	1,2,4,5
		3	3.6	1	1,2
		4	4.36	2	
		5	5.40	1,2,3,4,5,	1,2,3,4,5
W2002-2-4	Apply paragraph styles	3	3.6,3.18	1,3,4,5	1,3,4
		6	6.35		
W2002-3	**Formatting Documents**				
W2002-3-1	Create and modify a header and footer	3	3.54	2,3,4,5	1,2,3,4
W2002-3-2	Apply and modify column settings	4	4.23	1,2,3,4,5	1,2,3,4,5
W2002-3-3	Modify document layout and Page Setup options	2	2.18,2.28	1,2,3	
		3	3.27	5,6	4,3
		4	4.43	1,2,3,4,5	1,2,3,4,5
		5	5.28	1,2,3,4,5	1,2,3,4,5

Standardized Coding Number	Activity	Lab	Page	Lab Exercises Step-by-Step	On Your Own
W2002-3-4	Create and modify tables	3	3.45,3.51 3.48,3.50	5,6	1,2,3,4
		5	5.13	1,2,3,4,5	1,2,3,4,5
		6	6.21	3	
W2002-3-5	Preview and print documents, envelopes, and labels	1	1.61,1.62	1,2,3,4,5	
		2	2.55,2.57	1,2,3,4	
		3	3.65		1,2,3,4
		4	4.43	1,2,3,4,5	1,2,3,4,5
		5	5.59,5.63	1,2,3,4,5	1,2,3,4,5
W2002-4	**Managing Documents**				
W2002-4-1	Manage files and folders for documents	3	3.14		
W2002-4-2	Create documents using templates	1	1.7		
		5	5.4	1,2,3,4,5	1,2,3,4,5
		6		1,2,3,4,5	1,2,3,4,5
W2002-4-3	Save documents using different names and file formats	1	1.28,1.44		
		WT	2	2,3	
		4	4.15,4.23 4.29,4.36 4.40,4.43	1,2,3,4,5	1,2,3,4,5
		5		1,2,3,4,5	1,2,3,4,5
		6		1,2,3,4,5	1,2,3,4,5
W2002-5	**Working with Graphics**				
W2002-5-1	Insert images and graphics	1	1.55	2,3,4,5	2,3,4,5
		4	4.5,4.19	1,2,3,4,5	1,2,3,4,5
		5	5.9	1,2,3,4,5	1,2,3,4,5
W2002-5-2	Create and modify diagrams and charts	5	5.32	1	3
		6	6.27		
W2002-6	**Workgroup Collaboration**				
W2002-6-1	Compare and merge documents	WT2	2.12	1,2,3	
W2002-6-2	Insert, view, and edit comments	WT2	2.8,2.16, 2.19	1,2,3	
W2002-6-3	Convert documents into Web pages	WT		2,11	2,3
		6	6.9	1,2,3,4,5	1,2,3,4,5

Excel Reference 2

Excel Core Certification

Standardized Coding Number	Activity	Lab	Page	Lab Exercises	
				Step-by-Step	On Your Own
Ex2002-1	**Working with Cells and Cell Data**				
Ex2002-1-1	Insert, delete, and move cells	1	1.36,1.37,1.53	1,2,3,4,5	1,2,3,4,5
		3	3.14	1,2,3,4,5	1,2,3,4,5
		4	4.41		
Ex2002-1-2	Enter and edit cell data including text, numbers,and formulas	1	1.15–1.23,1.39, 1.42,1.59	1,2,3,4,5	1,2,3,4,5
Ex2002-1-3	Check spelling	3	3.4	1,5,6	
Ex2002-1-4	Find and replace cell data and formats	3	3.31		
Ex2002-1-5	Use automated tools to filter lists	6	6.19,6.29	1,2,3,4,5	1,2,3,4,5
Ex2002-2	**Managing Workbooks**				
Ex2002-2-1	Manage workbook files and folders	1	1.28	1,2,3,4,5	1,2,3,4,5
		4	4.16	1,2	1
		6	6.17	5	
Ex2002-2-2	Create workbooks using templates	1	1.5		
		4	4.9–4.18	1,2	1
Ex2002-2-3	Save workbooks using different names and file formats	1	1.26	1,2,3,4,5	1,2,3,4,5
		4	4.16	1,2	1
Ex2002-3	**Formatting and Printing Worksheets**				
Ex2002-3-1	Apply and modify cell formats	1	1.54–1.60	1,2,3,4,5	1,2,3,4,5
Ex2002-3-2	Modify row and column settings	1	1.48	1,2,3,4,5	
		3	3.35	1,2,3,4,5	
		5	5.46		
Ex2002-3-3	Modify row and column formats	1	1.24–1.26,1.49	1,2,3,4,5	
Ex2002-3-4	Apply styles	1	1.61	1,2,3,4,5	
Ex2002-3-5	Use automated tools to format worksheets	5	5.10	2,3	2,3,4,5
Ex2002-3-6	Modify Page Setup options for worksheets	2	2.51	1,2,3,4,5	
		3	3.44,3.47	1,2,3,4,5,6	
		6		1,2,3,4,5	1,2,3,4,5
Ex2002-3-7	Preview and print worksheets and workbooks	1	1.69	1,2,3,4,5	1,2,3,4
		6	6.33	1,2,3,4,5	1,2,3,4,5

Standardized Coding Number	Activity	Lab Exercises			
		Lab	Page	Step-by-Step	On Your Own
Ex2002-4	**Modifying Workbooks**				
Ex2002-4-1	Insert and delete worksheets	3	3.27	1,3,4,5,6	2,3,4
Ex2002-4-2	Modify worksheet names and positions	3	3.20,3.27	1,3,4,5,6	2,3,4
Ex2002-4-3	Use 3-D references	3	3.24	1	
Ex2002-5	**Creating and Revising Formulas**				
Ex2002-5-1	Create and revise formulas	1	1.39,1.41,1.46		
		3	3.11,3.14	1,2,3,4,5,6	1,2,3,4
Ex2002-5-2	Use statistical, date and time, financial, and logical functions in formulas	1	1.42	1,2,3,4,5	1,2,3,4
		3	3.11	1,2,3,4,5,6	1,2,3,4
		4	4.39	1	
		5	5.33	1,2,3,4,5	1,2,3,4,5
Ex2002-6	**Creating and Modifying Graphics**				
Ex2002-6-1	Create, modify, position, and print charts	2	2.7–2.22,2.49	1,2,3,4,5	1,2,3,4,5
Ex2002-6-2	Create, modify, and position graphics	1	1.65–1.68	1,2,3,4,5	5,On the Web
Ex2002-7	**Workgroup Collaboration**				
Ex2002-7-1	Convert worksheets into Web pages	6	6.38	5	5,On the Web
Ex2002-7-2	Create hyperlinks	6	6.12		
Ex2002-7-3	View and edit comments	5	5.41	3,5	

Reference 2: MOUS Skills

www.mhhe.com/oleary

Access Reference 2

Access 2002 Core Certification

Standardized Coding Number	Activity	Lab	Page	Lab Exercises Step-by-Step	Lab Exercises On Your Own
Ac2002-1	**Creating and Using Databases**				
Ac2002-1-1	Create Access databases	1	AC1.8	1,2,3,4,5	1,2,3,4,5
		6	AC6.57		
Ac2002-1-2	Open database objects in multiple views	1	AC1.25	2,3,4	
		2	AC2.40	1,2,3,4,5	1,2,3,4,5
		3	AC3.16,AC3.39	3	
Ac2002-1-3	Move among records	1	AC1.36	1,2,3,4,5	1,2,3,4,5
		2	AC2.6	1,2,3,4,5	1,2,3,4
Ac2002-1-4	Format datasheets	2	AC2.30		
Ac2002-2	**Creating and Modifying Tables**				
Ac2002-2-1	Create and modify tables	1	AC1.10,AC1.23	1,2,3,4,5	1,2,3,4,5
		2	AC2.8	1,2,3,4,5	1,2,3,4
		4	AC4.8–4.20	1,2,3,4,5	1,2,3,4,5
Ac2002-2-2	Add a predefined input mask to a field	4	AC4.9	1,2,3	3,4
Ac2002-2-3	Create lookup fields	4	AC4.14	1,4	
Ac2002-2-4	Modify field properties	1	AC1.18	1,2,3,4,5	
		2	AC2.8	1,2,3,4,5	
		4	AC4.8,AC4.20	1,2,3,4,5	2,3,4
Ac2002-3	**Creating and Modifying Queries**				
Ac2002-3-1	Create and modify select queries	3	AC3.12	2,3,4,5	
Ac2002-3-2	Add calculated fields to select queries	4	AC4.33,AC4.34		
Ac2002-4	**Creating and Modifying Forms**				
Ac2002-4-1	Create and display forms	2	AC2.32	1,2,3,4,5	1,2,3,4
Ac2002-4-2	Modify form properties	5	AC5.25,AC5.36	1,2,3,4,5	1,2
Ac2002-5	**Viewing and Organizing Information**				
Ac2002-5-1	Enter, edit, and delete records	1	AC1.27,AC1.47	1,2,3,4,5	1,2,3,4,5
		2	AC2.39	1,2,3,4,5	1,2,3,4
Ac2002-5-2	Create queries	3	AC3.11	2,3,4,5	2,3,4

Standardized Coding Number	Activity	Lab	Page	Lab Exercises	
				Step-by-Step	On Your Own
Ac2002-5-3	Sort records	2	AC2.27		
Ac2002-5-4	Filter records	3	AC3.4	1	1
Ac2002-6	**Defining Relationships**				
Ac2002-6-1	Create one-to-many relationships	4	AC4.50	2	
Ac2002-6-2	Enforce referential integrity	4	AC4.53	2	
Ac2002-7	**Producing Reports**				
Ac2002-7-1	Create and format reports	3	AC3.31	3,4,5	3,4
Ac2002-7-2	Add calculated controls to reports	6	AC6.27	1,2,3,4,5	2,3,4,5
Ac2002-7-3	Preview and print reports	3	AC3.45	3,4,5	3,4
Ac2002-8	**Integrating with Other Applications**				
Ac2002-8-1	Import data to Access	4	AC4.25		
Ac2002-8-2	Export data from Access	WT2	ACWT2.2	1,2,3	
Ac2002-8-3	Create a simple data access page	WT2	ACWT2.5	1,2,3	

PowerPoint Reference 2

MOUS Skills

PowerPoint Comprehensive Certification

Standardized Coding Number	Activity	Lab	Page	Lab Exercises	
				Step-by-Step	On Your Own
PP2002-1	**Creating Presentations**				
PP2002-1-1	Create presentations (manually and using automated tools)	1 4	1.7 4.5,4.6	1,2,3,4,5	1,2,3,4,5
PP2002-1-2	Add slides to and delete slides from presentations	1 2 4	1.33,1.35 2.8,2.37 4.8	1,2,3,4,5 1,2,4,5	1,2,3,4,5
PP2002-1-3	Modify headers and footers in the slide master	2	2.31	1,3,4	
PP2002-2	**Inserting and Modifying Text**				
PP2002-2-1	Import text from Word	4	4.4	5	2
PP2002-2-2	Insert, format, and modify text	1 2	1.14–1.25, 1.30,1.41–1.44 2.5,2.9	1,2,3,4,5 1,2,3,4,5	1,2,3,4,5 1,2,3,4,5
PP2002-3	**Inserting and Modifying Visual Elements**				
PP2002-3-1	Add tables, charts, clip art, and bitmap images to slides	1 2 3 4	1.45–1.50, 1.67,1.73 2.8	1,2,3,4,5 1,2,4,5 1,2,3,4,5 1,2,3,4,5	3 5 1,2,3,4,5 1,2,3,4,5
PP2002-3-2	Customize slide backgrounds				
PP2002-3-3	Add OfficeArt elements to slides	2 4	2.19,2.38 4.21	5 1,2,3,4,5	1,2,4 1,2,3,4,5
PP2002-3-4	Apply custom formats to tables	2 4	2.10–2.17 4.16	1,4 4	
PP2002-4	**Modifying Presentation Formats**				
PP2002-4-1	Apply formats to presentations	2 3	2.25,2.30,2.33 3.11	1,2,3,4,5 1,2,3,4,5	1,2,3,4,5 1,2,3,4,5
PP2002-4-2	Apply animation schemes	2	2.42,2.46		
PP2002-4-3	Apply slide transitions	2 3 4	2.44 4.30	2,5 1,2,3,4,5	5 1,2,3,4,5 1,2,3,4,5

Standardized Coding Number	Activity	Lab	Page	Lab Exercises Step-by-Step	On Your Own
PP2002-4-4	Customize slide formats	2	2.26	4,5	1,2,3,4,5
PP2002-4-5	Customize slide templates	2	2.24	4,5	
PP2002-4-6	Manage a slide master				
PP2002-4-7	Rehearse timing	3	3.51		
PP2002-4-8	Rearrange slides	1	1.34	2	
		2	2.37	2	
PP2002-4-9	Modify slide layout	2	2.17	1,2,3,4,5	1,2,3,4,5
		3	3.3	1,2,3,4,5	1,2,3,4,5
		4	4.12	1,2,3,4,5	1,2,3,4,5
PP2002-4-10	Add links to a presentation	4	4.40		
PP2002-5	**Printing Presentations**				
PP2002-5-1	Preview and print slides, outlines, handouts, and speaker notes	1	1.52	1,2,3,4,5	1,2,3,4,5
		2	2.60	1,2,3,4,5	1,2,3,4,5
		WT	14	1,2,3	
PP2002-6	**Working with Data from Other Sources**				
PP2002-6-1	Import Excel charts to slides	WT	8	3	
PP2002-6-2	Add sound and video to slides	2	2.43		
		4	4.27	5	1,2,3,4,5
PP2002-6-3	Insert Word tables on slides	WT	4	1,2	
PP2002-6-4	Export a presentation as an outline	3	3.48	1,2,3,4,5	1,2,3,4,5
PP2002-7	**Managing and Delivering Presentations**				
PP2002-7-1	Set up slide shows	4	4.31,4.37	1,2,3,4,5	1,2,3,4,5
PP2002-7-2	Deliver presentations	1	1.39		
		2	2.47		
		3	3.51	1,2,3,4,5	1,2,3,4,5
		4	4.37,4.50,4.54		
PP2002-7-3	Manage files and folders for presentations	4	4.53		
PP2002-7-4	Work with embedded fonts	4	4.34		
PP2002-7-5	Publish presentations to the Web	4	4.51		
PP2002-7-6	Use Pack and Go	4	4.32	1,2,3,4,5	1,2,3,4,5
PP2002-8	**Workgroup Collaboration**				
PP2002-8-1	Set up a review cycle	WT2	WT2.4		
PP2002-8-2	Review presentation comments	WT2	WT2.8		
PP2002-8-3	Schedule and deliver presentation broadcasts	WT2	WT2.21,WT2.25		
PP2002-8-4	Publish presentations to the Web	WT2	WT2.21,WT2.25		

Index

AVERAGE, EX1.42, WD5.20
Avg, AC6.10
AVI files, PP4.28
Axis titles, PP3.34, PP3.35

Background, WD5.37, WD6.17,
   PP3.10
Background color, AC2.30,
   AC2.31, PP2.15, PP2.16
Backspace key, EX1.16, EX1.18,
   PP1.17
Backup, AC4.52, AC4.53
Balance design template, PP2.23
Bar charts, EX2.5, EX2.20,
   WD5.32, PP3.25
Beam design template, PP2.23
Best Fit, AC1.41
Bitmap files (.bmp), EX1.65,
   WD1.55, AC1.31, PP1.46
Blank lines, WD1.13
Block layout style, WD2.31
.bmp files, EX1.65, WD1.55,
   AC1.31, PP1.46
Bold, EX1.56, WD1.50
Border drop-down menu, WD5.31
Border style, WD4.14
Borders and shading
   (paragraphs), WD4.30-WD4.32
Borders and Shading dialog box,
   WD4.14
Borders/lines, AC6.20-AC6.22
Bound control, AC3.42
Bound object, AC1.31
Branch, PP3.39
Break dialog box, WD3.26
Browse dialog box,
   AC1.32-AC1.34
Browser, EX6.38, PP4.51
Browsing; *see* Setting up
   presentation for browsing
Bubble charts, EX2.5, EX2.31
Bubble size, EX2.31
Builds, PP2.41, PP2.45
Bulleted items
   demoting, PP1.22, PP1.23
   5 by 5 rule, PP1.24
   format, PP1.16
   moving, PP1.19
   promoting, PP1.23
   removing bullets, PP1.44,
   PP1.45

Bulleted items (continued)
   Word, WD2.46-WD2.48
Bullets and Numbering dialog
   box, WD5.42
Buttons, WD6.47

Calculated-control expression,
   AC5.34
Calculated controls,
   AC5.34-AC5.46
   control reference,
   AC5.42-AC5.45
   creating, AC5.34, AC5.35
   Expression Builder,
   AC5.37-AC5.42
   reports, AC6.27-AC6.30
   setting control properties,
   AC5.36, AC5.37
   summing across reports,
   AC6.28-AC6.30
   testing the control, AC5.45,
   AC5.46
   text box control, AC6.27
Calculated field, AC4.33
Calculations
   Word, WD5.19-WD5.24
   calculated field, AC4.33-AC4.35
   multitable query, AC4.31,
   AC4.32
Capitalizing first letter of word,
   PP1.16
Caps Lock, EX1.19
Caption, WD3.41, WD3.42
Cascaded windows, EX4.20
Case sensitive, EX6.20, WD2.21
Category-axis title, EX2.6, PP3.26
Category names, EX2.6
Cell, EX1.7, WD3.45, AC3.16,
   PP2.8, PP3.30
Cell alignment, EX1.49-EX1.51
Cell reference. *See* Reference
Cell selector, EX1.7
Cell shading, WD5.26, WD5.27
Center, PP2.13
Center alignment, PP3.23
Center Section, EX3.48
Centering across a selection,
   EX1.53
Centering page vertically, WD3.27,
   WD3.28
Changing worksheet data,
   EX2.34, EX2.35

Character effects, EX1.56,
   WD1.50-WD1.52
Character formatting, WD1.45
   color highlighting, WD2.41,
   WD2.42
   copying formats (Format
   Painter), WD2.43, WD2.44
   PowerPoint, PP1.41
   Styles and Formatting task
   pane, WD2.44, WD2.45
   underlining text, WD2.42,
   WD2.43
Character spacing,
   WD4.11-WD4.13
Character Spacing tab, WD4.13
Character string, AC2.11
Character styles, WD3.6
Chart elements, EX2.6,
   EX2.24-EX2.26
Chart gridlines, EX2.6
Chart location, EX2.15, EX2.16
Chart object, EX2.12
Chart Options dialog box, PP3.35
Chart titles, EX2.6, EX2.23,
   EX2.24
Chart toolbar, EX2.13
Chart Type button, EX2.18,
   EX2.19
Chart Type dialog box, EX2.21
Chart types, EX2.5,
   EX2.18-EX2.22
Chart Wizard, EX2.8-EX2.13
Charts, WD5.32-WD5.40,
   PP3.24-PP3.38
   arrows, EX2.38, EX2.39
   axis titles, PP3.34, PP3.35
   background color, WD5.37
   basic parts, WD5.33
   changing the type,
   EX2.18-EX2.22
   changing values, EX3.42
   changing worksheet data,
   EX2.34, EX2.35
   Chart Wizard, EX2.8-EX2.13
   clustered-column, WD5.39
   color, EX2.33
   color/format of data series,
   WD5.38, WD5.39
   color of columns, WD5.37,
   WD5.38
   combination, EX2.30, EX2.31
   copying, EX2.29